Fundamentals of American Law

FUNDAMENTALS OF AMERICAN LAW

New York University School of Law

General Editor: ALAN B. MORRISON

Oxford University Press ·

Oxford University Press, Great Clarendon Street, Oxford OX2 6DP

Oxford New York
Athens Auckland Bangkok Bogota Bombay
Buenos Aires Calcutta Cape Town Dar es Salaam
Delhi Florence Hong Kong Istanbul Karachi
Kuala Lumpur Madras Madrid Melbourne
Mexico City Nairobi Paris Singapore
Taipei Tokyo Toronto Warsaw

and associated companies in
Berlin Ibadan

Oxford is a trade mark of Oxford University Press

Published in the United States
by Oxford University Press Inc., New York

First published 1996
Paperback reprinted 1997, 1998

British Library Cataloguing in Publication Data
Data available

Library of Congress Cataloging in Publication Data
Data available

ISBN 0–19–876404–9
ISBN 0–19–876405–7 (Pbk)

Printed in Great Britain
on acid free paper by
Bookcraft Ltd., Midsomer Norton, Somerset

EDITOR'S PREFACE

The importance of American law in today's world cannot be overstated. The problem is not that we need more American lawyers; rather, law is so vital to so much that is done that law is too important to be left to lawyers just as war is too important to be left to generals.

This book is written to supply the needed fundamentals of American law to at least four distinct audiences: (1) lawyers from other countries who deal with American lawyers and who need to understand the basics of our system; (2) American business people, government officials, and others whose work regularly involves legal issues and who want to understand the law—and lawyers—better than they now do; (3) college students who may be considering a career in the law or simply wish to learn about our legal system; and (4) general readers who recognize that an appreciation of American law is an important part of being an educated person. Some chapters will be of greater interest to one group than to another, but the core of the book will appeal to all audiences.

The idea for this book came to me in the law library at the Fudan University in Shanghai China in May 1989. I was giving a series of lectures on American law and government at the University under the auspices of the Fudan Foundation and I wanted to see what books the library had on American law. What I found—or more precisely did not find—led to this book.

Because books from the West were expensive, most of the library was donated, and many of the books were second-hand and out-of-date. But of greater significance was the fact that the law books were like those one might find in an American law school library—treatises and textbooks like those I had used when I was in law school. The problem was that they were much too detailed for use outside the United States, they assumed a knowledge of our legal and political culture that was almost certainly lacking, and they never pulled together in a coherent fashion, in a modest number of pages, the basic principles in a given area of the law. In short, they were not written for an audience of foreign lawyers and law students.

After I returned home, I investigated further to find out whether it was Fudan's library that was missing the critical volume, or whether there was no book that filled the need. Rather quickly I discovered that Fudan was in the same situation as most other places, since the few books on the general subject of American law were quite elementary, written more than 20 years before, and not directed at what I saw as the target audience.

I knew that I did not have the time, let alone the expertise, to write a book that would give foreign lawyers all the basics that they need to deal with their American counterparts. I tried to interest faculty members at several law schools in the project, but there were no takers. Finally, in 1993, when I was visiting the summer home of my close friend and Dean of New York University Law School, John Sexton, I told him of my idea, and he said yes almost immediately. NYU was then well along in its ambitious and exciting venture to create a truly Global Law School, as the accompanying Foreword by Professor Norman Dorsen explains. John immediately saw this book as a vital component of the plan to make NYU's name recognized as the leader in the field.

Although I had been reluctant to take on any significant role in the project, he persuaded me that it would not be done without me and that I should become the manager and general editor, using top NYU faculty in each subject to write a chapter. Since I had been an NYU adjunct professor since 1986 and was scheduled to teach civil procedure the next spring, I could find no excuse not to do it, other than my full time job at the Public Citizen Litigation Group, a public interest law firm that I had co-founded with consumer activist Ralph Nader in 1972.

Nearly 7 years have passed since I first conceived of this book, but the basic concept has not changed. The goal is not to make the reader an expert in any area of American law, let alone every subject in the book. Rather, our aim is to introduce our audience to the fundamentals of the American legal system so that they can discuss legal problems intelligently with American lawyers when they need to do so. Thus, each chapter includes both the basic rules, referred to in the United States as 'black letter law', and the rationale behind those rules.

Law is not simply a compilation of rules, randomly arrived at, but a system which seeks to achieve certain societal ends by particular means. Unless one understands what those ends are, and how the makers of the rules believe they are reaching their goals, it is impossible to comprehend any legal system. While the purpose of the book is not to persuade other countries to adopt our legal system, either in whole or in part, we recognized that some readers would want to consider that option. Therefore, we wanted to be sure that readers understood *why* certain rules exist, and in that particular form, so that they could make an independent judgment about whether our reasons for creating a particular legal structure are acceptable in their society as well as ours.

Our other challenge was to make the book understandable to those not schooled in American law. We wondered whether some of the leading scholars in their fields could condense what they knew into a single chapter that would lay out the basic concepts, without all of the details that are so important in the actual practice of law. And could they do so in language that would be comprehensible to our audience? I didn't know, but, quite by chance, found out very quickly that the answer was 'yes'.

Professor Lawrence King had agreed to write the bankruptcy chapter, but he was going on sabbatical in the spring semester 1994, when the bulk of the work was originally scheduled to be done. Instead of waiting until he came back, Professor King wrote his chapter before he left. When it was done, I knew we could achieve our goal since he had made one of the most difficult subjects readily accessible to his audience. And these same characteristics would also make the book useful for law firms, especially those in general practice, when they encounter subject areas outside their normal practice, or when young lawyers need an introduction to a subject that they have not taken in law school.

As the work on the book progressed, I began to recognize that the volume had a wider audience than we had originally envisioned, including many here in the United States. Law is not just for lawyers; it affects virtually everyone. Among those most affected by the law are business people, especially those at the top of major companies, who encounter law and lawyers almost every day. We found that, for the most part, law was not taught at all in business schools; and where it was, it was only as a 'business law' course, lacking the kind of theory and sophistication that the book offers, as well as dealing with much more limited subject areas. In essence, American business executives have the same needs regarding American lawyers as do foreign lawyers: to understand what they are talking about and why 'the law' requires, forbids, or permits one option or another. Thus, for both audiences, we have included a chapter on how the legal profession operates and what the responsibilities of a lawyer are to a client—matters that lawyers rarely discuss with those whom they are supposed to serve.

We also realized that many college students take courses in the law, either out of general interest or because they are considering becoming lawyers. Together with a general audience, for whom the book would broaden their horizons, but without any specific use in mind, this became another group of readers. To make the book more attractive to that group, we added two chapters that had originally been omitted as not of primary focus for our non-United States audience: criminal law and family law. Now that we have included these subjects, we can truly say that *Fundamentals of American Law* is a comprehensive treatment of the American legal system.

Nothing in the law is static, as the yearly flood of court decisions, statutes, and rules makes clear. The final editing of this book was completed in the fall of 1995, and we have made every effort to be as up-to-date as possible. We know, of course, that, before the first copy is off the presses, there will be new developments that a practicing lawyer would take into account in giving advice or planning strategy. Thus, the book is not intended to provide detailed information to be used by American lawyers, especially in areas where they regularly practice. Rather, it focuses on the fundamentals of American law that rarely change, and then only very slowly. For these reasons we feel confident that a broad range of readers can rely on this book to learn the basic approaches to American law.

This preface would not be complete without a few words of appreciation for those who made this book possible. Dean Sexton saw the possibilities that others missed and he provided the support, both moral and financial, to carry out the project, even before we had a publisher. As with so much else at NYU Law School, it would not have happened without him.

The book also owes much to two others from NYU, Professor Norman Dorsen and Adjunct Professor Gregory H. Fox. Beyond writing the Foreword describing the Global Law School program, which he heads, Norman served as a back-up editor and valued counselor in this endeavor. Greg helped enormously in the early phases of the project, especially in critiquing the early drafts of many of the chapters. Both of them made my job much easier.

In the end, what makes this book so different from others that have attempted to provide an introduction to the American legal system is that the chapters were all written by experts, who spent countless hours giving a clear and concise explanation of a subject that they have spent most of their professional lives mastering. All of them were involved with many other projects, yet they all devoted the time and thought needed to make this book the valuable and important work that we had hoped it would be. Their contributions are a credit to themselves and to NYU Law School.

Alan B. Morrison

CONTENTS

14. Commercial Law

17. Bankruptcy and Other Insolvency Remedies

LIST OF CONTRIBUTORS

R. LEA BRILMAYER
Benjamin F. Butler Professor of Law, New York University

NORMAN DORSEN
Frederick I. and Grace Stokes Professor of Law, New York University

ROCHELLE C. DREYFUSS
Professor of Law, New York University

SAMUEL ESTREICHER
Professor of Law, New York University

HARRY FIRST
Professor of Law, New York University

STEPHEN GILLERS
Professor of Law, New York University

MARTIN F. GUGGENHEIM
Professor of Clinical Law, New York University

GRAHAM HUGHES
Professor of Law, New York University

JAMES B. JACOBS
Professor of Law, New York University

LAWRENCE P. KING
Charles Seligson Professor of Law, New York University

MICHAEL KLAUSNER
Professor of Law, New York University

CHARLES L. KNAPP
Max E. Greenberg Professor of Law, New York University

SYLVIA A. LAW
Elizabeth K. Dollard Professor of Law, Psychiatry and Medicine, New York University

ALAN B. MORRISON
Adjunct Professor of Law, New York University

WILLIAM E. NELSON
Joel and Anne Ehrenkranz Professor of Law, New York University

BURT NEUBORNE
John Norton Pomeroy Professor of Law, New York University

DONALD J. RAPSON
Adjunct Professor of Law, New York University

LAWRENCE G. SAGER
Robert B. McKay Professor of Law, New York University

DEBORAH H. SCHENK
AAA–CPA Olincy Professor of Law, New York University

BERNARD SCHWARTZ
Edwin D. Webb Professor of Law, Emeritus, New York University; Chapman Distinguished Professor of Law, University of Tulsa

HELEN S. SCOTT
Professor of Law, New York University

JOHN E. SEXTON
Dean and Warren E. Burger Professor of Law, New York University

STANLEY SIEGEL
Professor of Law, New York University

RICHARD B. STEWART
Emily Kempin Professor of Law, New York University

FOREWORD: THE GLOBAL LAW SCHOOL PROGRAM

NORMAN DORSEN

The diverse essays in this book are united on a central theme: in the twenty-first century the world will become smaller and increasingly interdependent through transforming developments in transportation and communication. At the same time, law—specifically the rule of law—will be critically important for promoting economic relationships and for safeguarding national and human rights. It is no longer appropriate, if it ever was, for the United States, or indeed any nation, to view its legal system in isolation. And if law has become international and cross-cultural, tomorrow's lawyers must gain insight into the laws of many countries.

This book is a notable contribution to the new world system because it presents in clear terms the core doctrines of American law, as well as a sophisticated view of the American legal system as an ongoing process. Practitioners and professors, business people and students, indeed anyone here or abroad who seeks transnational understanding will profit greatly from the chapters of my colleagues.

The book should also be viewed in a larger context—as part of a new, multi-faceted effort, which is well under way, to establish at New York University School of Law the first truly global law school program.

To appreciate this development in legal education, it should be compared to the usual pattern. Reflecting the internationalization of law, American law schools in recent years have enrolled foreign students and American students have studied abroad. As a result, many schools now present an array of traditional and interdisciplinary courses in public international law, private international law, comparative law and related subjects. It is also common for American law schools to invite overseas professors to visit for a semester or year, just as American law teachers often spend a period at a foreign law school. In addition, conferences are held each year on topics of international importance, and there are increasing links between the law libraries of American law schools and those abroad. New York University Law School has long been a leader in these activities, all of which expand understanding among countries and peoples.

But these efforts fall far short of the current need. As Vice Chancellor Duncan Rice of New York University recently said, traditional programs, however admirable, 'do not integrate an international mindset into the work' of academic institutions. In other words, what has occurred to date in American law schools represents a 'peripheral model of internationalism,' rather than a structure that expresses globalism in every part of the enterprise.

Seeking to break through the customary boundaries, NYU Law has launched two new programs, each unique in concept and each requiring a major commitment of resources; taken together they will create a new form of law school. The first, the global faculty program, will add to NYU's faculty each year about twenty leading law professors from around the world. The arrangements with these professors depart from the usual mode of international visits, which, however pleasant and useful, are almost always one-shot affairs and, with rare exceptions, represent the only formal tie between the law school and the visitor. The NYU plan, which was inaugurated in 1994, fully integrates international faculty into the law school's academic program and the related activities of faculty, together, that largely define the institution.

Most important, many of NYU's global law faculty are long term members of the community, returning each year to offer courses and seminars. As such, they develop the scholarly relationships and perspectives that can come from such an ongoing commitment. Further, the courses taught by the global law faculty cut across the entire curriculum and are available to all NYU law students, not merely those who anticipate careers as international lawyers. Since the twenty members of the global law faculty annually teach hundreds of students, both foreign and domestic, they have a striking impact upon the legal education at NYU and play an increasingly visible role in its intellectual life.

For example, a German corporations law expert might be asked to teach or co-teach a comparative corporations course that would be offered in addition to the basic course. Students taking the special course would not only gain a deeper understanding of corporations generally but would also be able to understand American corporate law better by viewing it from a transnational perspective, including exploration of alternative approaches. This methodology enables students who are interested in practicing corporate law to be better prepared to meet their clients' needs in an increasingly internationalized law practice, and it provides the next generation of legal scholars with tools to construct imaginative new regimes for business associations.

The argument holds in other areas. Constitutional law deals with political and legal issues that most countries encounter. Having a Japanese scholar, for example, teach a course in comparative constitutional law or co-teach parts of the basic constitutional law course brings out aspects of American law that might be culturally hidden from American faculty and students. The argument is even stronger with advanced classes that specialize in particular doctrines, like freedom of expression or separation of powers. Many of the issues that Americans may overlook are central to the debates of other countries, and vice versa. Familiarity with the treatment elsewhere of hate speech, for instance, can help constitutional law practitioners and scholars to anticipate current controversies and frame solutions that otherwise might not occur to Americans.

There also are ample opportunities for members of the global law faculty to teach imaginative new courses, including seminars focusing on comparative research in a foreign legal system that are taught in their own language. Such seminars not only assist students to enhance their language ability and to monitor developments in the law of another country, but also permit the increasing number of bilingual students to explore a foreign legal system in the most effective way, through ideas expressed in the native tongue rather than through a translation in which something of the original is inevitably lost.

In short, the aspiration is to go beyond the conventional supplementation of an American legal education through a dose of comparative or international law. To be sure, traditional courses often provide a different perspective on a familiar legal problem. But they also tend to reinforce a conception that foreign law is peripheral, lurking permanently on the outskirts of American law. NYU is encouraging a curriculum and a pedagogy that assist students to recognize that their professional and intellectual lives have a global or non-United States aspect whatever their chosen specialty.

The second feature of the global law school program is the Hauser Scholars Program, which provides up to twenty full scholarships each year for leading graduate law students throughout the world to come to NYU. Each year, this elite cadre will join American counterparts in a laboratory of international diplomacy, business, and culture to hone skills, to learn from each other, and to develop working relationships that will last a lifetime as they become the legislators, judges, ambassadors, and policy-makers of tomorrow's world.

A special committee of eminent scholars, international lawyers, business leaders, and government officials chooses the winners, after an extensive and multi-levelled competition. Sir Robert Jennings, former President of the International Court of Justice, chairs the committee, which seeks individuals with intellectual and leadership ability and a capacity to participate productively in a multi-national community of scholars and practitioners. Hauser Scholars receive full tuition, room and board, travel expenses, and a nominal stipend to permit them access to the myriad opportunities afforded by residence in New York City.

Once at NYU, Hauser Scholars are integrated into the life of the law school. They take most of their classes with American students, and they are invited to partake in extra-curricular activities. The Scholars also participate in a range of special program activities and events. These include weekly meetings featuring talks by faculty, alumni, and other guest speakers; visits with prominent figures in the community; and an annual conference organized around a topic of international interest and designed to encourage graduates to return to Washington Square to reconnect with their colleagues.

Along with existing programs for international students at NYU, the new strategies for Hauser Scholars over time will create a world network of academics and practitioners who have shared a special learning experience and who will have developed valuable bonds with each other.

In launching the first global law school program NYU has capitalized on a unique advantage: a spectacular residential campus in New York City—the legal and economic center of the world, the headquarters of the United Nations, and the site of hundreds of diplomatic missions and dozens of organizations like the Council on Foreign Relations, the Asia Society, and the Lawyers Committee for Human Rights. NYU itself rests in a celebrated neighborhood, Greenwich Village, which fosters an informality and intimacy that provide a genuine sense of shared community. Many of the law school's faculty and 90 percent of its students live in modern residential buildings within walking distance of the campus. With world leaders and important figures from law, politics, and business just a few minutes away (and often on campus), no better setting exists for building and transmitting a global experience.

Fundamentals of American Law is an integral part of the global law school program at NYU. Its basic introduction to American law for lawyers, business people and students throughout the world will enable them to converse with their American counterparts and effectively translate American legal ideas to their clients. The book should therefore contribute significantly to the ultimate objective of NYU's global law effort—to facilitate the capacity of law to address social problems and satisfy human needs.

TABLE OF CASES

TABLE OF LEGISLATION

INTRODUCTION

JUSTICE WILLIAM J. BRENNAN, JR.

When the faculty of New York University School of Law invited me to introduce this book to foreign lawyers, college students, American business executives, and others with a curiosity about the American legal system, I must confess that I felt a bit out of my element. It has been nearly 70 years since I was a business student at Wharton. And for almost 50 years, I have been removed from the practice of law in the hustle and bustle of an ever-changing world.

Over the decades much has changed. The law is far more intimately interwoven into our lives and businesses today than it was when I was studying business and advising business executives. In those days, federal, state, and local legislatures had little to say about an employer's obligations to employees or to the environment. The tax code and securities rules were just a sliver of their current size. And administrative agencies were few and limited in power.

All that has changed in the intervening decades. Today's lawyers and the clients they advise must be aware of a tangle of regulations from a veritable alphabet soup of federal agencies and regulatory schemes—EEOC, SEC, FDA, EPA, NLRB, OSHA, ERISA, CERCLA, to name just a few—and their state counterparts. A single major transaction, such as the acquisition of a factory, could implicate labor regulations, securities regulations, employment regulations, occupational safety regulations, environmental regulations, tax regulations, and commercial laws, most of which were nonexistent or marginally relevant in my day.

Similarly, the practice of law has evolved into a very different trade from the one that I plied. When I represented my last client, law practice was essentially a local matter. When drafting a contract for one of my New Jersey clients, I might have worried about New York law, but it would never have dawned on me to wonder about the ramifications of foreign law on the transaction. Nor could I have imagined that a lawyer a world away might care to know about the American rule on, say, the enforceability of a clause of that contract or the tax consequences of the transaction. Even in my years as a judge, I gave scarcely a thought to global implications of American law. Of course, I hoped that our Constitution, and particularly our Bill of Rights, would serve as a beacon of human rights for the world to follow. But I did not contemplate the possibility that our nation's judicial pronouncements or legislation would have much impact on the rest of the world.

In the past decade or two, all that has also changed. Where international commerce was once limited to a handful of well worn trade routes, economic transactions have spun an intricate web across the world. The push of a button can beam information, technology, and investment capital as easily to Tokyo as to Topeka. And a captain of industry in New York is as likely to send goods or services to Santiago as to San Francisco. Modern merchants span cultural and language divides seemingly as wide as the oceans between them.

This global marketplace is the setting for innumerable transactions. Some are between private parties. Some involve a governmental entity as either a party to the transaction, an intermediary, or a regulator. Whether or not the parties are aware of it, each transaction is governed by some set of legal rules. Increasingly, those rules are American laws.

This book, which would have had little utility to college students, businesspersons, or foreign lawyers of my time, except perhaps as a passing curiosity, is an extraordinarily useful compendium of the fundamentals of the American legal system. The circumstances in which this book will be of value are as varied as the forms of commercial transactions. A business executive contemplating a transaction should know when it is time to call a tax specialist or an expert in employment law. The same executive should be aware that a seemingly innocuous change in benefits or in the manner of disposing of waste might trigger consequences within the jurisdiction of several agencies.

Similarly, when negotiating with an American party, a foreign lawyer must appreciate that American law will often dictate the range of options that are available to his or her American counterpart. If, for example, a South African corporation wants assurances from the board members of its American counterpart, it might be important to understand the limits of board power. Or if an American party to a contract will be taxed under the United States tax code, it would be helpful to know what could influence the tax liability. Or if a multinational conglomerate wishes to move against a United States competitor, it would certainly want to appreciate its potential tort or antitrust liability. These will be issues of primary concern to American lawyers involved in any international transaction. Without an understanding of why American lawyers advise their clients as they do, the foreign lawyer could overlook crucial aspects of a transaction and will negotiate less effectively on the client's behalf.

The purpose of the book, as the title declares, is to introduce the 'fundamentals' of the American legal system. This book does not pretend to be an exhaustive treatise on each of the areas of American law that might be relevant to our colleagues in other nations. The foreign lawyer's role ordinarily demands less detailed knowledge. Ordinarily, the foreign lawyer must feel confident conversing with an American counterpart about the legal constraints on business or other decisions of the principals involved and conveying this information to the client clearly and accurately. Definitive guidance on the specifics of American law is usually left to an American lawyer retained for expertise in a particular area of American law.

Each of the substantive chapters of this book has a dual objective. The first is to outline the tenets of the field—what Americans might call the 'black letter law.' The second is to sketch the legal theories and social policies that inform these rules. Because American law in many of the areas covered is constantly evolving, an understanding of basic policies can help the observer understand how a development relates to the larger body of established doctrine and perhaps even chart future changes.

The most cursory review of this book will impress upon the reader the monumental changes in law that developed over the past 200 years since our Constitution was ratified, and, indeed, even over my 34 years on the Supreme Court. In the early years of the republic 'American' law was, in fact, largely English common law. It was transplanted by a group of former colonial subjects who had begun their revolution in order to secure their 'rights as Englishmen'. In the nineteenth century, legal innovation occurred mostly at the state level, as common law courts adapted old doctrines to the circumstances of a new and growing nation. In this century, the momentum of reform began to shift from the states to the federal government, as new regulatory agencies and new constitutional restraints on state action augured a coming supremacy of federal law. Many areas of law discussed in this book, such as environmental, workplace safety, and securities regulation, are thoroughly modern phenomena introduced in this century by federal legislation.

The opening chapters help explain the two fundamental forces behind these remarkable changes. Chapter 1, covering the common law method of analysis, should leave the reader with the sense that much of the law, at least that which is made by judges, is not cast in stone. Chapter 2 describes the federal structure, which promoted further experimentation and growth, as well as the separation of powers, which allocates distinct functions and roles among the three branches of the federal government—the legislative, executive, and judicial branches. Each level of the intricate hierarchy of American government plays an important role in generating and interpreting legal norms. While it is a tenet of federalism that national law must reign supreme over contrary local law, laws promulgated at the various levels of government often complement rather than contradict each other. As a result, American lawyers must be well versed in rules generated by federal, state, and municipal bodies in order to render competent advice to their clients. And they must also be aware of which powers are solely within the province of one branch and which are shared, in order to assess the ability of a government agency to deliver on a promise.

One can scarcely overstate the significance of the federal structure to practicing lawyers or the meteoric growth of federal law in modern times. At the turn of the century, for example, a lawyer advising a client on a real estate purchase would need to be conversant in the law of conveying real property and little else. A modern lawyer, by contrast, would be committing malpractice if she failed to advise her client on such issues as zoning restrictions, environmental controls, municipal 'set aside' requirements, and tax consequences. Some of this new law is federal, some state, and some local. Some may be overlapping, requiring multiple filings of essentially the same information before different governmental agencies. To ascertain the relevant norms, a lawyer would need to consult a variety of statutory compilations, case reports, and other research tools. All this information must then be synthesized into a coherent plan of action for the client.

The dispersal of law-making competence over several different layers of government complicates the practice of law, to be sure. But it is nevertheless a great strength of our legal system. Smaller governmental units tend to be more responsive to local concerns, and the large number of entities promulgating new norms promotes legal innovation. I wholeheartedly endorse Justice Louis Brandeis's view of the fifty states as 'laboratories of democracy'—a phrase that could be easily applied to any entity in the federal system seeking to address social problems through legal reform.

Reigning supreme over all laws promulgated by any branch of government at any level is the federal Constitution and the Bill of Rights. Together, they constitute our nation's single most important contribution to the world. The Constitution grants the federal government the authority to operate in particular areas. More importantly, though, it limits what any governmental body at any level may do.

The Constitution's limitations are multifaceted, encompassing relations between the legislative, executive, and judicial branches of the federal government; between and among the states and the federal government; and between and among individuals and the state and federal governments. Some of these limits are mentioned explicitly in the constitutional text. Most, however, have been developed over time by a federal judiciary that plays an active role in interpreting broad phrases of the Constitution, such as 'due process' and 'equal protection of the laws'.

American courts interpreting these and other phrases are empowered to strike down legislative or executive acts. This power stems from the belief, fundamental to our democracy, that for all the good that may come from state intervention in the lives of citizens, government intrusion can infringe liberty. In keeping with this principle, the Constitution demands a strong justification for most governmental actions, particularly those potentially affecting the core of liberties protected by the Bill of Rights. It is the expectation that this mechanism will be used frequently and vigorously that has led Americans to view their Constitution as the ultimate touchstone of legitimacy for every area of our law, whatever its source or subject.

The foreign attorney, college student, or business executive encountering the American legal system is thus presented with a dual agenda. The first task is to become acquainted with the substance of legal doctrines that are increasingly complex and interrelated. Coming to understand American law should be an especially informative process for readers in developing countries, or in countries just now making the transition to market economies, for whom areas such as securities regulation, corporate law, and bankruptcy are as new in their conception as in their detail. The second task—more subtle, but equally important—is to understand the American legal system as an ongoing process, one substantially more fluid than the large body of fixed doctrine described in this book might lead one to believe. Many core doctrines are indeed permanent, but so is an underlying belief in the capacity of the law to change and expand to meet new social conditions. It is my hope that this admirable collection will assist its readers in accomplishing both tasks and provide a true introduction to the 'Fundamentals American Law'.

I

GENERAL PRINCIPLES

1

COMMON LAW SYSTEMS

GRAHAM HUGHES

I. Introduction

American legal systems, and all others that have grown from English roots, are characterized as 'common law', in contrast with the systems of continental Europe that are derived from Roman law and are called 'civil law' systems. England never absorbed Roman law principles and methodology, but developed its law from singular, native sources which, with the spread of English social culture, have become the foundation of the law in most English-speaking countries, including the United States.

The earliest idea of the common law was advanced by the English kings' judges some 900 years ago in an attempt to create a national legal system and to consolidate royal power through the centralization of the administration of justice. The national, royal courts proved very attractive to litigants because of their relative freedom from corruption and their ability to enforce judgments on a national basis through the executive power of royal officials. The law they applied was said to be 'common', because it allegedly represented customs common to the whole kingdom, in contrast with rules applied only locally, or with the law in ecclesiastical courts that were applying a foreign system. The common law thus had a unifying, state-building aspect which had both a practical and an ideological appeal.

What were the origins of this emerging common law? While there were some royal statutes even from the earliest times, the primary sources were not legislative. The common law was declared by the judges, although it was certainly not wholly invented by them. While its identification with the general customs of the nation was certainly exaggerated, there is no doubt that much of it consisted of a blending of Anglo-Saxon customary rules and principles with northern French practices and procedures familiar to the governing Anglo-Norman elite. In the process of selecting customary rules and practices from two cultures, from a very early date the judges displayed the practical genius of common law culture in building a structure of acceptable and efficient rules and principles. For, while the judges stated that the law existed already and that they were merely discovering or declaring it, there can be no doubt that in early times the process was a highly creative one of choosing and elaborating. To take one example, the common law judges held that primogeniture (the exclusive inheritance of real property by the oldest son, when there were male children) was part of the common law, although it is clear that, before the courts took this position, primogeniture was in fact only one mode of inheritance for certain kinds of military land-holding, competing with older English customs of equal division and other forms of inheritance.

The early centuries also exhibited an important phenomenon that has always continued to characterize common law systems. England developed at a very early date a powerful group of learned lawyers (the Bar), who enjoyed a high status and who were regarded as virtual equals by the judges. The arguments these barristers, as they were called, addressed to the courts are preserved in ancient law reports. They rely heavily on appeals to the authority of particular earlier decisions of the courts (precedent), which are treated as being worthy of the greatest respect if not absolutely binding. At the same time there is vigorous argument among the lawyers and the judges about the best way of understanding earlier decisions in the light of general considerations of efficiency and justice. In this way the law developed through a dialogue between judges and lawyers, with the courts often adopting the reasoning and language urged upon them by the members of the Bar.

Through this process of ongoing argument and adjudication, the common law became not merely a collection of individual authoritative decisions, but also a body of principles and concepts of public policy expressed and repeated by judges from one generation to another. From the earliest days, the common law did not show slavish respect for individual decisions, but sought to uncover the general principles and policy that best expressed the development of a line of cases in an area. So, in the nineteenth century, an English judge defined the common law as 'a system which consisted in applying to new combinations of circumstances those rules which we derive from legal principles and judicial precedents'.[1]

In this way, through the interaction of the judges and lawyers, the common law in its early centuries laid the foundations of the modern Anglo-American law of contracts, torts (civil wrongs), criminal law and the law of real property (interests in land). While there has been later statutory intervention in all these areas, the underlying governing principles and style of argument and decision-making are still those worked out long ago in the emerging years of the common law.

As commercial activity increased and became more sophisticated, an important additional field of jurisdiction was acquired by the common law. Disputes between commercial buyers and sellers, and those engaged in other commercial transactions, were traditionally resolved by arbitration under customary rules developed by traders (the 'law merchant'). Always anxious to increase their jurisdiction, and always willing to incorporate reasonable and convenient customs, the common law courts in the eighteenth century absorbed the customs of the law merchant and soon became the forum for commercial litigation and for developing and modernizing this body of law. When large sections of commercial law were later codified, as in the English Sale of Goods Act 1893 and the twentieth century American Uniform Commercial Code, although some reforms were introduced, much of the statutory content represented a restatement of common law principles.

One other fundamental theme must be noticed in the early evolution of the common law. While the common law evolved in the royal courts and was enforced by royal officers, its fundamental justification from the first identified itself with the idea and the ideal of the traditional and binding customs of the English people.

Doctrines of absolute royal sovereignty, that were a part of continental European Roman law systems, were rejected by common law theory. As conflicts between King and Parliament grew sharper in the seventeenth century, the common law judges became leading advocates of the Parliamentary position, and the great Chief Justice Coke observed in 1611 that the King 'hath no prerogative but that which the law of the land allows him'.[2]

Early declarations of the liberty of the subject and of restrictions on royal power (such as the famous Magna Carta [Great Charter] of 1215) came to be seen as part of the common law tradition. The result was that, in the English civil war in the seventeenth century between King and Parliament, the common law lawyers for the most part were on the Parliamentary side

---

[1] Per Lord Wensleydale in *Mirehouse* v. *Mennell*, 131 Eng. Rep. 482, 8 Bing. 490.
[2] *Case of Proclamations*, 77 Eng. Rep. 1352, 1354; 12 Co. Rep. 74, 76 (1611).

whose victory strengthened the view that the common law was an embodiment of fundamental liberties and human rights.

This ideological aspect had a powerful influence on the American colonies in their war of independence against England. The Americans invoked their rights under the common law as against royal prerogatives and saw themselves not as rebels, but as upholding the true and best traditions of their English heritage. Rights and privileges that later came to be embodied in the United States Constitution, such as the general requirement that no one may be deprived of life, liberty, or property without due process of law, can be traced back to Magna Carta and the general principles of the common law.

II. The Reception of the Common Law in America

When the English colonized North America, eventually overcoming competition from the French and other nations, foremost among the many practices and institutions that they imported was the common law. Since the common law was used as an ideological weapon in the American struggle for independence, the severing of links with England brought little change in the basic structure of the legal system. The content and method of the common law were absorbed into American social culture and have never been displaced.

This reception of the common law in the United States was greatly stimulated by the publication of what is surely the most influential treatise in the history of Anglo-American law. In the late eighteenth century an English judge, Sir William Blackstone, published four volumes entitled *Commentaries on the Laws of England*. Blackstone combined great talent as a systematizer and expounder of the common law with great literary grace and style. His treatise gave the common law a modern presentation in an orderly and attractive manner, whereas before it had been accessible only in thousands of cases in the law reports and in ancient and out-of-date institutional works. The development of the law was also brilliantly linked by Blackstone with the constitutional and political history of England.

Blackstone's work was enormously popular, particularly in the United States, where law libraries were few and incomplete, and where a single, compendious presentation of the law greatly enhanced the prestige and accessibility of common law doctrine. As one commentator put it:

It is the advent of Blackstone which opened the eyes of American scholars to the broader field of learning in the law. He taught them, for the first time, the continuity, the unity, and the reason of the Common Law—and just at a time when the need of a unified system both in law and politics was beginning to be felt in the Colonies. [3]

Blackstone's work insured the continued reception of the common law from the American colonies into the constituent states of the new American Republic. Each state has a large measure of sovereignty, subject to the national application of federal statutes and the requirements imposed nationally by the United States Constitution. Thus, it has been inevitable that the common law has not developed in exactly the same way in different states. At one time or another a state may have a judiciary and a political climate that is relatively liberal or relatively conservative when compared with the majority of states. The economic and social interests to which the judiciary must pay attention in a state with a largely agricultural economy may be very different from those that obtain in a highly industrialized state with a very large urban population. Thus, although a single common law was originally exported from England to America, a number of factors has led to the development of different common law rules in different states, notably in such areas as torts and criminal law.

For example, courts in an agricultural state may have felt local pressure to develop a strong form of liability for nuisances that interfered with the exploitation of land for agricultural puposes, while courts in an industrial state may have countenanced weaker rules of liability in this area in order not to burden emerging industrial enterprises with heavy costs. That different judges, operating under different social conditions, should develop the common law from an original stock of rules and principles in rather different ways is hardly surprising. What is more important is the continued uniformity of the common law techniques of litigation and decision-making.

It should be noted that, while each set of state courts has inherited the law-making power of the common law judicial tradition, this is not true of the United States federal courts. These courts are creatures of the United States Constitution, possessing only jurisdiction and powers expressly conferred by that Constitution. But, in practice, this does not produce any striking difference in the adjudicatory style of the federal courts. For example, the Constitution confers power on federal courts to decide maritime and admiralty cases. In exercising this power, the federal courts have always drawn upon ancient common law precedents in the maritime area. Again, federal courts are empowered to decide cases in which the parties are citizens of different states but, in such cases, the federal court must apply the law of the

---

[3] Warren, *A History of the American Bar*, p. 177.

state whose law governs the dispute. In this capacity the federal court sits as if it were a court of that state, which means that it must seek to apply the state law in a traditional common law manner, drawing upon common law techniques of interpretation and development where the state law is unclear.

Also, it should be emphasized that, in applying statutory federal law, the federal courts over time have naturally built up a large body of precedent and thus tend to proceed in a traditional common law manner. This is particularly evident in the interpretation of the Constitution, where the Supreme Court, while strictly bound by constitutional provisions, often confronts a case where the broad and vague constitutional language does not point to an obvious resolution. In these cases, the Court relies heavily on its own precedents and previous opinions in a classical common law manner.

III. The Growth of Legislation and Regulation

In the nineteenth century, the increasing complexity of commercial and social life created a growing need for intervention and regulation by government, both at the state and federal levels. This phenomenon led to a massive increase in legislative activity, a tendency that has intensified greatly in the twentieth century.

Modern regulation would be impossible to effect and implement with the old, pure common law method of slowly building rules and principles through authoritative judicial decisions in individual cases. If we consider the need to create schemes of regulation that will bring order and safety into the aviation industry, or the need in so many areas for regulatory codes that will reduce environmental pollution, it is apparent that this aim can only be realized through the drafting of codes by a central authority that can study a whole field of problems and attempt to advance a unified set of solutions. Such codes must go through several stages—initial drafting by committees, assisted by technical experts, submission to legislative committees for scrutiny and finally enactment by a legislative body. In turn, the legislative body must generally empower continuously-operating government entities, such as the Environmental Protection Agency or the Food and Drug Administration, to draft more detailed, but equally binding regulations.

These typical forms of law-making activity in the modern regulatory state could never be accomplished by the slow and fragmentary resolution of individual disputes by appellate courts. Judicial decision-making is, by its nature, designed to resolve immediate and particular claims made by a party under existing law, and the courts lack the power, the expertise, and the personnel to promulgate broad schemes of regulation. Indeed, any such attempt would be seen as an illegitimate usurpation of the legislative prerogative.

In the United States much of this regulatory rule-making is federal in nature—embodied in statutes of the United States Congress and regulations of federal agencies and departments. Its subject matter and content seem very far removed from the simpler concerns of the common law in older times, but it would be mistaken to conclude that the importance of the common law has been destroyed. There are several senses in which the common law system is still sharply recognizable and very vital.

IV. The Continued Vitality of the Common Law

Common law rules and principles in a modern, developed form still govern important areas of litigation between private parties—in the law of torts (civil wrongs) and in contractual relations. Again, while all states have codes of criminal law and criminal procedure, their most general elements are for the most part codifications and refinements of ancient common law concepts. If this is true of the content of substantive rules, it is even more true of the nature of legal institutions and processes. The adversary mode of civil trial, with the proceedings dominated by the presentation of the case by private attorneys representing the parties, the use of a jury and the consequent strictness of rules as to what can be admissible evidence—all these are essential features of a common law tradition. In criminal procedure, ancient common law institutions, such as the grand jury (the body that files a formal charge), and the highly adversarial mode of trial, still dominate the scene, while common law protections for the accused, such as the privilege against self-incrimination and the prohibition on double jeopardy, have been translated into guarantees contained in the United States Constitution.

One of the purest areas of common law, remaining to a great extent untouched by legislation, is the law of torts. The history and present condition of this branch of the law provide a good illustration of the nature of the common law and its ability to adapt to modern life.

In its earliest days the common law developed a simple remedy for simple wrongs when the king's courts began to issue three types of writs (a writ was a royal command directing a person to come to answer a complaint in the king's court)—for trespass to land, trespass to goods, and trespass to the person. The first two offered remedies for intrusions on land or for improper seizure of another's goods, while trespass to the person provided a remedy for intentionally and directly inflicted physical injury in the nature of assault and battery. The elements of direct and intentional infliction were useful in justifying the jurisdiction of the king's courts since they had aspects of a criminal attack on the person and so were a breach of the king's peace.

However, difficulties soon developed as plaintiffs sued for injuries that were not inflicted directly, or were not malicious or intentional, but rather were the result of a defendant's negligent conduct. No doubt in part from a desire to do justice, surely combined with a desire to increase their jurisdiction, the common law courts soon adapted the early trespass writs to accommodate allegations of harm caused indirectly or through negligence. While the full process was a slow one, by the early nineteenth century, both in England and in the different jurisdictions of the United States, the common law courts had developed a remedy for negligent infliction of harm with most of the modern elements in place.

The increasing complexity of modern life never ceases to pose fresh problems. In the action for negligence that had grown out of the old writ of trespass, the burden of proof was fully on the plaintiff. In negligence cases (which soon constituted the great majority of torts suits) this burden was often difficult if not impossible to discharge since the details of how the accident came about (why the boiler burst, why the train was derailed, why the airplane crashed) were either impossible to demonstrate or else were peculiarly within the knowledge of the defendant.

Once again the common law displayed its adaptability. The judges effectively relaxed the burden of proof in many cases by relying on a legal maxim, *res ipsa loquitur*, (Latin for 'the matter speaks for itself'). Under this approach, whenever the activity in question was under the control of the defendant and the accident was of the kind that usually does not happen without negligence on the defendant's part, these circumstances would suffice to meet the plaintiff's initial burden of proof, requiring the defendant to respond by showing that he had acted with due care in all respects. In this way the nineteenth century common law of torts began to move forward to a plaintiff-oriented approach, less preoccupied than in the past with notions of moral responsibility, thereby preparing the way to deal with modern concerns about equitably distributing loss in an industrialized society of large-scale commercial distribution of goods and services.

In this century there has been a mass of litigation in the United States concerned with injuries from defective products. The early common law could find no reason to offer a remedy in the absence of direct contractual relations between the manufacturer or seller of a product and the injured plaintiff. But many plaintiffs had no direct relationship with the manufacturer and perhaps not even with a vendor. They were third parties into whose hands a product had come or perhaps even bystanders injured by a defective vehicle.

Without any legislative intervention, common law courts made a great leap forward by developing a general theory of duty of care in torts, under which manufacturers were held to have a legal obligation to use all due care to ensure that their products would not injure anyone who could reasonably be foreseen to be a likely user or to be otherwise within the zone of risk defined by the product's defect. As a result, in modern times a sweeping concept of liabilty has been developed, conceived in the common law tradition by the courts acting alone.

However, the common law has not been a perfect law-making instrument, always able to devise new concepts and theories to adapt the law to modern conditions. Its history has been uneven, and there are examples of its failure to abandon old and obstructive, even unjust, positions. Tort law again serves very well as a source of illustration. The old common law rule was that, if the plaintiff had in any way contributed to an accident by her own negligence, she could recover nothing even if the defendant's negligence was the major causal factor. Some jurisdictions in the United States managed to modify or even abandon this position by judicial decisions within the common-law tradition and arrived at a position of 'comparative negligence', under which a negligent plaintiff would be granted relief, but with the modification that her damages would be reduced by an amount commensurate with her share of the fault.

However, in many states the courts felt too tightly bound by the weight of common law precedent to make such a change, or took the position that the change was too radical to be made by judicial action. In these states reform came through statute.

Again, some forms of novel claims presented in recent decades, for example, claims of racial discrimination in housing, or of sexual harassment in the workplace, were too innovative for the common law to absorb comfortably. In these areas, legislation has intervened to expand the scope of possible civil suits for damages. Private common law litigation to recover damages for civil wrongs has also been affected profoundly by the impact of insurance and, in the field of employment, by the development of Workers Compensation statutes, which offer a statutory scheme of compensation for job-related injuries without the burdens of proof and great expense of private litigation.

Nevertheless, by and large the common law of torts has displayed a remarkable flexibility to adapt to modern social complexities. As injuries from defective products came to constitute a large part of torts litigation, the common law forged ahead and developed doctrines of semi-strict liability, virtually guaranteeing a remedy for a plaintiff once a causal connection could be shown between the injury and a defect in the product. In this way tort law came to approximate an insurance system, in which industrial and commercial enterprises had to bear the burden of injuries to purchasers, users, and third parties as part of the cost of doing business.

Even more difficult complexities were resolved by some creative courts. A person who was injured when a medical drug or device turned out to be unreasonably dangerous often faced the difficulty that, after the passage of a considerable time, she might be unable to prove which manufacturer's products she had used when, as often happens, virtually identical drugs were produced by a number of companies. To meet this difficulty, some common law courts have permitted the plaintiff to join as co-defendants all substantial manufacturers of the product, who will then pay the damages in proportion to their share of the market, even though the plaintiff could not show which particular manufacturer had produced the harmful product she had used.

V. Precedent and the Growth of the Law

Such innovative judicial creativity demonstrates the frequent boldness of the common law tradition. In this sense the common law system has always contained a paradox. Its formal ideology offers strong allegiance to the notion of the binding force of precedent, on the theory that a legal system must protect settled expectations which would be dangerously disturbed if the highest courts were free to abandon positions that they had earlier declared with authority. This approach appears to carry a strongly conservative commitment to the status quo and to relegate the task of making important changes in the law to the legislature.

However, as the examples from the law of torts have shown, at least in some areas common law courts have sometimes acted in a radical and sweeping way to adapt ancient rules to modern needs. How can these apparently contradictory aspects of the common law tradition be reconciled? The answer moves us into theoretical jurisprudence, into legal philosophy, and into a discussion of how to explain the general concept of law. While the common law pays deference to the importance of precedent and *stare decisis* (an obligation to follow the rules laid down in earlier cases), at the same time, at its deepest theoretical level, the common law has never regarded individual cases as representing a final expression of the law on a particular point.

The starting point here must be a consideration of what exactly the common law has meant by adherence to precedent and fidelity to the maxim of *stare decisis*?

What legal proposition a decided case stands for is by no means obvious. Only the decisions of appellate courts carry authority, but these courts consist of three, five, seven or even nine judges. Appellate judges in common law systems are very conscious of their reponsibilty to present lower courts with opinions that offer guidance in future cases, and part of the common law tradition consists of an effort to fashion appellate opinions with this goal in view. In the highest appellate courts an important technique for achieving this aim is by producing, whenever possible, an 'opinion of the court', to which at least a majority of judges adheres. In this way, even when there may be dissents or individual expressions of opinion in concurrences, there is a single opinion that represents the authoritative views of a majority of the court.

But this hardly resolves the difficulty of stating with precision the 'holding' (*ratio decidendi*) of an appellate court—the core of the opinion which represents the propositions of law that will be binding on lower courts. First, even when the result is joined in by all the judges, different strands of reasoning may appear in the opinions of different judges, who are free to explain the decision in their own way and often do. Second, propositions of law are obviously always connected with the facts to which they are declared to be applicable. Since it is a vital part of the common law tradition that courts cannot declare authoritative legal generalities in the abstract, but only in relation to the facts of the dispute that they are adjudicating, the holding of a case can only be stated in terms of its essential facts. But what facts are essential or most important is neither preordained nor obvious. To some extent the opinion of the court may reveal what facts it considered to be essential, but the opinion will often leave room for disagreement.

Even when we have come to a decision about identifying the essential facts, we are left with the even more difficult problem of deciding how broad or how narrow are the propositions of law contained in, or that can be extracted from, the court's opinion which can be thought of as necessary for the decision of the case on the basis of the facts found to be essential. This problem is complicated by the tendency of American courts to write opinions at considerable length, in which the main issues are revisited, with a variety of pronouncements and the proffering of different lines of reasoning, some of which may appear to be much broader than others.

An example may be helpful here. At a time when the duty of care imposed on manufacturers to ultimate consumers was unclear, an appellate court had to decide a case in which a man bought his companion a lemonade contained in an opaque bottle.[4] When she had poured most of the liquid into a glass and drunk some of it, the woman discovered the decomposing remains of a snail at the bottom of the bottle. She became very ill and sued the manufacturer of the lemonade. The appellate court ultimately decided in her favor. But what should we take to be the holding in the case?

---

[4] *McAlister (Donoghue)* v. *Stevenson*, [1932] A.C. 562 (House of Lords: Scotland).

At an absurd level of specificity, we could say that the case stands for the proposition that manufacturers of lemonade in opaque bottles are liable to people who become ill after drinking the beverage and then discovering a decomposing snail in the bottle. But, while such a fact-specific approach to the holding is intuitively ridiculous, it is much harder to decide to what level of generality we should ascend in uncovering the precedential authority of the decision. We might pitch this at the highest level of generality by postulating that all manufacturers of goods are liable to any person who is injured by defects in the product. But various modifications are possible. The holding in the case could be confined to food and drink products; it could be understood to be confined to a class who might be called 'consumers', as opposed to all third parties; it could be understood to apply only to cases where (as with the opaque bottle) the consumer had no reasonable opportunity to discover the defect. Under this last modification the holding would only extend to cases where consumers are exposed to traps or hidden dangers, and where they are entirely free of negligence in failing to discover the defect.

In searching for a 'holding' among these propositions of law of lesser or greater generality, considerable help will be derived from the manner and style in which the opinion of the court is written. But, as already suggested, the tendency of American courts to write at considerable length, with diffuse discussion of the legal issues, almost always permits debate about the exact dimensions of the holding.

The solution is to abandon any notion that the holding in a case is a definite entity that can be discovered by applying some infallible formula. A better approach is to understand that the application of the doctrine of precedent in the common law is a process of arriving at what a court perceives as the best understanding of a flow of judicial activity over time. In the long run, it is not the individual case that matters so much, but rather the understanding that modern courts give to a line of cases—the principles and policies that they have extracted from them and in the light of which they now read them. There would be no doctrine of precedent with any meaning if judges did not pay some decent respect to the earlier decisions of authoritative appellate courts. On the other hand, the law would become unduly rigid if courts could not interpret the holdings of earlier decisions with a degree of latitude that permits them to inject their own understanding of what will best serve justice or efficiency. The chains of precedent must not bind too tightly, and the doctrine of *stare decisis* is not unyielding. Indeed, at times an appellate court will openly abandon the reasoning of earlier decisions by overruling them, when the results they appear to dictate now seem inequitable or imprudent.

The correct statement of the doctrine of precedent, therefore, is that it imposes an obligation to seek the best understanding of the most basic principles that a line of cases expresses. The common law's fidelity is to principle and not to the isolated decision. The examples given earlier from the law of torts again serve to demonstrate this point. When the common law courts introduced the broad concept of a general duty of care in negligence, they did not present this as a novel intellectual construct. Rather, they canvassed earlier case law in the area, and then declared that these prior decisions, when analyzed as a field of law, pointed irresistibly to a movement, the next step of which must rationally be the generalization of a duty of care in broad terms. Thus, the common law is best understood as a movement of particular decisions towards a general set of principles that are equipped to do justice in changing conditions. This notion is beautifully expressed in the famous observation of an eighteenth-century Scottish judge, Lord Mansfield, who wrote that 'the common law works itself pure'[5] from case to case.

VI. The Institutions and Method of the Common Law

In a modern system, that is increasingly dominated by legislation and regulation, one of the most enduring legacies of the common law, and the most distinctive characteristic of common law systems, is a cluster of methods of adversarial presentation in litigation, of argument, and of decision-making, discussed in greater detail below.

Perhaps the most conspicuous feature of the common law heritage is the dominant role played by lawyers and the relatively retiring role played by judges. This may appear paradoxical in a system which we have said consists of judge-made law, but, as noted above, the common law system has always been a collaboration between judges and lawyers, with the latter playing a leading role.

We see this phenomenon in both the criminal and the civil law. In criminal law a trial is conducted by the prosecutor and defense lawyers, who choose what evidence to present. Judges have no investigating role and do not compile any preliminary dossier with respect to the defendant or the circumstances of the crime. Virtually all questioning of witnesses is conducted by the lawyers, with each witness being examined by the party who calls him and then cross-examined by the lawyer for the other party. The judge intervenes with questions to a very small extent.

In this way it is the lawyers who control the information presented and the

---

[5] *Omychund v. Barker*, 26 Eng. Rep. 15, 24; 1 A. and K. 22, 23 (1744).

record that is eventually compiled. (If the accused chooses to remain silent, she cannot be questioned at all since she is protected by the privilege against self-incrimination). A verdict of guilty or not guilty is returned by a jury of ordinary citizens who are instructed as to the applicable law by the judge.

This method, which is usually called 'adversarial,' in contrast with European systems, often called 'inquisitorial,' places great power in the hands of the lawyers and is a prime characteristic of common law systems. The judge plays a neutral and somewhat detached role as an 'umpire' or 'referee', being primarily concerned with making legal rulings, which frequently concern the admissibilty of evidence, since all American systems operate with complex rules which tightly control the testimony and other material that may be presented to a jury.

In civil cases the control exercised by the lawyers is equally extensive. Complex civil cases often entail lengthy pre-trial battles for information in which each side attempts to obtain discovery of documents from the other and to examine potential witnesses and parties under oath. Each side will try to learn as much as possible and to reveal as little as possible. Certainly, disputes as to what may be discovered, or as to what lengths examination of a witness may go, will, in the end, have to be submitted to a judge for resolution, but the tactics, the strategy, and most of the operational decisions are drawn up and conducted by the lawyers.

Civil cases, too, are often litigated before a jury and are also governed by complex rules of evidence. The record that is compiled, and the evidence to which the jury listens, are thus the construct of the lawyers, with the judge essentially serving as a necessary referee when the lawyers disagree.

The production of authoritative decisions in appellate opinions is, just as much as the trial, closely shaped by common law traditions. The appellate court cannot stray outside the 'record' (the pleadings, exhibits and transcript of the proceedings in the court below), and these, as we have seen, are wholly the product of the parties' lawyers working in a strongly adversarial manner. So strong is this tradition, that a party cannot generally rely on any issue that was not raised in a timely fashion in the court below. Appellate courts, except in cases of egregious error that led to fundamental injustice, take the position that any issue not timely raised in the earlier proceedings has been lost by 'procedural default.' Similarly, for the most part, an appellate court can only consider errors that have been urged by the appellant in her appellate 'brief' (the written argument for reversal of the decision below). Thus, an appellate court does not enjoy the power to conduct a free-ranging inquiry into the propriety of the decision in the court below, but is constrained by rules that lead to a tight and limited review, which is essentially framed by the actions of lawyers both at the trial and appellate levels.

VII. Interpretation of Statutes

By far the greater part of modern litigation and adjudication consists of the interpretation and application of statutes, regulations, and, very centrally in the American system, both the Constitution of the United States and, in state courts, the Constitution of the individual state. At first sight, these might seem to be tasks that are essentially alien to the common law tradition and ones to which that tradition has little to contribute.

But, in truth, the common law tradition contributes a great deal to the interpretation of legislation and regulation. In the first place, older statutes are often either simple codifications of common law positions or restatements of the common law with some reforming features. In such cases, the content of the common law is either wholly or partly preserved, and the courts will rely on common law precedent in interpreting the statute. For example, a murder statute may briefly reiterate key common law terms with respect to the necessary mental element for the crime, such as 'malice' or 'intent' or 'recklessness.' In filling out the meanings of these statutory terms in marginal cases, the courts will turn to a heritage of common law elaboration of these concepts.

Secondly, if a statute or regulation contains a modern innovation, it is the nature of the common law method to search for older common law analogies and often to rely upon them directly or, at least, to be influenced by them in reading the new provision. For example, to aid in the enforcement of modern schemes of regulation, it has become customary for the relevant statute to confer subpoena power (the power to compel the production of documents or to compel a person to give testimony under oath) upon a government department or agency. This has become an indispensable tool in the investigation of possible violations of administrative regulations, and such subpoena power is held and widely exercised by a host of governmental organs, such as the Securities and Exchange Commission, the Antitrust Division of the Justice Department, the Environmental Protection Agency etc. In interpreting such agency powers, the courts have tended to rely closely upon familiar common law doctrine concerning the traditional subpoena power of the grand jury when investigating possible criminal conduct. In a number of early cases the courts had to consider whether an agency must make any preliminary showing of relevance or need for information before it could exercise its subpoena power. Relying on centuries of precedent with respect to the grand jury, the conclusion ultimately reached was that agencies and government departments need make no such showing, but enjoyed the large freedom of inquiry traditionally associated with the grand jury.[6]

---

[6] *United States* v. *Morton Salt Co.*, 338 U.S. 632 (1950).

Thirdly, while the common law has always given unqualified recognition to the supremacy of the legislature, it has at the same time managed to preserve its traditional adjudicatory style with respect to the application of legislation. This is particularly evident in the United States where legislation is always subject to judicial review on the ground that it contravenes provisions of the federal or a state Constitution. More generally, 400 years ago the common law itself propounded a method of statutory interpretation. This exhortation to the judges in an old case[7] directed them to inquire what was the common law before the statute was passed, what was the defect in the common law that the statute was designed to remedy, and what was the 'true reason' for the statutory remedy. If we translate this ancient directive into modern terms, it can be perceived as a subtle defense of the common law tradition, not at all questioning the authority of the legislature, but at the same time insisting on the judicial power to search a statute in terms of the general store of legal principles developed by the common law for the best understanding of its policy goals.

Thus, the law is perceived as a whole in which statutes must be read in the light of a historical development of relevant principles by the common law courts.

Finally, and most important, the common law method inexorably imposes itself on the whole process of statutory interpretation. For, with the passage of time, statutory provisions become themselves the subject of a gathering body of case law in the appellate courts. In this way an important secondary jurisprudence of a purely common law nature comes into being, since, while the statute remains the original source of law, the appellate decisions interpreting it themselves have authority within the doctrine of precedent. Thus, almost as if it were a pure common law subject, the process of deciding cases under a statute often resolves into a familiar style of analyzing and synthesizing the cases that have accumulated in that area. The policy of the statute and the principles that govern its application are, in the end, extracted from a body of case law that has attached itself to the statute, and the court's opinion often consists for the most part of a discussion of previous judicial decisions in the area. Of course, all legal systems pay some attention to earlier decisions of appellate courts in such a context, but the distinctiveness of the common law method is that these decisions from the highest courts are strongly authoritative and become the principal guide in the search to determine how the statute should be understood.

---

[7] The maxims on which this is based are contained in *Heydon's Case*, 76 Eng. Rep. 637; 3 Co. 7 (1584).

VIII. The Future of the Common Law

The previous discussion should make clear that common law systems preserve a singular identity, which will endure with continued vitality in several senses. The actual content of important segments of American law represents continuous development from centuries of common law building of rules and principles through unalloyed judicial decision-making.

These areas notably include all the basic elements of liabilty and defense in the criminal law, most of the law of torts, the underlying general principles of the law of contracts, and a good deal of the basic concepts of property law. Many statutory intrusions have taken place in all these areas. In some cases statutes merely codify traditional common law positions with some modicum of reform; but, in others, while statutes may be sharply innovative in their particular impact, they still leave the underlying body of common law principle largely undisturbed.

Secondly, the common law method produces a mode of approaching law that permeates American legal education and therefore shapes the mindset and modes of analysis that distinguish the American lawyer.

This almost 1,000 year tradition is characterized by close attention to the individual appellate decision, by a concentration in legal scholarship on an analysis of judicial argument and decision-making, and by emphasis on the control of litigation through the lawyer's skilful use of legal tactics. While legislation and regulation are obviously a primary source of law in modern jurisprudence, the common law lawyer is trained to be aware that, in the end, judicial interpretation will be decisive and therefore to marshal and deploy the most effective techniques for bringing questions before the courts and persuading them to take a desired view of the statute.

Finally, the basic institutions and personnel of the legal system—the courts, the style of adversary joinder, the prominence of lawyers, the relatively retiring role of the judge, the basic rules of criminal and civil procedure and the rules of evidence—have all evolved through centuries of common law development, even though some of the rules are now codified. Thus, in spite of the dominant role of regulation and legislation in contemporary American legal systems, the content, the institutions, and the techniques of the common law still stamp American law with a distinctive aspect that provides a high degree of cultural legal unity in the English-speaking parts of the world.

2

THE SOURCES AND LIMITS OF LEGAL AUTHORITY

LAWRENCE G. SAGER

I. Introduction: Federalism and Separation of Powers

The distribution and limitation of legal authority in the United States is complex. Much of this complexity is a result of a federal structure that distinguishes government in the United States from most of the world's national legal systems. To a degree that may escape the notice of the casual observer versed in other legal systems, the United States remains a federal legal system, with each of the fifty states of the national union seized of largely independent legal authority, and the federal government, in turn, possessed of a sprawling legal authority overlapping that of the states. This feature of law in the United States is complicated still further by a tradition of localism within the respective states, pursuant to which important legal authority is often delegated to a diverse structure of local governmental entities.

In addition to the essentially hierarchical or *vertical* questions of legal authority posed by federalism in the United States, there are the *horizontal* questions of the distribution of authority among the different branches of government at any given level. Government in the United States is organized around the concept of a division of authority among the executive, legislative, and judicial branches. Questions of the distribution of authority among these branches are in some contexts taken very seriously, and are themselves the source of close and complex legal doctrine; this is especially but not exclusively so at the level of the federal government, where 'separation of powers' issues have from time to time been the object of important constitutional concern.

While there is nothing unique about the recognition of the division of governmental functions, there are two features of government in the United States that are unusual in this respect. First, unlike the parliamentary governments in almost all modern democratic states, the federal government (as well as those of the states) has a separately elected chief executive who presides over the executive branch of government. Secondly, the United States has for most of its history had a robust tradition of judicial enforcement of its Constitution.

Together, the vertical questions of federalism and the horizontal questions of separation of powers give shape to the complex structure of legal authority in the United States. An understanding of these structural features should offer the reader a sense of the tone or flavor of legal events in the United States.

II. The Basic Allocation of State and Federal Authority

A. *The Organic Legal Authority of the States*

The states are fundamental building-blocks of legal authority in the United States. Each state has its own constitution and laws, and the organic source of state authority is conceived as arising from these state constitutions. The federal Constitution pervasively presumes the existence of the states, and it is clear that the states could not be abolished or fundamentally reshaped without doing violence to the scheme of governmental authority contemplated by the Constitution. The organic power of the states is understood to be coextensive with the 'police power', that is, the power of government over its citizens generally. Federal constitutional limitations on state authority, accordingly, are understood to function as subtractions from the general warrant of the police power enjoyed by the states.

Cities, towns, counties, and other governmental entities inferior to the states are understood to be the delegates of state authority. The legal status of these municipal entities is largely a function of state constitutional and statutory law. As a result, there is considerable diversity among the states as to the form and authority of local governments.

B. The Limited (In Theory) Authority of the Federal Government

In contrast to the organic police power authority of the states, the federal government is understood to be a government of 'enumerated powers', which enjoys only that authority specifically granted to it by the various provisions of the federal Constitution. The enumerated powers structure of federal authority is implicit in the first three articles of the federal Constitution,[1] which read naturally as specific and limited grants of authority to the federal government; it is also stated explicitly in the Tenth Amendment to the Constitution, which provides that 'The powers not delegated to the United States by the Constitution, nor prohibited by it to the States, are reserved to the States respectively, or to the people'.

In principle, accordingly, all federal legislation is open to question on the grounds that it exceeds the enumerated and apparently rather narrow domain of federal legislative authority. But the realities of a national economy, and the overwhelming sense of national authority and responsibility that has come to dominate American constitutional law, have had the effect of removing most if not all legal barriers to the exercise of federal legislative authority. This is particularly true in the commercial contexts that are most likely to interest the foreign consumer of law in the United States; there, the authority of the United States Congress is for practical purposes as broad as that of the states.

Article I, Section 8 of the Constitution grants the United States Congress power, inter alia, 'To regulate Commerce with Foreign Nations, and among the several States, and with the Indian Tribes'.[2] This base of federal legislative authority, commonly known as 'the commerce clause', has from time to time been construed relatively narrowly; but for the last half century it has been seen as an all but limitless source of power to regulate commercial activity. The predicate terms of this grant of power have been construed broadly, and any federal legislation that substantially affects interstate commerce has been held to constitute a regulation of it. The result has been that legislation directed at very local commercial activities has been sustained as an exercise

---

[1] Article I concerns federal legislative power, Article II executive power, and Article III judicial power.
[2] Article I, Section 8 [3].

of commerce clause authority,[3] as has legislation the obvious end of which is social justice rather than economic efficiency.[4] In part, this result has been supported by reference to the general grant of authority with which Article I, Section 8 concludes, giving Congress the power, 'To make all Laws which shall be necessary and proper for carrying into Execution the foregoing Powers'.[5] In practice, 'necessary and proper' has been read as though the word 'necessary' was not included.

It would be best to assume that any federal regulation of commercial activity will be upheld as an exercise of commerce clause authority. There may, of course, be other constitutional or statutory objections to federal regulation, but a challenge based on the limits of Congress' enumerated power is unlikely to succeed. This picture may not be entirely static. In April 1995, the Supreme Court reversed a 60-year old tradition of deference to Congress as to the scope of the federal government's commerce clause authority, and invalidated a federal law which barred the possession of firearms in the vicinity of a school; the Court held that Congress had exceeded its commerce clause authority.[6] The Supreme Court thus may be in the midst of a reconsideration of this area of constitutional jurisprudence. For the moment, however, challenges to the federal regulation of commercial activity on this ground remain poor bets.

We have focused on the commerce clause because of the broad base for the exercise of federal authority it has become. But there are other important grants of authority to Congress as well. These include the power to levy taxes and spend money for the general welfare, to create federal courts inferior to the Supreme Court, to provide for military forces, and to declare war.

C. The Relationship Between State and Federal Authority: The Supremacy Clause

1. The primacy of federal law

Despite the pervasive commitment to the place of the states in the American constitutional scheme, the states are ultimately subordinate to federal

---

[3] See, e.g., *Russell* v. *United States*, 471 U.S. 858, 105 S.Ct. 2455 (1985), where it was assumed to be within Congress' authority to make it a federal crime for an individual to attempt to set fire to a two-unit apartment building that he rented to others; and *Wickard* v. *Filburn*, 317 U.S. 111, 63 S.Ct. 82 (1942), where the Supreme Court upheld legislation specifying a wheat quota that applied to wheat grown wholly for consumption on the producing farm.

[4] See, e.g., *Katzenbach* v. *McClung*, and *Heart of Atlanta Motel, Inc.* v. *United States*, 379 U.S. 241, 85 S.Ct. 348 (1964), both of which upheld civil rights legislation banning racial discrimination in public accommodations. See also *Equal Employment Opportunity Commission* v. *Wyoming*, 460 U.S. 226, 103 S.Ct. 1054 (1983).

[5] Article I, Section 8.   [6] *United States* v. *Lopez*, 115 S.Ct. 1624 (1995).

authority, in both theory and fact. The heart of this subordination is Article VI, Section 2 of the federal Constitution, the 'supremacy clause':

This Constitution, and the Laws of the United States which shall be made in Pursuance thereof; and all Treaties made, or which shall be made, under the Authority of the United States, shall be the supreme Law of the Land; and the Judges in every State shall be bound thereby, any Thing in the Constitution or Laws of any State to the Contrary notwithstanding.

Pursuant to the supremacy clause, otherwise valid federal laws are superior to conflicting state and local laws. The lowest federal legal stipulations are lexically prior to the highest state provisions. Thus, for example, a valid discretionary act by a single federal administrative official will prevail over a conflicting provision enshrined in a state constitution. When federal law prevails, it is said to 'preempt' the conflicting state provisions.

There is, of course, a conceptual bootstrap imbedded in the supremacy clause: as a federal constitutional provision announcing the supremacy of federal law, the supremacy clause assumes the underlying priority of federal authority, at least when that authority is expressed in the Constitution itself. But as a matter of history and practice, the Constitution has prevailed, supremacy clause and all, and the principle of federal supremacy is uncontroverted in modern law.

2. Preemption controversies

Two questions arise in cases where there is a possibility of the federal preemption of state law. First, federal legal authority is itself limited by the federal Constitution, and only valid federal enactments can preempt conflicting state provisions. As we have already seen, however, to the extent that a challenge to federal action is based on the limits of the enumerated powers of the federal government, it is likely to fail. Second, there is the question of whether a particular state legal provision is actually in conflict with federal authority. In contrast to the question of enumerated federal power, this question is often a close and controversial one.

Consider the following situation: Congress has passed legislation requiring that cigarette manufacturers include on each package of cigarettes a warning statement, which reads 'WARNING: THE SURGEON GENERAL HAS DETERMINED THAT CIGARETTE SMOKING IS DANGEROUS TO YOUR HEALTH'. Now, suppose that long after the effective date of this legislation, an individual who is suffering from lung cancer sues the company whose cigarettes she has smoked for many years; the essence of her claim is that the cigarettes were negligently manufactured, tested, and marketed, that the company in question failed to warn her of the danger in smoking its cigarettes, and further, that the company actively misrepresented the safety or danger involved in smoking its cigarettes. She sues in the state where she resides (which is where she bought and smoked the cigarettes) and invokes the law of that state as the basis of her various claims. The cigarette company argues that all state law on the question of a cigarette manufacturer's liability to smokers was preempted by the federal legislation requiring warning labels, and hence that there can be no State law liability for harms suffered by the plaintiff after the effective date of the federal legislation.

The company's claim is that Congress has 'occupied the field' of responsibility and liability for the manufacture of cigarettes, that is, that Congress has taken over the entire area, and ousted the states of authority. The resulting legal issue is characteristic of many contested claims of preemption under the supremacy clause. Formally, the question of whether Congress has occupied a particular field of regulation is one of intent, but it is often the case that Congress is silent, either through inadvertence or political expedience. As a practical matter, the question often becomes the counterfactual one of whether a sensible Congress embarked on lawmaking in the area in question would have preferred exclusive authority over the area or would have welcomed the parallel regulatory efforts of state and local governments.

Even when Congress has expressly addressed the question of preemption, and attempted to oust the states of at least some authority, it may speak in terms that leave details of the preemption in doubt. The actual cigarette warning label legislation, for example, did contain an express provision preempting state authority; faced with the question of the scope of the preemption, the Supreme Court was sharply divided, and ultimately ruled that some but not all state law claims were preempted.[7] Thus, while the principles underlying preemption are simple and absolute, their application in a particular case is often wrapped with interpretive difficulty.

3. Derivative principles of federal supremacy

From the unquestioned primacy of federal law, two additional, unsurprising restrictions on state authority have been derived. First, unless Congress grants the states explicit permission to do so, they may neither tax nor regulate the federal government in any of its various manifestations.[8] Second, while the states generally may tax and regulate persons or companies who

---

[7] See *Cipollone* v. *Liggett Group, Inc.*, 505 U.S. 504, 112 S.Ct 2608 (1992).

[8] Chief Justice John Marshall, famously justifying the immunity of the federal government from unconsented-to state taxation: 'The power to tax is the power to destroy'. *McCulloch* v. *Maryland*, 17 U.S.(4 Wheat.) 316, 431 (1819).

work for the federal government as employees or private contractors, they may not do so under circumstances that substantially impede the federal government in the pursuit of its diverse projects.

D. The Continued Importance of State and Local Law

In the face of a constitutional tradition that bestows essentially unlimited authority on the national legislature and concedes unequivocal priority to national law, one might expect to discover that basic lawmaking in the United States had become nationalized in the current era. But this is far from true. To a surprising extent, the basic components of modern life—the family, business relationships, civil and criminal liability for injurious conduct, control of the use of land, and the ownership and transmittal of property—continue to be guided in many or most respects by state rather than federal law.

Indeed, the decentralization of law in the United States presses past the states themselves to local communities and special districts inferior to the states. There are durable conventions of local governance in the United States that may surprise the stranger to our legal practices. This tendency towards localism is at its most extreme in the context of land use regulation. Remarkably, regulatory authority over the use of land in the United States is largely vested in individual cities and towns. While regional entities have been developed in some states to coordinate aspects of the use of land, and some land resources (such as coastal areas bordering oceans) have been made the object of state-wide authority or even interstate or national authority, these are limited exceptions to a pervasive pattern of local regulation. In some metropolitan areas, accordingly, dozens of local governmental entities—which may have considerably divergent interests and agenda (as well as dramatically varying degrees of experience and sophistication) share responsibility for shaping the development of land resources in their region.

E. The Allocation of Judicial Authority

The distribution of judicial authority between the states and the federal government parallels that of legal authority generally. The federal Constitution presumes the existence of state courts, and contemplates the possibility that the only federal court would be the United States Supreme Court. Unless explicitly divested of their authority by federal legislation, state courts have subject matter jurisdiction (competence) to hear almost all legal controversies, state and federal, within the geographic sphere of their authority. In practice, the United States Congress has left this omnivorous state judicial authority intact in all but a few narrowly defined areas where it has made federal judicial jurisdiction exclusive.

In contrast, the subject matter jurisdiction of the federal courts is limited. The federal Constitution[9] circumscribes the jurisdiction that the federal judiciary can enjoy at its maximum; confers on Congress discretion to create or not to create federal courts subordinate to the Supreme Court; and permits Congress, if it does create such courts, to give them only part of the available federal jurisdiction. While the Constitution specifies the existence of the Supreme Court, and confers all federal jurisdiction on that Court, it permits Congress to make substantial exceptions to this constitutional specification of jurisdiction. The limits on federal judicial jurisdiction are thus two-fold: there are constitutional limits on the maximum jurisdiction that can be enjoyed by the federal courts, and Congress can further limit that jurisdiction by withholding portions of it in the case of the lower federal courts or withdrawing portions of it in the case of the Supreme Court.

Congress has in fact created a substantial federal judiciary, but neither the Supreme Court nor the lower federal courts have ever enjoyed the full scope of their constitutionally defined jurisdiction. Over the years Congress has created a complex web of federal jurisdiction, the details of which are beyond the scope of our discussion here. For our present purposes, it is sufficient to observe that there are two primary bases of federal jurisdiction: 'diversity' jurisdiction and 'federal question' jurisdiction. Diversity jurisdiction[10] involves controversies between the citizens of one state and those of another, or between the citizens of the United States and those of another country, where the amount in controversy exceeds $50,000. Federal question jurisdiction[11] involves cases where issues of federal law are presented, with no minimum amount required. For a federal question case to originate in the federal courts the case must actually 'arise' under federal law, a requirement that has spawned an arcane jurisprudence of its own; for a case originating in the state courts to be within the appellate jurisdiction of the Supreme Court, it need merely to present an issue of federal law.

Because of the broad jurisdictional authority of the state courts, plaintiffs whose cases arise under federal law or satisfy the diversity of citizenship

---

[9] Article III, Section 2 [1] reads as follows:

> The judicial power shall extend to all Cases, in Law and Equity, arising under this Constitution, the Laws of the United States, and Treaties made, or which shall be made, under their Authority;—to all Cases affecting Ambassadors, other public Ministers and Consuls;—to all Cases of admiralty and maritime Jurisdiction;—to Controversies to which the United States shall be a Party;—to Controversies between two or more States;—between a State and Citizens of another State;—between Citizens of different States;—between Citizens of the same State claiming Lands under the Grants of different States, and between a State, or the Citizens thereof, and foreign States, Citizens or Subjects.

[10] 28 U.S.C. § 1332.   [11] 28 U.S.C. § 1331.

requirements can elect to bring those cases in either state or federal court. Should the plaintiff in a diversity or federal question case elect to proceed in state court, federal legislation permits the defendant to 'remove' the case to federal court in almost all circumstances.[12] Accordingly, where a case arises under federal law or involves appropriately diverse parties, either party can place the case in federal court.

Some idea of the interplay among the elements of federal authority we have addressed so far is provided by the Foreign Sovereign Immunities Act.[13] That act:

(1) grants foreign governments immunity from suit in state or federal courts in the United States, subject to several exceptions, of which the most important concerns actions 'based upon a commercial activity carried on in the United States by the foreign state'; and

(2) provides for non-exclusive federal jurisdiction over any actions that satisfy one of the exceptions, whether the plaintiff is a citizen of the United States or a citizen of a foreign nation.

The granting of immunity to foreign governments is relatively unexceptional: Congress has power to act in this area by virtue of its authority over foreign commerce and foreign relations more generally, and the supremacy clause permits it to oust the state courts of jurisdiction they would otherwise have under state law to entertain actions against foreign states. The granting of federal jurisdiction over actions to which the statutory immunity is inapplicable is more complex. Under Article III, federal judicial authority includes actions between 'a State or the Citizens thereof, and foreign States'; this alone would permit Congress to extend federal jurisdiction to actions against foreign governments brought by citizens of the United States. But the Foreign Sovereign Immunities Act has been interpreted to permit citizens of other countries to bring suit against foreign nations in the federal courts of the United States, which exceeds the permissible scope of diversity jurisdiction. As to this more provocative extension of jurisdiction, the Supreme Court has held that, since every action against a foreign government must satisfy one of the exceptions to the general statutory grant of immunity, any qualifying action against a foreign government 'arises under' federal law and falls within the federal question jurisdiction of the federal courts.[14]

---

[12] The exception is a diversity case in which a defendant tries to remove a case from the courts of her own state; in a such case, the purpose of diversity jurisdiction—to protect a litigant from prejudice—is inapt, and removal is not permitted.

[13] 28 U.S.C. § 1330.

[14] See *Verlinden B.V.* v. *Central Bank of Nigeria*, 461 U.S. 480, 103 S.Ct. 1962 (1983).

III. Protection From the Burdens of Multi-State Legal Authority

To the foreign lawyer or entrepreneur contemplating commercial activity in the United States, the decentralized structure of legal authority may seem daunting. Since each state has independent legal authority over matters within its legal boundaries, the possibility of inconsistent, unanticipated, and burdensome regulations, liabilities, and tax obligations immediately arises. There are, however, elements of our federal legal tradition which limit the scope of these hazards.

A. *The Tradition of Uniform Laws*

The first of these protective shields in the federal system of laws in the United States is the substantial tradition of uniform laws. The terms of uniform laws are proposed by national commissions of interested and expert parties, typically after extensive hearings and deliberations.[15] The proposed laws are then proffered to the legislatures of the states, for adoption as state law. The object of the exercise is simple and obvious: to avoid the inefficiencies and injustices of disparate regimes of state law. The disruption of robust commercial activity is an obvious concern in this context, and, not surprisingly, the Uniform Commercial Code is the most prominent example of uniform lawmaking among the states.[16] But uniform laws play an important role in non-commercial multi-state settings as well, such as the making and modification of child custody arrangements.[17]

Uniform laws retain their status as state enactments. Not all states may adopt them of course, and those states who do elect to adopt them may change or delete some provisions.[18] Further, as state laws, uniform laws are in principle and practice open to divergent interpretations by various state courts, even when their formal texts are identical in relevant respects. But state courts in the United States tend in general to treat each other's judg-

---

[15] The National Conference of the Commissioners on Uniform State Laws is comprised of persons chosen by the Governors of each of the states; since 1892, the Commission has proposed more than 200 uniform acts, which have had a mixed reception among state legislatures.

[16] Other important uniform laws in the commercial context include the Uniform Partnership Act, the Uniform Limited Partnership Act, and the Uniform Arbitration Act.

[17] The Uniform Child Custody Jurisdiction Act (UCCJA) was promulgated in 1968 by the National Conference of Commissioners on Uniform State Laws, and has been adopted in every state without substantial modification.

[18] The Uniform Commercial Code (UCC) itself has been adopted by every state except Louisiana, and by the District of Columbia, Guam, the Northern Mariana Islands, and the Virgin Islands. There are, however, non-uniform modifications in many of these jurisdictions.

ments and opinions with the respect due to members of a broader national legal community, and uniform laws promote in state judges a particularly strong sense of being embarked on a common national endeavor. The Uniform Commercial Code and its less prominent uniform legal siblings have significantly reduced the costs of federalism in the United States.

B. *Constitutional Limits on the Reach of State Court Jurisdiction and Choice of Law*

Multi-state enterprises face two overlapping risks. First, they are exposed to divergent substantive responsibilities and liabilities from state to state. Secondly, they are exposed to the adjudicatory authority of the courts in a multiplicity of states. These two forms of exposure are connected of course, but only imperfectly. A state court undertaking to resolve a controversy with multi-state implications has to decide which state's law to apply, and there is an understandable and legitimate tendency of a state court to prefer its own law in such a case. But this is only a tendency, and there are many cases where state courts elect to apply the law of other states.

Elementary concerns of fairness—reflected in the American constitutional tradition by the insistence on 'due process'—require that there be some limits on these forms of multi-state exposure. In particular, it seems wrong that someone be subjected to the legal authority of a state under circumstances where:

(a)   they have undertaken no activities that led in some natural or reasonable way to their being under the aegis of the state in question and

(b)   it would have been difficult or impossible for them to have anticipated that they would fall under the aegis of that state.

Being forced to litigate in the unfamiliar courts of a distant state with which one has little or no contact is burdensome. Presumably, it is still worse to be exposed to substantive responsibilities and corresponding liabilities which could neither be avoided or planned for. Perhaps somewhat perversely, the Supreme Court has imposed significant constitutional limitations on the authority of state courts to adjudicate controversies with which they have only attenuated connections, but has been less vigilant in its restriction of the decision of a state court to apply the law of a state which has only attenuated connections to the controversy at issue.

The exact scope of the authority of state courts to adjudicate remote controversies involving persons and entities not physically present in the state is not entirely clear (and perhaps never will be, given the fact-sensitivity of the question); but a general picture can be sketched. The ultimate inquiry is whether the extension of a state court's jurisdiction over a defendant who is not physically present is consistent with 'fair play and substantial justice'.

This general inquiry proceeds at two levels. First, and more narrowly, the question is whether a non-resident state defendant has 'purposefully directed' its activities towards the residents of the forum state, and thus has established the requisite 'minimum contacts' with a state.[19] The Supreme Court appears divided on important details of what constitutes purposeful direction; in particular, it is unclear whether merely placing one's goods in a stream of commerce that may ultimately wash up onto the shore of some state market is sufficient, or whether a more direct purposeful reach towards a state is required.[20] In any event, if there is not the requisite purposeful direction and ensuing minimum contacts, the state may not extend its jurisdiction over the defendant.

Even if this first requirement is satisfied, there remains the more general, second question: given the totality of the circumstances in this particular case, would the extension of jurisdiction be consistent with fair play and substantial justice? Thus, for example, where a Japanese manufacturer of tire valves was being sued in the California courts on a cross-complaint by a Taiwanese manufacturer of tires which used its valves, the Supreme Court held that—even if the purposeful-direction/minimum-contacts test were satisfied—forcing the Japanese manufacturer to defend the action in California was not consistent with fair play and substantial justice.[21]

On the whole, the Supreme Court has been more generous to choice-of-law decisions by state courts, respecting these decisions when the state whose law is chosen has any meaningful contact with the pertinent aspect of the controversy.[22] But there are limits, and arbitrary and attenuated applications of a state's law will be struck down.[23] Constitutional doctrine in this area aside, the threat of arbitrary choice of law decisions is somewhat muted by circumstance. On the whole, states are not apt to choose to apply the laws of other states absent some good reason to do so; and where an unconnected court is seeking to adjudicate the controversy and apply its own law, the limits on adjudicatory authority that we have just discussed apply.

---

[19] See, e.g. *Burger King Corp.* v. *Rudzewicz*, 471 U.S. 462, (1985). For the origins of the minimum contacts infrastructure of this doctrine, see *International Shoe Co.* v. *Washington*, 326 U.S. 310, (1945).

[20] See the divided opinion of the Supreme Court in *Asahi Metal Industry Co., Ltd.* v. *Superior Court of California, Solano County*, 480 U.S. 102, (1987).

[21] *Asahi Metal Industry Co., Ltd.* v. *Superior Court of California, Solano County*, 480 U.S. 102, (1987).

[22] See, e.g. *Allstate Ins. Co.* v. *Hague*, 449 U.S. 302, (1981).

[23] See, e.g. *Phillips Petroleum Co.* v. *Shutts*, 472 U.S. 797, 105 S.Ct. 2965 (1985).

C. The Negative Commerce Clause

The final protection from the burdens of multi-state legal authority involves what is often called the 'negative' or 'dormant' commerce clause. The commerce clause proper, authorizes Congress to 'regulate Commerce with foreign Nations, and among the several States'.[24] Neither it nor any other provision of the Constitution is explicitly directed to the converse proposition, that the states are to some degree restricted in their authority to regulate interstate commerce. But such restrictions have been implied, in service of a viable national economy. It is these restrictions that comprise the negative commerce clause.

Doctrine in this area is somewhat ungainly, but is reasonably well captured by the observation that the states are barred from:

(1) discriminating against interstate commerce;
(2) unduly burdening interstate commerce; and
(3) inappropriately taxing interstate commerce.

The first of these restrictions is robust and relatively clear; the second is neither robust nor clear; and the third has produced a distinct and arcane body of doctrine, generally quite favorable to reasonable exercises of state taxing authority.

A state discriminates against interstate commerce when it makes the out-of-state character of a transaction or enterprise the gravamen of regulatory disadvantage, and does so for protectionist reasons. Thus, for example both of the following would be discriminations against interstate commerce: a state permits the burial of in-state garbage at designated sites, but prohibits the burial of out-of-state garbage because it wishes to restrict the amount of garbage buried in the state;[25] or, a state permits the sale of certain fish or live-stock within its borders, but prohibits the export of these products because it wishes to limit the overall amount of sales.[26] Even when the out-of-state character of a transaction or enterprise is not the explicit gravamen of regulatory disadvantage, if the regulation in question operates to the effective disadvantage of out-of-state interests and apparently has been enacted for protectionist reasons, the law will be treated as a prohibited discrimination against interstate commerce. Thus, a state that has produce grading and labelling requirements which substantially disadvantage out-of-state agricultural competition, and which seem unnecessary to any non-protectionist state interest, has discriminated against interstate commerce.[27]

---

[24] See text accompanying notes 2–6 supra.
[25] See *Philadelphia* v. *New Jersey*, 437 U.S. 617, 98 S.Ct. 2531 (1978).
[26] See *Hughes* v. *Oklahoma*, 441 U.S. 322, 99 S.Ct. 1727 (1979).
[27] See *Hunt* v. *Washington State Apple Advertising Commission*, 432 U.S. 333, 97 S.Ct. 2434 (1977).

There are two major and somewhat anomalous exceptions to the prohibition on state discrimination against interstate commerce. First, where the state is acting as entrepreneur instead of regulator, it may prefer in-state economic interests; thus, a state which is buying materials for its own purposes may prefer in-state sellers, and a state which is manufacturing and selling a scarce commodity of some sort may prefer in-state buyers. Secondly, the United States Congress can take whole areas of commerce and exempt them from what otherwise would be constitutional limitations on state authority. So if Congress declares, for example, that the insurance industry is not part of interstate commerce for these purposes, the states may then freely regulate the insurance industry, even to the extent of discriminating against out-of-state commercial interests.[28]

The second negative commerce clause limitation on the state regulation of interstate commerce is the prohibition of state regulations that 'unduly burden' interstate commerce. Such a rule could be very strong constitutional medicine indeed, inviting the federal judiciary to review virtually every piece of state commercial regulation to inquire whether it seemed an inappropriate restriction of free enterprise. But the Supreme Court long ago renounced this role as inappropriate to a judiciary in a democratic state, and concerns for the flow of interstate commerce are not sufficient to overbear this salutary judicial restraint. Accordingly, with very few exceptions, only rather extreme circumstances have prompted the modern judiciary to find that a challenged state regulation unduly burdens interstate commerce. In practice, the following circumstances have characterized most of the handful of cases where the finding of undue burden was made[29]: first, the burden has been directly on the *transportation of goods in interstate commerce*; secondly, the challenged state regulation has been *inconsistent with national practice generally*, and thirdly, the challenged state regulation has appeared to be *unsupported by any significant regulatory concern*.[30] This is an unusual confluence of circumstances, and the undue burden doctrine is not likely to figure prominently on the state regulatory landscape.

The third restriction on state authority concerns the taxation of interstate commercial enterprises. Obvious concerns dominate this area: if every state

[28] But the Supreme Court may be losing its commitment to this proposition in extreme cases. In *Metropolitan Life Ins. Co.* v. *Ward*, 470 U.S. 869, (1985), the Court struck down a state law than taxed in-state insurance companies at a lower rate than out-of-state insurance companies. Federal legislation exempted the insurance industry from consideration as interstate commerce, and the Court respected this by setting aside questions of the negative commerce clause; but it reached instead to the equal protection clause and invalidated the legislation on this ground.

[29] A prominent modern exception is *Edgar* v. *MITE Corp*, 457 U.S. 624, (1982), where the Supreme Court held that a state's anti-takeover statute unduly burdened interstate commerce, despite the absence of these three factors.

[30] See, e.g. *Kassel* v. *Consolidated Freightways Corp. of Delaware*, 450 U.S. 662, (1981); *Raymond Motor Transp., Inc.* v. *Rice*, 434 U.S. 429, (1978); *Bibb* v. *Navajo Freight Lines, Inc.*, 359 U.S. 520, (1959).

that had some remote contact with a multi-state enterprise could tax the enterprise without limit, the cumulative burden on such enterprises would be crushing; and, as between states that have a real connection to a particular multi-state enterprise, there is some need for a fair distribution of the tax potential of that enterprise. Although this area has produced a notoriously intricate body of rules and outcomes, the essential principles that have guided doctrine are fairly easy to state. First, the taxing state must have an appropriate 'nexus',—that is, contact—with the multi-state enterprise; the classic nexus is where the multi-state enterprise has been the beneficiary of state facilities or services towards which it has made no contribution. Secondly, the tax imposed by the state must be fairly apportioned to the enterprise's contact with the state. For example, a road tax on a multi-state vehicle might be keyed to miles travelled or to the number of days in the year the vehicle was in the state; or a corporate income tax might be keyed to the percentage of a multi-state enterprise's total earnings that were attributable to activities within the state or some other determinant like the percentage of total employee hours or compensation attributable to employees who work in the state. On the whole, the Supreme Court has been generous to state taxation schemes that seem to represent good-faith efforts to apportion a multi-state enterprise's tax liability.[31]

Special issues may arise with regard to the state taxation of multinational commercial enterprises. The Supreme Court has recognized the negative implications of the 'foreign commerce clause', and imposed two additional restrictions on states that tax multinational enterprises: first, a state may not tax a multinational enterprise when to do so would create a substantial risk of *international* multiple taxation; and secondly, a state may not tax such an enterprise when to do so would impair the ability of the United States to speak with a single voice in foreign affairs. In addition, state attempts to tax multinational enterprises may encounter special problems of federal preemption, given the presence of treaties or conventions that bear on the area of commerce in question.[32]

IV. The Distinct Character of Separation of Powers Issues in the United States

The broad structural features of the national government in the United States are relatively straight-forward, and may be familiar to many readers. At the

---

[31] See, e.g. *Barclays Bank PLC* v. *Franchise Tax Bd. of California*, 114 S.Ct. 2268, (1994).

[32] For a failed attempt to invoke these restrictions which nonetheless offers a good summary of contemporary law, see *Itel Containers Intern. Corp.* v. *Huddleston*, 113 S.Ct. 1095 (1993).

apex of executive authority is the President. Technically, the President is elected by special electors in each state who are in turn elected by the population at large. Each state is entitled to a number of electors based on the number of Representatives and Senators it has in Congress. In practice, the presidential electors are invisible and irrelevant: voters select the presidential candidate of their choice and in all but the most extraordinary of circumstances the electors are bound to vote for the candidates to whom they are pledged. Once elected, the President serves a fixed term of four years and may serve only two such terms.[33]

The legislative authority in the United States rests with Congress, which is composed of two houses. The Senate is composed of two persons from each state, elected at-large from within the state and serving staggered 6-year terms, with approximately one-third of the body elected every 2 years. The composition of the Senate represented a politically crucial compromise in the structure of the national government, and was intended to give each state, however large or small its population, an equal voice. The principle of equal representation among the states, in fact, is the only provision of the Constitution which purports to be unamendable except with consent of all the states. The House of Representatives, in contrast, is composed of representatives elected from geographic districts within each state. The number of representatives varies according to the population of each state, and representatives serve terms of 2 years.

State governments mirror the federal government in many important respects, including the existence of a single, seperately elected chief executive officer (called the 'Governor' at the state level), and the existence in all but one state of a bi-cameral legislative body. Accordingly, some federal concepts and questions of the 'separation of powers' variety may also arise at the state level.

A. The American Presidency and the Collision of Executive and Legislative Functions

The President of the United States is a unique figure. Unlike heads of state in parliamentary systems, the President is directly elected by the whole of the people, not secondarily by the legislative representatives of the people; he thus enjoys an independent and exclusive national political mandate.

[33] Like other 'Civil Officers of the United States', the President can be removed from office if he or she is impeached (that is, charged) with the commission of 'Treason, Bribery, or other high Crimes and Misdemeanors' by the House of Representatives and then convicted of that charge by two-thirds of the Senate. Article II, Section 4; Article I, Sections 2 and 3.

Unburdened by direct political responsibility to the legislature, he and he alone represents the people with a single voice in affairs of state. Conversely, he cannot be assured of legislative support: given the essentially two-party system that has long characterized politics in the United States and the distinct constituencies of members of the House of Representatives and the Senate, it is entirely possible that the President will confront a Congress in which one or both houses is dominated by his sworn political adversaries.

This structural detachment of the executive and legislative branches makes clashes of judgment and will between them entirely possible, and puts a special premium on an understanding of the domains of each. Simple formulae, on the order of 'the legislature makes law and the executive executes that law', are so far off target in many contexts as to be all but useless. True, in the classic situation, national legislative authority in the United States is ultimately located in the combined will of the two houses of Congress. However, the President has a substantial hand in proposing legislation, and may veto legislation; the House of Representatives and the Senate, in turn, can override the President's veto by two-thirds majorities. This basic model fails to capture many important legal circumstances in the United States, circumstances in which the intersection of executive and legislative responsibility is more complex and the division of authority between these branches is often murky.

The problem is not simply one of description or categorization. In the United States an important constitutional precept holds that the powers of the three branches of government must be kept sufficiently separate to facilitate the capacity of each branch to blunt the possibility that another branch will abuse its authority. Hence the twinned notions of 'separation of powers' and 'checks and balances'. Our commitment to this constitutional strategy of dispersed and counterpoised authority has at times collided with more general exigencies of modern governance, with rather complex and unstable results.

This is especially true in three broad and important areas of modern political life. First, in foreign affairs, the special authority of the President often is directly rivalrous with what elsewhere would plainly be the province of Congress; and as the twentieth century draws to a close, of course, there are few domains of government that are not tinged with multi-national implications. Second, as government in the United States has given onto what is often spoken of as the 'regulatory state', the burdens of a sprawling and detailed regulatory authority has made the neat division of executive and legislative impracticable, and has spawned a neither-fish-nor-fowl legal animal, the 'administrative agency'. Third, efforts by Congress to assure its own fiscal prudence and more generally, to assure the legality of executive officials' behavior, have led to inventive mechanisms for overseeing governmental conduct; ironically, these mechanisms themselves arguably are inconsistent with the tenets of separation of powers. We will sample separation of powers issues in each of these contexts.

B. Multi-National Agreements and the Domestic Law of the United States

1. Treaties

Early in the life of the Constitution, the question of the status of treaties in the domestic law of the United States put a strain on the simple model of legislative lawmaking. The Constitution vests treaty-making authority directly with the President, subject to the 'Advice and Consent' of two-thirds of the Senate present at the time of the ratifying vote. This places treaties in the joint authority of the executive and legislative branches, conceding primacy to the President and cutting the House of Representatives out of the picture altogether.[34] An understandable concession to the need in world affairs for the unity of voice and leadership provided by the office of the President, this is a far cry from the basic lawmaking model contemplated by the Constitution.

Note, however, that it need not follow from this expressly defined authority to make treaties that the resulting agreements will have the status of legislation in the domestic legal affairs of the United States. Treaties could be understood as having legal bite only in the domain of international law, as promises binding only in the sense that international law can bind sovereign states, to be fulfilled if necessary by subsequent legislation. Suppose, for example, that the United States and Canada enter into a treaty intended to protect certain migratory birds; specified in the treaty are prohibitions on hunting and sharp restrictions on the logging of trees vital to the species. Such a treaty could be understood as binding on each nation as a matter of international law and as a practical matter of ongoing cooperation, and yet, as having no direct effect on the domestic law of the United States absent legislation implementing the agreed upon restrictions. On this understanding, the treaty itself could not be the basis of domestic legal action taken to prevent or redress hunting or logging activities which contravened its terms. Conversely, the treaty could be understood as having the status of domestic legislation as well as that of international commitment. Neither outcome is

---

[34] It should be remembered that the political composition of the House of Representatives and of the Senate may vary dramatically: representation in the House of Representatives is based on the population of each state, while each state has two representatives in the Senate, regardless of population.

unproblematic: in the former case, nations negotiating with the United States would recognize that its treaty-making authority is inevitably discontinuous with its lawmaking authority, to the detriment of international trust; in the latter, the President's foreign affairs power would remake the Constitution's preferred model of lawmaking in a growing number of areas, especially in an era of global politics.

Early on, the Supreme Court settled the question of the authority of treaties. Relying on the supremacy clause—which we discussed earlier—the Supreme Court held that treaties have exactly the status of federal legislation. Hence, treaties can indeed alter domestic legal outcomes, and they are pre-emptive of conflicting state laws; indeed, like other federal enactments, treaties can displace earlier, inconsistent federal law.

Not all treaties operate in this fashion, however. Some treaties may be understood as promises to change domestic law through the ordinary legislative channels, rather than as agreements intended to directly consummate such change. Treaties that directly effectuate domestic legal consequences are called 'self-executing', and those that contemplate subsequent legislation are called 'non-self-executing'. The interpretative question of a treaty's status in this regard falls first to the President, who has to decide whether to seek supporting legislation; in default of subsequent legislation, it will fall to the judiciary to determine whether a treaty is self-executing or not.

The status of treaties as exactly on a par with other federal laws is a two-edged sword, of course. Just as self-executing treaties can displace prior federal legislation, so too can subsequent federal legislation displace the domestic law consequences of extant treaties. Thus, the capacity of the United States to bind itself domestically by multi-national agreement is ultimately limited to the ongoing support of Congress.[35]

There is an interesting and somewhat obscure interaction between the substantive scope of the ordinary lawmaking authority of Congress and that of the treaty-making authority shared by the President and the Senate. The Supreme Court has held that the President with the requisite support of the Senate can enter into treaties regarding matters not otherwise within the enumerated powers of Congress; self-executing treaties, on this account, can overreach the enumerated powers of Congress, and non-self-executing treaties can confer on Congress power to enact subsequent legislation that it otherwise would not have.[36] But it is important to note that this proposition was embraced by the Supreme Court at a time when there were sharp

[35] But note two wrinkles on this: first, if Congress were to try to enact legislation in conflict with an extant treaty, the President could exercise his veto, of course, which would have to be overridden by a two-thirds vote of each house; and second, subsequent legislation can efface the domestic effect of a treaty, but not the international obligation of the United States.

[36] *Missouri v. Holland*, 252 U.S. 416 (1920).

limitations on federal legislative authority, limitations that have been abandoned and, to a large extent, look artificial in retrospect. Some of the Court's generosity may have been a recognition of the limiting nature of then extant doctrine, from which a broad view of the treaty-making authority could effectuate a rescue.[37] In an era when federal legislative authority is far more generously defined, both the force and importance of this proposition is diminished.

2. Executive Agreements

Considerably less clear is the status of multi-national agreements entered into by the President without Senate approval. These 'executive agreements' are fairly common, and their capacity to bind the nation as a matter of international law is unquestioned; what is questioned is the status of such agreements as a matter of the domestic law of the United States.

It is helpful at the outset to distinguish three groups of executive agreements. The first are those agreements that are entered into by the President alone, but which are subsequently endorsed by a Joint Resolution of the two houses of Congress; these seem to be tantamount to treaties for all relevant purposes. The second are those agreements which concern matters within the exclusive competence and authority of the President, like the appointment and receiving of ambassadors; these have the unquestioned force of any other presidential act within this domain. The third are those agreements that do not satisfy the narrow conditions of either of the first two categories; these are the agreements whose status in the domestic law of the United States is problematic.

The status of executive agreements of this third sort remains somewhat obscure. To date, the Supreme Court has been equivocal: on the one hand, the Court has emphatically concluded that executive agreements of this sort displace conflicting state laws;[38] but on the other it has left open the possibility that such agreements are powerless to displace prior federal laws.[39] This requires some clarification. The idea, presumably, is not that the same exec-

---

[37] Justice Holmes wrote for the Supreme Court in the case in question, which upheld a treaty with Great Britain for the protection of birds migrating between the United States and Canada: 'Here a national interest of very nearly the first magnitude is involved. It can be protected only by national action in concert with that of another power. The subject matter is only transitorily within the State and has no permanent habitat therein. But for the treaty and the statute there soon might be no birds for any powers to deal with. We see nothing in the Constitution that compels the Government to sit by while a food supply is cut off and the protectors of our forests and our crops are destroyed'. *Missouri v. Holland*, above, 252 U.S. at 435.

[38] *United States v. Belmont*, 301 U.S. 324 (1937).

[39] See *United States v. Guy W. Capps*, 204 F.2d 655 (4th Cir. 1953), aff'd on other grounds 348 U.S. 296 (1955).

utive agreement can lead an odd dual life, overriding conflicting state laws
while simultaneously yielding to conflicting federal laws. This would be non-
sensical: if an extant federal statute mandates 'X', and a subsequent executive
agreement requires 'not-X', then a state contemplating legislation with
regard to x would be under conflicting federal mandates, and presumably the
statute would apply (if indeed executive agreements of the third type cannot
override extant federal legislation). Thus it would make no sense in this situation to say that the executive agreement in question could displace conflicting state laws.

The idea must be, instead, that there exist areas of governmental concern
that are not within the exclusive domain of the President, but within which
he may act in accord with other nations, and within which—even in the
absence of the support of the Senate or Congress as a whole—he may effectuate changes in domestic law by virtue of his multi-national executive agreements. But in these areas, the authority of the President is at the sufferance
of Congress, and he can be ousted from that authority by contrary legislative
mandate. When Congress has spoken, or by its silence in context indicated
its intent, the President is not free in these areas to contravene the will of
Congress. The situation is reminiscent of the 'zone of twilight' invoked by
Justice Jackson of the Supreme Court in a well-known case concerning the
attempt by President Truman to take over the operation of steel mills threatened by labor disputes in the midst of the Korean War:

When the President acts in absence of either a congressional grant or denial of
authority, he can only rely upon his own independent powers, but there is a zone of
twilight in which he and Congress may have concurrent authority, or in which its
distribution is uncertain. Therefore, congressional inertia, indifference or quiescence
may sometimes, at least as a practical matter, enable, if not invite, measures on independent presidential responsibility.[40]

Missing from this account is a conceptual delineation of this area of intermediate authority. It seems unlikely that it is as broad as the range of the
treaty-making authority enjoyed by the President when he secures the two-
thirds consent of the Senate, but there is no obvious alternative frame of
authority upon which to draw for these purposes.

C. *The Legislative Veto*

The Great Depression that overtook the United States and much of the rest
of the world at the close of the second decade of this century permanently

---

[40] *Youngstown Sheet & Tube Co.* v. *Sawyer*, 343 U.S. 579, 637 (1952).

remade the face of national lawmaking. The effort to recover from that economic catastrophe and to put in place mechanisms designed to prevent its recurrence and cushion individuals from its most drastic consequences was seen as requiring more nimble, expert, and ubiquitous governmental oversight than could be provided by Congress alone. Hence the birth in the United States of the 'regulatory state', in which substantial legislative authority is delegated to the executive branch itself, or to quasi-independent 'administrative agencies', to make what are called rules or regulations, but which look and operate very much like laws enacted by Congress.

The dramatic growth in the United States of an administrative bureaucracy seized of substantial legislative authority has radically reshaped the distribution of power among the branches of the federal government; indeed, arguably it has created a fourth—rather anomalous—branch of government. It has also spawned an elaborate corpus of law of its own, which is the object of Chapter 6 of this book. But one recent controversy, concerning the legislative veto, is instructive here because it offers a window on modern separation of powers jurisprudence in the Supreme Court, and may force a substantial revision of the way Congress and the administrative leviathan it has created do business with one another.

In its early scrutiny of national regulatory responses to the collapse of the economy, the Supreme Court flirted with the development of constitutional doctrine that would curb the breadth of administrative delegations of congressional authority. These early doubts were quickly withdrawn, however, and the regulatory state has been openly embraced by the Supreme Court for the last half century. Recently, the Court has revisited the delegation question, and found constitutional fault with the legislative veto, a mechanism used by Congress in conjunction with the delegation of legislative authority in over two hundred different statutes.

That the legislative veto should become the victim of the Supreme Court's revived interest in the question of congressional delegation of lawmaking authority is somewhat ironic, since Congress devised the mechanism precisely to maintain ongoing legislative oversight of its administrative delegees. What the legislative veto amounts to is simply this: Congress delegates administrative authority, but retains the capacity to revoke that authority in individual cases by some expedient mechanism short of full legislative reconsideration. The circumstances of the case which prompted the invalidation of the legislative veto by the Supreme Court—*I.N.S.* v. *Chadha*, 462 U.S. 919 (1983)—are illustrative. Congress had given the Attorney General authority to suspend the deportation of individuals under certain limited circumstances involving special hardship. Congress also specified, however, that the Attorney General should report any suspended deportation to both houses of Congress, and further, that either house could dissolve the suspension by the enactment of a simple, unilateral resolution.

The Supreme Court held that this legislative veto was unconstitutional, and did so in terms that indicate that any comparable effort by Congress to retain summary authority over the delegees of its authority is similarly infirm. The Court's rationale was blunt and somewhat startling: the question of whether to suspend the deportation of a deportable alien was in its essence a 'legislative' decision; Congress can make legislative decisions only under the full-dress circumstances of ordinary lawmaking; both houses must concur in supporting the legislative outcome, and that outcome must in turn be presented to the President for the possible exercise of his authority to veto the legislation.

The full implications of this decision are not easy to assess. The legislative veto provisions in all federal regulatory schemes are now unconstitutional; that much is pretty clear, and may make the *Chadha* case the statistical champion of constitutional decisions. With this sweeping outcome, some creative forms of federal lawmaking are now off-limits. But the illegality of the legislative veto does not prevent Congress from exercising on-going oversight of its delegees in ways that ultimately depend on orthodox legislative action. Thus, for example, Congress presumably can insist that a delegee of it authority report its intention to act in certain ways to Congress, and then wait a specified period before formally acting, during which time Congress could revoke or override its delegation of authority by ordinary legislative act.

The deep question about the Court's invalidation of the legislative veto is whether it will ultimately lead to a revival of constitutional doubts about the broad delegation of congressional authority to the executive branch and to administrative agencies. The Court's dependence in *Chadha* on the somewhat questionable notion that decisions like the suspension of a deportation can confidently be characterized as 'essentially legislative', combined with its insistence on a bicameral legislative process and presentment of legislation to the President for veto, could without much intellectual difficulty be read as leading to questions about the numerous decisions being made daily by the administrative delegees of Congress' authority. Most of these decisions, no doubt, are also essentially legislative, and none of them are being made by both houses of Congress and the President in the prescribed way.

On the other hand, the regulatory state is deeply entrenched in the United States, and it is hard to imagine that the Supreme Court is prepared to embark on the radical course of dismantling the machinery that drives so much of government. Moreover, there is some reason to believe that Congress' delegations to itself in the form of the legislative veto were particularly conducive to unreflective and unaccountable governance, since they were in lieu rather than in furtherance of full congressional oversight, and often gave on to at least the appearance of irresponsible decision-making. In the end, the demise of the legislative veto is apt to be a relatively minor crimp in the option set of Congress as it presides over the modern regulatory state.

D. *The Appointment and Removal of Executive Officials*

Chada with its invalidation of the legislative veto is not the only separation of powers difficulty encountered by Congress as it has experimented with novel mechanisms of governance in response to the exigencies of modern political life. An area where these difficulties have been especially pronounced concerns constitutional requirements for the appointment and removal of executive officials.

The Constitution requires that 'Officers of the United States' be appointed by the President, with the consent of the Senate.[41] In contrast, the Constitution is silent with regard to the *removal* of executive branch appointees. The Supreme Court, however, has inferred from the general precept of separation of powers the existence of substantial limitations on congressional arrangements for removal. The jurisprudence of these limitations is somewhat complex and possibly unstable, but its general thrust is easily captured: the Court is distinctly uneasy about any arrangements for the removal of executive branch officers that gives Congress control over such officers and hence raises the specter of parliamentary government.

The potential collision between these restrictions on appointment and removal (and, indeed, separation of power principles more generally) and novel governance mechanisms crafted by Congress to cope with the exigencies of modern government is realized in a number of recent Supreme Court cases. We will consider two which are illustrative of this collision.

Bowsher v. *Synar*[42] involved Congress' attempt in the mid-1980s to impose more-or-less ironclad budgetary restraints on the entire federal government to the end of reducing the growth of the national debt. Pursuant to the legislation in question, the Comptroller General of the United States played a pivotal role in communicating technical data concerning an excessive deficit to the President, along with detailed spending reductions proposals that would eliminate the statutory excess. Upon receiving these proposals the President was required to issue an order mandating the specified reductions to congressionally authorized spending.

---

[41] The same constitutional provision—Article II, Section 2—explicitly provides for the appointment of 'inferior Officers', permitting Congress to vest authority over their appointment 'in the President alone, in the Courts of Law, or in the Heads of Departments'.

[42] 478 U.S. 714(1986).

While the budget control legislation was new, the office of the Comptroller General—in whom much authority over its execution devolved—had been created more than a half century earlier. Pursuant to that early legislation, the Comptroller General can be removed from office either by formal impeachment proceedings or by joint resolution of Congress; the latter avenue of removal can be on very general statutory grounds, including 'inefficiency' and 'malfeasance'.

The Comptroller General's vulnerability to impeachment posed no constitutional difficulty: impeachment is an elaborate and formal process involving a decision to charge an official with 'Treason, Bribery, or other high Crimes and Misdemeanors',[43] by the House of Representatives and a decision to convict the official so charged by the Senate. It is expressly provided for in the Constitution, narrow in its scope, and casts the Congress in an essentially adjudicatory role. But the vulnerability of the Comptroller General to removal on general policy grounds (as in 'inefficiency') was seen by the Supreme Court as constitutionally fatal. In the Court's eyes, this provision gave Congress far too much control over the Comptroller General, and hence, over functions that belonged to the executive branch. This, for the Court, was a violation of the constitutional demand that executive authority remain separate from legislative control.

Neither the sharp scrutiny nor the arguably somewhat rigid analysis of the Supreme Court in *Bowsher* were in evidence in *Morrison* v. *Olson*.[44] There, the stakes on both sides of the question—that is, both the need for novel governmental machinery and the threat posed by that machinery—seemed higher. *Morrison* involved the elaborate and quite novel mechanism created by Congress for the *ad hoc* appointment of 'independent counsel' to investigate and prosecute alleged violations of federal criminal laws by high-ranking federal governmental officials. The perceived need for such independent counsel was the concern that the Attorney General might decline to vigorously pursue such criminal investigations and prosecutions on political grounds.

Under the independent counsel legislation, the Attorney General of the United States is called upon to make initial findings that an independent counsel is warranted. Once these findings are made, a special court of federal judges called the 'Special Division' is convened. The Special Division is authorized to appoint an independent counsel, to define the range of his or her prosecutorial authority, and to terminate his or her office once it finds that all investigations are sufficiently complete to warrant such termination. Once granted by the Special Division, the authority of the independent counsel can be terminated by Congress, but only by formal impeachment, as described

---

[43] Article II, Section 4.   [44] 487 U.S. 654(1988).

above; the Attorney General can remove an independent counsel but only under very narrow conditions, subject to judicial review, and justified in mandated reports to both the Special Division and to Congress. While in office the independent counsel is empowered to act entirely independent of supervision by the Attorney General or other members of the executive branch.

In *Morrison* v. *Olson* the Supreme Court upheld the independent counsel legislation against constitutional attack on separation of powers grounds. To the complaint that provisions for appointing independent counsel did not satisfy the constitutional requirements for the presidential appointment of federal officers, the Court replied that independent counsel qualified as 'inferior officers' within the meaning of the Constitution, and hence could be appointed by the Special Division.[45] The finding of 'inferior' status for these purposes rested on the vulnerability of independent counsel to removal by the Attorney General (albeit under very restricted conditions), on the limited duties of independent counsel, and on the limited scope of independent counsel's authority. To the complaint that the restrictions on the Attorney General's power to remove independent counsel was an unconstitutional limitation on the President's power to preside over the executive branch, the Supreme Court emphasized that unlike the situation in *Bowsher* v. *Synar* (discussed above), Congress had not itself assumed the power of removal, and found that the independent counsel provisions did not in this respect impermissibly interfere with the authority and responsibility of the President. To the more general complaint that the precept of separation of powers was being violated, the Court responded in parallel fashion, stressing that this was not a case where Congress was attempting to seize executive authority for itself.

V. The Robust Constitutional Judiciary

The most provocative aspect of the separation of powers among the branches of government in the United States is the robust role of the judiciary in the legal and political life of the nation. The heart of this role is the institution of 'judicial review', which empowers the courts, under the leadership of the Supreme Court, to measure governmental conduct against the terms of the Constitution and to invalidate that conduct if it is deemed inconsistent with the Constitution.

Chief Justice John Marshall's famous decision in *Marbury* v. *Madison*[46] pro-

---

[45] See n. 41 above.   [46] 5 U.S. 137 (1803).

vided the conceptual foundation for the power of judicial review. In its essence, *Marbury* rested on three propositions:

(a) that the Constitution is law, not merely an enshrinement of a set of political ideals;
(b) that the Constitution is supreme law, and overrides any conflicting source of law within the legal system; and
(c) that judges have the same responsibility and authority with regard to the Constitution as they do with regard to other sources of law.

On this account, judges engaged in judicial review are behaving as judges have always behaved; they are interpreting the legal norms that bear on the controversy before them, and resolving conflicts among those sources according to other (meta) norms that determine the priority among the first-order norms. According to *Marbury*, what makes the situation in the United States remarkable is the adoption of a written Constitution that is best understood as having the status of positive and supreme law.

One important consequence of *Marbury*'s emphasis on judges doing as judges have always done as the basis for judicial review is that the power of the federal judiciary to engage in judicial review is limited to circumstances where an actual legal case has appropriately engaged the court's attention. There are a variety of rather arcane doctrines that combine to define the structural circumstances that confer adjudicatory authority on a court. The essence of these doctrines is this: there must be an injured party whose ongoing injury (1) is distinct from the population at large, (2) flows from the conduct complained of, (3) is of the kind to which the legal norm in question is addressed, and (4) is likely to be ameliorated by the relief requested of the court; alternatively, there must be a party imminently threatened by an injury meeting these specifications. In practice, most controversies about the content of the Constitution will produce some number of parties who satisfy these requirements, and one or more of those parties is likely to seek judicial intervention on his or her behalf. Hence the constitutional judiciary, though limited to the traditional judical role of conflict resolution, is likely to find itself in the midst of most constitutional issues of note.

However unexceptional the impulse behind judicial review may be, the results of the response to that impulse are dramatic in their impact on the division of authority among the branches of government in the United States. When a federal court declares some facet of government practice to be unconstitutional, that conclusion cannot be displaced by the ordinary political process. With very few exceptions—such as the capacity of Congress to permit the states to regulate interstate commerce in a fashion that would otherwise be unconstitutional, as we discussed above—judicial interpretations of the

Constitution cannot be displaced by contrary legislation. Some sitting state court judges are subject to the pressure of standing for re-election, but the force of precedent and the deep tradition of an independent judiciary combine to minimize the effect of this vulnerability. All federal judges, including justices of the Supreme Court, are nominated by the President and confirmed by a majority of the Senate. Once appointed, they enjoy life tenure, with the guarantee of an undiminished salary, subject only to impeachment on grounds of egregious misconduct.

An unpopular judicial interpretation of the Constitution by a state court or lower federal court judge can be overturned by a higher court of course, but ultimately the Supreme Court will speak to a constitutional controversy of any great importance, and its judgment is binding on the entire legal system. Eventually, the Supreme Court may overrule its own prior judgments, aided perhaps by a change in the composition of the Court. Changes in the political climate of the nation do affect the judiciary, of course. Presidents choose their federal judicial nominees and the Senate considers these nominees through a lens forged in part by political concerns. Judges themselves are part of the political culture, and are not immune in either theory or fact from the changes in political sensibilities that characterize their times. But there is a substantial buffer between judges—especially federal judges and those state judges who do not have to turn to the electorate to stay in office—and immediate political pressures. The mantle of office has had striking results on the justices of the Supreme Court, many of whom have greatly surprised the President who appointed them, usually very much to the good.

The ultimate political response to an unpopular decision of the Supreme Court, in theory, is the amendment of the Constitution. But the procedures for amending the Constitution are burdensome,[47] and the tradition of constitutionalism in the United States is deep. In practice the Constitution has proven very difficult to amend, and only a very few amendments can be understood as reactions to unpopular decisions by the Supreme Court.

Thus, judgments of the Supreme Court are often quite durable, and may have a dramatic impact on the course of legal and political events. This is especially so because the Constitution is terse, and often general and abstract in its commitments; hence the responsibility for interpreting that document

---

[47] Under Article V of the Constitution, there are four possible sequences by which the Constitution can be amended: (1) two-thirds of both houses of Congress can propose an amendment, which three-quarters of the state legislatures ratify; (2) two-thirds of the States can apply for a constitutional convention, which Congress then convenes by ordinary vote. This convention can then propose an amendment, which three-quarters of the state legislatures ratify; (3) two-thirds of both houses of Congress can propose an amendment, which special conventions in three-quarters of the states ratify; (4) two-thirds of the States can apply for a constitutional convention, which Congress then convenes by ordinary vote. This convention can then propose an amendment, which special conventions in three-quarters of the states ratify. In practice, only the first method has been utilized.

sometimes implicates wide-ranging judicial judgment, notwithstanding the mounting constraint of prior judicial decisions. This is most obviously true of the Constitution's liberty-bearing provisions: ideals like 'due process', 'equal protection', 'freedom of speech' and the 'free exercise [of religion]' are open to competing understandings at the deepest level. Even after comparatively stable accounts of the basic meaning of these ideals are arrived at, their application to specific facts can be difficult and provocative. Hence deeply important and highly controversial decisions have helped shaped major features of the social and political culture of the United States: an abiding insistence on open political discourse, the racial desegregation of schools and other public facilities; the abolition of prayer exercises in schools and the complex adjustment of the relationship between church and state elsewhere; the insistence that state legislatures be drastically redesigned to equalize the population base of each elected representative; and the recognition of the right of women to elect an abortion—all these significant and sometimes fractious commitments are embodied in decisions of the United States Supreme Court.

The responsibility and license implicated in the judicial interpretation of the open-textured provisions of the Constitution does not stop with the liberty-bearing provisions of that document. Thus, for example, the various meanings ascribed to the commerce clause—which we have addressed at some length above (see p. 33)—are the products of judicial interpretation. Indeed, many of the basic structural features of federalism and separation of powers in the United States are the product not of the text or history of the Constitution *per se*, but rather, the product of well-established judicial judgment.

In one important respect, the judicial interpretation of the liberty-bearing provisions of the Constitution may be conceptually different from the judicial enforcement of structural provisions like the commerce clause. Some observers of the Supreme Court's modern understanding of the commerce clause—an understanding which concedes to Congress the authority to enact virtually any legislation connected with commercial activity in the United States—see in the Court's generosity to Congress not so much a judgment about the appropriate meaning of the clause, as a judgment about the appropriate arbiter of that meaning. These observers think that the Supreme Court is leaving the question of the appropriate scope of the commerce clause to Congress itself, while actively policing certain areas of personal liberty. This is a plausible interpretation of judicial practice, but one which complicates the understanding of constitutional law in the United States. If some constitutional decisions are analytical judgments of content, while others are institutional judgments of role, then the jurisprudence of the Constitution is considerably more complex than surface appearances may suggest.

The robust role of the judiciary in interpreting the Constitution means at least this: a full understanding of the complex structure of government in the United States cannot be read off the face of the Constitution directly; such an understanding requires familiarity with the corpus of constitutional decisions by the Supreme Court as well. In the United States, the judiciary is a major player in the structuring of fundamental aspects of law and justice.

VI. Conclusion

The structure of legal authority in the United States is complicated twice over: first, by the vertical distribution of authority between the states and the national government; and secondly, by the horizontal distribution of authority among the branches of the federal government. Even more-or-less routine commercial transactions in the United States can spawn complex legal issues implicating concerns of federalism or separation of powers, and many of the areas of law considered in subsequent chapters of this book have been shaped by these concerns. The aim of this chapter has been to provide the reader who is otherwise unfamiliar with the legal system of the United States a general understanding of these structural themes.

3

COURTS

ALAN B. MORRISON

I. Introduction

There is no one court system in the United States, nor even two—one federal and one state. Instead, there is the principal federal system, and some satellites and offshoots, and then there is a system for each of the fifty states, plus one for the District of Columbia and one for each of the territories. Because many state systems are similar to each other, they can be described generally, with the principal variations noted. Since even American lawyers are rarely familiar with the details of the court systems in more than a few states, this chapter is intended to give the reader an overall sense of both the federal and state systems and the principal areas where they differ.

II. Methods of Selecting Judges

One key variable among courts is the method of selection for the judges and the length of their terms of office. There are three general selection methods employed, with some minor variations. The first is appointment, which applies to the principal judges in the federal system: the Justices of the Supreme Court, the Circuit Court Judges (the principal appellate judges), and the District Court Judges (the principal trial judges). All of them are appointed by the President, and their appointments approved by the Senate, a process known as advice and consent. Article III of the Constitution gives those federal judges life tenure (subject to removal only if they have committed a serious offense) and a guarantee against salary reduction. Other federal judges who sit on specialized courts, such as the Tax Court and the Court of Federal Claims, or who perform specialized functions (bankruptcy judges) are also appointed by the President, but they do not have life tenure, although their terms of office are quite long, usually 15 years.

Some states use the appointment method for some or all of their judges, but almost no state judges have life tenure, unlike federal judges who can serve as long as they are able. Instead, state judges are appointed for terms of various lengths, often with mandatory retirement at an age such as 70. Typically, especially for positions on the highest court in a state, the appointment will be made by the governor, but lower court judges in some places are appointed by local officials, such as the mayor. In some states that use the appointment method, there are formal nominating commissions, composed of leading lawyers and others, that give the appointing official a list of names, at least three per vacancy and sometimes more, and the choice must be made from those on the list. This variation is thought to improve the quality of the judges chosen and to take some of the politics out of the process.

The second method is election, like other public officials, such as the governor, the attorney general, or state legislators. In some states, some judges are elected and others appointed, while in other states, all of the judges are elected. Terms vary from as short as 4 years to as long as 15 years, with judges in the higher courts tending to have longer terms. Among the electing states, there are two general approaches. Under one, all judicial races are considered nonpartisan, which means that a candidate does not run on a party ticket, and the parties do not endorse specific candidates; under the other, judges are treated like other office seekers, and they run with the support of their political party.

The third method of selection combines the other two: the judge is appointed, and then after several years, she or he runs in what is called a 'retention election': there is no opposing candidate, but the voters have a chance to say 'no' to a sitting judge whom they do not like, as they sometimes do.

III. Division of Judicial Workload

In the federal system, with the exception of administrative law judges who are generally not considered judges because they are part of the administrative side of the government, most judges are generalists: they handle any type of case within the federal system. However, because federal courts are quite limited in the kinds of cases that may be brought there, see Chapter 2, it is somewhat artificial to call them courts of general jurisdiction. At the trial court level, there is at least one federal district court within each state, with some states having as many as four separate districts. Overall, there are more than 90 districts and 630 district judges. Above the district courts are the twelve courts of appeals, with a total of approximately 170 judges, that hear appeals from district courts within their region and from certain administrative rulings.

Within the federal system, there are some judges, such as those whose work is limited to tax or bankruptcy, as well as those who sit on the Court of Federal Claims noted in section II above, who are not generalists under any definition of that term. There is also one court of appeals—known as the Federal Circuit—that has a more limited subject matter mandate, but in those areas where it hears appeals—patents, certain claims against the United States, and most personnel matters involving individual federal employees—its jurisdiction is exclusive.

In the state systems, there tend to be more subject matter divisions of authority than in the federal system and, except for certain specialized courts, most courts are local, rather than statewide, in their reach. For states that have courts of limited jurisdiction, some will draw the line between civil and criminal cases, with some trial judges handling one or the other on a permanent basis. Quite often, states will have family courts that will exclusively handle cases involving matters such as divorce, adoption, and child neglect; in some places, probating of wills and related matters falls within the ambit of the family court, while in others there is a separate court for those cases. In some jurisdictions the family court will handle cases involving juveniles charged with criminal acts as part of their responsibility, while others will have separate juvenile courts.

There are some other fairly common patterns in dividing up the judicial workload in the states. Every state has a small claims court, with informal procedures and prompt adjudication for cases involving relatively small amounts, varying from a ceiling of $1000 up to $5000, with one state (Tennessee) allowing claims up to $15,000 if the county has a population of 700,000 or more. Many states have separate courts for traffic offenses and for less serious criminal matters. Often states will set up special courts for some categories of claims against the government, generally with the right of appeal to a higher court of general jurisdiction. Many states have more than one level of appellate review, with a right to a single appeal, and review in the highest court only by permission of the court, a process known as *certiorari*.

IV. Parallel Systems of Adjudication

In essence, there are two parallel system of adjudication. Most cases in the federal court, except those involving the federal government, could also be maintained in state courts, with the party filing the case having the initial choice. If a case which could have been brought in a federal court is instead filed in state court, the other side may 'remove' it to federal court, but must do so within a relatively short time frame. Once a case is in the federal system, it may be transferred to another federal trial court for the convenience of parties and witnesses; similar provisions generally apply within a state, but not between states or between state and federal courts.

Because federal courts have limited jurisdiction, very few state cases could ever be heard in a federal court. The principal exception is that any state court case that raises an issue of federal statutory or constitutional law is eligible for review by the United States Supreme Court, but only on the federal question presented. Since most defendants in criminal case have some claim that the state has violated their federal constitutional rights, they will often seek Supreme Court review, but it is rarely granted. Despite the prominence of the federal system, only about 280,000 civil and criminal cases, plus another 858,000 bankruptcy cases (most of which are resolved without any court involvement) are filed in it each year, compared to approximately 27.5 million civil and criminal cases filed in all state and local courts annually. In addition, each year there are 4.5 million domestic, 1.7 million juvenile, and over 55 million traffic cases filed. Since the average federal case tends to be much more complicated than the typical state court action, the ratios are somewhat misleading as to the workloads of the respective court systems, but they do make clear that the state and local courts are where most cases are brought.

A final warning: terminologies vary widely, and so even courts with the same name do not necessarily perform the same functions in every state. The most prominent example of name confusion is the New York State Supreme Court. Not only is it not the highest court in the state, but it is the lowest court of general jurisdiction in New York, and it is where most civil and criminal cases are tried.

4

LITIGATION

ALAN B. MORRISON

Scarcely any political question arises in the United States that is not resolved, sooner or later, into a judicial question.[1]

Although there are many people who believe that de Tocqueville's statement about the willingness of Americans to sue is overstated, there are also some who think it's understated; at the very least, it seems clear that Americans utilize their court systems, described in the previous chapter, a great deal. This chapter attempts to provide a framework for litigation in the United States; it does not begin to cover the kinds of materials found in a typical course on procedure.

There are basically two sets of court systems in the United States: the federal court system and one for each of the states, plus the District of Columbia and the various possessions and territories, such as Puerto Rico, Guam, and the Virgin Islands. Although there are both statutory and constitutional limits on the kinds of cases which can be heard in the federal system—unlike state courts, which have general jurisdiction over all state law and some federal law matters—this chapter will focus on the federal court system for a number of reasons. First, it has now become the model for many but not all state systems. Secondly, foreign governments, companies, and individuals can usually elect to use the federal system to sue (or can be sued by) United States citizens whenever the case involves more than $50,000, and the federal system is generally thought to be more favorable than the state systems for

[1] Alexis de Tocqueville, 1 *Democracy in America* 280 (1835) (1948 ed.).

most aliens. Thirdly, the federal courts are also available for resolving questions of federal constitutional and statutory law, and many of the cases involving aliens will fall into that category. Procedural aspects of cases in the federal courts are governed by the Federal Rules of Civil Procedure, which, like the Federal Rules of Evidence, are issued by the United States Supreme Court. The most important Civil Rules will be noted in this chapter and cited as 'Rule . . .'.

Because this chapter is limited to civil cases, it omits the very large and important part of the business of both federal and state courts that involves criminal litigation. That is a separate and very complex subject, the basics of which are covered in Chapter 12. Nonetheless, there are three points worth noting about our criminal justice system:

(1)   the absolute right to trial by jury in all serious cases;
(2)   the right to have a lawyer, paid for by the Government if the accused cannot afford it, in all felony cases; and
(3)   the system is an accusatory one in which the State bears the burden of proving beyond a reasonable doubt that the accused is guilty, and the accused cannot be made to testify against himself, although he has an absolute right to testify on his own behalf if he chooses to do so.

I. Starting a Lawsuit

A lawsuit is begun by the filing of a complaint which need only be a short plain statement of the circumstances showing the basis for relief (Rule 8(a)). Filing is relatively inexpensive ($120), and the fee can be waived for those unable to afford it. There is no requirement that there be a detailed discussion of the law, or for that matter any mention of the specific laws relied on, although most complaints do include a statement of the legal basis for the claim, including any relevant statutes.

The complaint need not contain a detailed statement of the plaintiff's claim nor evidence to support it. Indeed, allegations can be made based on 'information and belief,' which is a standard requiring relatively little evidence for either the complaining party or its lawyer. There is, however, one provision, Rule 11, which requires the lawyer to make a reasonable investigation of the facts and law before filing any paper, including a complaint. The failure to do so may lead to a court imposing sanctions against the lawyer, which may include a monetary penalty and sometimes the payment of some of the attorney's fees of the opposing side.

Pleadings in the federal system are referred to as 'notice pleadings', which means that they are required only to give the opposing side a general idea of the nature of the claim that is sufficient to enable it to begin preparing its defense. The one exception is Rule 9(b), which requires that 'fraud or mistake shall be stated with particularity', but the Rule goes on to make clear that the exception is quite narrow by stating that 'malice, intent, knowledge and other conditions of mind of a person may be averred generally'.

The facts generally can be alleged in quite conclusory fashion and must only be sufficient such that, if they can be proven, they would entitle the plaintiff to the relief sought in the complaint. In most instances, that relief will be money damages, but even then the plaintiff may, but need not, specify exactly how much is being sought. In addition, other complaints may seek what is called 'equitable relief', typically an injunction, either a negative one—for example, forbidding the defendant from putting up a building or tearing one down; or affirmative—for example, requiring the defendant to turn over to the plaintiff specific property, such as stocks or bonds or a valuable antique.

In addition to the relative ease of filing a complaint, there is another aspect of American litigation that increases the number of lawsuits that are filed. Unlike some other legal systems, in the United States the parties to a lawsuit, with limited exceptions, pay for their own attorneys, whether they win or lose. This practice is known as the 'American Rule', in contrast to the rule in Great Britain where the loser generally pays the fees of the winner. Thus, if an individual sues a large company, and the company retains expensive lawyers, the individual will almost never have to pay for those lawyers even if the company prevails completely on the merits. There are some statutes, in areas such as civil rights and suits against the Government, that have exceptions to the general rule that each side pays its own legal fees. Those statutes authorize the courts to order the losing defendant (and in some exceptional circumstances, the losing plaintiff) to pay the other side's legal fees, in addition to other relief that might have been awarded. [2]

Furthermore, in the United States, there is what is known as the 'contingency fee', under which an attorney will receive a fee only if the client prevails by winning in court or by a favorable settlement. Although in theory the client is liable for the costs of the litigation (filing fees, transcript costs, etc., but not the fees of the other side's lawyer), most attorneys do not seek to collect those costs from their clients, in many cases because the clients do not have the money to pay any judgment the lawyer might obtain. This type of joint venture arrangement enables many individuals who cannot afford a lawyer to have their day in court.

---

[2] See e.g. 5 U.S.C. § 552(1) (4) (E); 42 U.S.C. § 1988.

The principal use of this type of fee is in personal injury cases where it is almost always employed. The typical contingent fee is one-third, although there are situations in which the percentage is higher for smaller recoveries and lower for very large awards. Although the use of contingent fees has been criticized, the basic concept is firmly entrenched because it is recognized as an important means of providing access to justice. Generally, the percentage charged is up to the parties, but there are some states that set maximum percentages, and there are efforts underway to restrict further the use and amount of contingent fees and to give clients more information and better bargaining leverage with their lawyers.

II. Responses to the Complaint

After the complaint is filed with the court, it must be provided to the other side, referred to as 'service' (Rule 4(d)). It is accompanied by a court document known as a 'summons', which is the legally binding notice from the court, and which, if not answered, will entitle the plaintiff to a judgment on the basis of the allegations in the complaint (Rule 55). The methods by which service is effected are rather complex, but, in general, they are designed to give reasonable assurance that the person who is summoned receives actual notice of the case. Receipt of the summons and complaint begins the time in which the defendant must respond to the complaint (Rule 12(a)). In most cases, a response is due within 20 days, but whatever the time allowed, it is often extended by agreement of the parties, or on request to the court, which almost always grants at least the first extension sought.

In responding to the complaint, the defendant has two basic choices. First, and the method employed in most cases, is to file an answer. The answer either admits or denies each of the allegations in the complaint, or indicates that the defendant has insufficient information to be able to do so, for instance, where a claim is made that the plaintiff suffered serious injuries, and the defendant is aware that an accident took place, but does not know the extent of any claimed injuries. The answer must contain all of what are known as 'affirmative defenses', which are assertions that there is some additional reason in law why, even if the plaintiff is correct in everything alleged, the defendant would still prevail. One of the most common defenses is the statute of limitations, which is the law that sets the time period within which a complaint must be brought or it will be dismissed as untimely. Generally speaking, those defenses, as well as other personal defenses that do not go to the merits of the plaintiff's claims—such as that the case has been filed in the wrong court, or the court has no personal jurisdiction over the defendant (see Chapter 8, Conflicts of Law)—must be included in the answer or they are considered abandoned (Rule 12(h)(1)).

If the defendant chooses to answer, the defendant may include with the answer any claims that the defendant has against the plaintiff. If those claims, which are referred to as 'counterclaims', arise out of the same transaction or occurrence as the original claim of the plaintiff, the defendant must include them or lose the right to bring them, not only in the present case, but in a future one as well (Rule 13(a)). A typical 'compulsory counterclaim', as it is called, would involve allegations that it was the plaintiff's negligence, not the defendant's that caused the accident and the injury to the defendant, or that it is the plaintiff not the defendant who breached the contract at issue in the case. The theory behind this rule is that the court systems, both federal and state, should have to deal with single transactions once and only once and that there is no good reason not to have the two claims decided in one proceeding. For counterclaims that are not compulsory (called 'permissive counterclaims') (Rule 13(b)), there must be a independent basis on which they could properly be brought in the federal system or else they will be dismissed, but they can be refiled in an appropriate state court.

The difference between an affirmative defense and a counterclaim, especially a compulsory one, is that the former is simply a reason to deny the plaintiff the relief that he seeks, whereas the latter is a request for relief by the defendant. Thus, for example in an automobile accident case, a claim that the plaintiff alone was negligent might be the basis of both an affirmative defense and, if the defendant was injured, a counterclaim. On the other hand, prevailing on a statute of limitations defense, for example, never gives rise to a counterclaim.

Secondly, instead of filing an answer, a defendant may ask the court, in a document known as a 'motion', to dismiss the complaint for a variety of reasons (Rule 12(b)). Those include personal defenses, such as the suit was filed in the wrong court, and, quite frequently, on the ground that the complaint does not state a valid legal claim. Motions of this kind are common and are a very important means by which the defendant can ask the court to decide that, even if the plaintiff can approve every fact alleged, he is still not entitled to win, because the law does not provide the relief requested. If a defendant prevails on such a motion, it can save a great deal of time and money by having the complaint dismissed at an early stage. In some cases the defendant may also move to dismiss based on an affirmative defense, such as the statute of limitations, and a victory on such a motion would have the same effect as a motion deciding that the complaint did not state a valid legal claim.

In some cases, a motion to dismiss is made because the plaintiff, or more accurately, the plaintiff's lawyer, has failed to include in the complaint an essential element of the legal cause of action. Usually, the plaintiff then recognizes the problem and adds the omitted allegations. In such cases, even if the motion is granted, the plaintiff is typically given the right to amend the complaint and include the allegations that the court finds are necessary. In general, most pleadings can be amended, and the courts usually allow that to occur on the theory that the pleading rules should not be traps that preclude either side from presenting its case, but rather should be used to assure that the other side has adequate notice of the nature of the claims at issue (Rule 15).

In many cases, however, the defendant does not assert simply that the plaintiff has left an element out of the complaint, but that the law is not on the plaintiff's side, and there is no legal basis for the lawsuit. In such instances, all of the facts alleged by the plaintiff are required to be accepted by the court as true, and the only proper grounds for debate involve the applicable law. If the trial court agrees with the defendant on the law, the plaintiff's only remedy is an appeal. Even in those cases in which the court allows the plaintiff to proceed, the motion may result in the case being narrowed and will have served to educate both sides and the court about the competing legal theories and arguments, which sometimes may lead to settlement.

This discussion has mentioned the key players in the litigation process—the judge and the opposing lawyers—but it is worth noting the precise roles and responsibilities of each. Under our codes of professional ethics, it is the lawyer's job to represent the client vigorously, and it is not his job to search out the truth. The theory of the system is that the clash of adversary counsel is the best method of bringing forth the truth, subject to certain requirements and limitations, such as the prohibitions against the destruction of documents, and against the offering of perjured testimony, and the requirement that lawyers must advise the court of legal authority of which they are aware which is controlling on the questions before the court, even if it is adverse to them. Stated another way, although a lawyer is considered 'an officer of the court', she is principally the champion of her client and has no responsibility for the other side or for seeing that justice is done.

On the other hand, the judge in the American legal system plays a more or less passive role by not independently seeking to gather facts or present legal theories, but accepts the presentations of the parties and makes a decision on that basis. Because of these different responsibilities, contacts with judges outside the presence of the other side are, except in extremely rare situations, strictly forbidden because they deprive the other side of the opportunity to present opposing arguments and facts to the judge.

III. Multi-Party Actions

So far the discussion has focused on lawsuits in which there is a single plaintiff and single defendant, but such simplicity is increasingly rare. Sometimes, the additional parties are other persons whom the plaintiff claims may be liable to him for some or all of his damages. Similarly, sometimes several individuals have claims against a single defendant, for example, the driver and two passengers in one automobile claim that the driver of another car was responsible for their injuries, and all three join as plaintiffs in the same lawsuit. By and large, rules for joinder of parties (Rule 20) and claims (Rule 18) are very permissive, on the theory that it is more efficient for the judicial system as a whole to handle a single controversy only once. And, when there is more than one defendant, they may make what are known as 'cross-claims' against one another (Rule 13(g)).

There are also a significant number of cases in which a person who is not named as either a plaintiff or a defendant in a lawsuit wishes to join the litigation, a process known as 'intervention' (Rule 24). In some circumstances, it is considered to be unfair to the excluded party to have the case determined without that party's presence. While the excluded party would still have the right to go to court against any of the existing parties, the completion of the first lawsuit could seriously prejudice the excluded party's rights, such as in those situations in which the court decided a contested legal issue that it was unlikely to revisit again in the future. In addition, in the second case, there may be prejudice from factors such as delay, resulting in memories fading or witnesses becoming unavailable, which further argue in favor of allowing any interested party to join the existing lawsuit. Although there are a variety of circumstances in which intervention is required or permitted, the courts generally take a practical approach to the issue and allow it where the excluded party has a good reason for joining and makes his request on a timely basis.

There are also cases, fewer in number, where a party has not been joined and has not requested intervention, but where the interests of justice counsel in favor of having the outsider in the lawsuit, so that the matter can be disposed of once, in a way that does not unduly prejudice the rights of either the present or absent parties. However, in some such situations, it is not possible to require the absent party to come in, either because the lawsuit is in a court that is distant from where the party resides, and the party cannot otherwise be required to participate, or because the party's participation would deprive the court of jurisdiction over the subject of the action (a problem in those cases brought in federal court on grounds of diversity of citizenship, which requires that the parties who are adverse to each other not be citizens of the same state). For a more general discussion of diversity and other bases for subject matter jurisdiction in the federal courts, see Chapter 2.

In situations where the interests of justice require that third parties be brought in, the court will attempt to join them (Rule 19). Where it cannot do so, it must decide whether to allow the suit to proceed without them and, if so, whether any measures can be taken to minimize the possibility of prejudice to both the existing and absent parties. Once again, as with intervention, the law requires the courts to take a practical approach and to try to find some way to minimize inconvenience and unfairness to all concerned.

The most common type of multi-party action is the class action, about which books have been written and which can only be described briefly in these pages.[3] In general terms, a class action is a lawsuit in which one or several named plaintiffs sue on behalf of a large group of people who are not formally named in the suit. Cases can proceed as class actions only if the court approves the class under the specific criteria set out in Rule 23. The class action device is authorized only where the named individuals have claims of fact and law in common with the other members of the class; where the class is too large to require all class members to be individual plaintiffs in the lawsuit; where the named individuals' claims are typical of those of the absent members; and where the named individuals and their attorneys will fairly and adequately represent the members of the class (Rule 23(a)).

Adequate representation is essential because, under the Due Process Clause of the Constitution, no one can be deprived of a legal claim unless that person has his or her day in court. Due process is served if another person in the same position brings a claim encompassing the claims of the class, *and* the court finds that the other person is able to represent everyone adequately. This principle is most often invoked in class actions where only the named plaintiffs are actually bringing the claims, and so the court must find that both the named parties and their lawyers are adequate representatives for those who are not present.

Once again, as with other forms of multi-party actions, the theory behind allowing class actions is one of efficiency; why should there be hundreds or thousands of lawsuits when one case can resolve the issues for one side or the other? The class action is most often used in cases in which there are a large number of persons with small claims, and it would be economically difficult, if not impossible, for each of them to retain their own lawyer, even on a contingent fee basis, to bring their own lawsuit. But by combining forces in a class action, the costs and attorneys' fees are shared among the entire class, and the matter can be efficiently brought to court.

---

[3] See e.g. *Newberg on Class Actions* (2nd ed. 1985).

Class actions, like individuals actions, can seek either money damages or injunctive relief or, in some cases, both. In cases involving money damages, which are brought under Rule 23(b)(3), the principal use is in areas of the law such as the purchase and sale of stock, where there is a common claim that the seller has committed a wrongful act, such as fraud, and that the buyers are entitled to damages. In such cases, the principal issue to be tried is the conduct of the defendant, and the damages to each class member can typically be determined by applying a formula to the number of shares of stock that each person had. Thus, in a process fairly typical of class actions, there would be a determination of the defendants' liability, followed by a more or less routine procedure to determine the damages for each class member. Until recently, other types of damage claims suffered by large numbers of individuals, such as persons harmed by a drug or other consumer product, have not been able to be brought as class actions. However, under some recent rulings, those cases can be maintained as class actions, at least where an overall settlement has been reached with the defendants so that most if not all of the contested issues do not have to be tried, at least on a class-wide basis.

In class actions principally seeking the payment of money damages, individual class members are entitled to notice that the case is pending, they have a right to be represented in the case by their own lawyer, and, most important of all, they have an absolute right to exclude themselves from the class (known as 'opting out') and to bring their own lawsuit (Rule 23(c)(2)). The right to opt out has made it difficult to maintain large numbers of personal injury damage claims as class actions because many individuals will exercise their right to bring their own cases, and thus the efficiency of the class action device is greatly reduced. The right to opt out is considered essential, especially in personal injury cases, because the circumstances of the injury and the nature of the injury suffered are likely to vary widely among class members, and for that reason these kinds of cases are generally considered not amenable to class-wide treatment.

One other essential feature of all class actions is that they cannot be settled by the parties without approval of the court (Rule 23(e)). The purpose of this provision is to be sure that the members of the class are not deprived of their claims unless they receive fair value for them and that the individual plaintiff, and equally if not more important, the plaintiff's attorney, are not paid handsomely by a defendant, who then provides little or no benefit to the remaining members of the class. Thus, the approval process includes an examination of the reasonableness of the amounts paid (or the value of the other relief accorded) to the members of the class, as well as of the lawyers' fees. Court supervision over attorneys' fees is highly unusual and occurs only in class actions and in other similar types of cases, such as stockholder derivative suits described in Chapter 13, or where the client is for some reason, such as youth or disability, unable to make an informed judgment about whether the fee that the lawyer seeks is fair.

The second basic type of class action, brought under Rule 23(b)(2), is that seeking injunctive relief. One very common type of lawsuit in this grouping involves claims by employees that their employer has unfairly discriminated against them on grounds such as race or gender. Typically, the action will seek a court order requiring an end to the discrimination in hiring, promotion, or firing practices of the company, although some complaints may also seek restitution or other monetary relief. Another typical class action of this type would be a claim that the Government was improperly denying benefits under a specific government program to a large group of individuals, and the complaint seeks to correct that practice for the future, coupled, in some cases, with a request for the payment of back benefits. One of the principal differences between injunctive classes and damage classes in the federal courts is that there is no right to opt out of an injunctive class, on the theory that, in general, there is likely to be an identity of interests among the members of such a class. In addition, in many cases the relief sought requires the restructuring of the way in which the defendant conducts its business or an agency of government operates a program, such that it would be impractical, if not impossible, for the defendant to be subjected to conflicting orders based upon different results in different cases. Like damage class actions, cases seeking injunctions can be settled only with approval of the court.

IV. Discovery

In the early days of the American legal system, a party had to prove its case with evidence that it obtained on its own, without help from the other side. In many cases, this put one side at a considerable disadvantage. For instance, in situations involving a defective product, almost all of the information concerning the design or manufacture of the product would be in the control of the defendant, while on the other hand, all of the evidence regarding the extent of the plaintiff's injury would be under the plaintiff's control. Absent some means to alter this imbalance, the result might well be a decision that would be unjust, and, perhaps more commonly, there would be major surprises on both sides as new evidence was brought forth for the first time at trial.

That theory of litigation has now changed radically, and a process known as 'discovery' permits each party to determine, before trial, the basis on which the other will attempt to support its position on the facts and law at trial. Subject to certain privileges, such as the attorney-client privilege, which prevents the other side from asking a lawyer about communications between the client and the lawyer, or the attorney work-product privilege, which precludes an adversary from asking for the work papers of the lawyer and persons working with her on the case, all information in the possession of the other side must be made available (Rule 26). It is not a basis for objecting to a discovery request that the information sought is not admissible evidence, so long as it 'appears reasonably calculated to lead to the discovery of admissible evidence', (Rule 26(b)(1)), which is not a very difficult test to pass. This result is a very sensible one since most cases settle, generally after some or even a great deal of discovery. As a result, the fruits of discovery are often used as bargaining chips against the other side, or as reasons to compromise your own position when settlement is discussed.

Not surprisingly, there are often disputes about what information is relevant, but in the discovery phase the courts are reluctant to deny a request on relevance grounds. However, courts will tend to look more carefully at issues of relevance when the person from whom the information is sought also claims a privilege, or alleges that to provide the information would be extremely burdensome. It is not a proper basis to refuse to supply information that it will be helpful to the other side or harmful to your case.

In some cases where a party objects to producing certain documents, or answering certain questions, the court will require the information to be produced, but will prohibit the party receiving it from making it public (unlike most evidence produced in a lawsuit), at least until it is needed for trial or for a motion (Rule 26(c)). Such orders are known as 'protective orders', and they are quite common, especially in product liability litigation, where the defendant claims that trade secrets or other commercially valuable information may not be disclosed. Although a judge may approve such an order only if she finds 'good cause' to do so, many plaintiffs' lawyers will agree to broad protective orders to avoid litigation and to speed up the discovery process.

There are three principal methods of discovery. The first, known as 'interrogatories', consist of written requests to the other side to answer questions, under oath, within 30 days (Rule 33). Interrogatories are considered very useful at obtaining objective information from the other side, at a quite modest cost, since the only expense is the writing of the questions. They are particularly useful when the other side is an organization, such as a corporation or government agency, because the rules require the organization to make reasonable inquiries to all persons in the organization who might have information about the subject, and it cannot simply respond based on one person's knowledge or lack of it. The principal difficulty in using interrogatories is that, if the question is not precisely phrased, clever counsel on the other side can respond in a way that, while literally true, does not provide information of the kind that the requesting party was actually seeking and would have obtained if the question had been framed slightly differently. In addition, because the answers are prepared by lawyers, although signed by the client, they generally include only basic factual information, presented in the light most favorable to the answering party.

A variation on the interrogatory is the 'request to admit' (Rule 36), under which one party states a proposition and the other is required to admit it or explain why it is not true. In some cases the two are simply rephrasings of each other — 'how fast were you going' is only a small step from being asked to admit that you were driving over 75 miles per hour. In others, the request can be used to authenticate a document, and they save time and money in not having to prove that it is genuine. However, like interrogatories, requests to admit can produce responses that meet the technical requirements of the Rule, but are not very helpful. Thus, in most cases, interrogatories are used instead of requests to admit since they are generally more flexible and take about the same amount of effort and expense to propound.

Secondly, each party can request that their opponent produce documents or other physical evidence (including computer and other electronic files) relating to the subject of the lawsuit (Rule 34). Similar production can be obtained from persons who are not parties, but who have relevant documents, etc., by use of a subpoena issued under Rule 45. Requests for production are extremely powerful tools for finding out the evidence on which the other side will rely, but once again their utility is based on the ability of the questioner to frame the inquiry precisely. To avoid this problem, many requests for production, as well as interrogatories, are stated in extremely broad terms to be sure that all of the relevant information is provided. The result in some cases is that large amounts of unnecessary information are produced at a high cost to the party providing it.

Defendants often object to broad requests, calling them 'fishing expeditions', but there is a countervailing interest on the other side in assuring that defendants do not withhold important information because the question is not phrased with sufficient precision. Information produced in the discovery process can generally be used by the receiving side as evidence at a trial, and the failure to produce documents or to respond to questions may result in the inability of the answering person to offer such evidence on its own behalf, unless there was a valid excuse for the failure to produce it during discovery.

The third method of obtaining discovery is by asking questions under oath to a witness, who may be the other party, an employee of the other party, or a person with no stake in the lawsuit, such as an eyewitness to an accident (Rule 30). Both sides have the right to be present during the proceeding, referred to as a 'deposition', which must be recorded either by a stenographer or on videotape. One obvious advantage of a deposition is that it allows for follow-up questions and assures that any doubts about the meaning of an answer can be pursued immediately. During a deposition, the memory of the witness as to the relevant events is tested, and the witness is often asked to explain documents which she either wrote or received. Evidence obtained at depositions from the other side is admissible at trial, but evidence from witnesses supporting your side may be admitted only in limited circumstances, principally those in which a witness does not testify at trial, either because the witness cannot be found, is dead, or cannot be compelled to attend the trial because she lives in a place distant from the courthouse (Rule 32(a)). Because of the costs of recording, the fact that lawyers on both sides must attend the entire deposition, and because travel is often involved, depositions are generally much more expensive than interrogatories or requests for production, and therefore are used less often by parties with limited litigation resources.

This summary only scratches the surface of the discovery process, which has become the focal point of most litigation, especially in large cases. It is often time-consuming, expensive, and intrusive, but it is nonetheless universally recognized as essential, to a greater or lesser degree, to assure that the facts come out and are not hidden by one side or the other. Not only does discovery enable the parties to learn the facts which the other side has that are favorable to them, but it also enables them to learn the facts that are favorable to their opponents. This latter aspect is a particularly important factor because most lawsuits do not go to trial but are settled, and lawyers and clients can make informed determinations about whether to settle and, if so, on what basis, only when they know the strengths and weaknesses of their case and those of their opponent. Thus, while discovery is often criticized because of the burdens it imposes, a reasonable amount of discovery is essential if informed decisions are to be made about settlement. The problem is drawing the line between reasonable and excessive discovery.

V. Summary Judgment

The principal purpose of a trial is to resolve disputed issues of fact. In many lawsuits, however, because the facts are not in serious dispute, there is a method by which those cases can be resolved without a trial, but after a full opportunity for presentation of the opposing points of view. Most often, 'motions for summary judgment' are made by defendants, but in some cases the plaintiff will move for summary judgment on her own, or cross-move at the time that the defendant moves. In some cases a party will move for partial summary judgment, such as a motion by defendant to strike one claim of several, or a motion by plaintiff to strike an affirmative defense, such as one based on the statute of limitations.

In many cases, the defendant will file a motion for summary judgment under Rule 56, asserting that the facts are not in dispute and that it should prevail as a matter of law, offering evidence from its witnesses, documents, and answers obtained in discovery to support its version of the case. In many cases, the plaintiff will be unable to respond because she has not had the opportunity to take discovery, and the courts in such instances are required to give the plaintiff a reasonable opportunity to gather evidence from the defendant and third parties to support her version of the case (Rule 56(f)). But at some time, after reasonable discovery has been allowed, the defendant is likely to refile the motion, perhaps with additional evidence, and ask that the court dismiss the plaintiff's complaint on the ground that, based on the applicable law and the facts that the plaintiff has established, the plaintiff has no legal claim. Note that on motions for summary judgment, unlike a trial, there is no live testimony, and no right to cross-examine a witness, although that may have happened previously on a deposition. Statements from parties and witnesses (known as 'affidavits') are submitted in written form, sworn to by the person asserting the facts, and based on that person's knowledge and hence ability to testify at trial as to those facts.

Several points should be noted about this process known as summary judgment. First, motions for summary judgment can be made by either side with respect to all or parts of the case, for example, in support of, or opposition to, one theory or one affirmative defense. Thus, granting a motion for summary judgment may not always dispose of the entire case, but it can at least narrow the issues.

Secondly, the question presented on a motion for summary judgment is whether, under the undisputed facts, one side is entitled to prevail as a matter of law. In some ways this is similar to the inquiry at the motion to dismiss stage, since in both situations the focus is on the validity of the opposing party's legal theory. But there is one substantial difference: unlike at the motion to dismiss stage, where all the plaintiff's factual allegations are assumed to be correct, at this stage the plaintiff must have evidence to support her factual allegations, or at least to refute those of the defendant. Thus, for example, a claim that the defendant negligently manufactured a product would survive a motion to dismiss, even without supporting proof, but the claim would not survive a motion for summary judgment where the defendant offered evidence of care in the manufacture, and the plaintiff offered no relevant counter evidence. In both motions, the focus is on the applicable law; the motion to dismiss assumes that the facts set forth in the complaint can be proven, but, on a motion for summary judgment, the facts are those in the evidence that the moving party has presented to the court.

A motion for summary judgment is properly used to decide disputed issues of law; it may not be used to decide disputed issues of fact. Thus, for instance, in an automobile accident case, if the plaintiff has testified that the defendant drove through the intersection when the defendant's light was red, and the defendant testifies that the light was green, it would be improper to decide a motion for summary judgment in favor of either party because there is a disputed issue of fact that must be resolved at trial. That is so even if there were ten witnesses on one side and only one on the other.

Although courts are forbidden to grant motions for summary judgment where there are disputed issues of fact, that limitation applies only where the disputes relate to facts that are relevant to the legal issues in the case. Thus, in the previous example, the color of the light at the intersection is obviously relevant, but the color of the jacket that the plaintiff was wearing, or the color of the defendant's eyes, even if they are in dispute, would not be relevant to the issue of negligence that the court or jury must decide. In these examples, deciding relevance was very easy, but in many cases the issue of relevance will be the central question under the applicable law. In those cases, the dispute will be principally about whether particular facts are relevant to the case, not whether there is a genuine dispute about them. But even where there is a factual dispute about a relevant issue, there is a *genuine* dispute only if there is some evidentiary basis on both sides to support their position. At the summary judgment stage, neither side is permitted simply to assert the contrary of the opponent's position, but must supply some evidence to support that conclusion.

VI. Trial

A very small percentage of the cases filed are actually tried in United States courts—state or federal. Some cases are simply withdrawn without any attempt at proceeding; others are dismissed either on the motion of the defendant to dismiss or for summary judgment; a very large portion are settled with the plaintiff obtaining some, but less than all, of the relief sought in the complaint; and the remainder, generally about 10 percent, go to trial. Some cases are settled for relatively modest sums, where the plaintiff has little chance of prevailing, but the defendant is willing to pay something simply to avoid further costs and attorney's fees. Most of the settlements, however, are based on the assessments of the parties that there are risks on both sides, and that a settlement is in the interest of everyone, rather than risking an all or nothing verdict at trial.

One aspect of American trials has made all litigants conscious of the risks of litigation: the role of the jury. In the federal system, both parties have a right to a trial by a jury, composed of between six and twelve persons, on all claims involving money damages (Rule 38). The Seventh Amendment to the United States Constitution guarantees the right for claims in excess of $20 'in suits at common law' where there was a right to trial by jury, which includes personal injury and breach of contract claims. In the more than 200 years since the Seventh Amendment became law, many new types of actions have been created, and the courts have held that, even if the cause of action is new, if it is of the type for which there would have been a jury trial in 1789, then the claim is one for which there is a right to a jury trial today, even if the claim was first created in 1989. Although the Seventh Amendment applies only to trials in federal courts, most state constitutions contain similar rights to trial by jury.

Juries are picked from the lists of eligible voters in the geographic area covered by the court, and the members serve for relatively brief periods of time, as an obligation of their citizenship. They are compensated, but only minimally, and they are often asked to decide extremely difficult and important disputes. The larger panels of potential jury members are selected by lot, from which individual jurors are excused if there is some reason to believe they would not be impartial—such as being a friend or a relative of a party or of a lawyer in the case. In addition, there is an opportunity for each side to exclude up to three other jurors without specific cause, in winnowing the larger group down to the actual jury, plus one or two alternates.[4] Generally, lawyers use this right, known as a 'preemptory challenge', to remove potential jurors whom they believe would be more favorable to the other side. The Supreme Court has recently limited preemptory challenges to assure that jurors are not excluded based on considerations such as race or sex.

At the trial, which is open for any person to attend (subject to space limitations), the parties present their documentary evidence and witnesses in court, rather than through affidavits, with the plaintiff going first, followed by the defendant, and then any rebuttal by the plaintiff. The party calling the witness asks questions first and then the other side is allowed to question ('cross-examine') the witness. Judges are permitted to ask questions of any

---

[4] 28 U.S.C. § 1870.

witness, but they generally refrain from doing so, especially in jury trials. At the conclusion of the evidence, each side's lawyer is entitled to summarize its case in an effort to persuade the jury to accept its version of the facts. Then the court gives the jury instructions, which are a translation of the law into terms that the jury can understand and apply, and the jury then leaves the courtroom, to discuss the case and vote in secret. In federal courts, the verdict must be unanimous, but in many states the verdict may be by majority of jurors. In most cases the jury will issue a general verdict—'we find that the defendant was not negligent', or 'we find the defendant liable and award plaintiff $100,000'—and in some cases the jury will be asked to answer specific questions, and the judge will then apply the law, a process known as a 'special verdict' (Rule 49). One reason for using special verdicts, especially in complex cases, is to be certain that the jury follows the law, instead of deciding the case on its notions of justice, or because it does not understand the judge's instructions on the legal rules that apply.

The task of the jury is to decide all factual issues. Among the most significant are issues of credibility—whom to believe when there is sharply contrasting testimony. Another vital role of the jury is setting damages, which is particularly significant where the plaintiff has sustained a physical injury, and she seeks compensation for pain and suffering, a determination which is obviously not subject to a precise numerical calculation. It is particularly because of the wide discretion given jurors on setting the amounts of damages that many cases are settled, rather than risking either a very high or a very low verdict.

While the jury controls the determinations of fact, the judge remains in control of the law. The judge's role is evident in several ways. First, at the conclusion of the plaintiff's case, the judge is often asked to rule that the plaintiff has failed to put on sufficient evidence to establish her claim as a matter of law, even if all disputed factual issues on which evidence has been presented are resolved in her favor (Rule 50(a)). That motion, formerly known as a 'motion for a directed verdict', now referred to as a 'motion for judgment as a matter of law', is similar to a motion for summary judgment; it resolves the legal issue in favor of the defendant based upon the evidence presented at trial, whereas the motion for summary judgment is decided based on the evidence presented before trial. In either case, if there are genuine disputed issues of material fact, the court may not grant the motion.

Secondly, in a number of cases, the court will be in doubt as to whether to grant such a motion, but often will deny it and allow the defendant to put on its case and then have the jury reach its decision. If the jury decides in favor of the defendant, then the motion becomes moot. But if the jury rules in favor of the plaintiff, the court has the right to review the situation again, this time also considering the defendant's case, in determining whether there was sufficient evidence to permit the jury to find for the plaintiff (Rule 50(b)). If the judge concludes that there was insufficient evidence on the plaintiff's side, then it may enter a judgment in favor of the defendant, despite the contrary result reached by the jury. The court's power to overturn a jury verdict can also be exercised in favor of a losing plaintiff, but that occurs much less often because generally juries show more sympathy to injured plaintiffs than to defendants. Thus, although the jury is said to be the ultimate arbiter of factual disputes, the court retains the power to assure that the jury does not abuse this power by making unjustifiable factual findings that have the effect of negating the law.

The court has another alternative, to grant a new trial where it believes that, while the evidence may have been legally sufficient, it would be unfair to allow the judgment to stand because the great weight of the evidence pointed to a different result. Such a ruling is often made in cases where the damages are believed by the court to be excessive, or in a few cases inadequate, in which case there would be a retrial only on the issue of damages, but not on liability. The court can also make its ruling on a new trial conditional, by saying to the parties, for example, 'if you are willing to accept $100,000, instead of the $200,000 that was awarded, I will not order a new trial; otherwise there will be a new trial on damages'. It is then up to the parties (which generally means the winning side) to decide whether to accept that offer (known as a remittitur) since the court cannot force them to do so; it can simply order a new trial if they do not.

Although many trials are before juries, there are some cases in which there is no right to trial by jury (such as claims against the United States for personal injuries) or in which the parties may choose to have the case resolved by the judge. While it would be an unusual case in which a person injured in an accident would elect to have the case tried by a judge rather than a jury, there are cases in which both parties prefer a judge for a number of reasons. Among these are the complexity of the case; the fact that the judge may be highly regarded by everyone and/or be very familiar with the case by having ruled on motions along the way; the fact that the case can be presented more quickly before a judge than before a jury; or that for a variety of logistical reasons, the case must be tried in segments, and the judge is better able to handle the stopping and starting than would a jury. But if one party has properly demanded a jury trial, both sides must consent before the case can be tried by a judge alone (Rule 38(d)).

If a case is tried by a judge, the trial proceedings are generally similar to those before a jury, except that the judge will often admit evidence that might be kept from the jury on grounds of relevance or possible prejudice. At the end of the case, or often several weeks thereafter, the judge will issue a ruling in which she is required to make findings of fact and conclusions of law, which are more detailed than a decision by a jury. In many cases, the judge will ask the parties to submit proposed findings, sometimes before trial and sometimes after trial, to assist the court and to sharpen the issues.

VII. Appeals

In the federal court system and in most state courts, the party that loses is entitled to at least one appeal as a matter of right. In addition, in the federal system, a party who loses an appeal may request that the United States Supreme Court hear the case, but review is discretionary in virtually all cases, and the Court hears less than 3 percent of all the cases in which it is asked to rule. The percentage of cases given a second level of review is somewhat larger in most state court systems, but even then it is still relatively rare in civil cases. Cases from state courts can reach the Supreme Court, on a discretionary basis, but only if they present questions of federal statutory or constitutional law.

In general, a person in the federal system has a right to appeal an adverse ruling only at the conclusion of the case. This principle, known as finality, is different from the practice in many state courts where many rulings made during the course of the proceeding, referred to as 'interlocutory decisions', may be appealed at that time, as well as at the end of the case. There are a few exceptions to the finality rule in the federal courts, such as the granting or denying of a request for a preliminary injunction which would remain in effect until the trial can be held, as well as certain other matters which as a practical matter would be unreviewable at the end of the case if they are not reviewed when they are made.

On the appeal, the issues to be decided are principally questions of law, which are decided 'de novo': i.e., the appeals court takes a full and fresh look at the legal issues and will not affirm the decision unless it independently concludes that the trial court made the right rulings. Even when the appeals court finds that the trial judge has made an error, for example, the jury instructions were mistaken in some respect, the judgment may still be upheld if the error is found to be harmless in light of all the circumstances. As it is sometimes put, a party is entitled to a fair trial, not a perfect trial.

Although appellate rulings are generally limited to questions of law, there are two exceptions. First, a party, most often a defendant, will argue that there was insufficient evidence to support the plaintiff's case, and thus as a matter of law the jury should not have been permitted to reach the verdict that it did. Appeals courts will entertain such contentions, not to decide whether the jury was correct in its findings, but only whether, under the law, there was enough relevant evidence to permit the jury to decide the question in favor of the prevailing party. Thus, if a reasonable jury could have reached a conclusion that this jury did, the appeals court will not disturb the verdict simply because it would have reached the opposite result. That power, though rarely exercised, is essential to assuring that juries do not take the law into their own hands by finding facts necessary to produce the outcome they desire.

Secondly, where the facts are found by a judge instead of a jury, an appeals court will overturn a finding if it concludes (as it rarely does) that the trial judge was 'clearly erroneous'. Appeals courts are more willing to reverse a judgment because there was a failure to produce any evidence on a critical point, because the law as given to the jury was incorrectly stated, or because the plaintiff's factual proof did not entitle it to prevail under the existing law. But even these reversals are relatively rare.

There is a third category of issues arising on appeals in which the trial court is almost never overruled. They involve exercises of the court's discretion on matters such as whether additional discovery should be stopped because it has become unduly burdensome, whether further cross-examination should be allowed of a witness, or whether a particular juror should have been excused for cause. In all of those instances the trial judge is exercising her informed discretion about how best to handle the case, and the appeals court, largely in recognition of the need to allow the trial judge flexibility and of her ability to assess first hand all the relevant factors, almost never finds that the trial judge abused her discretion, which is the standard for issues such as these.

Unlike the trial court where there are live witnesses, appeals are decided entirely on the factual record developed in the district court. The losing party writes a document known as a 'brief', which is often as much as 50 pages in length, and the prevailing party then responds, with a brief of similar length, followed by a relatively short reply by the appealing party. The case is assigned to a panel of three judges of the court of appeals who generally, but not in all cases, hear an oral presentation by the lawyers and have the opportunity to ask questions about it. Following oral arguments, which generally last someplace between a half an hour and an hour, the judges discuss the case in private and, some time later, issue a ruling. Until the appeals courts became very busy, there used to be a written opinion explaining the decision in most cases, but that is becoming increasingly less a part of appellate practice. Now, especially when the court affirms the decision below, there is often only a one or two sentence order, sometimes with a brief explanation accompanying it. In perhaps half of the cases, the court issues a lengthy opinion, but that number is decreasing, and in some courts the percentage is far less than that. If a judge disagrees with the result she may write a dissenting opinion, which occurs fairly often. In addition, a judge who may agree with the result may disagree, at least in part, with the rationale in the majority opinion, and may write a 'concurring' opinion that expresses his preferred rationale.

Although statistics are somewhat misleading, or at least inconclusive, the party who prevails in the trial court wins in well over half, and probably close to two-thirds to three-quarters, of the cases appealed. Thus, a party who loses a case in a trial court must give serious thought to whether the appeal is worth the time, the money for lawyers' fees and preparing the record, and additional effort, even where the ruling appears to be wrong or unjust.

VIII. Conclusion

The cautionary note in the preceding paragraph about taking an appeal could properly be applied to all litigation. The process is often expensive, time-consuming, and the outcome uncertain, which is why so many cases are settled and not decided by a judge or jury. Nonetheless, the relative ease of starting a lawsuit, the availability of the contingent fee arrangement, and the opportunity for discovery reflect a general willingness, if not an actual preference, for allowing those who believe they have a claim to seek redress in the courts. Indeed, the First Amendment right to petition the Government for a redress of grievances includes the right to go to court, subject only to reasonable restrictions on access, which may explain why there is so much litigation in this country, especially in contrast to most other societies.

No one believes that the present system cannot be improved, but the concept of access to justice through the court system is firmly entrenched in the culture and laws of the United States and is likely to remain there.

5

AN OVERVIEW OF THE BILL OF RIGHTS

BURT NEUBORNE

I. Introduction

Since even democratically elected governments are capable of violating individual rights, the founding generation insisted that the original text of the Constitution be expanded to include a catalogue of immutable rights that no government could ever ignore. The result was the adoption in 1791 of the first ten amendments to the Constitution—the Bill of Rights—designed to preserve religious liberty; free speech; personal privacy; private property; and procedural fairness against the power of the democratic majority. In the aftermath of a tragic Civil War (1861–1865), fought primarily over slavery, the Constitution was further amended by adding what many have called a second Bill of Rights—the Thirteenth, Fourteenth and Fifteenth amendments—designed to protect equality by outlawing slavery, guaranteeing equal protection of the laws, and assuring the right to vote to members of racial minorities. The protections of the Bill of Rights were expanded yet a third time in the twentieth century when the right to vote was assured to women by the Nineteenth Amendment (1919) and to youths 18 and over by the Twenty-fifth (1970).

Broad as the protections of the modern Bill of Rights are, however, they are not boundless. Most importantly, the Bill of Rights, standing alone, does not protect individuals against misuse of private power. With the important exception of the prohibition against slavery in the Thirteenth amendment, the provisions of the Bill of Rights protect the individual against the government, not against other individuals.[1] Nor does the Bill of Rights guarantee economic or social rights. The document concentrates, instead, on preserving the personal and political rights needed for the proper functioning of a tolerant political democracy, leaving the economic and social arena to the free play of democratic judgment.

The Bill of Rights does not simply catalogue rights, trusting the legislature, the executive, and the electorate to respect them. Rather, the Constitution establishes an institutional enforcement mechanism—judicial review—that vests life-tenured, politically-insulated federal judges (culminating in the Supreme Court) with the power and duty to enforce the Bill of Rights against all government officials—federal, state and local. State judges, many of whom are elected, also measure state and local government action against the guarantees of the Bill of Rights. The result is a nationwide network of judges—state and federal; elected and appointed—engaged in constant surveillance of the activities of the governing majority to assure that the individual rights described in the Bill of Rights are respected in everyday life.

Since the Constitution, including the Bill of Rights, necessarily speaks at a high level of abstraction, its text is often ambiguous. Reasonable people can, and often do, disagree vigorously about its precise meaning. American judges seek to resolve such disagreements in the course of deciding actual 'cases and controversies' brought by aggrieved individuals claiming that a particular exercise of government power violates the Bill of Rights. It is in the process of deciding such disputes that the American judiciary draws the critical line between the domain of the individual and the power of the state. In deciding a constitutional case, an American judge reads the Bill of Rights with the help of judicial precedents—written opinions issued by judges in earlier constitutional cases. Applying the rule of *stare decisis* (respect for precedent), a judge seeks to decide a contemporary constitutional case in a way that is logically consistent with the most analogous past precedents.[2] While there are 'easy' constitutional cases, where a consensus reading of judicial precedent and constitutional text render one outcome clearly preferable, 'hard' constitutional cases often force judges to choose among several plausible readings of precedent and/or text. Much of the intellectual richness of American constitutional law flows from disagreements over the proper approach to such

---

[1] In the modern era, Congress has enacted a significant body of legislation designed to protect constitutional values against private interference. Much of the Congressional activity has been aimed at race and gender discrimination by private persons.

[2] The most important recent discussion of the role of precedent in constitutional adjudication took place in the joint opinion of Justices O'Connor, Kennedy and Souter in *Planned Parenthood* v. *Casey*, 505 U.S. 833 (1992).

'hard' cases. Some judges and academics argue that a literal reading of the constitutional text, using dictionary meaning as a guide, is the most appropriate way to decide a constitutional case. Others argue that the original intentions of the framers should be a primary source of guidance. Yet others argue that a search for morally superior principles embedded in the text and past judicial precedent should guide a judge. And some argue that ambiguities should be resolved in accordance with the felt necessities of the age. The precise meaning of the Bill of Rights is, therefore, the result of a three-cornered partnership stretching back more than 200 years uniting the text written by the founding generation, the interpretive efforts of generations of judges past, and an evolving reading of the constitutional text by the current generation of American judges.

The original Bill of Rights (the first ten amendments) codifies thirty-one ideas.[3] The first six ideas describe an ideal commonwealth of respect for individual conscience, mutual toleration and democratic self-government. The next twenty-three ideas, spread over the Second through Eighth

---

[3] These are:
1. no establishment of religion (1st);
2. free exercise of religion (1st);
3. free speech (1st);
4. free press (1st);
5. free assembly (1st);
6. petition for redress of grievances (1st);
7. right to keep and bear arms (2nd);
8. no quartering troops (3rd);
9. no unreasonable searches (4th);
10. no unreasonable seizures (4th);
11. necessity of warrant on probable cause (4th);
12. specificity of warrant (4th);
13. grand jury indictment in serious cases (5th)
14. no double jeopardy (5th);
15. no compulsory self-incrimination (5th);
16. no deprivation of life, liberty or property without due process of law (5th);
17. no taking of property for private use (5th);
18. no taking of private property for public use without just compensation (5th);
19. impartial criminal jury trial (6th);
20. speedy and public trial (6th);
21. criminal venue—vicinage (6th);
22. notice of criminal charges (6th);
23. right of confrontation (6th);
24. compulsory process for criminal defendants (6th);
25. counsel in criminal cases (6th);
26. civil jury trial (7th);
27. no excessive bail (8th);
28. no excessive fines (8th);
29. no cruel and unusual punishments (8th);
30. enumerated rights do not preclude other rights (9th);
31. powers not delegated to national government are reserved to states and people (10th).

See R. Perry, (ed.), *Sources of Our Liberties* (American Bar Foundation, 1959) at 427–9 for a similar effort to catalogue the contents of the Bill of Rights. See also Eugene V. Hickok, (ed.) *The Bill of Rights: Original Meaning and Current Understanding* 218 (1991).

Amendments, respond to a series of threats to the First Amendment's ideal commonwealth, providing structural antidotes for each perceived danger. The last two ideas, codified in the Ninth and Tenth Amendments, guide future readers about how to resolve ambiguities inherent in any effort to use words to describe rights and define powers.

II. The First Amendment: The Founders' Ideal Commonwealth

What we now call the First Amendment was once third. When Congress proposed the original version of the Bill of Rights in 1789, it consisted of twelve amendments. The first two were alterations of the original Constitutional text. One revised the apportionment formula for the House of Representatives; the other imposed a ban on raising Congressional salaries during the term of office. When neither the apportionment nor the salary amendment commanded enough votes for ratification,[4] the third-ranked amendment emerged as the First.

Despite the equivocal numerology, though, the First Amendment amply deserves its place of honor at the head of the Bill of Rights, uniting for the first time the indispensable pre-conditions to a tolerant democratic society: freedom to believe, freedom of speech, and freedom to engage in collective action. The First Amendment parallels the life-cycle of a democratic idea—a journey from individual belief to collective political action. It opens with protection of freedom to believe, proceeds to freedom to communicate one's beliefs to others, and culminates in the protection of collective action needed to turn beliefs into law.

A. The Religion Clauses: The Freedom to Believe

The two religious freedom clauses—establishment and free exercise—flow directly from the experience of the Founders. Many settlers emigrated to the New World to escape attempts to use the power of the state to force adherence to a dominant religion. The Founders sought to prevent a repetition of the old-world pattern by building a constitutional 'wall' between church and state.

---

[4] Only recently, the ban on raising Congressional salaries finally garnered a sufficient number of state ratifications to qualify as an integral part of the Constitution.

One side of the 'wall', codified in the 'free exercise clause', prevents government from penalizing individual exercises of religious conscience. The other, codified in the 'establishment clause', prevents zealots from using government as an engine to advance religious dogma. Thus, the religion clauses assure both freedom *of*, and freedom *from*, religion.

In a series of 'easy' constitutional cases the Supreme Court has refused to permit religious belief to be used as a test for public office. In *Torcaso* v. *Watkins*,[5] the Court invalidated a law requiring office holders to believe in God, while in *McDaniel* v. *Paty*,[6] the Court struck down a law barring clergy from holding political office. The religion clauses have, however, presented the Court with many 'hard' cases, requiring the courts to resolve clashes between the wishes of the political majority and the claims of individual religious conscience.

1. The free exercise clause

Early attempts to enforce the 'free exercise clause' were unsuccessful. For example, in *Reynolds* v. *United States*,[7] the Supreme Court rejected a challenge to criminal laws banning polygamy by Mormons, despite arguments that consensual polygamy was a tenet of the Mormon faith. In the twentieth century, however, the judiciary has developed a formidable body of precedent protective of individual religious freedom. The modern 'free exercise' era begins in 1963 with the Supreme Court's ruling in *Sherbert* v. *Verner*,[8] that it would violate the free exercise clause to deny a Seventh Day Adventist unemployment benefits merely because she refused to work on her Sabbath. *Sherbert* was applied and expanded in *Wisconsin* v. *Yoder*,[9] when the Supreme Court granted the Old Order Amish a partial exemption from compulsory education laws because modern education violated their religious beliefs.

Under the analysis in *Sherbert* and *Yoder*, government must demonstrate a compelling need before it may penalize an individual for acting in accordance with religious belief. When such a compelling need has been shown, the modern Court has upheld laws that are claimed to burden religious conscience. For example, in *United States* v. *Lee*,[10] the Court declined to exempt Amish businessmen from paying social security taxes for their Amish employees, despite the fact that paying the taxes violated Amish religious scruples.[11]

In *Oregon Employment Division* v. *Smith*,[12] a bitterly divided Supreme Court appeared to modify the *Sherbert* test. In *Smith*, the Court upheld the

[5] 367 U.S. 488 (1961). [6] 435 U.S. 618 (1978). [7] 98 U.S. 145 (1878).
[8] 374 U.S. 398 (1963). [9] 406 U.S. 205 (1972). [10] 455 U.S. 252 (1982).
[11] See also *Jacobson* v. *Massachusetts*, 197 U.S. 11 (1905)(no religious exemption from compulsory vaccination); *Prince* v. *Massachusetts*, 321 U.S. 158 (1944) (no religious exemption from child labor laws).
[12] 494 U.S. 872 (1990).

punishment of a government worker who had been fired for smoking peyote, an illegal hallucinogenic drug, as part of a Native American religious ceremony, holding that since the government interference with the employee's religious worship was not intentional, Oregon was required to demonstrate merely a rational, as opposed to a compelling, need for its action. After *Smith*, the Court appears to distinguish between intentional interferences with religion, which continue to be governed by the stringent *Sherbert* test of compelling need; and unintentional interferences, which are subject to a more permissive test that asks merely whether the government action is rational.[13]

In *Church of the Lukumi Bablu Aye, Inc.* v. *City of Hialeah*,[14] the Supreme Court's first post-*Smith* free exercise case, the Court invalidated a local ordinance banning ritual animal sacrifice because the ban intentionally treated religious activity (ritual animal slaughter) worse than similar non-religious activity (slaughtering animals for food), and was an obvious effort to drive the Santeria cult (an Afro-Cuban religion) out of town.

2. The establishment clause

If the free exercise clause is designed to protect freedom *of* religion, the establishment clause is an effort to guarantee freedom *from* religion. The clause was originally aimed at preventing the emergence of an official church supported by an involuntary tax on all citizens. Not suprisingly, the establishment clause has always been viewed as barring government from singling out a favored religious denomination for preferential treatment. *Larson* v. *Valente*,[15] (condemning 'denominational preferences'). In recent years, the Supreme Court has held that the clause bars government efforts to advance religion generally, even when all religions are treated alike. See for example *Allegheny County* v. *ACLU*.[16]

The current Court applies a three-pronged test in all establishment clause cases that was initially proposed in *Lemon* v. *Kurtzman*,[17] asking whether a challenged government practice: (1) has a secular purpose; (2) has the effect of unduly advancing religion; or (3) results in excessive entanglement of church and state. A positive answer to *any* of the three questions dooms the government practice. In recent years, several Justices have argued that the *Lemon* test should be abandoned in favor of a test that permits greater efforts by government to 'accommodate' the religious desires of the majority.

Where government, in aid of a secular purpose, aids both religious and

---

[13] Congress, believing that the analysis followed in *Smith* fails to provide adequate protection to minority religions, enacted the Religious Freedom Restoration Act of 1992, requiring courts to use the compelling state interest analysis of *Sherbert* in all free exercise cases.

[14] 113 S.Ct. 2217 (1993).   [15] 456 U.S. 228 (1982).

non-religious groups, the establishment clause is not violated merely because a government benefit is incidentally conferred on religion. For example, in *Everson* v. *Board of Education*,[18] the Court upheld a New Jersey law that provided free bus transportation to students in religious schools because it was part of a free school bus plan open to all. Recently, in *Zobrest* v. *Catalina Foothills School Dist.*,[19] the Court approved the provision of a government-paid sign-language interpreter for a deaf student attending a parochial school, noting that similar services would be available to students in secular schools.

On the other hand, where the Court perceives an effort to use government power to advance religious ends, especially in public school settings, the Court has repeatedly condemned the attempt as violative of the establishment clause. In *Engel* v. *Vitale*,[20] the Court outlawed the widespread practice of beginning each public school day with an official non-denominational prayer. In *Abington Township* v. *Schempp*,[21] the Court prohibited the official reading of the Bible as part of public school opening ceremonies. And, in *Lee* v. *Weisman*,[22] the Court ruled that beginning a high school graduation ceremony with an official prayer violated the establishment clause.[23]

Most recently, in *Board of Education* v. *Grumet*,[24] a fragmented Supreme Court struck down an effort by New York State to authorize an orthodox Jewish community to operate a public school system for its learning disabled children, holding that the authorization constituted a discriminatory delegation of governmental power to a religious institution.[25] In *Lamb's Chapel* v. *Center Moriches School District*,[26] the Court ruled that a school board must allow groups wishing to engage in religiously oriented speech the same opportunity to use after-school facilities granted to secular groups. The Court's insistence that religious speech receive equal treatment with secular speech culminated in *Rosenberger* v. *University of Virginia*,[27] where the Court ruled that the University of Virginia was obliged to fund a newspaper published by a student religious group on the same terms enjoyed by secular student publications.

The Court has adopted a strict approach to government efforts to provide

---

[16] 492 U.S. 573 (1989). [17] 403 U.S. 602 (1971). [18] 330 U.S. 1 (1947).
[19] 113 S.Ct. 2462 (1993). [20] 370 U.S. 421 (1962). [21] 374 U.S. 203 (1963).
[22] 505 U.S. 577 (1992).

[23] When prayer in school is wholly student-initiated, not part of the formal school day, and non-coercive, lower courts have tended to permit the practice.

[24] 114 S.Ct. 2481 (1994).

[25] Less direct efforts to introduce officially-sanctioned religious practices into the public schools have also been rebuffed by the Court, e.g. *Stone* v. *Graham*, 449 U.S. 39 (1980) (invalidating law requiring display of Ten Commandments in public school classrooms); *Wallace* v. *Jaffree*, 474 U.S. 38 (1985) (invalidating law compelling moment of silence because intended to reintroduce prayer into classroom); *Edwards* v. *Aguillard*, 482 U.S. 578 (1987) (invalidating law requiring teaching of 'scientific creationism' as effort to impose religious doctrine on curriculum).

[26] 113 S. Ct. 2141 (1993). [27] 115 S.Ct. 2510 (1995).

financial assistance directly to religious schools. Government aid in a form that can potentially be used to promote religious values (even in the context of teaching secular subjects) is forbidden, while non-discriminatory government aid to students in a form that cannot be used to promote religion is permitted. For example, the Court has held that the mere presence of public school teachers in a religious school violates the establishment clause, even when the teachers do nothing more than provide remedial services in secular subjects. See *Aguilar v. Felton*.[28]

In a similar series of fact-sensitive opinions, the Court has banned the public display of religious symbols by the government in a manner that implies government endorsement of the symbols, *County of Allegheny v. ACLU*;[29] but has upheld government display of a Christmas Nativity scene when the presence of non-religious symbols, such as reindeer and candy-canes, render the message a predominantly secular one. See *Lynch v. Donnelly*.[30] Private individuals may display religious symbols on public property, as long as the site is open on a non-discriminatory basis to other persons wishing to display both religious and secular symbols.

One of the great intellectual challenges facing the religion clauses today is the treatment of secular conscience. If religious conscience is treated appreciably more generously by the government than similarly-binding secular conscience, does the discrimination in favor of religious conscience constitute an establishment of religion? If, on the other hand, in an effort to treat secular and religious conscience equally, the government ignores the demands of both, does the refusal to respect religious conscience constitute a violation of the free exercise clause? Finally, if the claims of both secular and religious conscience must be equally respected, will it be possible to have laws binding on everyone, or will virtually all controversial rules be subject to some form of conscientious objection? See generally *Welsh v. United States*,[31] (construing the grant of religious conscientious objection from the draft to apply to certain secular beliefs); *United States v. Seeger*,[32] (broadly construing what constiutes a 'religious' objection).

B. The Speech and Press Clauses

1. Obstacles to the effective protection of speech and press

The First Amendment devotes all of fourteen words to preserving freedoms of speech and press: 'Congress shall make no law . . . abridging the freedom of speech, or of the press . . .'.

---

[28] 473 U.S. 402 (1985).   [29] 492 U.S. 573 (1989).   [30] 464 U.S. 668 (1984).
[31] 398 U.S. 333 (1970).   [32] 380 U.S. 163 (1965).

The literal text purports to bind only Congress, not the President or the FBI; it purports to govern only laws, not regulations; it says nothing about binding states or localities; it says nothing about voting, running for office or the critical right of political association, and is silent on the right of hearers to receive information. It never even attempts to define what 'abridging' means, or what constitutes 'the freedom of speech' or 'of the press'.[33]

Nor is the historical record more promising. For the first 140 years of the Republic, the free speech clause played a relatively minor role in the nation's life. Early political struggles were marred by censorship and intolerance, culminating in the Alien and Sedition Acts and the jailing of dissenting newspaper editors;[34] censorship was widespread during the Civil War period in both the North and the South;[35] labor organizers were routinely jailed during the late nineteenth and early twentieth centuries;[36] opponents of World War I were jailed or deported for their opposition to conscription;[37] political radicals were jailed or deported during the 'Red Scare' of the early 1920s;[38] public school teachers were prosecuted for teaching Darwinian evolution;[39] James Joyce's *Ulysses* was banned from the United States during the 1930s, and the system of free expression was badly battered during the McCarthy era of the 1950s.[40] It was not until 1927 that the first state criminal conviction was reversed by the Supreme Court on free speech grounds, *Fiske* v. *Kanasas*,[41] (reversing conviction of political radicals for advocating industrial revolution); and it was not until 1965 that an act of Congress was invalidated under the First Amendment. *Lamont* v. *Postmaster General*,[42] (invalidating statute interfering with receipt of controversial political material mailed from abroad).

Free speech protection in the United States is, moreover, complicated by the lack of a consensus theory of why we care about protecting speech. Two theories currently vie for acceptance. One, associated with Alexander Meikeljohn,[43] argues that government interference with the free flow of information prevents the public from making informed democratic choices.

---

[33] Although occasional efforts have been made to create a separate jurisprudence for the press clause, most notably by Justice Stewart, the Court's usual approach has been to collapse the press clause into the speech clause, treating the two as a unified protection of communication. See Stewart, 'Or of the Press', 32 *Hastings L.J.* 631 (1975).

[34] See generally Levy, *Legacy of Suppression* (Harvard U.P., 1960); Smith, *Freedom's Fetters* (Cornell U.P., 1956).

[35] See Nye, *Fettered Freedom: Civil Liberties and the Slavery Controversy, 1830–1860* (Mich. St. U.P., rev. ed. 1963).

[36] See Preston, *Aliens and Dissenters: Federal Suppression of Radicals 1903–1933* (Harvard U.P., 1963).

[37] Chafee, *Free Speech in the United States*, 37–41, 51–52, 100–01 (Harvard U.P., 1941).

[38] Roche, *The Quest for the Dream*, 66–68 (Macmillan, 1963).

[39] *Scopes* v. *State*, 154 Tenn. 105, 289 S.W. 363 (1927).

[40] See Chafee, *The Blessings of Liberty* (Lippinoff, 1956). [41] 274 U.S. 380.   [42] 381 U.S. 301.

[43] See Meiklejohn, 'Free Speech and Its Relationship to Self-Government' (Harper, 1948), reprinted in *Political Freedom* (1960). The most powerful metaphor associated with Meikeljohn's approach is that of a free market in ideas in which speakers compete with each other for acceptance by the majority.

He notes that government officials cannot be trusted to control the flow of information because they have a vested interest in persuading the electorate to keep them in power. A second theory, associated with Tom Emerson,[44] argues that free speech is protected, not merely because it is vital to the proper functioning of democratic institutions, but because self-expression is an essential component of human dignity. Emerson argues that speech should be protected, not merely because it makes democracy work better, but because it is a betrayal of the human spirit to suppress individual efforts at self-expression. Modern approaches to free speech are often untidy amalgams of the two theories that fail to acknowledge the tension between an 'instrumental' and a 'dignitary' vision of free speech.

Despite the inauspicious omens of a fragile text, a troublesome history, and the lack of a consensus theory, 75 years of sustained, pragmatic effort by American lawyers and judges has generated a body of precedent interpreting the free speech clause that provides extraordinary protection to free speech in the contemporary United States.

2. Free speech doctrine and the Holmes–Brandeis opinions

The modern free speech clause begins with the celebrated opinions of Justices Holmes and Brandeis in the 1920s.[45] Although Holmes and Brandeis often wrote in dissent, their ideas have triumphed and dominate contemporary free speech law. Their perception that a free market in ideas is essential both to democracy and to individual liberty is the cornerstone of the modern Bill of Rights.

Four fundamental insights about free speech emerge from the Holmes–Brandeis legacy. First, government may never be allowed to censor speech merely because it disagrees with the speaker's viewpoint. Under the Holmes–Brandeis approach, the truth or falsity of an idea is a matter for the individual judgement of free men and women, not the government.

Secondly, since free speech occupies a place of honor in our hierarchy of values, government must demonstrate an interest that transcends ordinary day-to-day concerns before resorting to censorship. In modern parlance, any government interest in censorship must be 'compelling'.

Thirdly, there must be an extremely close causal connection between speech and the harm that it allegedly causes before government can suppress it. Mere speculation, or even plausible fear, cannot justify censorship. In

---

[44] Emerson, *The System of Freedom of Expression* (Vintage Books, 1970).

[45] e.g. *Schenck* v. *United States*, 249 U.S. 47 (1919); *Abrams* v. *United States*, 250 U.S. 616, 627 (1919) (Holmes and Brandeis dissenting); *Whitney* v. *California*, 274 U.S. 357, 372–78 (1927) (Brandeis and Holmes, concurring).

Holmes' timeless phrase, speech must create a 'clear and present danger' of harm before it can be suppressed.

Finally, in modern terms, government must use the 'least restrictive alternative' to regulate speech. Government may not resort to censorship if alternative forms of regulation exist that adequately protect the government interest.

Each of the four Holmes–Brandeis ideas has given rise to an elaborate body of modern free speech doctrine.

3. Modern free speech doctrine: content neutrality

The most eloquent statement of the free speech principle in all of American law was triggered by an effort to force school children to affirm a particular viewpoint: *West Virginia State Board of Education* v. *Barnette*.[46] In *Barnette*, a young Jehovah's Witness was suspended from school for refusing to participate in the compulsory flag salute that began each school day. In words that continue to resonate today, Justice Jackson wrote:

> If there is any fixed star in our constitutional constellation, it is that no official, high or petty, can prescribe what shall be orthodox in politics, nationalism, religion, or other matters of opinion or force citizens to confess by word or act their faith therein. If there are any circumstances which permit an exception, they do not now occur to us.[47]

The refusal to permit government to censor on the basis of viewpoint has ripened into a broad rule that subjects so-called 'content-based' speech restrictions to withering judicial scrutiny. In *R.A.V.* v. *City of St. Paul*,[48] for example, a five-person majority of the Court invalidated a local ordinance forbidding hate speech because the ordinance was premised on disagreement with the speaker's viewpoint.

The Supreme Court views so-called content-based speech regulation with such suspicion that laws capable of being used to censor on the basis of viewpoint are invalid, even if no intent to use them in that way has been shown. See *Simon & Schuster, Inc.* v. *Members of the New York State Crime Victims Board*,[49] (attempt by New York State to impound the proceeds of a convict's crime-related writings in order to make them available to his victim for restitution invalid as content-based); *Arkansas Writers' Project, Inc.* v. *Ragland*,[50] (tax rates keyed to magazine content unconstitutional as content-based); *Minneapolis Star & Tribune Company* v. *Minnesota Comm'r of Revenue*,[51]

---

[46] 319 U.S. 623 (1943). [47] Ibid. at 64. [48] 505 U.S. 377 (1992).
[49] 502 U.S. 105(1991). [50] 481 U.S. 221 (1987). [51] 460 U.S. 575 (1983).

(newspaper tax rates keyed to circulation unconstitutional as content-based); *Police Dep't. of City of Chicago* v. *Mosley*,[52] (picketing rules distinguishing between labor picketing and other subject matter unconstitutional as content-based).

In contrast to its hostility to content-based regulation of speech, the Court has been more sympathetic to so-called 'content-neutral' efforts to regulate the 'time, place or manner' of potentially disruptive speech. For example, the Supreme Court has upheld 'content neutral' parade permit statutes, as long as they do not vest too much discretion in local officials. Compare *Cox* v. *New Hampshire*,[53] (upholding narrowly drawn permit statute), with *Shuttlesworth* v. *Birmingham*,[54] (invalidating imprecise permit statute that invited discriminatory application). In *Ward* v. *Rock Against Racism*,[55] the Court upheld a New York City regulation requiring the use of government-selected 'sound mixers' at noisy rock concerts in Central Park. The *Ward* Court set out a four part test to measure the legality of such 'content neutral' 'time, place or manner' speech restrictions. First, the regulation must apply without regard to substantive content; second, it must be 'narrowly-tailored'; thirdly, it must advance a 'significant' government interest; and, fourthly, it must permit adequate alternative means of communication.

The difficulty of determining whether a speech regulation is content-based or content-neutral is illustrated by the Court's closely divided opinion in *Turner Broadcasting, Inc.* v. *FCC*.[56] Four members of the *Turner* Court argued that a Congressional statute requiring cable broadcasters to transmit the signals of over-the-air television stations was content-based and, thus, subject to the most rigorous level of judicial scrutiny. The five-member majority disagreed, holding that a regulation may treat categories of speakers differently without being labelled content-based, as long as little risk exists that the regulation will be used to control what the speakers say. See also *Leathers* v. *Medlock*,[57] (upholding differential tax rate because no risk of content manipulation).

The Court's reliance in recent years on its content-based approach has been subjected to two lines of criticism. First, since much legitimate regulation of speech is inevitably related to its content (obscenity, libel and commercial speech are three examples), it is increasingly difficult to separate legitimate from illegitimate speech regulations using a content-based metric. More fundamentally, critics have argued that the Court's content-based decisions penalize regulators for attempting to draw fine lines, inducing them to ban more speech than necessary in order to avoid being charged with engaging in content-based discrimination.

---

[52] 408 U.S. 92 (1972).　　　[53] 312 U.S. 569 (1942).　　　[54] 394 U.S. 147 (1969).
[55] 491 U.S. 781 (1989).　　　[56] 114 S.Ct. 2445 (1994).　　　[57] 499 U.S. 439 (1991).

Despite the criticisms, the first step in a modern free speech analysis is to determine whether a government regulation picks and chooses among speech or speakers on the basis of viewpoint or content. If it does, the regulation must satisfy 'strict scrutiny', requiring the government to prove an overwhelming social necessity for the regulation. If it does not, the regulation is subjected to 'intermediate scrutiny', requiring a lesser showing of need.

4. Modern free speech doctrine: interest balancing

The Holmes–Brandeis insistence that the government's interest in censorship must transcend the ordinary day-to-day concerns of government has evolved into the First Amendment 'balancing' doctrine, under which judges weigh the government's asserted interest in censorship against society's profound commitment to free speech. In the absence of a truly 'compelling' governmental interest that counterbalances the nation's commitment to free speech, censorship is forbidden.

An early, non-controversial example of balancing was the Court's refusal to recognize a desire for clean streets as a sufficient justification for censorship. *Schneider v. State*[58]; *Niemotko v. Maryland.*[59] Most recently, a unanimous Supreme Court ruled in *City of Ladue v. Gilleo*,[60] that a town's interest in promoting aesthetics was not sufficiently compelling to justify the banning of virtually all signs from a community. More difficult exercises in balancing include *Texas v. Johnson*,[61] and *United States v. Eichman*,[62] where the Supreme Court overturned convictions for burning the American flag as an act of protest because the government was unable to articulate a sufficiently 'compelling' government interest.

The most attractive aspect of the balancing approach is its candor. A judge engaged in 'balancing' openly reviews the various justifications for censorship proffered by the government and publicly weighs them against free speech. But the balancing metaphor should not lull an observer into thinking that a scientific measurement is taking place. Balancing is a subjective doctrine that invites a judge to establish a hierarchy of values with little or no external guidance. In the hands of judges sympathetic to free speech values, the balancing test results in significant protection. Thus, in *Cohen v. California*,[63] one of the Supreme Court's most sophisticated balancing opinions, the Court invalidated the conviction of a youth for displaying a 'Fuck the Draft' slogan on his jacket because a hearer's anger, hurt feelings, or sensibilities do not generate a sufficiently strong governmental interest to warrant censorship. Whether the controversial speakers have been civil rights

---

[58] 308 U.S. 147 (1939).
[59] 340 U.S. 268 (1951).
[60] 114 S.Ct. 2038 (1994).
[61] 491 U.S. 397 (1989).
[62] 496 U.S. 310 (1990).
[63] 403 U.S. 15 (1971).

demonstrators in the South, or Nazis seeking to march through a Jewish neighborhood, in the absence of a showing of face-to-face insults tending towards violence, the modern Court has 'balanced' hurt feelings and anger against free speech and has refused to permit the suppression of speech merely because it is highly offensive to hearers.

On the other hand, when a judge's subjective values are less protective of speech, balancing can lead to a lower level of free speech protection. In *CCNV* v. *Clark*,[64] for example, the Supreme Court 'balanced' the right of homeless demonstrators to stage a 'sleep-in' protest in Lafayette Park across the street from the White House against the government's interest in maintaining a clean and attractive park and upheld the ban.

5. Modern free speech doctrine: 'clear and present danger'

The Holmes–Brandeis insistence that government prove a close and demonstrable relationship between speech and the harm it allegedly causes has given rise to the Supreme Court's most celebrated speech doctrine, the 'clear and present danger' test.[65] Unlike the Supreme Court's earlier test, which had allowed speech to be censored if it had a mere 'bad tendency' to lead to something undesirable, the 'clear and present danger' test requires government to prove a close causal relationship between the speech in question and the feared evil. Mere speculation or even reasonable apprehension will not suffice.

The leading modern Supreme Court application of the 'clear and present danger' test took place in *Brandenburg* v. *Ohio*,[66] when the Court reversed the criminal conviction of a racist speaker because the government was unable to prove that his words were imminently likely to lead to unlawful acts. *Brandenburg* has been read to provide extremely broad protection to abstract political advocacy, even when the advocacy is of unlawful action. For example, using the *Brandenburg* analysis, the Supreme Court has overturned convictions for hyperbolic threats to the President;[67] threats to engage in disruptive demonstrations[68] and highly charged political rhetoric threatening violence.[69]

[64] 468 U.S. 288 (1984).

[65] The 'clear and present danger' test was initially articulated by Justice Holmes in *Schenck* v. *United States*, 249 U.S. 47 (1919), affirming a conviction for activity that would almost certainly be viewed as protected today. The first case in which the Court used the doctrine to invalidate a conviction on First Amendment grounds was *Stromberg* v. *California*, 283 U.S. 359 (1931), striking down a state conviction for displaying a red flag. [66] 395 U.S. 444 (1969).

[67] *Watts* v. *United States*, 394 U.S. 705 (1969) (reversing a conviction for saying 'If they ever make me carry a rifle, the first man I want to get in my sights is [the President]').

[68] *Hess* v. *Indiana*, 414 U.S. 105 (1973)(reversing conviction for statement during demonstration against the bombing of Cambodia that 'we'll take the fucking street later').

[69] *National Association for the Advancement of Colored People* v. *Claiborne Hardware Co.*, 458 U.S. 886 (1982)(setting aside civil damage award based on statement to crowd at public meeting that 'necks would be broken' if boycott of white businesses were ignored).

On the other hand, the potential weakness of the 'clear and danger' test is illustrated by *Dennis* v. *United States*.[70] In *Dennis*, the Supreme Court upheld the convictions of leaders of the American Communist Party for conspiracy to teach and advocate the overthrow of the government, despite the government's failure to demonstrate that the defendants' political activities had actually created an imminent danger of lawless action.

In order for the clear and present danger test to provide effective protection, judges must be prepared to require the government to prove—not merely to assert—that the speech in question actually creates a clear and present danger. As *Dennis* attests, in times of national hysteria, even the Supreme Court may lack the will to put the government to its proof.

The clear and present danger test has also been used to analyze the First Amendment status of speech likely to provoke a hearer to violence. Where such speech merely causes hurt feelings or anger, the balancing test, discussed above, has been used to protect the speech value. But where face-to-face insults, or incitement to imminent lawless action, are highly likely to provoke an imminent violent reaction, the Court has declined to grant the speech First Amendment protection. In Holmes' words, the First Amendment does not protect the right to shout fire falsely in a crowded theater. Thus, in *Chaplinsky* v. *New Hampshire*,[71] the Court affirmed a conviction for using 'fighting words' in calling someone a 'damned fascist' and a 'God-damned racketeer'. The modern Court has applied the 'fighting words' doctrine narrowly, limiting it to words that have a direct tendency to cause acts of violence by the person to whom, individually, the remark is addressed. *R.A.V.* v. *City of St. Paul* (see section II B3 above), at 414, (White J., concurring in judgment).

6. Modern free speech doctrine: 'least restrictive means'

Finally, the Holmes–Brandeis requirement that government may resort to censorship only when there is no less drastic means of protecting its interests has evolved into a body of doctrine that explores the necessity for censorship. For example, in *Schneider* v. *State*,[72] the Supreme Court invalidated laws banning leafletting in an effort to avoid litter, noting that less drastic means existed to assure clean streets. In *Sable Communications Co* v. *FCC*,[73] the Court invalidated a flat ban on sexually-explicit telephone messages designed to protect children because Congress had failed to consider less drastic means of shielding children from the messages. Most recently, in *City of Ladue* v.

---

[70] 341 U.S. 494 (1951).   [71] 315 U.S. 568 (1942).
[72] 308 U.S. 147 (1939).   [73] 492 U.S. 115 (1989).

Gilleo,[74] the Court observed that means less drastic than complete prohibition exist to protect a community inundated with signs.

The 'least restrictive means' doctrine has been criticized because it permits judges to second-guess legislators on the efficacy of alternative forms of regulation. Responding to such criticism, the Court has relaxed the doctrine in some areas—notably commercial speech—to require merely a reasonable fit between means and ends. See *Board of Trustees of the State University of New York* v. *Fox*.[75]

7. Modern free speech doctrine: categorization

A fifth body of doctrine, unrelated to the Holmes–Brandeis opinions, seeks to use categorization as a means of regulating speech. Instead of asking whether a communication may be censored under the clear and present danger test, the balancing test or some other substantive doctrine, courts have occasionally resorted to labelling as a technique of regulation. For example, obscenity is deemed unprotected by the First Amendment because the Court has labelled it as non-speech. See for example *Roth* v. *United States*;[76] *Miller* v. *California*.[77] It is entirely possible that obscenity might be banned under the clear and present danger or the balancing tests. The government has never been put to its proof, however, because the Court has branded obscenity as non-speech and, thus, has short-circuited the analysis.

Similarly, in the area of defamation and libel, the Court uses categories to distinguish between false speech about public figures or public issues, which gives rise to liability only if the speech is consciously false or delivered with reckless disregard for the truth, and so-called 'private figure' libel, which gives rise to liability if it is negligently false. See generally *New York Times* v. *Sullivan*;[78] *Gertz* v. *Robert Welch, Inc.*[79] Unlike the use of labels in the obscenity area, though, the public/private libel categories are related to a principled effort to provide enhanced protection for speech that contributes to democratic choice.

In yet another effort at categorization, commercial speech is recognized as entitled to free speech protection, but at a lower level than non-commercial speech. Until 1976, advertising and other speech that merely proposes a com-

---

[74] 114 S.Ct. 2038 (1994).   [75] 492 U.S. 469 (1989).   [76] 354 U.S. 476 (1957).

[77] 413 U.S. 15 (1973). The Court's most recent attempt to define obscenity in *Miller* describes obscenity as: '. . . works which, taken as a whole, appeal to the prurient interest in sex, which portray sexual conduct in a patently offensive way, and which, taken as a whole, do not have serious literary, artistic, political or scientific value.'

The most candid definition of obscenity was Justice Stewart's observation that while he could not define obscenity, he knew it when he saw it. *Jacobellis* v. *Ohio*, 378 U.S. 184, 197 (1964).

[78] 376 U.S. 254 (1964).   [79] 418 U.S. 323 (1974).

mercial transaction was not protected by the First Amendment. In *Virginia State Board of Pharmacy* v. *Virginia Citizens Consumer Council*,[80] the Court recognized that the flow of commercial information was necessary to the proper functioning of a free market economy. Accordingly, commercial speech was afforded a degree of First Amendment protection. In *Central Hudson Gas & Electric Corp.* v. *Public Svc. Comm'n*,[81] the Court set out a four-pronged test in commercial speech cases. First, the Court asks whether the speech is truthful and the commercial activity is lawful. If so, the government must demonstrate three things:

(1) a 'substantial' interest in regulating the speech;
(2) a showing that the regulation will 'directly and materially advance' the government's interest; and
(3) the existence of a 'reasonable fit' between the regulation and the advancement of the government's interest.

In contrast to its use of definitional techniques to restrict speech in the obscenity area and to limit speech in the commercial speech area, the Court has been generous in defining speech to include a variety of non-verbal communication techniques, ranging from picketing to nude dancing, although it has often granted non-verbal speech a lower level of protection. Thus, wearing a black armband to protest the war in Vietnam;[82] burning or otherwise altering the flag;[83] wearing military uniforms in a skit;[84] as well as marching, picketing and other forms of 'body rhetoric', have been granted significant levels of free speech protection.[85] But, as the Court's decision upholding a ban on nude dancing and the Court's affirmance of a conviction for publicly burning a draft card demonstrate, the Supreme Court often treats communicative action far less protectively than 'pure speech'.[86]

Given the welter of doctrines and theories, modern free speech doctrine is dizzyingly complex. Political speech is viewed as the core of the First Amendment and receives the highest level of protection, whatever the doctrinal formulation. Religious speech is treated as highly protected, verging on equality with politics. Aesthetic and scientific speech are both viewed as critical to a free society and receive substantial, though slightly less intense, protection, especially when the speech involves sexually explicit material.

---

[80] 425 U.S. 748 (1976).   [81] 447 U.S. 557 (1980).

[82] *Tinker* v. *Des Moines School District*, 393 U.S. 503 (1969).

[83] *Spence* v. *Washington*, 418 U.S. 405 (1974); *Texas* v. *Johnson*, U.S. (1989).

[84] *Schacht* v. *United States*, 398 U.S. 58 (1970).

[85] *Thornhill* v. *Alabama*, 310 U.S. 88 (1940); *Edwards* v. *South Carolina*, 372 U.S. 229 (1963).

[86] *United States* v. *O'Brien*, 391 U.S. 88 (1968) (draft card burning); *Barnes* v. *Glen Theater, Inc.*, 501 U.S. 560 (1991) (nude dancing).

Commercial speech is viewed as a necessary corollary of a free market, but is generally viewed as less deserving of full protection.[87] Modes of speech, whatever the content, involving potentially disruptive forms of behavior, like parading, mass demonstrations and loud music, are entitled to significant protection, but may be subjected to reasonable, 'content-neutral' 'time, place and manner' restrictions. Face-to-face insults dubbed 'fighting words', obscenity, and a small slice of private figure libel are entitled to no protection at all. Not bad for fourteen words.

8. Modern free speech doctrine: procedural protections

(a) *Prior restraints.* In addition to substantive protections, the modern Supreme Court has developed a formidable body of procedural rules that provide important protection to controversial speech.

First, and most importantly, the Supreme Court has repeatedly invalidated 'prior restraints'—efforts to require advance permission from the government in order to speak. The Court has required that even 'unprotected' speech be dealt with by 'subsequent punishment' after it is uttered, not by a prior restraint that forbids the utterance. The first case to reverse a prior restraint was *Near* v. *Minnesota*,[88] setting aside a court order banning the publication of a newspaper for one year as a punishment for libel. The most dramatic application of the prior restraint doctrine in recent years was in *New York Times* v. *United States*,[89] when the Supreme Court rejected the government's attempt to enjoin publication of the 'secret' Pentagon Papers containing embarrassing information about the nation's Vietnam policy. Several members of the Court suggested that publication of 'secret' material might be the basis for subsequent punishment, but agreed that prior restraint was improper. The Court has, however, upheld narrowly-tailored injunctions designed to prevent demonstrators from engaging in unlawful efforts, as part of a protest, to block access to abortion clinics, stressing that the injunctions were necessary to protect the rights of third-persons. See *Madsen* v. *Womens' Health Center*.[90]

(b) *Overbreadth and vagueness.* The Court forbids 'overbroad' laws that purport to ban both protected and unprotected speech. When an overbroad speech regulation is likely to be applied in a significant number of constitutionally protected settings, the Court treats the regulation as absolutely void, even in those settings where a narrowly drawn regulation would have been

---

[87] For example, while political speech is protected by the First Amendment regardless of its truth, false or misleading commercial speech receives no protection at all.

[88] 283 U.S. 697 (1931).   [89] 403 U.S. 713 (1971).   [90] 114 S.Ct. 2516 (1994).

constitutional.⁹¹ For example, in *Board of Airport Commissioners v. Jews for Jesus, Inc.*,⁹² the Court ruled that a flat ban on all political activity in an airport was overbroad, even though a narrowly drawn restriction on particular activity might have been lawful. The overbreadth doctrine is designed to force government to draft narrow and precise regulations when free speech is at stake. The price of sloppy drafting is the total invalidation of the regulation.

The Court also forbids vague laws that vest officials with too much discretion over who is permitted to speak. As with overbreadth, the 'void-for-vagueness' doctrine forces the government to draft careful and precise rules in the speech area. For example, in *Shuttlesworth v. Birmingham*,⁹³ the Court invalidated a local parade permit ordinance because it vested the local police chief with too much power to decide who would and who would not be permitted to conduct a parade.

(c) *First Amendment equality*. The Court imposes strict requirements of equality in the First Amendment area. As we have seen, efforts to treat speakers differently because of the content of their speech trigger lethal scrutiny, even when the government motive is benign. For example, an attempt to tax large newspapers at a different rate than small newspapers in order to help the small papers, was invalidated in *Minneapolis Star & Tribune Co. v. Minnesota Comm'r of Revenue*,⁹⁴ because it was capable of content-based abuse. The First Amendment equality doctrine acts as a powerful prophylactic against the temptation to single out unpopular speech for discriminatory regulation.

(d) *First Amendment due process*. The Supreme Court requires a judicial hearing before a prosecutor or a policeman can seize a book or a movie as allegedly unlawful or otherwise act to take speech out of circulation. See *Marcus v. Search Warrant*.⁹⁵

C. Collective Action: Assembly, Association, and Petition

The First Amendment text closes with two ideas designed to protect resort to collective action designed to transform personal belief into political reality—free assembly and petition for redress of grievances. As with the press clause, the Supreme Court has tended to collapse the assembly and petition clauses into the speech clause. For example, Supreme Court opinions dealing with mass demonstrations—classic exercises of free assembly—have tended to analyze the cases in terms of speech rather than assembly. See for example *Edwards v. South Carolina*.⁹⁶

---

⁹¹ The leading modern overbreadth opinion is *Broadrick v. Oklahoma*, 413 U.S. 601 (1973).
⁹² 482 U.S. 569 (1987).   ⁹³ 394 U.S. 147 (1969).   ⁹⁴ 460 U.S. 575 (1983).
⁹⁵ 367 U.S. 717 (1961).   ⁹⁶ 372 U.S. 229 (1963).

Ironically, the most significant Supreme Court development in the area of collective action has been the recognition of a non-textual right of free association. A crucial line of cases pioneered by Justice Harlan expanded free speech protection beyond the six ideas in the literal First Amendment text to include a seventh non-textual idea—freedom of association—because, in the Court's view, freedom to associate is integral to the advancement of political ideals. In the modern era, the Court has protected free association as though it were speech, forbidding hostile legislatures from demanding the membership lists of controversial organizations[97] and insulating political activity against burdensome regulation.[98] Most importantly, except for high-ranking policy-making jobs, the government may not consider political belief or affiliation in deciding whether to hire or promote a public employee. See for example *Elrod* v. *Burns*; *Branti* v. *Finkel*; *Rutan* v. *Republican Party*.[99]

Although 75 years of sustained judicial effort have resulted in a formidable body of precedent protective of free speech, it would be a serious mistake to view the area as intellectually static. In fact, free speech doctrine is in a constant state of flux, as judges seek to cope with changing technology and mores.

For example, the recent acknowledgement that the First Amendment protects the interests of hearers (as well as speakers) has introduced a new variable into First Amendment law. In some settings—a consumer's right to receive commercial information, for example—the recognition of a hearer's 'right to know' has expanded free speech protection. In others—a homeowner's right to be free from 'focused picketing' at his residence, for example—acknowledging the hearer has resulted in a dilution of the speaker's rights. See *Frisby* v. *Schultz*,[100] (limiting 'targeted' residential picketing). A new generation of scholars have focused on the impact of speech on hearers to argue that violent pornography and hate speech should be censored because of the impact it makes. Initial judicial reaction has been protective of the speaker, while recognizing that racist and sexist speech, especially on the job, can constitute a violation of laws guaranteeing equal

---

[97] *NAACP* v. *Alabama ex rel Patterson*, 357 U.S. 449 (1958); *NAACP* v. *Button*, 371 U.S. 415 (1963). See also *NAACP* v. *Claiborne Hardware Company*, 458 U.S. 886 (1982).

[98] e.g. *Anderson* v. *Celebreze*, 460 U.S. 780 (1983)(ballot access); *Meyer* v. *Grant*, 486 U.S. 414 (1988) (paid petition circulators); *Eu* v. *San Francisco County Democratic Committee*, 489 U.S. 214 (1989) (internal party regulations).

Although some members of the Court have suggested that fundamental political rights, like voting and running for office, should be protected as quintessential forms of collective political action, the Court's voting cases continue to rest primarily on the Fourteenth Amendment fundamental rights/equality principle, which was introduced into American law by the second Bill of Rights, discussed in section V below. *Illinois State Board of Elections* v. *Socialist Workers Party*, 440 U.S. 1 (1979).

[99] 427 U.S. 347 (1976); 445 U.S. 507 (1980); 497 U.S. 62 (1990).

[100] 487 U.S. 474 (1988).

employment opportunities for women and racial minorities. See *Meritor Savings Bank* v. *Vinson.*[101]

Similarly, dramatic changes in technology are forcing the courts to re-examine the ground rules surrounding government regulation of the media. In *Turner Broadcasting Co.* v. *FCC,*[102] the Court propounded a three-tier theory of media regulation. Newspapers and magazines, as purely private speakers, receive the highest level of protection.[103] Radio and television broadcasters, because of the inherent scarcity of the broadcast spectrum, are subject to regulation, but continue to enjoy significant protection from government efforts to dictate content.[104] Cable broadcasters, free from the scarcity rationale, but recognized as 'gatekeepers' on the information highway, are subject to an intermediate level of regulation that provides strong protection against efforts to regulate content, but that allows the government to assure that the 'gatekeeper' role is not abused by preventing others from access to the technology.[105]

Thirdly, an almost universal dissatisfaction with the laws governing campaign finance makes it the subject of intense debate. To what extent may, or should, the personal wealth of candidates or contributors be regulated in the context of a political campaign? Current First Amendment doctrine permits the imposition of limits on campaign contributions, but forbids efforts to control the use of a candidate's personal wealth, or the independent expenditure of funds by supporters.[106]

Disagreement over the First Amendment's role in campaign financing and regulation of the media are examples of the ongoing concern over the effect of resource imbalance on the proper operation of a free market in ideas. May government ever silence a voice that is too strong in an effort to equalize the speech market? May weak speakers receive government subsidies? If so, who gets them, and what strings go with the subsidies?[107] May broadcasters be required to provide free, or cut-rate, air time to candidates? What is the government's proper role as a political speaker? May government seek to distinguish between regulating the content of speech and regulating access to the

---

[101] 477 U.S. 57, 65 (1986).   [102] 114 S.Ct. 2445 (1994).

[103] *Miami Herald Pub. Co.* v. *Tornillo*, 418 U.S. 241 (1974) (no right of access to newspapers).

[104] *Red Lion Broadcasting Co.* v. *FCC*, 395 U.S. 367 (1969) (upholding 'fairness doctrine); *FCC* v. *Pacifica Foundation*, 438 U.S. 726 (1978) (upholding FCC ban on indecent language during periods when children in audience).

[105] *Turner Broadcasting Co.* v. *FCC*, 114 S.Ct. 2445 (1994).

[106] *Buckley* v. *Valeo*, 424 U.S. 1 (1976). Compare *Austin* v. *Michigan Chamber of Commerce*, 494 U.S. 652 (1990) (upholding ban on corporate expenditures on behalf of candidate during election campaign), with *First Nat'l Bank of Boston* v. *Bellotti*, 435 U.S. 765 (1978) (invalidating ban on corporate expenditures on behalf of issues during referendum).

[107] Compare *FCC* v. *League of Women Voters*, 468 U.S. 364 (1984) with *Rust* v. *Sullivan*, 500 U.S. 173 (1992).

technology used to amplify it? These free speech questions, and many more, await the attention of the American judiciary in the years to come.

III. The Fourth Through Eighth Amendments: Control of the Law Enforcement Function

The Founders understood that the utopian polity sketched in the First Amendment was, and is, a fragile one. In an effort to defend it, they surveyed the perceived dangers to their ideal commonwealth, painstakingly ranked them by seriousness, organized them chronologically and provided twenty-three precisely targeted structural antidotes in the Second through the Eighth Amendments.

The most immediate danger envisioned by the Founders, both in terms of impact, chronology and likelihood, was armed subversion. That is why the all-important description of the ideal commonwealth in the First Amendment is immediately followed in the Second and Third by two structural protections against armed subversion—a guaranty of the individual's right to bear arms and a protection against the quartering of troops. While the Second Amendment continues to play a role in debates over gun control, the Founders' fear of armed subversion has, thankfully, never materialized. Accordingly, neither the Second nor Third Amendments have played significant roles in American constitutional law.

With the threat of armed subversion dealt with by the Second and Third Amendments, the Founders turned to the next most serious set of perceived threats to their ideal commonwealth—government abuse of the law enforcement power. Law enforcement proceeds through four chronological stages: (1) investigation; (2) formal accusation; (3) adjudication; and (4) punishment. The twenty-one ideas embodied in the Fourth, Fifth, Sixth, Seventh and Eighth Amendments are a carefully organized set of structural protections designed to guard against abuse at each stage of the process.

A. The Fourth Amendment and the Investigative Phase

The Fourth Amendment regulates the investigative phase, preventing the police from intruding on personal privacy in the absence of probable cause. Like almost all of the provisions of the Bill of Rights, the Fourth Amendment now applies to the states as the result of the 'incorporation' process described in section V A below, although it was originally aimed solely at federal power.

Pursuant to the so-called 'exclusionary rule' imposed by the Supreme Court in *Mapp* v. *Ohio*,[108] evidence obtained by the police in violation of the Fourth Amendment may not be used in any criminal prosecution — state or federal—even if the illegality resulted from a good faith error by the police. Not surprisingly, intense controversy surrounds the exclusionary rule. Proponents cite the rule as evidence of the nation's commitment to constitutional government and argue that no other technique exists to enforce the Fourth Amendment effectively. Critics argue that criminals should not go free merely because the police make a good faith mistake.

Since the Fourth Amendment applies only to 'unreasonable searches or seizures', many police investigatory techniques that do not involve physical interference with person or property (such as visual surveillance, seizure of evidence in plain view, and non-coercive interrogation of witnesses) are not governed by its strictures. But, once investigatory activity intrudes upon an individual's privacy by subjecting him to a search of his property or a restraint of his freedom of movement, Fourth Amendment protections come into play.

The precise point at which unregulated 'investigation' ripens into a Fourth Amendment 'search or seizure' is difficult to define. For example, under current law, while wiretaps or listening devices constitute a search, photographs taken from an airplane flying over a suspect's home do not. Similarly, while any restraint on freedom of movement constitutes a seizure, randomly-sited roadblocks aimed at deterring drunk driving do not. The difficulty of distinguishing between a legitimate interrogation and a forbidden seizure has given rise to an intermediate category, the 'street stop', which may take place on the basis of an 'articulable suspicion' that is less than 'probable cause', but more than a mere hunch. A street stop may be accompanied by a limited pat down or frisk designed to safeguard the police officer.

Under the Fourth Amendment, law enforcement activity that rises to the level of a 'search or seizure' must be predicated on 'probable cause' that evidence of criminal activity will be uncovered or that the target is guilty of a crime. While the precise definition of probable cause remains elusive, it connotes a level of reasonable belief that is greater than mere suspicion, but less than certainty.

Ideally, the decision that probable cause for a search or seizure exists should be made by a neutral magistrate in the process of deciding whether to issue a search or an arrest warrant. Whenever possible, therefore, law

---

[108] 367 U.S. 643 (1961).

enforcement officials are under a duty to seek a judicial warrant before carrying out a search or seizure. Failure to obtain a warrant may render a search or an arrest unlawful, even if the police possessed clear probable cause. The warrant requirement is particularly important in connection with arrests, especially those carried out at night at a person's dwelling.

Despite the strong preference for advance determination by a magistrate, many, perhaps most, searches or seizures take place in the absence of a warrant, either because the need for immediate action makes it impossible to seek a warrant, or because the search falls within one of several judicially recognized exceptions to the warrant requirement, the most important of which are searches incident to lawful arrests; searches conducted under 'exigent circumstances', where delay would impose an unacceptable risk of flight or the destruction of evidence; seizures of evidence in 'plain view'; and seizures of persons in 'hot pursuit'. In such cases, probable cause is tested after the fact, usually in the context of a motion by the accused to exclude the evidence.

Under existing precedent, if a magistrate makes a good faith mistake in the issuance of a warrant, the evidence may, nevertheless, be used; but if a policeman makes a good faith error in carrying out a warrantless search or seizure (either because probable cause did not exist, or because no warrant was obtained), all evidence uncovered as a result of the unlawful search or seizure remains excludable.

B. *The Fifth Amendment and Formal Accusation*

The Fifth Amendment governs the formal accusation phase. Once the investigation has narrowed its focus to a particular target (often after an arrest), the Fifth Amendment requires the prosecution to persuade a grand jury (traditionally a group of twenty-three citizens) to indict the defendant in any serious case. The grand jury originally was viewed as a check on prosecutorial abuse, by requiring a showing of probable guilt before formal charges could be brought. In order to shield the privacy of the accused and the safety of witnesses, the grand jury traditionally hears the prosecution's case in secret. Not even the accused's lawyer is permitted to be present. Indeed, an accused may not even know that he is the subject of a grand jury proceeding. Many believe that the contemporary grand jury no longer acts as a check on prosecutorial power. Rather, the ability of a grand jury to compel testimony in secret has evolved into a powerful prosecutorial tool. Since the grand jury clause of the Fifth Amendment is one of the few provisions of the Bill of Rights that is not binding on the states, several states have replaced the grand jury with a preliminary hearing process that permits both sides to participate.

The 'double jeopardy' clause of the Fifth Amendment prevents the government from prosecuting a defendant more than once for the same offense. A defendant is generally deemed 'in jeopardy' once a jury has been selected and the taking of evidence begins. Thus, once a criminal trial begins, the prosecution may not terminate it in order to begin again. There are, however, two important practical exceptions to the ban on multiple prosecutions. If the jury 'hangs' (is unable to reach a verdict), a subsequent re-trial does not violate the double jeopardy clause, since the proceedings are deemed to be a continuation of the first trial. Moreover, if a defendant succeeds in overturning a conviction on appeal, or if the trial court declares a mistrial at the defendant's urging for reasons other than prosecutorial misconduct, double jeopardy does not bar a re-trial since the defendant is deemed to have waived his objection to a second trial.

The double jeopardy clause bars multiple prosecutions or multiple punishments for the same offense, even though additional evidence of guilt has been discovered. But, it is occasionally difficult to determine whether multiple prosecutions involve the same offense, especially when the same evidence may 'prove' more than one crime. Generally, double jeopardy bars the same sovereign from re-prosecuting for all lesser-included offenses and for different offenses that could have been charged, but permits the use of evidence used in an earlier case in a new prosecution for a different offense, especially when the second prosecution is carried out by a different sovereign. Thus, despite double jeopardy, under the American system of federalism, each sovereign (state or federal) may prosecute a defendant on the same facts, if the sovereign can demonstrate a unique interest that was not adequately present in the initial prosecution. Thus, a defendant acquitted in a state court of assault or murder may be re-tried in a federal court for violating federal civil rights laws, despite the ban on double jeopardy.

The most celebrated protection of the Fifth Amendment is the ban on compulsory self-incrimination, empowering an individual (but not a corporation) to refuse to answer any question or provide any information to the government that creates a risk of criminal prosecution. No inference of criminal guilt may be drawn from an individual's decision to invoke the right to remain silent, although invocation of the Fifth Amendment by a government official in response to questions about official duties may be used as a basis to suspend her.

The right to remain silent was originally designed to shield religious dissenters from being forced to swear an oath to support the dominant religion. More recently, it has been seen as a device to prevent torture or coerced confessions. In one of its most controversial criminal procedure decisions, the Supreme Court ruled that a confession is coerced if it was obtained after an accused has indicated a desire to remain silent, or if the police fail to inform a suspect of his right to remain silent and his right to court-appointed counsel. See *Miranda* v. *Arizona*.[108] As with the Fourth Amendment, statements taken in violation of the Fifth Amendment (including the prophylactic rules laid down in *Miranda*) cannot be used as evidence (or as a help to the police in seeking evidence) in any criminal prosecution.

Once the government has completed the accusatory phase by assembling sufficient evidence to charge an individual with a crime, a strong temptation exists to avoid the cumbersome formalities of the adjudicatory phase by proceeding directly to punishment. It is at this point of great temptation that the Founders inserted the 'due process' clause, forbidding the government from depriving a person of life, liberty, or property without due process of law. The structural placement of the due process clause at the close of the accusatory phase suggests that its initial purpose was important, if modest: to assure that government officials did not jump from formal accusation to punishment without adhering to the norms of adjudicatory fairness set forth in the Sixth Amendment. But the growth of the administrative state has added an important new role for the due process clause. As administrative regulation grew in importance, the due process clause assured that basic norms of procedural fairness were applicable to the regulatory process. Since the due process clause of the Fourteenth Amendment has been the principal vehicle for growth, the modern due process clause will be discussed in section V below under the Fourteenth Amendment.

The Fifth Amendment closes with limits on the government's power to take private property without a public purpose, although in recent years the idea of a public purpose has been very broadly construed by the Supreme Court. For example, taking property and turning it over to private investors in order to stimulate the re-development of run-down areas has been held to be a public purpose. The clause also requires the payment of 'just compensation' for the taking of property (for example, to build a highway or a state office building).

The public purpose and just compensation clauses, thus, complement the due process clause by explicitly removing the government's power to punish opponents by seizing their property. The troublesome line between valid regulation and improper taking has caused the Court much difficulty, discussed more fully in Chapter 11, Property. See for example *Nollan* v. *California Coastal Comm'n*,[109] (invalidating unreasonable conditions imposed on property owner seeking zoning variance); *Dolan* v. *Tigard, Ore*,[110] (invalidating disproportionate conditions imposed on property owner seeking zoning variance).

---

[108] 384 U.S. 436 (1966).   [109] 483 U.S. 825 (1987).   [110] 114 S.Ct. 2309 (1994).

C. The Sixth and Seventh Amendments and the Adjudicatory Phase

The Sixth and Seventh Amendments govern the trial phase. Once the government has lodged formal charges against an accused (typically by grand jury indictment in a criminal case), the Sixth Amendment guarantees an accused a fair hearing on the question of guilt or innocence by requiring:

(1) adequate notice of the charges;
(2) trial in the geographical setting where the crime allegedly took place;
(3) the right to confront and to cross-examine witnesses;
(4) compulsory process to obtain defense witnesses;
(5) the assistance of counsel (without charge, if necessary, in criminal cases); and
(6) trial by an impartial jury.

The Sixth Amendment is one of the earliest efforts to unite the minimum components of a fair hearing in a single document. While its norms explicitly apply only in criminal cases, the Sixth Amendment's fundamental concerns with notice and the right to a fair hearing have provided the principal model for procedural due process of law generally. Two sets of protections are, however, unique to the Sixth Amendment.

First, the Supreme Court has interpreted it to require free court-appointed counsel in any case involving potential incarceration if the suspect cannot afford a lawyer. See *Argersinger* v. *Hamlin*.[111] The *Miranda* decision requires the police to inform a suspect of the right to a free lawyer before any effort at interrogation. The Supreme Court has not, however, extended the absolute right to a free lawyer to civil or administrative proceedings governed by the due process clause. Typically, in proceedings governed by the due process clause, an individual must make a preliminary showing that a free lawyer will be of real help before one will be appointed. Without a lawyer, it is often very difficult for an indigent individual to make such a showing. The potential for unfairness is somewhat abated by the existence of government-funded neighborhood legal services offices where poor people can obtain free lawyers, at least for certain issues. Unfortunately, in recent years, Congress has placed numerous restrictions on Legal Services lawyers and seriously cut back on funding.

The second unique aspect of the Sixth Amendment is its assurance that no defendant can be found guilty of a crime unless a so-called 'petit' (as opposed

[110] 114 S.Ct. 2309 (1994).   [111] 407 U.S. 25 (1972).

to 'grand') jury agrees that the government has proved the charges beyond a reasonable doubt.[112] Traditionally, the petit jury in a criminal case consists of twelve persons, with a unanimous vote required to convict. Failure to reach a unanimous verdict for conviction or acquittal results in a 'hung' jury, often leading to another trial. The traditional twelve-person/unanimous jury remains the norm at the federal level and in most states. Recently, however, the Supreme Court has permitted twelve-person juries to convict on less than a unanimous vote (nine votes), and has upheld the use of unanimous six-person criminal juries.

The criminal jury plays a powerful role in American law. Although a judge can direct a jury in a civil case to reach a particular verdict if the evidence seems overwhelming, the Supreme Court has interpreted the Sixth Amendment as forbidding a directed verdict of guilty, while permitting a directed verdict of not guilty. Thus, a jury of ordinary citizens can exercise an absolute veto—often called jury nullification—over any effort to convict a defendant of a criminal charge, but cannot convict a defendant if the judge believes that it would be unreasonable to do so.

The importance of the jury raises serious concerns about who serves as a juror. Ideally, the jury is chosen from a body of citizens (called the venire or array) chosen at random from the population. Lawyers and the judge question members of the venire in order to select the final jury. Members of the venire who display bias or some other disqualifying characteristic may be disqualified (or 'challenged') for 'cause'. In most cases, moreover, counsel may 'peremptorily' challenge a fixed number of prospective jurors on the basis of hunch or intuition.

From the beginning, concerns have arisen over efforts to manipulate the make-up of a jury. The so-called 'venue and vicinage' clause of the Sixth Amendment (guaranteeing trial at the place where the crime was allegedly committed) was inserted to assure that the site of a criminal trial is not unfairly manipulated to affect the make-up of the jury. Since the adoption of the Fourteenth Amendment, moreover, the Supreme Court has attempted with varying degrees of success to prevent the exclusion of racial minorities from jury service. More recently, the Supreme Court has invalidated state rules impeding women from serving on juries. The Court's preoccupation with assuring a truly representative jury culminated recently in an extraordinary series of cases prohibiting the use of peremptory challenges in both civil and criminal cases on the basis of the race or gender of the prospective juror.

[112] Although the reasonable doubt requirement is not set out explicitly in the Sixth Amendment, the Supreme Court has interpreted the due process clause as requiring proof beyond a reasonable doubt in all settings where incarceration for unlawful conduct is possible, even in juvenile delinquency proceedings that are not formally subject to the Sixth Amendment because they are deemed non-criminal. *In re Gault* 387 U.S. 1 (1967).

The Seventh Amendment guarantees trial by jury in most civil cases in federal, but not state, courts; although most states have constitutional provisions similar to the Seventh Amendment. The Supreme Court has interpreted the civil jury guaranty as freezing the law as it was applied in England in 1789. Thus, if a case would have qualified for a jury trial in the 'law' courts of Westminster in 1789, it qualifies for a jury trial in the United States in 1995. Conversely, if an action would have fallen on the 'equity' side of English practice in 1789, it may be tried by a judge. When confronted with causes of action that did not exist in 1789, the Court asks whether they are more analogous to old fashioned 'law' or 'equity' claims. Applying the historical test, actions in federal court seeking money damages must be tried by a jury unless the parties waive the Seventh Amendment; while actions seeking injunctive relief do not require a jury. Where both damages and an injunction are sought, the preliminary stage of the case (seeking interim injunctive relief) may be tried before a judge, but the final disposition of contested factual issues must be made by the jury.

Unlike the Sixth Amendment jury right which forbids a directed verdict of guilt, judges may freely direct verdicts in favor of either party under the Seventh Amendment if, at the close of the evidence, no reasonable jury could find otherwise.

D. The Eighth Amendment and the Punishment Phase

The Eighth Amendment provides protection during the punishment phase, banning excessive fines and cruel and unusual punishments and assuring that bail will not be set unreasonably high, since the Founders realized that unfair denial of bail results in punishment before trial. Where an indigent accused is unable to post bail, he must remain incarcerated until trial, unless the court agrees to release him on his own recognizance. Recently, the Court has upheld the concept of preventive detention, which permits the denial of bail to defendants who can be shown to pose a threat to the community if released pending trial.

The ban on cruel and unusual punishment was originally intended to prevent physical mutilation and torture. Its contemporary meaning, especially in the context of the death penalty, is a matter of intense controversy. A majority of the Court has refused to hold that the death penalty constitutes cruel and unusual punishment. Instead, the Court has imposed a series of procedural rules designed to assure the fair application of the death penalty. Despite statistics purporting to show racial disparities in the application of the death penalty generally, the Court has declined to intervene in the absence of a particularized showing that race played a role in a specific case.

The Court has, however, interpreted the contemporary cruel and unusual clause as imposing a principle of proportionality on the sentencing process in extreme circumstances. Accordingly, it has struck down efforts to impose the death penalty for anything except murder and has set aside extremely long prison sentences that were wholly disproportionate to the severity of the offence.

IV. The Ninth and Tenth Amendments: The Enigma of the Closing Amendments

Controversy surrounds current efforts to interpret the Ninth Amendment, which provides that 'the enumeration of certain rights shall not be construed to deny or disparage others retained by the people'. Some argue that it has no more legal force than an 'ink blot'. Others read its delphic text as an invitation to protect so-called 'unenumerated rights', rights deemed essential to the idea of ordered liberty that are not explicitly described in the text of the Bill of Rights. Most importantly, an expansive reading of the Ninth Amendment is said by some to be the source of a constitutional right to reproductive autonomy, often characterized as part of a constitutional right to privacy.

In *Griswold* v. *Connecticut*,[113] the Supreme Court struck down a Connecticut statute that banned the use of contraceptives by married persons, holding that it violated a constitutional right to privacy located by various Justices in the First Amendment, the due process clause of the Fourteenth Amendment, the 'penumbras and emanations' of the Fourth and Fifth Amendments, and the open-ended language of the Ninth Amendment. Justice Goldberg, speaking for Chief Justice Warren and for Justice Brennan, wrote an influential concurrence in *Griswold* identifying the role of the Ninth Amendment as the guardian of unenumerated rights.[114]

Griswold's protection of reproductive autonomy was expanded beyond marriage in *Eisenstadt* v. *Baird*,[115] when the Court struck down a Massa-

---

[113] 381 U.S. 479 (1965).

[114] *Griswold* was foreshadowed by the Supreme Court's invalidation of a compulsory sterilization law in *Skinner* v. *Oklahoma*, 316 U.S. 535 (1942), and by Justice Harlan's influential dissent in *Poe* v. *Ullman*, 367 U.S. 497, 541–42 (1961), an earlier case under the Connecticut law that had been dismissed on procedural grounds.

[115] 405 U.S. 438 (1975).

chusetts statute banning the distribution of contraceptives to unmarried persons, and in *Carey* v. *Population Services International*,[116] invalidating a ban on the commercial sale of nonmedical contraceptives.

The Court's reproductive autonomy opinions culminated in its historic abortion decisions in *Roe* v. *Wade*,[117] and *Doe* v. *Bolton*,[118] holding that the constitutional right of privacy was 'broad enough to encompass a woman's decision whether or not to terminate her pregnancy'.

Justice Blackmun's opinion for seven Justices[119] in *Roe* v. *Wade* permitted virtually no government-imposed restrictions on abortion during the first trimester of pregnancy because the state's interest in potential life was overborne by the individual's privacy interest in reproductive autonomy. Somewhat greater state controls over abortion were permitted during the second trimester, generally to preserve the health of the mother. During the third trimester, after the fetus had quickened and was capable of life outside the womb, Justice Blackmun held that the state's interest in protecting imminent life could be overborne only by a serious threat to the life or health of the mother.

The Court's decision in *Roe* was among the most controversial in its history. Critics concentrated on the profound moral disagreement over whether a fetus should be viewed as a living 'person', and on the lack of a clear textual source for a constitutional right of reproductive autonomy. Proponents of a constitutional right of privacy, including reproductive autonomy, have cited the First Amendment (freedom of intimate association); the Ninth Amendment (unenumerated right to privacy); the due process clause of the Fourteenth Amendment (substantive due process including a fundamental right of personal autonomy); the equal protection clause of the Fourteenth Amendment (reproductive autonomy as a necessary component of women's equality); and the emanations and penumbras of the Fourth and Fifth amendments, as potential textual sources. Critics of *Roe* point to the essentially subjective nature of the reading all five textual sources.

The controversy over *Roe* raged for 20 years, dominating the judicial selection process and resulting in a steady erosion of Supreme Court support from the original 7–2 vote to a point where five members of the Court appeared to harbor serious doubts about its correctness. See *Webster* v. *Reproductive Health Services*.[120]

The constitutional battle over abortion culminated in an extraordinary separate opinion by Justices O'Connor, Souter and Kennedy in *Planned*

---

[116] 431 U.S. 678 (1977).   [117] 410 U.S. 113 (1973).   [118] 410 U.S. 179 (1973).

[119] Justice Rehnquist and Justice White dissented in *Roe* v. *Wade*, arguing that the issue should be left to the political process.

[120] 492 U.S. 490 (1989).

Parenthood v. *Casey*,[121] declining to overrule *Roe* v. *Wade*. While the separate opinion in *Casey* appears to contemplate a somewhat greater degree of state regulation of abortion, the pro-*Roe* votes of Justices O'Connor, Souter and Kennedy, coupled with the continuing support for *Roe* by Justices Blackmun and Stevens, appear to have ended the current struggle to overrule the constitutional right to an abortion, especially since the two Justices appointed by President Clinton after the *Casey* opinion—Justices Ginsburg and Breyer—have both endorsed a constitutional right to an abortion.[122]

Roe v. *Wade* was, however, the high water mark for the constitutional right of privacy. In the years following *Roe*, civil rights lawyers were unable to require the government to fund abortions for poor women, even though the government agreed to pay for pregnancy and birth. See *Harris* v. *McRae*.[123] And, in *Bowers* v. *Hardwick*,[124] the Court, by a vote of 5–4, declined to extend constitutional privacy protection to homosexuals charged with consensual sodomy in the home. Current debates over constitutional privacy center on whether it assures a constitutional right to refuse medical treatment and, even, to commit suicide. See *Cruzan* v. *Director, Missouri Dept. of Health*.[125]

The Tenth Amendment has likewise stirred controversy, if not the passion that has surrounded debates over the Ninth Amendment. Some have argued that the Tenth Amendment should be read as a broad protection of federalism, placing judicially-enforceable limits on the central government's power to impose rules on the states. In *National League of Cities* v. *Usery*,[126] five members of the Court used the Tenth Amendment to overrule Congress' decision to impose minimum wage requirements on all state and municipal employees. *National League of Cities* ushered in a decade of intense debate over whether it was possible for the judiciary to identify the essential elements of state power that lie beyond the reach of Congress. In *Garcia* v. *San Antonio Metropolitan Transit Authority*,[127] the Court overruled *National League of Cities* by a 5–4 vote. Justice Blackmun's opinion for the majority suggested that the federalism constraints of the Tenth Amendment were not judicially enforceable. Instead, he argued, states must look to Congress to vindicate their interests. Critics of *Garcia* charged that the Court was abdicating its responsibility to interpret the Bill of Rights. Supporters of the decision argue that Congress is better suited to make the fine judgments needed to balance the national interest against the local concerns of the states.

A curious inconsistency often exists between approaches to the Ninth and

---

[121]   505 U.S. 833 (1992).

[122]   Justice Ginsburg has urged a reappraisal of the intellectual underpinnings of *Roe*, suggesting equality as a stronger rationale. Justice Breyer unequivocally endorsed the constitutional right to an abortion at his confirmation hearing before the Senate Judiciary Committee.

[123]   448 U.S. 297 (1980).   [124]   478 U.S. 186 (1986).   [125]   497 U.S. 261 (1990).

[126]   426 U.S. 833 (1976).   [127]   469 U.S. 528 (1985).

Tenth Amendments. Many critics who urge a broad reading of the Ninth Amendment applaud the *Garcia* Court's reluctance to interpret the Tenth broadly. Conversely, the adherents of a broad reading of the Tenth Amendment often criticize the Court for attempting to read the Ninth Amendment broadly. Several scholars have sought a middle position, arguing that the Ninth and Tenth Amendments are really canons of construction, instructing judges how to read the text of the Constitution. The Ninth Amendment is said to be a direction to read the rights-bearing clauses broadly, while the Tenth is a warning to read the power-granting clauses narrowly.

V. The Thirteenth, Fourteenth, and Fifteenth Amendments: Equality and the Second Bill of Rights

The original Bill of Rights provided historic protection for religious conscience; free expression; collective action; private property; fair procedure; and personal autonomy. It remains the bulwark of individual freedom at the core of American law. It was, however, radically incomplete. In large part because the nation, in 1787, accepted the moral blights of slavery and the subordination of women, the original Bill of Rights was silent on the issue of equality. While the protection of individual rights of conscience and expression in the First Amendment, and the efforts to control the law enforcement apparatus in the Fourth through Eighth Amendments, were limited protections of equality, since they protected the weak from the strong, the lack of an explicit equality guarantee in the Bill of Rights was a fundamental flaw. It took a bloody Civil War, fought primarily over the issue of slavery, to correct it.

With the Union's victory in 1865, the so-called 'Reconstruction Congress' proposed three amendments to the Constitution designed to fulfill the promise of equality to the newly freed slaves—the Thirteenth, Fourteenth, and Fifteenth Amendments. The Thirteenth Amendment abolished slavery and peonage. Although occasional instances of forced labor persisted into the twentieth century, especially for migrant agricultural workers, the command of the Thirteenth Amendment has generally been heeded without the necessity for widespread judicial interpretation.

The Fifteenth Amendment guaranteed the right to vote to members of racial minorities, especially newly freed slaves. Tragically, the promise of the ballot was denied, often by violence. It was not until the 1960s that the

Fifteenth Amendment was vigorously applied by the courts to protect the children and grandchildren of slaves from continuing disenfranchisement. And, even then, the Court adopted a narrow construction of the Amendment to ban only intentional discrimination, leaving rules that have the effect (if not the intent) of disenfranchising racial minorities in effect. It was not until the passage by Congress of the Voting Rights Act of 1965, and its expansion in 1982, that the promise of broad political participation regardless of race was made a reality. The inexcusable hundred year lag between the making of the promise of color-blind access to the ballot in the Fifteenth Amendment and the enforcement of the promise is a graphic reminder that the mere existence of a paper promise to protect rights is meaningless without the societal commitment to protect them.

While the Thirteenth and Fifteenth Amendments were critical components of the addition of equality to the Bill of Rights, the heart of the second Bill of Rights was the equal protection and due process clauses of the Fourteenth Amendment, prohibiting states from denying any person equal protection of the laws or depriving any person of life, liberty, or property without due process of law.

A. The Due Process Clause

The due process clause of the Fourteenth Amendment has played three transforming roles in the evolution of American law. In its least controversial form, it extends the guarantee of procedural fairness enforceable against the federal government under the Fifth Amendment to actions of state and local governments. As the administrative state has evolved in the twentieth century, the promise of uniform procedural fairness at every level of government has provided Americans with an important source of constitutional protection. Although the precise attributes of procedural due process vary with the setting, they include fair notice, an opportunity to be heard, a right to retained counsel, and access to a neutral arbiter.

In its most controversial form, the due process clause of the Fourteenth Amendment (as well as its federal cousin in the Fifth) has been viewed as a source of substantive rights against governmental intrusions into economic markets and personal autonomy. In its initial manifestation, the idea of 'substantive due process' was used to invalidate efforts to regulate the *laissez faire* economy in the early years of the twentieth century. State and federal laws regulating prices, wages, or hours of work were often deemed to deprive person of liberty or property without due process of law, even in those settings where the law was enacted with scrupulous procedural regularity, and where the persons whose rights were allegedly violated (the workers) actually benefitted from the law. Examples of the use of substantive due process to invalidate efforts to regulate the economy include *Lochner* v. *New York*,[128] (invalidating law setting maximum work week for bakers) and *Adkins* v. *Children's Hospital*,[129] (invalidating minimum wage law). Opposing the growth of substantive due process, Justice Oliver Wendell Holmes, Jr., dissenting in *Lochner*, bitterly argued that the Fourteenth Amendment 'does not enact Mr. Herbert Spencer's Social Statics'.

Justice Holmes' ideas ultimately triumphed in *West Coast Hotel* v. *Parrish*,[130] when the Court, confronted with the economic realities of the Great Depression (1929–1939), and a growing political assault on the Court itself, upheld minimum wage legislation. By 1949, the Court unanimously and without controversy announced that it had repudiated the era of economic substantive due process, leaving regulation of the economy to the political branches. See *Lincoln Federal Labor Union* v. *Northwestern Iron and Metal Co.*[131]

With the demise of economic substantive due process, modern cases seeking to protect property rights have centered on whether a regulation constitutes a 'taking' without adequate compensation. Until very recently, it has been almost impossible to challenge economic regulations as uncompensated takings. The current Court has shown somewhat more interest in the issue. See section III B above.

The demise of economic substantive due process did not, however, eliminate the idea that the due process clause has a substantive component. It merely changed its subject matter from economic rights to personal liberties. The modern Supreme Court has invoked substantive due process to protect personal liberty values ranging from reproductive autonomy; to the right to marry; to the right of families to live together. For example, in *Moore* v. *Village of East Cleveland*,[132] Justice Powell explicitly invoked substantive due process to invalidate a law prohibiting a grandmother from living with her grandchildren if they are not siblings. Similarly, the substantive aspect of the due process clause played important roles in *Griswold* and *Roe*. See also *Zablocki* v. *Redhail*,[133] (invalidating restraint on right to marry). Substantive due process methodology remains intensely controversial, however, precisely because of its historic connection with the *Lochner* era and the lack of objective standards to measure judicial behavior.

Thirdly, and perhaps most importantly, the due process clause of the Fourteenth Amendment has acted as the conduit through which the substantive provisions of the original Bill of Rights were made binding on state and local governments. As originally enacted, the first ten amendments to

---

[128] 198 U.S. 45 (1905).   [129] 261 U.S. 525 (1923).   [130] 300 U.S. 379 (1937).
[131] 335 U.S. 525, 535 (1949).   [132] 431 U.S. 494 (1977).   [133] 434 U.S. 374 (1978).

the Constitution were binding solely on the national government. See *Barron v. Mayor of Baltimore*.[134] State and local governments were to be constrained, if at all, by state Bills of Rights. Beginning in 1925, however, the Supreme Court began to read the due process clause of the Fourteenth Amendment as 'incorporating' provisions of the Bill of Rights, thus making them directly applicable against the states. See *Gitlow v. New York*,[135] (free speech clause of the First Amendment applicable against states through Fourteenth Amendment due process clause).

In the years after *Gitlow*, arguments raged over whether the due process clause 'selectively' incorporated only the most important aspects of the Bill of Rights, or whether it incorporated the entire document word for word. While the Supreme Court has clung to a selective incorporation theory, the reality has been the steady incorporation of virtually every provision of the Bill of Rights against the states, with the exception of the grand jury clause of the Fifth and the civil jury clause of the Seventh. The struggle over incorporation can be traced through *Palko v. Connecticut*,[136] (arguing for selective incorporation); *Adamson v. California*,[137] (adhering to selective incorporation by 5–4 vote). The movement toward full incorporation can be traced through *Malloy v. Hogan*,[138] (incorporating self-incrimination clause); *Griffin v. California*,[139] (overruling *Adamson*); *Benton v. Maryland*,[140] (overruling *Palko* and incorporating the double jeopardy clause); and *Duncan v. Louisiana*,[141] (incorporating jury trial clause of Sixth Amendment).

B. The Equal Protection Clause

In the modern era, while members of racial minorities continue to be the paradigm class protected by the equal protection clause, the clause has evolved into a broad charter of equal treatment that reaches beyond race to protect women, aliens, illegitimates and other 'discrete or insular minorities' who have historically been short-changed in the political process. As with the rest of the Bill of Rights, however, its protections run only against the government. Private acts of discrimination must be dealt with, if at all, by legislation at the federal, state or local level.

---

[134] 7 Pet. (32 U.S.) 243 (1833).
[135] 268 U.S. 652 (1925).
[136] 302 U.S. 319 (1937).
[137] 332 U.S. 46 (1947).
[138] 378 U.S. 1 (1964).
[139] 380 U.S. 609 (1965).
[140] 395 U.S. 784 (1969).
[141] 391 U.S. 145 (1968).

1. Racial discrimination

The history of the equal protection clause in the nineteenth century is, sadly, largely a history of judicial failure. Reflecting a national lack of will, the Supreme Court failed to enforce the Thirteenth, Fourteenth, and Fifteenth Amendments well into the twentieth century. See for example, *The Civil Rights Cases*,[142] (invalidating Congressional efforts to ban private discrimination); *Plessy* v. *Ferguson*,[143] (upholding laws mandating racial segregation). The result was the persistence of a regime of state enforced racial apartheid in much of the United States well into the twentieth century.

The United States even fought a war against Hitler's racial madness with black and white troops prevented by law from fighting side by side. In 1951, the State of Texas did not allow interracial boxing matches. In Florida, white and black students were forbidden by law from using the same editions of a school textbook. In Arkansas, white and black voters could not enter a polling place in each other's company. In Alabama, a white female nurse was forbidden to care for a black male patient. Six states required separate bathroom facilities for black and white employees, and a like number forbade white prisoners from being chained to blacks. In seven states, tuberculoses patients of different races could not be treated in the same facility. In eight states, all forms of public recreation—parks, playgrounds, swimming pools, beaches, fishing ponds, boating facilities, athletic fields, amusement parks, racetracks, pool halls, circuses, theaters and auditoriums—were racially segregated by law. Ten states required segregated waiting rooms for all forms of public transportation. Ten states banned interracial marriage and imposed harsh penalties on interracial sexual relations. Eleven states ordered black passengers to ride in the rear of the bus and to give up their seats to whites. Fourteen states segregated railroad passengers by race. Twenty-one states and the District of Columbia—the seat of the national government—operated public schools that were segregated by race as a matter of law.

The story of the effort to redeem the unfulfilled promise of equality in the Fourteenth Amendment begins with the Supreme Court's assault on government-imposed racial apartheid in *Brown* v. *Board of Education*.[144] The *Brown* opinion is majestic in its simplicity. It rejects the idea that 'separate' can be 'equal'. Legally imposed segregation, held Chief Justice Warren, imposes

---

[142] 109 U.S. 3 (1883). [143] 163 U.S. 537 (1896).

[144] 347 U.S. 483 (1954). A companion opinion in *Bolling* v. *Sharpe*, 347 U.S. 497 (1954), invalidated public school segregation in the District of Columbia, a federal enclave that is not subject to the Fourteenth Amendment, which applies only to 'states'. The *Bolling* Court held that the protection of equality in the equal protection clause was applicable against the federal government through the due process clause of the Fifth Amendment, a doctrine known as 'reverse incorporation'. See section V A above, for discussion of the incorporation doctrine.

a badge of inferiority on members of the excluded group and deprives them of the equal protection of the laws. Ninety-seven years after the moral disaster of *Dred Scott*,[145] the Supreme Court's decision in *Brown* began the redemption of the nation's long-delayed promise of equality.

Brown was followed by a burst of Supreme Court activity that eliminated government imposed racial segregation from every aspect of American life. Laws mandating racial segregation (known as Jim Crow laws) on municipal golf courses were invalidated in 1954 and 1955; and on public beaches and in bathhouses in 1955. Laws requiring blacks to sit in the back of the bus were struck down in 1956, in connection with the Montgomery bus boycott, a mass movement that introduced the nation to a young pastor named Martin Luther King, Jr., and a woman of courage and dignity named Rosa Parks, whose refusal to give up her seat to a white man triggered the boycott. In 1958, the Court invalidated laws mandating the segregation of parks and playgrounds. In 1962, segregation in public restaurants at airports was overturned by the Court. In 1963, the Court invalidated segregated courtrooms throughout the South. In 1964, the Court invalidated laws requiring racially separate records for voting, taxation and property ownership and finally outlawed the poll tax. In 1966, segregation in public libraries was outlawed. In 1967, laws banning interracial marriage and miscegenation were struck down—60 years after their initial validation by the Supreme Court. In 1968, prison segregation was outlawed, and laws requiring candidates to be listed on the ballot by race were invalidated.

Unfortunately, enforcement of *Brown* itself languished. In 1964, after 10 years of 'all deliberate speed'—the standard announced by the Court for implementing desegregation—only 2.14 percent of black children residing in the South attended integrated schools. The lack of meaningful progress toward implementing *Brown* caused the Court to reassess its remedial strategy. Beginning in 1963, the Court issued a number of warnings that progress in implementing *Brown* was intolerably slow. In 1968, the Court abandoned its 'all deliberate speed' approach in favor of a command to take affirmative steps 'now' 'to convert to a unitary system in which racial discrimination would be eliminated 'root and branch'. By October 1969, the Court was insisting that even a 4-month delay in implementing 'integration now' was too long. Within 5 years of the adoption of the new remedial posture in 1969, virtually all Southern school districts were racially integrated.

Political opposition to the Court's energized remedial stance was intense. Within a year of the *Charlotte-Mecklenburg* decision upholding forced busing

[145] In *Dred Scott* v. *Sandford*, 60 U.S. 393 (1856), Chief Justice Taney, in an ill-starred effort to avert the Civil War, held that African-Americans could not be full-fledged 'citizens'. Section 1 of the Fourteenth amendment explicitly overrules *Dred Scott* by guaranteeing state and federal citizenship to all persons born or naturalized in the United States.

to achieve racial integration, fifty-nine constitutional amendments banning bussing were introduced into Congress. Congress responded in 1972 and 1974 by enacting a law curbing the remedial authority of the courts in bussing cases. Although the courts ignored the statute when bussing was deemed necessary to eradicate the effects of past unlawful segregation, popular opposition to bussing took its toll. In 1974, Chief Justice Burger ruled in *Milliken* v. *Bradley*,[146] that federal courts could not order inter-district bussing to relieve segregation unless both districts had been guilty of operating segregated schools. The opinion rendered it virtually impossible to desegregate many inner-city schools because the white school population had migrated to the suburbs. Coupled with Justice Rehnquist's opinion for the Court in *Pasadena City Board of Education* v. *Spangler*,[147] casting doubt on whether school segregation caused by the cumulative effect of private decisions (referred to as 'de facto' segregation) was unlawful, *Milliken* brought the Court's remedial phase in *Brown* to a close. Legally imposed segregation had been extirpated 'root and branch', but the Court was unwilling or unable to forge remedies for segregated public schools caused, not by law, but by the cumulative effects of private decisions.

Thus, the promise of *Brown* was only partially fulfilled. Today, ironically, Southern schools are better integrated than their Northern counterparts, where residential segregation is reflected in numerous all-black minority schools providing the segregated education that *Brown* sought to eliminate.

Racial minorities—especially blacks—are the paradigm 'discrete and insular minority' protected by the Fourteenth Amendment. Even before *Brown*, the Supreme Court had applied the Fourteenth Amendment to invalidate overt discrimination on the basis of race. For example, as early as *Strauder* v. *West Virginia*,[148] the Court invalidated a state law forbidding blacks from serving on juries. By the time of *Brown*, the Court had evolved an analytical model that subjected laws burdening members of a racial minority to an exacting standard of judicial review, often called 'strict scrutiny'. Under 'strict scrutiny', a law will be upheld only if the state demonstrates a 'compelling state interest' that cannot be advanced by 'any less drastic means'. The government has been able to meet 'strict scrutiny' in a case alleging a burden on a racial minority only once, in the infamous setting of the internment of Japanese-Americans during World War II. See *Korematsu* v. *United States*.[149]

Ordinarily, however, 'strict scrutiny' is fatal to laws burdening racial minorities. See, for example *Yick Wo* v. *Hopkins*,[150] (racially discriminatory

---

[146] 418 U.S. 717 (1974).   [147] 427 U.S. 424 (1976).   [148] 100 U.S. 303 (1880).
[149] 323 U.S. 214 (1944). The internment of the Japanese-Americans during World War II is conceded to have been an improper surrender to fear and racism. Congress has apologized to the survivors and voted monetary reparations.
[150] 118 U.S. 356 (1886).

application of licensing law violates Fourteenth Amendment); *Loving* v. *Virginia*,[151] (laws forbidding interracial marriage invalid under Fourteenth Amendment); *Palmore* v. *Sidoti*,[152] (invalidating loss of custody based on remarriage to black man); *Batson* v. *Kentucky*,[153] (invalidating racially motivated peremptory jury challenges).

The use of 'strict scrutiny' to protect racial minorities is, however, subject to three significant limitations. The first is that the Fourteenth Amendment protects only against 'state action', although government assistance or enforcement of private discrimination can satisfy the state action requirement in some circumstances. See *Shelley* v. *Kramer*,[154] (judicial enforcement of private racially restrictive covenants constitutes state action). Standing alone, the equal protection clause provides no protection against racial discrimination by private parties. For examples of the Court's struggle to define 'state action' in the context of allegations of racial discrimination. *Terry* v. *Adams*,[155] (pre-primary election by private club constitutes state action); *Burton* v. *Wilmington Parking Authority*,[156] (privately owned restaurant in public bus terminal constitutes state action); *Moose Lodge* v. *Irvis*,[157] (grant of liquor license does not make private club state actor).

Secondly, the Supreme Court has limited the scope of the Fourteenth Amendment to intentional acts of discrimination. See *Washington* v. *Davis*,[158] (Fourteenth Amendment forbids only purposeful discrimination). Inadvertent acts having a discriminatory impact must, ordinarily, be dealt with by legislation.

Thirdly, although the Fourteenth Amendment was undoubtedly enacted in an effort to aid members of racial minorities, one of its unanticipated modern roles has been to limit the government's ability to enact race-based plans designed to assist racial minorities at the expense of the white majority—plans often referred to as 'affirmative action'. Applying 'strict scrutiny' to the 'benign' racial classification in government-imposed affirmative action plans, the Court has upheld race-based affirmative action plans designed to redress past discrete acts of discrimination, but has refused to uphold affirmative action plans designed to redress so-called societal discrimination. For cases dealing with the constitutionality of race-based affirmative action plans, see for example, *Regents of Univ. of California* v. *Bakke*,[159] (upholding preferential admissions plan); *Richmond* v. *J.A. Croson*,[160] (invalidating City Council plan for racial set-asides in local construction contracts); *Shaw* v. *Reno*,[161] (rejecting gerrymandering on basis of race in order to create minority-controlled

---

[151] 388 U.S. 1 (1967).
[154] 334 U.S. 1 (1948).
[157] 407 U.S. 163 (1972).
[160] 488 U.S. 109 (1989).

[152] 466 U.S. 429 (1984).
[155] 345 U.S. 461 (1953).
[158] 426 U.S. 229 (1976).
[161] 113 S.Ct. 2816 (1993).

[153] 476 U.S. 79 (1986).
[156] 365 U.S. 715 (1961).
[159] 438 U.S. 265 (1978).

district); *Adarand Constructors, Inc.* v. *Pena*,[162] (requiring all government affirmative action plans to satisfy strict scrutiny).

2. Discrimination on bases other than race

The Warren Court's egalitarian revolution was not confined to race. Two weeks before his historic opinion in *Brown*, Chief Justice Warren ruled in *Hernandez* v. *Texas*,[163] that the Fourteenth Amendment outlawed discrimination on the basis of national origin as well as race. Chief Justice Warren's opinion for a unanimous Court in *Hernandez* set forth a theory of fluid constitutional protection of groups suffering from community prejudice.[164] Laws burdening such victim groups create 'suspect classifications' warranting 'strict scrutiny' and almost certain invalidation under the Fourteenth Amendment.

In *Levy* v. *Louisiana*,[165] the Court added illegitimacy to its list of 'suspect classifications', and struck down a Louisiana law denying illegitimate children the right to bring a damage action for the death of their mother. Unfair treatment of illegitimate children was invalidated in cases like *Weber* v. *Aetna Casualty & Surety Co.*,[166] and *Trimble* v. *Gordon*,[167] involving the rights of illegitimates to inherit under intestacy laws; but classifications based on legitimacy have been sustained by the Court when they did not appear motivated by irrational prejudice. See *Matthew* v. *Lucas*.[168]

Alienage was added as a suspect classification in 1971, when the Court struck down a federal statute confining public assistance payments to citizens. See *Graham* v. *Richardson*.[169] Two years later, the Court invalidated laws barring aliens from public employment and the practice of law. See *Sugarman* v. *Dougall*;[170] *In re Griffiths*.[171] See also *Hampton* v. *Mow Sun Wong*,[172] (invalidating federal ban on employment of aliens) and *Bernal* v. *Painter*,[173] (invalidating state ban on alien serving as notary public). But the Court has upheld statutes excluding aliens from serving as police officers and public school teachers because of the supposed sensitivity of the jobs. See *Foley* v. *Connelie*,[174] (police); *Ambach* v. *Norwick*,[175] (public school teachers).

The Court has taken a more deferential posture to federal (as opposed to state) efforts to regulate the immigration process. See *Matthew* v. *Diaz*,[176]

---

[162] 115 S.Ct. 2097 (1995). [163] 347 U.S. 475 (1954).
[164] Justice Warren's theory is drawn from footnote 4 of *Carolene Products*, recognizing that special care should be taken when dealing with laws burdening 'discrete and insular minorities' that have been the target of historic prejudice. *Carolene Products Co.* v. *United States*, 304 U.S. 144, 152 n.4 (1938).
[165] 391 U.S. 68 (1968). [166] 406 U.S. 164 (1972). [167] 430 U.S. 762 (1977).
[168] 427 U.S. 495 (1976). [169] 403 U.S. 365 (1971). [170] 413 U.S. 634 (1973).
[171] 413 U.S. 717 (1973). [172] 426 U.S. 88 (1976). [173] 467 U.S. 216 (1984).
[174] 435 U.S. 291 (1978). [175] 441 U.S. 68 (1979). [176] 426 U.S. 67 (1976).

(Medicaid eligibility of alien may be conditioned on permanent residence or continuous stay of 5 years); *Fiallo* v. *Bell*,[177] (upholding failure to grant illegitimate children of natural father preferred immigration status enjoyed by children born in wedlock).

By far the most important addition to the list of victim groups entitled to heightened protection under the Fourteenth Amendment was 'gender'. Women were granted the vote in the United States in 1919, 49 years after racial minorities had been enfranchised by the Fifteenth Amendment. Legally, however, women continued to be treated in a discriminatory manner, reflecting a general societal acceptance of sexual stereotyping. The nineteenth century Supreme Court had upheld laws barring women from becoming lawyers and from voting, stating that 'the paramount destiny and mission of woman are to fulfill the noble and benign offices of wife and mother'. See *Bradwell* v. *State*.[178] As recently as 1948, the Supreme Court had upheld laws banning women from working as bartenders as a 'preventive measure' to protect them against temptation. See *Goesaert* v. *Cleary*.[179]

Since women constitute a majority of the population, the modern Court found it difficult to characterize them as a 'discrete and insular minority' requiring 'strict scrutiny' protection from majoritarian abuse. Accordingly, gender was never explicitly added to the list of 'suspect classifications', despite the urgings of four of the Justices. Instead, the Court applied what it characterized as a form of 'intermediate scrutiny' to laws drawing distinctions on the basis of gender, striking them down when they appeared to reflect a stereotypical view of a women's role. In *Reed* v. *Reed*,[180] the Court's first major gender discrimination decision since the 19th century, Chief Justice Burger invalidated an Idaho law favoring men for appointment as the administrator of an estate, holding that it was based on a stereotypical view of women. The Court followed with a series of decisions striking down gender-based distinctions in access to military health benefits; computation of social security benefits; and eligibility for old age insurance.[181]

The effect of the Court's gender discrimination opinions was to sweep away virtually all governmental disabilities imposed on women. See *Craig* v. *Boren*;[182] *Mississippi University for Women* v. *Hogan*.[183] On the other hand, the Court explicitly upheld gender classifications when they were designed to remedy past discrimination against women. As with the race cases, though, there was a limit to the Court's remedial energy. For women, that point was

[177] 430 U.S. 787 (1977).

[179] 335 U.S. 464 (1948).

[181] See *Frontier* v. *Richardson*, 411 U.S. 677 (1973); *Stanton* v. *Stanton*, 421 U.S. 7 (1975); *Schlesinger* v. *Ballard*, 419 U.S. 498 (1975); *Weinberger* v. *Wiesenfeld*, 420 U.S. 636 (1975); *Califano* v. *Goldfarb*, 430 U.S. 199 (1977).

[182] 429 U.S. 190 (1976).

[178] 16 Wall. (83 U.S.) 130 (1873).

[180] 404 U.S. 71 (1971).

[183] 458 U.S. 718 (1982).

reached when the Court declined to view the exclusion of pregnancy from government health benefits as a form of sex discrimination, although the Court did strike down refusals to permit pregnant teachers to continue working past the fifth month of pregnancy. Compare *Geduldig* v. *Aiello*,[184] (declining to recognize discrimination on basis of pregnancy as 'based upon gender' for purposes of Fourteenth Amendment review), with *Cleveland Bd. of Education* v. *LaFleur*,[185] (invalidating mandatory leave policies forcing teachers to leave classroom after fifth month of pregnancy).

The mentally retarded constitute an anomalous group for the purposes of the Fourteenth Amendment. Although the Court has not granted them formal heightened review status, the Court has subjected statutes burdening them to careful scrutiny. See *City of Cleburne* v. *Cleburne Living Center*,[186] (invalidating failure to grant zoning variance to group home because decision based on stereotypical thinking).

Efforts to expand the category of 'suspect classification' to age, poverty and sexual preference have ended in failure. See *Massachusetts Bd. of Retirement* v. *Murgia*,[187] (declining to apply heightened scrutiny to age classifications); *James* v. *Valtierra*,[188] (declining to apply heightened scrutiny to poverty classification); *Bowers* v. *Hardwick*,[189] (declining to recognize substantive due process or privacy rights of homosexuals charged with criminal sodomy in the home).

3. Fundamental rights review

In addition to expanding the list of 'suspect classifications', the Warren Court extended its egalitarian philosophy by categorizing certain rights as 'fundamental'. Once a right was deemed 'fundamental', any attempt by the government to discriminate in its enjoyment became subject to the same Fourteenth amendment 'strict scrutiny' that generally dooms a 'suspect classification'. For example, by characterizing voting as a 'fundamental' right, the Court was able to provide substantial protection for the right to vote and the right to run for office, despite the lack of any textual protection for voting in the federal constitution. In reapportionment cases, beginning with *Baker* v. *Carr*,[190] the Court used a strict equality analysis to require all legislative bodies, with the exception of the United States Senate (whose malapportioned composition is mandated by the Constitution itself), to be equally apportioned on the basis of one-person one-vote. Similarly, beginning with *Carrington* v. *Rash*,[191] (invalidating a ban on voting by servicemen in Texas

---

[184] 417 U.S. 484 (1974). [185] 414 U.S. 632 (1974). [186] 473 U.S. 432 (1985).
[187] 427 U.S. 307 (1976). [188] 402 U.S. 137 (1971). [189] 478 U.S. 186 (1986).
[190] 369 U.S. 186 (1962). [191] 380 U.S. 89 (1965).

elections) and *Kramer* v. *Union Free School District*,[192] (invalidating a requirement that a voter in a school board election either own real property or be the parent of a school-age child), the Court applied strict scrutiny to invalidate restrictions on the right to vote and to run for office, reasoning that fundamental rights could not be granted to some, but not others, in the absence of a showing of overwhelming need. For representative cases utilizing strict scrutiny equal protection analysis to protect the right to vote, see *Dunn* v. *Blumstein*,[193] (invalidating state and local durational residence requirements for voting); and *Williams* v. *Rhodes*,[194] (invalidating restrictions on third-party candidates).

The Court's effort to label certain non-textual constitutional values as fundamental has generated substantial controversy. As the voting cases demonstrate, the net effect of the technique is to create a non-textual substantive right. Critics argued that fundamental rights analysis was merely substantive due process in a different form because the choice of what right to call fundamental was subjective. Supporters argued that laws mandating unequal access to important rights was exactly what the Fourteenth Amendment was designed to prevent.

When the dust cleared, three non-textual rights—voting; travel and procreation had been elevated to fundamental status. Efforts to further expand the category of fundamental rights failed in *San Antonio Independent School District* v. *Rodriguez*,[195] when the Court declined to recognize education as a 'fundamental' right.

4. Rational basis scrutiny

In the Fourteenth Amendment equal protection cases that do not involve either a suspect classification or a fundamental right, the Court has adopted a deferential standard of review, asking only that a legislative judgment be rationally based. See, for example, *Vance* v. *Bradley*;[196] *U.S. Railroad Retirement Board* v. *Fritz*.[197] Even at the level of rational basis scrutiny, however, the Court has refused to permit unfair treatment of weak groups based on irrational stereotypes. Thus, in *City of Cleburne* v. *Cleburne Living Center*,[198] the Court, claiming to apply rational basis review, struck down a refusal to permit a group home for the mentally retarded, holding that the community's objections were based on irrational stereotypes.

[192] 395 U.S. 621 (1969).   [193] 405 U.S. 330 (1972).   [194] 393 U.S. 23 (1968).
[195] 411 U.S. 1 (1973).   [196] 440 U.S. 93 (1979).   [197] 449 U.S. 166 (1980).
[198] 473 U.S. 432 (1985).

VI. Conclusion

As an experiment in the use of law to protect individual liberty, the Bill of Rights is a great success story. But the continued success of the Bill of Rights is always in doubt. Respect for liberty is notoriously fragile, and 'parchment' protections of the individual have crumbled more often than we care to admit. In the end, no set of institutional safeguards can make a people free if they lack the will and the courage to be free. Eloquently simple and carefully organized, the Bill of Rights lights a path to freedom—but the people must choose to walk it.

6

ADMINISTRATIVE LAW

BERNARD SCHWARTZ

In the American conception, administrative law is concerned with powers and remedies and answers the following questions:
(1)   What powers may be vested in administrative agencies?
(2)   What are the limits of those powers?
(3)   What are the ways in which agencies are kept within those limits?[1]

In answering these questions, American administrative law deals with the delegation of powers to administrative agencies; the manner in which those powers must be exercised (emphasizing almost exclusively the procedural requirements imposed on agencies); and judicial review of administrative action. These form the three basic divisions of American administrative law: delegation of powers, administrative procedure, and judicial review. This chapter will seek to present an overview of these three subjects, focusing on the federal system, which applies to federal as contrasted with state or local agencies, which have similar principles applicable to them. Its aim is to enable the reader to understand the essentials of a system that is, in many ways, so different from those in other countries.

---

[1] Compare Griffith and Street, *Principles of Administrative Law* (Pitman, 2nd ed. 1957) 3.

I. Administrative Agencies

First something should be said about the American administrative agency and its place in the constitutional system. According to the Federal Administrative Procedure Act (as we shall see, now the basic statute in American administrative law) ' "agency" means each authority . . . of the Government of the United States other than Congress, [and] the courts . . .'.[2] This definition equates the agency with the executive branch; under it, every governmental organ outside of the legislature and the courts, except the President and his close personal advisers,[3] is an administrative agency.

This definition is too inclusive for our purposes. Traditionally, American administrative law was not concerned with every government agency exercising executive powers; its concern was primarily with those aspects of administrative authority that affect private rights and obligations. Indeed, there are major functions performed by agencies in the executive branch that are not part of what is ordinarily considered administrative law.

(1)   Among the most significant functions performed by government is military defense. Military agencies are, however, mainly outside the scope of American administrative law. Except under conditions of martial law, the instruments of national force are turned against the outside world. American administrative law is concerned with agencies whose powers are turned inward against private persons or property.

(2)   What is true of the military is true of agencies engaged in the administering of foreign affairs. They also normally do not affect private rights and obligations.

(3)   There are governmental organs engaged in 'housekeeping' functions, such as maintenance of quarters, custody of records, personnel matters, and fiscal management. These functions involve matters of internal administration, whose effect is within the government, rather than upon private rights and obligations.

It should, however, be noted that in exceptional cases, action of these agencies may affect private rights and obligations in a manner that subjects them to administrative law principles—e.g. where a citizen is deprived of the right to travel by refusal of a passport. These borderline cases apart, American administrative law is not interested in agencies vested with the above functions. Almost all of their activities are consequently not part of administrative law.

(4)   During this century, governmental agencies have been established in the United States to operate public services previously operated exclusively

---

[2] 5 U.S.C. § 551.   [3] *Franklin* v. *Massachusetts*, 112 S. Ct. 2767 (1992).

by private enterprise. The outstanding example is the Tennessee Valley Authority. Agencies of this type affect the private community, but their impact is more economic than legal. In the main, they are governed by principles of law similar to those that govern private corporations engaged in comparable activities, rather than by administrative law principles.

This leaves us with two principal kinds of governmental organs:

Regulatory agencies. Present-day administrative agencies are vested with authority to prescribe generally what shall or shall not be done in a given situation (similar to what legislatures do); to determine whether the law has been violated in particular cases and to proceed against the violators (just as prosecutors and courts do); to admit people to privileges not otherwise open to members of the public (as the British Crown once could do); and even to impose fines and render what amount to money judgments. Agencies vested with these powers are usually called 'regulatory agencies' because their activities impinge upon private rights and regulate the manner in which those rights may be exercised. To American administrative lawyers, this is the best-known type of agency; its prototype is the Interstate Commerce Commission, set up as an independent agency in 1887, to regulate the nation's railroads. Today, the agency with the most pervasive mandate is the Environmental Protection Agency (EPA).

Agencies administering benefits programs. There is another group of agencies vested with the authority to dispense benefits for promoting social and economic welfare, such as pensions, disability and welfare grants, and government insurance. The American system of social welfare includes programs of old age, survivors, and disability insurance; medical benefits; aid to families with dependent children; supplementary security income; veterans' pensions and other benefits; and workers' compensation. Agencies that administer these programs include the Social Security Administration, the Health Care Financing Administration, and the Department of Veterans Affairs.

Administrative lawyers initially concentrated on the regulatory agency—for the natural reason that it serves to restrict private rights. It is in this area, accordingly, that the law is more fully developed. An imposing edifice of formal administrative procedure has been constructed, patterned upon, but different from, the adversary procedure of the courtroom. When American jurists speak of the judicialization of the administrative process, it is essentially the regulatory process to which they are referring.

Recent years have, however, seen a substantial shift in the center of gravity toward the non-regulatory area. The Welfare State has converted an ever-growing portion of the community into government clients; Americans, both individuals and businesses, are coming increasingly to live on public largess. For more and more of them, government is coming to represent a primary source of income and other economic benefits. This has necessitated a tremendous expansion of non-regulatory agencies. Quantitatively, the work of the Social Security Administration completely dwarfs that of a regulatory agency like the EPA.

The consequence is a shift in importance from regulatory to non-regulatory administration. Although many lawyers may still not realize it, the growing point of administrative law today is in the non-regulatory area. It is, indeed, the manner in which non-regulatory agencies function that will largely determine whether American administrative law will successfully meet the needs of society at the end of the twentieth century.

II. Independent Agencies and Separation of Powers

The Interstate Commerce Commission type of independent agency remains an important feature of the American administrative process. Such agencies are independent because they are not in any executive department and, most importantly, their members cannot be removed from office by the President except for cause during their prescribed terms which are generally about 5 years. Their constitutional position has, however, recently been challenged. High members of the Reagan administration, particularly the Attorney General (the chief federal legal officer), asserted that the independence of these agencies was contrary to the separation of powers established by the United States Constitution. They urged that agencies carrying out the law must be agents of the Executive and could not be set up as independent bodies outside the executive departments and not subject to the President's unlimited power to remove executive officers appointed by him. There are other officials, such as the Administrator of the Environmental Protection Agency or the Secretary of Agriculture, who perform similar regulatory functions, but who serve at the pleasure of the President and can be removed at any time, for any reason.

The federal courts have rejected the claim that the independent agencies are unconstitutional. In the 1935 *Humphrey* case,[4] the Supreme Court decided that the President could be restricted in his power to remove a member of the Federal Trade Commission, an ICC-type independent agency, to instances where he had good cause to do so. More recently, in 1986, the Court expressly stated that it was not 'casting doubt on the status of "independent" agen-

---

[4] *Humphrey's Executor* v. *United States*, 295 U.S. 602 (1935).

cies'.[5] Then, in 1988, the Court specifically upheld a statute that limited the President's power to remove an independent counsel, appointed to investigate and prosecute high-ranking officials, to removal for cause.[6] This decision confirms the *Humphrey* holding that Presidential removal power over the independent administrative agencies may constitutionally be restricted to removal only for cause. As a federal appeals court put it, in rejecting a challenge to the constitutionality of the Federal Trade Commission's independent position, the recent Supreme Court decisions only confirm the continuing vitality of the *Humphrey* precedent.[7]

III. Delegation

Administrative power is as old as American government itself. The very first session of the First Congress enacted three statutes conferring important administrative powers. Well before the setting up of the Interstate Commerce Commission (ICC) in 1887—the date usually considered the beginning of American administrative law—agencies were established which possessed the rule-making and/or adjudicatory powers that are usually considered to be characteristic of the administrative agency. Modern American administrative law, nevertheless, may be said to start with the Interstate Commerce Commission, the archetype of the contemporary administrative agency in the United States. It has served as the model for a whole host of federal and state agencies that were vested with delegated powers patterned after those conferred upon the first federal regulatory commission.

Conscious use of the law to regulate society has required the creation of an ever-growing administrative bureaucracy. The ICC has spawned a progeny that has threatened to exhaust the alphabet in the use of initials to characterize the new bodies. Nor has the expansion of administrative power been limited to the ICC-type economic regulation. A trend toward extension into areas of social welfare began with the Social Security Act of 1935. Disability benefits, welfare, aid to dependent children, health care, and a growing list of social services have since come under the guardianship of the administrative process.

During the past quarter century, a new generation of administrative agencies has also been created. These agencies have been a direct product of the increased concern with consumer and environmental protection that has so

---

[5] *Bowsher* v. *Synar*, 478 U.S. 714 at 725 (1986).
[6] *Morrison* v. *Olson*, 487 U.S. 654 (1988).
[7] *FTC* v. *American Natl. Cellular*, 810 F.2d 1511 (9th Cir. 1987).

changed American public law in recent years. The leading agencies among this newer breed are the Environmental Protection Agency, Occupational Safety and Health Administration, and the Consumer Product Safety Commission.

These agencies promote social, rather than economic, goals. They issue regulations to protect public health and safety and the environment. Virtually every economic activity is affected in some way by federal health, safety, and environmental regulations. In fact, the traditional area of economic regulation in the United States is now dwarfed by the growing fields of social health and welfare and environmental concern.

The first prime task of American administrative law was to legitimize the vast delegations of power that had been made to administrative agencies, particularly at the time of President Franklin D. Roosevelt's New Deal. Two 1935 decisions of the Supreme Court[8] struck down the most important early New Deal statute on the ground that it contained excessive delegations of power because the authority granted under it was not restricted by what the American courts call a 'defined standard'.

The requirement of a defined standard in enabling legislation was imposed by the American courts in order to ensure against excessive delegations. The delegation of power must be limited—limited either by legislative prescription of ends and means, or even of details, or by limitations upon the area of the power delegated. The statute must, in other words, contain a framework within which the administrative action must operate; in the Supreme Court's recent words, it must lay down an 'intelligible principle' to which the agency is directed to conform.[9] The 'intelligible principle' serves the function of ensuring that fundamental policy decisions will be made, not by appointed officials, but by the body directly responsible to the people, the legislature. As a federal judge has put it: 'At its core, the doctrine is based on the notion that agency action must occur within the context of a rule of law formulated by a legislative body'.[10] If there is no guideline in the statute to limit delegations of power, the administrative agency is being given a blank check to make law in the delegated area of authority. In such a case, it is the agency, rather than Congress, that is the primary legislator.

Despite these considerations, it must be conceded that, during the past half century, the American courts have moved away from the strict view that laws delegating power must be invalidated unless they contain limiting standards. The 1935 cases are the only ones in which delegations have been invalidated

---

[8]   *Schechter Poultry Corp.* v. *United States*, 295 U.S. 495 (1935); *Panama Refining Co.* v. *Ryan*, 293 U.S. 388 (1935).

[9]   *Mistretta* v. *United States*, 488 U.S. 361 (1989).

[10]   Wright, 'Beyond Discretionary Justice' (1972) 81 *Yale L.J.* 575 at 583.

by the Supreme Court. Since then, delegations have been uniformly upheld by the federal courts. Broad delegations have been the characteristic Congressional responses to the endemic crises of the contemporary society. As new crises have arisen, the tendency has been to deal with them by delegating broad power to the Executive. When inflation threatens to get out of hand, Congress gives the President power to stabilize prices, rents, and wages. Though there is nothing in the statute beside the bare delegation of stabilization power, the courts rushed to sustain the grant, reading into the statute an implied standard which Congress did not bother to put into the statute.[11] When an energy crisis or some other emergency arises, the unchallenged solution is to confer vast chunks of authority on the President, with no attention given to the need to guide or limit the power delegated.[12] The result is that 'the principle that the Constitution prohibits Congress from delegating its legislative authority is essentially nugatory, for little is [now] required of Congress when it wants to obtain the assistance of its coordinate branches'.[13]

There has, however, been a countervailing tendency which should be noted. American judges themselves have begun to express dissatisfaction with the trend toward wholesale delegations unrestrained by defined standards. Thus, in a 1993 case, a federal judge declared:

> A jurisprudence which allows Congress to impliedly delegate its criminal law-making authority to a regulatory agency . . .—so long as Congress provides an 'intelligible principle' to guide that agency—is enough to make any judge pause and question what has happened. Deferent and minimal judicial review of Congress' transfer of its . . . lawmaking function to other bodies, in other branches, calls into question the vitality of the tripartite system established by our Constitution.[14]

In 1974, the Supreme Court itself repeated the rule that a delegation of power must be accompanied by discernible standards.[15] In 1980 and 1981, then Justice, now Chief Justice, William Rehnquist stated that he would rule that the law at issue was invalid because it contained an excessive delegation of legislative power.[16] Some of the most distinguished American judges, speaking off the bench, have called for revival of meaningful limitations on

---

[11] *Amalgamated Meat Cutters* v. *Connally*, 337 F. Supp. 737 (D.D.C. 1971).

[12] e.g. Emergency Petroleum Allocation Act, 87 Stat. 627 (1973); Federal Energy Administration Act, 88 Stat. 96 (1974).

[13] *United States* v. *Mills*, 817 F.Supp. 1546 at 1552 (N.D. Fla. 1993).   [14] *Ibid.*

[15] *National Cable Television Assn.* v. *United States*, 415 U.S. 336 at 342 (1974).

[16] *Industrial Dept.* v. *American Petroleum Inst.*, 448 U.S. 607 at 675 (1980); *American Textile Mfrs.* v. *Donovan*, 452 U.S. 490 at 543 (1981).

delegation of power.[17] It is true that these judicial statements have not yet had effect on the case law. But they are significant, as an indication of judicial dissatisfaction which may foreshadow a movement back to the days of enforcement of the defined standards requirement.

Mention should also be made of renewed legislative efforts to control the exercise of delegated powers. The most significant legislative technique developed in this connection was what came to be called the 'legislative veto'—exercised through statutory provisions empowering one or both Houses of Congress to disapprove delegated agency decisions by passage of an annulling resolution. The technique is derived from the practice of 'laying' delegated legislation before Parliament, subject to annulment by resolution of either House, which has long been an established feature of English administrative law. However, in a 1983 case, the Supreme Court decided that the 'legislative veto' technique violates the constitutional requirement of separation of powers.[18]

IV. Administrative Procedure

American administrative law has been based upon Justice Frankfurter's oft-quoted assertion that 'the history of liberty has largely been the history of the observance of procedural safeguards'.[19] The American system, more than any other, has emphasized administrative procedure (the procedural requirements imposed upon what continental jurists term the active administration). The starting point in such emphasis has been the constitutional demand of due process. 'When we speak of audi alteram partem—hear the other side—we tap fundamental precepts that are deeply rooted in Anglo-American legal history',[20] precepts that are now a command, spoken with the voice of due process.[21] But American law has gone far beyond the constitutional minimum. Building upon the due process foundation, the law has constructed an imposing edifice of formal procedure. The consequence has been a virtual judicialization of American agencies; from the establishment of the Interstate Commerce Commission to the present, much of the American administrative process has been set in a modified judicial mold.

---

[17] See Douglas, *Go East Young Man* (Random House, 1974) 217; Wright, n. 10 above, at 582–6.
[18] *Immigration and Naturalization Service* v. *Chadha*, 462 U.S. 919 (1983).
[19] *McNabb* v. *United States*, 318 U.S. 332 at 347 (1943).
[20] *In re Andrea B.*, 405 N.Y.S.2d 977 at 981 (Fam. Ct. 1978).
[21] *Caritativo* v. *California*, 357 U.S. 549 at 558 (1958).

A. Rule-Making

One must, however, note that application of the due process requirement in specific cases depends upon the function being exercised by the given administrative agency. In particular, the crucial dividing line is that between rule-making (the common American term for exercise of what in English administrative law are termed powers of delegated legislation) and adjudication. Rule-making is the administrative equivalent of the legislative process of enacting a statute, under which agencies announce the standards that will apply in the future such that compliance with them is as mandatory as compliance with a statute. Equally important, not only is the public bound by an agency's rules, but the agency must follow them itself,[22] which sometimes is quite inconvenient for the agency. Agencies engaged in rule-making are, as a general proposition, no more subject to constitutional procedural requirements than is the legislature engaged in enacting a statute. This means that agencies are freed from the necessity of imitating courts when they are functioning as sublegislatures; except for specific statutory requirements, the procedure to be followed in rule-making is largely a matter for the agency concerned. Unless a statute requires otherwise, a rule or regulation will normally not be invalid because of agency failure to hold a hearing or to consult or otherwise seek, before promulgation, the views of those affected.

However, the Federal Administrative Procedure Act (APA) (a statute enacted by Congress in 1946, which imposes general procedural requirements on all federal administrative agencies) does impose procedural requirements upon rule-making. In general, it may be said that the APA provides for a system of antecedent publicity before agencies may engage in substantive rule-making. General notice of any proposed rule-making must be published in the *Federal Register* (the official publication in which federal administrative regulations are published). The agency must then afford interested persons the opportunity to participate in the rule-making process through submission of written data, views, or arguments, with the opportunity to present them orally in some, but not most cases, with all relevant matter so presented to be considered by the agency.

Rule-making under the APA is often called 'notice and comment' rule-making. The APA does not mandate anything like a formal hearing prior to rule-making. All that it requires is that the agency publish the notice of proposed rule-making and give interested persons an 'opportunity' to participate. The purpose is to work a democratization of the rule-making process without destroying its flexibility by imposing procedural requirements that

---

[22] *Reuters v. FCC*, 781 F.2d 946 at 951 (D.C. Cir. 1986).

are too onerous. It may be true, as Justice Jackson pointed out in a famous opinion, that most people have neither the time nor the interest to read the 'voluminous and dull' *Federal Register*.[23] But those subject to administrative authority tend to be members of trade, business, professional, or other organizations interested in the subject areas of a particular agency, which regularly scan the *Register* for relevant notices of proposed rule-making and then, after alerting their members, send in materials supporting the organization's view to the agency concerned.

Notice and comment rule-making under the APA has been criticized as not providing enough procedural safeguards, especially where there are factual premises that are needed to support a rule. Although some courts tried to impose stricter procedures, the Supreme Court aborted this line of cases in *Vermont Yankee Nuclear Power Corp.* v. *Natural Resources Defense Council*.[24] In that case, the lower court had struck down a rule dealing with the uranium fuel cycle in nuclear power reactors because of inadequacies in the procedures employed in the rule-making proceedings. The agency had complied with the APA notice and comment requirements, but the appellate court held that more should be required in order to facilitate full ventilation of the issues. The Supreme Court reversed on the ground that the APA lays down the only procedural requirements for informal rule-making. To require more, said the Court, would 'almost compel' the agency to conduct all rule-making proceedings with the full panoply of procedural devices normally associated only with adjudicatory hearings.

The Supreme Court decision means that, if agencies are to be required to follow stricter procedures than those imposed by the APA, such requirements will have to be imposed by Congress, or by the agencies themselves, but not the courts. It is, however, unlikely that the APA will be amended to require more than notice and comment procedures in most rule-making. Recent years have seen a tremendous expansion of rule-making power in America. Both Congress and the courts have fostered the trend toward rule-making. But that does not mean that rule-making should be moved in a judicialized direction. To do so would defeat the principal advantages of the rule-making process—flexibility and informality.

B. Adjudicatory Procedure

If the general principle governing rule-making in the United States is that due process does not require formal procedures before regulations are promul-

---

[23] *Federal Crop. Ins. Corp.* v. *Merrill*, 332 U.S. 380 at 387 (1947).   [24] 435 U.S. 519 (1978).

gated, the constitutional principle governing administrative adjudications is the opposite one. The requirement of due process has been interpreted as requiring a formal adversarial hearing—what has come to be called an evidentiary hearing—before administrative decisions which adversely affect private individuals may be made. It is with regard to adjudicatory decisions that the American administrative process has, as already noted, been set largely in the judicial mold.

This means that, before an administrative decision which adversely affects an individual may be made, that person has a right to an evidentiary hearing, which means 'a hearing closely approximating a judicial trial.'[25] Included in that right is the right to:

(1) notice, including an adequate formulation of the subjects and issues involved in the case;

(2) present evidence (both testimonial and documentary) and argument;

(3) rebut adverse evidence, through cross-examination and other appropriate means;

(4) appear with counsel;

(5) have the decision based only upon evidence introduced into the record of the hearing;

(6) have a complete record, which consists of a transcript of the testimony and arguments, together with the documentary evidence and all other papers filed in the proceeding; and

(7) have the agency explain the basis for its decision—an important means of assuring agency adherence to the law, within the broad discretion given on fact, policy, and even legal issues.

Comparative observers have criticized the American requirement of a full hearing with a formal record before administrative adjudications. How can administration be carried on effectively if every administrative decision which affects private rights must be preceded by a trial-type hearing? This question was addressed to the present writer when he testified in 1956 before the Franks Committee investigating administrative law in Britain. Does not the right to a full hearing 'tend to gum up the administrative works?'—this was the query asked by a British barrister.

The answer given was a negative one:

> . . . in our experience the rights which individuals have are not insisted upon in every case . . . It does not happen in that way for various reasons, in part the question of expense, in part the fact that there is no point really at issue and therefore no point in going through the formality of a hearing. I have seen the

---

[25] *Mathews v. Eldridge,* 424 U.S. 319 at 325 (1976).

figures in some agencies, and in none of them are full rights insisted upon in more than five per cent of the cases. That is what makes the thing workable.[26]

The individual's right to a full hearing does not mean that a full 'day in court' must automatically be held in connection with every trifling dispute with which an agency has to deal. If the right to a formal hearing were insisted upon in every case where it exists, it would virtually paralyze administration. But the fact is that the right is asserted in only a very small percentage of the cases. The leading official study of American administrative law noted that hearings were held in less than 5 percent of the cases disposed of by federal regulatory agencies.[27] In non-regulatory agencies the percentage of hearings is even smaller. During the 1992 fiscal year, the Department of Health and Human Services processed over 100 million claims; in that period some 250,000 HHS hearings were held.

The constitutional right to due process gives the individual affected a right to an evidentiary hearing. Like other constitutional rights, the right to be heard can be waived.[28] The vast bulk of agency decisions are made without resort to formal proceedings, because the right is waived most of the time.

Three important developments with regard to American adjudicatory procedure should be noted. The first is the extension of the right to an evidentiary hearing from the older field of regulatory administration to the burgeoning benefactory apparatus of the Welfare State. Before 1970, the latter was still beyond the due process boundary, since there was a constitutional right to procedural safeguards only in cases where the administrative decision adversely affected the individual in his rights. If the individual was being given something by government to which he had no preexisting 'right', he was being given a mere 'privilege' and was 'not entitled to protection under the due process clause'.[29]

All this was changed by the landmark decision in *Goldberg* v. *Kelly*,[30] which held that public assistance payments to an individual might not be terminated without affording that person an opportunity for an evidentiary hearing. The Court specifically rejected the rule that there was no right to a hearing because public assistance was a mere 'privilege'. 'The constitutional challenge', declared the Court, 'cannot be answered by an argument that public assistance benefits are a "privilege" and not a "right" '. It is no longer accurate to think of welfare benefits as only privileges. 'Such benefits are a matter of statutory entitlement for persons qualified to receive them'. In this sense, they are 'more like "property" than a "gratuity" '.[31]

[26] Committee on Administrative Tribunals and Enquiries: *Minutes of Evidence* 1034 (1956).

[27] *Report of the Attorney General's Committee on Administrative Procedure* 35 (1941).

[28] *National Indep. Coal Operators Assn.* v. *Kleppe*, 423 U.S. 388 (1976).

[29] *Gilchrist* v. *Bierring*, 14 N.W.2d 724 at 730 (Iowa 1944).   [30] 397 U.S. 254 (1970).

[31] *Ibid.* at 262.

The same reasoning applies to other cases involving social welfare benefits, particularly those under the Social Security Act—the federal statute which provides for extensive programs of old age, survivors, disability, and medical insurance, as well as aid to families with dependent children, supplemental security income, and other social welfare programs. The Supreme Court has, however, held more recently that, with regard to some of these federal benefactory programs, not involving dire need, the required evidentiary hearing may be held after the payments to the individual concerned have been terminated by the administration.[32]

Secondly, the Supreme Court has recently been following a cost-benefit approach to the question of the particular procedures to be required in an administrative proceeding, or at least at an early stage of the process. The Court has indicated that that question is to be determined under a tripartite test that requires the balancing of:

> (a) the private interests affected; (b) the risk of an erroneous determination through the process accorded and the probable value of added procedural safeguards; and (c) the public interest and administrative burdens, including costs that the additional procedures would involve.[33]

The Court has used the cost-benefit test to decide that the exclusionary rule (which bars the admission of illegally seized evidence in a criminal trial) does not apply in an administrative hearing to determine whether an alien should be deported.[34] The Court's analysis concludes that the costs involved in applying the rule in such an administrative proceeding far exceed the benefits to be secured from excluding the evidence in the given case. The decision has been criticized as reducing basic rights to the level of the counting house, but it has been followed by other American courts.

The third important development with regard to American adjudicatory procedure concerns the important changes made in the processes of hearing and decision in federal agencies by the Administrative Procedure Act (APA). Unlike the first two, which are based on the Constitution, and thus apply to state agencies also, the APA is limited to federal entities, although most states have similar laws applicable to their agencies. The APA set up within each agency a corps of independent hearing officers originally called hearing examiners. These examiners, who were given powers comparable to those of judges in the courts, were to preside over evidentiary hearings. Under the APA, examiners were empowered to issue initial decisions, which became the decisions of the agencies concerned unless those decisions were appealed.

---

[32] *Mathews* v. *Eldridge*, 424 U.S. 319 (1976), with retroactive payments if the individual prevails at the hearing.

[33] *United States* v. *Raddatz*, 447 U.S. 667 at 677 (1980).

[34] *Immigration and Naturalization Service* v. *Lopez-Mendoza*, 468 U.S. 1032 (1984).

What the APA did was to set up within each agency the equivalent of first-instance and appellate tribunals. The first-instance level was to be at the hearing stage, before an independent hearing official vested with the power to make a decision, subject to appeal to the agency heads, who were thus relegated to the appellate level. More recently, there has been a further judicialization of the trial level. The hearing officers provided under the APA have evolved into an administrative judiciary, endowed with authority to make binding decisions (subject to appeals to the agency heads) in adjudicatory proceedings. In 1978, Congress confirmed this development by a statute which expressly changed the title of APA hearing examiners to administrative law judges.

The evolving system of American administrative justice brings to mind an opinion of the Supreme Court over 40 years ago, which referred to the distinction between American law, in which one system of law courts applies both public and private law, and the practice in a continental European country such as France, which administers public law through a system of administrative courts separate from those dealing with private law questions.[35] The French administrative courts are specialized tribunals that review the legality of administrative acts. Although proposals have been made for establishment of comparable American administrative courts, the French concept of administrative reviewing courts has largely remained foreign to American administrative lawyers.

Under the federal APA, however, the American system has taken its own path toward establishment of an administrative judiciary—but, in the American version, an administrative trial judiciary. The evolution of hearing officers under the APA, culminating in their judicial status as administrative law judges, set the pattern for the developing system of American administrative justice. In particular, we can project a continuing increase in the size of the administrative judicial corps. When the APA provisions went into effect, the federal agencies employed 197 examiners. In 1992, there were over 1,200 administrative law judges in thirty federal agencies; over 70 per cent (850) were in the Social Security Administration, reflecting the impact of that agency's mass justice upon the administrative process. Only the fiscal squeeze of recent years has prevented the number from rising substantially higher. The Social Security Administration alone projects an administrative law judge corps of well over 1,000 in the next decade. In the next century, we can predict that there may well be a federal administrative judiciary running into the thousands and administrative law judges in ever-increasing numbers dispensing both regulatory justice and the mass justice of an expanding Welfare State.

[35] *Garner* v. *Teamsters Local 776*, 346 U.S. 485 at 495 (1953).

V. Judicial Review

A. Availability

Judicial review is the balance wheel of American administrative law. It enables practical effect to be given to the basic theory upon which administrative power is based: 'When Congress passes an Act empowering administrative agencies to carry on governmental activities, the power of those agencies is circumscribed by the authority granted'.[36] The responsibility of enforcing the limits of statutory grants of authority is a judicial function: when an agency oversteps its legal bounds, the American courts will intervene. Without judicial review, statutory limits would, to paraphrase the famous English writer Thomas Hobbes, be naught but empty words.

The overriding principle with regard to judicial review in the American system is that in favor of the availability of review. 'Indeed, judicial review of . . . administrative action is the rule and non-reviewability an exception which must be demonstrated'.[37] In federal administrative law, the original English common law system of review has been superseded by an elaborate statutory system. Federal statutes creating administrative agencies generally provide for judicial review of the acts of those agencies. 'The mere failure to provide specially by statute for judicial review is certainly no evidence of intent to withhold review'.[38]

The leading case is *Stark v. Wickard*.[39] Under it, the omission of review provisions by the legislature gives an administrative agency no immunity from the normal judicial scrutiny of the legality of its actions. In another case the Supreme Court stated that 'judicial review of a final agency action by an aggrieved person will not be cut off unless there is persuasive reason to believe that such was the purpose of Congress'.[40] Mere legislative silence is not such 'persuasive reason'; it indicates only that the legislature intended to leave the individual to the general review remedies available in American administrative law—the non-statutory remedies derived from English law, as well as that under the federal Administrative Procedure Act, since there is a general provision for judicial review in the APA.[41] To hold otherwise would be contrary to the *ultra vires* theory upon which the American system is based, under which administrative power is limited to the authority granted by statute. 'The responsibility of determining the limits of statutory grants of

---

[36] *Stark* v. *Wickard*, 321 U.S. 288 at 309 (1944).   [37] *Barlow* v. *Collins*, 397 U.S. 159 at 166 (1970).
[38] *Administrative Procedure Act: Legislative History* 275 (1946).   [39] 321 U.S. 288 (1944).
[40] *Abbott Laboratories* v. *Gardner*, 387 U.S. 136 at 140 (1967).
[41] *Ortego* v. *Weinberger*, 516 F.2d 1005 at 1009 (5th Cir. 1975).

authority in such instances is a judicial function entrusted to the courts . . . by the statutes establishing courts and marking their jurisdiction'.[42]

A similar result is reached even when a statute contains a provision which appears to prohibit judicial review. Thus, in an important case, the Supreme Court held that judicial review was available despite the fact that the statute provided that the challenged administrative decision 'shall be final'.[43] This is the approach that is normally followed where American statutes provide for administrative finality: 'Tolerance of judicial review has been more and more the rule against the claim of administrative finality'.[44] As the Supreme Court has stated, 'We begin with the strong presumption that Congress intends judicial review of administrative action'.[45] A finality provision alone is not enough to justify preclusion, though a literal reading might support such a result. 'Examples are legion where literalness in statutory language is out of harmony either with constitutional requirements . . . or with an Act taken as an organic whole'.[46]

In the American system at least, interpretation of such provisions to prohibit all judicial review might raise a difficult constitutional question. In the oft-quoted words of one of the most famous American judges, Justice Louis D. Brandeis, 'The supremacy of law demands that there shall be an opportunity to have some court decide . . . whether the proceeding in which the facts were adjudicated was conducted regularly'.[47] In American administrative law, where an administrative order impinges directly upon personal or property rights, 'there is a constitutional right of judicial review'.[48] As an American court has put it '. . . the courts could not be divested of their constitutional obligation to afford due process of law, even in the face of legislation purporting to eliminate such judicial consideration of decisions of administrative bodies'.[49] The Constitution does not permit the legislature to shield administrative agencies from all judicial review.

What has just been said is illustrated by a recent Supreme Court case on the matter, where the statutory provision appeared categorically to preclude all judicial review of specified administrative decisions. Petitioner, a civilian naval security guard, suffered from bronchitis and had been retired by the Navy. The relevant agency denied his disability claim, and the denial was upheld by the Merit Systems Protection Board. The lower court held that the review action was barred by the statutory preclusion provision, which pro-

---

[42] 321 U.S. at 310.   [43] *Shaughnessy* v. *Pedreiro*, 349 U.S. 48 (1955).
[44] Douglas J., dissenting, in *Union Pac. R. Co.* v. *Price*, 360 U.S. 601 at 619 (1959).
[45] *Barlow* v. *Collins*, 397 U.S. 159 at 166 (1970).
[46] *Oestereich* v. *Selective Service Bd.*, 393 U.S. 233 at 238 (1968).
[47] *St. Joseph Stock Yards Co.* v. *United States*, 298 U.S. 38 at 84 (1936).
[48] *Blount* v. *Metropolitan Life Ins. Co.*, 677 S.W.2d 565 at 569 (Tex.App. 1984).
[49] *County Council* v. *Investors Funding Corp.* 312 A. 2d 225 at 255 (Md. 1973).

vided that agency determinations 'concerning [disability determinations] are final and conclusive and are not subject to review'.

The Supreme Court reversed, holding that the statute was not intended to bar all review. Instead, judicial 'review is available to determine whether "there has been a substantial departure from important procedural rights, a misconstruction of the governing legislation, or some like error 'going to the heart of the administrative determination' " '.[50]

B. Scope

Before dealing with the scope of judicial review itself, it should be noted that, where there is an agency record, the review proceeding is essentially an appellate proceeding, and review is limited to the record made before the agency. Where the agency has heard evidence, the reviewing court's decision is not based upon evidence produced at a trial in court, but upon the evidence presented before the agency.[51] The focal point for review is the administrative record already in existence, not a new record made in the reviewing court. The only evidence that may be considered is evidence that was before the agency. Evidence may not be received by the reviewing court even if it was wrongfully excluded by the agency or is newly discovered evidence. If the court feels that such evidence should be heard, it should remand the case for it to be received before the agency.

When the American courts review administrative acts, the overriding consideration is that of deference to the administrative expert. The result has been a theory of review that limits the extent to which the discretion of the expert may be scrutinized by the non-expert judge. The basic approach was one stated by the Supreme Court a half century ago: 'We certainly have neither technical competence nor legal authority to pronounce upon the wisdom of the course taken by the Commission'.[52]

The consequence has been a theory of review by the courts which provides for only limited review where questions of fact are at issue—the theory being that it should be the primary responsibility of the administrative expert to find the facts in a given case. The courts may review administrative adjudications of fact only to determine whether they are supported by substantial evidence. As explained by an English observer, '. . . the scope of judicial review over administrative action is limited to . . . whether or not the findings of fact underlying the administrative conclusion are based upon substantial

---

[50] *Lindahl* v. *OPM*, 470 U.S. 768 at 791 (1985).
[51] See Schwartz, *Administrative Law* (Little, Brown, 3rd ed. 1991) § 10.2.
[52] *Board of Trade* v. *United States*, 314 U.S. 534 at 548 (1942).

evidence'.[53] As interpreted by the Supreme Court, substantial evidence means 'such relevant evidence as a reasonable mind might accept as adequate to support a conclusion'.[54]

The 'substantial evidence rule' (as it is called) tests the rationality of administrative determinations of fact; it is a test of the reasonableness, not the rightness, of administrative factual determinations.[55] All that is needed is evidence which a reasonable person would accept as adequate to support the determination. Different terminology is used when facts found in a rule-making are challenged; in such a case the reviewing court is said to review whether the agency rules are 'arbitrary, capricious, or an abuse of discretion'. This standard is essentially one of reasonableness; under it, the agency is given great latitude.

In two early cases—those involving so-called 'constitutional facts'[56] and those involving 'jurisdictional facts'[57]—the Supreme Court indicated that the courts might more fully review the administrative determinations and determine their correctness on their own. More recently, the Court has receded from these statements and indicated that even determinations upon which constitutional rights and jurisdiction depend are to be reviewed only under the substantial evidence test—i.e. the reviewing courts are to determine only the reasonableness, not the rightness, of these administrative determinations.[58]

Mention should also be made of the so-called *Chevron* doctrine (after a case of that name),[59] which now governs review of administrative interpretations of statutes. Statutory interpretation is, of course, governed primarily by legislative intent: if Congress has clearly said what a statute means, its intent must be followed. The *Chevron* doctrine applies when a statute is ambiguous—i.e. its meaning is not made clear in the language or legislative history of the statute. Under *Chevron*, the administrative agency, not the reviewing court, has the primary role in giving meaning to the statute. The agency's statutory interpretation is to be upheld if it is *reasonable*, even if it is not *right*, in the sense that the court would interpret the statute in the same way.[60] *Chevron* requires the courts to give effect to a reasonable administrative interpretation of a statute unless that interpretation is inconsistent with a clearly expressed Congressional intent.

Chevron has been criticized as inconsistent with the very basis of the law of

---

[53] Wade, 'Foreword' to Schwartz, *American Administrative Law* (Pitman, 1950) vi. (italics omitted).

[54] *Consolidated Edison Co.* v. *Nat'l. Labor Relations Bd.*, 305 U.S. 197 at 229 (1938).

[55] *Matter of Otero Elec. Co-op.*, 774 P.2d 1050 at 1053 (N.M. 1989).

[56] *Ohio Valley Water Co.* v. *Ben Avon Borough*, 253 U.S. 287 (1920).

[57] *Crowell* v. *Benson*, 285 U.S. 22 (1932).

[58] For a discussion of the cases, see Schwartz, *Administrative Law* n. 50 above §§ 10.23, 10.28–10.29 (3rd ed. 1991).

[59] *Chevron* v. *NRDC*, 467 U.S. 837 (1984).   [60] *INS* v. *Cardoza-Fonseca*, 480 U.S. 424 at 454 (1987).

judicial review.[61] From almost the beginning of administrative law in the United States, review has focused upon two main questions: that of jurisdiction and that of proper application of the law. The American courts have left questions of fact and policy for the administrator, subject only to limited review. Ensuring that agencies remain within the limits of their delegated powers and that they have not misconstrued the law has, on the contrary, been conceived of as a judicial function. Yet, under the *Chevron* doctrine, both statutory construction and the determination of agency jurisdiction are taken from the reviewing court and vested primarily in the administrator.

On the other side, however, reference should be made to a 1974 important extension in the scope of review by the Supreme Court of California, which has developed a rule of broad review in cases involving fundamental rights. As stated by the California courts, its rule is that:

> if the order or decision of the agency substantially affects a fundamental vested right, the trial court, in determining . . . whether there has been an abuse of discretion because the findings are not supported by the evidence, must exercise its independent judgment on the evidence and find an abuse of discretion if the findings are not supported by the weight of the evidence.[62]

The California rule is a direct consequence of the increasing judicial vigilance to protect individual rights and the growing disenchantment with the claims of administrative expertise. The California court has asserted that, when an agency decision affects a fundamental right, full review is appropriate because 'abrogation of the right is too important to the individual to relegate it to exclusive administrative extinction'.[63] The result is a substantial broadening of the scope of review, which may set a pattern for other American courts in coming years.

From a broader point of view, the California approach may be seen as an indication of the changing attitude of many American courts toward the administrator. There has been increasing articulation of judicial doubts about the desirability of the trend toward narrow review of administrative authority. According to a leading federal judge, it is no longer enough for the courts regularly to uphold agency action 'with a nod in the direction of the "substantial evidence" test, and a bow to the mysteries of administrative expertise'.[64] A more positive judicial role is demanded by the changing character of administrative litigation:

---

[61] See Schwartz, *Administrative Law*, n. 50 above, § 10.36.
[62] *Strumsky v. San Diego Employees Retirement Assn.*, 520 P.2d 29 at 31 (Cal. 1974).
[63] *Ibid.* at 33. For

> [C]ourts are increasingly asked to review administrative litigation that touches on fundamental personal interests in life, health, and liberty ... To protect these interests from administrative arbitrariness, it is necessary ... to insist on strict judicial scrutiny of administrative action.[65]

The same judge asserts that the American system is now at a watershed: 'We stand on the threshold of a new era in the history of the long and fruitful collaboration of administrative agencies and reviewing courts'.[66] The expression of judicial doubts about the desirability of the trend toward limited judicial review is most suggestive for the future of American administrative law.

Despite such expressions, the dominant theme in the scope of review is still that of *Chevron* deference. Under it, there is now limited review not only over administrative determinations of fact, but also over agency interpretations of law. *Chevron* deference assimilates review of questions of statutory interpretation into review of questions of fact. Indeed, according to a federal court, the *Chevron* doctrine all but does away with the law-fact distinction that has been so basic in American administrative law.[67]

VI. Freedom of Information

'Publicity', said Justice Brandeis, 'is justly commended as a remedy for social and industrial diseases. Sunlight is said to be the best of disinfectants; electric light the best policeman'.[68] Americans firmly believe in the healthy effects of publicity and have a strong antipathy to the inherent secretiveness of government agencies. One manifestation of this is the refusal of the courts to accept extreme claims of executive privilege and allow the Government, by its mere fiat, to suppress evidence needed by parties to legal proceedings.[69] The judicial attitude in this respect was strongly reaffirmed in *United States* v. *Nixon*,[70] where the claim of the President to an unreviewable privilege to withhold evidence was rejected.

In the same spirit, Congress in 1966 enacted the Freedom of Information Act (FOIA). Before then, the people's 'right to know' was a journalistic slogan rather than a legal right. The 1966 statute changed this since it gave any person, with no showing of any specific need, a legally enforceable right of access to government files and documents. The only exceptions are those nine exemptions contained in the Act, which were written by Congress, and

---

[65] *Environment Defence Fund* v. *Ruckelshaus*, 439 F.2d 584 at 597–8.   [66] *Ibid.* at 597.
[67] *National Fuel Gas Supply Corp.* v. *FERC*, 811 F.2d 1563 (D.C. Cir. 1987).
[68] *The Words of Justice Brandeis* 151, Goldman ed. (Henry Schuman, 1953).
[69] *United States* v. *Reynolds*, 345 U.S. 1 (1953).   [70] 418 U.S. 683 (1974).

not by the agencies whose records are being sought. The FOIA effects a profound alteration in the position of the citizen vis-à-vis government. No longer is the individual seeking information from an administrative agency a mere supplicant. In signing the new law, the President said, with pardonable inaccuracy, that it entitled Americans to 'all the information that the security of the Nation permits'.[71]

This is not the place for a detailed analysis of the Freedom of Information Act. Some understanding of its basic thrust is, however, essential to those interested in American administrative law. As stated by the Attorney General, the policies behind the act are as follows:

(1) that disclosure be the general rule, not the exception;
(2) that all individuals have equal rights of access;
(3) that the burden be on the government to justify the withholding of a document, not on the person who requests it;
(4) that individuals improperly denied access to documents have a right to seek injunctive relief in the courts;
(5) that there be a change in government policy and attitude.[72]

The key FOIA provision for attaining these goals provides that, on request for identifiable records, each agency shall make the records promptly available to any person. If they are not so made available, the federal district courts are given jurisdiction to enjoin the agency from withholding records and to order the production of records improperly withheld from a complainant. In the court action, the normal rules governing actions against agencies give way in two vital respects. The normal rules are (a) that agency acts have a presumption of validity, and the individual challenging them has the burden of proving their invalidity and (b) that the scope of review of challenged agency action is limited. Under the key provision of the FOIA, (i) the court shall determine the matter de novo, and (ii) the burden is on the agency to sustain its action in withholding information.

This means that the complainant does not have to overcome any presumption in favor of the correctness of the agency's action. All a complainant must allege in an action under the FOIA is that he made a request for identifiable records which the agency turned down. The burden then shifts to the agency to justify its refusal. It can normally meet this burden only by showing that the records involved fall within one of the nine exceptions excluded from the statute. The whole purpose of the statute 'was to reverse the self-protective attitude of the agencies'.[73] Disclosure was made the

---

[71] *Attorney General's Memorandum on the Public Information Section of the Administrative Procedure Act*, 21 Admin. L.2d (P & F) 201 (1967).

[72] *Ibid.* at 203–4.

[73] *Consumers Union* v. *VA*, 301 F.Supp. 796 at 799 (S.D.N.Y. 1969), *appeal dismissed*, 436 F.2d 1363 (2d Cir. 1971).

general rule, and only information specifically exempted by the act may now be withheld. Where the records called for in a given complaint do not come within the exceptions, the court must order their production—there is no residual discretion to withhold beyond that given by Congress.[74]

[74] *Consumers Union* v. *VA*, 301 F.Supp. 796 at 799 (S.D.N.Y. 1969), *appeal dismissed*, 436 F.2d 1363 (2d Cir. 1971).

7

THE AMERICAN LEGAL PROFESSION

STEPHEN GILLERS

I. A Statistical Portrait

One facet of the American legal profession that surprises many observers, including American lawyers, is its size. It is big and growing bigger, both absolutely and relative to the American population.

In 1970, there were about 350,000 American lawyers. By 1983, that number had increased to 600,000, and in 1992, there were 750,000. Although the American population is also growing, the lawyer population is growing faster. In 1970, the lawyer-to-population ratio was 1/572. It was 1/310 in 1990. By the end of the century, the ratio is expected to drop below 1/275. From 1963 to 1974, the number of law school graduates tripled (from about 9,000 to 27,000) and then increased another 55 percent by 1993, when American law schools awarded 42,000 law degrees.

The composition of the profession is also changing because of the increase in women and minorities. This change can be seen clearly when we look at legal education. In 1963, of the nearly 47,000 law students enrolled in the 135 law schools then accredited by the American Bar Association, only 3.7 percent were women. In 1994, when 129,000 students were enrolled at 177 accredited law schools, 43.7 percent of the student body were women. Minority enrollment in American law schools has also advanced. In 1977, 5,300 African-American students were enrolled in American law schools. By

1994, that number increased to 9,680. Corresponding numbers for Hispanic students are 2,531 (1977) and 6,772 (1994), and for Asian and Pacific Island students, 1,382 (1977) and 7,196 (1994).

II. Entering the Profession

Americans become lawyers through a process that is fairly uniform in all American jurisdictions. Lawyers are admitted by the courts of the jurisdictions in which they wish to practice. Although these jurisdictions include not only the 50 American states, but also Washington D.C., Puerto Rico, Guam, and the Virgin Islands, the word 'states' will be used to refer to them collectively. With minor exceptions, the prelude to admission consists of college graduation, law school graduation, a bar examination, and review by a character committee. Unlike some other nations, there is no apprenticeship period required before a person who meets these qualifications may begin to practice law, even on his or her own. At one time, many American states required applicants for admission to their bars to be residents of the state, but in 1985, the United States Supreme Court invalidated that requirement.[1]

Nearly all states require that applicants for admission have graduated from a law school approved by the American Bar Association. Some states, like California, also admit graduates of locally accredited law schools, but these graduates are often unable to gain admission to the bars of other states. A lawyer admitted in one state is not thereby entitled to practice law in another state. A New York lawyer who sets up practice in Ohio without gaining admission to the Ohio bar will violate Ohio's unauthorized practice of law rules. These rules forbid persons who are not admitted to the state bar to render legal advice in the particular state except incidentally to their home state practice, as described below. Lawyers who want to practice in federal courts are generally admitted based on their admission to the bar of a state court. No separate examination is required.

The existence of more than 50 state bars has caused some problems for lawyers admitted in one or two states who want to practice nationwide. Technically, they can even be forbidden to advise on their own state's law or on federal law while physically in a state in which they are not admitted to practice. This is because that state has not found them competent and fit to advise clients, even though their home state has. However, for practical reasons, states tend to overlook the fact that lawyers giving legal advice within

---

[1] *Supreme Court of New Hampshire* v. *Piper*, 470 U.S. 274 (1985).

their borders may not be admitted to the bar of the state, so long as the lawyer's presence in the state is transitory and the advice is incidental to the lawyer's practice in his or her home state. This tolerance allows clients whose legal problems are national to hire a single law firm to represent them without having to obtain additional lawyers in each state in which they need assistance.

A lawyer admitted in one state can also gain admission to the bar of some other states by motion. This means that the lawyer asks the court to let him or her join the bar of that state without taking its bar examination. About half of American jurisdictions recognize motion admission. Many of these states require that the applicant have practiced for a minimum number of years in their home state, generally 5, before applying. The Supreme Court has ruled that when a state does allow motion admission, it cannot limit that advantage to lawyers who reside in that state, although it can require lawyers to practice full-time in the admitting state.[2] The prohibition against favoring one's own citizens is based on a constitutional guarantee that citizens of each state shall enjoy 'all Privileges and Immunities' of citizens of other states.

In states that do not have motion admission (or if a lawyer does not qualify for motion admission), admission requires passage of the customary bar examination or in some states a shorter examination for applicants who are already admitted to the bar of another state.

The character examination for bar applicants is intended to ensure that dishonest and mentally ill individuals are not licensed to practice law. Only in a few states will a conviction for serious crime *automatically* exclude an applicant from the bar. States may not impose a political test for admission to their bars, although they can ask applicants to swear or affirm that they will 'support the Constitution of the United States' and of the admitting state.[3]

About two dozen American jurisdictions permit graduates of foreign law schools to take their bar examinations, although here the rules vary significantly. For example, some states permit admission of a foreign law school graduate only if the applicant's country follows a common law tradition. Some states require at least one year of attendance at an American law school. The American Bar Association publishes an annual guide to the bar admission requirements of each of the American jurisdictions, which lists the requirements for foreign law school graduates.[4] An applicant who otherwise

---

[2] *Supreme Court of Virginia* v. *Friedman*, 487 U.S. 59 (1988). *Goldfarb* v. *Supreme Court of Virginia*, 766 F.2d 859 (4th Cir.), *cert. denied*, 474 U.S. 1986 (1985).

[3] *Law Students Civil Rights Research Council* v. *Wadmond*, 401 U.S. 154 (1971).

[4] See *Comprehensive Guide to Bar Admission Requirements* (1993–94), published by the American Bar Association Section of Legal Education and Admission to the Bar and the National Conference of Bar Examiners. Single copies of this publication can be obtained without charge by writing to ABA Order Fulfillment Department, 750 N. Lakeshore Drive, Chicago, Illinois 60611.

qualifies for bar admission in a state may not be excluded because he or she is not an American citizen.[5]

III. Regulating the Profession

State regulation of the legal profession does not end with admission to practice. Rather, it continues for all of the lawyer's professional life. Although the machinery of lawyer regulation varies from place to place, American jurisdictions are alike in all important respects.

Perhaps the most significant difference among the various jurisdictions is the role of bar associations. Of the several national bar associations in the United States, the American Bar Association (ABA) is the most prominent, counting close to half of American lawyers among its members. But the American Bar Association is a private organization. Although it is highly influential, it has no governmental authority. For example, the ABA publishes 'model' documents prescribing ethical rules for American lawyers. These documents are suggestions only. American states are free to adopt them, modify them, or reject them entirely. As it happens, all American states have adopted one or another version of ABA model ethics documents, although often with significant changes.[6]

Every state has a state bar association. In some states, these (like the ABA) are private organizations, which lawyers are free to join or refuse to join. However, in most states, membership in the state bar association is mandatory. Mandatory bar membership exists, for example, in California, Florida, and Texas, but not in New York, Illinois, and Massachusetts.

States that require state bar membership may treat the state bar as part of the lawyer regulatory machinery. The state courts may then use the state bar in any of a number of ways, including in connection with professional discipline, continuing legal education, and the promulgation and interpretation of ethics rules. Beyond the state bars, many cities and counties also have bar associations, in which membership is entirely voluntary.

American courts uniformly deem the regulation of the legal profession to be within their special province. They look with great suspicion on any effort by state legislative bodies to make rules about the profession, including admission to it and for the discipline of lawyers. Courts often declare that they have *inherent* and exclusive authority to govern the lawyers they admit

---

[5] *In re Griffiths*, 413 U.S. 717 (1973).

[6] The three major ABA ethics documents discussed here are: *The Model Rules of Professional Conduct* (RPC); *The Model Code of Professional Responsibility*; and *The Model Code of Judicial Conduct*.

to practice. Nearly always, this authority ultimately resides in the highest court of a state. (In New York, intermediate appellate courts share authority to regulate the profession.) Courts derive this inherent authority either from language in their state constitutions or from the separation of powers doctrine, which envisions that the three branches of state government—executive, legislative and judicial—each has a particular area of power, that judicial authority encompasses the regulation of the bar, and that this authority cannot be invaded by the other branches.

The judiciary's authority to govern the practice of law extends to the definition of the practice of law, which is typically very broad. It includes advice or representation in which legal rules are applied to the client's particular problem or matter. Appearances in a court or other tribunal, drafting a contract or other document that defines rights and duties, and counseling on the likely consequences of contemplated activity are all law practice. A piece of legislation that purported to grant persons who were not members of the bar of the state the authority to perform a task that a state high court deemed the practice of law would violate a state's constitution unless the court were willing to defer to or share power with the legislature, which is possible but not likely.

Some work sounds like it should be law practice under this definition but is not. The only explanations for this discrepancy are historical ones or the political power of a particular group. For example, accountants are permitted to give advice on one of the most complex of American statutes—the Internal Revenue Code—and may even represent tax clients before the Internal Revenue Service and the United States Tax Court. Also, a host of professionals negotiate for clients without being deemed to practice law, although in theory they cannot draft a contract based on the negotiation. These professionals include literary agents, real estate brokers, and investment bankers.

Every state's judiciary has adopted ethical rules governing the behavior of lawyers admitted in that state. These substantially derive from suggestions by the American Bar Association. The ABA promulgated its first ethics code in 1908, called *The Canons of Professional Ethics*. In 1970, after a number of amendments over the years, the ABA promulgated a new document called *The Code of Professional Responsibility*. Shortly after it did so, all American jurisdictions, which had previously adopted the *Canons* (often modified), switched to the *Code* (also often modified). In 1983, the ABA adopted a third document to replace the *Code*, called *The Rules of Professional Conduct*. So far about three-fourths of American jurisdictions have adopted the *Rules* (again with modifications).

Whether a state has adopted the *Code* or the *Rules* or some amalgam of the two, lawyers who practice within the state are expected to obey the particular rules adopted in their state. Failure to do so can result in professional discipline, discussed below.

Ethics rules cover a gamut of matters. They describe a lawyer's confidentiality obligations; his or her obligation to avoid conflicts of interest; the lawyer's duty to keep a client informed of the status of a matter; and the lawyer's duty of loyalty. Many of these rules are duplicated in the substantive law of fiduciary duty. A fiduciary is someone who occupies a position of trust toward another person. American lawyers are fiduciaries in their relationship to their clients. Many of the obligations that American law imposes on fiduciaries reappear as ethical obligations of lawyers. The ethical rules are not limited to a restatement of fiduciary duties, however. They also address such issues as lawyer advertising, the organization of law firms, and details about conflicts of interest peculiar to the role of lawyer.

Although the details of the disciplinary apparatus differ from place to place, its overall operation is much the same everywhere. Disciplinary authorities are under the control of the courts, sometimes with the assistance of the state bar association. If a disciplinary authority receives a complaint about lawyer wrongdoing—or discovers evidence of such wrongdoing on its own—it can open an investigation, which can lead to a charge. A lawyer charged with wrongdoing has a right to a hearing before an impartial judge or decisionmaker. The lawyer is entitled to notice of the charges; to be represented by counsel; to subpoena witnesses and evidence; to cross-examine opposing witness; and to testify in his or her own defense. Generally, disciplinary authorities are empowered to impose minor discipline, such as a private reprimand, while major discipline, such as disbarment, suspension from practice for a period of time, or public censure, is the responsibility of judges.

Although disbarment sounds like it lasts forever, most jurisdictions allow a disbarred lawyer to reapply for admission after some period of time, generally 6 or 7 years. However, readmission is certainly not automatic and not even probable.

In all states, lawyers who are convicted of criminal conduct will become the subject of discipline. If the crime is serious, which includes all felonies, many jurisdictions will automatically disbar the lawyer without need for any additional hearing. If the crime is less serious, it may, but need not, serve as the basis for discipline.

Once the disciplinary process identifies probable cause to believe that a lawyer acted unethically, most states follow the ABA recommendation and open the process (including any hearing) to public view. Until that point, however, the process is generally confidential in order to protect lawyers from baseless accusations. A minority of states, including New York, do not permit the public to see the process unless and until a court, after a hearing, has decided that the lawyer deserves serious discipline. The rationale for this secrecy is that revelation of an investigation can cripple a lawyer's career and is therefore only appropriate in the event of a finding of serious wrongdoing. At least one state, Oregon, opens the disciplinary process from the time a grievance is filed, even before a decision is made whether the grievance has merit. Whether the disciplinary system should be kept secret and the degree of secrecy, if any, are currently subjects of much debate in America.

IV. Malpractice and Related Claims

If a lawyer's performance of legal work is negligent, and a client is harmed as a result, the client will have an action for malpractice. The action may allege a breach of contract or a tort. A breach of contract claim will essentially say that the client hired the lawyer to perform a service, that the lawyer agreed to perform it, and that the lawyer failed to perform it competently. A tort claim will allege that the lawyer's conduct in performing a legal service was negligent. Often it does not much matter whether the client's claim is based on tort or contract, but sometimes it does. For example, the statute of limitations might be longer for one kind of claim than another. Also, tort claims can result in remedies unavailable for breach of contract actions, including punitive damages and damages for emotional distress.

When a client sues a lawyer for malpractice, the client must prove that the lawyer's negligence or breach of contract resulted in harm to the client in order to recover damages. However, even if the client is not harmed, the client may be able to get back all or part of the fee the client has paid to the lawyer.

When a client claims that a lawyer is guilty of malpractice in connection with a litigation, the client will ordinarily have to prove that he or she would have won the litigation. For example, assume a client hires a lawyer to sue a third party for breach of contract. Assume the lawyer neglects to file the lawsuit in time, and as a result the claim is lost. The client may sue the lawyer for missing the statute of limitations on his claim. In order to win the malpractice claim against the lawyer, the client will have to prove not only that the lawyer breached a duty to the client in missing the statute of limitations, which in this case should be easy, but also that the client would have won the underlying breach of contract action had the lawyer filed it on time, which is often much harder.

A distinct, though partly overlapping, theory of recovery against a lawyer is based on breach of fiduciary duty, under which lawyers owe their clients a very high degree of trust. A lawyer cannot put her own interests above those of a client in connection with a matter in which the lawyer is representing the client. Nor may the lawyer favor one client over another in such a matter. Thus, a lawyer who, for example, uses confidential client information to gain an advantage for himself, at the expense of the client, violates his fiduciary duty. A lawyer who frustrates the goals of one client in the area of representation, in order to advance the goals of another client, will also violate fiduciary duty. A lawyer who takes advantage of a client's dependency to persuade a client to give him or her a gift, or to make his or her relatives a beneficiary in the client's will, violates the lawyer's fiduciary obligation.

Lawyers may be liable not only to their clients, but also to third parties who are injured by their clients if the lawyer helped the client cause the injury. A lawyer who helps a client commit fraud on a third party will be liable along with the client. But traditionally, absent complicity in a client's fraud, a lawyer would not be liable to a third party injured by the fraud, not even if the lawyer negligently failed to discover the fraud. This is because, courts have said, there is no client-attorney relationship between the third party and the lawyer. Absent such a relationship, or *privity* as it is sometimes called, a lawyer would not be professionally responsible to a third party.

In the last 30 years, however, courts have increasingly been willing to make exceptions to the privity requirement and to hold lawyers liable to non-client third parties on one or another theory. For example, assume a client asks a lawyer to write a will in which the client wants to leave $50,000 to her friend Joe. The lawyer writes the will, but errs and the bequest to Joe fails. The failure is not discovered until the client has died and can no longer correct the error or sue. Can Joe sue the lawyer? Most jurisdictions that have addressed this issue say that Joe can sue because he is the beneficiary of one of the client's objectives in hiring the lawyer. Another example of a situation in which courts overlook the absence of privity is when a lawyer is asked to prepare an opinion that the lawyer knows the client will give to a third party to induce the third party to do something. If the lawyer acts negligently in reaching his opinion, the lawyer will be liable to the third party for negligent misrepresentation even though there is no attorney-client relationship with the third party. This is because the lawyer can foresee the reliance of the third party on the lawyer's opinion.

The circumstances under which lawyers will be liable to third parties absent privity are many and depend on the applicable state law. Some states are generous in allowing third party claims against lawyers, and others are quite reluctant to do so.

Not every mistake by a lawyer amounts to professional malpractice or negligence. Lawyers sometimes make errors of judgment that will not be actionable. A lawyer is not a guarantor of the accuracy of his or her work; her responsibility is to exercise the same degree of care, skill, and judgment as other lawyers practicing in the lawyer's state. If the lawyer claims to be a specialist, however, the lawyer will be required to exercise the higher degree of care and skill that specialists are expected to have.

V. Court Sanctions

In addition to discipline and the risk of civil liability, a lawyer who acts improperly in a litigation can be sanctioned by the court. Sanctioning rules have been adopted in many states and in the federal system. Perhaps the most attention has focused on a federal rule called Rule 11 of the Federal Rules of Civil Procedure. That Rule played almost no role in American litigation until 1983, when it was strengthened considerably and sanctions then became common. They became so common in fact that the Rule was amended in 1993, to narrow its sweep, although the Rule retains significant force.

Rule 11 now states that a lawyer who signs, files, submits, or advocates based on a pleading or other document submitted to the court, thereby certifies the following to the court:

(1) that the document is not presented for an improper purpose 'such as to harass or to cause unnecessary delay or needless increase in the cost of litigation';[7]

(2) that the legal argument made in the document is 'warranted by existing law or by a non-frivolous argument for the extension, modification, or reversal of existing law or the establishment of new law';[8]

(3) that factual allegations 'have evidentiary support' or are likely to have support after investigation;[9] and

(4) that denials of allegations have evidentiary support or 'are reasonably based on a lack of information or belief'.[10]

Violation of rules like this one can result in monetary sanctions. While most monetary sanctions for violations of Rule 11 have been relatively small—several thousands of dollars or less—some have been very high, in the hundreds of thousands of dollars. Several have exceeded one million dollars. Under the recent amendments, the likelihood of large awards is significantly reduced but not eliminated.

---

[7] Rule 11(b)(1), Federal Rules of Civil Procedure.   [8] Rule 11(b)(2).   [9] Rule 11(b)(3).
[10] Rule 11(b)(4).

VI. Right to Counsel

Civil liability, judicial sanctions, and discipline are the three dominant mechanisms for ensuring that lawyers comply with their professional obligations, including their obligation of competence, and for providing remedies in the event of misconduct or incompetence. A fourth mechanism deserves mention.

The Sixth Amendment to the United States Constitution guarantees criminal defendants in state and federal courts 'the assistance of counsel'.[11] The Supreme Court has held that this guarantee requires that counsel be 'effective'.[12] Persons accused of a serious crime (one that can result in incarceration) have a right to a lawyer paid by the state if they are unable to pay for their own lawyer.[13]

The constitutional right to the effective assistance of counsel protects criminal defendants only. Civil litigants generally have no constitutional right to a free or an effective lawyer, although statutory regimes in all jurisdictions strive to provide free counsel to indigents in certain matters, such as divorce and claims for state benefits.

What must a criminal defense lawyer—whether retained privately or provided by the state—do to fulfill the constitutional obligation of 'effective' counsel? The Supreme Court has held that counsel becomes ineffective if his or her advice is not 'within the range of competence demanded of attorneys in criminal cases'.[14] The test is 'an objective standard of reasonableness'.[15] Although the Court has refused to be more specific in its statement of the test, it has given examples of things that must be done and not done:

> Representation of a criminal defendant entails certain basic duties. Counsel's function is to assist the defendant, and hence counsel owes the client a duty of loyalty, a duty to avoid conflicts of interest. From counsel's function as assistant to the defendant derive the overarching duty to advocate the defendant's cause and the more particular duties to consult with the defendant on important decisions and to keep the defendant informed of important developments in the course of the prosecution. Counsel also has a duty to bring to bear such skill and knowledge as will render the trial a reliable adversarial testing process.[16]

A defendant who can prove that his or her counsel was constitutionally ineffective may be entitled to a new trial. The courts, however, have not made

---

[11] *McMann* v. *Richardson*, 397 U.S. 759 (1970).
[12] *Ibid.* at 771, n.14. *Cuyler* v. *Sullivan*, 446 U.S. 335 (1980).
[13] *Gideon* v. *Wainwright*, 372 U.S. 335 (1963).
[14] *Strickland* v. *Washington*, 466 U.S. 668 at 687 (1984).   [15] *Ibid.* at 688.   [16] *Ibid.*

the constitutional guarantee terribly demanding. It is rare for a court to find that a criminal defense lawyer has rendered ineffective assistance. But it does happen if, for example, a defense lawyer has spent no time preparing the case, interviewed no witnesses, and conferred with his or her client hardly at all.

Where a defendant establishes that counsel was constitutionally ineffective, the defendant will be entitled to a new trial only if he or she can also show that 'there is a reasonable probability that, but for counsel's unprofessional errors, the result of the proceeding would have been different. A reasonable probability is a probability sufficient to undermine confidence in the outcome'.[17] Where the defendant can show this, he or she will have demonstrated 'prejudice' sufficient to warrant a new trial.

VII. Conflicts of Interest

Ethics rules for lawyers forbid conflicts of interest. While the conflict rules are complicated, essentially they have two specific aims. First, they ensure that lawyers will not act disloyally to a current or former client. Secondly, they ensure that a current or former client's confidential information will not be misused.

The conflict rules distinguish between current and former clients. The rules are more demanding in their statement of obligations to current clients. A lawyer may not act *adversely* to a current client. For example, if a lawyer is representing Company A in connection with tax planning, that lawyer cannot also sue Company A, even if the lawsuit is on a wholly unrelated matter. Similarly, if the owner of the office building in which Company A has its headquarters wants to sue Company A for breach of the lease, Company A's tax lawyer cannot represent the owner.

Furthermore, the tax lawyer's conflict is *imputed* to all other lawyers in his or her firm. This means that all other lawyers in the tax lawyer's firm are deemed to have the same obligations as the tax lawyer. Another way to think about this is to imagine that all firm lawyers are treated as a single lawyer. If a single lawyer in a firm has a conflict, then, ordinarily, every other lawyer in the firm has the same conflict.

The conflict rules also protect former clients, but less extensively. If a firm has represented Company A on tax matters and has concluded its representation of the company, the firm may later represent a new client against Company A. However, the new matter cannot be factually related to the

---

[17] *Ibid.* at 693.

former matter. This rule aims to protect Company A's confidential information. If in the prior representation the law firm would likely have acquired information that would be useful to Company A's opponent in the new matter, then the law firm may not represent the opponent because the risk is too great that the firm will use that information to A's disadvantage. Furthermore, entirely apart from protection of information, a lawyer may not attack the work that the lawyer rendered to a client. For example, if a lawyer has negotiated a contract for a client, he or she may not later represent a new client who wants to challenge the validity or scope of that very contract.

There are other specific situations in which lawyers have conflicts that will prevent them from representing a client on a particular matter. For example, a lawyer cannot prepare a document giving the lawyer or a relative of the lawyer 'any substantial gift from a client, including a testamentary gift, except where the client is related' to the recipient of the gift.[18] This rule ensures that lawyers will not be tempted to exercise their dominance over clients to persuade them to make gifts to the lawyer or his or her relatives. It does not however, prevent a lawyer from recommending to the client that the lawyer be appointed executor or counsel to the client's estate, which can sometimes be lucrative positions.

Similarly, lawyers are permitted to enter business transactions with clients, whether or not in the area of the lawyer's representation, but only when certain client-protective measures are taken. First, the transaction must be 'fair and reasonable to the client', and its terms must be disclosed to the client 'in writing . . . in a manner which can be reasonably understood by the client'. The client has to be given a chance to obtain 'the advice of independent counsel'. And the client must consent to the transaction in writing.[19] These duties are based on the recognition that lawyers who enter business transactions with clients generally have an advantage. The advantage flows from the fact that the client is dependent on the lawyer's legal skills, including perhaps in the very business transaction, and the fact that the lawyer has a good deal of information about the client as a result of the representation, whereas the client does not have equivalent information about the lawyer. Ethics rules recognize that once an attorney and a client have established a professional relationship, the lawyer has a fiduciary duty to the client. That duty does not allow the lawyer to deal with the client as though their relationship were 'arms' length', but requires instead that the lawyer exercise special care to ensure that the client is treated fairly.

Another prominent issue in the area of lawyer conflicts of interest falls

---

[18] RPC Rule 1.8(c).   [19] RPC Rule 1.8(a).

under the rubric 'revolving door'. The 'revolving door' is a metaphor for the common practice of lawyers who move between government service and private practice. Many American lawyers spend several years in government service in order to gain expertise in a particular area of law and to obtain an important resumé credential. Ethical rules and statutory law limit the ability of government lawyers to exploit their government connections once they enter or reenter private practice. While a lawyer is free to use his or her general knowledge about the government agency or department in which the lawyer worked, the rules prevent the lawyer from working in private practice on any specific matter for which the lawyer had substantial responsibility while with government.[20]

Assume a lawyer is investigating Company X on behalf of the government. The lawyer then leaves the government and goes into private practice. The lawyer will not be allowed to represent Company X on the other side of the government's investigation unless the government consents. But the disqualification is even more extensive than that. Ordinarily, the lawyer will not be allowed to represent other clients against Company X if the other clients' claims against Company X are the same or substantially similar to the government's investigation of Company X. The reason the lawyer is not permitted to do this is to prevent the lawyer from profiting from what he or she learned about Company X while having special access to government information.

The revolving door rules also ensure that government lawyers do not choose the targets of their investigation because they anticipate being able to use their accumulated knowledge about those targets on behalf of private interests once they leave government and enter private practice. If lawyers are forbidden to represent clients in the areas of their investigation after they leave government, we can have greater confidence that they will choose areas of investigation without regard to the anticipated benefit to themselves when they subsequently return to private life.

American rules generally do not impute the conflicts of former government lawyers to other lawyers in their firms so long as the former government lawyers are screened from participation in the particular matter. For example, although the lawyer who investigated Company X while at the government cannot represent Company X against the government, or represent another private client against Company X on a similar matter, the lawyer's colleagues at his or her new firm are not conflicted. If a conflict were imputed

---

[20] See generally RPC Rule 1.11. Federal criminal statutes prohibit former government employees (including lawyers) from representing clients on matters that they handled 'personally and substantially' while in government or over which they had 'official responsibility' within one year before leaving government. Certain former government employees are disabled for designated periods of time (generally one year) from representing clients on any matter before their former agencies. See 18 U.S.C. § 207.

to the former government lawyer's new colleagues, law firms might be reluctant to hire former government lawyers for fear that the firms would then be prevented from accepting many clients and might even have to give up some current clients. A reluctance to hire former government lawyers for this reason could very well cause lawyers to refuse to go into government service in the first place, for fear that they would become unemployable in the area of their specialty when they return to private life.

VIII. Confidentiality

A hallmark of the American legal system is its protection of information a lawyer gains about a client. This value is reflected in the rules regarding conflicts of interest where the protection of client confidences is one of the major goals.

There are actually two separate but overlapping doctrines of confidentiality in American jurisprudence. One doctrine derives from the rules of evidence. It posits that communications between lawyers and clients (or agents of the client) are *privileged*. Communications between individuals and certain other persons are also generally privileged—for example, those between spouses, between a doctor and a patient, or between a member of the clergy and a penitent. Privileges are largely the product of state or federal statutory or common (i.e. judge-made) law. The various American jurisdictions are not uniform in the privileges they will recognize or in the scope of protection they will give to particular communications. But all recognize the lawyer-client privilege.

Whether statutory or judge-made, the lawyer-client privilege enables a client and a lawyer to refuse to reveal communications between them. No judge can order the revelation unless some exception to the privilege applies. An exception would apply, for example, if the client has waived the protection of the privilege by previously revealing the content of the communication, or if the communication was in furtherance of a crime or fraud.

Not only individuals, but also corporations and other entities, including governments, enjoy the attorney-client privilege. Obviously, corporations cannot obtain legal advice from their lawyers except through their agents, including officers and employees. These communications between corporate agents and the company's lawyer are generally protected as privileged.[21]

In addition to the evidentiary attorney-client privilege, information that

---

[21] *Upjohn Co.* v. *United States*, 449 U.S. 383 (1981).

lawyers obtain about a client, whether from a client or its agents or from any-one else, is protected in another way. The lawyer must treat this information as *confidential*. The lawyer may not use or reveal confidential information except in certain narrow circumstances. The scope of information protected as confidential includes, but is much broader than, the scope of the informa-tion protected as privileged. In the former category is information gained from *anyone* about the client, not only information from the client and its agents. In the latter category is information gained from the client and its agents. When information is protected as confidential, a lawyer may not vol-untarily reveal the information except if it benefits the client to do so, or if another exception applies; but unless the confidential information is also privileged, the lawyer cannot refuse to disclose it if ordered to do so by a court.

States vary widely in identifying the exceptions under which a lawyer may or must reveal confidential information. These exceptions to the duty to maintain client confidences are hotly debated among American lawyers. While it is not possible to catalog all of the exceptions here, three broad cat-egories can be defined.

The ABA *Model Rules* permit, but do not require, a lawyer to reveal confidential information 'to prevent the client from committing a criminal act that the lawyer believes is likely to result in imminent death or substantial bodily harm'.[22] Some jurisdictions go further and *require* a lawyer to reveal such information in order to protect the intended victim. Some jurisdictions permit (or in a few cases require) a lawyer to reveal a client's prospective financial or property crimes as well.

In addition, all jurisdictions permit a lawyer to reveal client confidences to establish the lawyer's right to a fee or to enable a lawyer to defend herself. The ABA *Model Rules* identify this exception to confidentiality this way: A lawyer may reveal client confidences:

> to establish a claim or defense on behalf of the lawyer in a controversy between the lawyer and the client, to establish a defense to a criminal charge or civil claim against the lawyer based upon conduct in which the client was involved, or to respond to allegations in any proceeding concerning the lawyer's repre-sentation of the client.[23]

So, for example, if a lawyer is charged with a disciplinary violation arising out of a representation, he or she can use client confidences in self-defense. The same is true if a lawyer is sued for malpractice or charged with criminal

---

[22] RPC Rule 1.6(b)(1).   [23] RPC Rule 1.6(b)(2).

conduct. And a lawyer can also use client confidences to the extent reasonably necessary to establish her right to a legal fee.

In one specific area of practice, many courts are especially insistent on a lawyer's obligation to reveal client confidences: when the client has made a false statement in the course of a litigation. For example, in civil litigation in the United States each side is entitled to gather information from its opponent before trial. One way of getting information is to question one's opponent under oath, known as a deposition. If a lawyer learns that his or her client has lied on a material point during a deposition, and the client declines to correct the lie, in most states the lawyer will have to do so. The same is true if a client (or other witness called by the lawyer) lies during a trial. The lawyer's obligation to correct the lie is superior to the confidentiality obligation, even if it means revealing confidential information.[24] In some states, however, the confidentiality obligation is seen to be more important than the duty to correct the lie. In those states, the lawyer either has to withdraw from the representation or, if that is not possible, take pains not to do anything in the representation that will help the client take advantage of the lie.

IX. Adversary Justice

Drawing on British antecedents, American justice relies on an adversary system. This is true in both civil and criminal cases. Under this system, the parties to a litigation, represented by counsel, largely conduct their own investigations and determine the issues to be decided by the judge or jury. The judge and jury are relatively passive, hearing the evidence and making a decision according to the applicable law. The judge has additional responsibilities to superintend the progress of the litigation and to ensure that procedural rules are honored. But the judge does not conduct a factual investigation on his or her own. The judge relies on the lawyers to produce the relevant information and to challenge the information produced by the opposing lawyers.

The adversary system proceeds on the assumption that parties to a lawsuit are in the best position to determine its scope and content in a way that will generate substantial justice. After all, they are the ones who will have to live with the result, and so they are seen to have the greatest interest in affecting it.

One consequence of this theory is that, with a few exceptions, lawyers in an adversary contest have no obligation to parties or interests other than their

---

[24] See RPC Rule 3.3(a) and (b).

own clients. If a lawyer were to discover information that would be helpful to an opponent but harmful to his or her client, that lawyer would ordinarily have no duty to reveal the information and would indeed have an obligation not to reveal it unless (improbably) a court rule required the lawyer to do so.

Consequently, justice, or the right result, is not the responsibility of either lawyer. Each lawyer's responsibility is to help his or her own client get the best result possible for the client, whether or not it is the fairest result in an abstract sense. This system is justified on the theory that, when two or more lawyers singlemindedly pursue the interests of their individual clients, the confrontation will lead to the most just result. If it is not a perfect result, many contend that it is at least better than the result any other system of justice is likely to produce.

In addition, supporters of the American system argue that it respects the autonomy of clients by putting them in control of their own cases. By autonomy, they mean respect for the individual and the right of the individual to make important decisions affecting his or her life. If the state takes control of the scope and content of the litigation, the individual's personal autonomy is seen to be compromised, and the individual is less likely to respect the outcome.

American justice is not undiluted adversary justice; there are limits. Most prominently, in criminal cases prosecutors are required to provide the defense with any information which tends to exculpate the defendant.[25] For example, if a prosecutor discovers a witness whose story would help the defendant, the prosecutor must reveal the identity of that witness. If one of the prosecutor's own witnesses has made a deal with the government in exchange for his testimony, the prosecutor must reveal that deal to the defense, which can then use it to undermine the credibility of the witness.

There are other ways in which adversary justice is tempered. For example, any lawyer who learns that her own witness or client has committed perjury may not seek to exploit the false evidence to the client's advantage. The lawyer, as we saw above, might actually have a duty to reveal the false testimony to the court.[26] Similarly, civil litigation rules permit each side to conduct discovery, or a pre-trial investigation, of the other side. An advocate may not fail to produce information properly requested in discovery although the information will hurt the client's chances of winning at trial.

One attribute of the adversary system deserves special mention. Although a lawyer cannot lie or allow a client to lie, a lawyer (other than a prosecutor or other government lawyer) is free to encourage the factfinder (judge or

---

[25] *Brady* v. *Maryland*, 373 U.S. 83 (1963).

[26] *Nix* v. *Whiteside*, 475 U.S. 157 (1986), held that it did not violate a criminal defendant's right to effective assistance of counsel for a state to impose a duty on the defense lawyer to reveal intended client perjury.

jury) to reach a wrong conclusion. Lawyers sometimes protest that they don't know what the right conclusion is because they don't *know* the truth, but sometimes they do know the truth because of what their client has told them or because of what their investigation has produced. Nevertheless, even if a lawyer knows a fact to be true, she is free to argue that a court should find the fact to be false, or at least that it has not been proved, so long as the evidence could support the lawyer's argument. A lawyer is also free to cross-examine a witness in an effort to discredit the witness in the eyes of the judge or jury even if the lawyer knows the witness is telling the truth.

Although the American theory of adversary justice is most pronounced in civil and criminal litigation, it also influences other kinds of legal services. For example, as a general rule, a lawyer who is negotiating a contract for a client has no duty to provide the opposing side with information helpful to it, nor to correct the other side's possible misapprehensions of fact or law. However, as with litigation, a lawyer cannot lie about a material fact, and if a lawyer's client has lied about such a fact in a negotiation, the lawyer must insist that the client correct the lie before the lawyer can continue to represent the client. If the client refuses, in nearly all states the lawyer's ethical duty to protect the client's confidential information is superior to his or her duty to warn the other side. This means the lawyer will have to withdraw from the representation. When he does, the lawyer is also free in most states to disavow any opinion or the accuracy of any document he has previously provided. In this way, the other side is likely to be alerted to a problem.

X. Legal Fees

Lawyers who are retained by private clients are generally free to negotiate their fees with the client. Since, with few exceptions, lawyers' fees are not subject to government control, the range of fees for legal services in the United States is quite wide. Some private lawyers work for as little as $50 or $60 an hour. At the other extreme, some lawyers charge as much as $500 or $600 hourly.

Beyond the market, ethical rules require lawyers to charge fees that are 'reasonable'. Rarely does a court find a fee unreasonable, but it does happen from time to time. Factors courts consider in determining reasonableness include the lawyer's experience; the novelty of the legal problem; customary fees in the locality; the results the lawyer obtained; the time and labor required to perform the legal service; and whether the fee is contingent.

A contingent fee is one to which the lawyer will be entitled only if certain events occur. Contingent fees are common in personal injury actions in the United States. They also occur in other kinds of matters but are generally forbidden for public policy reasons in criminal cases and in matrimonial cases. The theory behind contingent fees is that they enable individuals without funds to hire a lawyer by promising the lawyer a part of their recovery. Because the lawyer takes the risk that the client will not prevail, in which case the lawyer will get no fee, courts allow lawyers who work on contingency to receive more for a service than might be reasonable if the fee were certain.

Contingent fees have drawn much criticism, especially when the lawyer's risk is low or practically non-existent. Some claims are virtually certain to result in recovery. The only uncertainty is the precise amount. Many would put passenger deaths in airline accidents in this category. Because of the potential for abuse, courts place some limits on the percentage that lawyers may charge as contingent fees. These limits are most common in personal injury cases, where the maximum contingency is usually about one-third of the client's recovery. Lately, some American jurisdictions have imposed limits on legal fees in malpractice actions against doctors and other health care providers.

Fees need not be contingent or hourly. Many lawyers charge fixed fees for particular tasks. For example, a lawyer may charge a fixed dollar amount for writing a simple will or to do the legal work associated with the purchase or sale of a home.

Except for contingent fees, only a few states require that fee agreements between lawyers and clients be in writing. The reasons contingent fee agreements must be in writing are, first, to ensure that the lawyer clarifies what, if any, expenses of the litigation will be deducted from the recovery before the lawyer's contingent percentage is applied, and secondly, because sometimes the agreement is required to be filed in court. Further, a writing makes it clear that the lawyer is working on a contingency and will not later be able to bill the client if he loses.

Generally, a client has the absolute right to fire his lawyer. The main exception to this is where the client is in litigation and discharging the lawyer will disrupt the court's calendar. A lawyer, by contrast, has no absolute right to withdraw from representing a client. The lawyer needs a good reason, such as the failure of the client to pay bills or the client's insistence that the lawyer act improperly. A lawyer who represents a client in court also needs the judge's consent to withdraw. When a client fires a lawyer, or a lawyer properly withdraws, the client will have to pay the lawyer for the work she has already done. The basis for the payment will usually be the retainer agreement or sometimes, as when the lawyer was working on a contingent fee, the reasonable value of the lawyer's services. Even when a lawyer withdraws improperly, or is discharged with cause, some courts will require the client to pay him the value of the services actually provided, but other courts will deny all compensation.

XI. Lawyers Employed by Corporations

In some countries, lawyers are not permitted to be salaried employees of their clients on the theory that it would compromise the lawyer's independence. But in the United States, many lawyers are employed by corporations. They receive salaries and have only one client—the company. Many corporations choose to have lawyers 'in house', as these lawyers are described, because they find it cheaper than to parcel out their legal work to law firms.

An in-house lawyer (like a law firm lawyer working on retainer to a corporation) is required to recognize that his or her client is the corporation and not its officers and directors.[27] Nevertheless, because the corporation can only operate through its officers and directors, the lawyer must take direction from these corporate control persons and give his or her advice to them.

Where a lawyer—either in-house or outside—believes that officers and directors of a corporation or similar entity are behaving unwisely or improperly, the lawyer's job is to protect the corporation, which is the client. Exactly what the lawyer does to protect the corporation depends on the nature of the questionable conduct. If the lawyer merely believes that an officer or director is making an unwise business judgment, the lawyer may seek to have that judgment reviewed, but in the end, business judgments are not for the lawyer, but for the officers and directors of the company.

However, if the lawyer believes that the officers and directors are violating their legal obligations to the company, or are violating the law in a way that could be attributed to the company, then the lawyer has certain additional responsibilities. If the violation 'is likely to result in substantial injury to the organization', the lawyer must try to protect it.[28] Among the things a lawyer can do are to seek reconsideration of the matter; advise that a separate legal opinion be sought for presentation to the appropriate authority in the organization; or refer 'the matter to higher authority in the organization, including, if warranted by the seriousness of the matter, referral to the highest authority that can act on behalf of the organization as determined by applicable law'.[29]

Generally, that highest authority will be the board of directors of the orga-

---

[27] RPC Rule 1.13(a).   [28] RPC Rule 1.13(b).   [29] *Ibid.*

nization. If, despite the lawyer's efforts to end the particular violation, it nevertheless continues, the lawyer may resign but ordinarily may not reveal the wrongdoing to outsiders, not even to the shareholders of the organization.[30] This resolution of the lawyer's responsibility is the dominant one in the United States although some states, and many commentators, believe it is not the best resolution. In the view of some, lawyers for corporations should, under certain circumstances, be entitled to report misconduct to outsiders, including government regulators, especially when the misconduct threatens the very existence of the corporate client or serious harm, such as physical injury, to others.

XII. Marketing Legal Services

In the last two decades, there has been something of a revolution in the United States concerning rules governing lawyer advertising. Until the mid-1970s, virtually all efforts by lawyers to bring themselves to the attention of the public through paid advertisements were prohibited. Lawyers who disregarded these prohibitions could be and were disciplined. In this earlier era, lawyers could do little more than put their name in the telephone book and list their firms in multi-volume lawyer directories that were consulted mainly by other lawyers.

That all changed in 1977, when the Supreme Court held, by a 5-4 vote, that a legal clinic's newspaper advertisement was protected by the free speech guarantee of the First Amendment to the United States Constitution.[31] The term 'legal clinic' is itself relatively recent. A legal clinic is often another name for a private law office, but it suggests an office whose fees are more likely to be affordable by and whose services are more likely to be aimed at middle-class and low-income consumers.

After the Supreme Court's ruling, protection for lawyer advertising increased exponentially. Although the Supreme Court has never extended its ruling to the electronic media, in fact all states permit lawyers to advertise on radio and television. Some states, however, recognizing what they perceive to be the enormous power of the electronic media, have imposed strict limits on their use. For example, in Iowa, Florida, and some other states lawyers who advertise on television and radio may not use dramatizations.

The Supreme Court has also protected lawyers who want to advertise through the mail. Letters sent to potential clients, even persons whom the

---

[30] RPC Rule 1.13(c).   [31] *Bates v. State Bar of Arizona*, 433 U.S. 350 (1977).

lawyer knows to need legal services, enjoy constitutional protection. Thus, a lawyer who learns that a company has been sued or that a person's home has been threatened with foreclosure may write to that company or person offering his or her services.[32] Newspaper advertisements directed at a potential client group have also been protected. In one case, the Supreme Court ruled that the First Amendment protected a lawyer who advertised in a newspaper for clients who had used a particular pharmaceutical product and who may have been injured as a result.[33]

One important restriction that states might constitutionally impose on legal (and other professional) advertising, whether through the mail or in print, are prohibitions against false and misleading messages or assertions of fact that cannot be verified. For example, law firms can be prohibited from describing themselves as the 'best' firm in a particular area. The Supreme Court has also upheld (albeit by a 5-4 vote) a Florida rule, present in some other states too, that forbids lawyers to send mail solicitations to accident victims or their families during the first 30 days after the accident. The Court stressed the state's interest in protecting the privacy of the recipient and reputation of the bar. The dissent stressed the need of potential clients to receive legal help while the evidence is still fresh.[34]

The Supreme Court has permitted states to ban in-person solicitation of prospective clients, at least in some circumstances.[35] In-person solicitation occurs when a lawyer actually approaches or telephones a potential client to solicit business. The Supreme Court has accepted the argument that these in-person solicitations are fraught with so many dangers of overreaching that a categorical prohibition is constitutionally proper. However, the Court has intimated that its willingness to tolerate categorical prohibitions on in-person solicitation might not extend to situations in which the prospective client is sophisticated and not inclined to make a rash decision.[36] For example, while a state might forbid lawyers to visit the homes of accident victims uninvited, a state might not be able to prohibit lawyers from in-person solicitation of a possible business client. In the latter circumstance, the danger of the lawyer overwhelming the judgment of the prospective client may be viewed as too low to tolerate a blanket prohibition.

Although lawyer advertising is protected under the First Amendment's free speech guarantee, it is deemed 'commercial' rather than 'political' and does not enjoy as much protection as the speech the Constitution tradition-

---

[32] *Shapero* v. *Kentucky Bar Association*, 486 U.S. 466 (1988).

[33] *Zauderer* v. *Office of Disciplinary Counsel*, 471 U.S. 626 (1985).

[34] *Florida Bar* v. *Went For It, Inc.*, 115 S.Ct. 2371 (1995).

[35] *Ohralik* v. *Ohio State Bar Association*, 436 U.S. 447 (1978).

[36] *Edenfield* v. *Fane*, 113 S.Ct. 1792 (1993) (accountant has constitutional right to solicit business clients by phone).

ally protects. That is why a state can prohibit false or misleading lawyer advertising, but not false or misleading political speech. In the area of litigation, however, efforts by lawyers and clients to organize and present claims that further the ideological beliefs of the lawyers or clients will enjoy greater protection than the commercial speech of lawyers who are just looking to attract business. Consequently, when lawyers for public interest organizations like the American Civil Liberties Union or the National Association for the Advancement of Colored People seek clients, including through in-person solicitation, in order to bring significant legal cases, states may not interfere. The non-commercial nature of these efforts immunizes them from the state's regulatory authority over commercial speech.[37]

Likewise, when clients band together to purchase legal services at lower cost than any one client would pay on her own, their effort is protected by the First Amendment. In a series of opinions culminating in 1971, the Supreme Court held that states could not prevent union members from using group purchasing power to secure legal representation in connection with their workers' compensation and allied claims. The Court held that 'collective activity undertaken to obtain meaningful access to the courts is a fundamental right within the protection of the First Amendment'.[38]

Many Americans, including many lawyers, believe that the extensive appearance in the American media of lawyer advertisements has come to cheapen the profession and has led to an 'overcommercialization' of law practice and an overemphasis on profit. Certainly, any viewer of late-night American television can see legal advertisements that many consider starkly inconsistent with the view of law as a learned profession. Nevertheless, the Supreme Court over the last two decades has removed from state regulatory bodies the power to prohibit lawyer advertisements entirely, to ban those in bad taste, or even to exercise control over their content in most situations.

XIII. The Judiciary

Except for some minor courts in a few jurisdictions, all American judges are members of their state's bar. Federal judges are appointed by the President with the consent of the United States Senate. State judges are chosen in many ways. Most states elect all or the majority of their judges. In some states, all, most, or some judges are appointed, generally by a chief executive officer like the governor of the state or a mayor.

---

[37] *In re Primus*, 436 U.S. 412 (1978); *N.A.A.C.P.* v. *Button*, 371 U.S. 415 (1963).
[38] *United Transportation Union* v. *State Bar of Michigan*, 401 U.S. 576 at 585 (1971).

Once appointed or elected, judges are regulated in three important ways. First, just as the American Bar Association promulgates a model ethics code for lawyers, it also has a model ethics code for judges, called *The Code of Judicial Conduct*. The latest version of the *Code* was adopted in 1990. While the movement among the states to adopt this latest version has been slow, the earlier version, adopted in 1972, is not much different. Every state has adopted the 1972 *Code*, although frequently with amendments.

The Code of Judicial Conduct addresses many facets of a judge's work and life. Judges are instructed to 'avoid impropriety and the appearance of impropriety in all of the judge's activities'.[39] A judge's judicial duties 'take precedence over all the judge's other activities'.[40] A judge must conduct all extra-judicial activities so that they do not 'cast doubt on the judge's capacity to act impartially as a judge; demean the judicial office; or interfere with the proper performance of judicial duties'.[41] Full-time judges may not practice law.[42]

The 1990 (but not the 1972) judicial conduct code also forbids judges to join organizations, including clubs, that practice 'invidious' discrimination on the basis of 'race, sex, religion or national origin'. An organization invidiously discriminates if it excludes women, minorities, or others arbitrarily.[43]

American law is especially concerned with equal treatment in the courtroom. Judges are instructed (in the 1990 *Code*) to:

> require lawyers in proceedings before the judge to refrain from manifesting, by words or conduct, bias or prejudice based upon race, sex, religion, national origin, disability, age, sexual orientation or socioeconomic status, against parties, witnesses, counsel or others.[44]

Just as lawyers can be disciplined, so can judges for violation of the ethics codes that govern them. As with lawyers, there is a range of punishments for unethical conduct by judges. At one end are private reprimands or reprovals. At the other end is removal from the bench. In between are public censure and suspension from service for a period of time. As a rule, the decision about whether to discipline a judge is made by other judges in a state. However, federal judges serve for life unless impeached by Congress. They cannot be removed or suspended from office by other judges. They can, however, be publicly reprimanded.

A second way in which judges are regulated is through law. Federal law presents a good example. A federal statute states the circumstances under which a federal judge has a disqualifying conflict of interest.[45] These circumstances are fairly representative of the rules in many states.

---

[39] *Code of Judicial Conduct* (1990), Canon 2 (CJC Canon).   [40] CJC Canon 3(A).

[41] CJC Canon 4(A).   [42] CJC Canon 4(G).   [43] CJC Canon 2(C).

[44] CJC Canon 3(D)(6).   [45] 28 U.S.C. § 455.

Judges may not sit if they have 'personal bias or prejudice concerning a party'.[46] But even if the judge is in fact entirely unbiased, he or she may not sit if it could reasonably appear to a fair observer that the judge has an interest in the matter. Appearances count. Federal law defines certain circumstances in which such an interest will disqualify a judge because of appearances. For example, if a judge or certain close relatives of the judge has 'a financial interest in the subject matter in controversy or in a party to the proceeding, or any other interest that could be substantially affected by the outcome of the proceeding', the judge is disqualified.[47] Similarly, a judge is disqualified if before going on the bench, the judge or any of his associates in private practice worked on the matter.[48] If the judge was a government employee before going on the bench and worked on the matter in that capacity, he or she is also disqualified.[49]

Aside from ethics rules and legislation, the Due Process Clause of the United States Constitution may forbid a judge to sit. In one case, a judge on a state supreme court cast the deciding vote (and wrote the opinion) in a case, while at the same time the judge had his own case pending on the same issue. The opinion the judge wrote enabled him to obtain a favorable settlement in his own case. The Supreme Court held that the judge's participation in the case violated the Due Process Clause whether or not the judge was influenced in his vote by his interest in advancing his own case. The Constitution:

> may sometimes bar trial by judges who have no actual bias and who would do their very best to weigh the scales of justice equally between contending parties. But to perform its high function in the best way, 'justice must satisfy the appearance of justice'.[50]

XIV. The Future: More Competition

While no one's crystal ball is clear enough fully to predict what lies in store for the American legal profession, one trend appears likely.

The profession is facing increased competition from many sources. Most obviously, increased competition will come from the steady increase in the number of American lawyers. But other sources also loom. The pressure is growing to allow legal technicians (or paraprofessionals) to handle routine, largely non-discretionary tasks, like drafting simple wills and uncontested

---

[46] 28 U.S.C. § 455(B)(1).   [47] 28 U.S.C. § 455(b)(4).   [48] 28 U.S.C. § 455(b)(2).
[49] 28 U.S.C. § 455(b)(3).   [50] *Aetna Life Insurance Co.* v. *Lavoie*, 475 U.S. 813 at 825 (1986).

divorces. This is how a very large number of American lawyers now earn their livings. Businesses like banks and accounting firms have shown interest in providing legal advice to clients as part of a broader package of banking or accounting services. Foreign law firms will increasingly see the American legal market as a profitable source of clients. They can be expected to continue to open branch offices in the United States and to employ American lawyers to provide advice on American law both in the United States and abroad. Technological advances in computers and communication will, in turn, make it easier for these and other competitors to mount credible challenges.

American lawyers have long been protected by rules that limit the 'supply side' of the market. These rules have restricted those who may wish to sell knowledge of the law although they are not lawyers. They have also limited the ability of non-lawyers to invest capital in the law industry. Only lawyers could do that. But computers and advances in communication, coupled with the increasing globalization of the law industry, may erode many of those rules. Even if these developments do not force their formal repeal, they may begin to make them less important as practical constraints on the law market. It is too soon to tell, but it is not too soon to speculate.

8

CONFLICT OF LAWS

LEA BRILMAYER

The question of how to integrate the legal powers of competing jurisdictions is always a sensitive one, and so it should come as no surprise that, from one legal culture to another around the world, the rules that regulate jurisdictional integration are some of the most complicated and confusing to be found. In many countries, the subject is referred to as 'private international law', but in the United States the preferred term is 'conflict of laws.' Included under this heading are the rules and principles for regulating when a court may assert authority over the person of the defendant (personal jurisdiction); whether it should apply its own law or the law of some other state (choice of law); and when it is obliged to respect the legal decisions of other states (judgments enforcement).

The subject takes on added complexities in the United States because the country is divided into fifty semi-sovereign entities with substantial law-making powers of their own.[1] One such complexity—the division of authority between the states and the federal government—is addressed in Chapter 2, dealing with federalism. But even once questions of the proper allocation of power between the state and federal governments are laid to rest, numerous jurisdictional issues remain. The central conflict of laws question in

---

[1] In addition to the fifty states of the United States, their are other jurisdictional entities whose existence poses problems for the conflict of laws. Native American groups, for example, have substantial legal powers over group members and over activities occurring within reservations; the District of Columbia has powers that in some respects are similar to those of the states; and military law is properly applicable to certain sorts of disputes but not others. While conflict of laws for the District of Columbia is treated substantially the same as conflict of laws for the states, some of these other jurisdictional entities raise distinct and highly specialized conflict of laws problems that cannot be addressed in this chapter.

American jurisprudence concerns how power is to be divided between the states themselves. But there are also problems of the scope of state authority when a dispute has international implications. And there are problems of the scope of federal authority in international disputes, as well. To add to the complexity, each of these sets of issues has both constitutional and non-constitutional dimensions, which typically means a layer of federal constitutional oversight on top of state or federal authority, whether legislative or common law. Due to the federal nature of the American system, conflict of laws takes on a bewildering range of different problems and provides an intimidating array of different answers.

We will start with the question of personal jurisdiction, then turn to choice of law, and finally address problems of judgments enforcement. In each of these areas, we will first describe the standard conflicts doctrines that deal with relations between two states of the United States; then consider what difference it makes that a state law case heard in state court has international dimensions; and finally address the special issues arising when it is federal (rather than state) authority that competes with the authority of a foreign nation. To some degree, similar principles animate the entire range of conflicts doctrines. The basic principles are a prohibition on state overreaching at the expense of non-citizens and an obligation to respect the co-equal sovereignty of other states. By and large, these principles prohibit a state from exercising legal authority over individuals who have inadequate connections with the state. Spelling out what counts as an adequate connection is a large part of the job.

I. Personal Jurisdiction

The first issue, for obvious reasons, is determining whether a court has jurisdiction over the person of the defendant. This question must come first because without such power the court is simply not entitled to proceed. In addition, if a court renders a judgment in the individual defendant's absence, then the defendant is entitled to later challenge the judgment for lack of jurisdiction when the plaintiff seeks to have the judgment enforced.[2]

Personal jurisdiction must be distinguished from two related notions, venue and *forum non conveniens*. Venue rules allocate business within the sovereign's own court system in cases where personal jurisdiction concededly exists; the sovereign admittedly has legitimate power over the defendant, and

---

[2] See e.g. *Baldwin v. Iowa State Traveling Men's Ass'n*, 283 U.S. 522, 524–527 (1931).

must simply decide which of its many courts is the most appropriate place to conduct the litigation. *Forum non conveniens* is somewhat more similar to personal jurisdiction because both deal with cases in which the forum's connection with the defendant is somewhat attenuated; the question is not (as with venue) which of the sovereign's courts is the most appropriate, but whether exercise of the sovereign's authority is appropriate at all. For this reason, *forum non conveniens* and personal jurisdiction issues often arise in the same cases.

Forum non conveniens and personal jurisdiction must nevertheless be distinguished. *Forum non conveniens* dismissals are granted where the court does, doctrinally speaking, have a right to hear the case; personal jurisdiction does exist. The court nonetheless chooses not to exercise the right because it believes that some other sovereign's courts would be substantially more appropriate. The judge exercises his or her discretion to dismiss because the witnesses and evidence are mostly located elsewhere; because hearing a case with so few local connections would be an unreasonable burden on the court system or on the community members who would be called to serve as jurors; because the judge would have difficulty apply an unfamiliar law; or because some other state has a local interest in having the trial conducted there.[3] *Forum non conveniens* motions are not granted unless some suitable other forum exists, and for this reason defendants are often required to waive statute of limitations or personal jurisdiction defenses in those other forums as a condition for prevailing. Because *forum non conveniens* is a discretionary doctrine, a judge's decision will only be reversed on appeal if the decision was an abuse of discretion. The law of *forum non conveniens* varies from state to state, with some states having virtually abolished the doctrine so that if jurisdiction exists, the judge is obligated to exercise it.

Personal jurisdiction, in contrast, is not a discretionary doctrine. States have so-called 'long arm statutes' which prescribe the circumstances in which their courts may or may not exercise the power to adjudicate. In addition to these state law limits on a court's power to adjudicate, there are federal constitutional limits on the reach of state court authority. For several reasons, it is these federal constitutional limits that will comprise our primary focus below. First, because state laws vary, it is hard to generalize about what they require; when dealing with an exercise of authority by an Iowa court (for example) one must simply look up the specific provisions of Iowa law. Secondly, some states have essentially done away with state law limits on personal jurisdiction altogether, by adopting long arm statutes that provide that personal jurisdiction exists in their courts to the limits allowed by the federal

---

[3] The two most important interpretations of the *forum non conveniens* doctrine in American courts are *Gulf Oil Corp.* v. *Gilbert*, 330 U.S. 501 (1947) and *Piper Aircraft* v. *Reyno*, 454 U.S. 235 (1981).

Constitution.[4] Thirdly, even when state law limits do exist, they are not an adequate basis for Supreme Court review, for the federal Supreme Court does not concern itself with matters of state law. For this reason, most of the important historical cases address federal constitutional limitations, and in particular the limits on personal jurisdiction placed by the Fourteenth Amendment.

A. The Fourteenth Amendment Due Process Clause

The Due Process Clause of the Fourteenth Amendment provides that no person shall be deprived of property without the due process of law.[5] From virtually the time of the amendment's adoption, it has operated as a limitation on a state's right to adjudicate cases with which it has only a slight connection. Because the traditional categories have continued to influence today's thinking about constitutional limits on personal jurisdiction, it is worth a brief digression to trace the way the law developed historically.

At one time, there was a strict conceptual distinction between jurisdiction based on the presence of property (*in rem* jurisdiction) and jurisdiction based on the defendant's connections with the forum (*in personam* jurisdiction.)[5] Where the defendant owned property in the forum, it was not necessary to demonstrate that any further forum contact existed. Indeed, under the traditional view, it was not even necessary to show that the litigation had any connection to the forum property. This allowed states a fair amount of power over absent defendants in precisely those states where the prevailing party would be likely to try to enforce the judgment anyway. This compensated for the fact that notions of what should count as adequate connection for *in personam* jurisdiction were rather limited. *In personam* jurisdiction was rather difficult to establish, virtually requiring that the defendant reside in the forum or be served with process there. Over time, the permissible bases for *in personam* jurisdiction were expanded to include contacts such as engaging in tortious activity in the forum; non-resident motorist statutes paved the way by specifying jurisdiction over defendants involved in local automobile accidents.

The two different strands of due process analysis were united in 1976 in the landmark case of *Shaffer v. Heitner*.[6] There, the Supreme Court announced that henceforth all assertions of state court jurisdiction had to be evaluated

---

[4] See e.g. Cal. Civ. Proc. Code sec. 410.10 (West 1973); Wyo. Stat. sec. 5-1-107(a) (1977).

[5] For a more detailed discussion of the development of the law of personal jurisdiction, see Lea Brilmayer et al, *An Introduction to Jurisdiction in the American Federal System*, ch. 1 (Michie Co., 1986).

[6] 433 U.S. 186 (1977).

according to a single standard. The test was to be whether the defendant had sufficient 'minimum contacts' with the forum such that exercising adjudicatory authority would not offend traditional notions of fair play and substantial justice.[7] The defendant's ownership of property in the forum was not necessarily irrelevant in determination of whether personal jurisdiction existed; property might count as a forum connection in the same way as any other factor. What changed, however, was that ownership of property was no longer automatically enough.

Everything now turns, then, on the existence of 'minimum contacts'. Some cases are fairly straightforward, such as those in which the defendant agrees to jurisdiction, either in advance or at the time of the lawsuit.[8] But the existence of minimum contacts in other situations is more uncertain, and the additional proviso that the minimum contacts must be such as to satisfy traditional notions of fairness does not clarify matters very much. Here, one must keep in mind another distinction of some historical importance, which has retained its utility to a greater degree than the *in rem / in personam* distinction. That distinction is the difference between contacts that are related to the controversy and contacts that are unrelated.

Consider a hypothetical individual from Illinois who drives briefly into Iowa, becomes involved in an auto accident while there, and is sued. She has only one connection with the forum—the accident—but that contact, clearly, is an important one. It is the central focus of the litigation. The fact that she drove into the state (or even that she was involved in an accident there) does not, however, mean that she should be subject to suit in Iowa for any cause of action whatsoever. If a mail order business from California that shipped goods to her at her home in Chicago claims that she never paid for them, they cannot simply point to the fact that she once drove into Iowa as a basis for bringing suit in that state. The Iowa accident is not related to that litigation. The distinction between related and unrelated contacts (or, as it is sometimes phrased, between litigation that arises out of the forum connection and litigation that does not) has given rise to a distinction between so-called 'specific' and 'general' jurisdiction.[9]

---

[7] This standard was borrowed from the earlier case of *International Shoe* v. *Washington*, 326 U.S. 310 (1945). The most recent Supreme Court ruling on what fairness and reasonableness require is *Asahi Metal Industry Co., Ltd.* v. *Superior Court*, 480 U.S. 102 (1987).

[8] States sometimes require consent as a precondition for doing business in the forum, and sometimes they treat this as consent to general jurisdiction. The sorts of choice of forum clauses typically found in commercial contracts usually only give rise to jurisdiction over causes of action related to the contract. The Supreme Court upheld choice of forum clauses in *National Equipment Rental* v. *Szukhent*, 375 U.S. 311 (1964).

[9] The distinction was first explained in Von Mehren and Trautman, 'Jurisdiction to Adjudicate: A Suggested Analysis', 79 *Harv. L. Rev.* 1121 (1966). For a more recent discussion, see Brilmayer, 'How Contacts Count', 1980 *Supreme Court Review* 77.

If a defendant has very extensive connections with some particular state, then she will be subject to suit there on any cause of action whatsoever. Since the defendant in our hypothetical lives in Chicago, for example, she will be subject to 'general jurisdiction' in the courts of Illinois. In those states where she has fewer contacts, however, she will only be subject to 'specific jurisdiction,' that is, jurisdiction in cases arising out of or related to those forum contacts. Two obvious problems arise: how does one tell whether a particular connection is sufficiently 'related to' a dispute so that only the smaller showing of contacts required for specific jurisdiction must be shown? Secondly, once one decides whether specific or general jurisdiction is at issue, how does one determine whether some particular set of contacts is enough?

On the first question, many problems are certainly easy enough to classify. In our hypothetical example, the automobile litigation is clearly on one side of the line and the contract dispute clearly on the other. But others are more puzzling; the courts have not agreed on the difficult problems, and the Supreme Court has given no guidance at all. For example, does the sending of similar products into the forum, which do not themselves cause injury, count as related contacts? Assume that a manufacturer's allegedly defective products are said to have caused an injury to a plaintiff who wishes to sue in New Jersey. It would be clear that the injury would count as a related contact if it had taken place there. But what if the injury actually occurred in Pennsylvania, and the asserted basis for New Jersey jurisdiction is that the products that the manufacturer sent into New Jersey were essentially similar to the one that caused the injury being sued on?

Another situation that is difficult to classify involves actions in the forum that have some bearing on how the incident in question unfolded, but are not strictly speaking of legal relevance to the dispute. If the only connection between a defendant ski resort and the forum is that the defendant placed advertisements in newspapers there, which resulted in the plaintiff travelling to the resort and being injured, does this suffice for jurisdiction? It depends in part on whether the advertisements are related to the controversy, and without a clear idea of what 'related to' means, this question is difficult to answer.

Once this first difficulty is resolved, others remain. The problems that plague specific jurisdiction are somewhat different from those that plague general jurisdiction, but they are equally substantial. Few cases of specific jurisdiction are as easy as the one where the defendant drives into the forum and becomes involved in an accident there. More typical are situations where the defendant sends something into the forum, or allows something to be taken into the forum, and the object produces injury.[10] These are sometimes

---

[10] See e.g. *World Wide Volkswagen* v. *Woodsen*, 444 U.S. 286 (1980).

referred to as 'stream of commerce' cases, for the defendant released a product into the stream of commerce and the product, so to speak, drifted downstream to another state, where the tortious consequences occurred. The issue is often framed in terms of 'foreseeability' that the product would make its way into the forum. In such cases, the result will turn on the degree of control that the defendant exercised in the product's eventual path into the forum; if the control was direct as opposed to passive, or if the product's eventual location was more attributable to the defendant's activities than to the plaintiff having taken it there, then the chances of obtaining jurisdiction are increased.

When the subject is general jurisdiction, the issues tend to revolve more around whether the overall quantity of contact is sufficient. Certain contacts are automatically sufficient for general jurisdiction: residence, domicile, place of incorporation, principle place of business, and service of process while present in the forum. Where these automatic factors are not present, the contacts that do exist must be amassed and weighed to determine whether they are sufficiently 'systematic', 'continuous' or 'substantial'.[11] The decisions tend to be highly fact specific, involving an ad hoc weighing of connections such as time spent in the forum, whether the defendant had bank accounts or an office there, whether the defendant made sales or purchases there, and so forth.

B. Jurisdiction Over International Cases

So far we have been assuming that the competing sovereigns are states of the United States. But what difference would it make if the alternative forum were a foreign nation? In most respects, the law of personal jurisdiction takes little notice of the fact that a case has international dimensions. While the Supreme Court has occasionally suggested that international cases might require a different analysis,[12] it has never elaborated on what the different consequences might be. Consider first the situation where a state court must decide whether to assert jurisdiction over an international dispute. One might think that the greater stature accorded a foreign nation might make a state more reluctant to assert jurisdiction, but such has not been the case. As far as Due Process is concerned, it is hard to see what difference it makes that the alternative forum is Peru rather than Pennsylvania.

The relevance of the international aspects of a dispute is somewhat clearer

---

[11] See *Helicopteros Nacionales de Colombia* v. *Hall*, 466 U.S. 408 (1984); *Perkins* v. *Benguet Consol. Mining Co.*, 342 U.S. 437 (1952).

[12] *Asahi Metal Industry Co., Ltd.* v. *Superior Court*, 480 U.S. 102 (1987).

when the authority of federal courts under their federal question jurisdiction is at issue. As a general rule, federal courts do not have distinctive long arm statutes of their own; under the federal Rules of Civil Procedure, they are charged with applying the long arm statutes of the states in which they sit. For this reason, it usually does not matter whether a case is heard in state or federal court.[13] But in a few types of federal substantive cases, state long arm statutes are pre-empted by special congressionally provided long arm statutes. Where one of these special federal statutes is at stake, the court will evaluate the defendant's contacts with the nation as a whole rather than simply with the particular state. Obviously, the existence of such a statute will make it easier to obtain jurisdiction over defendants who are foreign nationals, and whose contacts with the United States may be widely scattered across the country. However, the special long arm statute must be explicitly provided by Congress; a court will not simply infer from the fact that a federal substantive law controls, that aggregation of the defendant's nationwide contacts is permissible.

II. Choice of Law

As with personal jurisdiction, choice of law is best explained by starting with choice between the laws of two or more states; after explaining interstate choice of law, we will return to the distinctive problems posed by cases with international elements.

There are two important elements to interstate choice of law: the state law and the federal constitutional dimensions. Personal jurisdiction also, as we noted, has both state law and federal constitutional dimensions. But the state law elements of personal jurisdiction are dictated by individual state long arm statutes that vary from state to state; generalization is impossible. State law on choice of law is different in that there are several important schools of thought on the subject, with individual states tending to fall into one category or another. For this reason, the best way to approach state choice of law is to examine the different schools of thought that have influenced the development of choice of law theory. Here, the theories of legal academics have exerted substantial influence, with the competing approaches offering differ-

---

[13] On the importance of state long arm statutes in federal court cases based on federal question jurisdiction, see *Omni Capital International* v. *Rudolf Wolff & Co.*, 484 U.S. 97 (1987). There, the Supreme Court held that the state statute governed because there were no sufficiently explicit Congressional instructions to the contrary.

ent jurisprudential understandings of what the choice of law process is all about.[14]

The traditional approach was embodied in the *First Restatement of Conflict of Laws*, published in 1934 and written largely by Joseph Beale, a Harvard law professor who also wrote an influential treatise expounding his views.[15] An intellectual descendant of Joseph Story and Ulrich Huber, Beale believed that choice of law rules should be designed to enforce the vested rights that parties acquired when they engaged in legal transactions in particular territorial locations. Thus, for example, if the parties entered into a contract within the state of New Jersey, their contractual rights vested in New Jersey, and every other state was duty bound to enforce these legal rights on the parties' behalf. Beale's theory is referred to either as 'the vested rights theory' or as 'territorialism', because in enforcing vested rights the courts of other states respected the territorial sovereignty of the states where the relevant acts occurred. It was designed to promote certainty, predictability and harmonious relations between the states in the interstate system.

Central to this approach to choice of law analysis was a process known as 'characterization'. Before it could be determined where the rights vested, it was necessary to determine what kind of legal rights were alleged. Some cases posed contracts problems, others torts problems, and still others problems of property law. Different rules governed these different sorts of problems. To determine where contract rights vested, one needed to know where the contract was formed. An offer by itself does not constitute a contract; an acceptance is also necessary, and so the contract was formed where the acceptance took place. Analogously, to determine where a tort occurred, one needed to know the location of the last act necessary to complete the legal requirements of the tort. Typically, this was the place of the injury. Property problems were governed by the law of the place where the property was located. These rules were shortened into Latin maxims; for contract, *'lex loci contractus'*, for tort, *'lex loci delictus'*, and for property 'the *situs* rule'.

Beale's system purported to cover every sort of legal problem that might arise, and the *First Restatement* provided a complicated set of detailed rules for dealing with all manner of legal disputes. Beneath the tidiness of the several hundred rules, counter-rules, and exceptions, however, lurked a reality that was far more complex. In particular, there were many cases which it proved impossible to characterize as one legal sort rather than another. If a borrower pledges real property located in one state as guarantee for a loan negotiated

---

[14] A more complete description of the various choice of law theories and their historical antecedents is found in chs. 1 and 2 of Lea Brilmayer, *Conflict of Laws* (Little, Brown, 2nd ed, 1995).

[15] There were other methods, also, for avoiding the application of foreign law, such as the *renvoi* doctrine which allowed the court to apply the choice of law rules of the selected state rather than its substantive law. That state's choice of law rules might point back toward the substantive law of the forum.

in another, is this a property problem or a contract problem? Products liability raises issues of both tort and contract; and if the purchase occurs in one state but the injury in another, which rule prevails? These ambiguities offered judges intent on evading rules the opportunity to justify whichever result they wished. Characterization came to be known as an 'escape device' by which judicial manipulation was effectively encouraged and legal certainty undermined.

Perhaps most prominent of these escape devices were those that gave the judge an excuse to apply the law with which he or she was most familiar and comfortable, and which would probably therefore be perceived as 'the most just': forum law. Room for the application of forum law was built in the *First Restatement* system in several ways. One was that forum law applied on all matters of procedure. Viewed in the abstract, this principle is unexceptional; the forum should dictate the conduct of lawsuits in its own courts. The problem came when the judge had to decide whether some particular borderline issue was procedural or not. Numerous rules with apparently substantive aspects, such as the proper amount of damages, were characterized as 'procedural' when some judge simply wished to avoid a foreign rule that seemed objectionable. A second example of a rule favoring forum law was the 'public policy exception.' Under this rule, the forum might decline to apply a foreign rule that would otherwise be applicable on the grounds that it was offensive to some strong held public policy, such as prohibition on gambling contracts.[15]

Rigid in theory, complicated in application, but nonetheless easily manipulable in practice, the *First Restatement* system came under increasing criticism from scholars in the 1950s and 1960s. The critics claimed that 'vested rights' and 'territorialism' were wrongheaded from start to finish; that the goal of choice of law should be to effectuate the policies that the competing states had embodied in their substantive laws. While numerous talented academics blazed the trial towards intellectual rejection of the traditional way of thinking, none was more important than Brainerd Currie, who argued for a 'state interest' approach to choice of law that would better identify those policies and put them into practice.[16] Currie argued that for each contending state, the judge was to determine whether the policy underlying its law would be advanced by application to the facts at hand; if so, the state was said

---

[14] A more complete description of the various choice of law theories and their historical antecedents is found in chs. 1 and 2 of Lea Brilmayer, *Conflict of Laws* (Little, Brown, 2nd ed, 1995).

[15] There were other methods, also, for avoiding the application of foreign law, such as the *renvoi* doctrine which allowed the court to apply the choice of law rules of the selected state rather than its substantive law. That state's choice of law rules might point back toward the substantive law of the forum.

[16] Brainerd Currie's essays were collected and published in 1963, in his *Selected Essays on the Conflict of Laws* (Duke U.P.). Chapter 4 of that book outlines his basic position, and is the foundation for the description that follows.

to have an 'interest' in having its law applied. If only one state had an interest, the case was a 'false conflict', and the law of the only interested state should be applied. If several states had interests then the case was a 'true conflict', and the forum should favor its own law. If no state had an interest, then the case was 'unprovided for', and the forum, again, should apply its own legal rule.

The key to putting this advice to work, of course, was in the determination of whether the policy underlying a legal rule would be advanced by application. Take an ordinary contract rule; what is its purpose? In most cases, rules providing for enforcement of contracts are motivated by a desire to protect the expectations of the parties entering into them by requiring the unwilling party to carry out his or her promises. Determining the underlying policy of substantive rules is sometimes complicated, but in this respect interest analysis calls for nothing more than what domestic disputes require, namely that the judge interpret the statute as best as possible in conditions of uncertainty. The next step is somewhat more controversial, however. Would the policy be advanced by application of the rule to a particular interstate case? Here Currie tended to assume that a policy would be advanced only if its application would work to the advantage of a local resident. Thus a rule calling for enforcement of certain sorts of contracts would give rise to application of the rule only if the party who sought enforcement of the contract was a forum resident.

This conclusion has struck some critics as far from self evident. Why assume that the policies underlying a contract rule are advanced by application of the rule to the advantage of local creditors rather than by application of the rule to contractual relationships formed within the state? The answer cannot be that this is what the legislature that adopted the rule wanted, for two reasons. First, Currie admitted at times that legislatures typically have no particular wishes about the territorial range of their statutes. Secondly, Currie's adherents have insisted that where legislatures actually do have a preference this will not give rise to an 'interest' unless the legislature happens to prefer the result that interest analysis considers rational in light of the substantive policy.[17] There is, in other words, only one rational way to set territorial scope once a particular substantive policy is chosen. Interest analysts are convinced that the particular territorial range they have in mind is in some sense the only sensible and appropriate one in light of the underlying substantive policies, but their arguments tend to take this as a matter of faith, offering no clear explanation for why they believe this to be so.

Many critics have suggested that interest analysis imputes a kind of

[17] See, e.g., Allo, 'Methods and Objectives in the Conflict of Laws: A Response', 35 *Mercer L. Rev.* 565 (1984).

parochialism to state legislatures that is as unrealistic as it is unattractive.[18] When academics insist on defining interests in terms of helping local residents, this may do injustice to the evenhandedness of actual legislative preferences as well as also raising issues of discrimination that must be taken seriously in a nation committed to the equal treatment of outsiders. Another form of parochialism occurs once the forum identifies a true conflict. If it then automatically proceeds to apply forum law at the expense of outside interests, this hardly seems to treat other coequal sovereigns with equal concern and respect. Still another common concern is that because it is impossible to determine the residence of those with whom one interacts—and, therefore, to determine which states will have interests—individuals cannot predict in advance which state's laws they will be subjected to. The unpredictability of interest analysis is compounded by the fact that different courts will not necessarily apply the same law; for in true conflicts or unprovided for cases, the forum is advised simply to apply its own rule of decision.

As many scholars and judges have been dissatisfied with Currie's version of interest analysis as with the Bealean *First Restatement* system it sought to replace. When the American Law Institute decided to revisit the subject in the 1960s, it aspired to produce a new restatement that would combine the insights of the modern learning with the traditional appeal of the old. In the minds of many, however the final version of the *Second Restatement of Conflicts*, published in 1971, was faithful to neither. Interest analysts complained that the new *Restatement* clung to its predecessor's format of black letter rules when it should have moved to a more freewheeling and modern, if amorphous, policy analysis. Traditionalists complained that it was just as unpredictable and chaotic as the interest analysis that was its chief modern competitor. What is the *Second Restatement* approach, and what are its strengths and weaknesses?

The *Second Restatement of Conflicts* retained the *First Restatement*'s division into different types of legal problems: tort, contract, property, and so forth. The unifying element, however, was not a Bealean theory of vested rights but a set of seven considerations listed in its Section 6 which were designed to help identify the state of 'most significant relationship'. These are:

(a)   the needs of interstate and international systems;
(b)   the relevant policies of the forum;
(c)   the relevant policies of other interested states and the relative interests of those states in the determination of a particular issue;
(d)   the protection of justified expectations;

[18] See, e.g., Ely, 'Choice of Law and the State's Interest in Protecting Its Own', 23 *Wm. and Mary Law Rev.* 173 (1981).

(e)   the basic policies underlying the particular field of law;

(f)   certainty, predictability, and uniformity of result; and

(g)   ease in determination and application of the law to be applied.

Some of these factors reflect modern conflicts concepts (particularly those that emphasize policy) but the factors that speak of protecting party expectations and systemic values have a more traditional ring. Section 6 itself gives little guidance on how to combine these factors.

The proper way to apply this list of competing considerations is illustrated, instead, in the sections that follow, which are divided into different chapters for each of the various substantive topics. For each subject (for example, contract) there are a small number of general sections setting out the basic principles and then a number of subsidiary rules spelling things out in greater detail. The main contracts sections, for example, are Sections 187 and 188. Section 187 deals with choice of law clauses in contracts. It provides that such clauses will normally be given effect, except where the law chosen would violate a mandatory provision (that is, one that cannot be varied by contract) of the law that would otherwise apply. If the chosen law contradicts a mandatory provision, it will still be applied unless either the chosen state has no reasonable connection with the dispute or its law violates a fundamental policy of the state with a greater interest. All in all, the *Second Restatement* takes a relatively permissive view of the parties' power to choose the applicable law. After the general sections on choice of law in contract, the *Restatement* addresses specific issues such as insurance contracts, with directions about which state's law will usually apply, absent exceptional circumstances.[19]

There are other competitors in the race to gain the allegiance of the state courts, such as Leflar's so-called 'better law' theory which invites the judge to decide, in part, based on which law is perceived to be the better one.[20] But the main contenders, today, are the *First Restatement* (which still has the largest number of adherents), the *Second Restatement* (which is in second place) and interest analysis (which in its pure form has rarely been adopted, but which has asserted a substantial intellectual influence on other modern theories.)[21] For obvious reasons, it is impossible to describe American choice of law theory as a general matter. When faced with a particular legal problem, one's first task is to determine which choice of law approach is followed by the state that will be litigating the case, and then attempt to apply that approach to the problem in question.

---

[19] See *Second Restatement* Section 193, providing that the law of the principle location of the insured risk shall in most cases govern insurance contracts.

[20] Professor Leflar set out this better law theory in his article 'Conflicts Law: More on Choice Influencing Considerations', 54 *Cal. L. Rev.* 1584 (1966).

[21] For a survey of the approaches that different states follow, see Herma Hill Kay, 'Theory Into Practice: Choice of Law in the Courts', 34 *Mercer L. Rev.* 521 (1983).

A. *Constitutional Limitations*

Adding to the complexity of different conceptual visions of choice of law in the state courts is an additional layer of federal oversight. Even if one state decides that its law should be applied, this is not the end of the matter, for the federal Constitution must also be satisfied. There are two constitutional provisions that bear on the choice of law process. Most important is the Due Process Clause of the Fourteenth Amendment, which we encountered earlier (see section I A above), in the discussion of personal jurisdiction. Also implicated is the Full Faith and Credit Clause, Article IV Section 1 of the Constitution, which states that 'Full Faith and Credit shall be given in each State to the public Acts, Records, and judicial Proceedings of every other State.' By and large, these two provisions have been interpreted as coterminous; except for the fact that the Full Faith and Credit Clause has no application in international cases, the requirements they impose are virtually identical.[22]

What seems to be required by both is that the defendant have 'a significant aggregation of contacts [with the forum], creating interests', such that applying local law would not be fundamentally unfair.[23] The case in which this test was developed, *Allstate Insurance Company* v. *Hague*, demonstrated how minimal this requirement is in practice. The plaintiff's deceased husband had been riding on a motorcycle in Wisconsin. All of the parties to the accident were from Wisconsin, all of the vehicles had been garaged there, and the insurance contract had been written in Wisconsin as well. Nonetheless, the Supreme Court permitted Minnesota was permitted to apply its law because the widow later moved to Minnesota, the insurance company wrote other unrelated policies covering Minnesota risks, and the decedent had been employed there (although he was not killed in the course of his employment or while commuting). Seven years later, the Court affirmed the traditional rule that a state might apply its local law to all 'procedural' issues; at stake in that dispute was the applicable law on statutes of limitations.[24]

Few cases at the Supreme Court level address the constitutional limits on choice of law, and for this reason it is difficult to draw specific guidance about what the constitutional threshold requires. Vague language about aggregations of contacts, interests, and fundamental unfairness provide lawyers with little guidance. It seems quite likely that all of the factors that would be relevant under one or more of the various state law choice of law methodolo-

---

[22] See *Home Ins. Co.* v. *Dick*, 281 U.S. 397, 410–411 (1930) (Full Faith and Credit need not be given to the laws of Mexico). On the similarity of the two clauses' scopes in interstate cases, see e.g. *Allstate Ins. Co.* v. *Hague*, 449 U.S. 302, 308 n.10 (1981)(plurality opinion.)

[23] *Allstate Insurance Co.* v. *Hague*, 449 U.S. 302, 312–313 (1981) (plurality opinion).

[24] *Sun Oil Co.* v. *Wortman*, 486 U.S. 717 (1988).

gies—traditional territorial connecting factors and modern domiciliary factors alike—probably all count toward satisfying the constitutional standard. It also seems quite likely that, for the indefinite future, the Supreme Court will exercise only minimal scrutiny over state choice of law decisions.

B. *International Choice of Law*

What difference should it make that a court is choosing between the law of a state and a foreign country rather than between the law of two states? One might think that at that point international law would come into play, for international law puts limits on a nation's authority to apply its law at the expense of other nations.[25] This instinct would be reinforced by the fact that in the United States international law has the status of federal law, which is, of course, the supreme law of the land under the Supremacy Clause.[26] Thus, while the Supreme Court has held that Congress may if it chooses decide to ignore international law limits, there is no comparable reason to confer this power on the states. If international law has the status of federal statutory law, then Congress can override it as it would override an earlier statute; but the states have no power to override federal statutes at all.[27]

For reasons that are not at all apparent, however, international law has not been thought relevant to the choice between foreign country law and the law of a state of the United States. The issue seems never to have been directly addressed.[29] Instead, choice between state law and foreign law has been treated exactly the same as choice between the laws of two states, in both its state law and its constitutional dimensions. The sole exception is a minor one, dealing with constitutional limitations. As already noted, the Full Faith and Credit Clause does not protect the prerogatives of foreign nations; but since that clause has essentially the same scope as the Due Process Clause (which does apply when the alternative law is that of a foreign nation) little follows from this difference as a practical matter.

The fact that choices between state and foreign nation law are treated exactly like interstate cases is especially striking given another fact: choice between federal law and the law of foreign nations is treated quite differently.

---

[25] These limits are described in Chapter 4 of the *Restatement (Third) of Foreign Relations Law*.

[26] *The Paquete Habana*, 175 U.S. 677 (1900); *Banco Nacional de Cuba v. Sabbatino*, 376 U.S. 398 (1964).

[27] On the power of Congress to override international law, see *The Chinese Exclusion Case*, 130 U.S. 581 (1889); *Head Money Cases*, 112 U.S. 580 (1884).

[28] This phenomenon is discussed in Brilmayer and Norchi, 'Federal Extraterritoriality and Fifth Amendment Due Process', 105 *Harvard L. Rev.* 1217 (1992).

[29] For a discussion of the cases and an argument that the Fifth Amendment Due Process Clause ought to apply, see Brilmayer and Norchi, n. 29 above.

Again, nowhere is there an explanation for this pattern; the cases do not discuss it, it being largely taken for granted. The distinctive nature of federal law/foreign law choice of law is illustrated both in its constitutional and non-constitutional dimensions. As a constitutional matter, no court has ever explicitly held that the Due Process Clause applies to federal extra-territoriality; and this is so despite the fact that the clause quite clearly applies to state law cases with international dimensions.[29]

As a non-constitutional matter, the special nature of federal extra-territoriality is also clear. First, state law cases with international overtones are governed by the *Restatement of Conflicts*, just as interstate cases are. In contrast, federal law cases with international overtones are governed by the *Restatement of Foreign Relations Law*. Secondly, international law is assumed to be applicable to federal extra-territoriality cases even though, as just noted, it has not been thought relevant in state law cases. This means that the standard for choosing between the law of a foreign nation and the law of a state is different from the standard for choosing between the law of a foreign nation and federal law. In particular, with a small number of exceptions, federal extra-territoriality is more closely regulated than application of state law to international disputes. This is because unless Congress otherwise so states, it is presumed to have legislated consistently with international law, and because international law standards are more restrictive than some versions of modern choice of law theory.[30]

The general principle for federal extra-territoriality is that legislation should be construed unless otherwise indicated to apply only to activities occurring within United States territory unless otherwise indicated.[31] This rebuttable presumption has been applied to numerous United States regulatory statutes, from legislation requiring overtime pay for more than eight hours of work, to antidiscrimination law.[32] Closely aligned with this 'territoriality' principle in theory, but much more expansive in practice, is the theory known as 'impact territoriality'.[33] Impact territoriality allows application of United States law (such as for example antitrust legislation) where an individual acting outside the United States has caused consequences within. Impact territoriality is the theory that has provoked the most friction with foreign governments, who point out that activities considered entirely innocent abroad, and undertaken primarily with an eye to their foreign con-

[30] For a federal extra-territoriality case relying on international law to interpret the scope of federal legislation, see *Lauritzen* v. *Larsen*, 345 U.S. 571 (1953).

[31] See, e.g., *Foley Bros. Inc.* v. *Filardo*, 336 U.S. 281 (1949).

[32] *Foley Bros.* v. *Filardo* (see n. 31 above) involved overtime legislation. *E.E.O.C.* v. *Aramco*, 499 U.S. 244 (1991) involved the extra-territorial reach of antidiscrimination law; its result, however, has been overruled by explicit statutory language in 42 U.S.C. §§ 2000 e(f), 2000e-1.

[33] Impact territoriality is recognized in Section 402(1)(c) of the *Restatement (Third) of Foreign Relations Law*.

sequences, might nevertheless be punished in American courts, sometimes (as the antitrust example suggests) by the imposition of a treble damages remedy.[34]

Of less concern to foreign governments is the 'domiciliary principle', whereby the United States asserts authority to apply its law to its own citizens, even when they are acting abroad. There are some situations in which United States laws have been interpreted in this manner, but not a large number.[35] 'Passive personality' would permit the application of local law whenever a local person has been injured abroad. It is considered somewhat dubious under international law and has rarely been applied by American federal courts, although the similarities between it and state law interest analysis should be noted.[36] Finally, universal jurisdiction allows any state to punish offenders of particular universal norms such as the prohibition on piracy or the slave trade, regardless of whether a jurisdictional nexus links the offense to the enforcing state's territory or people. Two federal anti-terrorism statutes purport to apply virtually universally, but their jurisdictional provisions have not yet been substantially challenged in American courts.[37]

Because Congress has rarely specified the territorial reach of its statutes, courts have typically been able to limit jurisdictionally dubious results by interpreting statutes so as not to flout international law. This does not mean that United States application of its laws has not been aggressive; in circumstances it has, but only with regard to certain statutes such as the antitrust laws. Federal extra-territoriality, at any rate, has clearly not been much influenced by modern choice of law thinking.[38] With its emphasis on territoriality, it more nearly resembles the *First Restatement* approach to state choice of law that most academics find largely discredited.

III. Judgments Enforcement

As with personal jurisdiction and choice of law, judgments enforcement is a blend of state and federal law, derived from statutory, constitutional and

---

[34] Impact territoriality was upheld as applied to antitrust laws in *Hartford Fire Insurance Co.* v. *California*, 113 Sup. Ct. 2891 (1993).

[35] See, e.g., *Blackmer* v. *United States*, 284 U.S. 421 (1932).

[36] Passive personality is cited in Section 402 comment (g) of the *Restatement*.

[37] Universal jurisdiction is discussed in Section 404 of the *Restatement*. The statutes in question are the Hostage Taking Act, 18 U.S.C. 1203 (1988) and the Anti-hijacking Act of 1974, 49 U.S.C. 1472(n) (1988).

[38] For an argument that it should have been, however, see Kramer, 'Vestiges of Beale: Extraterritorial Application of American Law', 1991 *Supreme Court Review* 179.

common law sources. When operating within a single state, the rules prescribing how much respect a judgment must be accorded are predominantly state law, usually common law. These rules tells who should be bound by a judgment; how long a judgment should remain enforceable; what bases exist for resisting judgments enforcement (collateral attack); and when issues are sufficiently similar to those already litigated that re-litigation should be foreclosed.[39] There are, admittedly, some federal constitutional limitations. Due process, for example, prohibits the enforcement of a judgment against an individual who did not have adequate notice and opportunity to defend.[40] But intrastate judgments law is, basically, state law, going under the labels 'collateral estoppel', '*res judicata*', or 'issue preclusion' and varying in its precise contours from one state to another.

The most significant federal issues enter the picture when the judgment is sought to be enforced in a state other than the one where it was rendered. The basic principle requiring states to enforce one another's judgments is a constitutional one; it is found in the Full Faith and Credit Clause, which we have already briefly discussed in the choice of law context (see section II A above). The Full Faith and Credit Clause says that 'full' faith and credit must given to the judgments of other states, but how much credit is 'full'? Does the enforcing state have to give a judgment the maximum enforcement that is consistent with the Due Process Clause, allowing only those defenses to the judgment that the federal constitution requires? What if the enforcing state allows certain additional defenses as a matter of state law; can it also allow those defenses when the judgment comes from out of state? Or should it only allow the defenses that the rendering state would itself recognize? The constitutional provision does not specify which of these three alternatives defines the credit that is due.

By federal statute, however, Congress does seem to have addressed this problem. Shortly after the Constitution itself was adopted, Congress provided in what is now 28 U.S.C. 1738 that the enforcing state must give a judgment the same credit as the rendering state would.[41] If taken literally, the Full Faith and Credit Clause squarely chooses the third of these alternatives. It would seem that the enforcing state need only consult the judgments law of the state where the judgment was initially handed down, and can thereby easily determine who should be bound; how long the judgment will remain enforceable; what issues can be relitigated and by whom, and so forth. In fact

---

[39] Such questions are deal with in the *Restatement of Judgments*.
[40] *Mullane* v. *Central Hanover Bank and Trust Co.*, 339 U.S. 306 (1950).
[41] 'Acts, records, and judicial proceedings' of any state 'shall have the same full faith and credit in every court within the United States . . . as they have by law or usage in the courts of such States, . . . from which they are taken.'

though, as is usually the case with things that seem simple, actual practice is more complex.

Obviously, the enforcing state can refuse enforcement if the rendering court had no personal jurisdiction and the defendant did not appear, or if the defendant never received adequate notice. This is not really an exception to the principle that the enforcing state must give the same respect as the rendering state, however, because in such circumstances the rendering state is itself barred from enforcing the judgment by the Due Process Clause. A potentially more interesting problem arises when the enforcing state refuses enforcement on the grounds that its statute of limitations for judgments enforcement has passed, even though the judgment is still enforceable in the state that rendered it. The Supreme Court has held that second states may do so; and while this seems to contravene the literal wording of the statute, at least it is directly parallel to the choice of law rule that the state may always apply its own statute of limitations.[42] The Supreme Court precedents seem to hold that a state may not refuse enforcement on the grounds that the underlying cause of action violates the enforcing state's local public policy.[43] Neither may it refuse enforcement by citing jurisdictional defects that the parties had an adequate opportunity to raise and litigate in the first proceeding, and this is true regardless of whether the jurisdictional issues were actually raised or not.[44]

The question occasionally arises whether the enforcing state may give the judgment more effect than the rendering state would. In particular, this problem can be raised where the enforcing state is less restrictive than the rendering state about who is entitled to rely on the judgment, for some states hold that the only parties who can rely on a judgment are those who would have been bound had the decision gone the other way. To this point, there seems to be no good reason why a state should not give a judgment more effective than it would have where handed down.[45] Some of the most difficult cases have involved mass accidents, in which the potential preclusive effect of a judgment is substantial because of the large number of plaintiffs, but in which the facts vary slightly from one plaintiff's case to another and it is not clear whether the first plaintiff's victory should automatically control.

---

[42] *Roche* v. *McDonald*, 275 U.S. 449 (1928); *Watkins* v. *Conway*, 385 U.S. 188 (1966).

[43] See e.g. *Fauntleroy* v. *Lum*, 210 U.S. 230 (1908). Compare, however, the plurality opinion of Mr. Justice White in *Thomas* v. *Washington Gas Light*, 448 U.S. 261 (1980), which recognized the importance of the enforcing state's public policy in a worker's compensation case.

[44] *Chicot County Drainage Dist.* v. *Baxter State Bank*, 308 U.S. 371 (1940).

[45] See, e.g., *Hart* v. *American Airlines*, 61 Misc. 2d 41, 304 N.Y.S. 2d 810 (Sup. Ct. 1969).

A. *International Judgments Enforcement*

In judgments enforcement, adding international factors to a dispute brings about a bigger difference that in either the personal jurisdiction or the choice of law context. The reason has already been cited: full faith and credit does not apply to foreign legal rules or judgments in the same way as it applies to domestic ones. This leaves foreign judgments holders more dependent on the sufferance of the local judge, who will apply a comity based analysis to determine whether the judgment warrants respect. [46]

The comity standard offers a judge a great deal more discretion in making the enforcement decision than the relatively cut and dried standard provided in the interstate judgments statute. Except where specific rules are provided by international treaty or convention, the judge is free to take a number of factors into account. One is the type of legal system in which the judgment was first handed down. While American judges do not expect foreign judges to conform to the precise procedural standards that would apply in an American court, there must have been some adequate opportunity for the losing party to present his or her case, and the decision-maker must have been relatively fair and impartial. It was once assumed that reciprocity was a requirement for international judgments enforcement; that American courts would not enforce a judgment from a nation that would not, itself, enforce American judgments. While the original Supreme Court case establishing the reciprocity requirement has not been overruled, lower courts have increasingly assumed that American law does not require penalizing the innocent individual who just happens to come from a country that chooses not to recognize American judgments.[47]

IV. Conclusion

Conflict of laws is already confusing enough without the many added complexities that are unavoidable in a federal system such as that of the United States. A unified system would only have a single set of issues to address, as opposed to the American issues of federal/state relations, state/state relations, state/foreign country relations, and federal/foreign country relations.

---

[46] See *Hilton* v. *Guyot*, 159 U.S. 113 (1895).

[47] *Hilton* v. *Guyot* (see n. 46 above) is the source of the reciprocity requirement; for cases suggesting that it is no longer valid, see *Tahan* v. *Hodgson*, 662 F. 2d 862 (D.C. Cir. 1981); *Bank of Montreal* v. *Kough*, 612 F. 2d 467 (9th Cir. 1980)(no reciprocity requirement under the Uniform Enforcement of Money Judgments Act).

Because so much of the important law-making power in the United States has effectively been left in the hands of the states, foreign lawyers face a virtually impenetrable thicket of competing legal rules from different sources. This makes conflict of laws more confusing in systems such as the American one; but also far more important to understand.

II

STATE BASED LAWS

9

CONTRACT LAW

CHARLES L. KNAPP

I. Introduction

In the United States, contract law is the term generally used to describe the body of rules applying to the formation, performance, and termination of private consensual agreements. In the Anglo-American system, contract law has traditionally been a common law area, with judicial decisions in individual contract disputes serving as precedents for the decision of later similar cases. Statutes of various kinds (federal, state or local) are apt to be important in defining the rights and duties of parties to particular types of private agreements, but with the exception of the *Uniform Commercial Code*, there is no statute with implications for contract law in general. In the American federal system, contract law is an area generally governed by state rather than federal law. Although it has been traditional to teach and write about contract law as though it were a single body of rules applicable uniformly throughout the nation, in fact any dispute involving contract enforcement will be resolved in accordance with the contract law of the particular state whose law governs the transaction.

A. Relation to Other Areas of Law

Contract law is 'private' law, in several senses: it provides a mechanism for the enforcement of rights created by agreement between two or more private parties; the standards of behavior it enforces are the obligations defined by the parties themselves, in their agreement; and the usual remedy for breach of contract is compensation payable to the party who has been injured by the other party's non-performance. By contrast, tort law deals typically with transactions (or at least encounters) between private persons, and provides private remedies, but the standards of behavior it enforces are 'public' ones, defined by the state. Criminal law also deals often with encounters between private parties, but is purely 'public' law; it enforces standards of behavior created by the government rather than by the parties themselves, and its sanctions are not private remedies but public ones—typically, fines and/or imprisonment.

Although the principles of basic contract law underlie any enforcement of rights created by private agreement, it is common for such agreements also to be governed by other more particular bodies of law. Some of these are rules of commercial law, like those found in the *Uniform Commercial Code* (UCC, or 'the Code'), which governs such commercial devices as checks and negotiable instruments, secured transactions, bills of lading and warehouse receipts. Others are specialized bodies of law applicable to particular types of agreement, such as the sale of various types of corporate securities, commercial financing and other types of lending (particularly in the consumer market), and the formation and administration of collectively-bargained labor contracts.

Other bodies of general common law may also be important in the resolution of contract disputes. For example, the question whether the actions of one person, ostensibly acting on behalf of another, will serve to bind the latter to an agreement is often crucial in deciding how or whether that agreement will be enforced. Contract law does not directly address such questions, and answers must be found in rules of corporate law or general principles of agency.

B. Sources of Contract Law

As contract law is primarily common law, its rules are to be found (at least in theory) in the aggregate of judicial decisions handed down over the years by courts deciding similar disputes. Because the body of accumulated decisions is so vast as to make it impractical (even in the age of computers) for lawyers and judges actually to review all past decisions which might conceivably serve as precedents for later decision-making, certain conventional sources have been developed from which lawyers and courts can discover the general rules ordinarily governing contract disputes. One of these is a peculiarly

American institution, the 'restatement' of law. Sponsored and officially promulgated by the American Law Institute, restatements are attempts by prominent attorneys and scholars to distill from the body of decided cases the general principles of law in a given area, and to state them in concise form, accompanied by explanatory commentary and illustrations of their application. There have been two general restatements of contract law; the first was officially promulgated in 1932 and the second in 1979. Although the 'blackletter' rules of the *Restatements of Contracts* may resemble statutory provisions in form, they are not statutes; indeed they are not 'law' at all in the sense of being binding on any court. The *Restatements* do serve, however, as 'persuasive authority' for the rules which they express, and are often cited and quoted by American courts to justify their decisions.

Although it remains generally true that contract law is common law, it has in recent years been greatly influenced by the provisions of the UCC, in particular Article 2 of the Code, dealing with sales of goods. As conceived by Professor Karl Llewellyn, its principal original drafter, Article 2 contains not only rules applying specifically to goods transactions (such as rules governing shipment, inspection, and the risk of loss), but also provisions susceptible of wider application, such as the Code's definition of 'good faith', or its proscription of 'unconscionability'. Modern courts often look to the UCC as a source (at least 'by analogy') of general contract law, and its influence can clearly be seen in the provisions of the Restatement (Second) of Contracts.[1]

While a general consensus can often be reliably identified with respect to particular rules of contract law, there is less consensus among members of the legal community as to the general goals which contract law should serve. For practicing attorneys and judges, a principal goal of contract law is to provide a relatively stable body of rules which can serve as a reliable guide for parties entering into various commercial transactions in ordering their conduct to accomplish predictable legal results. The extent to which contract law actually does that is another question; many have contended its uniformity and predictability is more apparent than real, with courts exercising their manifold powers of discretion to reach often unpredictable results.

Beyond providing a legal environment of stability and predictability, a variety of other goals for contract law have been suggested. Some see it as an expression of the moral values which society seeks to advance.[2] Others

---

[1] The 'official' version of the UCC is drafted and promulgated by the American Law Institute (ALI), an organization composed primarily of judges, lawyers and academics, dedicated to the improvement of the law. However, the Code becomes binding law only as it is adopted by the legislatures of the various American jurisdictions. Article 2 of the UCC is currently being revised by the ALI, a process which will probably take several years. When that revised version is completed, it is likely to be adopted by all or most states, but that process will also take some time.

[2] e.g. Charles Fried, *Contract as Promise* (Harvard U.P., 1981).

envision contract law as a vehicle—perhaps not a particularly effective one—for achieving a modest degree of social justice or even redistribution of resòurces.[3] Commentators who apply the mode of analysis known as 'law and economics' have seen contract law as a means by which society achieves an 'efficient' allocation of its resources.[4] Such issues of underlying principle may emerge only infrequently in the written decisions of courts, but they clearly play a role in the process by which the rules of contract law are formed and re-formed over the years.

II. Sources of Obligation

A. *Promissory Commitment*

As we have seen, the essential function of contract law is to enforce obligations undertaken by private agreement. In order to know what types of agreements will constitute 'contracts', one must consider the bases on which agreements are characterized as enforceable in American law. The first element of such an agreement is an expression of commitment on the part of at least one of the parties (typically, all of them) to render some designated performance in the future. Such a commitment, or 'promise',[5] may be conditioned on the occurrence of one or more events, but it must nevertheless evidence a fixed intention to perform should such conditions be fulfilled. Expressions of intention which do not rise to the level of a promise are unlikely to be enforced under the rules of contract law. On the other hand, the mere making of a promise does not necessarily impose a legal duty of performing it, because not all promises are regarded as enforceable. For the promise to be legally enforceable, some additional factor must be present in the transaction or the surrounding circumstances.

B. *Promises Under Seal*

As we will see below, it is not generally true in American law that a promise must be in written form to be enforceable. However, the presence of writing may have legal effect in various ways. One of those is the possibility that a

---

[3] e.g. Duncan Kennedy, 'Distributive and Paternalist Motives in Contract and Tort Law, with Special Reference to Compulsory Terms and Unequal Bargaining Power', 41 *Md. L. Rev.* 562 (1982).

[4] e.g. Robert L. Birmingham, 'Breach of Contract, Damage Measures, and Economic Efficiency', 24 *Rut. L. Rev.* 273 (1970).

[5] *The Restatement* uses the term 'promise'. *Restatement (Second) of Contracts* §2(1) (1979). *The Restatement (Second) of Contracts* will be cited below as 'R2'.

written promise may be made 'under seal'—with a certain formality that by itself gives the writing a particular legal status.[6] Historically, sealed writings were of great importance in English and American law, but today in America the presence of a seal is apt to have little effect.[7] At most it may give rise to a rebuttable presumption that the requirement of consideration (discussed below) has been met.[8]

C. Consideration

Originally, in English law no remedy was available for the non-performance of a purely 'executory' agreement—i.e. one in which no performance on either side had taken place. Where the plaintiff had performed its side of the agreement, however, some compensatory damage remedy would be assessed against the non-performing defendant. Gradually, courts came to enforce promises in cases where performance had not been fully rendered on either side—agreements still executory. In such a case, the court would identify the factor—the 'consideration'—in the case which impelled it to regard the promise as enforceable. Eventually, it came to be said that a promise would not be enforced unless it was given for 'consideration,' and a variety of tests were employed for ascertaining the presence of consideration.

One traditional test for consideration is the 'benefit/detriment' test. If the promisor has received some benefit for the making of the promise, or if the promisee has suffered some detriment in connection with its making, the promise will be regarded as 'supported by consideration'. The detriment or benefit involved need not have substantial economic value, however; this notion was traditionally expressed in the saying that even a 'peppercorn' would satisfy the test for consideration. Another version of the consideration requirement (endorsed by both *Restatements of Contracts*) is the 'bargained-for exchange' test: if a promise was bargained for and given by the promisor in exchange for either a performance or a promise of performance in return, the promise is deemed to have been given for consideration.[9] Generally, the effect of the consideration requirement is to distinguish between exchange agreements and purely donative, or 'gift', promises, granting enforcement

---

[6] Originally, the term 'seal' referred to a dab of sealing wax, into which had been impressed a signet ring or other device. Eventually, the requirement of a seal could be satisfied merely by use of the words 'under seal' or their Latin equivalent, handwritten or even preprinted on a document.

[7] The *Uniform Commercial Code* provides that presence of a seal has no effect with respect to contracts for the sale of goods. UCC, 1991 Official Text (cited below as UCC), §2–203. Corporate documents are still customarily authenticated by use of a 'corporate seal', which is typically an impression on the paper, produced by a metal device.

[8] See generally R2 ch. 4, topic 3, 'Contracts under Seal', Introductory Note.   [9] R2 §71.

only to the former. Most commercial agreements (being exchanges) would therefore qualify for enforcement; many promises made in a non-commercial setting (such as promises between family members) would not, because they do not involve any exchange.

While it remains generally true today that the presence of consideration is a basis for enforcing a promise, it is also true that virtually all agreements calling for some performance on both sides are likely to be regarded as 'supported by consideration'. Occasional exceptions may be found in cases where the promises of one party are so qualified as to really make no substantial commitment at all—to be 'illusory' promises, at best. In that situation, the illusory promise would be too weak to enforce, while the promise given in return would be unenforceable because not supported by consideration.[10] In many such cases, however, the implied obligations and other 'default rules' of contract law (discussed below) might supplement the expressed terms of the agreement and 'fill in the gaps' to make it enforceable.[11]

D. *Reliance by the Promisee (Promissory Estoppel)*

In Section 90 of the first *Restatement of Contracts*, an alternative basis for enforcement was identified. Building on prior case law, Section 90 declared that, even where no consideration was present, a promise might be enforced where the promisee had changed position in reasonable reliance on the promisor's apparent commitment to perform, so that injustice would now result unless the promise were enforced. In a non-exchange setting, 'unbargained-for reliance' could thus serve as a substitute for consideration, to make a promise binding. This principle of reliance-based enforcement, often referred to as 'promissory estoppel' (because of its supposed similarity to the earlier-developed doctrine of 'equitable estoppel'), was initially employed primarily in non-commercial cases, often involving intra-family donative promises or charitable subscriptions. (A leading case involved a grandfather's promise to pay his granddaughter $2,000, expressed in a promissory note; in reliance on the note, his granddaughter quit her job—as he apparently had hoped she would—and remained unemployed for several months.[12])

Eventually, promissory estoppel came to be applied to promises which, while gratuitous (i.e. not made in exchange for any specified performance in return), were made in a commercial setting.[13] Some writers have suggested

[10] R2 §77, Comment *a*.
[11] A well-known early decision using this approach is *Wood* v. *Lucy, Lady Duff-Gordon*, 222 N.Y. 88; 118 N.E. 214 (1917).
[12] *Ricketts* v. *Scothorn*, 57 Neb. 51; 77 N.W. 365 (1898).
[13] e.g. *Universal Computer Systems, Inc.* v. *Medical Services Assn.*, 628 F.2d 820 (3d Cir. 1980).

that the principle of reliance-protection underlies the enforcement of virtually all promises, including those which are made as part of exchange agreements (and are thus 'supported by consideration' in the conventional sense).[14] Whether reliance does play such a pervasive role in contract law, it clearly provides one of the principal bases on which enforcement of a promissory commitment may be grounded.

E. Restitution (Unjust Enrichment)

Since the early days of English common law, the defendant's prior receipt of benefits from the plaintiff has furnished a basis for imposing on the defendant a duty to pay for those benefits. This principle of 'restitution' may provide a basis for computing damages in an ordinary contract case; it might also furnish a reason for enforcing an express promise to pay for benefits received, even in a case where the ordinary requirement of 'consideration' has not been met[15]; it could even impel the court to find that an implied promise of payment had been made, in the absence of any express promise to that effect. The principle of restitution—sometimes referred to as the prevention of 'unjust enrichment'—is also a basis for the imposition of legal obligation in many cases where the defendant has made no promise at all (either express or implied) to pay for those benefits. Although cases of the latter type are sometimes referred to as 'quasi-contractual', they really fall outside the domain of contract law, and are properly seen as examples of pure restitution, which is itself a separate body of common law.[16]

III. Contract Formation

A. Offer and Acceptance

Contract law has traditionally conceptualized the process by which enforceable agreements are made as a process of 'offer and acceptance'. This model of the agreement process does not apply to cases where gratuitous promises have become enforceable solely by virtue of the promisee's unbargained-for

---

[14] Lon L. Fuller and William R. Perdue, Jr., 'The Reliance Interest in Contract Damages I', 46 *Yale L.J.* 52 (1936).

[15] A well-known case in this area is *Webb* v. *McGowin*, 27 Ala. App. 82, 168 So. 196 (1935), enforcing a promise of lifetime payments made by the promisor in gratitude for the promisee's saving of his life (at the cost of severe personal injury to the promisee).

[16] See generally the *Restatement of Restitution* (1936).

reliance; it also does not accurately describe the actual process of negotiation by which many exchange agreements are made. Nevertheless, 'offer and acceptance' remains the conventional model of the contract-making process in American law.

When two parties are contemplating entering into a contractual relationship, one of them (probably after some initial period of preliminary negotiations) may become an 'offeror' by making the other party an 'offer'. This is simply a proposal for entering into an agreement for the exchange of performances, made with sufficient certainty and finality that the other party (the 'offeree') can properly infer that his own assent is all that is necessary to conclude the bargain.[17] Except as may be required by some applicable Statute of Frauds (discussed in section III C below), there is no requirement that an offer be made in any particular form: it may be written or oral, formal or informal. Nor is it necessary for the offer to include an express statement of the offeror's intent to be legally bound. It is sufficient that the offer manifests the offeror's commitment to performance of the proposed exchange, subject to the offeree's assent in return.

That expression of assent is ordinarily referred to as the offeree's 'acceptance' of the offer. So long as it sufficiently manifests assent to the bargain proposed by the offeror, an acceptance may be in any form, unless the offer itself specifies that a particular mode of acceptance is necessary. (In this respect, as in many others, the offeror is traditionally said to be 'master of the offer'.) Typically, an offer will propose that the parties exchange reciprocal commitments to perform in the future. Agreements of this type, involving an exchange of promises, are often referred to as 'bilateral' contracts.

Sometimes an offer provides that the offeror's promise of performance will be exchanged only for the offeree's actual performance, rather than a mere commitment by the offeree to render some future performance. (Examples could include the offer of a reward for the finding of some lost item, or a promise to pay a broker's commission to the offeree should she succeed in procuring a buyer for the offeror's property.) In such cases the offeree's performance of the specified act is also regarded as an acceptance of the offer, and the resulting contract (formed by exchange of a performance for a promise) is referred to as a 'unilateral' contract.[18] Frequently, the offeror appears to contemplate that acceptance will be by a promissory communication from the offeree, but it is nevertheless reasonable to infer from the language or the circumstances that the offeree's immediate performance could also be an appropriate mode of acceptance. In such cases the offeree may

---

[17] R2 §24.

[18] For discussion of bilateral and unilateral contracts in modern law, see Mark Pettit, Jr., 'Modern Unilateral Contracts', 63 *B.U.L. Rev.* 551 (1983).

accept either by making a promise of performance or by actually rendering performance.[19]

The offeree's ability to bring a contract into existence by an appropriate communication of assent is often called the 'power of acceptance'. If the offer itself puts a time limit on the exercise of that power, this will control, and an acceptance will be ineffective unless made within the specified time period. In the absence of such a provision, the power of acceptance created by an offer will last (unless earlier terminated) for a 'reasonable time' in the circumstances.[20] A power of acceptance may also be terminated by the offeror's death or incapacity, or by the offeree's making of a rejection or a counter-offer of her own.[21]

The most difficult problems in this area, however, are likely to be created by the offeror's attempt to terminate the power of acceptance by withdrawing his offer. In Anglo-American law, offers are generally regarded as 'revocable' by the offeror at any time until the offeree has made an effective acceptance. This is the case when the offer itself specifies that it may be withdrawn at any time; it is also true when the offer is silent on the subject of revocability. Indeed, it has traditionally been held that until acceptance takes place, an offer may be freely revoked even though the offer by its terms purports to be irrevocable, either generally or until some stated time. The principal exception to this rule of unlimited revocability has been in cases where, in exchange for some 'consideration' (usually money), the offeror has agreed to enter into an 'option contract', promising to keep the offer open for some specified period. The presence of consideration makes this promise of irrevocability binding, and until the promised period of irrevocability has expired, the offeree may effectively accept, even if the offeror attempts to revoke.[22]

There are other factors which may limit the offeror's freedom to revoke at will. One is the possibility that an applicable statute so provides, such as Section 2-205 of the UCC, known as the 'Firm Offer' section. This rule, which applies only to written offers by 'merchants' to buy or sell goods, provides that an offer which states that it is irrevocable (or 'firm') will indeed *be* irrevocable, for up to 3 months, despite the absence of any consideration.

Another factor which may limit an offeror's freedom to revoke is the possibility that the offeree has relied on the offer in some substantial way, so as to make it unjust to permit the offeror to revoke without first giving the offeree an opportunity to accept. In such a case, the court may hold that the offer became at least temporarily irrevocable as a result of that reliance. This result, which is another application of the principle of 'promissory estoppel' discussed above, was first articulated in a well-known case involving a

---

[19] R2 §§32, 50.   [20] R2 §41.   [21] R2 §36.   [22] R2 §§25, 37.

subcontractor's attempt to withdraw a subcontract-bid on which the general contractor had relied when it prepared and submitted its own bid on the general contract.[23] The principle of that case has been frequently applied in cases with similar facts, but although endorsed by the Restatement (Second),[24] it has yet to be widely applied in other contexts.

B. Incomplete Agreements

As suggested earlier, the offer/acceptance model of the agreement process is probably not accurate in many cases. For instance, complex agreements are often hammered out over time through a process of negotiation involving the exchange of 'drafts' to which neither party is yet fully committed, but which represent attempts to memorialize those terms on which agreement apparently has been reached, as well as proposing other terms for addition to the agreement. When this negotiation process reaches successful fruition and a complete, enforceable contract has been produced, it may be impossible with any accuracy to label either party as the 'offeror' or 'offeree' in the sense described above.

Sometimes, however, this agreement-making process does not produce a single, complete, and detailed agreement to which both parties are clearly committed. One common problem stems from the tendency of commercial parties to use standardized forms for many types of recurrent transactions. If both parties have their own form for a given type of transaction, each party may simply transmit its own form to the other; even though the two forms do not agree in all their terms, the parties may not think it worthwhile to bargain out all their differences. If the parties instead proceed to perform, and a dispute later develops, a court may be faced with the dilemma of either ruling that no contract exists (because of the failure to agree on a single expression of its terms) or having to choose between two competing sets of standardized (or 'boilerplate') terms. One effort at resolving this dilemma is found in Section 2-207 of the UCC , which attempts generally to preserve such contracts by providing rules for choosing between competing terms. Although many cases have applied the provisions of Section 2-207, its application is often awkward and problematic, and the section is widely regarded as only a partially successful solution to this 'battle of forms' problem.

Another problem of incomplete agreement is the so-called 'agreement to agree', where the parties have reached and memorialized an agreement on many terms of their contemplated exchange, at the same time agreeing also

---

[23] *Drennan v. Star Paving Co.*, 51 Cal. 2d 409; 333 P.2d 757 (1958).   [24] R2 §87(2).

to continue bargaining toward a more complete and detailed agreement. Although courts of an earlier day were inclined to dismiss the possibility that such a partial agreement could have any binding effect at all, more recently commentators and judges have begun to see the possibility of enforcing such 'contracts to bargain' in various ways.[25] A prudent attorney involved in such negotiations should therefore counsel the client that any such agreement to agree (a 'letter of intent', for instance) should contain an express statement of intention either to be bound or *not* to be bound, in order to minimize the risk of a later dispute on the issue.

C. Formal Requirements: the Statute of Frauds

In American law, there is no general rule requiring contracts to be in writing and signed in order to be legally binding. In theory, important contracts—perhaps involving large sums of money—can be made by the most informal of writings or even orally and still be enforceable, provided the trier of fact (a jury or a judge, depending on the nature of the case) believes the proponent's evidence of the contract's existence and its terms.

Having said that, it is necessary to add two cautionary notes. The first is simply practical advice: a prudent attorney will be aware that the chances of legal enforcement of any contract are far greater if that contract is embodied in a signed writing. Secondly, in every state there are statutes which impose a writing requirement for certain types of contracts. These statutes are all modeled after an early English statute, and are usually referred to, as that statute was, as 'the Statute of Frauds'.[26] Generally, these statutes provide that contracts of certain designated types, although lawful, can not be enforced unless the plaintiff seeking enforcement can show that the agreement is embodied in a writing signed by the other party. Failure to satisfy the requirements of an applicable Statute of Frauds is likely to leave the aggrieved party with no effective legal recourse, should the other party fail to perform as promised.

The list of contracts to which the typical Statute of Frauds applies[27] is far from exhaustive of the wide variety of contracts which potentially exist, and does not include some important types, such as contracts for the performance of services (unless the statute's 'one year clause', discussed below,

---

[25] See generally Charles L. Knapp, 'Enforcing the Contract to Bargain', 44 *N.Y.U.L. Rev.* 673 (1969); E. Allan Farnsworth, 'Precontractual Liability and Preliminary Agreements: Fair Dealing and Failed Negotiations', 87 *Colum. L. Rev.* 217 (1987). A recent example is *Teachers Insurance & Annuity Assn.* v. *Tribune Co.*, 670 F. Supp. 491 (S.D.N.Y. 1987).

[26] e.g. N.Y. Gen. Oblig. L. §5–701. See generally R2, ch. 5.

[27] An enumeration can be found in R2 §110.

applies). The statute does, however, apply to a great number of commercially important transactions, including sales or leases of land, contracts for the sale of goods, and many contracts of suretyship (promises by one party to guarantee the payment of debts incurred by another). The typical Statute of Frauds also applies to 'any contract not to be performed within one year of its making'. This latter provision has historically been subjected to narrow judicial construction, but the safest approach is to assume that any long-term contract that contemplates performance over a period longer than a year *from the making of the contract* will come within the statute's scope, and will thus be unenforceable in the absence of a writing.[28]

The writing requirement is that of a 'memorandum' or other writing, signed by the party against whom enforcement is sought (often referred to in the statute as 'the party to be charged'). Jurisdictions vary in their application of this requirement; some require the writing to contain a full statement of all the terms of the agreement, while others are less demanding. (The Statute of Frauds now applicable to sales of goods is Section 2-201 of the UCC, which imposes a less stringent standard.) The requisite writing need not be formal, and may consist of two or more documents referring to the same transaction; even a letter or other memorandum signed at a later time may satisfy the statutory requirement if it sufficiently admits the existence of the asserted agreement.

Proponents of the Statute of Frauds have justified it as providing an effective barrier to the enforcement of spurious agreements, trumped up by unscrupulous plaintiffs to oppress innocent defendants (hence the title 'Statute of Frauds'). Courts have not been especially hospitable towards the Statute of Frauds over the years, apparently because in many cases it has appeared to the judge that its strict application would permit the defendant unjustly to escape obligations actually assumed in an agreement truly made with the plaintiff, thereby having the effect of perpetrating a fraud, rather than preventing one. This judicial attitude has resulted in a tendency to construe the statute narrowly, so as to restrict the scope of its application. It has also produced some judicially-created exceptions to the statute, permitting enforcement of an oral agreement in many cases where 'part performance'[29] or a change of position in reliance by the plaintiff[30] was demonstrated. The principle of 'promissory estoppel', discussed in section III A above in connection with the consideration requirement, thus plays a role here as well.[31]

---

[28] See R2 §130.   [29] R2 §129, Comment *a*.   [30] R2 §139.

[31] For a discussion of the various applications of the promissory estoppel principle in the *Restatement (Second) of Contracts*, see Charles L. Knapp, 'Reliance in the Revised *Restatement*: The Proliferation of Promissory Estoppel', 81 *Colum. L. Rev.* 52 (1981).

IV. Identifying the Contract

In its definitional provisions, the *Uniform Commercial Code* distinguishes between 'agreement' and 'contract'. The former, it states, is the parties' actual agreement ('bargain of the parties in fact'), while the latter is the collection of rights and duties ('total legal obligation') that arise from it, including any implied by law.[32] In order to know what the contract of the parties is, therefore, the court must first ascertain their true agreement, and then apply relevant rules of law to determine its legal effect. The starting point in any contract dispute will thus be to discover what the parties in fact agreed to do. This involves first identifying the terms of their agreement, and then if necessary interpreting those terms to determine their meaning in the circumstances. In cases where the parties have adopted a formal written document to express their agreement, this process of discovery and interpretation may be complicated by the 'parol evidence rule' (discussed in section IV B below), which restricts the use of certain kinds of evidence when those conflict with or depart from the parties' agreement in writing. Once the agreement has been found and interpreted, the court can determine its legal effect. In some cases, terms not expressed or even implied in the parties' agreement will be included in their contract, by operation of law.

A. Finding and Interpreting the Agreement

Obviously, the primary vehicle for expressing an agreement is language—'express' terms that the parties have selected to define their performance obligations. Express terms may be in writing, or they may be oral. Virtually any agreement, however, will have at least some terms that are not expressed in the language of the agreement at all, but can nevertheless fairly be implied as part of the agreement in fact. The UCC identifies several places where such terms might be found. They may be seen in the parties' own performance of the agreement at issue: a 'course of performance' indicating what the parties themselves understand their agreement to require (or permit).[33] Implicit terms may also be discovered from the parties' prior performance of similar transactions between them: a relevant 'course of dealing'.[34] Or, they may be found in the commercial setting in which the parties have dealt: 'trade usages' common to that context.[35] Generally, both the Restatement (Second) and the UCC regard all of these as relevant and appropriate sources for discovering

---

[32] UCC §1-201(3), (11).   [33] UCC §2-208.   [34] UCC §1-205(1).   [35] UCC §1-205(2).

the agreement of the parties.[36] In contrast to courts of an earlier day, which often confined their attention to the parties' written agreement in isolation from its context, judges today are admonished by modern contract and commercial law to approach the agreement as best they can, not merely through the eyes of the hypothetical 'reasonable man' (or woman), but through the eyes of the parties themselves, equipped with an understanding of the parties' own dealings with each other and the commercial context in which they have operated.

Course of performance, course of dealing, and usage of trade are regarded both as sources of substantive terms and also as aids to interpretation of the agreement. (A word employed by the parties may well mean one thing in ordinary speech, for instance, and quite another thing in a particular trade.) There are also a number of conventional maxims—often phrased in 'legal Latin' language—that are sometimes useful as aids to interpretation. Examples include *ejusdem generis* (a general term will be interpreted in light of specific examples) and *expressio unius exclusio alterius* (express inclusion of some specific items implies the exclusion of other, similar items which have not been expressly included). Probably the most potent maxim of interpretation is *omnia praesumuntur contra proferentem*, which calls for construing ambiguity against the drafter of the agreement.[37] This latter maxim is particularly likely to be used in interpreting 'contracts of adhesion', where all the terms of the agreement have in effect been dictated by the stronger party, often through use of a form contract, such as those typically employed by banks or insurance companies.[38]

B. *Effect of a Writing—the 'Parol Evidence Rule'*

Like the Statute of Frauds, which denies enforcement to certain types of contracts unless expressed in a signed writing, the 'parol evidence rule' reflects a belief that written evidence is more trustworthy than oral testimony.[39] (Although the rule can result in the exclusion of certain types of written evidence as well, its principal operation is to prevent the use in litigation of certain types of oral, or 'parol', evidence.) The rule in its traditional form excludes any evidence of oral agreements made before (or contemporaneously with) the parties' adoption of a formal written statement of their agreement. This exclusion is justified on the premise that the writing was intended by the parties to be the complete and exclusive statement of the rights and

---

[36] See generally UCC §§1-205, 2-208; R2 §§202, 203, 222, 223.   [37] R2 §206.

[38] See the discussion in *Joyner* v. *Adams*, 87 N.C. App. 570; 361 S.E.2d 902 (1987).

[39] See generally R2 ch. 9, topic 3. An excellent discussion of the parol evidence rule can be found in E. Allan Farnsworth, *Contracts*, (Little, Brown, 2nd ed. 1990) §§7.2–7.6.

duties created by their agreement, and should not therefore be supplemented or varied in court on the basis of some asserted oral agreement.

Courts and commentators differ greatly in their view of the proper scope of the parol evidence rule. There seems general agreement on the notion that it should be applied to exclude extrinsic evidence in cases where the parties have intended their written agreement to be a 'completely integrated' one—a final and complete statement in writing of all the terms of their agreement.[40] The question is how to know when the parties had such an intent. Some courts will look for that intention only in the writing itself (within its 'four corners', as this approach is sometimes phrased), and are likely to assume that any written agreement that looks complete on its face was intended as a final integration, not to be contradicted or even supplemented by oral evidence of some other agreement. (This is particularly likely if the writing contains a 'merger clause', stating that the writing represents a final and complete integration of the parties' agreement.) Other courts may be willing to consider extrinsic evidence of surrounding circumstances before deciding whether the agreement was intended to be an 'integrated' one, and therefore subject to the exclusionary parol evidence rule.[41] For our purposes it is enough to suggest that it is always risky to rely on an oral agreement that departs in any respect from a formal written agreement. Even if there are numerous credible and disinterested witnesses to the making of that oral agreement, the parol evidence rule may well preclude consideration of that evidence if a dispute should arise.

This cautionary note must be balanced, however, by the fact that the parol evidence rule has a number of exceptions. The principal one is that evidence of surrounding circumstances is always admissible to explain or interpret the writing. This exception will certainly apply where the writing is ambiguous on its face ('patently' ambiguous); many courts will permit the use of extrinsic evidence to reveal (and then to explain) a 'latent' ambiguity as well. Evidence of *later* oral agreements is also not excluded by the parol evidence rule (since the theory of the rule is that the parties' writing was intended to summarize and replace all *earlier* agreements).[42]

Although it seems to many observers to belong to an earlier, 'classical' period of American contract law, the parol evidence rule continues to be applied, and is included (albeit in somewhat weaker form) in both the

[40] R2 §§209, 210.

[41] For a recent illustration of these competing points of view in operation, see the majority and dissenting opinions in *Hershon v. Gibraltar Bldg. & Loan Assn., Inc.*, 864 F.2d 848 (1989).

[42] The parties' original written agreement might expressly provide that it could not be modified except by a writing signed by the parties. The common law of contracts did not regard such a provision as effective, because the parties were seen as always having power to alter it merely by later agreement to that effect. The *Uniform Commercial Code* provides that, with certain limitations, such a clause is to be given effect. UCC §2-209(2).

Restatement (Second) and the UCC.[43] It seems likely, however, that the parol evidence rule survives today principally as a device for controlling the flow of information to a jury. If the judge can be convinced of the trustworthiness of the evidence of a supplementary oral agreement, there is likely to be some doctrinal basis on which its admission as evidence could be justified, allowing the jury to take it into account.

C. *Terms Implied by Law*

We have already seen that courts often find the agreement of the parties to consist both of express terms and of terms which can fairly be implied from the parties' express agreement and the surrounding circumstances. There is another type of term which can also be regarded as 'implied', but which stems not so much from an attempt to understand what the particular parties may have meant, as from the law's belief that agreements made by parties in such circumstances should ordinarily be regarded as having particular legal effects. These are terms implied by law, rather than in fact. Some such implied terms are mandatory, and will be included in the contract even if the parties have expressly agreed otherwise. More commonly, contract terms implied by law may be displaced by express agreement to the contrary, and will function only in the absence of the parties' agreement otherwise. (Terms of the latter sort are often referred to in this computerized age as 'default rules', applying only 'in default' of contrary agreement.) The common law rule that a power of acceptance will continue for a 'reasonable time' unless the offer specifies otherwise is such a default rule, as are many of the UCC rules governing sales of goods.[44]

Some terms implied by law add substantive obligations to the parties' agreement. Examples include 'implied warranties' in the sale of goods—warranties that the goods will be 'merchantable',[45] that in some cases they will be fit for the particular use for which the buyer intends them,[46] and that the seller has and can convey legal ownership of the goods ('good title').[47] Such implied obligations can be displaced by express agreement (although that is likely to require clear provision to the contrary, and perhaps compliance with other requirements as well[48]); otherwise they will become part of the parties' contract by operation of law.

---

[43] UCC §2-202.

[44] UCC §1-102(4), Comment 3 ('general and residual rule is that the effect of all provisions of the [UCC] may be varied by agreement').

[45] UCC §2-314.   [46] UCC §2-315.   [47] UCC §2-312.

[48] e.g. UCC §2-316(2), which imposes certain formal requirements for an effective disclaimer of implied warranties.

Other terms implied by law do not add performance obligations, but qualify the manner in which the parties are to perform the obligations specified in their agreement. Implied obligations of this latter sort include duties of cooperation and of 'good faith'.[49] The notion of good faith includes at least 'honesty',[50] and also may require 'commercial reasonableness' and 'fair dealing'.[51] Sometimes a party, while not required by the contract to achieve a particular result, will be subject to an implied obligation to at least use 'best efforts' to do so.[52] These standards of performance may seem vague, but the courts can and will give content to them as circumstances require.[53] While judges of an earlier day may have regarded the role of the law to be merely one of enforcing the parties' express agreement, a modern American court is more likely (through use of such devices as the implied obligations of good faith and fair dealing) to police the conduct of the parties in making and performing agreements, with an eye toward reaching results that reflect the court's notions of justice and fairness.

V. Defenses Against Enforcement

Until now we have dealt primarily with the process of contract formation. That is only the beginning of the story, however. Even if the court finds that the negotiation process has been successfully completed, that there is consideration (or some effective substitute), and that any applicable writing requirement has been met, there may still be grounds on which the defendant might claim that the agreement does not compel her performance. One could be the plaintiff's own non-performance, as discussed in section VI below. There are other contract doctrines, however, which may be invoked by a defendant to argue either that the agreement ought not to be regarded as binding at all (may be 'avoided') or that her further performance should be 'excused'. Although more than one of these defenses might be raised in a given case, they can generally be divided into three basic types: bargaining misconduct; unfair bargain; and change in circumstances.

---

[49] UCC 1-203; R2 §205.   [50] UCC §1-201(19).   [51] UCC §2-103(1)(b); R2 §205.
[52] UCC §2-306(2).
[53] e.g. *United States ex rel. Crane Co.* v. *Progressive Enterprises, Inc.*, 418 F. Supp. 662 (E.D. Va. 1976), in which the defendant asserted that the contract modification by which defendant agreed to pay a higher price to plaintiff for its goods was procured by plaintiff's bad faith threat to breach, and therefore unenforceable under UCC §2-209. The court concluded, however, that defendant was the party guilty of bad faith, by virtue of its failure to protest at the time what it later claimed were extortive tactics on the part of the plaintiff.

A. *Bargaining Misconduct*

Since a contract should be a product of the freely given consent of the parties, the common law has generally been receptive to defenses against enforcement based on assertions of coercion or deception by the party seeking enforcement. Obviously, any exchange agreement is likely to be in part the result of market forces or other extrinsic circumstances, and also may reflect inequality in the bargaining strength of the parties; to that extent it will not be the product of untrammeled free will. These circumstances are not ordinarily thought of as defects in the bargaining process; they are simply inherent in a market economy where individuals of unequal strength compete in an arena governed by 'freedom of contract'. There are, however, a number of types of bargaining conduct that go beyond the permissible exercise of superior bargaining power, rendering any resulting agreement potentially unenforceable by the party who employs them.

The most obvious form of improper bargaining is physicial intimidation: force, or threats of force, to life or property. The common law has gone beyond that simple 'gun to the head' stage, however, recognizing that other types of coercion may be equally improper means of procuring 'assent' to a proposed contract. Threats of unfounded litigation, of the commission of some crime or tort, or even of breach of contract may amount to such 'duress' as will render any agreement so procured avoidable by the aggrieved party.[54] (Many cases have found improper duress where the supplier of goods or services under an existing contract threatened to withhold timely performance unless the other party agreed to a price increase, particularly at a time when procuring an alternate source of supply was unfeasible and the possible consequences of interrupted performance were dire.[55]) Even if the defendant does convincingly assert that a contract (or a contract modification) was procured by improper threats, however, the court may also consider whether the defendant had any reasonable alternative to submitting to those threats. If she did, the contract may still be enforced.[56] The case law in this area is still developing, and further types of 'economic duress' are likely to be identified in future cases.

Another closely related basis for avoidance is one party's exercise of 'undue influence' over the other.[57] This is not mere high-pressure selling, but something more: the exercise of unfair persuasion by a stronger, 'dominant' party over a weaker, 'subservient' one. This relation of dominance may stem from

---

[54] R2 §§175, 176.
[55] e.g. *Austin Instrument, Inc.* v. *Loral Corp.*, 29 N.Y.2d 124; 272 N.E.2d 533 (1971).
[56] e.g. *Tri-State Roofing Co.* v. *Simon*, 187 Pa. Super. 17; 142 A.2d 333 (1958).
[57] R2 §177.

the presence of a 'fiduciary' relationship between the parties, formal or informal, or it may be based on physical or emotional factors.[58] Whatever the source, it results in the weaker party's submission to the stronger party's pressure for agreement. Unlike duress, where the coerced party is likely to be aware of what is going on and yet be powerless to resist, undue influence is likely to persuade the weaker party (at least temporarily) that the proposed contract is indeed in his best interests.

Duress and undue influence both involve strong persuasion designed to induce acquiescence, but they do not necessarily involve lying or deception. (Indeed, a bargainer exercising duress is apt to be very frank about his intentions, while someone applying undue influence may be deceptive only about his professed fidelity to the other party's welfare.) Lying and deception may furnish independent grounds for avoidance, however. If a contract is induced by a misrepresentation of fact which is either 'fraudulent' (knowingly or recklessly made with intent to deceive) or 'material' (likely to induce reliance), or both, the resulting contract may be avoided by the party so misled.[59] If the misrepresentation was intentional (and perhaps even if merely negligent), it might also give rise to an action for damages in tort;[60] in this respect tort and contract law substantially overlap, although their measures of damages may differ.

Traditionally, remedies for misrepresentation were not extended to cases where, rather than lying about a particular fact, the party with greater knowledge simply kept silent. No general duty to disclose existed, even where it was clear that the other party was ignorant of the fact being withheld, and would probably be materially affected by knowledge of it. More recently, however, numerous decisions and commentaries have embraced the principle that in some cases silence is the legal equivalent of a misrepresentation—that there may be, in effect, a duty to disclose material facts in certain circumstances. (The seller of real property, for instance, may have a duty to disclose a hazardous condition on the land, where this fact is unknown to the prospective buyer and would not be discoverable by reasonable inspection.[61]) Improper non-disclosure may exist where the silent party's prior words or conduct have contributed to the other party's mistaken belief, and also in cases where the parties have a fiduciary relationship. However, there is also considerable authority for the more far-reaching proposition that disclosure of material facts may sometimes be required simply because justice and fair dealing demand it.[62]

---

[58] e.g. *Odorizzi v. Bloomfield School District*, 246 Cal. App. 2d 123; 54 Cal. Rptr. 533 (1966).

[59] R2 §§162, 163, 164.   [60] *Restatement of Torts (Second)* §§525, 552 (1976).

[61] *Sorrell v. Young*, 6 Wash. App. 220; 491 P.2d 1312 (1971).

[62] R2 §161; e.g. *Hill v. Jones*, 151 Ariz. 81; 725 P.2d 1115 (1986) (termite infestation in residence sold by defendant to plaintiff, known to defendant but not disclosed).

B. Unfair Bargain

Traditionally, contract law in its 'classical' form did not purport to impose any requirement that an exchange agreement be fair in order to be enforceable. The doctrine of consideration is generally held to require the presence of a genuine exchange (in substance, not just in form), but it traditionally disclaims any attempt to weigh the relative values of the things exchanged. This non-interventionist attitude of contract law was particularly suited to the more unbridled form of *laissez-faire* American capitalism of the late nineteenth and early twentieth centuries, encouraging actors in the economic marketplace to make the best deals they could, with confidence that those deals would be enforced, no matter how one-sided.

More recently, American legal institutions have taken a somewhat different approach. While still adhering to the general notion of 'freedom to contract', both courts and legislatures have deemed it appropriate to 'police' bargains against the possibility of extreme overreaching. This change of attitude has been particularly evident with respect to consumer transactions, where imperfections in the market-place and imbalances of bargaining power have been thought to justify extensive regulation of sales and financing activity. Over the past 30 years or so, much federal and state legislation has been directed toward the end of protecting consumers in the market-place.

This shift in the law has not been a complete reversal, however. The common law of contracts still has no general rule by which otherwise enforceable agreements may be avoided simply on the ground of inequality of the values exchanged. However, there has been a recent resurgence of the notion—rooted in older equity tradition—that an 'unconscionable' contract or term ought not to be enforced. Section 2-302 of the UCC endorses this approach, and the Restatement (Second) has followed suit.[63] Numerous recent cases have applied this principle to relieve a party from contract provisions thought to be oppressive and unfair. Most of these cases have involved consumers. (One well-known early case involved a contract between a 'door-to-door' salesperson and a non-English-speaking buyer for the purchase of a home freezer, at a price found by the court to have been three times its reasonable value.[64]) However, the unconscionability doctrine has also been applied in some disputes between business organizations.[65]

Although extensive commentary has attempted to define the concept of unconscionability, the term remains somewhat amorphous. The consensus

---

[63] R2 §208.   [64] *Jones v. Star Credit Corp.*, 59 Misc. 2d 189; 298 N.Y.S.2d 264 (1969).

[65] *Construction Associates, Inc. v. Fargo Water Equipment Co.*, 446 N.W.2d 237 (N.D. 1989) (holding defendant pipe-seller's disclaimer of warranty and limitation of liability ineffective when plaintiff contractor/buyer would be otherwise left with no effective remedy for defects in pipe already laid).

of courts and commentators appears to be that mere inequality of exchange is not enough to justify invocation of the unconscionability doctrine; the bargain at issue must be so unbalanced as to be substantially 'unfair', and there must also be some respect in which the bargaining process was defective.[66] This defect might be the presence of deceptive practices, or knowing exploitation of a party ill-equipped to protect himself; it might even be found in a market environment which left the weaker party with no alternative but to accept an unfairly onerous bargain.[67] The concept of unconscionability has far-reaching potential, but has generally been kept within rather narrow boundaries. The issue is ordinarily considered one for decision by 'the court' (i.e. the judge), and judges have by and large been restrained in their exercise of this power. The mere existence of this doctrine, however, may to some extent serve as a deterrent to the more egregious forms of commercial oppression and overreaching.

C. Change in Circumstances

Since contracts are by definition devices for making enforceable commitments to future performance, one would assume that ordinarily a contract will be enforced even if circumstances have changed between the time of its making and the time agreed upon for performance. Indeed, one of the reasons parties make contracts in the first place is to protect themselves against adverse changes in market conditions. If at the time a contract is being negotiated it appears that some substantial change in market conditions is likely to take place, the parties may respond in a number of ways—by shortening the contract's duration, for instance, or adjusting the price or other terms to reflect the uncertainty factor, or providing a mechanism in the contract itself for later modification or even termination. Or they might simply refrain altogether from contracting for future performance, dealing only on a current basis.

Not every change in circumstances is foreseeable, however, and even ones that are foreseeable might not be dealt with in the contract—there is after all a limit to the time and energy that can be put into drafting for possible alter-

---

[66] Frequently cited is the two-part test enunciated in the leading case of *Williams* v. *Walker-Thomas Furniture Co.*, 350 F.2d 445 (D.C. Cir. 1965): 'absence of meaningful choice on the part of one of the parties together with contract terms which are unreasonably favorable to the other party'. In his seminal article, 'Unconscionability and the Code—The Emperor's New Clause', 115 *U. Pa. L. Rev.* 485 (1967), Professor Arthur Leff suggested a similar dichotomy: 'procedural unconscionability', involving various defects in the bargaining process, and 'substantive unconscionability', a grossly unfair bargain.

[67] e.g. *Henningsen* v. *Bloomfield Motors, Inc.*, 32 N.J. 358; 161 A.2d 69 (1960) (holding auto manufacturer's warranty disclaimer and limitation of liability ineffective where all auto manufacturers imposed similar onerous terms, making it impossible for buyer to 'shop around' for better warranty terms).

native contingencies. Over the years, Anglo-American contract law has developed a set of doctrines which give limited relief in some cases where one party to a contract has been adversely affected by later developments, not expected when the contract was made. These doctrines include mistake, impossibility, impracticability, and frustration of purpose.

Sometimes a contract is made on the basis of an assumption of fact that is simply not true—a 'mistake', not discovered until sometime later. The mistake might be a 'mutual' one, shared by both parties, or it might be 'unilateral'—one party being mistaken, but the other simply having no knowledge or opinion about the matter.[68] A number of decisions in both English and American courts have allowed avoidance in such cases, provided the mistake was important enough and the parties had not so changed position that avoidance would be unjust in the circumstances. Earlier decisions involving relief for mistake tended to ask whether the mistake went to the 'essential nature' of the subject of the contract.[69] The modern tendency in some cases is first to assess the 'materiality' of the fact at issue and then to decide the case in terms of which party 'bears the risk' of a material mistake.[70]

The 'mistake' cases involve changed circumstances only in the sense that the situation is later discovered by the parties to have been different than they supposed when the contract was made. Several other doctrines have been developed for cases where later events affect the performance of a contract. These include cases where it has become literally 'impossible' to perform the contract according to its terms, often because of the death or destruction of a person or thing necessary for performance.[71] (The leading English case of this type involved the burning down of defendant's music hall before the date when plaintiff had contracted to rent it.[72])

A related but broader doctrine permits excuse of a party whose performance has become 'impracticable'—not literally impossible, but substantially more difficult (and probably more expensive) than originally contemplated.[73] (In the leading American case, a buyer of gravel from a gravel pit was excused from further performance when it had taken all the gravel above the water level, because removal of the remaining gravel was much more expensive and involved different technology.[74]) And even if performance is not impossible or

[68] R2 §§152, 153.

[69] e.g. *Sherwood* v. *Walker*, 66 Mich. 568; 33 N.W. 919 (1887), the well-known 'barren cow' case, in which the court permitted the seller of a cow to rescind the contract of sale where it appeared that the cow, which the parties had assumed to be incapable of breeding, was in fact 'with calf' at the time of contracting, making its value much greater than the contract price.

[70] R2 §154. See, e.g. *Lenawee County Bd. of Health* v. *Messerly*, 417 Mich. 17; 331 N.W.2d 203 (1982), applying the 'risk allocation' approach of R2 §154, and implicitly disapproving the result in *Sherwood* v. *Walker*, n.69 above.

[71] R2 §§262, 263; UCC §2–613 (destruction of goods).

[72] *Taylor* v. *Caldwell*, 122 Eng. Rep. 309 (K.B. 1863).   [73] R2 §261.

[74] *Mineral Park Land Co.* v. *Howard*, 156 P. 458 (Cal. 1916).

even impracticable, it may occasionally be excused where circumstances have so drastically changed that the contemplated exchange of performances will no longer be of any value to one of the parties—its purpose thus being 'frustrated'.[75] (One who agrees to rent a room to watch a coronation procession may be excused from performance by 'frustration of purpose' if the king's illness forces cancellation of that event.[76])

Although the Restatement (Second) retains separate treatment of the above doctrines, Section 2-615 of the UCC combines the notions of impracticability and frustration into a more general concept—'occurrence of a contingency the non-occurrence of which was a basic assumption on which the contract was made'. Despite approving commentary by the drafters of the Code, the principle of Section 2-615, like its common law forebears, is 'more honored in the breach than in the observance'—frequently invoked but seldom determinative of the outcome.[77]

VI. Performance

If the parties have succeeded in creating an enforceable contract, and none of the grounds for avoidance or excuse described above is present, then the stage is set for legal enforcement if one of the parties should fail to perform as promised. In general, any unexcused failure to perform when performance is due is regarded as a 'breach of contract', and will entitle the other party to some remedy. In section VII below, we will consider the range of remedies available for breach of contract. In this section, however, we focus on the threshold question: When does a present duty of performance exist? Of course, the parties' agreement is apt to state with more or less precision when the respective performances should take place, and performance will not be due before the stated time (although earlier repudiation might amount to a breach, as discussed in section VI B below). But there are two other factors that might keep an obligation from becoming a present duty of performance: the duty of performance may be expressly conditioned on the occurrence of one or more events, which have not yet occurred; or, performance by one party may be seen as a necessary prerequisite to the existence of a present duty of performance by the other (in which case the latter party's duty to perform is in effect conditioned on performance by the former).

[75] R2 §265.

[76] These were the facts of the leading English case, *Krell* v. *Henry*, [1903] 2 K.B. 740 (C.A.).

[77] For a recent general discussion of these matters, see John D. Wladis, 'Impracticability as Risk Allocation: The Effect of Changed Circumstances Upon Contract Obligations for the Sale of Goods', 22 *Ga. L. Rev.* 503 (1988).

A. *Express Conditions*

At the time of contracting, each party may well foresee circumstances in which it would not be able or willing to render the performance called for by the contract. Some of these may be circumstances in which the law itself would provide an excuse for non-performance. (Recall the doctrines of impossibility, impracticability and frustration, discussed above; these might well be supplemented by a more general *force majeure* clause in the agreement, broadening the grounds for excuse to include various events beyond the parties' control, such as war, strikes, accident, or 'Acts of God'.) But others may be peculiar to the transaction. A prospective buyer of real property, for instance, may be willing to commit generally to the purchase, and yet not want to run the risk of having to perform if she is unable to get financing for the bulk of the purchase money. Or perhaps the buyer only wants to own the property in question if she can use it in a particular way. In such a case, if the seller agrees, their contract might 'condition' the buyer's duty to make the purchase on the happening of some specified event—the obtaining of a mortgage loan, or the grant of a use permit from the local zoning authority, by some designated date. If the contract expressly imposes a condition on one party's obligation, then that obligation will not become a present duty of performance until either the conditioning event has occurred (in which case the condition has been 'fulfilled', or 'satisfied'), or the condition has for some reason been 'excused' (in which event its occurrence is no longer a condition to the duty of performance). (The party whose duty is subject to a condition is sometimes referred to in this context as the 'obligor'; the other party would then be called the 'obligee', the one to whom an obligation is owed.) Ordinarily, the conditioning event must occur *before* a duty arises; for this reason such conditions are sometimes referred to as 'conditions precedent'. Occasionally a contract provides that the occurrence of a specified event will discharge a present duty of performance under the contract; a condition of this sort may be called a 'condition subsequent'.

Of course, principles of interpretation must often be applied in order to determine what event will satisfy the condition. (Continuing the example above, if a mortgage loan were available to the buyer, but only at higher-than-ordinary interest rates, would that be sufficient to satisfy the condition?) But assuming that the contract's meaning can be ascertained, the duty will not generally be held to arise unless the condition has occurred exactly as called for in the contract. Ordinarily, this will afford the obligor the protection she wished against the specified risk, while not prejudicing the interests of the obligee—who did, after all, agree to that provision in the contract, thus assuming the risk that the non-occurrence of the conditioning event would keep the obligor's duty from ever ripening into a present duty to perform.

Occasionally, however, insistence on strict fulfillment of a condition may appear unjust in the circumstances. Suppose an insurance company expressly conditions its payment obligation under an accident insurance policy on its receiving a notice of claim from the policy-holder ('the insured') within 30 days after the accident. In that case, timely filing of a proper notice would probably be seen as a condition precedent to the insurer's duty of payment under the policy. Suppose the insured is indeed injured in an accident, but does not file her notice of claim until the 35th day. Should that be fatal to the claim? Consider the following alternate additional circumstances:

(a) Filing of the notice was delayed because the insured was in a coma, unconscious, for 31 days after the accident.

(b) On the 28th day after the accident, the insurance company's agent told the still-recuperating insured, 'Don't worry if your notice of claim is a few days late; you need more time to get back on your feet'.

(c) When the notice was filed on the 35th day, the company's agent said 'I see this notice is a little late, but don't worry; that's no problem'.

(d) The policy calls for notice to be given on a form provided by the insurer, but the insurance company, although earlier requested to do so by the insured, failed to provide appropriate forms until the 33rd day.

In each of these cases, the conditioning event (notice within 30 days) has not occurred. In each case, however, the insurer might nevertheless be liable to pay on the policy, because the condition of timely notice is likely to be excused for the following reasons:

(a) Delay in giving notice may be excused by impossibility, because the condition will be seen as 'non-material' and substantial forfeiture would result from strict enforcement.[78]

(b) The obligor (the insurer) 'waived' the condition in advance, and failed to retract that waiver before the obligee (the insured) had relied on it by delaying her filing until the stated due date had passed.[79]

(c) The obligor waived the condition after the time for its occurrence had passed, and the condition, being deemed 'non-material', should therefore be excused.[80]

(d) The obligor in effect kept the conditioning event (timely giving of notice) from happening; this 'prevention' justifies excuse of the condition.[81]

---

[78] R2 §§229, 271.   [79] R2 §84(2).   [80] R2 §84(1).   [81] R2 §245.

B. *Effect of Other Party's Non-performance*

Often, the question whether one party is under a present duty of performance will depend on the extent to which the other party has performed her side of the bargain. Assuming the agreement imposes obligations on both parties, some of which remain unperformed on each side, a number of questions may be raised:

(a)   When may one party suspend performance because of the other's non-performance?

(b)   Must one party's performance be completed or at least 'tendered' before the other party comes under a present duty to perform?

(c)   At what point will non-performance by one party release the other party entirely from further obligation?

To illustrate these issues in context, consider the case of a builder, B, who contracts to build a house for C on C's land for a total price of $100,000. The contract expressly provides that construction is to be completed on or before a designated date, but is silent as to the time when payment must be made. When will payment by the owner be due? The common law worked out a series of conventional rules to govern the order of performance, if the contract itself did not expressly answer that question. In a case like this, the law would presume that the building had to be completed before the price was payable—that completion of the construction work by the builder was, as it is sometimes put, a 'constructive condition' to the owner's duty of paying the price.[82] In contrast, in a sale of goods, where the performances can be simultaneously rendered, the law would presume that a 'tender' of delivery of the goods was necessary before payment would be due, and vice versa.[83] In other words, the performance by each party would have to be at least offered before the other party had a present duty to render its performance in return. (This situation is sometimes referred to as one of 'concurrent constructive conditions'.) The common law approach would mean, in our building contract example, that unless the parties agreed otherwise, B would have to build C's house entirely 'on credit', trusting C to honor her obligation to pay upon completion. Since builders in the real world are usually not so trusting (nor so well capitalized), any actual contract like the one between B and C is likely to provide for installment payments as the work progresses, plus an initial payment in advance of any construction, to enable the builder to finance its operations.

Suppose therefore that our hypothetical B–C contract calls for an initial

---

[82] R2 §234. e.g. *Stewart v. Newbury*, 220 N.Y. 379; 115 N.E. 984 (1917).
[83] UCC §§2-507(1), 2-511(1).

payment of 10 percent of the contract price, with further payments of 20 percent when the foundation is completed, 40 percent when the roof is on, 20 percent when interior carpentry is completed, and the remaining 10 percent on satisfactory completion of all work including plumbing and electricals. C makes the first three payments as promised, but after B has completed the interior carpentry, C does not make the payment then due. This may be because C is temporarily short of cash, because C has suffered severe financial reverses, or because C claims that B's performance is somehow defective. C's non-payment raises a number of questions, the answers to which will depend on the surrounding circumstances.

First, is C presently obligated to make the payment? The answer is yes, unless B's performance is defective in some important respect. The contract provides that payment is due on completion of this stage of the builder's performance, which is a question of fact. If B's performance conforms to the contract exactly, then C owes the money, and would be liable to B in a lawsuit for that sum. B's performance might not literally conform to the contract in every respect, however, yet still be seen by a court as 'substantial', conforming except in relatively unimportant, 'non-material' respects. (Perhaps B used for the interior framing a different type of wood than specified, but one which is just as strong and durable as the type called for in the contract.[84]) In that case C would be liable to B for that installment payment, but B's recovery would be subject to an offset in favor of C for the cost or value of the defect in performance. (In the above example, that offset might be little or nothing.) It might be, however, that B's performance is not substantial, being defective in material respects. (Perhaps B used a different and less durable type of lumber for the rafters of the house than was specified in the contract.) In that case C is entitled to withhold the payment, pending at least 'substantial performance' by B. (In this case that could mean replacing the defective rafters with conforming ones.[85])

Suppose in the first scenario above C refuses to make the fourth payment due, claiming a defect in performance, but in fact B's performance to date conforms to the contract, and C owes the money. If C persists in refusing to pay, B is probably entitled to suspend any further performance pending payment, either because the breach by C is regarded as 'material' (involving not merely a delay in payment but also a refusal to admit that the payment is due), or because C's refusal to pay this large a portion of the contract price when due justifiably makes B 'insecure' about C's willingness to honor her contract obligations, and justifies B's refusal to perform further unless C either performs or gives 'adequate assurances' that she will perform in the

[84] This is a variation of the leading case, *Jacob & Youngs, Inc.* v. *Kent*, 230 N.Y. 239; 129 N.E. 889 (1921).
[85] For an enumeration of the various factors affecting materiality, see R2 §241.

future.[86] (If C is temporarily short of cash, C may be able to provide sufficient assurances of future payment; if C has suffered severe financial reverses, however, this may not be the case, and B may be justified as treating the contract as terminated by material breach.)

So long as B has merely suspended performance pending payment by C, C can 'cure' her breach by making that payment, and thereby reinstate B's duty to continue performing. At some point, however, B may wish to call it a day, and move on to some other project with a more reliable customer. If B notifies C that he elects to treat her breach as material and as terminating his further duty of performance, C at that point will have lost the ability to reinstate B's duty of performance. Also, B will—if he chooses to pursue it—have a cause of action against C for 'total breach' of their contract.[87] (B's possible remedies are discussed in the section VII below.)

The above example involves the effect of non-performance at a time when performance is due. That may have the effect of suspending or discharging the other party's continued performance under the contract. If one party 'repudiates' a duty *before* performance is presently due by declaring that she cannot or will not perform as promised, that repudiation may have the same effect as a present total breach.[88] Continuing with our hypothetical B–C construction contract, suppose that C makes her initial payment to B under their contract, but before B has begun construction, C notifies him not to proceed with construction, either because financial reverses will prevent her from paying for the construction, or because she has simply changed her mind about the project. Assuming—as seems likely—that in either case there is no factor which would excuse C from her obligations under the contract, B may treat C's 'anticipatory' repudiation of her obligation as the equivalent of a present material breach, terminating his obligation to proceed with performance (which obligation would otherwise have been triggered by C's initial payment), and entitling him to damages for total breach.

VII. Remedies for Breach of Contract

A. *Goals of Contract Remedies*

Fundamental to any discussion of contract remedies is the premise upon which the remedial principles of contract law are commonly said to be based: contract law exists not to punish non-performers for failing to live up to their

---

[86] R2 §251; UCC §2-609.   [87] R2 §§242, 243.   [88] R2 §253; UCC §2-610.

obligations, but only to redress the injuries caused by such failure. Many would agree that making a promise of performance creates a moral duty of performing it, particularly when that promise was made with the deliberation and formality that frequently accompany the making of contracts. It also seems indisputable that decisions by judges and juries about which party is in breach, and what the remedy should be for that breach, are likely to be affected by their judgments about the moral quality of the parties' conduct. Nevertheless, at least since Oliver Wendell Holmes, the conventional wisdom has been that contract law is centrally concerned not with preventing breach of contract, but only with setting the price the breaching party should pay in order to redress the resulting injury to the other party.[89] For this reason, 'punitive' or 'exemplary' damages, designed to punish the breaching party, are seldom awarded in contract cases; only when the breacher's conduct also amounts to a 'tort', or at least has tortious characteristics (deception bordering on fraud, perhaps), will such damages be assessed.[90] For the most part, the wronged party has to be content with such money damages as are available under conventional rules to compensate her for the injury actually suffered.

Developments in recent years have to some extent altered this picture of contract law as indifferent to the moral character of breach. On the one hand, modern law places more stress on the character of the parties' performance, often speaking in terms of 'honesty', 'good faith', and 'fair dealing'. This may enable the court to take morality—at least 'business morality'—into account more directly than had been called for by the conventional rules of classical contract law. There are even recent decisions which treat 'bad faith' breach of contract as the equivalent of a tort, justifying punitive damages.[91] Such cases are still the exception, but they do indicate a greater willingness to take the moral character of the parties' behavior into account in assessing both the existence and the consequences of breach of contract.

On the other hand, modern commentators of the 'law and economics' school have strenuously argued that not only should the law be indifferent to the morality (or immorality) of the decision to breach a contract, it ought in some cases actually to encourage breach. Sometimes, they argue, society will be better off if one party breaches a contract in order to enter into another, more beneficial, one; even if the breaching party pays full compensatory

---

[89] Holmes expressed it thus: 'The only universal consequence of a legally binding promise is that the law makes the promisor pay damages if the promised event does not come to pass. In every case it leaves him free from interference until the time for fulfillment has gone by, and therefore free to break his contract if he chooses'. Oliver Wendell Holmes, *The Common Law* 236 (Mark DeWolfe Howe ed. (Little, Brown, 1963)).

[90] R2 §355.

[91] e.g. *Seaman's Direct Buying Service, Inc.* v. *Standard Oil Co. of California*, 36 Cal.3d 752; 686 P.2d 1158 (1984).

damages for breaching the first contract, he may still be economically better off by making and performing the second one instead. In a case like this, it is asserted, breach is 'efficient', because the breaching party is better off, the other party is no worse off, and society as a whole benefits by having wealth redirected towards a more highly valued use.[92] Such commentators argue that contract law should attempt to deter only 'inefficient' breaches, being neutral—or even providing incentives to breach—in cases where breach would be efficient.

B. Interests Protected

Commentators beginning with Professor Lon Fuller in 1936 have analyzed the remedial aspects of contract law in terms of the 'interests' to be protected.[93] Fuller identified three interests deserving of legal protection: expectation, reliance, and restitution. The 'expectation interest' is the plaintiff's expectation of gain from performance of the contract as promised. Protection of that interest involves putting the plaintiff into the position she would have been in if the contract had been fully performed on both sides, by awarding her the economic equivalent of the gain she would have realized. The 'reliance interest' is the plaintiff's interest in being put into the position she would have been in, had the contract not been made; this involves compensating her for detrimental changes of position made in reliance on the contract being performed. The 'restitution interest' is the plaintiff's interest in being compensated for injury resulting from the defendant's 'unjust enrichment'. Its protection entails compelling the defendant to return or pay for benefits received by virtue of the contract which it would be unjust for him to retain without compensation. The Restatement (Second) employs these concepts in discussing the purpose and nature of contract remedies, as do most modern courts and commentators.[94]

To illustrate and contrast the three remedial interests defined above, let us return to the example of a building contract between builder B and owner C. Suppose that C unjustifiably refuses to make the 20 percent progress payment due when B has completed the interior carpentry work on her house. Assuming that C's refusal amounts to a material breach of contract, entitling B to full contract damages, what remedies would be required to compensate him for the injury to each of the three interests defined above?

[92] Richard A. Posner, *Economic Analysis of Law* (Little, Brown, 4th ed. 1992) 119.
[93] Lon L. Fuller and William R. Perdue, Jr., 'The Reliance Interest in Contract Damages I', 46 *Yale L.J.* 52 (1936).
[94] R2 §344; see generally, Robert E. Hudec, 'Restating the "Reliance Interest"', 67 *Cornell L. Rev.* 704 (1982).

Protection of B's *restitutionary* interest involves making the breacher compensate the other party for any enrichment received and retained for which compensation has not already been made. On the facts assumed, B has already received 70 percent of the price in progress payments, but has done another part of the work for which he has not yet been compensated. One way to compensate B for the injury to his restitutionary interest would be simply to award the amount of the next progress payment due, on the assumption that this represented the parties' valuation of the amount of work that would be done at that point. That amount might be too high or too low, however. A more precise restitutionary approach would be to award B the 'reasonable value' of all the construction done so far, offset by the aggregate payments already received from C.

Requiring C to compensate B for benefits received by C will also have the effect of compensating B for his actions in *reliance* on the contract, to the extent that those actions have also served to benefit C. Suppose, however, that at the time of C's breach, B had also purchased and worked on some of the plumbing and wiring to be installed in the house, but had not yet installed any of it. C would not at that point have been 'enriched' by this latter work, and yet B would be injured to the extent that B's outlay for material and labor could not now be salvaged for use on some other project. If B's 'reliance interest' is to be fully protected, C should be required to compensate B for these expenses as well.

Protection of only the restitutionary and reliance interests will not fully compensate B for C's breach, however, if protection of the *expectation* interest is the goal. This requires putting B into the position he would have been if performance on both sides had been completed as promised. That would have entailed full payment by C, but it also would have required full performance by B. This means that, in computing the amount of B's lost expectation, the court must take into account not only the value of the performance that defendant C would have rendered, but also what it would have cost plaintiff B to earn that performance. Thus, in cases like this one involving a partially performed construction contract, the usual formula for computing expectation damages is to award the builder damages measured by the *full (unpaid) contract price*, *minus* what it would have cost the builder to finish building the house—his *cost of completion*. Such an award automatically protects all three of the remedial interests defined above: in effect, it requires the owner to pay for any enrichment she has already received; it also compensates the builder for any additional reliance expenditures already incurred; and it awards the builder the profit he would have made on the contract if it had been fully performed—his expectation of gain. (Of course, B in our case would be entitled to only one measure of damages for any given breach by C;

the point of this example is that an award of expectation damages in such a case automatically compensates for injury to the restitution and reliance interests as well.)

C. *Rules Governing Damage Awards*

To this point, we have considered only the award of money damages as a potential remedy for breach of contract. They are not the only possible remedy, of course. Sometimes the law will compel a contracting party to do exactly what he promised to do, by an order of 'specific performance'. Specific enforcement is not the norm, however; special rules, discussed in section VII D below, govern its availability. And in any case, the plaintiff may prefer not to endure the inevitable delay involved in specific enforcement, electing instead to proceed immediately to make a substitute contract with some third party, and seeking damages only if necessary to compensate her for the breach. For these legal and practical reasons, money damages will generally be the remedy sought by the plaintiff in a breach of contract suit. These are governed by a number of general principles, as well as some which are specific to the type of damages involved.

Generally, all damage awards are subject to the requirements of 'causation' and 'certainty'.[95] The plaintiff bears the burden of showing that the injury for which redress is claimed did actually result from the defendant's breach, and of showing the monetary amount of such injury with reasonable certainty. The type of injury complained of must also have been 'foreseeable' to the defendant at the time the contract was made.[96] (In the leading English case, the owner of a mill complained that delay in delivery of a crankshaft necessary for the operation of his mill had caused lost profits for which the defendant carrier ought to compensate the miller. Even though the injury was in fact caused by the defendant's delay, and the amount of lost profits might have been proved with sufficient certainty, those damages were held not recoverable, because not foreseeable to the carrier at the time of contracting.[97]) Although foreseeability may be regarded as a requirement for all contract damage awards, there are many types of 'general damages', the foreseeability of which is simply presumed as a matter of law. Only in the case of 'special' or 'consequential' damages must the plaintiff actually prove that the defendant knew (or had reason to know) of the likelihood of such injury resulting from breach.

Another general limitation on the recovery of money damages is the plain-

[95] R2 §§346, 352.   [96] R2 §351.   [97] *Hadley* v. *Baxendale*, 156 Eng. Rep. 145 (1854).

tiff's 'duty to mitigate' her damages. The doctrine of mitigation expresses the general principle that the plaintiff ought not to recover for harm which she could have avoided by the exercise of reasonable effort.[98] ('This is sometimes also referred to as the doctrine of 'avoidable consequences'.) When a breach of contract occurs, the mitigation doctrine in effect requires the plaintiff to refrain from further action which will have the effect of increasing her injury and to act reasonably to ameliorate the effects of that injury. The damage recovery will be limited both by the extent to which mitigation of damages actually does occur, and also by the extent to which it appears it reasonably *should have* occurred.

This principle is expressed in a variety of more particular rules, depending on the type of case. Thus, in a sale of goods case, the disappointed buyer may only recover damages measured by the extent to which it has to pay more than the contract price to purchase substitute equivalent goods in the market.[99] The wrongfully discharged employee may recover her compensation for the remainder of the contract period, but subject to an offset for the amount she earns (or reasonably *could* have earned) by taking a comparable job with some other employer during that period.[100] And the seller of land whose buyer repudiates the contract may recover the difference (if any) between the contract price and the market value of the land. (Sale to another buyer at a lower price may furnish evidence of that difference.[101])

If these requirements are met, full expectation damages should be available for the breach of any contract (unless the parties have provided for some other remedy in the contract, a possibility discussed in section VII E below). Often, however, the full amount of plaintiff's expectation injury cannot be proved with sufficient certainty. (Sometimes, for example, the 'cost of completion' of a construction contract is deemed to be too dependent on unknowable factors to be computed with sufficient certainty, precluding the computation of plaintiff's lost expectation of profit.) In such a case, the plaintiff may at least be entitled to a full measure of reliance damages. (The contractor plaintiff referred to above should thus recover at least the cost of all the construction work actually done so far.) Reliance damages are also sometimes awarded to the plaintiff in cases involving 'promissory estoppel', discussed earlier in this chapter. Indeed, there is some authority for the proposition that reliance damages should be the maximum award in promissory estoppel cases.[102] Most courts appear to feel otherwise, however, awarding conventional expectation damages even in promissory estoppel cases.[103]

---

[98] R2 §350.   [99] UCC §§2-712, 2-713.   [100] R2 §350, illus. 8.
[101] *Kemp v. Gannett*, 50 Ill. App. 3d 429; 365 N.E.2d 1112 (1977).
[102] *Wheeler v. White*, 398 S.W.2d 93 (1965).
[103] A recent discussion of these issues can be found in Edward Yorio & Steve Thel, 'The Promissory Basis of Section 90', 101 *Yale L.J.* 111 (1991).

Restitutionary damages play a less important part in compensating breaches of contract than do reliance or expectation damages; they have greater significance for their role in related situations. Ordinarily, as the preceding discussion has indicated, the plaintiff in a breach of contract case will attempt to recover full expectation damages. If that fails, a full measure of reliance damages will be sought, which will ordinarily compensate the restitution interest as well (and perhaps more). A pure restitutionary remedy is thus likely to be the last resort of a plaintiff seeking damages for breach of contract.

There are other situations, however, in which the plaintiff's claim is not based on breach of contract, and expectation damages are not an available remedy. One of these is avoidance of a contract for some reason not involving breach on either side, such as mutual mistake. Where neither party has committed an actionable breach, expectation damages cannot be recovered. It may well be, however, that one party has rendered some performance for which the other has not yet given performance in return. The contract itself might fix a rate for compensating such a partial performance; if not, restitutionary principles would call for awarding the performing party at least the reasonable value of the benefit it had conferred.[104]

Another case where restitution furnishes an appropriate remedy is the contract which is unenforceable under the Statute of Frauds because no signed writing was ever executed. If one party has partly performed under that agreement, this will sometimes make the whole contract enforceable, on a 'part performance' or 'promissory estoppel' basis. If it does not, however, the performing party should at least be compensated for any performance she has actually rendered, on the principle of restitution.[105]

Besides its role in compensating for breach of contract and redressing injury occasioned by avoidance or unenforceability of contract obligations, the principle of restitution also plays a role in other situations not involving consensual obligations. For example, if the clerk in a store mistakenly gives you a 100 dollar bill in change rather than the 20 you are entitled to, you may not have promised expressly or even impliedly to repay the 80 dollar over-payment. Nevertheless, you are obligated to do so, under the principle of restitution for unjust enrichment.[106]

D. Specific Enforcement

The limitations on the availability of specific enforcement in American law come from the early English law on which American common law was

---

[104] R2 §§376, 377.   [105] R2 §375.   [106] *Restatement of Restitution* §163 (1936).

founded. The English law courts originally did not order specific performance, but only awarded money damages for breach of contract. When the
court of 'equity' conducted by the King's Chancellor began to give remedies
for breach of contract, it would order specific performance in certain types of
cases, but only if the remedy which might have been awarded by a law court
was regarded as insufficient to fully compensate the plaintiff for the breach.
Although very few American jurisdictions today retain separate courts of law
and equity, it still remains true that specific performance of a contract is generally said to be available only when the 'remedy at law'—i.e. the damage
remedy—is 'inadequate'.[107]

Certain conventional rules have grown up to identify the cases where
specific relief is available. Probably the most important is the traditional rule
in both English and American law that cases involving land are appropriate
candidates for specific enforcement, on the theory that each piece of land is
'unique'.[108] Sales of goods have traditionally qualified for specific performance where the goods are regarded as unique (family heirlooms, valuable
paintings and the like); modern law also allows this remedy in cases where
the goods are not available in the market, or can not be obtained commercially at the times or in the quantities promised under the contract.[109]

Generally, employment contracts have not been regarded as specifically
enforceable in American common law. Enforcement against the employee is
thought to involve possible violation of the American Constitution's prohibition of 'involuntary servitude'.[110] Beyond that, specific enforcement against
either employee or employer has traditionally been thought undesirable for
policy reasons. Modern statutes, however, often provide for reinstatement of
an employee discharged in violation of some statutory provision, such as the
statutes which prohibit racial, religious, or other discrimination by employers. Reinstatement may also be an available remedy under collectively bargained labor contracts. Another exception to the general rule withholding
specific enforcement of employment contracts is applied in cases involving
athletes, entertainers, and other 'unique' employees. While not willing to
order specific performance by the employee, courts in such cases may be willing to grant to the employer a kind of negative specific enforcement, by an
'injunction' ordering the employee not to perform similar services during the
contract period for a competitor of the employer.[111]

In general, the plaintiff seeking specific enforcement of any contract will
have the burden of persuading the court that this extraordinary remedy
should be granted. Beyond a showing that other remedies are for some

---

[107] R2 §§359, 360.   [108] R2 §360, Comment *e*.   [109] UCC §2-716.

[110] U.S. Const. amend. XIII.

[111] *Washington Capitols Basketball Club, Inc.* v. *Barry*, 304 F. Supp. 1193 (N.D. Cal. 1969).

reason inadequate, this may entail a showing that the contract is not unfair, that specific enforcement does not involve undue difficulties of supervision on the court's part, and that the plaintiff herself has not been guilty of inequitable conduct—or, as it is often phrased, she comes into court with 'clean hands'.

E. Agreed Remedies

If the parties foresee the possibility that one side or the other might fail to perform as promised, they may wish to specify in their agreement itself what remedies should be available in the event of its breach. As we have seen, the principle of freedom of contract is reflected in the fact that many implied rules of contract law are 'default rules', which apply only if the parties have not agreed otherwise. This is not the case with the rules governing remedies, however. Traditionally the freedom of the parties to specify their own remedies has been limited by the courts' oversight of the remedial process, and many such provisions have been struck down by courts as unenforceable.

We have seen that there are a variety of factors to be considered in computing the damages recoverable by a successful plaintiff in a breach of contract case: the damages must be certain in amount; the plaintiff must have mitigated damages; and the injury must have been foreseeable. If one party anticipates difficulty in meeting those requirements in the event of a breach by the other, it may negotiate a 'liquidated damages' clause, fixing either an amount or a formula for computing the amount of damages in the event of breach. Such a clause will be enforced if the amount of damages that would be incurred in the event of such a breach is likely to be difficult to ascertain, and the amount fixed appears reasonable. (Thus, it is common in construction contracts to provide that, in the event of a delay in completion, damages shall be assessed in a fixed amount per day; in the absence of such a clause, the plaintiff might have difficulty demonstrating exactly the types and amount of injury caused by the delay.[112]) A liquidated damage clause will not be upheld, however, where the damages fixed by it appear so large as to go beyond any reasonable compensation for the injury inflicted by the breach. Such a clause will be seen as designed not merely to provide fair compensation for breach, but to coerce the other party into performing, and will therefore be characterized as a 'penalty', remitting the plaintiff to whatever damages she can show under the rules of law governing damage awards.[113]

Sometimes the agreement limits a party's liability for damages in the event

---

[112] *Dave Gustafson & Co. v. State of South Dakota*, 83 S.D. 160; 156 N.W.2d 185 (1968).
[113] R2 §356.

of breach. This may take the form of putting an upper monetary limit on damages, or of excluding certain types of damages. For instance, it is very common to exclude or limit 'consequential damages' by contract, since these damages are likely in many cases to be much larger than the values involved in the contract itself. (Thus, consequential damages caused by defective goods might include lost profits caused by the defects; such damages could easily exceed the contract price of the goods.) It is also common for sellers of goods to attempt to exclude express or implied warranties of quality (to the extent that the UCC rules permit such exclusions). Generally, exclusions and limitations of liability do not present the 'penalty' problem described above, because they do not by their nature present the risk of overcompensation. The risk they present is rather one of *under*compensation—that the injured party will get little or no redress for the injury inflicted by breach. Such provisions are not favored in law, and may be narrowly construed, but they are not likely to be regarded as unenforceable *per se*. If both parties understand and agree to limitations of liability, this is regarded as an acceptable example of freedom of contract at work. For this reason, many modern commentators have argued that courts should be less quick to impose their own views of what is reasonable in this area. Efficiency will be better served, say many legal economists, if the parties themselves are allowed to fix the allocation of risks between them, including the risk of liability for non-performance.[114] Like a number of other areas in contract law, the debate is over what limits, if any, the law should impose on the parties' freedom to contract.

---

[114] Charles J. Goetz and Robert E. Scott, 'Liquidated Damages, Penalties and the Just Compensation Principle: Some Notes on an Enforcement Model and a Theory of Efficient Breach', 77 *Colum. L. Rev.* 554 (1977).

10

TORTS

SYLVIA A. LAW

Tort law determines when a person who suffers injury can obtain redress from the actor who caused the harm. Torts are private legal actions in which one person seeks a remedy, usually money, for damages caused by another. As Professor Hughes observes in Chapter 1, tort law is the classic common law subject, developed by judges in the context of resolving concrete disputes. The common law tradition is built upon social custom and experience, rather than upon abstract ideals or universal principles. The creation of tort law is highly decentralized and dynamic. Diversity amongst the states is far greater in tort law, than, for example, in contracts or criminal law, where national uniform acts and model codes, promulgated by national professional associations and adopted by state legislatures, now dominate the law.

The harms people cause one another are as diverse as human experience. The losses currently protected by American tort law include injury to life, health, family members, physical integrity, property, peace of mind, reputation, procreative capacity, and opportunity for advantageous trade relations. The concept of injury, like all of tort law, varies from state to state, and it has contracted and expanded in response to changing social experience and perception.

The central question in each tort case is: 'when should the law require people to pay for injuries they cause to others?' In answering that question, the law takes into account the many purposes served by tort liability including:

(a)   compensation for the person injured;
(b)   deterrence of accidents or behavior thought to be socially unreasonable;
(c)   assigning costs of accidents to the activities that generate them;
(d)   social recognition of moral right and wrong.

These objectives of tort law often conflict. If compensation is the primary goal, the law should not necessarily care whether or not the actions causing the injury were reasonable or moral. A child injured at birth is no less deserving of compensation to care for her in the future because the doctors and hospital exercised great care than if they acted carelessly. In either case, *someone* will have to bear the costs; the question is who should it be. If compensation is our sole social purpose, it is probably more efficiently achieved through social insurance. Conversely, if deterrence of unreasonably risky behavior is the law's primary goal, social response should turn on the probability of injury rather than the happenstance of whether the injury happens to be unusually grave or fortunately trivial. Further, all of the reasons supporting tort liability conflict with a social desire to promote enterprise, innovation, and economic progress, free from excess concern about potential liability for injury to others.

Although most tort law is developed by judges in the process of deciding disputes about particular injuries, legislatures, both state and federal, also contribute to the development of tort principles in several ways. First, legislatures set regulatory or criminal standards for reasonable behavior, and those standards are adopted by common law courts. For example, at one time there were no fixed speed limits for carriages and autos. Common law judges and juries made individualized determinations about what was reasonable in all circumstances. As state legislatures adopted rules for the regulation of traffic, common law courts used those legislative rules to determine what was reasonable.

Legislation impacts on tort law in yet a second way. Legislatures can reverse common law courts' judgments, rejecting either particular rules or supplanting a whole area of the law. For example, as we discuss later (see section II A below), in the 1920s most state legislatures rejected the common law approach to workplace accidents and substituted an administrative system of workers' compensation. In the federal system, Congress can override both state legislatures and state courts. For example, when Congress sought to promote the private development of nuclear power, it encouraged business to undertake this project by providing a system of limited no-fault compensation to replace state tort liability.[1] For another example, when Congress

---

[1] *Duke Power Co. v. Carolina Environmental Study Group, Inc.*, 438 U.S. 59 (1978).

requires uniform federal warnings about the dangers of particular products, it sometimes preempts state laws that impose different warning requirements.[2]

American tort law includes three basic types of conduct giving rise to liability: negligence, intentional torts, and strict liability. In each area, tort law has been an historic battlefield of changing social concepts of a good society and strong economy. While the branches intertwine, each classically grapples with particular questions, and each typically is invoked to deal with distinctive human problems. The rest of this chapter will discuss these three major branches of tort liability and then consider some contemporary disputes about tort law.

I. Negligence

Negligence is the most common means of establishing liability in American tort law. Auto accidents, medical malpractice, injuries caused by slippery floors or broken stairways—all are governed by negligence principles. This section first discusses some of the legal rules that govern negligence cases, and then examines how negligence principles have been applied and modified in some common human situations: workplace injuries, auto accidents, and medical malpractice.

A. Reasonable Care

'Negligence' has a common sense and a legal meaning which includes both *inadvertence*—not paying attention in a situation in which a reasonable person would do so—and *imprudence*—taking a risk that a reasonable person would not take. A common definition of negligence is that:

> **The degree of care demanded of a . . . person is the resultant of three factors: The likelihood that his conduct will injure others, taken with the seriousness of the injury if it happens, and balanced against the interest that he must sacrifice to avoid the risk.**[3]

---

[2] *Cipollone* v. *Liggett Group*, 505 U.S. 504 (1992) (federal law on warnings about the dangers of cigarettes preempts state law, but other state tort claims, based on fraud or negligence, remain).

[3] Learned Hand, *Conway* v. *O'Brien*, 111 F.2d 611, 612 (2nd Cir. 1940), *rev'd on other grounds*, 312 U.S. 492 (1941).

The formula's appearance of precision is misleading. 'Seriousness' and 'likelihood' of injury are not easily quantified. The interests which must be sacrificed to avoid the risk are numerous, varied, and often impossible to value objectively. Striking a balance among these factors is a complex task.

Since the formula does not apply itself, the courts call on a venerable fiction of tort law—the reasonable person—to apply the formula through the instructions given by the judge to the jury, which applies it to the particular facts of the case. The negligence concept asks, 'Did the person who caused the injury behave as a reasonable person would have?' Take a concrete case. Would a reasonable person drive seventy miles an hour on a two-lane road on a rainy night? If the interest to be sacrificed to avoid the risk of a collision is the desire to get home to watch a favorite TV program, a reasonable person would not take the risk. But if the driver was rushing to the hospital with a person suffering a heart attack, the interest to be sacrificed in avoiding the risk of accident is escalated, and probably a reasonable person would speed. We all engage in this process every day, in governing our own conduct and in judging the actions of others. Negligence is deeply grounded in common experience and common sense.

Common sense intuition is informed, guided and constrained by legal rules. The most important rule defining the meaning of negligence is that 'in most cases reasonable prudence is in fact common prudence.'⁴ But what is common prudence? Ordinary people are not always prudent, common practice is not always wise. Does that fact excuse us from liability in negligence when our imprudence results in injury to others? No! As one English wit put it, the reasonably prudent person is:

> always thinking of others; prudence is his guide, and 'Safety First' . . . his rule of life . . . He is one who invariably looks where he is going, and is careful to examine the immediate foreground before he executes a leap or bound; who neither star-gazes nor is lost in meditation when approaching trapdoors or the margin of a dock; . . . who never mounts a moving omnibus and does not alight from any car while the train is in motion . . . who never drives his ball till those in front of him have definitely vacated the putting green . . . who . . . uses nothing except in moderation and even while he flogs his child is meditating only on the golden mean.⁵

In all United States jurisdictions, the common law definition of the reasonable person is a person on good behavior. The reasonable person is a construct. If someone is injured, no state allows a defense for the 'accident prone', the incompetent, or the person just not paying attention. On the

---

⁴ *The T. J. Hooper*, 60 F.2d 737 (2nd Cir. 1932).
⁵ A. P. Herbert, *Uncommon Law*, (Methuen, 7th ed. 1952), pp. 1–6.

other hand, the common law does accommodate young people and those with physical disabilities, demanding only that they perform as a reasonable person would in their particular situation. Although the 'reasonable person' standard is idealized, judges and juries evaluate the conduct of ordinary people involved in everyday activities and regularly make judgments about what a reasonable person would do in a given situation.

The task becomes more difficult when we move away from ordinary life situations to the actions of people and organizations involved in complex enterprises. Consider, for example, the question of whether a reasonable railroad runs broad-gauge cars on a narrow-gauge track. What does the jury, or even the judge, know about running a railroad? Not much. How can they evaluate the seriousness or likelihood of risks created by this practice, or the interests which must be sacrificed to keep narrow-gauge cars on narrow-gauge tracks? Common experience does not help. How can judges and juries acquire the knowledge needed to evaluate whether a reasonable railroad runs broad-gauge cars on a narrow-gauge track?

One obvious approach is to ask a person engaged in the railroading business. From the mid-nineteenth century until the 1930s, the 'custom of the industry' largely determined what constituted negligence in cases involving facts and judgment beyond the personal experience of ordinary people. Railroads charged with negligence for causing injury to a person by running a broad-gauge car on a narrow-gauge track could defend themselves by simply showing that this was customarily done in the railroading business. As one court addressing this precise issue in 1890 said:

> Even if the practice had been shown to be dangerous, that would not show it to be negligent. Some employments are essentially hazardous . . . All the cases agree that the master is not bound to use the newest and best appliances . . . 'Reasonably safe' means safe according to the usages, habits, and ordinary risks of the business . . . No man is held by law to a higher degree of skill than the fair average of his profession or trade . . . Juries . . . cannot be allowed to set up a standard which shall, in effect, dictate the customs or control the business of the community.[6]

This view, highly protective of industry and deferential to industry judgment, prevailed until the 1930s. At that time, however, many began to argue that there was a need for greater legal incentives for safety. In 1932, Judge Learned Hand was presented with a case in which two boats went down at sea while being towed by a tug that did not have a radio receiver. If the tug had a radio, it could have received warnings of the impending storm and put

---

[6] *Titus v. Bradford B. & K.R. Co.*, 136 Pa. 618, 626, 20 Atl. 517, 518 (1890).

into port. Even though radios had rapidly become popular with the baseball- and music-loving public, most tugboats did not have them. The cost of a radio was small, and the risks involved in operating at sea without a current weather report were large. Judge Hand held that the tug company was negligent in failing to provide a radio:

> [I]n most cases reasonable prudence is in fact common prudence; but strictly it is never its measure; a whole calling may have unduly lagged in the adoption of new and available devices. It never may set its own tests, however persuasive be it usages. Courts must in the end say what is required; there are precautions so imperative that even universal disregard will not excuse their omission.[7]

This has become the classic statement of the effect of industry custom in determining what conduct is negligent. The practices of the industry are highly relevant. They show what is possible. For example, if some tugboats have radios and others do not, it is clearly possible to use them. Industry custom provides evidence of industry knowledge of the state of the art. Most important, custom shows how other knowledgeable people have struck the balance between the costs of accidents and the cost of avoiding them. Although industry custom is important and relevant, it is not determinative. Normally, courts must make an independent judgment as to whether the industry has acted reasonably, generally after hearing expert testimony, in striking the balance between the risk of injury and the costs of avoiding the risks.

B. Causation in Fact

In addition to proving that the defendant acted negligently, the injured person must establish that the defendant's negligence caused the plaintiff's injury. Causation, like reasonable care and the prudent person, is a common sense concept that has meaning in ordinary language as well as in the law. Causation is also tremendously controversial.

Take a simple example. The plaintiff, running to catch a train, is injured when he falls down the stairs. The stairs are poorly lit, and the stair treads are worn. The man is obese and carrying several large packages. He persuades the jury that the railroad acted unreasonably in failing to light the stairs and repair the treads. But can we say that the railroad's negligence 'caused' his injury?

---

[7] *The T. J. Hooper*, 60 F.2d 737, 740 (2nd Cir. 1932).

The answer depends largely on the way in which the question is framed. The man would argue that the worn treads and lack of lights greatly increased the chance of injury, that a fall was perfectly foreseeable, and that it was precisely the failure to guard against this risk that made the railroad's conduct unreasonable. The railroad would argue that, given his weight, the packages, and the rush, he might well have fallen, whatever the condition of the treads and the light. The railroad will assert that the fall and the lack of lights were merely coincidental. Both the man and the railroad can find legal support for the approach they urge to the causation question.[8] The question of whether the defendant's action in fact caused the plaintiff's injury is decided by the jury. While the question is posed as a factual matter, the legal standards used to determine cause 'in fact' are often influenced by perceptions of social policy. For example, resolution of the 'factual' issue of causation is often influenced by the jury's judgment of the gravity of the defendant's fault.

C. Proximate or Legal Causation

Once the plaintiff has established that the defendant acted unreasonably and that the defendant's conduct 'in fact' injured the plaintiff, a second issue of causation arises. Plaintiff must show that the defendant's actions were the 'legal or proximate' cause of the plaintiff's injury. This is a question of policy and law, to be resolved by the court. Many verbal formulae have been offered to define the limits of proximate cause. Was the injury the *direct* consequence of the defendant's negligence? Was the plaintiff's injury foreseeable? A much admired standard, offered by Judge Cardozo of the New York Court of Appeals, connects concepts of negligence and causation. 'The risk reasonably to be perceived defines the duty to be obeyed . . .'[9] The issue is basically one of social policy: is it fair to hold the negligent defendant accountable for the plaintiff's injury?

Consider a concrete example. The defendant parks his car near a school yard and leaves the keys in it. Some young women notice the keys, take the car for a joy-ride, and quickly collide with an elderly man crossing the street. The elderly man sues the owner. (The young women would certainly be liable, but as a practical matter, car owners are usually insured and people who steal typically are not.) Tort law would find little difficulty in concluding that the defendant was unreasonable in leaving his keys in the car. Further, it

[8] See William L. Prosser, John W. Wade, Victor E. Schwartz, *Cases and Materials on Torts*, 284–7, (West Pub., 8th ed. 1988).
[9] *Palsgraff* v. *Long Island R.R. Co.*, 248 N.Y. 339, 162 N.E. 99 (1928).

seems fair to say that the defendant's negligence 'in fact' caused the old man's injuries: 'but for' the defendant's unreasonable act of leaving the keys in the car, the old man would not have been injured. On these facts, there seems no strong policy reason to deny liability.

But change the facts. The young women take the car, give it to a friend, who drives it across the country. Several weeks later, the friend uses it in a robbery of a drive-through restaurant. The restaurant argues that the owner is responsible for the robbery because, 'but for' his negligence in leaving the keys in the car, the robbery would not have occurred. In the second situation, most courts would deny liability—the connection between the defendant's negligence and the plaintiff's injury is just too far removed. How far is too far is, of course, a question on which reasonable people disagree.[10]

In the nineteenth century, narrow and demanding concepts of causation often led to the conclusion that the defendant had not caused the plaintiff's injury. General cultural concepts led to a search to identify a single cause for any phenomenon. In the twentieth century, science and culture have increasingly seen causation as a matter of statistical probability and as deriving from multiple sources.[11] Further, as society and the law have become more sympathetic to plaintiffs' needs for compensation and society's need to deter unreasonable behavior, concepts of causation have expanded.

D. Joint and Several Liability

Complex problems arise where more than one defendant negligently causes the plaintiff's injury. Suppose, for example, that two negligent drivers collide and injure an innocent pedestrian. Under joint and several liability, 'where two or more causes combine to produce . . . a single result, incapable of division on any logical or reasonable basis, and each is a substantial factor in bringing about the harm . . .' the plaintiff may sue any responsible defendant and recover 100 percent of his or her damages.[12] A right of contribution permits a defendant who has paid a disproportionately large share of the plaintiff's liability to recover the overpayment from a defendant who has paid a disproportionately small share of this liability.[13] In most United States jurisdictions each defendant's contribution is determined on the basis of comparative fault, although some courts and statutes allocate liability on the basis of pro rata shares. These rules with respect to joint and several liability and con-

---

[10] Cornelius J. Peck, 'An Exercise Based on Empirical Data: Liability for Harm Caused By Stolen Automobiles', 1969 *Wisc. L. Rev.* 909.

[11] Morton Horowitz, *The Transformation of American Law*, (Harvard U.P., 1977).

[12] *Restatement of Torts*, Section 433A.   [13] *Restatement of Torts*, Section 886A(1).

tribution confront parties with difficult strategic choices in deciding whom to sue and when and how to settle.[14]

E. Vicarious Liability

While negligence law most often imposes liability on the basis of individual 'fault', since the eighteenth century, the concept of vicarious liability has held some people responsible for the injuries negligently caused by others. For example, employers are financially responsible for the injuries caused by the negligence of their employees, during the course of their employment. The employer's liability is not premised on 'fault' in failing to train or supervise the employee, but is rather a form of strict liability, holding those with power to control responsible for the wrongdoing of those who work for them. Complex questions arise as to whether the negligent worker was doing the employer's business or 'on a frolic', and whether the person who caused injury was an employee or an independent contractor.

F. Plaintiff's Conduct

If both the plaintiff and the defendant act unreasonably, it is difficult to conclude that the defendant 'caused' the plaintiff's injuries. The nineteenth century common law rules, which sought to identify the single cause of the plaintiff's injury and to protect enterprise and activity, required that the plaintiff establish both that the defendant acted unreasonably and that the plaintiff was without fault.[15]

In an initial round of reform, common law courts reallocated this burden of proof and required that, just as the plaintiff must establish the defendant's negligence, so too the defendant must establish the plaintiff's contributory negligence. Under the traditional principles, if the plaintiff was contributorily negligent, recovery was barred.

In many cases the contributory negligence bar appeared unfair, particularly where the negligence of the defendant was grave, while the negligence of the plaintiff was trivial. In the 1960s, this led courts and legislatures to abandon the rule that the plaintiff who was contributorily negligent could recover nothing and to replace it with a principle that says, if both the defendant and the injured plaintiff are negligent, the plaintiff's damages should be proportionally reduced. Various states have adopted different approaches for

[14] For a good recent discussion see Lewis A. Kornhauser and Richard L. Revesz, 'Settlements Under Joint and Several Liability', 68 N.Y.U. L. Rev. 427 (1993).

[15] Brown v. Kendall, 60 Mass. (6 Cush.) 292 (1850).

determining the amount of the reduction. Some states give the jury large freedom to determine the relative fault of plaintiff and defendant and to award damages accordingly. For example, the jury could find that the plaintiff's negligence was 90 percent responsible for her injuries and require the defendant to pay 10 percent of the damages. Other states require that the plaintiff persuade the jury that the defendant's fault was more responsible for the injury. So, for example, if the jury finds that the defendant was 51 percent at fault, the plaintiff recovers 51 percent of her damages, but if the defendant was only 49 percent at fault, the plaintiff recovers nothing.

Comparative negligence, allocating responsibility between plaintiffs and defendants, is similar to the joint and several liability rules for allocating responsibility among various defendants. In both instances the comparative approach achieves greater fairness at the cost of greater complexity.

G. *Duty*

While 'reasonable care' and the 'reasonably prudent person' provide the unifying themes of negligence law, in some cases questions arise as to whether the defendant has a duty to the plaintiff that gives rise to an obligation to act reasonably. The classic example asks whether people have an obligation to throw a rope to a drowning person. Many believe that people have an ethical obligation to throw the rope, at least where the threat of injury is grave and rescue can be accomplished at no great cost or inconvenience. Nonetheless, the common law traditionally drew sharp distinctions between action and inaction and held that people have no affirmative duty to help one another. However, the common law said, that when a person acts, he or she must exercise reasonable care, even though no person is affirmatively obligated to help another. Historically, the principle was based on a strong version of rugged individualism. Perhaps the no-duty principle has surfaced, in part, from a perception that, in contemporary American society, the publicly expressed needs of our fellow citizens are so vast that a legal obligation to be responsive to them would entail excessively large costs.

The no-duty for inaction principle has always been riddled with exceptions. *Undertakings* sometimes give rise to duties. Even though the good Samaritan has no duty to help the drowning person, if she attempts to do so and bungles the job, liability may result if she has not acted as a reasonable person would have. *Special relations* between a plaintiff and defendant sometimes give rise to duties. For example, landowners have affirmative duties to tenants, guests, and even some trespassers. Teachers have duties to students, jailers to prisoners, and so forth.

The no-duty principle is not limited to situations where the defendant fails to help. For example, sometimes the defendant has no duty because the plaintiff 'has assumed the risk' of injury. Suppose the plaintiff goes to a baseball game and chooses to sit in a seat that is not screened from the field. Plaintiff is hit by a foul ball. Most courts will say that plaintiff 'assumed the risk'. The defendant park owner had no duty to protect this plaintiff against the obvious risk of balls leaving the playing field. Or take another example: the plaintiff buys a ticket to ride the defendant's roller-coaster. The plaintiff is badly frightened and suffers a heart attack. Again, most courts will say that plaintiff 'assumed the risk'. The defendant had no duty to protect the plaintiff against the obvious risks—indeed the attraction—of the roller-coaster.

H. Injury

A final legal issue in negligence cases defines the harms for which the law will provide redress. Most tort cases seek redress for physical harm to person or property. The law requires that the negligent defendant pay the plaintiff the actual costs required to put him back in the position he would have been in had the accident never occurred. The goal is to 'make the plaintiff whole'. Such damages typically include medical expenses, repair and replacement costs, and lost earning capacity. In fixing actual damages, the defendant must take the plaintiff as he finds him. Hence, the negligent defendant who injures a high-earning plaintiff must pay much more to compensate for lost earning capacity than the negligent defendant who injures someone who is poor. So too, if the defendant injures a hemophiliac plaintiff and he bleeds to death as a result of the injury, the defendant has no right to object to being held fully liable, even though most people would have recovered from the accident.

In addition to providing compensatory damages for physical harm to person or property, tort law requires that the defendant compensate the plaintiff for pain and suffering. These damages, which can often be quite large, compensate for a variety of interests other than discomfort. For example, if a worker with a desk job loses his leg, he may be unable to show that his earning capacity has been damaged. Nonetheless, the law recognizes that he has suffered a grievous loss that goes beyond medical expenses and earning capacity. This loss is compensated through pain and suffering damages, which are inherently subjective and made more so because the jury assesses them. In the American legal system, each party bears their own legal costs. Even where the defendant is found negligent, she is not required to pay the plaintiff's lawyer. Many people believe that pain and suffering damages serve a useful, informal function of helping the successful plaintiff to pay her lawyer. However, because these damages are difficult to quantify and are sometimes quite large, they are controversial.

Tort law sometimes protects economic and commercial interests, beyond the losses that result from property damage or personal injury. Plaintiffs can recover for the pecuniary losses attributable to misrepresentation or fraud. Tort law protects contractual remedies against the promisor, but also tort remedies against a third party who induced a breach of contract.[16] Further, tort law sometimes protects, not existing contracts, but advantageous relationships that the plaintiff hopes to maintain or enter into with third parties.[17] Finally, tort law sometimes provides common law remedies to supplement the legal protection of valuable information provided by the law of patents, copyrights, tradenames, or trademarks.

In rare cases, a tort plaintiff may also recover punitive or exemplary damages. Such damages are not designed to compensate the plaintiff for the losses suffered at the hands of the defendant, but rather to deter the defendant from the repeated commission of wrongful conduct or to punish the defendant for some wrong deliberately and flagrantly committed. Punitive damages are quasi-criminal. Simple negligence does not support punitive damages. Rather, the plaintiff must prove conscious wrongdoing, by clear and convincing evidence. Sadly, there are cases in which plaintiffs can meet these demanding standards.[18] Cases awarding punitive damages are rare in American tort law, and for this reason command press attention.

In the twentieth century, the law has expanded the range of harms for which plaintiffs can seek compensation and the range of plaintiffs who may make claims. The traditional common law rule was that tort claims were personal actions that died with the plaintiff. Hence if the negligent defendant caused the plaintiff's death, he or she could not be held liable. Legislatures in every state have reversed this rule and created statutory actions for 'wrongful death'. These claims recognize that surviving family members suffer a serious loss that deserves compensation and that the goal of encouraging reasonable behavior can be better achieved by imposing liability when negligent conduct results in death.

Under the dynamic, case-by-case method of the common law, courts have recognized harms not traditionally protected by the law. For example, courts have recognized that reproductive capacity is an important human interest

---

[16] *Lumley* v. *Gye*, 11 Eng. Rep. 749 (1853), is the classic case.

[17] *People Express Airlines, Inc.* v. *Consolidated Rail Corp.*, 100 N.J. 246, 795 A.2d 107 (1985).

[18] See e.g. *Fisher* v. *Johns-Mansville Corp.*, 103 N.J. 643, 672, 512 A.2d 266, 281 (1986) ('Not only did [the defendant] fail to warn users of the serious health hazards associated with exposure to asbestos, it actually took affirmative steps to conceal this information from the public.')

that should be protected against negligent destruction.[19] As another example, courts have recognized that people's interests in reproductive choice demand that physicians provide information and referral when there is good reason to believe that a pregnant woman has suffered a disease or taken a drug that is likely to cause serious damage to her fetus.[20] Many states have recognized a cause of action for negligent infliction of emotional distress, although others have refused to do so.

On the other hand, sometimes the dynamic, socially responsive common law method leads courts to withdraw protection for injuries that were once vindicated by the law. Historically, the common law allowed a man to sue a man who seduced his wife or daughter. Changing social mores, including a recognition that the woman might be a responsible actor in such situations, and rejection of the notion that wives and daughters are a man's property, have led most courts to abandon protection against this harm.[21]

Injury to reputation is another interest that receives less protection today than was traditional at common law. Historically, the common law has provided strong protection for community and professional reputation. Actions for libel and slander allowed the plaintiff to recover damages for false statements that were damaging to reputation. Plaintiffs were not required to show that the defendant was negligent or had a bad intent. If printed comments were deemed 'per se' libelous, injury was presumed. Traditional common law concepts allow a defense of 'privilege' where there is a strong public interest supporting communication of information that is potentially damaging to reputation. For example, employers are privileged to give performance and character references on former employees, and merchants can share credit information about their customers. In the 1980s, litigation over employer references exploded and may now constitute a third of defamation suits.[22]

Beginning in 1964, the Supreme Court has held that the First Amendment guarantee of freedom of speech prohibits states from providing such broad remedies for libelous statements made about public officials or people who have assumed a significant public role.[23] The Court held that even statements that are untrue deserve some protection if 'free speech' is to have the breathing space it needs to survive'.

---

[19] See e.g. *Hawkins v. A.H. Robbins Co.*, 595 F. Supp. 1290 (D. Colo. 1984). Loss of male reproductive capacity has also been recognized as a protected interest. See e.g. *McCann v. Baton Rouge General Hospital*, 276 So.2d 259 (La. 1973).

[20] See e.g. *Procanik v. Cillo*, 97 N.J. 339 (1984).

[21] Wex Malone, *Torts: Injuries to Family, Social and Trade Relations*, pp. 80–1 (West Pub., 1979).

[22] Martha Middleton, 'Employers Face Upsurge in Suits over Defamation', *Natl. L. J.*, May 4, 1987.

[23] *New York Times v. Sullivan*, 376 U.S. 254 (1964).

II. Negligence Principles Applied to Some Common Activities

This section briefly explores how general negligence principles have been applied to some common activities. It underscores the historical development of the common law and the interaction between common law courts and other actors.

A. Workplace Accidents

The workplace, along with the highway, is the most common site of accidental injury. This was particularly true in the Industrial Revolution in the late nineteenth and early twentieth centuries, when technologies were new, workers were not unionized, and many industrial enterprises were hazardous.

The early tort law was not sympathetic to the claims of injured workers or their families. There was virtually no insurance, either public or private, to cushion the financial burdens of injury, illness, or unemployment. As we have seen, the law gave great deference to defendants' customs and discretion in determining what constituted due care. Even when the plaintiff could meet the formidable challenge of demonstrating that the defendant's conduct was negligent, the law gave the employer three powerful tools to defeat the worker's claim. First, the doctrine of contributory negligence (see section I F above) barred the worker from recovery if he was at fault in the slightest way. Secondly, the doctrine of assumption of risk (see section I G above) demanded that workers bear the burden of risks that were obvious or inherent in the enterprise. Finally, the 'fellow servant doctrine' held that workers, rather than employers, were responsible for any wrongdoing on the part of fellow workers.

The Progressive Movement of the 1910s sought wide-ranging workplace reforms, including protection of child workers, minimum wage and hour legislation, product safety laws, and protection for injured workers and their families.[24] These reformers documented the plight of injured workers and their families and sought legislative reform to replace tort remedies with a workers' compensation system that provided more certain benefits to injured workers. Many leading industrialists supported the plan. The workers' compensation benefits were typically modest, but they were predictable and less administratively costly than tort-based liability. Under workers' com-

---

[24] See Arthur Link, *Woodrow Wilson and the Progressive Era: 1910–1917*, 59 (Harper & Row, 1963 ed.).

pensation, covered workers receive a more secure right to payment, but give up their rights to sue in tort, including the right to collect damages for pain and suffering. Proposals that sought to retain tort liability, while limiting or abolishing employers' defenses, were rejected.

Between 1910 and 1921, workers' compensation was adopted in virtually every American state. As a practical matter, fault-based tort principles are not applicable to workplace accidents. In theory, workers' compensation would provide appropriate incentives for workplace safety by placing the costs of accidents on the industries that generated them. It is not clear that it has been effective in doing so, in part because the benefits provided in most states are very limited. In 1970, Congress adopted the Federal Occupational Health and Safety Act in an effort to use regulatory tools to promote workplace safety.[25]

B. Auto Accidents

Auto accidents generate the largest number of tort cases. Between 1970 and 1975, 24 states adopted some form of no-fault compensation for injuries caused by auto accidents. The movement for no-fault auto insurance was supported by many factors. First, steady increases in auto liability insurance premiums produced consumer dissatisfaction. Secondly, many influential legal and economic analysts demonstrated the waste and unfairness of applying ordinary negligence principles to disputes arising out of injuries caused by auto accidents because fault or negligence is often difficult to demonstrate in the auto accident context. Litigation costs accounted for large fractions of premiums while many deserving victims went uncompensated. Further, data showed an inverse relationship between serious harm to the accident victim and the proportion of economic loss recovered. Perhaps most strikingly, many people who were seriously injured received nothing under the negligence law. Many people also believed that the risk of liability added little deterrent to that provided by instincts for self-preservation and police enforcement of traffic regulations. Finally, the consumer and environmental movements produced a climate favorable to attempting alternative approaches.[26]

Even more than workers' compensation reform of tort law, no-fault auto insurance varies greatly from state to state. Some states seek to replace tort actions, in most cases by providing no-fault compensation and enacting high

---

[25] Pub. L. 91–596, 84 Stat. 1590. 29 U.S.C. 654 et seq.

[26] For a good overview of these issues and a collection of the works of some of the leading proponents of auto no-fault insurance, see Robert Rabin, *Perspectives on Tort Law*, esp. pp. 166–233, 283–91 (Little, Brown, 1990).

threshold limits that must be met in order to seek the more generous tort-based compensation. Other states simply added compulsory no-fault insurance to the common law negligence system in the hope that, if people could obtain some compensation for their physical injuries, they would not seek to engage in the difficult process of proving negligence.

Despite the no-fault reforms, auto accidents remain the largest single category of tort claims, and liability insurance premiums remain high. On the other hand, compulsory no-fault assures out-of-pocket compensation to many who might otherwise be unable to obtain any fault-based recovery.

C. Medical Malpractice

In the mid-1970s and the mid-1980s, medical malpractice premiums rose rapidly, and there was a widespread perception that the United States confronted a malpractice 'crisis'. This section discusses some changing characteristics of malpractice liability law and briefly describes competing theories about the causes of and cures for the perceived crisis.

Since the mid-1960s the numbers of malpractice claims filed, and the amounts of damages awarded, have increased more rapidly than tort claims generally, though these increases have slowed since the late 1980s. The extent and the causes of these increases are the subject to fierce dispute.[27] Nonetheless, knowledgeable observers would probably agree that one major cause of the increase in malpractice litigation is the abandonment of the traditional rule requiring the plaintiff to produce a local expert to testify that the defendant doctor was negligent. This section discusses that development in the law, and then summarizes other, more controversial, hypotheses about the increases in malpractice litigation and liability.

The role of community custom is much more weighty in medical malpractice law than it is in other types of negligence cases. As we have seen, the general tort rule is that community custom is highly persuasive in determining what is reasonable, but never fully determinative. By contrast, in medical malpractice actions, the plaintiff must demonstrate that the defendant did something that no reasonable physician would have done. Custom is not simply persuasive, but legally controlling. Further, while in many cases expert testimony is necessary as a practical matter to demonstrate that a defendant acted unreasonably, in a medical malpractice action, expert testimony that the doctor acted unreasonably is required by law. It is because of these differ-

---

[27] For a good summary of recent literature, see Peter H. Schuck, *Tort Law and the Public Interest: Competition, Innovation and Consumer Welfare* at pp. 24–7 (Schuck), 176–204 (Patricia M. Danzon) and 205–237 (Michael J. Trebilcock, Donald N. Dewess and David G. Duff) (Norton, 1991).

ences between the negligence principles applied to doctors and those applied to other actors, that it is more difficult to prove negligence against a physician than against other defendants.

Changes in medical and legal standards have significantly eased the burden of establishing that a physician is negligent. First, until the late 1960s, every jurisdiction required the malpractice plaintiff to present a physician from the local community, who could testify that the defendant physician violated the professional standards of the local community. The locality rule was premised on the understanding that a small-town doctor in a frontier community could not reasonably be held to the same standards as a specialist in a major urban teaching hospital. In practice, the locality rule made it very difficult for the injured patient to find a local doctor to testify against the defendant physician. Most doctors acknowledged that they would never testify against a local medical colleague, no matter how plain the negligence. This 'conspiracy of silence' made it very difficult for injured patients to obtain redress against a negligent doctor.

Since the 1960s, common law courts have rejected the locality rule. In a 1968 case, an anesthesiologist practicing in New Bedford, Massachusetts, argued that physicians from Boston should not be allowed to testify on behalf of a patient who was injured as a result of an allegedly excessive dose of anesthetic. New Bedford is a community of 100,000 people located fifty miles from Boston. The trial court upheld the doctor's defense that New Bedford doctors could not be held to Boston standards. The Massachusetts Supreme Court reversed, relying upon developments in transportation and communication, as well as the development of national professional standards.[28]

The medical profession itself has been the major force leading the movement toward national standards of education, knowledge, and skill. All physicians are educated at national medical schools and are certified and supervised by national professional boards. Specialists are certified by national specialty boards. In abandoning the locality rule, the common law simply followed the changing custom of the profession. Local factors, such as the facilities and equipment available to a physician, are still relevant in determining what constitutes due care. But 'objectively reasonable expectations regarding the physician's knowledge, skill, capacity for sound medical judgment and general competence are, consistent with his field of practice and the facts and circumstances in which the patient may be found, *the same everywhere*'.[29]

The erosion of the locality rule has made it significantly easier for an injured patient to establish medical malpractice. This is not because the legal

[28] *Brune v. Belinkoff,* 354 Mass. 102, 109, 235 N.E. 2d 793,797–98 (1968).
[29] *Hall v. Hilbun,* 466 So. 2d 856, 872 (Miss. 1985)

standard of care has been increased; it remains whether the physician did something that no reasonable physician would have done in the circumstances. The significance of the erosion of the locality rule is that, as a practical matter, it makes it easier for the patient to find an expert to testify.

Many other factors are thought to contribute to increases in malpractice litigation. Most knowledgeable observers believe that the consumer movements of the 1970s, a general increase in litigiousness, and changes in medical practice that erode intimate, life-long doctor-patient relations are factors encouraging injured patients to sue. Increases in medical knowledge and technology produce both important improvements in medical care and new opportunities for malpractice. Physicians tend to attribute increases in malpractice litigation to excessively attractive damage awards, particularly for pain and suffering damage; increasing numbers of lawyers available to bring such claims; contingent attorneys fees; and unrealistic patient expectations. Plaintiffs' lawyers focus on the fact that independent professional researchers find that negligent medical treatment quite commonly produces injury and a very small fraction of these cases result in malpractice litigation.[30]

Increases in liability insurance rates have sparked concern about tort liability. Insurance rates and liability experience are not, however, directly related. The profits or losses of insurance companies are affected by business and economic forces unrelated to claims, and these factors are reflected in insurance rates. Further, because hospitals and doctors are a much smaller group than, for example, auto drivers or home owners, it is exceptionally difficult to set accurate rates for malpractice insurance. Factors other than liability experience thus have a large influence on premiums.

Since the 1970s, every United States jurisdiction has adopted legislation to reform its medical malpractice law. The most common measures fall into two categories. Many states adopted rules to discourage litigation, including shortened statutes of limitations; restrictions on contingent fees for plaintiffs' attorneys; penalties for frivolous suits; and limits on expert witnesses. Second, many states limited the damages available to the successful malpractice plaintiff by imposing caps on damages, especially for pain and suffering, and requiring reductions for amounts that plaintiffs receive from other sources, for example, general health insurance. Evidence suggests that limits on damages, and particular rules requiring reductions for compensation received from other sources, have reduced malpractice litigation and recoveries.[31]

---

[30] Two recent professional studies show that one percent of patients admitted to hospital suffer negligently caused injuries, but that only 3–10 percent of those injured file suit. Patricia A. Danzon, *Medical Malpractice: Theory, Evidence and Public Policy* at 43 (Harvard U.P., 1985).

[31] *Ibid.* at 169, 170 (1985).

Malpractice tort reform has focused on reducing liability and insurance costs. It is fundamentally different from earlier tort reform in relation to workplace and auto accidents. Those earlier reforms sought a trade-off between the interests of plaintiffs and defendants. Malpractice reform, by contrast, seeks simply to shift risks and costs from defendants and their insurers to injured patients. While these reforms may serve a larger social good in the form of reduced premiums and consequently reduced medical care costs, they do not provide any off-setting benefits to the narrower class of injured patients. The one-sided nature of the bargain imposed by malpractice reform, and the fact that such laws treat injured patients less favorably than other tort plaintiffs, led some state courts to hold that some malpractice reform measures are unfair and unconstitutional.[32]

III. Intentional Torts

Unlike negligence, which asks whether the defendant's conduct was reasonable, intentional torts ask whether the defendant 'intended' to invade a legally protected interest of the plaintiff. Intent can be established either by showing that the defendant desired to bring about a prohibited consequence or that the defendant could foresee, to a substantial certainty, that such a consequence was likely to occur. The traditional common law protected individuals against battery, assault, false imprisonment and trespass to land or chattels. Battery includes *any* touching to which the plaintiff has not consented, though consent can sometimes be implied from social circumstances. For example, when a person seeks help from a physician and the nurse instructs the patient to undress and put on a robe, we all assume that the patient has consented to a basic physical examination. However, when the physician proposes intervention, negligence concepts require that the patient be given reasonable information to facilitate informed consent.

Assault is a threat to commit a battery, coupled with an apparent present ability to effectuate the threat. False imprisonment requires confinement to a physical place without the plaintiff's consent; no violence, malice, or physical injury is required, so long as the defendant intends to touch or restrain, without the plaintiff's consent. Contemporary common law courts have broadened the interests protected against intentional invasion. For example, the tort of intentional infliction of emotional distress provides a remedy where the defendant intentionally does something likely to cause extreme

---

[32] See e.g. *Lucas v. United States*, 757 S.W.2d 687 (Tex. 1988).

distress in an ordinary person. Plaintiffs may also recover damages against government officials who intentionally violate their constitutional rights. For example, a plaintiff may recover constitutional tort damages against a police officer who conducts an unreasonable search in violation of the Fourth Amendment, or against a jailer who administers punishment that violates the Eighth Amendment's prohibition against cruel and unusual punishment.[33]

Consent is the primary defense to an intentional tort. For example, when people agree to play football, arm wrestle, or box, the law assumes consent to the injuries that result, at least so long as everyone plays by the rules. Some unconsented to touchings or imprisonments are 'privileged'. For example, children cannot sue their parents for assault for spanking them, even though the child does not consent, because the parent is privileged to administer corporal punishment in moderate form. Students cannot sue boarding schools for false imprisonment for enforcing a curfew. The school's action is privileged. Similarly, many states give merchants a limited privilege to detain a person suspected of shop-lifting, for the purpose of investigation.

Often the interests protected by intentional torts are also protected by the criminal law. Every victim of burglary, robbery, battery, threatened assault, rape or virtually any other crime is entitled to bring a tort action against the person who injured them. But intentional torts are not limited to conduct defined as criminal. The law of intentional torts strongly affirms a zone of individual liberty and autonomy. For example, the law of battery protects the patient's right to refuse unwanted medical treatment and a woman's right to refuse unwanted carnal touches.

Tort suits for intentional wrongdoing on the part of private individuals are rare in American law. Defendants often lack resources, and liability insurance, if available, typically does not cover losses resulting from intentional wrongdoing. In addition, unless the plaintiff has suffered serious physical injury, provable damages are not likely to be sufficient to motivate a lawyer to accept the plaintiff's claim on a contingent fee basis.

---

[33] Bivins v. Six Unknown Named Agents of Federal Bureau of Narcotics, 403 U.S. 388 (1971) (4th Amendment); Carlson v. Green, 446 U.S. 14 (1980). However, imposition of damages for constitutional torts is an act of judicial prudence and courts will deny damages where special factors counsel hesitation in the absence of affirmative Congressional action. Bush v. Lucas, 462 U.S. 367 (1983) (given comprehensive statutory protection for Civil Service employees from arbitrary action by supervisors, court should not tamper with scheme by creating a constitutional tort damage remedy for first amendment violation).

IV. Strict Products Liability

In 1842, an influential English decision denied the possibility of tort liability when a negligently manufactured product causes injury. Even if the defendant acted unreasonably, and the injury to the plaintiff was foreseeable, liability for injuries caused by dangerous products was limited to contract remedies.[34] The rule—no tort liability for injuries caused by negligently manufactured products—represented an exception to the general negligence principles discussed above (see section I). Perhaps it can best be understood as a 'no-duty' rule; product manufacturers' duties were limited to those specified by contract.

As Professor Hughes explains in Chapter 1, common law courts long defined exceptions to the rule to allow recovery, particularly where the product was dangerous, injury occurred shortly after it had left the manufacturer's control, and it seemed probable that the manufacturer had failed to exercise reasonable care. Finally, in the landmark decision *McPhearson* v. *Buick Motor* in 1916, Judge Benjamin Cardozo held that the exceptions had swallowed the rule and that it was time to recognize a new rule, allowing a person injured by a product to recover upon showing that the manufacturer's negligence had caused the injuries.[35]

From 1916 to 1960, American common law courts applied negligence principles to claims by people injured by products against those who manufactured them. Injured people rarely prevailed. Manufacturers also developed warranties that strictly limited their liability to the purchasers of products. Injured plaintiffs confronted difficulty establishing that defects had been caused by the manufacturer, rather than the distributor, retailer or consumer. Most significantly, the concept that the ordinary customs of an industry are presumptively reasonable made it difficult for injured people to prove that manufacturers acted unreasonably in designing or manufacturing products. All these difficulties were exaggerated by the fact that, for plaintiffs, injury by a defective product was a once in a life-time experience, while manufacturers had the ability and incentive to mobilize experts and lawyers to defend multiple cases. It was virtually impossible to establish liability against the manufacturer of a dangerously defective product, in either contract or tort.

In the 1950s, influential scholars criticized this pattern. Contract scholars observed that manufacturers and sellers were capable of dictating terms to purchasers of consumer products and there was no reasonable opportunity for bargain. Torts scholars argued for broader manufacturer liability on

---

[34] *Winterbottom* v. *Wright*, 152 Eng. Rep. 402 (1842).
[35] 217 N.Y. 382, 111 N.E. 1050 (Ct. App. 1916).

grounds that manufacturers were much better able to both determine what safety precautions were efficient and to spread the costs of injuries caused by defective products.

In the 1960s, common law courts responded to these arguments. In 1960, the New Jersey Supreme Court considered a claim by a woman injured by a defective automobile recently purchased for her by her husband. *McPhearson* assured that she could sue for negligence, even though she had not directly contracted with the defendants. But the defendant retailer and the manufacturer asserted that the contract for sale eliminated their liability for personal injuries. The court's landmark decision, *Henningsen* v. *Bloomfield Motors*, held that the contract was against public policy.[36] The disparity of bargaining power between buyer and seller demanded that the *law* imply a non-waivable warranty to protect ultimate consumers and users against personal injuries resulting from defective products. In 1963, the California Supreme Court reached a similar result relying on tort principles, announcing in *Greenman* v. *Yuba Power Products* that manufacturers are strictly liable in tort for personal injuries caused by defective products.[37] In 1964, the prestigious American Law Institute affirmed these principles by announcing that sellers should be liable to buyers for injuries caused by products that are defective and unreasonably dangerous, even though the sellers have exercised all reasonable care in preparing the product.[38]

All states have adopted the principle that manufacturers are strictly liable for personal injuries caused by defective products. The defendant is liable if the product contains a 'defect' which renders it 'unreasonably dangerous' to the user or consumer. These include: (1) design defects, such as the use of inadequate materials or the absence of feasible safety devices; (2) defects which occur in a particular product because of errors or omissions in manufacturing, assembly, or processing; and (3) inadequate warnings or directions for use. As is typical in tort law, various states have adopted divergent approaches in applying these principles. Most states require that the plaintiff establish that the product is dangerous to an extent beyond that contemplated by the average user or consumer. In the case of design defects, this requires a balancing of the risk of injury and the costs of prevention similar to that used in negligence cases. Other states are more protective of injured plaintiffs and define a defective product as one that could have been manufactured differently so as to avoid the injury.

Like medical malpractice, products liability costs have increased dramatically in recent years, especially when the product is widely sold and a substantial number of people are injured by it. Manufacturers argue that liability

---

[36] 32 N.J. 358, 161 A.2d 69 (1960).   [37] 59 Cal. 2d 57, 377 P.2d 897, 27 Cal. Rptr. 697 (1963).
[38] *Restatement of Torts*, Section 402(a).

impairs their ability to compete in international markets and deters valuable innovation. Plaintiffs' advocates dispute these claims and argue that strict products liability provides appropriate incentives for safety and necessary compensation to injured people. As with medical malpractice, many states have adopted reforms that limit the damages that plaintiffs may recover for injuries caused by defective products, and have sought to lower the standards of care demanded of manufacturers for product safety.

V. Conclusion

American tort law is dynamic and responsive to changing social perceptions and values. On the one hand, many Americans believe that the law should provide compensation when one person or enterprise causes injury to another. On the other hand, many people believe that tort liability has become too expansive and that fear of liability imposes unreasonable constraints on human enterprise and innovation. Common law courts—in dialogue with legislatures, litigators, and ordinary people—will continue to seek to strike a wise compromise.

11

PROPERTY

WILLIAM NELSON

The United States is thought to be a nation in which private property is scrupulously protected from public seizure and control. However, much of the law of property, and hence this chapter, focuses on the powers of government that have the potential to erode that protection. Both federal and state constitutional law give government extensive power over private property. Moreover, state and local governments with some frequency have enacted legislation extending their power to its limits. After fully exploring the breadth of government's power, we shall return at the end of this chapter to the means by which property rights are protected.

Government, as we shall see, can exert power over property in three different ways. First, it can impose a tax on property. Real property taxes, in fact, constitute an important form of taxation in America, where most local governments derive the largest portion of their revenue from taxes imposed on lands and buildings within their jurisdiction. Secondly, government may use its power of eminent domain to seize individual pieces of property needed for public purposes, as long as it pays just compensation to the owner. Thirdly, government has enormous power to regulate how owners use their property.

This chapter is structured around an analysis of each of these three powers: taxation, eminent domain, and regulation. Before turning to the law of real estate taxation, however, it is necessary to make a few preliminary observations about who can own interests in property and about the nature of the interests they can hold.

I. The Nature of Ownership in America

Under the old common law, only subjects or citizens of a jurisdiction could own land within that jurisdiction. But now, by virtue of the Due Process Clause of the Constitution's Fourteenth Amendment, which provides that no person can be deprived of property without due process of law, it is settled that all persons may own property. All human beings, whether or not citizens of the United States, are considered legal persons and can therefore own land as individuals within the United States. Corporations, whether foreign or domestic, have also been defined as legal persons and thus may hold property, as may partnerships. The most prominent exception to the rule that any individual, corporation, or partnership may own property is that, on most Native American reservations, only members of the tribe may own land.

In addition to being owned by a single person—that is, by one individual, one corporation, or one partnership—property can also be held in co-ownership. Under the common law, many persons can simultaneously have property interests in the same tract of land. For example, two or more people can have identical undivided interests in the same land. Joint tenants, for example, are two or more persons who hold an undivided fractional interest in land and succeed to a proportional share of interests of any other joint tenants who predecease them. For example, if A, B, and C hold land that we shall call Blackacre as joint tenants, they each have an undivided one-third interest in Blackacre. All three must consent to every action taken in Blackacre's management, and if one of them dies, the other two will each succeed to one-half of the decedent's one-third interest. The joint tenancy can be severed if one or more of the joint owners seeks judicial intervention to partition the land, in which case the court will grant each co-owner a specific portion of the land to be held in severalty—that is, as the sole owner.

A very important subcategory of joint tenancy is the tenancy by the entireties. This form of tenancy arises when a husband and wife acquire property jointly; when one dies, the other succeeds to the land by survivorship, not inheritance. This fact can prove important if the surviving spouse is entitled to inherit some specified percentage of the decedent's estate, since anything acquired by survivorship will not be included in the specified percentage. The tenancy by the entireties can also become a serious obstacle to a creditor seeking to levy on only one rather than both spouses; all the creditor can obtain is an undivided half interest.

Joint tenancies and tenancies by the entireties must be distinguished from tenancies in common. Tenancies in common lack the feature of survivorship, which means that when one tenant dies, the heirs or distributees of that tenant, not the other tenants, acquire the deceased tenant's proportional interest in the land. Otherwise, tenancies in common have all the attributes of joint tenancies: in particular, each tenant has an undivided proportional interest in the property and must therefore share in the use and management of it, unless a court partitions the land at the request of one of the tenants.

Ownership of land can also be divided over time, with one person having the right to occupy the land or obtain rents from it in the present, and another having a comparable right in the future. The person with the current right is said to have a present interest; successors are said to have future interests. Someone who has the present right together with all possible future interests in perpetuity is said to have *seisin*, which is best defined as the right to possession under a valid claim of right, in *fee simple absolute*. In most American jurisdictions today, a grant of land to A without the imposition of any restrictions will be deemed to create a fee simple absolute.

A person can be seised of a *freehold* estate of less than perpetual duration. Any estate of indefinite duration is deemed to be one of freehold, as distinguished from a *leasehold* or estate for a definite term of years or months. One form of freehold is the *conditional fee*, such as would be created, for example, by a grant of land to A provided that the land be used for some specified purpose, such as a site for a single family residence. Logically, the condition attached to such a fee can be either a condition precedent or a condition subsequent. A condition precedent is one that must exist in order for the fee to come into and remain in existence, whereas a condition subsequent is one that will terminate an already existing fee if it should arise. A fee to which a condition precedent is attached, known as a *fee simple determinable*, is understood to come to an end automatically if the condition ceases to operate. A *fee on condition subsequent*, in contrast, is understood to terminate only if the person with power to enforce the condition subsequent exercises that power and thereby brings the fee to an end.

Historically although not doctrinally, a *fee tail*, which was a grant of land to a person and the heirs of his or her body that came to an end upon the decease of the family line of the grantee, was a sort of conditional fee. At common law, a fee tail could be transformed into a fee simple by a complex procedural device known as a *common recovery*. The fee tail has been abolished by statute in nearly all American jurisdictions. Most, although not all, legislation simply transforms existing *fee tails* into *fee simples*, at least after the initial heir specified in the original grant has been born.

A final form of freehold estate is the *estate for life*. Life estates are often created for specified individuals in wills and deeds providing for the intergenerational disposition of wealth. A device often used in such intergenerational transfers is the *trust*, whereby one person or entity—a trustee—holds assets for the benefit of another—the beneficiary—with the obligation of managing or investing the assets and turning the income over to the beneficiary.[1] Life estates can also be created by operation of law. At common law, for example, a wife upon her husband's death received *dower*, which is an estate for her life in one-third of all lands owned by the husband at any time during his life. A husband also had a life estate in the lands of his wife, even while she was alive. In light of societal and constitutional constraints of gender equality that have arisen over the course of the past century, common law devices like dower have been abolished in most American jurisdictions, and gender-neutral provisions, which vary from state to state, have been made by statute for the support of surviving spouses.

This brief survey of the mechanisms by which the common law system of estates makes possible the division of title into a variety of discrete interests should not, however, disguise the fact that most land in the United States is owned in fee simple absolute by single individuals, married couples, or corporations. In the following discussion of the scope of government's power over land through taxation, eminent domain, and regulation, we shall assume that we are dealing with lands that are so owned.

II. Taxation of Real Property

'The power to tax', as Chief Justice John Marshall wrote in *McCulloch* v. *Maryland*,[2] 'involves the power to destroy'. Indeed, the power of taxation is so potentially destructive that, if no limits existed on the power, government would not need a power of eminent domain in order to confiscate property; it would simply impose a confiscatory tax. Nor would any need exist for a power of regulation: government would have no need to prohibit or control unwanted uses of property through criminal or administrative sanctions if it could simply impose prohibitive taxes when it did not approve of the property's use. That is, there must be limits on the power of government to tax comparable to those that exist on its power to regulate property or to take it by eminent domain. Were it otherwise, government could simply attain its object of seizing or controlling property by resort to a tax.

Analysis must thus begin by considering the legal constraints on the taxing power, which are derived from the constitutional requirement 'that there should be equality in taxation'.[3] Equality, however, is not strictly applied. Rather, the Constitution requires only 'the seasonable attainment of a rough

---

[1] The use of a trust is not restricted to cases involving life interests.
[2] 17 U.S. 316 (4 Wheat. 1819).   [3] *Sioux City Bridge Co.* v. *Dakota County*, 260 U.S. 441 (1923).

equality in tax treatment of similarly situated property owners'.[4] Property owners whose situations are dissimilar can be classified into different groups and taxed at different rates, and the equality requirement demands only that such a classification 'rationally further a legitimate state interest'.[5] In reviewing cases of allegedly unequal taxes, the Supreme Court does not demand that 'a legislature or governing decisionmaker actually articulate at any time the purpose or rationale supporting its classification', as long as 'a purpose may conceivably' be imagined or ' "may reasonably have been the purpose and policy" of the relevant governmental decisionmaker'.[6] Even if a scheme of taxation 'appears to vest benefits in a broad, powerful, and entrenched segment of society', the courts will uphold its validity as long as they can draw 'any plausible inference that the reason for the unequal . . . practice was to achieve' some legitimate state purpose.[7] Included within the range of legitimate purposes are such interests as raising revenue, minimizing the administrative burden of tax collection,[8] and preserving the continuity and stability of local neighborhoods.[9]

Under this reasoning, courts have sustained legislation taxing corporations at a different rate from individual owners of property;[10] private businesses at a different rate from municipally owned businesses with which they competed;[11] and various types of businesses at different rates from each other and from farms.[12] They have also declared it appropriate to grant tax exemption or other favorable tax treatment to charities[13] and to business entities that will promote economic development or growth.[14] Most significantly, they have upheld tax authorities' customary practice of assessing real property only when a change occurs in ownership, or when new construction is added to the land or existing buildings, even when this customary practice has been legislated into positive law.[15] In a world in which inflation produces periodic increases in property values, the result of this customary assessment practice is to tax two neighbors who own identical real estate at unequal rates—the more recent purchaser at a higher and the more distant purchaser at a lower rate.

Even this brief survey makes it obvious that the constitutional requirement of equality in taxation amounts to a weak constraint on the legislative

---

[4] *Allegheny Pittsburgh Coal Co.* v. *Webster County*, 488 U.S. 336 (1989).
[5] *Nordlinger* v. *Hahn*, 112 S.Ct. 2326 (1992).   [6] *Ibid.*   [7] *Ibid.*
[8] See *New York Rapid Transit Corp.* v. *City of New York*, 303 U.S. 573 (1938).
[9] See *Nordlinger* v. *Hahn*, 112 S.Ct. 2326 (1992).
[10] See *Lehnhausen* v. *Lake Shore Auto Parts Co.*, 410 U.S. 356 (1973).
[11] See *City of Pittsburgh* v. *Alco Parking Corp.*, 417 U.S. 369 (1974); *New York Rapid Transit Corp.* v. *City of New York*, 303 U.S. 573 (1938).
[12] Cf. *Charleston Federal Sav. & Loan Ass'n* v. *Alderson*, 324 U.S. 182 (1945).
[13] See *Bell's Gap R.R.* v. *Pennsylvania*, 134 U.S. 232 (1890).
[14] See *Wein* v. *Beame*, 43 N.Y.2d 326, 372 N.E.2d 300 (1977).
[15] See *Nordlinger* v. *Hahn*, 112 S.Ct. 2326 (1992).

formulation of tax policy. Legislatures have been granted enormous freedom to tax different sorts of property owners unequally, and they have taken advantage of their freedom. Yet the power of legislatures is not untrammeled. Thus, the Supreme Court will occasionally strike down tax schemes that bear unequally on out-of-state business enterprises in comparison with in-state property owners,[16] while state courts have occasionally launched even broader attacks against unequal assessment systems.[17] Furthermore, as a practical matter, particular property owners who are singled out and taxed at a higher rate than the generality of people in their community will often be able to get their taxes reduced if they have the time and the money to protest. In closing, it can be said only that, while the constitutional requirement of equality does not give rise to a cohesive set of constraints on real estate taxation, nevertheless some vague constraints do exist. Similarly, while there is no coherent body of tax law that can be transposed to other areas where government impinges on private property rights, such as eminent domain and regulation, nonetheless the existence of at least these minimal constraints on taxation means that government power in those other areas can be constrained as well.

III. The Power of Eminent Domain

The Fifth Amendment to the Constitution, which is made applicable to the states by the Fourteenth Amendment, provides explicitly, '[N]or shall private property be taken for public use, without just compensation'.[18] On the basis of this text, American courts have uniformly held that the government may 'take' private property only if two requirements are met: (1) that the taking be for a public purpose, *and* (2) that just compensation be paid. The important question of whether a particular government regulation can become so oppressive as to amount to a taking is discussed below in section IV B1.

A. The Public Purpose Requirement

Nineteenth century case law made it clear that government could not seize the private property of one person for the purpose of giving it to another or

---

[16] See *Allegheny Pittsburgh Coal Co.* v. *Webster County*, 488 U.S. 336 (1989); *Sioux City Bridge Co.* v. *Dakota County*, 260 U.S. 441 (1923).

[17] See *Hellerstein* v. *Assessor of Town of Islip*, 37 N.Y.2d 1, 332 N.E.2d 279 (1975).

[18] United States Constitution, Amendment 5.

advancing another's interests,[19] and the old law occasionally is echoed in more modern cases.[20] But most recent cases, especially those in the Supreme Court, leave no doubt that government may take property from one individual and grant it to another when some public purpose exists for doing so.[21] Moreover, the recent cases have given the public purpose requirement an extremely expansive meaning.

Berman v. *Parker*[22] remains the leading case. In *Berman*, Justice Douglas wrote for a unanimous Court that:

> [t]he concept of the public welfare is broad and inclusive. The values it represents are spiritual as well as physical, aesthetic as well as monetary. It is within the power of the legislature to determine that the community should be beautiful as well as healthy, spacious as well as clean, well-balanced as well as carefully patrolled.[23]

Following that reasoning, courts have upheld takings for purposes of providing a factory site for industry,[24] of preventing a business from leaving a state or municipality,[25] of providing a fund with which to subsidize mass transit,[26] and of correcting maldistribution in the ownership of land.[27] In short, it appears that, as long as a legislature declares a purpose to be a public one, government may seize private property to further the purpose, and the judiciary will not interfere.[28]

B. The Just Compensation Requirement

Although substantial slippage has occurred during the past half century in judicial enforcement of the public purpose requirement, the second requirement in eminent domain cases—the requirement of just compensation—continues to be enforced rigorously. Rules specifying how to measure compensation are incredibly complex and cannot be elaborated here in detail. But several key concepts should be noted.

One is the principle that a condemnee is entitled to receive the value of the

---

[19] See *Taylor* v. *Porter*, 4 Hill 140 (N.Y. Sup. Ct. 1843).

[20] See *Estate of Waggoner* v. *Gleghorn*, 378 S.W.2d 47 (Tex. 1964).

[21] See *Hawaii Housing Authority* v. *Midkiff*, 467 U.S. 229 (1984); *Berman* v. *Parker*, 348 U.S. 26 (1954); *Poletown Neighborhood Council* v. *City of Detroit*, 410 Mich. 616, 304 N.W.2d 455 (1981).

[22] 348 U.S. 26 (1954).   [23] *Ibid.*

[24] See *Poletown Neighborhood Council* v. *City of Detroit*, 419 Mich. 616, 304 N.W.2d 455 (1981); *Yonkers Community Development Agency* v. *Morris*, 37 N.Y.2d 478, 335 N.E.2d 327 (1975).

[25] See *City of Oakland* v. *Oakland Raiders*, 32 Cal.3d 60, 646 P.2d 835 (1982).

[26] See *Courtesy Sandwich Shop, Inc.* v. *Port of New York Authority*, 12 N.Y.2d 379, 190 N.E.2d 402 (1963).

[27] See *Hawaii Housing Authority* v. *Midkiff*, 467 U.S. 229 (1984).

[28] See *Berman* v. *Parker*, 348 U.S. 26 (1954).

property taken as the property existed without regard to the program for which it was condemned. Thus, the fact that a run-down house will become part of a tract on which an expensive, new office complex will rise does not alter the amount due the owner. The same principle requires that the condemnation award be measured by the value of the property on the date on which the government became definitively committed to the project for which the land was taken rather than the date on which title was formally taken.[29] Of course, if general inflation in property values occurs between the two dates, the value as of the date of the government's commitment will have to be adjusted so that the condemnee receives the value as inflated.[30] Moreover, if government activity deprives an owner of the use of land prior to the date on which the government formally assumes title, the owner is entitled to compensation for the loss of income resulting from the government's activity.[31]

To the extent these rules fail to provide a condemnee with full value for what is condemned, courts will sometimes take further steps to ensure that the condemnee is not cheated. In *Riley v. District of Columbia Redevelopment Land Agency*,[32] for example, the jury had awarded the owner of a single-family home condemned in 1954 the sum of $7000, which was $3800 less than she had paid for it only 3 years earlier, and $1900 less than she still owed on her mortgage on the property. Although no procedural errors had occurred in the case and the jury had been properly instructed under preexisting law, the Court of Appeals nonetheless reversed the judgment below and granted a new trial. In essence, the reason for the reversal was that the court felt the damages too low and was seeking a means to make them higher.

It thus seems fair to conclude that, if the public purpose requirement is to some significant degree enforced with laxity, the just compensation requirement is to an equal degree enforced with rigor. While government can take anything by eminent domain that it wants, property owners whose lands are taken usually receive money equal in value to what they owned prior to government's intervention. The eminent domain power accordingly has never become a vehicle destructive of the private property system in America.

IV. Government Regulation of Land

We next turn to the subject of regulation. Before looking at specific regulatory programs, however, we need to examine two more general parameters which determine the scope of government's regulatory powers.

---

[29] See *United States v. Miller*, 317 U.S. 369 (1943).
[30] See *City of Buffalo v. J.W. Clement Co.*, 28 N.Y.2d 241, 269 N.E.2d 895 (1971).
[31] Cf. *First English Evangelical Lutheran Church of Glendale v. County of Los Angeles*, 482 U.S. 304 (1987).
[32] 246 F.2d 641 (D.C. Cir. 1957).

First, there are the parameters set by the law of taxation and the law of eminent domain. It is essential that government's powers to tax and seize property have limits comparable to those of the power to regulate. The reason is that, when the limitations on all three powers are comparable, government will choose to act pursuant to the power that maximizes some combination of efficiency and justice; on the other hand, if government has greater freedom to use one of the powers rather than the others, there will be a tendency to use it even at the expense of efficiency and justice. Thus, it is important to approach the law of regulation with the understanding derived from the prior sections that American governments possess extensive but nonetheless limited powers of taxation and eminent domain.

The second set of parameters that frame the law of regulation are derived from the leading 1851 case of *Commonwealth* v. *Alger*.[33] The *Alger* case was grounded on two assumptions about existing common law rules:

(1) that it was 'the right of society, in the midst of a populous settlement, to be exempt from the proximity of dangerous and noxious trades', and
(2) that it was 'the duty of the owner of real estate, in the midst of many habitations, to abstain from . . . using it' in a fashion 'dangerous to the lives, health, or comfort of the inhabitants of such dwellings'.[34]

Society could enforce its right through the law of public nuisance by a criminal prosecution against a property owner who posed a threat to public health or safety, while an individual owner could bring a private nuisance action against a neighboring owner who wrongfully interfered with his comfort. Unfortunately, as the case observed, this sort of 'general duty and obligation' was not 'fixed by a rule precise enough for practical purposes'.[35] Using as an example the issue of how closely a slaughterhouse could be built to dwellings in an inhabited area, the court in *Alger* noted that, although everyone could agree that a distance of 200 feet was too little and 2000 feet too great, distances between these extremes would produce disagreement. Because an 'authoritative rule, carrying with it the character of certainty and precision, [was] needed', the legislature was given power to enact a regulatory statute establishing 'a definite, known . . . rule which all can understand and obey'.[36]

In the 1992 case of *Lucas* v. *South Carolina Coastal Council*,[37] the Supreme Court reaffirmed the principle that the legislature may adopt regulatory laws in order to introduce a definite, certain, and precise rule on a subject already within the range of common law adjudication. As long as the legislature does

[33] 7 Cushing 53 (Mass. 1851).   [34] *Ibid.*   [35] *Ibid.*   [36] *Ibid.*
[37] 112 S.Ct. 2886 (1992).

not authorize any physical invasion of land, *Lucas* upholds the constitutionality of regulatory laws which 'inhere . . . in the restrictions that background principles of the State's law of property and nuisance already place upon land ownership' or which, 'in other words, do no more than duplicate the result that could have been achieved in the courts', even when such regulatory laws deprive a landowner of all value attributable to his land.[38]

As a consequence of the holdings of *Alger* and *Lucas*, which authorize legislative regulations consistent with results judicially attainable at common law, it becomes necessary to divide regulatory schemes into two categories:

(a)   those that codify or supplement common law principles, and
(b)   those that expand the common law.

As we shall see, no doubt exists about the appropriateness of the first category of regulation, but the second is the subject of significant constitutional challenge.

A. Regulatory Doctrines Parallel to the Common Law

1. Determining title to land

In any private property system, disputes will frequently arise about who owns a particular tract of land. In American law, such disputes are resolved in the courts by reference to doctrines that have their source in ancient statutes that have been elaborated by judges in detail, so that what exists today is a mixed body of common and statutory law. We shall examine these doctrines under three headings: (1) transfer of title, (2) recording of title, and (3) adverse possession.

(i) Transfer of title.   Today's methods of transferring title have their origins in three ancient Parliamentary statutes: the 1536 Statute of Uses, the 1677 Statute of Frauds, and the 1540 Statute of Wills. The form and language of modern deeds, which are used for *inter vivos* transfers, have their origins in the Statute of Uses and the Statute of Frauds, while the form and language of wills, which are used by an owner to convey property to others upon his or her death, have their origins in the Statute of Wills. Deeds and wills must follow the prescribed form, and typically are held void and ineffective if they do not. In addition to transfers by deed and will, land can be transferred by a judicial judgment or, if an owner dies without a will, by inheritance.

Deeds can be used for three different sorts of *inter vivos* transfers. First,

[38]   112 S.Ct. 2886 (1992).

deeds are used to convey title from a seller to a buyer. In these circumstances, several weeks or months before the *closing*, which is the time when title will be transferred, the buyer and seller will typically enter into a contract of sale for the land. Once the contract is executed, the buyer becomes the equitable owner of the land and, on payment of the full purchase price, the seller is obligated to execute a deed to the buyer.

Secondly, mortgage deeds are used to provide security to a creditor lending money to a buyer or owner of land. The *mortgagor* is the person who borrows money and, in return, gives the lender a conditional title in the property that can be transformed through foreclosure into a full title if the loan is not repaid; the person who gives money and receives the mortgage deed in return is the *mortgagee*. If money is lent to facilitate the purchase of land, the deed giving title to the buyer and the mortgage deed giving a conditional title to the lender will typically be exchanged at the same closing; at this time, the buyer is generally required by the lender to obtain a policy of title insurance for the protection of both his own and the lender's interest. The insurance, in effect, provides that the seller is the owner of the land and has the right to sell it, free of any claims of another; if not, the title insurance pays for the loss. Thirdly, a deed must be used when someone wishes to make a gift of land, without monetary consideration, either to some individual or to a charitable or other entity.

(ii) Recording of title. At common law, a deed was fully effective to transfer title from the grantor to the grantee. If, subsequent to the execution of a deed, a grantor gave a second deed to a second grantee, the second grantee received nothing, on the theory that the grantor at the time of the second deed had nothing left to give. In order to render titles more secure and to eliminate opportunities for fraud, legislatures in every American state have adopted recording acts, which provide registries of deeds where grantees can record their instruments and which change the common law rule of priority between recipients of successive deeds.

There are three types of recording acts. First is the 'race' type act, by which a grantee who records his deed has priority over all unrecorded or subsequently recorded deeds. Second is the 'notice' type statute, by which a grantee receives priority over all prior unrecorded deeds of which he had no notice; the subsequent grantee need not record his deed in order to enjoy his priority. Third is the 'race-notice' type, by which a grantee receives priority over all prior unrecorded deeds of which he had no notice, unless the prior grantee records his deed before the subsequent grantee does, in which case the prior grantee will regain his common law priority.

(iii) Adverse possession. At times, proof of a paper title derived from a properly recorded deed may prove impossible even for someone who is the actual

owner of land. This will be especially true of very old titles, where ancient documents required as evidence may have been lost or destroyed. For this reason, a person who has occupied land for the length of time provided in the state's statute of limitations for bringing actions for recovery of land can establish title by the doctrine of adverse possession, provided the following five elements are satisfied:

(1) the possession over the required period of time must be actual;
(2) it must be open and notorious;
(3) it must be exclusive;
(4) it must be continuous; and
(5) it must be such as would give the holder of the paper title or anyone else claiming the land a cause of action against the occupant throughout the prescribed statutory period.[39]

Even if an occupant has held land for less than the statutory period, the occupant's possession will be protected by the courts against all but someone who can establish a superior title.[40]

If adverse possession were seen as a device by which the legislature authorized taking property from true owners and giving it to others, it would be plainly unconstitutional. But this is not the way the courts have looked at the doctrine. Instead, adverse possession has been understood as a legislative device providing a clear rule for resolving difficult issues involving conflicting and uncertain evidence. As such, its constitutionality can be readily sustained under the holding of *Commonwealth* v. *Alger*.

2. Judicial and legislative regulation of competing land use

(i) Nuisance and zoning.   A centerpiece of the law of property is nuisance, by which courts resolve the rights of neighboring land owners who want to use their land in ways that burden each other. The paradigmatic nuisance case is one involving suit by a residential or agricultural user of land against an industrial polluter. Unfortunately, this paradigmatic case has no clear, paradigmatic resolution.

There are at least four possible approaches. The first is an environmentally protective one that favors natural land uses, like agriculture, over polluting uses, like industry. Arguably, the early common law favored natural over

---

[39] See *Belotti* v. *Bickhardt*, 228 N.Y. 296, 127 N.E. 239 (1920); A.J. Casner (ed.), 3 *American Law of Property* sec. 15.3 (Little, Brown, 1952).

[40] *Tapscott* v. *Cobbs*, 52 Va. 172 (1854).

industrial users, although this approach was in large part rejected during the course of the nineteenth century.[41]

Diametrically opposed is the second approach, which favors the more efficient of the competing land users. The leading case is *Boomer* v. *Atlantic Cement Co.*,[42] which involved the construction and subsequent operation of a cement plant in a previously established agricultural and residential community. The court nonetheless refused to grant an injunction against the cement plant, in which in excess of $45,000,000 was invested and which employed over 300 people, whereas the totality of permanent damages to all plaintiffs in the community amounted to only $185,000. The only relief it allowed was an award for damages, which could have had only a minor impact on the cement firm's profitability.

A third, legal realist approach sees nuisance law as policy driven and ultimately political. As the Rhode Island Supreme Court declared in litigation between a farmer and a corporate owner of an oil refinery, '[a] query arises as to whether the divergence of views expressed in . . . [nuisance] cases . . . do[es] not rest on public policy rather than legal theory'.[43] Pointing to an opinion of Justice Holmes approving the use of public policy as a basis for judicial decision-making, the court noted that analogous cases were typically decided on behalf of farmers in jurisdictions with a predominantly agricultural economy, whereas they were decided for industry in manufacturing jurisdictions. The Rhode Island court decided in favor of the refinery.[44]

A fourth approach, which was applied in the Massachusetts case of *Stevens* v. *Rockport Granite Co.*,[45] looks to the character of the neighborhood—to whether a pattern of land use 'has become so dominant as to impress its special character upon the community'.[46] At issue in the *Rockport* case was whether resort and summer residence development had as yet stamped the neighborhood in the vicinity of what is now Rockport with the character of a tourist resort; if so, the defendant's granite polishing business would have had to be closed down. In fact, however, the court found that summer residents had not so overwhelmed the community as to become their distinctive feature, and hence the granite business was allowed to remain in operation.

No clear resolution exists for the conflict among these approaches: each one has had its adherents in the past as well as the present. And, even if the conflict could be resolved, the law of nuisance would still be uncertain and ambiguous. The reason is that the application of nuisance law inevitably involves issues of public policy that, in a broad range of cases, tend to cloud legal doctrine.

[41] See Morton J. Horwitz, *The Transformation of American Law, 1780–1860*, at 31–34 (Harvard U.P., 1977).
[42] 26 N.Y.2d 219, 257 N.E.2d 870 (1970).
[43] *Rose* v. *Socony-Vacuum Corp.*, 54 R.I. 411, 173 Atl. 627 (1934).   [44] *Ibid.*
[45] 216 Mass. 486, 104 N.E. 371 (1914).   [46] *Ibid.*

One troublesome issue is the definition of what constitutes an inconsistent use. The cases have clearly established, for example, that use of property as a funeral home is inconsistent with the maintenance of at least some areas as residential districts and thus constitutes a nuisance.[47] In contrast, use of property as a half-way house for convicts, drug addicts, or the mentally disturbed, or as some other sort of social welfare center, is typically thought not to be a nuisance.[48]

The problem lies in accounting for these divergent results. Surely, convicted criminals, who statistically have a high rate of recidivism, pose a greater threat to the inhabitants of a residential neighborhood than do dead bodies, although both are likely to produce a reduction in the property values of adjacent residential structures. Arguably, the reason for permitting the operation of social welfare centers, but not funeral homes, in residential neighborhoods is that the welfare centers must be so located in order to accomplish their legitimate public welfare functions.

Still, one wonders why the particular neighborhoods in which they are located should alone bear costs that produce a benefit for the public at large. If, for example, state prisons were financed through taxation levied only on some municipalities or neighborhoods, no judge would hesitate to invalidate that scheme as an unconstitutionally unequal tax. For this reason, some courts have held that neighborhoods located beneath airport flightpaths ought to receive compensation for the resulting noise and vibration; their justification is that, although airports must be located near cities in order to serve their public purpose, it would be unequal and hence unfair to place the uncompensated burden of an airport only on particular neighborhoods when the benefits inure to a city as a whole.[49]

It seems impossible to distinguish the airport cases from the half-way house cases, except perhaps on the basis of some unexpressed judicial assumption that the public wants airports badly enough to raise added taxes for compensating property owners who suffer unique damages from their construction, but that if the public had to pay similar additional taxes for the construction of half-way houses and other welfare centers, these valuable entities would never be built. The law of nuisance may thus be reflecting some practical judicial sense of the limits that exist on their capacity to ensure that the public good is attained in a fair and equal manner.

Another troublesome issue that leads to judicial bending of doctrine occurs when both sides in a case involving inconsistent land uses have relied on legitimate expectations that their side would impose its land use on the

---

[47] See *Powell* v. *Taylor*, 222 Ark. 896, 263 S.W.2d 906 (1954).

[48] See *Nicholson* v. *Connecticut Half-Way House, Inc.*, 153 Conn. 507, 218 A.2d 383 (1966).

[49] See *Alevizos* v. *Metropolitan Airports Commission*, 298 Minn. 471, 216 N.W.2d 651 (1974).

other. *Spur Industries, Inc.* v. *Del E. Webb Development Co.*[50] was one such case. Spur Industries was maintaining a cattle feedlot with 20,000 to 30,000 head of cattle that produced over a million pounds of wet manure per day. When it was initially built, the feedlot was located over a mile away from the nearest residential community, but then Del Webb decided to expand its retirement community to within several hundred feet of the feedlot. Retirees who bought homes without appreciating the proximity of the feedlot learned after moving in that they could not live with the feedlot's odors, and litigation accordingly arose.

Both Spur Industries and the residents of the retirement community—that is, the two inconsistent land users—were innocent victims with every reason to expect that they could recoup the investments they had made in their property. Traditional nuisance doctrine gave the court no basis for chosing the interests of the one rather than the other, since the real culprit in the case was the Del Webb Co. It had taken advantage of cheap land prices in an agricultural area when it located its retirement community, and it had then sold houses to retirees without disclosing the harms they would suffer. Focusing on the misbehavior of Del Webb Co., the court wisely ignored traditional doctrine and crafted a damage remedy against it—a remedy that enabled the retirees to enjoy their homes and compensated Spur Industries for the costs of removing its feedlot operation to a new, more distant location.[51]

These cases demonstrate that the common law of nuisance, above all, is highly fact specific, as well as tied to a number of competing doctrinal approaches tending to produce inconsistent results. Nuisance is a classic subject on which investors seeking to commit capital to developmental ends must look forward to litigation in which results are utterly uncertain and unpredictable. Thus, it is an area that under the rationale of the *Alger* and *Lucas* cases calls for legislative regulation.

Such regulation has occurred under the rubric of zoning. In *Village of Euclid* v. *Ambler Realty Co.*,[52] the first case in which the Supreme Court passed on the constitutionality of zoning, the Court drew an explicit connection between nuisance and zoning, as it took the position that 'the common law of nuisances . . . [could] be consulted, not for the purpose of controlling, but for the helpful aid of its analogies in the process of ascertaining the scope of, the power' to zone.[53] *Euclid* seems to suggest that the purpose of zoning is the legislative regulation of competing land uses in circumstances in which a possible use of one tract of land might amount to a nuisance toward another tract.

Several early state cases supported this view; indeed, they held zoning ordinances unconstitutional when applied to properties that did not

---

[50] 108 Ariz. 178, 494 P.2d 700 (1972).   [51] *Ibid.*   [52] 272 U.S. 359 (1926).   [53] *Ibid.*

constitute a potential nuisance to neighboring properties. For example, in *Arverne Bay Construction Co. v. Thatcher*,[54] the New York Court of Appeals held a New York City ordinance unconstitutional when applied to prevent construction of a gasoline service station in an area in which the only other structures were a cow stable and an associated office, an incinerator, and an open sewer. Similarly, in *Vernon Park Realty, Inc. v. City of Mount Vernon*,[55] the same court struck down an ordinance that prohibited the owner of a parking lot in the middle of a business district from constructing stores and offices comparable to those already located in the district, even though the City badly needed continued operation of the parking facilities. In the court's view, the planned stores and offices were not inconsistent with existing patterns of land use in the district and thus could not be prohibited. Finally, in *Katobimar Realty Co. v. Webster*,[56] the New Jersey Supreme Court struck down an ordinance that prohibited construction of a shopping center on land zoned for light industry, which the municipality hoped would move into town and thereby improve its tax base. The land in question was located in the midst of other industrial and commerical uses, and the construction of a shopping center would have been perfectly consistent with those existing uses.

One older, classic view of zoning thus links it closely to the law of nuisance. As we shall see in sections IV B below, the legislative power to zone has expanded far beyond the prevention of inconsistent uses of land, even though the power had its origins in such prevention. But before we turn to ways in which the power to zone has expanded, we must turn to other bodies of ancient common law—the law of easements, covenants, and servitudes—which have given much structure to modern doctrines of land use regulation.

(ii) Easements, covenants, servitudes, and zoning.   Just as the common law system of estates in land made it possible to subdivide interests in land temporally, doctrines about easements, covenants, and servitudes make it possible to give different individuals varying kinds of spatial use interests in the same tract of land. And, just as the law of nuisance lies at the foundation of modern regulatory zoning, so too the law of easements, covenants, and servitudes lies at the base of much modern subdivision and zoning practice. Each of these ancient bodies of law must be addressed separately before turning to the modern doctrines which they have spawned.

Easements. An easement confers on its holder the right to make some specific, limited use of land owned by another. Typically, the person who benefits from an easement must be an owner of other land in the vicinity. As a formal doctrinal matter, the easement is understood to exist for the benefit of that other land and is said to be *appurtenant* to that land. The land to which

---

[54]   278 N.Y. 222, 15 N.E.2d 587 (1938).   [55]   307 N.Y. 493, 121 N.E.2d 517 (1954).
[56]   20 N.J. 114, 118 A.2d 824 (1955).

the easement is appurtenant is said to be the *dominant tenement*, while the land over which the easement lies is called the *servient tenement*.

Only limited categories of rights can take the form of an *easement appurtenant*. The owner of the dominant tenement can, for example, possess a right of way; a right to run a wire or pipeline; a right to support from adjacent property; a right to enjoy a specified view; or a right to enjoy access to light and air. Under older common law rules, the owner of the dominant tenement could also enjoy a right to harvest a specified type of natural growth of the servient tenement, such as berries or wood. In more modern times, owners of a dominant tenement have been permitted to use the servient tenement as a park.[57]

At traditional common law, *easements in gross*—that is, easements that were not attached or appurtenant to some dominant tenement—could not exist.[58] Today, however, courts have acknowledged that sound public policy requires individuals and corporations who do not own land in the vicinity of a servient tenement to maintain facilities such as railroads, utility lines, and pipelines over extended distances, and therefore the courts allow these very limited sorts of facilities to assume the legal form of easements in gross.[59]

Easements are full-fledged property rights fully equivalent to the common law estates in land examined above. As such, they can normally be created and transferred only in the same way as other property rights in land are created and transferred—by deed, by will, or by judicial judgment. They cannot be created or transferred orally.[60] Once created, easements are difficult to destroy. They exist for the benefit of the owners of the land to which they are appurtenant, and if the land is subdivided, all owners get to enjoy the easement,[61] unless their combined usage is so extraordinary or excessive as to be incompatible with the easement that was originally granted. When the owners of the dominant estate are no longer able to use the easement as originally intended, the easement will terminate. Easements can also be terminated by eminent domain taking, if just compensation is paid; or by abandonment, if an intent to abandon is proved. Otherwise, an easement endures in perpetuity unless it was created for a lesser period of time.

Like freehold interests in land, easements can also be created by a sort of adverse possession, which is known as *prescription*. An *easement by prescription* will be created by an adverse use of land for the required statutory period that is open and notorious and under a claim of right adverse to the land's

[57] See *Re Ellenborough Park*, [1955] All E.R. 38 (Ch. 1955); *Cottrell* v. *Nurnberger*, 131 W. Va. 391, 47 S.E.2d 454 (1948) (by implication).
[58] See *Boatman* v. *Lasley*, 23 Ohio St. 614 (1873).
[59] See *Geffine* v. *Thompson*, 76 Ohio App. 64, 62 N.E.2d 590 (1945).
[60] See *Cottrell* v. *Nurnberger*, 131 W. Va. 391, 47 S.E.2d 454 (1948).
[61] See *Martin* v. *Music*, 254 S.W.2d 701 (Ky. 1953).

owner.[62] Because of their special nature, certain kinds of easements cannot be created by prescription; in the case of such easements, it will typically be impossible for the person claiming the easement to show that he or she acted for the statutory period in a fashion adverse to the land's owner. Two examples are the easement of view and the easement of light and air;[63] neither can be created by prescription since people enjoying a view or enjoying light and air usually do not intend to assert any claim against their neighbors' lands while they are doing so.

Because of their special nature, easements can also be created in another fashion—*by implication of necessity*. Sometimes known as *easements by or of necessity*, they are in essence easements created by sensible construction of written instruments creating freehold interests in land. An example will illustrate. Suppose that an owner of a house and an adjacent tract of land, who brings electricity into the house along a wire that is strung across the adjacent land, sells the house in fee simple to a buyer without expressly granting in the deed of sale an easement to maintain the electric wire across the land that the seller retains. At least in the absence of evidence to the contrary, courts will make the reasonable assumption that the parties intended the buyer to continue bringing electricity into the house by the same means the seller had used, and they will imply the easement that the parties' attorneys had not expressly created.[64]

Covenants. A second device for dividing property rights in land among different interests is the *covenant running with the land*. A covenant running with the land should be distinguished from an ordinary covenant or contract. An ordinary contract is enforceable only by the parties or their personal successors, whereas a covenant running with the land is enforceable by whoever owns the land benefitted by the covenant. In the majority of American jurisdictions, any type of interest can be created as a covenant running with the land.

Only two requirements need to be met in most states for a covenant to run with the land. First, the parties who created the covenant must have intended it to run. Secondly, *privity of estate* must exist between the plaintiff and defendant in the lawsuit seeking to enforce the covenant.[65] This second requirement is an extraordinarily technical one which requires that the covenant at issue must have been created by the same instrument that transferred the land either benefited or burdened by the covenant. The privity requirement also demands that the parties to the lawsuit can trace specified interests in the land to the original parties to the transaction.

[62] See *Dartnell* v. *Bidwell*, 115 Me. 227, 98 Atl. 743 (1916).
[63] See *Parker* v. *Foote*, 19 Wend. 308 (N.Y. Sup. Ct. 1838).
[64] See *VanSandt* v. *Royster*, 148 Kan. 495, 83 P.2d 698 (1938).
[65] See *Neponsit Property Owners' Ass'n* v. *Emigrant Indus. Sav. Bank*, 278 N.Y. 248, 15 N.E.2d 793 (1938).

In a minority of American jurisdictions, most notably New York, a third requirement going back to the sixteenth century[66] must also be met in order for a covenant to run with the land: the covenant must *touch or concern* the land.[67] The precise meaning of this touching or concerning requirement is unclear, although in one leading case, the New York Court of Appeals sought to clarify it by holding that only *restrictive* covenants, not *affirmative* ones, can run with the land.[68] A restrictive covenant is one that limits the manner in which the burdened land may be used; an affirmative covenant is one that requires the owner of the burdened land to perform an act for the benefit of the owner of the second tract of land.

Subsequent New York cases suggest, however, that the touching or concerning requirement is no longer part of the state's law,[69] even though it remains available as a device for invalidating a covenant when a court, as a matter of policy, does not want to enforce it. In one case, for example, a lower court refused to enforce a covenant requiring a lessee of a gasoline service station to purchase only supplies refined by the lessor and gave as its reason the covenant's failure to touch or concern the land, not its inconsistency with public policy.[70]

Perhaps it would have been better if the court had rested its holding on an explicit policy ground, since, at least in the context of equitable enforcement of covenants, there exists a clear policy against enforcing covenants if it would be contrary to the public interest to do so. Thus, in one case, a court refused to enforce a covenant restricting competition,[71] while in another, a court refused to enforce terms incorporated into a residential subdivision which did not apply equally to all of the owners.[72] There is no question, however, that covenants drafted to create a scheme of common neighborhood development, applicable equally to all in the community will generally be enforced.[73] Indeed, in Houston, Texas, and in some smaller communities, such covenants are used as a substitute for zoning, which does not exist.

Related to the practice of not enforcing covenants which are contrary to public policy is the rule that courts will invalidate covenants when changed conditions in the neighborhood make continued enforcement unreasonable

---

[66] See *Spencer's Case*, 5 Co. Rep. 16a (K.B. 1583).

[67] See *Miller* v. *Clary*, 210 N.Y. 127, 103 N.E. 1114 (1913).   [68] *Ibid.*

[69] See *165 Broadway Building* v. *City Investing Co.*, 120 F.2d 813 (2d Cir. 1941); *Nicholson* v. *300 Broadway Realty Corp.*, 7 N.Y.2d 240, 164 N.E.2d 832 (1959).

[70]. See *Bill Wolf Petroleum Corp.* v. *Chock Full of Power Gasoline Corp.*, 70 Misc.2d 314, 333 N.Y.S.2d 472 (Sup. Ct. 1972).

[71] See *Shade* v. *M. O'Keeffe, Inc.*, 260 Mass. 180, 156 N.E. 867 (1927). But cf. *Hercules Power Co.* v. *Continental Can Co.*, 196 Va. 935, 86 S.E.2d 128 (1955), which upheld a covenant restricting competition when its purpose was to protect an industry's resource base, rather than its share of the consumer market.

[72] See *Petersen* v. *Beekmere, Inc.*, 117 N.J. Super. 155, 283 A.2d 911 (Ch. Div. 1971).

[73] See *Harrod* v. *Rigelhaupt*, 1 Mass. App. Ct. 376, 298 N.E.2d 872 (1973).

or at odds with the neighborhood scheme contemplated by those who had initially imposed the covenants.[74] At one level, the changed conditions rule is merely the application of a more general principle—that before enforcing a covenant, a court must always determine whether enforcement is in the public interest. This open-ended policy judgment is one that can only be made by a court, however; it cannot be delegated to an administrative agency.[75]

Servitudes. As we have seen, two requirements exist for the enforcement of a covenant running with the land: (1) the parties creating the covenant must have intended it to run, and (2) privity of estate must exist between the parties in litigation. If the privity requirement cannot be satisfied, a restriction can still be enforced if the party against whom enforcement is sought either knew of the restriction or ought to have known of it from examining the land records. So enforced, the restriction will be known as an *equitable servitude.*[76] Enforcement will be subject to all the public policy defenses to which enforcement of covenants is subject, as well as to standard equity defenses such as estoppel and laches.[77]

Zoning. Just as the basic structure of zoning law is parallel to and arguably grows out of nuisance law, other specific doctrines in the field of zoning grow out of the law of easements, covenants, and servitudes. One such doctrine requires every municipality to base its zoning ordinance on a comprehensive plan. The power to zone does not authorize a municipality to adopt an ordinance which, for example, makes all land within its boundaries available for residential or agricultural use, with the municipality then reserving power to allow other uses on a case-by-case basis, as appropriate.[78] Known by the epithet of 'spot zoning', such an approach to municipal land use regulation would violate the common law principle applicable to the law of covenants that a land use scheme should be applicable to the neighborhood as a whole and to all of its landowners equally. For analogous reasons, the requirement of a comprehensive plan has accordingly become a standard requirement of the law of zoning.

A second set of zoning doctrines for which parallels can be readily found in the law of covenants and servitudes arises in the rules allowing for variances. As we saw, courts will refuse to enforce the terms of covenants when conditions in the neighborhood have so changed as to render enforcement inconsistent with the scheme contemplated by the original convenanting

[74] See *Wolff* v. *Fallon*, 44 Cal.2d 695, 284 P.2d 802 (1955).
[75] See *Pulos* v. *James*, 261 Ind. 279, 302 N.E.2d 768 (Ind. 1973).
[76] See *Tulk* v. *Moxhay*, 2 Phillips 774 (Ch. 774); *Trustees of Columbia College* v. *Lynch*, 70 N.Y. 440 (1877).
[77] Estoppel occurs when a person, who has induced another to change his position to his detriment, is not permitted by a court of equity to take advantage of the change in position. Laches is the equitable equivalent of the statute of limitations; the doctrine bars a litigant from pleading a claim if unreasonable delay in advancing the claim has prejudiced his opponent.
[78] See *Rockhill* v. *Chesterfield Township*, 23 N.J. 117, 128 A.2d 473 (1957).

parties. Similarly, variances from strict application of a zoning ordinance are available to landowners who can show that they will suffer hardship through the use of their land in accordance with the scheme of the ordinance.[79] The hardship must result, however, from changes in the neighborhood that result in the ordinance's application to their land in a fashion different from that contemplated by its drafters. If, in contrast, an ordinance simply places land along a boundary between commercial and residential zones, with the result that an owner simply suffers the hardship which the first residential owner on the boundary of a commercial zone inevitably suffers—a hardship contemplated by the drafters of the ordinance, then a variance is inappropriate.[80]

Subdivision controls are a third set of practices which are related to the common law doctrines discussed above—this time to doctrines about easements. When a developer wishes to subdivide a large tract of land into individual lots to be sold as homesites, a municipality can require him to dedicate various kinds of easements that will be needed in the new community—easements for roads, utility lines, pipelines, and parks, for example. Arguably all that a municipal legislature is doing when it requires the dedication of such easements for eventual public use is making explicit the easements that courts would otherwise raise by implication of necessity if the developer sold off individual lots to prospective home buyers. Developers are normally willing to comply with municipal demands because the dedication of easements usually increases the value of the subdivided building lots that remain.

Some municipalities have gone even further and have required developers to make a cash payment to the municipal government in lieu of the reservation of land. Although the New York Court of Appeals upheld these cash payments in the leading case of *Jenad, Inc.* v. *Village of Scarsdale*,[81] the Supreme Court's recent reference to *Jenad's* standard as 'too lax to adequately protect' property rights[82] renders their constitutional validity doubtful.

B. Regulatory Doctrines Expanding the Common Law

1. Aesthetic regulation through zoning and environmental law

Much of contemporary zoning law, like other law regulating the use of land in the United States, can be readily justified on the theory set out in the old case of *Commonwealth* v. *Alger*[83] and the recent case of *Lucas* v. *South Carolina*

---

[79] See *Parsons* v. *Board of Zoning Appeals of New Haven*, 140 Conn. 290, 99 A.2d 149 (1953).
[80] See *Sullivan* v. *Board of Appeals of Belmont*, 346 Mass. 81, 190 N.E.2d 83 (1963).
[81] 18 N.Y.2d 78, 218 N.E.2d 673 (1966).
[82] *Dolan* v. *City of Tigard* 114 Sup. Ct. 2309, 2319   [83] 7 Cush. 53 (Mass. 1851) (see n. 33 above).

Coastal Council.[84] Zoning is frequently a regulatory substitute for what judges could achieve through common law adjudication under the rubric of nuisance, easement, and covenant doctrines. In recent decades, however, legislatures have undertaken an expansive role that has transformed zoning into a regulatory mechanism vastly broader than the common law, the courts have, in large part, sustained its constitutionality.

The expansion of municipal regulatory powers arguably began with already quoted dictum in the 1954 case of *Berman* v. *Parker*[85] declaring that Congress had authority in the District of Columbia to create a socially just and aesthetically pleasing community, as well as to protect health and safety and to legislate regulatory precepts in the area of nuisance. Although *Berman* was an eminent domain rather than a regulation case, its dictum became determinative in the regulatory field when the Court repeated it in *Village of Belle Terre* v. *Boraas*[86] and then added the following:

> A quiet place where yards are wide, people few, and motor vehicles restricted are legitimate guidelines in a land-use project addressed to family needs . . . The police power is not confined to elimination of filth, stench, and unhealthy places. It is ample to lay out zones where family values, youth values, and the blessings of quiet seclusion and clean air make the area a sanctuary for people.[87]

Boraas thereby made it clear that local governments may use their police or regulatory power both to promote their vision of social justice and to make their communities beautiful.

One of the earliest cases squarely to uphold zoning for purely aesthetic purposes was *People* v. *Stover*,[88] decided by the New York Court of Appeals in 1963. The case arose out of a tax protest by a resident who hung tattered and dirty clothing on a clothesline stretched across his front lawn. When the City responded with an ordinance that, with certain exceptions, prohibited clotheslines on front lawns, Stover ignored the ordinance. In appealing his conviction for violating the ordinance, Stover argued unsuccessfully that the ordinance was beyond the scope of the City's zoning power.

The case is important first because it illustrates the level of trivial detail to which American municipalities can descend in their zoning ordinances. It is even more important because the court upheld the ordinance solely 'as an attempt to preserve the residential appearance of the city . . . by banning insofar as practicable, unsightly clotheslines from yards abutting a public street'. The statute, 'based on what may be termed aesthetic considerations, proscribe[d] conduct which offend[ed] sensibilities and tend[ed] to debase the

[84] 112 S.Ct. 2886 (1992) (see n. 37 above).   [85] 348 U.S. 26 (1954) (see n. 22 above).
[86] 416 U.S. 1 (1974).   [87] *Ibid.*   [88] 12 N.Y.2d 462, 191 N.E.2d 272 (1963).

community'.[89] Here was a clear holding in a state court of the constitutionality of purely aesthetic zoning.

Two years later the City of New York took the mandate of the Court of Appeals in *Stover* to heart and adopted legislation to protect historic buildings and neighborhoods in order to foster 'civic pride in the beauty and noble accomplishments of the past' and to promote 'the use of historic districts, landmarks, interior landmarks, and scenic landmarks for the education, pleasure and welfare of the people of the city'.[90] The legislation authorized a Landmarks Preservation Commission to identify buildings of special aesthetic or historic character and to designate them as landmarks, which had the effect of prohibiting any alteration in their exterior without the Commission's consent.

The constitutionality of this legislation was brought before the Supreme Court of the United States in *Penn Central Transportation Co.* v. *City of New York*,[91] where the Court declared that the 'objective of preserving structures and areas with special historic, architectural, or cultural significance is an entirely permissible governmental goal' and therefore 'that States and cities . . . [could] enact land use restrictions or controls to enhance the quality of life by preserving the character and desirable aesthetic features of a city'.[92] More recent Supreme Court cases have adhered to this holding. In *Nollan* v. *California Coastal Commission*,[93] for example, the Court assumed that government had power to engage in 'scenic zoning' and in 'protecting the public's ability to see the beach',[94] while in *Keystone Bituminous Coal Ass'n* v. *DeBenedictis*,[95] the Court upheld the power of states 'to protect . . . the environment', even when no health or safety considerations were implicated in the protection.[96] The Court's most recent case—*Lucas* v. *South Carolina Coastal Commission*[97]—likewise upholds the constitutionality of regulatory legislation addressing 'ecological . . . and aesthetic concerns' provided the legislation does not have the effect of depriving any piece of 'land of all economically beneficial use'.[98]

With the advent of the environmental movement in the 1970s, much state and local legislation has been adopted for aesthetic rather than health and safety reasons. Although some environmental law aims at protecting the health and safety of the current generation, other laws strive to protect natural resources, such as beaches[99] and wildlife,[100] for the future. Environmental law of this sort, which has become widespread in most states, can

[89] *Ibid.*

[90] New York City Charter and Administrative Code, ch. 8-A, sec. 205–1.0(b) (1976).

[91] 438 U.S. 104 (1978). [92] *Ibid.* [93] 483 U.S. 825 (1987).

[94] *Ibid.* [95] 55 L.W. 4326 480 U.S. 470(1987). [96] *Ibid.*

[97] 112 S.Ct. 2886 (1992). [98] *Ibid.*

[99] See *State ex rel. Thornton* v. *Hay*, 254 Ore. 584, 462 P.2d 671 (1969).

[100]. See *Michigan Oil Co.* v. *Natural Resources Comm'n*, 71 Mich. App. 667, 249 N.W.2d 135 (1976).

only be seen as a kind of aesthetic regulation. Its constitutionality nonetheless was uniformly upheld until the Supreme Court in the 1992 case of *Lucas v. South Carolina Coastal Council*[101] and the 1994 case of *Dolan* v. *City of Tigard*[102] raised some significant questions.

At issue in *Lucas* was a regulation that prohibited the owner of two building lots on a South Carolina barrier island from erecting any permanent structure on them, thereby reducing the value of the lots from approximately the $1 million Lucas had paid for them to virtually nothing. Concluding that such a huge reduction in value might constitute a 'taking' for which just compensation is required, the Supreme Court remanded the case to the South Carolina courts with instructions that, if the purpose of the prohibition was to protect public safety by preventing flooding during storms and if the law was reasonably likely to carry out that purpose, it would be constitutional even though the regulated land was rendered worthless. On the other hand, the Court held that the regulation would be unconstitutional if the lower courts found its purpose to be the preservation of the shorefront in its natural state for the benefit of wildlife and future generations. While environmental protection for aesthetic ends might be legitimate, according to the Court, a regulation that destroyed all economic value would be equivalent to an eminent domain taking and could therefore be sustained only if government paid just compensation. There would be no taking, however, if the impact of the regulation was only to reduce slightly the value of the land.

Then in 1994, in *Dolan* v. *City of Tigard*, a 5–4 majority of the Court again applied this 'taking' analysis. At issue in *Dolan* was a requirement that a landowner dedicate land adjacent to a stream for flood control purposes and certain additional land for construction of a bicycle path to alleviate the added traffic that Dolan's expansion of her business would produce. Even though the Court recognized that these ends of public safety lay within the scope of state power envisioned by *Alger* and *Lucas*, the majority still found a taking had occurred, since there was insufficient evidence that there was a rough proportionality between the city's goals and the means used to achieve them.

In view of the fact that the municipality in the *Dolan* case was demanding that land be dedicated to its purposes without payment, the case is best understood as involving an uncompensated and hence unconstitutional taking. Indeed, the Court left no doubt in dictum that the city could prohibit the landowner from any construction that would actually increase the risk of flooding. Thus, the principle of *Alger* and *Lucas* upholding regulations for health, safety, and the prevention of nuisances appears to remain intact. But,

[101] 112 S.Ct. 2886 (1992).   [102] 114 Sup. Ct. 2309 (1994).

if government attempts to acquire title to land or if it engages in aesthetic regulations that substantially impair the value of property, the Court will declare
that a taking has occurred. The government's effort will thereupon be held
void as a regulation and will be upheld as an eminent domain condemnation
only if just compensation is paid.

2. Regulation for social justice

Suppose that the purpose of a regulatory scheme is the creation not of a beautiful, but of a just community. What then is the scope of government's regulatory power?

First, it is clear that government may not use its power to achieve otherwise illicit constitutional ends. It may not, for example, regulate to exclude
people of a particular race or ethnicity from a community,[103] nor may it
refuse to permit people living in traditional sorts of family relationships from
continuing to reside together.[104] Some cases have held that, in the absence of
a compelling state interest, government may not regulate land use by religious bodies at all,[105] although recent case law in the Supreme Court suggests the contrary.[106] Congress, however, has sought to restore the more
religion-protective standard in the Religious Freedom Restoration Act of
1993,[107] but its constitutionality has not yet been determined.

Inclusionary Zoning. Some state courts have ruled not only that government must not act to cause injustice, but also that it must act to promote justice. The leading case is *Southern Burlington County N.A.A.C.P.* v. *Township of
Mount Laurel*,[108] in which the Supreme Court of New Jersey held that most
municipalities have an affirmative, constitutional obligation to provide housing for miniorities and the poor. 'The basis for the constitutional obligation',
the Court declared, is that the state 'cannot favor rich over poor. It cannot legislatively set aside dilapidated housing in urban ghettos for the poor and
decent housing elsewhere for everyone else'.[109] The court thereupon called
upon the state legislature to make provision for low income housing in
municipalities throughout the state, and subsequently it sustained the statutory scheme which the legislature adopted.[110]

No other state has acted as strongly as New Jersey to provide low-income
housing, but others have taken at least some action to prevent localities from

---

[103] See *Village of Arlington Heights* v. *Metropolitan Housing Dev. Corp.*, 429 U.S. 252 (1977).
[104] See *Moore* v. *City of East Cleveland*, 431 U.S. 494 (1977).
[105] See *Westchester Reform Temple* v. *Brown*, 22 N.Y.2d 488, 239 N.E.2d 891 (1968).
[106] See *City of Seattle* v. *First Covenant Church of Seattle*, 499 U.S. 901 (1991); *Employment Division,
Department of Human Services* v. *Smith*, 494 U.S. 872 (1990).
[107] 107 Stat. 1488 (1993).   [108] 92 N.J. 158, 456 A.2d 390 (1983).
[109] *Ibid.*   [110] See *Hills Development Co.* v. *Township of Bernards*, 103 N.J. 1, 510 A.2d 621 (1986).

using their zoning power to exclude certain groups from their midst. Thus, Pennsylvania, for instance, has struck down exclusionary large-lot zoning[111] as well as prohibitions on the construction of multi-family apartment structures.[112]

So far the Supreme Court has not passed upon the constitutionality of statutes that regulate land use in order to achieve the legislature's vision of social justice. Read literally, *Lucas v. South Carolina Coastal Council*[113] would allow such legislation, just as it does aesthetic legislation, if its impact was merely to reduce but not totally wipe out property values. Legislation designed to achieve social justice is arguably more important than aesthetic legislation and more akin to health, safety, and nuisance regulation; for that reason, one might argue, it should be accorded the same broad scope as the latter sorts of regulation. With two new justices appointed to the Supreme Court since *Lucas*, replacing one justice in the majority and another in the dissent, it is difficult to predict how the Court will respond to such an argument.

Landlord and Tenant. The last three decades have witnessed an extraordinary transformation of the law of landlord and tenant in respect to residential leases. As late as the mid-1960s, the leasing of an estate for a specific term of years or months was viewed like any other transaction in land. The law's paradigm for the *leasehold* was the rental of argicultural land for a term of years, not the rental of urban apartments. Thus, no implied warranties of quality were attached to leaseholds, and renters entered into transactions under the principle of *caveat emptor*, or 'let the buyer beware'. In the absence of fraud or a tenant being forced to move out of an apartment, the tenant was obliged to continue paying rent even if living conditions in a dwelling were wholly unsatisfactory.

Changes started to occur in the late 1960s when judges began to see leaseholds of urban dwelling units through the lenses of a new paradigm, which taught that urban residential leases were equivalent to sales of consumer goods. On this basis, it was held appropriate to imply standard warranties from the law of sales into the rental of apartments. By the end of the decade, relying on analogies to the implied warranties of merchantability and fitness for intended purpose, judges had developed the implied warranty of habitability as an automatic element in leasehold transactions. By so implying the habitability warranty into residential leases, tenants obtained all the standard contractual remedies of damages, recission, and reformation.[114]

Other cases quickly expanded the implied warranty. In *Javins v. First National Realty Corp.*,[115] for example, the court made the warranty cotermi-

---

[111] See *Concord Township Appeal*, 439 Pa. 466, 268 A.2d 765 (1970).
[112] See *Girsh Appeal*, 437 Pa. 237, 263 A.2d 395 (1970).
[113] 112 S.Ct. 2886 (1992).
[114] See *Lemle v. Breeden*, 51 Haw. 426, 462 P.2d 470 (1969).
[115] 428 F.2d 1071 (D.C. Cir. 1970).

nous with the local housing code, with the result that any housing code violation by a landlord gave a tenant the full panoply of remedies for breach of contract. In *Edwards* v. *Habib*,[116] the same court upheld the right of tenants to report housing code violations to regulatory authorities and prohibited landlords from evicting tenants in retaliation for their reports. Meanwhile, other cases gave tenants the right to stop paying rent if the implied warranty of habitability was breached, with some cases basing the right on the common law[117] and others basing it on legislation.[118]

These various holdings came together in *Robinson* v. *Diamond Housing Corp.*,[119] which virtually obliterated the property rights of landlords in low cost rental housing. After the landlord had failed to remedy substantial housing code violations and the tenant had stopped paying rent, the landlord brought suit to evict her. She defended on the ground of her right to stop paying rent in the face of housing code violations, and the court upheld her defense. The landlord next tried to evict her on the ground that the code violations made her occupation of its building unlawful, but the court, following *Edwards*, held that a landlord could not evict a tenant for furnishing information to public authorities. Finally, the landlord tried to evict Mrs. Robinson in order to take her housing unit off the market, but the court ruled that this proceeding was poisoned by the two prior ones. It held that the landlord had to permit the tenant to continue occupying the unit without paying rent until the landlord either went out of business or made the required repairs.

Even though this decision had the effect of depriving the landlord of all economic return from its property, it nonetheless should pass constitutional muster under the *Lucas* analysis, since housing codes protect core health and safety interests rather than interests of an aesthetic nature. Precisely such an analysis led the New York Court of Appeals to sustain legislation permitting the City of New York to take over multiple dwelling units and devote rental income to repairs, without making any compensation to the owner.[120]

Another regulatory scheme that impinges enormously on the property rights of landlords is rent control. The rationale for rent control, however, is not the protection of tenants' health and safety, but rather the curing of market failures resulting from the shortage of rental housing and the consequent inequality of bargaining power of landlords and tenants—a rationale that also justifies other governmental interventions in the residential landlord-tenant relation. Since rent control only reduces but does not destroy the economic return of landlords, its constitutionality has been periodically upheld by the

[116] 397 F.2d 687 (D.C. Cir. 1968).
[117] See *Brown* v. *Southhall Realty Co.*, 237 A.2d 834 (D.C. Ct. App. 1968); *Marini* v. *Ireland*, 56 N.J. 130, 265 A.2d 526 (1970).
[118] See *Farrell* v. *Drew*, 19 N.Y.2d 486, 227 N.E.2d 824 (1967).   [119] 463 F.2d 853 (D.C. Cir. 1972).
[120] See *Matter of Department of Buildings of the City of New York*, 14 N.Y. 291, 200 N.E.2d 432 (1964).

Supreme Court, beginning as early as 1921,[121] even when the effect of rent control is to require some but not all landlords to subsidize particularly needy tenants.[122]

An important by-product of rent control is that it not only fixes rents, but also grants tenants and certain categories of people living with them, the right to occupy their apartments until the end of the rent control period. Indeed, specified individuals who have been living with a tenant by virtue of such legislation can even obtain a right to a new tenancy upon the death of the initial tenant. Surviving spouses are typical recipients of such a statutory right, but in New York the right has been extended to others, including homosexual partners, and its constitutionality has been upheld.[123]

Extensive as the power to regulate the property rights of landlords may be, the power is not unlimited. One significant limitation is that government may not compel an owner of private property to remain in business against its will. Thus, when New York City adopted a local ordinance prohibiting the demolition of single-room occupancy properties and obligating their owners to maintain them in habitable condition and lease them at controlled rents, the Court of Appeals in *Seawall Associates* v. *City of New York*[124] balked. While recognizing 'that government regulation—by definition—involves the adjustment of rights for the public good' in a fashion that '[o]ften . . . curtails some potential for the use or economic exploitation of private property', the court nonetheless found 'the constitutional guarantee against uncompensated takings is violated when the adjustment of rights for the public good becomes so disproportionate that it can be said that the governmental action is "forcing some people to bear public burdens which, in all fairness and justice, should be borne by the public as a whole".' Thus, the court concluded that the SRO ordinance ' "interfere[d] so drastically" with the SRO property owners' fundamental rights to possess and to exclude' that it amounted to an unconstitutional 'physical taking'.[125]

With the *Seawall* decision, the law of landlord and tenant looks quite similar to other bodies of law dealing with the regulation of private property. Except for *Seawall*, cases over the course of the past three decades have expanded the regulatory power of government to a vast extent. But government power is not unlimited, and when government transgresses its limits, courts will set its legislation aside.

Nor has government always legislated in the field of landlord and tenant to the full extent of its powers. In this regard, it is essential to observe that the

---

[121] See *Yee* v. *City of Escondido*, 112 S. Ct. 1522 (1992); *Bowles* v. *Willingham*, 321 U.S. 503 (1944); *Block* v. *Hirsch*, 256 U.S. 135 (1921).

[122] See *Pennell* v. *City of San Jose*, 485 U.S. 1 (1987).

[123] See *Braschi* v. *Stahl Associates*, 74 N.Y.2d 201, 543 N.E.2d 49 (1989).

[124] 74 N.Y.2d 92, 542 N.E.2d 1059 (1989).   [125] *Ibid.*

law treats residential and commercial leases quite differently. Normally no need exists to rectify inequalities in bargaining power between landlords and commercial tenants, who have adequate market power to protect themselves. For this reason, there is considerably less regulation of commercial than of residential leases, and courts are inclined to enforce the terms of commercial leases as the parties have written them.

V. The Ultimate Protection of Property Rights

Given the extensive power of governments in the United States to tax, condemn, and regulate property, the question arises why people continue to believe that private property remains sacred in America and still enjoys substantial immunity from government control. The answer is that the belief has much substance to it, as evidenced by three factors.

First and foremost is the protection that the political process affords to property rights. Americans in recent years have displayed outright hostility to taxation—hostility which not only keeps taxes low but also deprives government of the means to fund eminent domain takings and extensive regulatory programs. Moreover, Americans remain suspicious of regulatory programs, which they see as inefficient substitutes for the free market and as intrusive invasions of their right to make money and get rich. The result is that the political process rarely pursues policies that come close to the limits of its constitutional powers of taxation, eminent domain, and regulation and that, when legislatures act to the limits of their power, their legislation appears out of line with the public's expectations and sense of what is right, and may make those who support it politically vulnerable.

The second factor that makes protection of property rights real is that the courts, at least on occasion, do hold legislative interferences with property unconstitutional. Thus, there are limits on the constitutional power of government to tax, condemn, and regulate property. Although the limits are not entirely clear, they are nonetheless real.

It is precisely the lack of clarity of the limits, however, that constitutes the third factor facilitating the protection of property. When legislatures enact statutes near the limits of their constitutional power, the uncertainty of results makes litigation almost inevitable, and the inevitability of litigation, in turn, deters legislatures from even approaching the limits of their power. Here all three factors encouraging protection of property rights come into play: the political unpopularity of legislation interfering with property rights, the likelihood of litigation if legislation is passed, and the possibility that a court will ultimately strike the legislation down all combine to keep legislatures from pressing the limits of their power.

Thus, although property rights in America are not secured solely by law and the constitution, law and the constitution play their part. They give actors in the political process who oppose legislation that would impair property rights an added bargaining chip; they enable opponents to argue that legislators who vote to restrict property rights will suffer a heavy loss of popularity with the public without necessarily obtaining the regulatory or other objective they want. Law and politics thus combine to help guarantee that property is, indeed, scrupulously protected from public seizure and control.

12

CRIMINAL LAW, CRIMINAL PROCEDURE, AND CRIMINAL JUSTICE

JAMES B. JACOBS

I. Overview of the Systems

At the outset, American criminal law, criminal procedure, and criminal justice must be understood in terms of the division between the federal government and the states and the distribution of authority within each state among counties, cities and towns. Every state and the federal government has its own substantive criminal law (specifying crimes and defenses) and criminal procedure (specifying the stages of the criminal process from arrest through prosecution, sentencing, appeal, and release from prison). Congress passes federal criminal laws, which are enforced, prosecuted, adjudicated, and punished by federal law enforcement agencies, federal prosecutors, federal courts, federal prisons, and federal probation and parole systems. Each state legislature promulgates that state's criminal law which is enforced by state and county prosecutors, adjudicated in local and state-level courts, and punished in state prisons or local jails.

There are over twenty specialized federal law enforcement agencies, most

of which are in the Departments of Justice and Treasury. The most prominent federal law enforcement agencies are (in the Department of Justice) the
Federal Bureau of Investigation, the Drug Enforcement Administration, and
(in the Department of Treasury) the Bureau of Alcohol, Tobacco, and
Firearms, the Secret Service, and the Customs Service. These agencies have
their headquarters in Washington, D.C., and operate through field offices
around the United States (and in some cases, abroad).[1]

Federal prosecutors, called 'U.S. attorneys', are appointed by the President
for each of 94 judicial districts in the United States. They prosecute only federal crimes in federal courts. As presidential appointees, the U.S. attorneys
have a great deal of independence, but they are accountable to the U.S.
Attorney General, who heads the Department of Justice and who is a member of the President's cabinet. Within limits, each U.S. attorney establishes his
or her own prosecutorial priorities. Each U.S. attorney selects her own subordinates who hold the title of 'assistant U.S. attorney (AUSA)'. The majority
of AUSAs serve for less than 5 years and thereafter pursue careers in private
practice. A minority, however, become career prosecutors. (The U.S. attorneys handle most of the federal government's civil litigation as well as its
prosecutorial responsibilities.)

The Department of Justice's criminal division in Washington, D.C. provides assistance, expertise and some guidance and supervision to the U.S.
attorneys. The central office of the Department of Justice also includes special prosecutorial units with nationwide authority in such matters as organized crime, war crimes, anti-trust, and international drug trafficking; these
units usually work in co-operation with the U.S. attorneys.

Federal offenders who are sentenced to prison terms are incarcerated in
federal prisons administered by the Federal Bureau of Prisons, an agency
within the Department of Justice. These prisons are located throughout the
United States, but a defendant convicted in federal court may be incarcerated
in any federal prison; there is no right to incarceration near home. Less than
10 percent of all United States prisoners are incarcerated in federal prisons.[2]
Federal offenders who are sentenced to probation, and those who are
released on parole, are the responsibility of the Department of Probation and
Parole.

Most criminal justice activity is conducted under the auspices of state and
local governments.[3] Law enforcement at the state level is mostly decentral-

---

[1] For an overview of federal law enforcement see Norman Abrams and Sara S. Beale, *Federal Crime and
Its Enforcement* (West Publishing Co., 1993).

[2] The best source for criminal justice statistics is: *Sourcebook of Criminal Justice Statistics*, published annually by the National Institute of Justice, an agency within the Department of Justice.

[3] A good overview of the 'typical' American state-level criminal justice system is the President's
Commission on Crime & The Administration of Justice, *Challenge to a Free Society* (1968).

ized to the counties, cities and towns. The state police exercise authority over the major state highways and over unincorporated rural areas within the state. They often have other limited functions, including maintenance of criminal records. State attorneys general, unlike the U.S. Attorney General, usually have little or no prosecutorial authority, although they may be responsible for arguing criminal appeals and post-conviction petitions submitted to overturn convictions or set aside sentences.

Prosecution is a county-level function.[4] Most prosecutors, called 'district attorneys (DAs)', are elected. They have the authority to appoint their assistants (ADAs), but once in office, most of these subordinates are protected by civil service and thus cannot be fired (without good cause) when a new DA is elected. As with the AUSAs, most ADAs only serve for a few years and then leave for private law practice.

Each county has a jail which holds defendants awaiting trial as well as defendants convicted of minor crimes called 'misdemeanors' (crimes punishable by a maximum jail term of one year or less). Probation departments are usually organized at the county level as well. There are more than 20,000 independent police departments that belong to local government. Most of these departments, which serve small towns, are very small. However the big city police departments are huge. The New York City Police Department, the nation's largest, has approximately 38,000 officers. Defendants in state court who are convicted of felonies and sentenced to imprisonment, are incarcerated in the state-operated prison system, usually called the 'department of correction'. Parole is also a state responsibility.

II. Substantive Criminal Law

A. *State Substantive Laws*

While rooted in English common law, American substantive criminal law is statutory.[5] There are no common law crimes in the United States. In other words, the law of crimes is promulgated by the state legislatures (for each state) and by Congress (for the federal government). Most states, but not the federal government, have a comprehensive 'code' of substantive criminal law made up of general principles of criminal responsibility, laws defining the particular criminal offenses, and laws defining excuses and justifications.

---

[4] Thomas A. Mavet, Donald Casswell, Gordon P. MacDonald, *Fundamentals of Trial Technique* (Little, Brown, 1984).

[5] The standard treatise on American substantive criminal law is Wayne R. LaFave and Austin W. Scott, *Criminal Law*, 2nd ed. (West Publishing Co., 1986).

Criminal sentences, which are discussed later, are also prescribed by Congress and the state legislature.

The state legislatures can promulgate whatever criminal laws they like for their respective jurisdictions, subject only to federal and state constitutional limitations. Thus, for example, neither Congress nor a state legislature can pass a criminal law that punishes free speech because that would violate the First Amendment. The United States Constitution places a few other restrictions on the nature of substantive criminal law. For example, due process requires that criminal offenses be written, available and sufficiently definite so that the citizenry has notice of what conduct has been proscribed. The *ex post facto* clause (as against the federal government) and the due process clause (as against the states) prohibits applying criminal law to conduct that was innocent when it was performed. State constitutions may also impose certain additional restrictions on the legislature's authority to promulgate criminal offenses.

Two-thirds of the states have adopted in whole or in part the *Model Penal Code* (MPC) which was drafted in the 1950s and 1960s by the American Law Institute, a prominent law reform organization.[6] The MPC is the most influential work in American substantive criminal law. Its general principles cover:
(1)   the purposes of the criminal law;
(2)   rules governing interpretation of the code;
(3)   allocation of evidentiary burdens of proof; and
(4)   the requirement that punishment be proportional to the gravity of the offense.

The bulk of the MPC is devoted to general rules of criminal responsibility (e.g. culpability, voluntariness, causation, accomplice liability, mistake of fact, and mistake of law); specific definition of crimes (e.g. murder, assault, drug trafficking), and excuses and justifications (e.g. necessity, public duty, and duress).

One of the most deeply-rooted principles in American criminal law is that there can be no criminal responsibility without culpability or blameworthiness. Under the MPC, culpability, sometimes referred to as 'mens rea' or 'state of mind', is satisfied by a showing of intent, knowledge, recklessness, or negligence, all of which are carefully defined by the Code. Except in the case of minor offenses and some regulatory crimes, the MPC requires that there be a specified 'culpability' for every element of an offense (conduct, attendant circumstances, result).

Criminal codes set out the prohibitions that constitute the law of crimes—

---

[6] The Model Penal Code and Commentaries are available in a multi-volume work. See The American Law Institute, *Model Penal Code and Commentaries* (The American Law Institute, 1985).

offenses against the person (e.g. murder and rape); offenses against property (e.g. theft and arson); offenses against public order (e.g. disorderly conduct and rioting); offenses against the family (e.g. bigamy and incest); and offenses against public administration (e.g. bribery and perjury). In general, American criminal law 'grades' offenses into several different 'degrees' based upon culpability and extent of harm. For example, homicide is graded into two large categories, murder and manslaughter and, in many jurisdictions, those categories are subdivided into the specific offenses of first degree murder, second degree murder, voluntary manslaughter, and involuntary manslaughter. Similarly, most United States criminal codes contain several degrees of robbery, burglary, larceny, sale of drugs and so forth. The grade of offense affects either the sentence maximum, minimum, or both. Thus, the work of apportioning punishment is divided between the substantive law of crimes and sentencing law.

One of the most unusual features of American (as well as English) substantive criminal law is the law of conspiracy which, among other things, has been used in most 'political trials' and in most organized crime trials. The law of conspiracy makes it a crime to agree with another person to engage in criminal conduct.[7] Thus, conspiracy, like the law of attempts, punishes people for conduct that falls short of a completed offense. All that needs to be proved is that the defendant agreed to commit a criminal act in the future and that any member of the conspiracy took a step in furtherance of the plan. The agreement need not have been explicit or formal; nor is it required that all the co-conspirators agreed with one another as long as they agreed with one of the conspirators to further the goal of the conspiracy.

Under federal law, defendants can be convicted and punished for both the completed crime and for conspiracy to commit that crime. In addition, federal law makes each conspirator an accomplice in every offense committed by co-conspirators in furtherance of the conspiracy. Members of the same conspiracy can be joined at a single trial. Commentators have frequently criticized the law of conspiracy as amorphous and vague and for, in effect, allowing guilt by association.[8] The MPC's provision on conspiracy reins in the doctrine somewhat.

Although the federal system and a few states rely on common (court-made) law for justifications and excuses, most state criminal codes include statutorily defined excuses and justifications, including self defense; necessity; duress; public duty; involuntary intoxication, and insanity.[9] Self defense is the most often used defense, and it has generated a substantial jurispru-

---

[7] James Alexander Burke and Sanford H. Kadish, 'Conspiracy', in *Encyclopedia of Crime and Justice* (1983) 1:231.

[8] See Phillip Johnson, 'The Unnecessary Crime of Conspiracy', 61 *Calif. L. Rev.* 1137 (1973).

[9] See Paul H. Robinson, *Criminal Law Defenses* (West Publishing Co., 1984).

dence, comprised of judicial interpretations of statutes, concerning such questions as immediacy, proportionality, and the duty to retreat.

The most controversial defense is the insanity defense, although it is used only infrequently and rarely successfully.[10] Under the MPC, '[a] person is not responsible for criminal conduct if at the time of such conduct, as a result of mental disease or defect, he lacks substantial capacity either to appreciate the criminality of his conduct or to conform his conduct to the requirements of law'. A few states have abolished the insanity defense altogether. A number of other states have eliminated the 'lack of capacity to conform' prong of the insanity defense, thereby returning the law to the state that it was in when the English court first announced the insanity defense in the famous *McNaughten* case.[11]

Insanity has to be specially pled and, if successful, results in a 'not guilty by reason of insanity' verdict. (A few states have recently added a new plea and verdict—'guilty but mentally ill'—which results in a judgment of guilty and a recommendation for psychiatric treatment within the penal system.) Historically, a defendant found 'not guilty by reason of insanity' was committed indefinitely to a mental hospital. The defendant could remain longer in the mental institution than a prison sentence would have required had he been convicted of the offense. The Supreme Court, however, has sharply restricted the terms under which a person can now be held involuntarily in a mental institution.[12] The 'not guilty by reason of insanity' verdict in the case of John Hinckley, who attempted to assassinate President Ronald Reagan, led Congress to pass a federal insanity defense for the first time. (Previously each federal circuit court defined the appropriate insanity doctrine for that circuit.) It provides:

> It is an affirmative defense to a prosecution under any Federal statute that, at the time of the commission of the acts constituting the offense, the defendant, as a result of a severe mental disease or defect, was unable to appreciate the nature and quality or the wrongfulness of his acts. Mental disease or defect does not otherwise constitute a defense.[13]

At the heart of the jurisprudential debate about the insanity defense is a basic conflict between the meaning of insanity to the psychiatrist and its crim-

---

[10] See Norval Morris, *Madness and the Criminal Law* (The University of Chicago Press, 1982); Richard Bonnie, 'The Moral Basis of the Insanity Defense', 69 *Am. Bar Ass'n Journal* 194 (1983); Steven Morse, 'Excusing the Crazy', 58 *S. Cal. L. Rev.* 777 (1985).

[11] See *ibid.*

[12] See James W. Ellis, 'The Consequences of the Insanity Defense: Proposals to Reform Post-Acquittal Commitment Laws', 35 *Catholic University Law Review* 961 (1986). Also see Stanley S. Herr, *Legal Rights and Mental-Health Care* (Lexington Books, 1983).

[13] 18 U.S.C. §20(a).

inal law role in excusing a defendant from criminal responsibility. The various formulations of the insanity defense provide greater or lesser freedom for psychiatrists, testifying as expert witnesses for both sides, to explain their diagnosis of the defendant's mental condition at the time of the offense. Many lawyers and psychiatrists argue that the goal of the criminal justice system—to assess blame and mete out punishment—is fundamentally incompatible with the goal of the mental health system, which is to diagnose and treat. According to the critics, in criminal trials involving an insanity defense, the lawyers and the psychiatrists speak different languages. The problem is exacerbated by American criminal procedure which permits each side to call its own expert witnesses; the prosecution's psychiatrist tells the jury that the defendant was not insane at the time of the offense, and the defense's psychiatrist testifies that he was insane.

In recent years, a great deal of attention has been paid to a spate of so-called 'abuse excuses' like battered woman's syndrome, abused child syndrome, post traumatic stress disorder, and so forth.[14] These excuses have been put forward either (1) as a form of the insanity defense; (2) to establish a self defense rationale; or (3) to mitigate the degree of culpability through a general diminished capacity defense. The battered woman's defense has achieved a degree of success. Many courts permit expert testimony on this syndrome because of its relevance to the defendant's subjective belief in the necessity of defensive force.[15]

B. Federal Criminal Law

Which crimes are federal and which are state? There is no principled answer to this question. Indeed, criminal conduct cannot be sorted into these two baskets. Today, much serious anti-social conduct violates both federal and state criminal laws; if so, the perpetrator can be prosecuted by the federal government or by the relevant state (by one of its district attorneys). When a single act or course of conduct violates both federal and state criminal laws, it is even possible for both governments to prosecute because, under the 'dual sovereignty' doctrine, the double jeopardy bar does not apply to separate prosecutions by separate sovereigns (a dubious but nevertheless controlling rationale).

In theory, Congressional power is limited to the powers expressly enumerated in Section I of the Constitution. Offenses like counterfeiting United

---

[14] For an overview, see Stephen Morse, 'The "New Syndrome Excuse Syndrome" ', *Criminal Justice Ethics*, Winter/Spring 1995, pp. 3–15.

[15] See Holly Maguigan, 'Battered Women and Self-Defense: Myths and Misconceptions in Current Reform Proposals', 140 *U Pa. L. Rev.* 379 (1991).

States currency, illegally entering the United States, treason, and violation of constitutional and federal statutory rights are obviously within the federal government's core jurisdiction. But, utilizing its expansive powers under the commerce clause and other elastic provisions, Congress has passed federal criminal laws dealing with drug trafficking, firearms, kidnapping, racketeering, auto theft, fraud, and so forth. The Supreme Court has rarely found a federal criminal law unconstitutional, on the ground that Congress lacked authority to prohibit the conduct in question. However, in 1995 the Supreme Court did strike down a federal law making it a federal crime to carry a firearm in or near a school.[16] Although the majority opinion acknowledged that Congress's power under the commerce clause is vast, the power to regulate interstate commerce is primarily concerned with unconstitutional economic activities. The Court held that the Gun-Free School Zones Act, 'by its terms has nothing to do with "commerce" or any sort of economic enterprise, however broadly one might define those terms'.[17] This decision will have little if any effect on the threat of guns in and near schools since the states have the authority and the responsibility to deal with this problem.

The reach of the federal criminal law has grown inexorably throughout the twentieth century.[18] Today, federal criminal law can be used to prosecute many offenses that traditionally were regarded as a state responsibility. In practice, however, the significance of federal criminal law is greatly circumscribed by resource constraints. The FBI and other federal law enforcement agencies, as well as federal prosecutors, can investigate and prosecute only a small fraction of all the crimes that potentially fall within their purview.

One of the most powerful federal criminal laws is the Racketeer Influenced and Corrupt Organizations Act (RICO) which was passed in 1970.[19] Among other things, RICO makes it a crime to participate in the affairs of an enterprise through a pattern of racketeering activity. An enterprise can be a legal entity like a corporation, union, or government agency, or a wholly illegal entity like a street gang or organized crime syndicate. A pattern of racketeering activity is defined as the commission of any two (of a long list of) federal crimes or their state counterparts within a 10-year period. RICO is punishable by a 20-year maximum sentence, or for life if the violation is based on a predicate offense for which the maximum penalty is life imprisonment. RICO has made it possible to bring to trial whole organized crime syndicates that, even under expansive federal conspiracy law, could not previously have been tried together. Since the mid-1970s, RICO has been used to convict the

---

[16] *U.S.* v. *Lopez*, 115 S. Ct. 1624 (1995).
[17] *Ibid.* at 1630–1.
[18] See Norman Abrams and Sara S. Beale, *Federal Crime and Its Enforcement* (West Publishing Co., 1993).
[19] 18 U.S.C. §§ 1961–68 (1988).

leadership of practically every *cosa nostra* crime family in the United States.[20]

C. Federal and State Gun Control

The United States has the well-deserved reputation of being a violent society, at least in comparison with most other advanced industrial countries. Much of the violence is committed with handguns. In 1992, offenders armed with handguns committed over 900,000 violent crimes, accounting for the majority of all homicides and 13 percent of all crimes of violence.[21]

The lawful access of civilians to firearms is one of the best known and most controversial features of American society.[22] There are an estimated 200 million firearms in civilian hands, of which one-third are handguns. There is at least one firearm in approximately one half of all American households. Most of them never inflict harm, but are used for target shooting, hunting, and self defense. However, in the cities where crime rates are highest, firearms, especially handguns, exact a terrible human toll.

There is constant political conflict over what to do about the situation. Proponents of gun control blame the country's high rates of violent crime on the relatively free flow of firearms. Opponents of gun control stress that violence is perpetuated by criminals not firearms and that there would be even more violent crime if law-abiding citizens were disarmed and only criminals had guns. They further argue that individuals have a 'natural right' of self defense that should guarantee them the right of access to instruments necessary to protect themselves.[23]

The fierce political debate over gun control policy demonstrates the importance of constitutionalism and federalism, especially in the criminal justice context. The Second Amendment to the United States Constitution states:

> A well-regulated militia being necessary to the freedom of a free state, the right of the people to keep and bear arms shall not be abridged.

The meaning of this constitutional guarantee is constantly debated. Proponents of strong gun control laws emphasize the Amendment's preamble,

---

[20] For a study of RICO in action see James B. Jacobs, Christopher Panarella and Jay Worthington, *Busting the Mob: U.S. v. Cosa Nostra* (New York University Press, 1994).

[21] Jeffrey Roth, 'Firearms and Violence', National Institute of Justice, Research in Brief, February 1994.

[22] Franklin Zimring and Gordon Hawkins, *The Citizen's Guide to Gun Control*, (MacMillan Publishing Co. 1987).

[23] Gary Kleck, *Point Blank: Guns & Violence in America*, (Aldine DeGruyter, 1991).

arguing that it guarantees the people and the states an effective militia, today the national guard.[24] Gun control opponents (led by the National Rifle Association), emphasizing the second clause, argue that the Amendment was meant to guarantee every law-abiding individual the right to possess and carry a firearm.[25]

The Supreme Court has provided remarkably little assistance in interpreting the Second Amendment. There has only been one Supreme Court decision interpreting the Second Amendment in the twentieth century, and that over 50 years ago; it held that there is no constitutional right to possess a sawed-off shotgun.[26] But the Court also said, and gun control opponents emphasize, that the sawed-off shot gun was not the kind of personal weapon that the citizens needed or used at the time the Constitution was drafted. Thus, both sides claim support from the Supreme Court's decision.

In the nineteenth century, the Supreme Court held that the Second Amendment (and the rest of the Bill of Rights) applied only to federal governmental restrictions on the right to bear arms and, to this day, the Court has never held that the Second Amendment applies to state (as opposed to federal) infringement of gun owners' rights. Thus, the states are free to pass whatever gun control legislation they desire. However, the majority of state constitutions contain strong 'right to bear arms' provisions, protecting gun owners from at least certain types of gun controls.

Since no rights are absolute, even if the Second Amendment were held to guarantee the individual citizen's right to keep and bear arms, reasonable federal and state regulation would be permissible. Indeed, there already exists a substantial corpus of federal and state gun controls. The federal laws mostly aim at preventing the use of the mails to ship guns to persons other than federally licensed dealers. Unfortunately, from the controllers point of view, there are approximately 250,000 such dealers. There are no federal controls over secondary sales of firearms.

Federal law prohibits civilians from owning machine guns and 'destructive devices'. Recently, Congress also banned more than a dozen types of 'assault rifles'. And federal law has long made it a crime for an ex-felon to possess a firearm of any kind.

In late 1993 the federal Government enacted the 'Brady Law' requiring that, before a federally licensed dealer can sell a handgun, the dealer must notify the chief law enforcement officer in the jurisdiction of the impending sale, and give that official 5 days to determine whether the sale should be

---

[24] Andrew Herz, 'Gun Crazy: Constitutional False Consciousness and the Dereliction of Dialogic Responsibility', 75 B. U. L. Rev. 57 (1995).

[25] William van Alstyne, 'The 2nd Amendment and the Personal Right to Bear Arms', 43 *Duke L. J.* 1236 (1994).

[26] *United States* v. *Miller*, 307 U.S. 174 (1939).

stopped because the would-be purchaser is an ex-felon, drug user, mental defective, illegal alien, dishonorably discharged military person or an individual who has renounced United States citizenship.[27] The Brady Law requires that by 1998, the states implement a computerized 'instant background check' that would allow the firearms dealer or law enforcement officer to determine whether the would-be firearms purchaser falls into a prohibited class.[28]

Most gun control legislation in the United States is state law. However, the states are sharply divided on how they treat civilian ownership of firearms, especially handguns. Some states, especially in the West and South, where a rural 'gun culture' flourishes, provide for very liberal civilian access to firearms. In a few states (Florida, for example), citizens without a criminal record can easily obtain permits to carry concealed weapons.

At the other end of the spectrum, there are jurisdictions, especially cities, that practically outlaw all civilian gun ownership. In New York City, for example, there is a restrictive licensing system. A person can neither possess nor carry a handgun without a license that is issued by the police department. Such licenses are granted only for good cause and even then only after exhaustive investigation of the prospective licensee. They are notoriously difficult to obtain. By contrast, the black market in guns (as in drugs) is booming.

D. Juvenile Justice

Juvenile justice consists of a wholly separate criminal law and procedure.[29] In theory, this system of law and institutions, invented by progressive reformers at the turn of the twentieth century, operates 'in the best interest of the child'.[30] In practice, the system no longer reflects the idealism of its founders.

Juvenile justice is meted out in juvenile or family court, not the usual criminal court. The goal is not retribution or deterrence, but rehabilitation. The age that makes an offender eligible to be treated as a juvenile varies from below 16 to below 21 depending on the jurisdiction and, within a single jurisdiction, on the type of offense with which the offender is charged. Thus, there are statutes that permit (and in some cases mandate) treating a juvenile as an

---

[27] James B. Jacobs and Kimberly Potter, 'Keeping Guns Out of the Wrong Hands: The Brady Law and the Limits of Regulation', 86 *J. Cr. L. & Crim.* 101 (1995).

[28] 18 U.S.C. §922.

[29] See Frank W. Miller, Robert O. Dawson, George E. Dix and Raymond I. Parnas, *The Juvenile Justice Process* 3rd ed. (Foundation Press, 1985).

[30] The classic history is Anthony M. Platt, *The Child Saver: The Invention of Delinquency* (The University of Chicago Press, 1969).

adult if the offense is a homicide or other serious crime of violence. Generally, the juvenile justice system treats the accused more leniently than the adult system even though the former provides fewer procedural rights.

The juvenile who is arrested is brought to a juvenile detention center, separate from the adult jail and typically administered by a specialized agency of local or county government. In the majority of states, the juvenile has no right to bail. In these jurisdictions, the juvenile's pre-trial status depends solely upon a judge's determination of whether the juvenile should remain in custody pending trial to prevent flight or to protect the community from risk of the juvenile's commission of a future offense.

The juvenile defendant is not charged with a statutory offense, but with being 'delinquent'. However, he is entitled to counsel and to a presumption of innocence.[31] Juveniles have no right to trial by jury, but approximately one quarter of the states have enacted statutes providing for a jury trial option in juvenile cases. If the judge finds the juvenile defendant to be guilty (beyond a reasonable doubt), she may sentence the juvenile to probation or to an indefinite sentence in a juvenile correctional center or reformatory up to age 21, at which point the juvenile must be released. The juvenile may be released earlier at the discretion of the correctional authorities and subject to conditions which those authorities might impose.

The juvenile justice system has always stirred controversy. Many liberals have argued that juveniles should enjoy the same constitutional rights that apply to adults and have criticized the juvenile justice system for being paternalistic and authoritarian.[32] Conservatives have excoriated the leniency of the juvenile justice system, pointing out that young males under the age of 21 have the highest rates of offending. Despite the criticism, the juvenile justice system survives because there is no agreement on an alternative.

E. Rights of Victims

Historically, American criminal law ignored the victim.[33] To the extent that the victim had a role, it was limited to that of an ordinary witness. Indeed, rape victims had less standing than ordinary witnesses since their testimony had to be corroborated. In some jurisdictions, judges cautioned the juries

---

[31] The seminal Supreme Court decision on the rights of juvenile defendants is *In re Gault*, 387 U.S. 1 (1967). See also, *In re Winship* 397 U.S. 358 (1970).

[32] See Janet E. Ainsworth, 'Re-Imagining Childhood and Reconstructing the Legal Order: The Case for Abolishing Juvenile Court', 69 *N.C. L. Rev.* 1083 (1991); Barry C. Feld, 'Criminalizing the American Juvenile Court', in 17 *Crime and Justice: An Annual Review of Research* 197 (Michael Tonry ed., 1993).

[33] Abraham Goldstein, 'Defining the Role of the Victim in Criminal Prosecution', 52 *Miss. L. J.* 515 (1982).

that the rape victim's charges had to be considered skeptically or at least critically because of the propensity of some women to fabricate such charges. In the last two decades there have been major reforms in the law of rape, and these sexist rules have been eliminated. Indeed, many states have passed 'rape shield laws' which prevent the defense, with limited exceptions, from adducing testimony about the rape victim's prior sexual behavior.[34]

Today, an active crime victims' rights movement lobbies for legislation, communicates its views to prosecutors, and monitors court proceedings.[35] Many states have passed laws that permit the victim to make a 'victim's impact statement' at the sentencing stage of the proceedings. In some states there are also laws providing that restitution to the victim be the first claim on the convicted offender's funds, even before the criminal fine is paid. Some states give the victim a right to be informed about plea bargaining.

Finally, many jurisdictions have established 'victims services agencies' which provide counselling and material aid, and assist victims through each stage of the criminal justice process. Victims have always had a common law right of action in tort against the person who injured them, but this right has been of little practical use because so many criminals are indigent.

II. Criminal Procedure

Criminal procedure specifies:
(1) the rights of criminal suspects and defendants;
(2) the limitations on the conduct of police and other criminal justice personnel in investigating and prosecuting crime; and
(3) the rules and stages of the criminal process.

The sources of criminal procedure are constitutional, statutory, and judicial. Every state, and the federal jurisdiction, has its own criminal procedure rules.[36] The Federal Rules of Criminal Procedure are written by judicial advisory committees and promulgated by the Supreme Court, subject to amendment by Congress. The state criminal procedure rules are usually promulgated by the state legislatures. Of the twenty-three separate rights noted in the first eight amendments to the Constitution, twelve concern

[34] Vivian Berger, 'Man's Trials, Women's Tribulation: Rape Cases in the Courtroom', 77 *Colum. L. Rev.* 1 (1977); Susan Estrich, 'Rape', 95 *Yale L. J.* 1087 (1986); Stephen Schulhoffer, 'Taking Sexual Autonomy Seriously: Rape Law and Beyond', *Law and Philosophy* 35 (1992).

[35] See Diane Sank, David Kaplan, eds., *To Be A Victim: Encounters with Crime and Justice* (Plenum Press, 1991).

[36] See Wayne R. LaFave and Jerold H. Israel, *Criminal Procedure*, (West Publishing Co., 2nd ed. 1992).

criminal procedure. Before World War II, these rights were held only to protect the individual against the federal government. Since World War II, practically all of these rights have been 'incorporated' through the Fourteenth Amendment's due process clause and applied to state law enforcement as well. It is important to understand that, in constitutionalizing much of criminal procedure, the Supreme Court has set a 'floor', not a 'ceiling' on the accused's rights; the state legislatures and courts (interpreting state constitutions) are free to grant the criminal defendant more rights if they so wish. A number of states (e.g. New York) are substantially more protective of the rights of criminal suspects and criminal defendants than is the Supreme Court.

A. The Fourth and Fifth Amendments

In American legal parlance, 'criminal procedure' refers to the constitutional, statutory, and administrative limitations on police investigations—searches of persons, places and things, seizures, and interrogations—as well as to the formal steps of the criminal process. Both the Fourth and Fifth Amendments protect the citizenry, not just criminals and criminal suspects, from overreaching police activity. The Fourth Amendment provides that:

> The right of the people to be secure in their persons, houses, papers, and effects, against unreasonable searches and seizures, shall not be violated, and no Warrants shall issue, but upon probable cause, supported by Oath or affirmation, and particularly describing the place to be searched and the persons or things to be seized.

Interpretations of this single, albeit complex, sentence constitute an enormous and very difficult jurisprudence that cannot be summarized briefly.[37] The law reports are filled with fact-specific decisions on such questions as: what constitutes a search? a seizure? probable cause? When is a warrant necessary? When can a warrant be dispensed with? When must illegally seized evidence be suppressed?

For much of United States history, the Supreme Court gave primacy to the Fourth Amendment's second clause by:

(1) requiring the police to get a judicial warrant to carry out searches except in limited circumstances, and

(2) by requiring the police to have probable cause before conducting any kind of search or seizure and before effecting an arrest.

---

[37] The standard treatise on the Fourth Amendment is Wayne R. LaFave, *Search and Seizure: A Treatise on the Fourth Amendment*, (West Publishing Co., 2nd ed. 1987).

In other words, the probable cause standard contained in the second clause defined reasonableness for the purposes of the first clause. Thus, police searches and seizures had to be based upon probable cause, evidence that would justify a prudent person in believing that the suspect has committed, is committing, or is about to commit a crime, or that the property to be searched is connected to a crime and is located in the place to be searched.[38]

The purpose of a warrant is to put the judgment of 'a neutral and detached' magistrate between the police and the prospective targets of their searches, seizures, and arrests. In other words, the Fourth Amendment gives the courts certain supervisory authority over the police. It is for the courts to determine, before the fact if possible, when and how the police can search and seize, and when and whom they can arrest. The Constitution requires that the warrant application 'be supported by oath or affirmation, particularly describing the place to be searched, and the persons or things to be seized'. Having to fill out an application for a search warrant also forces the police to reflect on whether they have sufficient evidence to undertake a search. The written warrant application also constitutes a record that can later be reviewed on a motion by the defendant to suppress evidence on the ground that it was the result of an illegal search or seizure.

A search warrant is required for electronic surveillance.[39] The Omnibus Crime Control and Safe Streets Act of 1968,[40] a federal law, established a set of rules for electronic surveillance by federal, state, and local police. In order to conduct electronic surveillance (wire tapping or 'bugging'), the police must make a detailed application to a judicial officer.[41] If the request is granted, they will obtain authority to eavesdrop on the suspect's communications for a limited period of time, subject to various restrictions listed in the Act and, in some cases, to additional restrictions imposed by the judicial officer.

In the modern world plagued by street crime, much police activity involves quick reaction to crimes rather than a lengthy investigation culminating in a search. In the last two decades the Supreme Court has substantially relaxed both the warrant and probable cause requirements. The Court has promulgated a number of exceptions (e.g. exigent circumstances, plain view, consent of the party) to the warrant requirement. Perhaps most importantly, the Court has permitted the police to 'stop and frisk' suspects on mere suspicion rather than full-blown probable cause. Increasingly, the Court has shown a preference for the Fourth Amendment's first ('reasonableness') clause, sometimes treating the second ('warrant') clause as a subcategory of the more general requirement in the first clause.

---

[38] See *Brinegar* v. *U.S.*, 388 U.S. 160 (1949).
[39] See J. Carr, *The Law of Electronic Surveillance*, (C. Bowdman Co., 2nd ed. 1977).
[40] 18 U.S.C. §§2510–2520.   [41] 18 U.S.C. §§ 2510–2521.

The 'exclusionary rule' requires that evidence which has been obtained in violation of the Fourth Amendment be suppressed, that is, it may not be introduced into evidence as part of the prosecution's case against the accused. It may, however, be introduced to impeach the defendant. The exclusionary rule, imposed nationwide by the Supreme Court in 1961, has always been controversial.[42] The Supreme Court has taken the view that the exclusionary rule is the only way to make Fourth (and Fifth) Amendment rights meaningful.

The Fifth Amendment provides, among other things, that no person 'shall be compelled in any criminal case to be a witness against himself'. While the words of this amendment seem to be directed at the trial process, they also play a vital role in controlling police interrogations.[43] According to the famous decision in *Miranda v. Arizona*[44], once a person is placed in police custody, the police must tell him that:

(1)   he has a right to remain silent;
(2)   anything he says may be used against him;
(3)   he has a right to an attorney, and
(4)   if he cannot afford an attorney, one will be appointed for him free of charge.

Any confession obtained in violation of the *Miranda* rules must be suppressed, as must any other evidence obtained as a result of the tainted confession.

The '*Miranda* warnings' are a very controversial feature of constitutional criminal procedure.[45] Critics argue that the Supreme Court lacks authority to impose 'prophylactic rules' on the states and that *Miranda* unduly hampers law enforcement. Defenders argue that the Supreme Court has the power to prescribe rules to protect constitutional rights from infringement and that the *Miranda* warnings are not inconsistent with effective law enforcement.[46]

A substantial jurisprudence has developed around *Miranda* involving such questions as: when must the warnings be given? to whom? when must questioning cease? and when can questioning be reinitiated? This is a complex body of law that is quite fact-specific and not easily summarized, but some aspects are reasonably well established.

---

[42] See Report to the Attorney General, 'The Search and Seizure Exclusionary Rule, Feb. 26, 1986', reprinted in 22 *Univ. of Mich. J. of Law Reform* 573 (1989).

[43] See Joseph D. Grano, *Confessions, Truth and the Law* (The University of Michigan Press, 1993).

[44] 384 U.S. 436 (1966).

[45] See Report to the Attorney General, 'The Law of Pre-Trial Interrogation, Feb. 12, 1986', reprinted in 22 *Univ. of Mich. J. of Law Reform* 393 (1989).

[46] For further discussion of the Fourth and Fifth Amendments, see Chapter 5 on the Bill of Rights. Also see 'Interrogation and Confessions' in Wayne R. LaFave and Jerold H. Israel, *Criminal Procedure* (West Publishing Co., 1992) at 2907.

The police remain free to direct questions to people as long as they do not place them in 'custody' or cause them to feel unfree to move on. The police may also use informants or undercover agents to engage suspects in conversation without triggering the protections of the Fifth Amendment. As long as the warnings are given, *Miranda* does not prevent the police from interrogating or attempting to interrogate a suspect. But if the suspect indicates that he does not want to talk or that he wants an attorney, interrogation must cease immediately. Furthermore, the Fifth Amendment right to silence is a testimonial right. It does not protect the defendant from being compelled (by court order) to produce physical evidence (hair, urine, semen, fingerprints, etc.) which could be used to establish the defendant's guilt. Note also that the Fifth Amendment protects the individual from being compelled to serve as a witness against *himself*, but not against others. Moreover, if the Government is willing to grant the accused immunity, even his testimonial evidence can be compelled, but not used against him.

B. Pre-Trial

After an accused is arrested, he is 'booked' at the police station; his picture and fingerprints are taken and sent to the agency in charge of criminal records to verify identity and prior criminal record. The arrestee must be brought before a judge 'without unnecessary delay'. At this 'initial appearance', the judge will have a copy of the 'complaint', a written statement of the essential facts constituting the offense charged. On the basis of the complaint, the judge must determine whether there is probable cause to believe that an offense was committed and that the defendant committed it, in which case (if the complaint constitutes a felony) the accused is 'bound over' to answer formal charges, or (if the complaint constitutes a misdemeanor) the defendant may be asked to plead guilty or not guilty in the lower court.

1. Right to counsel

The right to counsel attaches at the point that the suspect becomes an accused, that is at the initiation of adversary judicial proceedings. If the accused is indigent, the judge assigns him a defense counsel at the first court appearance. *Gideon* v. *Wainwright* held that the government must appoint defense lawyers for indigents accused of felonies.[47] Later cases extended that ruling to cover all cases, felonies and misdemeanors, where the defendant

[47] 372 U.S. 335 (1963).

could be sent to jail or prison. In order to establish his indigency, the defendant must attest to his financial condition. In practice, judges rarely turn down or even question such petitions, and counsel is assigned in the large majority of cases.

There are two main schemes for providing lawyers to indigent criminal defendants. The first scheme is the public defender system. The public defender agency is a government-funded organization that operates like a large law firm with salaried staff attorneys, supervisors and support personnel. The public defender agency may represent all or some percentage of the indigent defendants in its jurisdiction. The second scheme is an 'appointed counsel' system whereby the judge appoints lawyers (from a list of those who wish to participate) to represent individual defendants for an hourly fee, paid by the Government, but only up to some maximum, usually between $1,000 and $2,000. Some jurisdictions use both systems. Both the public defender and the assigned counsel systems are typically plagued by inadequate resources to provide vigorous representation to the large numbers of indigent criminal defendants. Therefore, in many cases, representation is far from the ideal envisioned by the adversary system.

2. Bail and pre-trial detention

If the accused pleads not guilty, the judge must decide on pre-trial release and, if so, whether bail or other conditions ought to be imposed. Historically, the courts held that a defendant ought to be released unless he presented a risk of flight. Despite the presumption of innocence inferred from the due process clause and the right to be free from the imposition of 'excessive bail' (a right explicitly guaranteed by the Eighth Amendment), the Supreme Court has held that there is no right to pre-trial freedom or even to having bail set. (Bail is a sum of money paid by the defendant or someone on his behalf, to the court to guarantee that the defendant will appear at trial and not flee. If the defendant does flee, the bail is forfeited to the court.) If bail is set, it may not be excessive. But it has been held that an arrestee has no right to bail which he can afford to pay.[48] Typically, despite the supposed link between bail and assuring appearance at trial, judges set high bail for individuals arrested for serious offenses, undoubtedly because they are concerned about public safety, i.e. the defendant committing more crimes if released. These individuals remain in jail awaiting trial, sometimes for months, because they cannot meet the bail amount.[49]

A bail reform movement that began in the 1960s led most states to change

---

[48] See *Stack* v. *Boyle*, 342 U.S. 1 (1951).
[49] Wayne R. LaFave and Caleb Foote, 'Bail' in *Encyclopedia of Crime and Justice* (1983) 1:99.

their bail systems. The famous VERA Institute of Justice Bail Reform Project demonstrated that an accused's risk of flight could be reasonably well predicted by certain easily ascertainable information—prior record, family ties, employment, and so forth. The VERA researchers developed a risk assessment point score which was applied to each pre-trial detainee; utilizing the risk assessment score, the VERA staff made recommendations to the judge on release or detention. These recommendations proved to be reliable.[50] Over time, large cities throughout the United States implemented the VERA risk assessment procedure, and new 'pre-trial services agencies' emerged to conduct risk assessments and make recommendations on pre-trial release.

Many states abolished the bail bondsmen who had for generations flourished by charging criminal defendants a fee for posting their bonds. In the event that the defendants fled, the bondsman had extraordinary power to hunt them down and bring them back. Under the reforms, many defendants were given the opportunity to meet their bail by paying the court only 10 percent of the face amount. In addition, release 'on recognizance', i.e. no bail, just a promise to return, became more common. Finally, some jurisdictions adopted the practice of releasing defendants on a conditional pre-trial release supervised by the pre-trial services agency. In recent years, as researchers have demonstrated a strong link between drugs and crime, many defendants have been released on condition that they submit to regular drug testing (via urine analysis) that is conducted by the pre-trial services agencies. These reforms have resulted in the pre-trial release of a greater percentage of defendants, but in some jurisdictions the rate of failure to appear at trial exceeds 20 percent.[51]

In 1984, Congress passed the Bail Reform Act which establishes pre-trial release procedures for the federal system.[52] That Act requires that a defendant be released with the least restrictive conditions, consistent with the defendant's appearance at trial *and the safety of the community*. In theory, if the judge decides to grant bail, it should be in an amount that the defendant can afford to pay. In other words, under the Act, the purpose of bail is not to hold defendants in pre-trial custody, but to release them subject to a reasonable bond which is forfeitable if they fail to appear. The Act provides that if the judge determines, pursuant to a detention hearing, that no conditions will reasonably assure the defendant's appearance at trial or the safety of any person or the community, the defendant may be held in custody until trial. The Supreme Court upheld this controversial power of 'preventive detention'.[53]

---

[50] Charles Ares, Anne Rankin, and Herbert Sturz, 'The Manhattan Bail Project: An Interim Report on the Use of Pre-Trial Parole', 38 *NYU Law Rev.* 67–95 (1963).

[51] Bureau of Justice Statistics, 'Pretrial Release of Felony Defendants, 1992' (Nov. 1994) at 1.

[52] Bail Reform Act, 18 U.S.C. §§ 3142—3148.   [53] *U.S.* v. *Salerno*, 481 U.S. 739 (1987).

3. Formal accusation and the grand jury

If the arrestee is bound over for formal charging, the prosecutor's office must prepare formal charges. American prosecutors have extensive discretion over whether to charge, what to charge, and how many charges to bring. Most prosecutors' offices dismiss charges against a substantial percentage of arrestees at an early point in the process because
(1)   the arrestee's conduct did not constitute a crime;
(2)   while there is a crime, it is too insignificant to prosecute;
(3)   while there is a crime, it is not provable against this person at this point; or
(4)   while there is a crime, the prosecutor believes that 'pre-trial diversion' to a treatment or other program is the most appropriate disposition.

Until the trial begins, the prosecutor may voluntarily dismiss the charges against the accused without prejudice, and thus can bring new charges at a later point.

The Sixth Amendment provides that there shall be no criminal prosecution except upon indictment by a grand jury.[54] However, the Supreme Court has held that this is one of the few rights included in the Bill of Rights (the first ten amendments to the United States Constitution) that is not binding on the states. Thus, each state can decide for itself whether to utilize a grand jury to initiate the formal criminal proceeding. Where grand juries are used (about half the states), they are secret and hear only the prosecutor's evidence. In practice, the grand jury almost always follows the prosecutor's recommendations. Critics often charge that the grand jury no longer serves as an effective mechanism for screening out weak cases and ought to be replaced by a preliminary hearing before a judicial officer.

The grand jury can also serve as a powerful investigatory tool, one which has proven especially important in complex racketeering cases. While a prosecutor cannot compel a person to appear in his office and explain under oath what he or she knows about a criminal episode, the same end can be achieved by means of the grand jury. The grand jury has 'a right to every man's evidence'. Any person may be subpoenaed to appear before the grand jury and may be compelled to testify under oath; perjury can be prosecuted. Moreover, without even a showing of probable cause, the grand jury can order any person to produce relevant documents and papers.

In most states, a grand jury witness cannot have counsel present in the grand jury room. The witness can, however, invoke Fifth Amendment protection, and refuse to answer questions which could incriminate her in a

---

[54] See Sara S. Beale, *Grand Jury Law and Practice* (Callaghan, 1986).

crime. The prosecutor may, however, supplant the witness's Fifth Amendment right by an 'immunity' grant. The Supreme Court has held that a grand jury witness need only be given 'testimonial immunity'. This means that nothing said before the grand jury, nor any 'fruits' that grow out of what she said, can be used against that witness at any future criminal proceeding. Some states provide a broader 'transactional immunity', which prevents a future prosecution for any matter related to the subject of the witness's testimony, other than perjury before the grand jury.

The grand jury, usually comprised of twenty-three persons, may vote by simple majority to indict the accused for any number of offenses. The indictment is the formal accusatory instrument that transforms the accused into a 'defendant'. At his 'arraignment' the defendant is called upon to plead guilty or not guilty to each count in the indictment.

Those states, like California, that do not use a grand jury system initiate the formal criminal case with an 'information', a list of charges set out and formally sworn to by the prosecutor. (Even in the federal system, lesser offenses can be charged by informations as well as indictments.) In those states the defendant is entitled to a 'preliminary hearing' at which a judicial officer must find that there is probable cause to hold the defendant to answer the charges filed in the prosecutor's information. Sometimes, the defendant can use the preliminary hearing to discover testimony and evidence on which the prosecutor intends to rely.

The accused must be arraigned and formally charged within a short period of time. At arraignment, the judge reads the formal charges and asks the defendant to plead guilty, not guilty, or not guilty by reason of insanity to each one. Most states also permit a plea of *'nolo contendere'* (no contest) which, for practical purposes, is equivalent to a guilty plea. A plea of not guilty can subsequently be changed to a plea of guilty, and in some cases a plea of guilty can be withdrawn.

4. Pre-trial motions

The rules of criminal procedure provide that the defendant has a certain number of days to make pre-trial motions challenging the legal sufficiency of the indictment or information, or seeking the suppression of evidence. In addition, the defendant may move for limited 'discovery' of certain evidence held by the prosecutor. Under most states' rules, the defense, if it makes the request, has a right to a copy of any statements made by the accused, copies of scientific tests, and a list of the prosecution's witnesses. If requested, the prosecution has a constitutional duty to turn over to the defendant all exculpatory evidence in its files. The defense must likewise turn over to the prosecution scientific test results and, in some jurisdictions, witness lists. Moreover, in some jurisdictions the defendant must notify the prosecution in advance of its intent to rely on certain defenses such as an alibi or insanity.

The accused may obtain an evidentiary hearing on certain motions, for example to suppress tangible evidence on the ground that it was illegally seized; to suppress a confession on the ground that it was obtained in violation of *Miranda*; or to suppress identification testimony on the ground that the identification procedure employed by the police was improper. The hearing, at which witnesses testify and are cross-examined, looks like a trial, except that the judge, not the jury, decides the factual issues. In some cases, because the evidence is so vital, the outcome of a motion determines whether the defendant will be convicted (or, in some cases, even brought to trial). Denials of pre-trial motions are usually not appealable before trial, but if the defendant is convicted, they can be raised on appeal; even defendants who plead guilty can appeal unfavorable rulings on pre-trial motions.

5. Plea bargaining

The American practice of 'plea bargaining' is often misunderstood.[55] The practice might more accurately be referred to as a system of guilty plea 'discounts'.[56] More than 90 percent of convictions are obtained on pleas of guilty. For most defendants who plead guilty, there has been no 'bargaining'. Rather, the defendant has accepted an offer of a shorter sentence or a less serious charge (thereby protecting the defendant against the most severe punishment possible in his situation). Some jurisdictions (e.g. the federal system) have a tradition of charge 'bargaining', that is the prosecutor withdraws ('drops') the most serious charge, and the defendant pleads guilty to a lesser charge. In other jurisdictions (e.g. New York City) the judge explicitly offers sentencing discounts; for example, the defendant is promised a 3-year minimum, 5-year maximum prison term if he pleads guilty, but is told that he will face a 10–year minimum, 15-year maximum prison term if convicted at trial.

Some critics have (unsuccessfully) argued that the defendant's due process and trial rights are violated by what is, in effect, a threatened punishment for exercising constitutional rights. The majority of commentators and courts have preferred to see the system as granting a discount for guilty pleas, rather than as imposing a premium for exercising the right to trial.

The Supreme Court has explicitly upheld plea bargaining as long as certain

---

[55] See Graham Hughes, 'Pleas Without Bargains', 33 *Rut L. Rev.* 753 (1981).
[56] See Milton Heumann, *Plea Bargaining: The Experience of Prosecutors, Judges and Defense Attorneys* (University of Chicago Press, 1978).

procedures are followed.[57] If the defendant indicates a desire to plead guilty, the judge has to assure herself that the plea is knowing and voluntary and that it has a factual basis. Thus, she must be sure that the defendant understands the charges, knows that he is waiving his trial rights, and acknowledges guilt. While the acknowledgment of guilt is not a constitutional prerequisite to a plea of guilty, most jurisdictions require either such an acknowledgment or an explicit judicial finding that there is a factual basis to believe that the defendant is guilty. The Supreme Court has also held that, if a defendant is induced to plead guilty by prosecutorial promises of leniency, the prosecutor may not renege on the promise.[58]

The Federal Rules of Criminal Procedure require that the prosecutor reveal a plea agreement in open court. The prosecutor may agree to drop certain charges, not to oppose the defendant's sentencing argument, or to recommend a particular sentence. Federal prosecutors may not promise the defendant a particular sentence, since the federal courts treat sentencing as a judicial function. The judge has discretion to reject the agreement; if so, the defendant may withdraw the guilty plea. Neither the fact of the plea nor the content of the discussions leading up to the plea are admissible against the defendant in a subsequent trial. If the judge accepts the agreement, the defendant will obtain the deal promised him.

The prosecutor has two obvious reasons to support the plea bargaining system. The first is resources. The office is not staffed and supported with the expectation of going to trial on more than a fraction of the cases. The second is the certainty of obtaining a conviction that comes with the plea bargain. This is a valuable benefit to a prosecutor who is aware that, no matter how strong the case against the accused, there is always a risk, especially with jury trials, of an erroneous acquittal. In any event, the prosecutor may be conceding little, if anything, since the defendant may have been 'over-charged' (more counts than were realistically appropriate or likely to have been taken into account in sentencing) in the first place. The prosecutor may have only agreed to withdraw excess counts, leaving the defendant to plead guilty to a charge that adequately reflects the gravity of the offense.[59]

The judges support plea bargaining because of their over-burdened caseloads. The courts cannot possibly try more than a small fraction of the pending cases, especially in light of the unwieldy nature of the jury trial. Moreover, because judges are partially evaluated in terms of their ability to resolve their cases promptly, they have an incentive to encourage the parties to 'settle'.[60]

---

[57] See Rule 11, Federal Rules of Criminal Procedure, for the federal system's detailed procedures on the taking of a plea of guilty.

[58] *Santobello* v. *New York*, 404 U.S. 257 (1971).

[59] Albert Alschuler, 'The Prosecutor's Role in Plea Bargaining', 36 *U. Chi. L. Rev.* 153 (1989).

[60] Albert Alschuler, 'The Trial Judge's Role in Plea Bargaining, Part I', 76 *Colum. L. Rev.* 1059 (1976).

Both assigned and privately retained defense lawyers also have incentives to settle their cases. Like the prosecutors and judges, public defenders are chronically overburdened and short of staff. Their attorneys carry huge caseloads and cannot provide a well-prepared adversarial defense for more than a small fraction of the indigent defendants whom they represent. The court-appointed lawyers face a very limited maximum fee per case; thus, it is against their own financial interest to see a criminal case drag on. Likewise, the privately retained defense lawyers usually get paid in advance and keep the same (or nearly the same) fee whether or not their client goes to trial.[61]

Even though there is always a chance of acquittal at trial, the principal reason for the defendant to plead guilty is the perceived risk that he will receive a more severe punishment if convicted at trial. Indeed, the plea bargaining system is predicated upon the understanding that conviction after trial will result in a more severe sentence than conviction upon plea of guilty. Additional reasons for a defendant to plead guilty are: a plea will end the case right away while opting for trial may mean spending a year or more in pre-trial detention; pleading to some lesser charge might avoid forfeiture of his (or a relative's) home or car; pleading to a misdemeanor will avoid the collateral consequences of conviction of a felony (inability to get certain licenses, ineligibility for certain types of employment, loss of right to vote, and, for aliens, deportation) and will avoid laying the predicate for a habitual offender charge in the future; a guilty plea will spare one's family from watching and possibly having to participate as witnesses in a trial; and some defendants may wish to spare the victim the unpleasantness and indignity of being cross-examined (e.g. in domestic violence cases where the defendant knows the victim and may feel compassion for him or her or may hope for a future reconciliation).

In defense of plea bargaining, it is argued that, when the defendant is clearly guilty, it is wasteful for the criminal justice system to engage in an expensive fact-finding exercise. Supporters of plea bargaining further argue that the uncertainty of trial makes it rational for both sides to reach a compromise; after all, an innocent person bears a risk of being wrongfully convicted at trial and a guilty defendant may be wrongfully acquitted.

C. Trial

1. Speedy trial

Under the Sixth Amendment, the criminal defendant has a constitutional right to a speedy trial. There must not be 'undue delay' between arrest and

---

[61] Albert Alschuler, 'The Defense Attorney's Role in Plea Bargaining', 84 *Yale L. J.* 1179 (1975).

initiation of the adversarial process, between arrest and indictment, or between indictment and trial. The Supreme Court, however, has never specified a definite period of time which, if exceeded, violates this right. Every jurisdiction has a speedy trial law that establishes time constraints within which the prosecution and the courts must bring the defendant to trial. The federal Speedy Trial Act[62] provides that:

> In any case in which a plea of not guilty is entered, the trial of a defendant charged in an information or indictment with the commission of an offense shall commence within seventy days from the filing date . . .

The time constraints can be, and often are, waived or 'tolled' by the defendant who frequently needs more time to prepare his defense motions or desires to delay the case, perhaps hoping that witnesses will lose interest or that the evidence will grow stale. If the prosecution fails to abide by the time constraints, the judge must dismiss the case, either with or without prejudice to the charges being reinstated at a later date.[63]

2. Right to a jury trial

The Sixth Amendment guarantees a criminal defendant the right to a jury trial. However, like most rights, the jury trial right may be waived. The defendant may elect a 'bench' trial before a single judge (or, of course, the defendant may plead guilty, thereby waiving trial altogether). Most defendants have a better chance of acquittal by a jury. (One-fourth to one-third of jury trials end in acquittals.) But in some cases defendants may feel that a judge would be more likely to see the gaps in the prosecution case. In deciding whether to demand a jury trial, the defendant must also consider that a conviction after a bench trial is likely to be punished more leniently than a conviction after a jury trial.

If the defendant elects trial by jury, twelve jurors (plus several alternates) are empaneled in federal trials and in every state except two. The Supreme Court has held that, while the federal government is bound to a trial by twelve, the states are not.

'*Voir dire*', the manner in which the jury is chosen from among those summoned to court for jury service, has been much criticized. In the federal courts, the judge conducts most of the questioning to determine whether any prospective juror is so biased that she must be dismissed 'for cause'. In

---

[62] See 18 U.S.C. §§ 3161–3174.
[63] See Thomas W. Church and Milton Heumann, *Speedy Disposition: Monetary Incentives and Policy Reform in Criminal Courts* (State University of New York Press, 1992).

most state courts, the lawyers retain the authority to conduct the *voir dire*, and it takes much longer since they are looking for jurors likely to be biased in their favor. Each side may challenge a potential juror 'for cause' (bias); if the judge finds that the challenged juror is not likely to be impartial, that prospective juror must be dismissed. In addition, both sides have a number of 'peremptory challenges' which may be exercised to prevent a person from being seated as a juror; no reason need be given. However, neither the prosecutor nor the defense lawyer may dismiss a prospective juror for reasons of race, religion, or gender. Absent some significant pattern in the dismissals, it is not easy to determine the 'real reason' why a lawyer exercised a peremptory challenge.

The criticisms of the *voir dire* system include:

(1) it is time-consuming;
(2) it results in the dismissal of competent and unbiased jurors because the lawyers are searching for jurors biased in their favor;
(3) it is demeaning to the prospective jurors; and
(4) it permits the lawyers to influence the trial by arguing their cases surreptitiously in the context of juror *voir dire*.

In addition to the twelve jurors empaneled for trial, several alternate jurors are also chosen. The alternate jurors sit in court along with the twelve empaneled jurors and may be called upon to take the place of an empaneled juror who is dismissed or becomes ill during trial. In extraordinary (e.g. organized crime) cases, the identity of the jurors may be kept anonymous. In some jurisdictions, the jury is always sequestered during the deliberation period. Only very rarely are jurors 'sequestered' in a hotel throughout the entire trial so that they do not discuss the case with family or friends or read or view any media coverage of the case.

In the federal system and practically every state, the jury must reach a unanimous verdict, although this is not constitutionally compelled. A jury which cannot agree is called a 'hung jury'. In the event of a hung jury a 'mistrial' is declared, and the prosecution must decide whether to try the defendant again. There is no limit to how many times a defendant can be retried in order to achieve a unanimous verdict, but very few defendants are tried more than three times.

3. The right to a public trial

The defendant has a right to a 'public' trial. Thus, American courtrooms are open to the public, including journalists. Indeed, the Supreme Court has held that the defendant cannot waive the right to a public trial because the citizenry also shares this right; nor can a judge bar the press from writing about criminal trials. However, this does not mean that cameras (still, moving, or television) must be allowed in the court room. Some states, like California, have recently passed laws permitting live television coverage of criminal trials. Supporters argue that television coverage provides legal education for a vast public which otherwise might never see a criminal trial. Critics contend that the presence of television in the courtroom affects the conduct of the lawyers, judge, and jurors and alters the courtroom atmosphere. It remains to be seen whether the O.J. Simpson murder trial in Los Angeles, which was covered live by Court TV and other television stations in 1994–95, will convince more states and the federal courts to permit live television or whether it will convince California and the other 'tv states' to repeal their legislation.

4. The trial

The criminal trial is based upon demands and obligations imposed by the adversary system. The defense lawyer owes his client a duty of vigorous representation, whether or not he believes the defendant is guilty.[64] The prosecutor represents the state and the people, but also bears an ethical responsibility to act as a minister of justice.[65] Thus, the Justice Department's motto is, the 'United States wins its point whenever justice is done its citizens in the courts'.

There are technical rules governing the kinds of charges that can be joined together against the same defendant in a single trial. A defendant who was forced to defend at the same trial against a number of charges allegedly stemming from incidents which occurred in different places and at different times would be severely disadvantaged. The Federal Rules provide that:

> two or more offenses may be charged in the same indictment or information . . . if the offenses are of the same or similar character or are based on the same act or transaction or on two or more acts or transactions connected together or constituting parts of a common plan.

Similarly, two or more defendants cannot be tried together unless 'they are alleged to have participated in the same act or transaction or in the same series of acts or transactions constituting an offense or offenses'. Co-conspirators can always be joined together at the same trial. The RICO law, discussed in section II B above, provides even wider latitude for joining large numbers of criminal associates in the same trial.

---

[64] See Randy Hertz, Martin Guggenheim, and Anthony G. Amsterdam, *Trial Manual for Defense Attorneys in Juvenile Court* (The American Law Institute, 1991). See also American Bar Association, 'The Defense Function', in *Standards for Criminal Justice* (1980) 1: ch. 4.

[65] See American Bar Association, 'The Prosecution Function', in *Standards for Criminal Justice* (1980) 1: ch. 3.

The jury system requires a rather complex law of evidence because it is assumed that a lay jury is not able to properly weigh 'hearsay' (out-of-court statements not subject to cross-examination) and other types of evidence that may be unreliable or prejudicial. In addition, the rights of cross examination and due process prevent some kinds of hearsay statements from being introduced. Thus, the process of introducing testimony and documentary evidence at trial is punctuated with objections and arguments that can be very time-consuming.

The Constitution requires that, in order to find the defendant guilty, the fact-finder, whether jury or judge, must determine that the prosecution has proven every element of the offense beyond a reasonable doubt. This is the meaning of the oft-quoted maxim that the 'defendant is presumed innocent'. No facts necessary to establish the offense can be conclusively presumed against the defendant because that would deny the defendant's right to a trial by jury and to be considered innocent until proven guilty. The Constitution does not require disproof of all defenses beyond a reasonable doubt, but most jurisdictions do impose that onerous evidentiary burden on the prosecution. However, as previously noted (see section II A above), there has been some movement to reduce or even switch the burden of proof on the issue of insanity.

Both sides have the right to call their own witnesses and to subpoena witnesses who will not come to court voluntarily. The lawyers subject their own witnesses to direct examination and the other side's witnesses to cross-examination. The judge, but not the jurors, may ask the witnesses questions, but under the American adversary system, the lawyers ask practically all the questions and the judge acts as an impartial umpire. A witness may refuse on Fifth Amendment grounds to testify if she believes that the testimony could incriminate her. The prosecution may compel the witness to testify by granting immunity. The defense has no such power.

At the end of the prosecution's case, the defense routinely asks for a dismissal on the ground that the evidence is insufficient to establish a 'prima facie case'; that is, no reasonable jury could find guilt beyond a reasonable doubt. If the judge sustains the motion, the defendant is acquitted. If the judge rejects the motion, the defense proceeds to its case. The defendant has a right to testify as a witness as well as a right not to testify. If he chooses not to testify, no negative inference can be drawn by the trier of fact. If he does testify, he testifies as a sworn witness, and is subject to impeachment, cross-examination, and perjury charges for testifying falsely. Once the defendant elects to testify in his own behalf, he cannot invoke the Fifth Amendment privilege during cross-examination, but must answer every proper question put to him. If he refuses to answer or prevaricates, he can be held in contempt of court and punished by incarceration. Any witness, including the defendant, may be impeached by his previous record of felony and certain other convictions.[66] Therefore, a defendant with a serious criminal record may be dissuaded from testifying for fear that the jury will infer present guilt from previous convictions.

The defense need not, and often does not, put on a case; it may rest, hoping to have raised a reasonable doubt through its cross-examination of the prosecution's witnesses. After the defense rests, the prosecution may call rebuttal witnesses (and, in some jurisdictions, the defense has a similar opportunity). Finally, the lawyers make their closing arguments to the jury, each recapitulating the evidence in the light most favorable to its side. The defense will also renew its motion to dismiss the charges on the ground that the prosecution did not establish a prima facie case, giving the judge a last opportunity to acquit the defendant before submitting the case for the jury's deliberation.

If the judge rejects the defense motion to dismiss the charges, she then instructs the jury on the law, explaining what facts must be found beyond a reasonable doubt to sustain a verdict of guilty for each charge. The judge may not comment on the weight of the evidence nor try to evaluate the evidence in any way; nor, of course, can the judge 'direct a verdict' for the prosecution. In the federal system and practically all the states, the jury's decision must be unanimous; a lack of unanimity results in a hung jury and a possible retrial. The Supreme Court, however, has held that jury unanimity is not constitutionally required.

D. Post-Conviction

1. Sentencing

The legislatures, courts, probation departments, parole boards and, in some jurisdictions, sentencing commissions, all play a role in the sentencing process. In the first instance, criminal sentences, or at least the maximum permissible sentence for each offense, are prescribed by legislatures. State sentencing statutes vary considerably, and sometimes the same state has different types of sentencing statutes for different crimes. Throughout the twentieth century, most states had broad 'indeterminate' sentencing statutes which prescribe a minimum and maximum punishment for each offense; the sentencing judge may choose any sentence within the range.

---

[66] See Rule 609, Federal Rules of Evidence for the federal system's detailed treatment of using prior felony convictions to impeach a witness.

Sentence is imposed by the judge after a hearing at which the prosecutor and defense attorney argue for the sentence each thinks is appropriate. The defendant is usually given an opportunity to address the court prior to sentence. In some jurisdictions, the victim or the victim's representatives may address the court as well. The defense lawyer is likely to emphasize the defendant's remorse, family responsibilities, good job prospects and amenability to out-patient treatment in the community; the prosecution is likely to emphasize the defendant's prior criminal record, injuries to the victim and the victim's family, and the need to deter other would-be offenders. The judge will be advised by the probation department's report and recommendation based on its independent investigation of the defendant's background, prior criminal record, history of drug abuse, and so forth. The judge does not have to make formal factual findings and need not write an opinion explaining or justifying the sentence. As long as the sentence is within the statutory range, it cannot be appealed. Thus, historically, there has been very little common law jurisprudence on sentencing.

In the 1960s and 1970s there was a powerful political and intellectual attack on the 'rehabilitative ideal' which held that the purpose of imprisonment was rehabilitation and which gave judges wide discretion in sentencing and parole boards wide discretion over release from prison.[67] Liberals argued that it was oppressive and authoritarian to send or to keep offenders in prison for their own good. They argued that rehabilitation was a sham, and that, under the guise of benevolence, the state often exacted more punishment than the offender deserved. Moreover, they charged that vesting judges and parole boards with so much discretion produced grossly disparate sentences for similarly situated offenders, and that parole authorities sometimes used their discretion to punish political activists and prisoners who displeased the prison officials.[68]

Conservatives were happy to ally themselves with the attack on rehabilitation. They maintained that rehabilitation was a sham, because it did not work and that it resulted in releasing offenders (via parole) too soon, given the nature and gravity of their offenses and the threat they posed to the community. Both liberals and conservatives criticized the unfettered discretion of sentencing judges to impose sentences for any reason.

The result of the assault on the rehabilitative ideal was the launching of a sentencing reform movement that would take sentencing discretion away from judges and place it either in the hands of the legislature or in the hands of an administrative agency, usually referred to as a sentencing commission.

---

[67] See Francis A. Allen, *The Decline of the Rehabilitative Ideal: Penal Policy and Social Purpose* (Yale University Press, 1981).

[68] See Marvin E. Frankel, *Criminal Sentences: Law Without Order* (Hill and Wang, 1993).

A number of states passed 'determinative sentences' setting a specific sentence for each crime; others, as well as the federal government, passed mandatory minimum sentences for certain crimes, especially those involving illicit drugs. Minnesota was the first state to establish a sentencing commission which soon promulgated an elaborate sentencing grid specifying the sentence (within a very narrow range, e.g. 28–32 months) that an offender with each type of criminal background ought to receive for committing various grades of each offense.[69] In 1984, Congress passed a similar sentencing scheme for the federal system[70] requiring the issuance of Federal Sentencing Guidelines.[71] Judges may depart from the guidelines—either above or below—but only for certain limited reasons. Both the prosecution and the defendant can appeal the sentencing judge's decision to depart or not depart from the guidelines.

By the 1990s, the sentencing guidelines 'movement' seemed to have ground to a halt. In addition to the federal government and Minnesota, only a few states have implemented full-blown guideline regimes. Indeed, there now seems to be a counter-attack by advocates of individualized sentencing. Many federal judges argue that the guidelines do not allow them enough discretion to make appropriate distinctions in individual cases.

2. Sanctions

Probation is the most common sentence meted out by American criminal court judges. In effect, the defendant avoids prison as long as he keeps out of trouble and adheres to the rules, regulations, and reporting requirements of the probation department. The judge determines how long the probationary term will last; several years is not uncommon. The judge may also impose special conditions like participating in a treatment program, maintaining employment, or staying in school. The probation department decides how closely the offender ought to be monitored in terms of face to face contacts with probation officials and, increasingly, urine testing for illicit drug use. If the probation department determines that the probationer has violated the conditions of probation, it may seek to have the judge revoke probation and sentence the defendant to prison. So as to avoid the necessity of another sentencing hearing in the event of a probation violation, judges often set the sentence prior to allowing probation.

Imprisonment is a very widely used sentence; on any given day in the mid-1990s there were approximately 1.3 million persons in United States

---

[69] See Andrew von Hirsch, Kay A. Knapp, and Michael Tonry, *The Sentencing Commission and Its Guidelines* (Northeastern University Press, 1987).

[70] 18 U.S.C. §§ 991–998.   [71] *Ibid.*

prisons and jails. Each state has its own prison system, as does the federal government. The prison department, usually called the department of corrections, classifies (according to dangerousness, escape risk, age, and so forth) offenders placed in its charge and assigns them to an appropriate maximum-, medium-, or minimum-security penal institution. Likewise, the department has the authority to transfer the prisoner from one institution to another and to assign the prisoner to work assignments and educational and treatment programs. Prison officials also have the authority to punish prisoners for breaches of the prison rules; punishments include loss of privileges, confinement in 'punitive segregation', and loss of 'good time' (known elsewhere as remission or sentence reduction for good behavior in prison).

Prisoners do not forfeit all their constitutional rights. Since the 1960s, a prisoners' rights movement led by civil rights attorneys has caused the courts to become significantly involved in monitoring prison operations and conditions. Prisoners' rights lawyers have brought many successful lawsuits establishing at least limited rights of religion; free speech; access to reading material; correspondence; visitation; free access to the courts; and due process in the application of discipline. Perhaps even more importantly, civil rights lawyers have succeeded in practically every state in large-scale class action lawsuits alleging that the totality of prison conditions violates the Eighth Amendment's cruel and unusual punishment clause. Consequently, in a majority of states, the largest prison or the whole prison system operates under a judicially-supervised order to bring conditions and operations (including medical care, living standards, sanitation, food, and recreation) up to the constitutionally-mandated threshold.[72]

Forfeiture of property used in, related to, or constituting the proceeds of crime, has increased dramatically as a criminal sentence in recent years, especially in drug and organized crime cases. Typically, forfeiture laws provide that the judge may order, as part of the criminal sentence, that the defendant forfeit the instrumentality of the crime (including car, boat, plane, and even house) and/or the proceeds of his criminal activity (business, bank accounts, securities, etc.). RICO requires forfeiture of any interest that the defendant has acquired or maintained in violation of that law. In order to influence law enforcement priorities and to help bolster the budgets of beleaguered law enforcement agencies, many jurisdictions provide that the forfeited property may be kept and utilized by the law enforcement agency responsible for the investigation leading to the conviction.

Fines are less frequently imposed by United States courts than by courts in many other countries. When they are imposed, it is usually in addition to

---

[72] See James B. Jacobs, 'The Prisoners Rights Movement and Its Impacts', in J. Jacobs, *New Perspectives on Prisons and Imprisonment* (Cornell University Press, 1983).

other sanctions. Historically, the size of fines has been low, indeed, much lower than the amount a criminal lawyer would charge a fee-paying defendant. Recently, however, maximum fines have increased dramatically. When fines are imposed, the Supreme Court has held that a defendant cannot be imprisoned for failure to pay the fine, unless the failure is willful.

The prison-crowding crises, class action lawsuits, and spiralling costs occasioned by the four-fold increase in the number of prisoners over the last 20 years have stimulated a great deal of interest, for less serious offenses, in 'intermediate sanctions',[73] such as fines; restitution; community service; house detention with electronic monitoring; work programs; and 'boot camps' (prisons with a daily regime patterned after military basic training). Proponents argue that offenders should be sentenced to the least restrictive alternative given the offender's dangerousness and the seriousness of the offense. Intermediate sanctions sometimes also receive support from those who consider them an alternative to suspended sentences or to probationary sentences which provide very little monitoring and few conditions. Clearly, intermediate sanctions are being used more widely and will grow even more popular in the future, but they currently constitute only a small percentage of criminal sentences.

3. Capital punishment

Capital punishment seemed to be withering away in the United States in the 1960s.[74] Then, in 1972, the Supreme Court held in *Furman* v. *Georgia*, by a vote of 5–4 (but without a majority rationale), that all state death penalty statutes were unconstitutional.[75] Two justices found that the death penalty, under all circumstances, constituted cruel and unusual punishment in violation of the Eighth Amendment. Three justices found procedural problems with the statutes before the court. In their view, the capital punishment statutes left too much discretion in the hands of the jury and therefore made the imposition of the death penalty arbitrary and capricious.

In reaction to *Furman*, about two-thirds of the states and the federal government passed new statutes attempting to overcome the *Furman* procedural objections. Over the next 20 years, most of these statutes have been upheld, although the Supreme Court has limited capital sentencing in a number of ways.[76] While death penalty statutes cannot vest the jury with too much discretion, neither can they be mandatory or automatic; the jury has to have

---

[73] See Norval Morris and Michael Tonry, *Between Prison and Probation: Intermediate Punishment in a Rational Sentencing System* (Oxford University Press, 1990).

[74] See Franklin Zimring and Gordon Hawkins, *Capital Punishment and the American Agenda*, (Cambridge University Press, 1986).

[75] 408 U.S. 238 (1972).   [76] See *Gregg* v. *Georgia*, 428 U.S. 153 (1976).

discretion to show mercy. The death penalty can only be imposed for the taking of life. It can only be imposed after a separate penalty phase following the determination of guilt, and the defendant must be allowed to put all mitigating circumstances and factors before the jury. A few states allow the judge to override the jury's judgment on whether the death sentence should be imposed.[77]

Each year, hundreds of death sentences are imposed, but only about 20 executions take place. The number of death row inmates exceeds 3,000 as of mid-1995. Because offenders who have been sentenced to death have many avenues of appeal (direct appeals in state court and *habeas corpus* in federal court) they are often able to keep their case under review for many years. Many death sentences are eventually reversed or commuted. The majority of executions take place in just a few southern states: Florida, Georgia, Louisiana, and Texas. Some states, like Pennsylvania, have sentenced hundreds of people to death since the late 1970s, but have not carried out a single execution. California leads the nation in the number of inmates on death row, but as of fall 1995, has carried out only two executions. The federal government has not carried out an execution since 1963, but in its 1994 omnibus crime bill Congress specified dozens of new crimes which carry the death penalty.

4. Appeal and post-conviction remedies

The Constitution does not guarantee a convicted offender a right of appeal, but every jurisdiction allows at least one appeal as of right, and many states have two levels of appellate courts and two levels of as-of-right appeals. For some second level appeals, the court has the discretion to hear only those cases that it chooses. Because of the guarantee against double jeopardy, the prosecution may not appeal a not guilty verdict. Thus, an acquittal stands, even if it was based upon an egregious mistake by the judge in interpreting the law or upon an incomprehensible factual finding by the judge or jury.

Counsel is provided free of charge, at least for the first appeal.[78] Consequently, practically every defendant appeals his conviction, even if he has pled guilty. Most appeals allege prejudicial errors in the pre-trial and trial proceedings, and misapplication of law. Many trials contain errors of some kind, but not all errors require that the conviction be reversed. If the appeals court deems the error to be 'harmless' (i.e. it is clear beyond a reasonable

---

[77] See Robert A. Burt, 'Disorder in the Court: The Death Penalty and the Constitution', 85 *Mich. L. Rev.* 1741 (1987).

[78] See David Wasserman, *A Sword For the Convicted: Representing Indigent Defendants on Appeal* (Greenwood Press, 1990).

doubt that it did not affect the verdict), the conviction will not be overturned. The defendant may also appeal on the ground that the judge's or jury's verdict was plainly incorrect. The standard that the appellate courts apply is whether a rational jury could have convicted on the evidence before it. This is a difficult standard for the defendant to meet. Many defendants appeal on the ground that they received inadequate assistance of counsel in violation of their Sixth Amendment right to effective assistance of counsel. The Supreme Court has promulgated a tough standard for making out a constitutional violation on this ground.[79]

After a state offender's state court appeals have been exhausted, he may file a *habeas corpus* petition in federal district (trial level) court alleging that he is being held in state custody in violation of his federally guaranteed statutory or constitutional rights. The right of *habeas corpus* is guaranteed by the Constitution and implemented by a federal statute.[80] *Habeas corpus* authorizes the federal district court to review the same constitutional questions that the state appellate courts have already heard and rejected. If the federal judge finds a constitutional violation, she may order the offender to be freed. Whether the federal district judge rules in favor of the offender or not, the ruling may be appealed by either side to a federal appeals court and ultimately to the Supreme Court, which has discretion as to whether to hear the case. In some limited circumstances, an offender who was unsuccessful in the first *habeas corpus* proceeding may bring additional *habeas corpus* petitions alleging other constitutional violations, thus initiating the whole process anew. The existence of the *habeas corpus* right accounts, to a large extent, for the long period of time between the imposition of a death sentence and the actual execution. Both Congress and the Supreme Court have been attempting (over powerful civil liberties objections) to limit the ability of death-sentenced offenders to bring *habeas corpus* petitions.

5. Parole, remission and commutation

Traditionally, parole boards have played the major role in releasing offenders from prisons. Each state has its own parole board whose members are appointed by the governor. The parole board is usually one component of a large parole agency that supplies post-prison supervision to offenders released on parole. The point at which a prisoner is eligible for parole is a matter of state law, and there is considerable variation among the states. In a sentencing system in which the judge only specifies a maximum sentence,

---

[79] *Strickland v. Washington*, 466 U.S. 668 (1984).

[80] 28 U.S.C. §§ 2241–2254. See James S. Liebman and Randy Hertz, *Federal Habeas Corpus Practice and Procedure* (Michie, 2nd ed. 1994).

the prisoner might, for example, become eligible for parole after serving one-third of the sentence. The parole board, which typically meets in panels, holds brief interviews with the prospective parolees at the prison. The panel is generally interested in the prisoner's adjustment within the prison, but it will invariably consider the facts of the crime and the prisoner's previous record. If parole is not granted, the prisoner remains in prison and the matter of his parole will be reviewed again, usually annually or biannually. Some parole agencies have attempted to develop formal guidelines to achieve uniformity in parole decisions.

If the defendant is released, he remains on parole until the whole judicially-imposed sentence (minus good time) is served. The parole agency, like the probation department, may impose various conditions—treatment, urine testing for illicit drug use, schooling, avoiding certain people and places, etc. If the parole agency determines that the parolee has violated the terms of parole, an administrative hearing will be held by another subdivision of the parole agency, to determine whether parole should be terminated.

The prison authorities in each state have, according to state statutes, authority to award prisoners a certain amount of time off their sentences for good behavior (thus, the term 'good time').[81] This remission is usually about one-third of the prisoner's sentence although there is considerable variation from state to state. In practice, time off for good behavior is actually administered as time added on for bad behavior! In other words, the prisoner is presumptively granted all the good time to which he is entitled and only encounters the 'good time system' when the prison officials charge him with violating an internal prison rule for which good time can be taken away. The prisoner is entitled to due process in the imposition of such punishment. Good time that is forfeited can also be restored.

Good time always applies to the maximum sentence. For example, a 10 year sentence may be served (if all remission is awarded) in say, 6⅔ years. However, some states also apply good time to the minimum sentence, which has the effect of accelerating the prisoner's parole eligibility.

The conjoint operation of parole and remission means that on average prisoners serve less than 50 percent of their prison sentence, sometimes considerably less. Recently, in a period of rising concern about law and order, Congress has passed a 'truth in sentencing' law that would deny states certain discretionary federal funds for criminal justice unless the state makes its prisoners serve, on average, at least 85 percent of their judicially-imposed sentences. It remains to be seen whether and, if so, how the states will meet this requirement.

---

[81] See James B. Jacobs, 'Sentencing by Prison Personnel: Good Time', 30 *UCLA L. Rev.* 217 (1982).

One other development that merits attention is the increasing popularity of sentences of life imprisonment without possibility of parole. Many states now provide life sentences that permit neither parole nor remission. The notorious 'three strikes and you're out' legislation that has emerged in the 1990s provides for life imprisonment without parole for offenders who commit a third felony. What counts as 'three (felony) strikes' varies from jurisdiction to jurisdiction.

Finally, the governor of each state has the power to pardon or commute the sentences of offenders in that state. The President of the United States has similar authority for federal offenders. Frequently, the law provides for the appointment of a pardon board which sifts through petitions, conducts investigations, and makes affirmative recommendations to the executive. Governors, especially in the most prolific death sentencing states, are frequently called upon to commute a death sentence and are always the last hope before the execution takes place. Unlike many countries, general amnesties are not a part of American law or tradition.

13

CORPORATIONS AND OTHER BUSINESS ORGANIZATIONS

STANLEY SIEGEL

I. Forms of Business Association

This chapter will provide a brief overview of the forms of business association in the United States, including a discussion of the laws that govern their structure and the procedures to be followed for their organization. Detailed discussion will be limited to selected topics involving organization, operation, and reorganization of business corporations.[1]

---

[1] Few respectable texts on United States corporate law are shorter than 500 pages. This brief summary must, therefore, omit some subjects altogether and abbreviate the discussion of the remainder. Moreover, because American corporation law is, in fact, the law of 50 states (and the District of Columbia) as well as federal law, nearly every statement in this chapter is subject to variation—or even contradiction—by a statute, regulation, or rule in one or more of these jurisdictions.

A. Introduction

Business enterprises in the United States are organized principally in one of four forms: the *proprietorship*; the *general partnership*; the *limited partnership*; and the *corporation*. A fifth form, used originally in the nineteenth century, which may become increasingly important in the forthcoming years, is the *limited liability company*. The laws that govern establishment of each of these enterprises and the relationships among their participants are, with two important exceptions,[2] state laws. The choice of the form of the organization, as well as the choice of the state law under which it will be established, is made by the original organizers.

The largest business enterprises in the United States are, with few exceptions, corporations, most—though not all—of which are owned by large numbers of stockholders. However, for economic and organizational reasons, the proprietorship and partnership forms (as well as the limited liability company) remain very important. Probably the most significant reason for the continued use of partnerships is a particular feature of United States tax law: while the distributed income (dividends) of corporations is taxed twice (once at the corporate level, and once again at the stockholder level), the distributed income of partnerships is taxed only once.[3] Avoidance of this multiple tax burden is the principal reason why some forms of business, such as real estate enterprises (e.g. office buildings, rental apartment complexes, and shopping centers), motion picture production ventures, and natural resource exploration projects, are widely organized as limited partnerships.[4] Professional service organizations, including doctors, dentists, accountants, and lawyers are also often organized as partnerships, although a substantial number of professionals have established 'professional corporations' as a means of obtaining certain tax benefits and providing a degree of limitation of liability.

Start-up companies are often formed as proprietorships or general partnerships, and while many remain in those forms, those that become sizeable are often eventually incorporated. The various forms of business enterprise may be used as components of a larger structure, in which a corporation,

---

[2] The most important laws and regulations affecting the public issuance and trading of securities are federal, including the Securities Act of 1933, as amended, and the Securities Exchange Act of 1934, as amended. In addition, most states have enacted state securities laws (known generally as 'Blue Sky Laws') regulating the issuance of securities. These laws are the subject of Chapter 22.

Business associations are also heavily affected by income tax laws, the most important of which is the federal income tax. This subject is considered in Chapter 23.

[3] In fact, the income of partnerships is taxed directly to the partners *whether or not* it is distributed. However, the tax is imposed only once: when previously taxed income is ultimately distributed by the partnership, its partners do not pay any tax on the distribution. See Chapter 23, section VI.

[4] The limited partnership is used to allow limitation of liability of the passive investors. The general partner of these limited partnerships is often a corporation.

partnership, or limited liability company may be a parent, a subsidiary, or an intermediate holding company.

B. *The Applicable Laws*

Since an enterprise may be formed under the laws of any state irrespective of where it actually does business, the organizers can choose the laws under which it will be established and governed. In general, the enterprise will be recognized in all states, and the laws governing the relationships among its owners and managers will be the laws of the state of its organization.[5]

The basic law of partnerships, the Uniform Partnership Act, (the UPA) was drafted in 1914 and was adopted essentially verbatim by all but one state.[6] A revised form of the UPA was approved in 1992 (RUPA), and it is likely to be adopted by most of the states in the near future. A similar situation prevails with respect to the law of limited partnerships: the Uniform Limited Partnership Act of 1918 (the ULPA) was adopted by all the states, and the Revised (1976) and amended (1985) Uniform Limited Partnership Act (the RULPA) has replaced that law in all but a handful of states.[7] The general adoption of these statutes means that, with the exception of variations in state decisional law, the law of partnerships is approximately the same from state to state, and there is usually neither advantage nor disadvantage in establishing a general or limited partnership under the laws of any particular state.

The situation is very different with respect to corporations, as to which the governing statutes have from the outset varied substantially from state to state. Part or all of the Model Business Corporation Act or the Revised Model Business Corporation Act,[8] often with substantial variations, has been adopted by more than half the states, but many of the commercially most important jurisdictions—such as Delaware, New York, New Jersey, and

---

[5] The legal status of corporations and partnerships formed in other states is explicitly recognized by the statutes of each of the states. This is not the case with respect to limited liability companies, which are not recognized under the laws of some states.

The state corporation laws, with few exceptions, explicitly apply the law of the state of organization to internal affairs of corporations organized out of the state.

[6] The Uniform Laws are drafted under the direction of, and approved by, the National Conference of Commissioners on Uniform State Laws. They are then recommended for adoption by the state legislatures, which may adopt them in whole or in part, with or without variations.

[7] The RULPA is, however, less 'uniform' in its actual enactment than the original ULPA, since a number of states (like California) adopted the substance of the new law but modified its wording.

[8] The Model Business Corporation Act was drafted and has been periodically amended and revised under the auspices of the Committee of Corporate Laws of the Corporations Section of the American Bar Association. Although it does not have the status of a uniform law (such as the UPA and the RULPA), it has been used as a model in the drafting of many state corporation laws. The most recent version is entitled the Revised Model Business Corporation Act.

California—have enacted clearly different statutes. Historically, New Jersey, New York, and finally Delaware emerged as jurisdictions of choice for new incorporation, originally because of the increased permissiveness of their statutes. Delaware remains the state of incorporation of most corporations whose stock is listed on the New York Stock Exchange, as well as many other corporations, large and small. The reasons for this dominance are several, including the responsiveness of the Delaware legislature to changes in corporate problems and practice, the extensive body of interpretive case-law available to guide Delaware corporations, and the expertise and efficiency of the Delaware courts in deciding corporate cases.[9]

Although many of the differences among state corporation laws are merely of wording or procedure, some of the differences are importantly substantive. They concern, among other matters, voting procedures; required majorities; liabilities of directors and officers; and procedures for major corporate changes. The discussion in this chapter will be based on the latest version of the Revised Model Business Corporation Act, but important differences will be noted by citation to selected state statutes.[10]

II. The Process of Formation

A. *Proprietorships and Licensing Requirements*

A proprietorship, as such, requires no formation and is not recognized as a separate legal entity for such purposes as liability, property ownership and conveyancing, and taxation. And while all state laws require that the proprietor make a filing of any assumed business name that he or she may use, there is no general requirement that the business itself make a filing, nor is there a requirement that it obtain a license to do business or appoint an agent.[11] For tax purposes, the proprietorship does not file a separate tax return, but instead reports its net income as a component of the proprietor's personal taxable income.

---

[9] Delaware benefits from being the state of incorporation in a variety of ways, including revenues from filing fees and legal and administrative business generated by Delaware corporations. There is, however, relatively little *income tax* advantage to the state of incorporation, since income is generally allocated among the states in which the corporation does business, usually based on a three-part formula including the factors of payroll, assets, and sales.

[10] Citations to the corporation laws of each of the states, and comparative discussions of their provisions, may be found by reference to the *Revised Model Business Corporation Act Annotated*, a multi-volume work that is revised annually to reflect corporate law changes.

[11] The civil law institutions of the 'commercial register' (in which businesses of all types file certain information), and 'procurist' (a commercial agent with general authority to enter into transactions binding the business association), do not exist in the United States.

Nevertheless, many activities require licenses from one or more government agencies irrespective of the form in which they may be conducted. For example, doctors, lawyers, hairdressers, electricians, schools, restaurants, and many other professions, trades, businesses, and callings require licensure. The license and filing requirement in these cases applies to the *activity* rather than to the *business association*.

B. *The General Partnership*

A general partnership similarly requires no filing. As defined in the Uniform Partnership Act, a partnership is an association of two or more persons to carry on as co-owners a business for profit.[12] There is, in fact, no requirement that the partners enter into any formal written or oral agreement; the partnership is a residual form of business association that is presumed to exist when there is a sharing of the net profits of a business.[13] If the partners enter into an agreement, it may (subject to very few exceptions) contain whatever provisions the partners may wish to adopt concerning the conduct of the business and their rights and duties in relation to themselves and the partnership.[14] These include such matters as: division of profits and losses; payment of salaries or interest; allocation of control; admission and withdrawal of partners; and the duration of the partnership. If the partners do not enter into an agreement, or if the agreement is silent on certain matters, the Uniform Partnership Act specifies presumptive rules to be applied to the rights and duties among the partners[15] and with respect to those who deal with the partnership.[16]

Despite the lack of a filing requirement, a partnership under the original Uniform Partnership Act is, for most purposes, a legal entity.[17] Any remaining ambiguity on this subject is eliminated by the Revised Uniform Partnership Act, which explicitly declares that 'a partnership is an entity'.[18]

C. *The Limited Partnership and the Limited Liability Company*

The other business forms—limited partnership, limited liability company, and corporation—require filing as a condition of coming into existence. The participants who purport to carry on a business in any of these forms, but

[12] UPA § 6(1); RUPA §202(a).   [13] UPA § 7(4); RUPA § 202(c)(3).
[14] UPA § 18; RUPA § 103(a).   [15] See UPA § 18; RUPA § 401.
[16] See UPA § 9; RUPA § 301 (agency authority of partner).
[17] See, e.g. UPA §§ 8, 10 (partnership property).   [18] RUPA § 201.

who fail to file the required organizational document, are likely to be treated as general partners who are liable personally for the debts of the business.[19]

A limited partnership is formed by filing a 'certificate of limited partnership' with the appropriate state office, usually the Secretary of State. Most states require very limited information in this document: the name of the limited partnership; its address and agent for the service of legal process in the state; the names and business addresses of the general partners; and the latest date when the partnership will dissolve.[20] The partnership is formed as of the date of filing; it is therefore easily possible to form a limited partnership in the course of a single business day. Important matters relating to the partners' relative rights and duties are generally contained in the partnership agreement, a document that is not filed with the state and is not available for public inspection.[21]

Formation of a limited liability company similarly requires a routine filing of a certificate of formation, containing only limited information: the name of the company; the name and address of its agent for the service of legal process in the state; and the date of dissolution if the company has limited life.[22] The company comes into existence as of the filing, and as in the case of the limited partnership, details of its structure, organization, and operation are set out in other non-filed documents.

D. The Corporation

The simplicity and speed of the formation procedures described above serve as prelude to the process of incorporation, which in the United States is a much simpler, more rapid, and less demanding process than its counterpart in most of the civil law world. Creation of a corporation requires only the filing of a single document, generally called the 'articles of incorporation', signed in almost all jursidictions by a single person acting as the incorporator.[23] The articles may be as short as a single page, since the required contents include only the corporate name; the aggregate number of shares of each class of stock that the corporation is authorized to issue; the address of the corporation's registered office in the state; the name of its registered agent at

---

[19] Some protection against the rigors of this rule is provided in RULPA § 304.

[20] See RULPA § 201(a).

[21] See RULPA § 201, comment: 'the partnership agreement, not the certificate of limited partnership, has become the authoritative and comprehensive document for most limited partnerships . . .'.

[22] See, e.g., Del. Limited Liability Company Act, Del. Code Ann., Title 6, Ch. 18, §18–201.

[23] See, e.g. Revised Model Business Corporation Act ('RMBCA') § 2.01. A few states retain the requirement of having as many as three incorporators.

that office; and the name and address of the incorporator(s).[24] The articles of incorporation need not set out the powers or the purposes of the corporation, since these are granted in the broadest terms by the corporation law itself.[25] Most of the important structural aspects of the corporation—including the titles, duties and authorities of the corporate officers, the size of the board of directors, and the location and times of stockholders' meetings—are set out in the bylaws, which do not become part of the public records.[26] The doctrine of *ultra vires* has largely been eliminated in the United States. Therefore, the validity of a corporate action may not be challenged on the ground of lack of corporate powers, except in a stockholder action seeking an injunction or seeking (derivatively) damages from directors or officers, or in a proceeding by the state based on abuse of corporate authority.[27]

In sharp contrast with the general civil law structure, United States corporation laws impose no requirements of publication, minimum capital, minimum subscribed shares, appraisal or notarial approval. It is common practice for a corporation to be formed within a single business day. Filing of the articles is conclusive proof of existence of the corporation.[28] Most states provide that those who act as a corporation are personally liable for the debts of the enterprise incurred prior to filing.[29]

A corporation established in one state may conduct activities in all the states, but it is required to file as a 'foreign corporation' in all states in which its activities amount to 'doing business'. Whether the activities of the corporation in a given state represent 'doing business' or 'transacting business' in that state turns on the nature of those activities. For example, isolated transactions and interstate shipments do not fit within the filing requirements. Filing as a foreign corporation expressly subjects the corporation to service of legal process within the state as well as imposition of state income taxes.[30]

---

[24] See, e.g. RMBCA § 2.02(a). Other clauses, including provisions with respect to liability, control and any other matters not inconsistent with law, are permitted to be included in the articles. See, e.g. RMBCA § 2.02(b).

[25] See, e.g. RMBCA §§ 3.01 (purposes); 3.02 (general powers).

[26] See RMBCA § 2.06. Most states allow the bylaws to be adopted and amended either by the board of directors or by the stockholders. Most major corporations follow the former practice, thereby granting wider managerial discretion to the board.

[27] See, e.g. RMBCA § 3.04.   [28] See, e.g. RMBCA § 2.03(b).

[29] See, e.g. RMBCA § 2.04, and comment. The Revised Model Business Corporation Act imposes personal liability only upon persons who so acted with *knowledge* that there was no incorporation. Some decisional law, as cited in the comment, holds similarly.

[30] See, e.g. RMBCA § 15.01. Failure to file does not, however, impair the validity of any contracts of the corporation, nor does it result in the imposition of personal liability on the stockholders, officers, or directors. Rather, it disables the corporation from maintaining lawsuits in the courts of the state until filing has been made, and it subjects the corporation to penalties for non-filing, as well as potential tax penalties. See, e.g. RMBCA § 15.02.

E. Limitation of Liability

Among the most important characteristics of corporate status is immuniza-
tion of the stockholders from personal liability for the debts of the corporation.[31] This immunity is very strong in the United States; the concept of
'lifting the corporate veil' to impose liability on stockholders is sharply limited in most jurisdictions to three situations:

(1)   failure to observe required corporate formalities, such as issuance of
      shares, holding of corporate meetings, maintenance of a corporate bank
      account, and the like;
(2)   use of the corporation as a device to defraud creditors, usually by gross
      undercapitalization;[32] and
(3)   stockholder use of the corporation as an 'alter ego', or representation by
      the stockholders that they are conducting business in other than the cor-
      porate form.[33]

One important by-product of this view of limited liability is that, with very
rare exceptions, a parent corporation will not be held liable for the debts of
its wholly or partially owned subsidiary.

III. Raising of Capital

A. Sources of Capital

Corporations raise capital from three sources; equity, debt, and income
retention. New capital from outsiders is raised by the issuance of equity (in
the form of stock of one or more classes) and debt (in the form of bonds,
notes, and short-term obligations). Further capital is raised from the cash
generated by the net income generated from corporate operations, all or a
portion of which may be retained by the corporation to finance its continued
operations or expansion. The relative importance of each of these sources of
financing changes during the life-cycle of the corporation and is affected as

---

[31] Limitation of investor liability is also an important feature of limited partnerships (in which only the
general partner or partners are personally liable for enterprise debts) and limited liability companies. For
these entities as well, personal liability is unlikely if the appropriate statutory formalities have been
observed and if the entity is not used as a device to defraud creditors.

[32] The most widely cited cases under this heading were decided in California. See, e.g. *Automotriz del
Golfo de California S.A.* v. *Resnick*, 306 P.2d 1 (Cal. 1957); *Minton* v. *Cavaney*, 364 P.2d 473 (Cal. 1961).

[33] For commentaries on this subject, see Posner, 'The Rights of Creditors of Affiliated Corporations',
43 U. Chi. L. Rev. 527 (1976); Krendl & Krendl, 'Piercing the Corporate Veil: Focusing the Inquiry', 55 Den.
L.J. 1 (1978); Comment, 'The Alter Ego Doctrine: Alternative Challenges to the Corporate Form', 30
U.C.L.A. L. Rev. 129 (1982).

well by varying economic conditions. Issuance of stock is a crucial source of funds for the start-up company, and stock issuance is also associated with initial public offerings, certain acquisitions, and certain major financing plans. Debt is used routinely by both beginning and mature corporations to provide long-term and seasonal financing, to acquire assets or entire businesses, and as part of the normal credit cycle of acquiring assets or services. However, retention of income is in the aggregate the principal source of financing by mature corporations in the United States.[34]

B. *Authorization and Issuance of Stock*

Stock issuance must be authorized in the articles of incorporation, normally by number of shares and by class, designating the rights, preferences, and privileges of each class.[35] If additional stock is to be authorized, the articles of incorporation must be amended.[36] However, stock may be authorized in an amount substantially in excess of the number of shares initially issued, thereby avoiding for the foreseeable future any need to resort to further stockholder approval. Many states allow an alternative to initial specification of the rights, preferences, and privileges of all classes of stock in the articles of incorporation. These states provide statutory authorization for a provision in the articles of incorporation creating 'series preferred', a single class of stock that may be issued in series, the terms and conditions of which may be determined from time to time by the board of directors.[37] Series authorization affords the board of directors great flexibility in stock issuance, often particularly important to publicly-held corporations planning future acquisitions that may be financed by issuance of stock. Capital requirements often found in civil law countries—including minimal capital, minimum initial subscription for shares, and limited (e.g. 5-year) authorization of unissued shares—do not exist in the United States.

In the United States, a corporation may legally issue stock not only in exchange for cash but also in exchange for any form of tangible or intangible assets. These include such items as notes and accounts receivable, inventories, plant, equipment, patents, and goodwill.[38] No independent appraisal of these assets is required, and the judgment of the board of directors as to their

---

[34] For the past half-century, the source of more than half of the funds of nonfinancial corporations has been internal, primarily through retention of earnings and cash flows from asset dispositions. Within the last decade, self-financing in this form has ranged from slightly over 70 percent to well in excess of 90 percent of corporate funds. Debt generally provides the remaining funds. In fact, since 1980, nonfinancial corporations have in the aggregate *reduced* their contributed capital (primarily through stock redemption). Detailed statistics may be found in United States Federal Reserve Board, *Flow of Funds Accounts.*

[35] See, e.g. RMBCA § 6.01.   [36] See, e.g. RMBCA § 10.03.

[37] e.g. RMBCA § 6.02.   [38] See, e.g. RMBCA § 6.21(b).

value is binding in the absence of fraud.[39] The notes of the purchaser, however, are often excluded as permissible consideration.[40] Most statutes also permit the issuance of stock in exchange for services actually performed for the corporation, including services and expenses incurred in its organization,[41] although many prohibit issuance of stock in exchange for promised future services.[42]

The requirement of a fixed minimum consideration for initial stock issuance, whether in the form of a par value or a stated value, may be disappearing from United States law. California was the first state to eliminate completely the concept of par value and to delete from its corporation law all restrictions based on par value or stated capital.[43] The Revised Model Business Corporation Act has done the same.[44] However, other major corporate jurisdictions, including Delaware[45] and New York,[46] retain the concept of par value. Even in these states, the articles of incorporation may authorize stock without par value or with a low par value (e.g. $1 per share, or even 10 cents per share), which may be issued for essentially any consideration within the broad discretion of the board, without running afoul of the statutory requirements. In practical effect, therefore, the problem of 'watered stock' (stock issued for consideration of a value less than its par value) has largely disappeared in the United States.

C. Common Stock

Very often, new enterprises are capitalized entirely through the issuance of common stock. Common stock is the residuary equity investment in a corporation. It has the last right to receive dividends and the last right to receive distributions in liquidation. Creditors of every kind (including holders of bonds and debentures) and all preferred stockholders normally take priority over common stock. While common stock is generally voting, it may in most states be divided into voting and non-voting classes.

Common stock receives distribution of income in the form of dividends, at the discretion of the board of directors, and the courts have been extremely reluctant to interfere with board discretion concerning the payment of dividends.[47]

---

[39] See, e.g. RMBCA § 6.21(c).

[40] See, e.g. NYBCL § 504(b). By contrast, promissory notes are explicitly permitted as consideration under the Revised Model Business Corporation Act; RMBCA § 6.21(b).

[41] e.g. RMBCA § 6.21(b).

[42] e.g. NYBCL § 504(b). By contrast, the Revised Model Business Corporation explicitly permits the receipt of future services for the issuance of shares; RMBCA § 6.21(b).

[43] See Cal. Corp. Code §§ 400, 409.   [44] See RMBCA § 6.21.

[45] See Del. Gen. Corp. L. §§ 151(a), 153.   [46] See NYBCL §§ 501(a), 504(c), (d).

[47] See, e.g. RMBCA § 6.40(a).

D. Preferred Stock

Preferred stock is fundamentally a contract instrument, which may be issued with a wide variety of rights, preferences and privileges, including dividend preference and limitation; liquidation preference; redemption or conversion provisions; and variations in voting rights. Preferred stock is usually granted a stated annual preference in dividends, expressed either in dollar amount ('$8 preferred') or as a percentage of par or stated value or liquidation preference ('11% preferred'). The preferred dividend must be declared and paid annually as a precondition to the declaration and payment of dividends on common stock. The dividend preference is usually cumulative; if a preferred cumulative dividend is skipped in one year, no dividends on common stock may be paid until after that dividend and the current year's preferred dividend are paid.

In the United States, preferred stock also usually has a prior and limited right to the proceeds of corporate liquidation. Typically, preferred stock with a par or stated value is entitled to receive in liquidation, before any distribution is made to the common stock, its par or stated value plus any dividend arrearages.

Preferred stock may be created with a privilege of conversion into common stock or into another class of preferred stock. The conversion privilege, intended to make the preferred stock more attractive to potential investors, gives the stock a dual aspect. While it is held in its original form, it has all the characteristics of preferred stock. Upon conversion, it becomes common stock. The conversion privilege may be time-limited, and may be at a fixed or variable price. Preferred stock may also be redeemable, thereby providing the corporation with the option of eliminating the fixed dividend obligation at a future date.

Preferred stock is generally non-voting or partially voting. Although preferred stockholders generally do not vote in the election of the board of directors, they often gain the voting right when dividends have not been paid for a stated period.[48]

E. Debt

Debt of every kind may be issued by a corporation by resolution of the board of directors. The power to incur debt and to issue all forms of debt instruments (including bonds, secured debt, and convertible debt) is included

---

[48] The typical provision derives from the preferred stock listing requirement of the New York Stock Exchange. When four quarterly dividends have been omitted, the preferred stock becomes voting.

within the general powers granted by the corporation laws.[49] Corporations of every size incur short-term trade debt in connection with purchasing goods for sale or use, and acquiring services. A significant additional source of debt financing is bank borrowing, in the form of renewable short-term notes, demand notes or lines of credit. Certificated, tradeable debt (in the form of bonds or debentures[50]) is normally issued only by corporations whose stock is also publicly traded. Most bonds in the United States are issued in denominations of $1,000 principal amount, with interest payable semi-annually 'in arrears' (i.e. after the interest has accrued).

Stock and bonds in the United States are presently issued only in 'registered' form, with the ownership thereof noted on the books of the issuing corporation or its transfer agent. Publicly traded stocks and bonds are widely held 'in street name', the registered owner being a brokerage house or its nominee. Street name securities may always be traced to the equitable owners, and are in fact so traced for purposes of income taxation of dividends and interest and the exercise of voting and other rights.

IV. Control Structure—Stockholders

The normative structure for business corporations under American law is delegated management, in which stockholder participation is limited to voting on certain major corporate changes and electing the board of directors.

A. *Election of the Board of Directors*

For election of the board of directors, the voting procedure involves notice, a meeting, and a vote in person or by proxy for candidates for the board. Unless otherwise provided in the articles of incorporation, directors are elected by *plurality*, i.e. the candidates with the greatest number of votes are elected, whether or not they have received the approval of a majority of the voted shares.[51]

In the election of the board of directors, two voting mechanisms are generally allowed by state corporation laws: straight voting and cumulative

---

[49] See, e.g. RMBCA § 3.02(7).

[50] 'Bonds' generally have a security interest in specified corporate assets, such as land, building or equipment. 'Debentures' are unsecured, general obligations of the corporation.

[51] See, e.g. RMBCA § 7.28.

voting.[52] Under straight voting, each directorship position is treated as a separate election, with the result that each stockholder may cast no more votes in favor of any candidate than the number of voting shares that the stockholder owns. By contrast, under cumulative voting, candidates for the board effectively run 'at large', and each stockholder may cast in favor of any candidate all or any portion of his votes. One implication of cumulative voting is that it provides a degree of protection for proportional representation of voting shares.

While the statutory norm is annual election of the entire board of directors by the voting stockholders, most statutes allow provision in the articles of incorporation for staggered election of the board to multi-year terms. Most commonly, staggered election is statutorily limited so that each year no fewer than three directors stand for election. For example, the Revised Model Business Corporation Act permits staggered elections when the board consists of nine or more members, and allows division of the directors into either two groups (with 2-year terms) or three groups (with 3-year terms).[53] In the context of the tender offer explosion of the late 1980s, staggered election was widely used by publicly traded corporations as a device to protect against hostile takeover.[54]

Stockholders may cast their votes in person, at the stockholders' meeting, or by proxy.[55] Proxy voting is a routine necessity in publicly held corporations, and is heavily regulated by state and federal law and regulations. The subject of proxy regulation is discussed in Chapter 22, section IV.

B. Voting on Other Matters

Unless otherwise specified in the statute, the required vote for resolutions submitted for stockholder approval is a majority of the shares present at a meeting at which a quorum is present in person or by proxy.[56] By contrast, major corporate changes submitted for stockholder vote (such as amendment to the articles of incorporation, merger, or dissolution) require for approval the affirmative vote of a statutorily-specified majority of the outstanding voting shares. Shares that have no vote in the election of the board

---

[52] Some states, like California, mandate cumulative voting for the board. See Cal. Corp. Code § 708; compare Cal. Corp. Code § 301.5 (exception for listed corporations). Most permit either mechanism as specified in the articles of incorporation; however if the articles are silent, most states presume straight voting. See, e.g. RMBCA § 7.28(b).

[53] See, e.g. RMBCA § 8.06.

[54] See Lipton and Rosenblum, 'A New System of Corporate Governance: The Quinquennial Election of Directors', 58 *U. Chi. L. Rev.* 187 (1991).

[55] See, e.g. RMBCA § 7.22.

[56] See, e.g. RMBCA § 8.63 (stockholder approval of interested director transactions).

may be granted the vote on major corporate changes, either by the terms under which the corporation issued them or by statute when the corporate action under consideration affects the terms of their stock.[57]

C. Alternative Voting and Approval Provisions

A provision may be included in the articles of incorporation increasing the required stockholder vote for all or stated corporate actions.[58] Similar provisions can be made either in the articles of incorporation or the bylaws for greater-than-majority or unanimous consent of the board of directors on all or certain actions.[59]

Stockholder action may also be taken by unanimous written consent without a meeting.[60] Some states now permit attendance at a stockholders' meeting by telephonic or other electronic communication, and a few states permit action to be taken, or presume that action may be taken, by stockholders by majority written consent.[61]

D. Close Corporations: Voting Agreements

The formal voting and control structure specified by the state corporation laws was designed for corporations with widely distributed stock ownership. This structure is usually not well suited to 'closely-held' corporations, those with relatively few stockholders, many or all of whom are actively involved in the control and daily operations of the corporation. The distinction between a public corporation and a private corporation has been recognized in United States statutory and decisional law only in the latter part of this century. American law has no direct equivalent of the *Gesellschaft mit beschraenkter Haftung* (GmbH), a German innovation of the late nineteenth century that has been adopted with modifications throughout most of the civil law world.[62] In general, there is but a single form of business corporation in the United States, but it may be modified by agreement to carry out the particular purposes of its stockholders.

The initial attempts to create stockholder-controlled close corporations

---

[57] See, e.g. RMBCA § 10.03(e) (amendments); RMBCA § 11.03 (mergers and share exchanges). The voting requirements for these transactions are discussed in section VIII B below.

[58] See, e.g. RMBCA § 7.27(a).   [59] See, e.g. RMBCA §§ 8.24 (a) (quorum), (c) (vote).

[60] See, e.g. RMBCA § 7.04.

[61] See, e.g. Del. Gen. Corp. L. § 228 (authorized unless prohibited by the certificate of incorporation); Mich. Bus. Corp. L. § 407(1) (authorized if so provided in the articles of incorporation).

[62] The statutory close corporation, available in several states and discussed in section V C below, offers some of the features of the GmbH, but is fundamentally different in origin and structure.

were struck down by the courts on the ground that contractual interference with the normal statutory voting and control structure was forbidden; that voting agreements, control agreements, and attempts to eliminate the board or curtail its functions violated the statutory norm and were at least unenforceable and often void.[63] Eventually, the unique needs of close corporations were recognized by commentators, then by the courts, and ultimately by the legislatures.[64] Today, it is a rare state that does not explicitly recognize a multitude of control agreements and arrangements, including elimination of the board of directors and direct management by stockholders.

Two of the principal forms of control arrangements in close corporations are voting trusts and voting agreements. They are both valid and specifically enforceable.[65] A voting trust is, in fact, a trust: the corpus consists of the shares transferred to the trustee to be voted in accordance with the trust instrument. State laws tend to limit the term of a voting trust, most often to 10 years. Generally, a voting trust may be entered into by any group of stockholders, although a few state statutes require that all stockholders be given the opportunity to join the trust. In most jurisdictions, the existence and terms of a voting trust are matters of public record.

Although voting agreements are today universally recognized, the conditions of their validity and enforcement vary. In some states, there is no statutory assurance of validity and enforceability unless the agreement is among all stockholders. In some states, voting agreements (like voting trusts) are matters of public record, but in many others, such agreements may be entered into by any group of stockholders, without any disclosure.

E. Share Transfer Restrictions

The normal presumption of corporation law is that shares of stock are freely transferable. Restrictions on the free transfer of shares may be imposed for a variety of reasons, such as:

(1) assurance of registration exemption under federal or state securities laws;

(2) qualification for certain income tax treatment;

(3) legal limitations of ownership related to certain licenses or franchises;

---

[63] See, e.g. *Abercrombie* v. *Davies*, 130 A.2d 338 (Del. 1957) (invalidating a voting agreement among stockholders); *Long Park, Inc.* v. *Trenton-New Brunswick Theatres Co.*, 297 NY 174, 77 N.E. 2d 633 (1948) (invalidating a control agreement among stockholders).

[64] e.g. RMBCA § 8.01(c) (elimination of board of directors), § 7.31 (voting agreements), Model Statutory Close Corporation Supplement (close corporations); NYBCL § 620(a) (voting agreements), § 620(b) (control agreements); Del. Gen. Corp. L. §§ 341–356 (close corporations).

[65] See, e.g. RMBCA § 7.30 (voting trusts; term limited to 10 years); RMBCA § 7.31 (voting agreements permitted among two or more stockholders).

(4)   retirement, family, and estate planning; and

(5)   preservation of close corporation control arrangements.

Limitations on the free transfer of stock may be divided into two broad categories:

(i)   contractual or other limitations on transfer, in the form of options, consent requirements, limitations, or outright prohibitions on transfer: and

(ii) 'buy-sell agreements' that specify how, to whom, and at what price the stock will be transferred, and that impose corresponding requirements on one party to sell the stock and on the other to buy it.

The validity and enforceability of share transfer restrictions is universally recognized in the United States, generally by explicit provisions in the corporation statutes.[66] However, they may be imposed only upon consenting stockholders, either in the form of restrictions imposed as of the initial issuance of the stock, or by agreement or provision in the articles of incorporation consented to by the stockholder whose shares will be restricted.[67] Moreover, they are enforceable against would-be subsequent transferees only if notice of the restrictions appears on the share certificates.[68]

V. Control Structure—Directors and Officers

A. *The Board of Directors*

The corporation statutes specify that a corporation's business and affairs shall be run by or under the direction of the board of directors.[69] American corporations have a single board of directors; the German two-level structure consisting of a supervisory board (*Aufsichtsrat*) and a managing board (*Vorstand*) does not exist in the United States. In small corporations, the board itself manages, with the members often electing themselves as officers. The boards of larger corporations delegate management duties to officers and employees, retaining a supervisory rather than day-to-day managerial role. Larger corporations also routinely establish committees of the board.[70] Among these are usually the executive committee (which acts for the board between regular meetings); the audit committee (which supervises the inde-

---

[66] See, e.g. RMBCA § 6.27.   [67] See, e.g. RMBCA § 6.27(a).

[68] This requirement is imposed by Uniform Commercial Code § 8–204. It is often repeated in the corporation statutes. See, e.g. RMBCA § 627(b).

[69] See, e.g. RMBCA § 8.01(b).

[70] See, e.g. RMBCA § 8.25. For discussion of the increased role of board committees in publicly held corporations, see 'The Corporate Director's Guidebook', 33 *Bus. Law.* 1591 (1978); 'The Overview Committees of the Board of Directors', 35 *Bus. Law.* 1335 (1980).

pendent audit of the corporation and receives the auditors' report); and often an independent litigation committee.

The board elects and discharges officers, sets salaries, supervises day-to-day corporate operations, causes the issuance of corporate stock and bonds, authorizes payment of dividends, and initially approves actions to be submitted for stockholder approval. On these matters, the stockholders normally have no voice. Authority is, in effect, fully delegated to the board of directors, limited only by the stockholders' powers of election and removal of the board.

Board action is by meeting,[71] requiring notice[72] and the presence of a quorum of the board (normally a majority).[73] When a quorum is present, the vote of a majority of that quorum generally represents the action of the board of directors.[74] Many statutes now provide for director attendance at a board meeting by conference telephone call,[75] and it is a widespread practice to include that authorization in the corporate bylaws. Board action may also be taken by unanimous written consent.[76] In a few jurisdictions, board action by majority written consent is also possible.

B. *Officers*

Officers of the corporation, and by implication all other employees of the corporation, are appointed by or under the direction of the board of directors and serve at the pleasure of the board. The officers may therefore be removed at any time by the board, although officers so removed may have the right to damages or other remedies under their employment contracts.[77]

C. *Close Corporations: Control Agreements*

Under contemporary corporation statutes, it is possible by agreement to remove any or all of these powers from the board of directors—or to eliminate the board entirely—and to vest these powers directly in the stockholders or in their delegates. There are generally four statutory conditions to assuring the validity and enforceability of control agreements:

(1) *Unanimity.* In one form or another—whether by specific statutory

---

[71] See, e.g. RMBCA § 8.20.
[72] See, e.g. RMBCA §§ 8.22, 8.23.
[73] See, e.g. RMBCA § 8.24(a).
[74] See, e.g. RMBCA § 8.24(c).
[75] See, e.g. RMBCA § 8.20(b) (which authorizes such attendance unless otherwise provided in the articles of incorporation or the bylaws).
[76] See, e.g. RMBCA § 8.21(a).
[77] See, e.g. RMBCA §§ 8.43(b), 8.44(b).

requirement with respect to the agreement[78] or by requiring unanimous consent to a close corporation election as a condition of statutory validity of the agreement[79]—unanimous stockholder consent is generally required.

(2)   *Notice*. The statutes require that all stock certificates bear notice of the existence of the control agreement[80] or close corporation status.[81]

(3)   *Restricted transfer*. The statutes require, directly or indirectly, that restrictions be imposed on the transfer of shares, preventing non-consenting purchasers from acquiring shares.[82]

(4)   *Public record*. The statutes generally require that the agreement be the subject of public filing and record by providing that it must be included in the articles of incorporation (which are themselves publicly filed)[83] or by requiring election as a close corporation (requiring public filing) as a precondition of entering into a statutorily-sanctioned control agreement.[84]

One important consequence of entering into a control agreement is that the signatory stockholders become personally liable as directors for the actions removed from the board's discretion. This liability is not the equivalent of direct stockholder liability for the debts of the corporation, but rather is liability for the fiduciary obligations normally imposed upon directors.[85]

State corporation laws vary in the mechanisms that they authorize to effectuate close corporation control structures. Some states, like New York, include sections in the body of the business corporation law dealing with control agreements and other issues primarily of concern to close corporations.[86] Others have enacted separate codes or code chapters applicable to electing close corporations.[87]

The advantage of election as a statutory close corporation is that the close

---

[78] See, e.g. RMBCA § 7.32(b).

[79] See, e.g. Cal. Gen. Corp. L. § 158(b) (unanimous vote required for close corporation election), § 300(b) (validating control agreements by the stockholders of close corporations). Cf. Model Statutory Close Corp. Supp (MSCCS) § 3(b) (close corporation election by two-thirds class vote of stockholders), § 20(a) (unanimity required for control agreement among stockholders of close corporation).

[80] See, e.g. RMBCA § 7.32(c).   [81] See, e.g. MSCCA § 10.

[82] See, e.g. RMBCA § 7.32(c). Compare, e.g. NYBCL § 620(b)(2) (implying that transfer to a nonconsenting purchaser will invalidate the agreement) with RMBCA § 7.32(c) (avoiding invalidation by affording the purchaser the option to rescind the purchase or otherwise be bound to the agreement).

[83] See, e.g. NYBCL § 620(b). But see RMBCA § 7.32(b) which, by permitting the agreement to be included either in the articles or the bylaws (the latter of which is not publicly filed), validates agreements that need not be publicly filed.

[84] See, e.g. Cal. Gen. Corp. Law § 300 (b) (agreement among shareholders of a close corporation), § 158 (qualification as close corporation).

[85] See, e.g. RMBCA § 7.32(e), (f).   [86] See, e.g. NYBCL § 6.20(b).

[87] In the case of the Model Act, the Statutory Close Corporation Supplement is non-exclusive. Therefore control and other agreements may, depending on their terms, be enforceable under either the Supplement or the Act itself. See RMBCA § 7.32 (control agreements), Model Statutory Close Corp. Supp. (close corporations).

corporation statutes or chapters are all-inclusive, and the election permits all forms of agreements that the parties are likely to wish. Moreover, the close corporation statutes often provide dispute and deadlock provisions that may prove helpful in resolving problems of disagreement or oppression among stockholders.[88]

D. Deadlock and Oppression

Particularly in closely-held corporations, business or personal circumstances of the corporation or its stockholders may lead to sharp disagreement or deadlock over corporate policies, or to oppressive or illegal conduct by some of the stockholders. These problems may be resolved by agreement or by a variety of dispute-resolution techniques, including mediation or arbitration. When they cannot be resolved, judicially imposed remedies are available, the most well known of which is judicial dissolution upon the petition of aggrieved stockholders, based on deadlock or on oppressive or illegal actions by controlling stockholders. The statutes vary in their requirements of the petitioners,[89] in the substantive bases for the petition,[90] and in the standard to be applied by the court.[91]

Some state statutes provide for judicial appointment of a custodian or receiver in the case of deadlock or illegal or oppressive stockholder conduct.[92] A related but less drastic remedy is the appointment of a provisional director, authorized by several statutes, usually for close corporations.[93]

Some courts—even in the absence of specific statutory guidance—have fashioned remedies against deadlock, or oppressive or illegal conduct by controlling stockholders, based upon the same fiduciary principles applicable among partners.[94] A few states have added provisions to their corporation laws granting the court a wide range of remedial alternatives beyond the traditional remedy of dissolution. These include judicial invalidation of oppressive agreements, resolutions or by-laws, mandatory dividends, mandatory

---

[88] See, e.g. MSCCA §§ 40–43 (court actions to protect stockholders).

[89] See, e.g. RMBCA § 14.30(2) (any stockholder); MSCCS § 40 (any stockholder of a close corporation).

[90] See, e.g. RMBCA § 14.30(2) (deadlock; illegal, oppressive or fraudulent conduct; corporate waste); MSCCS § 40(a)(1) (illegal, oppressive, fraudulent or unfairly prejudicial conduct by directors or those in control), § 40(a)(2) (deadlock); NYBCL § 1104 (deadlock), § 1104-a (illegal, fraudulent or oppressive actions of those in control of the corporation).

[91] See, e.g. RMBCA § 14.30(2) (deadlock: irreparable injury threatened or suffered); MSCCS §§ 41–43 (court discretion); NYBCL § 1111 (court discretion; 'the benefit to the shareholders of a dissolution is of paramount importance'.)

[92] See, e.g. RMBCA § 14.32; MSCCS § 41(a)(6).

[93] See, e.g. MSCCS § 41(a)(7); Del. Gen. Corp. L. § 353.

[94] See, e.g. *Donahue* v. *Rodd Electrotype Co.*, 367 Mass. 598, 238 N.E.2d 505 (1975).

buy-out of one or more stockholders, and invalidation of salary plans and recovery of excessive salaries.[95]

E. *Control by Creditors*

Formal creditor control of the corporation, by means of voting rights, is permitted in some states[96] and forbidden in others.[97] However, operational control is often demanded and obtained by creditors, usually in the form of negative covenants providing that certain actions—such as incurring other debt, making substantial capital acquisitions, increasing dividends, changing the executive officers—may not be made without the consent of the creditor. Although the creditor is without power to prevent these actions directly, their implementation without creditor consent may represent a default of the loan instrument, giving the creditor the right to demand immediate repayment. In these circumstances, the creditor has an effective direct voice in control until such time as the corporation is in a position to repay the loan.

VI. Fiduciary Obligations and Standard of Care

The standard of conduct of corporate directors and officers, though phrased with wide variations among state statutes, has two components:
(1) the obligation to act in good faith, in the interests of the corporation; and
(2) the requirement to act with the care of an ordinarily prudent person in a like position, usually encompassed in the so-called 'business judgment rule'.[98]

Most statutes explicitly provide that directors and officers, in discharging their duties, may rely in good faith upon opinions, reports and information provided by corporate officers and by attorneys, accountants, and other experts.[99]

---

[95] See, e.g. MSCCS § 41(a).   [96] See, e.g. NYBCL § 518(c); Del. Gen. Corp. L. § 221.
[97] See, e.g. RMBCA § 7.21(a) and comment ¶ 2.
[98] See, e.g. RMBCA §§ 8.30(a) (directors); 8.42(a) (officers).
[99] See, e.g. RMBCA §§ 8.30(b) (directors); 8.42(b) (officers).

A. The Standard of Care

Director liability for failure of the 'business judgment rule' standard of care, though not unknown,[100] is uncommon. Normally, the courts will not question the directors' judgments if they acted on an informed basis, in good faith, and believing that their actions were in the best interests of the corporation.[101] Very rarely has this standard resulted in director liability except in cases of gross negligence, fraud, or bad faith.

In actual practice, exposure to liability for careless conduct is uncommon, since the state corporation laws permit indemnification and insurance of directors and officers against liability for conduct carried out in good faith and in the interests of the corporation.[102] Many states also permit a corporation to include a provision in its articles of incorporation eliminating or limiting the liability of directors except for intentional acts or the taking of personal financial benefits.[103]

The subject of directors' standard of care, as well as the related subjects of directors' liabilities and derivative suits, were among the areas of study of the Corporate Governance Project of the American Law Institute. That project, recently concluded after 15 years of study, generated much scholarship, many proposals for law reform, and considerable controversy. Its implications for American corporate law have yet to be judged.[104]

B. Transactions by Interested Directors

Before the corporation laws directly addressed this issue, it was widely held that the participation of an 'interested director' (i.e. a director with a financial or other personal interest in a proposed corporate transaction) in approving that transaction rendered it at least voidable, if not void *ab initio*. However, business reasons, as well as complex corporate ownership structures, may make an 'interested' transaction important to the operations of a corporation. Corporate statutes in the United States now explicitly eliminate the taint of voidness or voidability, subject to approval or fairness requirements applicable to the transaction.[105] The statutes generally provide that, if any

---

[100] Two recent examples of judicially-imposed liability are *Smith* v. *Van Gorkum*, 488 A.2d 858 (Del. 1985), and *Francis* v. *United Jersey Bank*, 432 A.2d 814 (N.J. 1981).

[101] See, e.g. *Aronson* v. *Lewis*, 473 A.2d 805 (Del. 1984).   [102] See, e.g. RMBCA §§ 8.50–8.58.

[103] See, e.g. RMBCA § 2.02(b)(4); Del. Gen. Corp. L. § 102(b)(7). These provisions, though widely enacted in state law, have not been universally adopted in corporate articles of incorporation.

[104] See American Law Institute, *Principles of Corporate Governance: Analysis and Recommendations* (1992). For analysis of the analysis, see 'Symposium on Corporate Governance', 48 *Business Lawyer* 1267–1507 (1993).

[105] See, e.g. RMBCA § 8.61(b).

one of three tests is met, the transaction is neither void nor voidable by virtue of director interest:

(1)   the transaction is approved by the board of directors or a committee of the board by a majority vote of disinterested directors, following disclosure of the material facts of the transaction and the director's interest;

(2)   the transaction is approved by stockholder vote, following disclosure of the material facts of the transaction and the director's interest; or

(3)   the transaction is fair as to the corporation as of the time it is approved or ratified.

Despite compliance with any of these tests, nondisclosure or misdisclosure, as well as fraud in the transaction, continue to be bases for judicial examination.[106]

An interesting question is whether stockholders who are interested in a transaction are disabled from voting in its favor. While stockholders may generally vote their own interests, a stockholder who is also a director may by statute[107] or by decisional law[108] be rendered incapable of voting in favor of an interested transaction, even in her capacity as a stockholder.

C. Derivative Suits

Legal actions brought on behalf of the corporation to recover amounts from third parties are, like other corporate acts, normally authorized by or under the authority of the board of directors. When the board does not act on a potential claim, or refuses to pursue it, a stockholder of the corporation may institute a 'derivative suit', seeking recovery by the corporation against the third party. Although the nominal plaintiff in a derivative suit is the stockholder, the real plaintiff—the party for which damages or other relief are sought—is the corporation itself. In some cases, a derivative suit is brought because the board of the corporation decides not to bring suit against an outside third-party. Far more frequently, however, the potential defendant is a member of the board of directors, or an officer, of the corporation whom the board does not wish to sue.

Derivative suits raise complex legal and procedural issues, some of which to this day remain the subject of disagreement among lawyers as well as among state laws. Three important questions are:

---

[106] e.g. RMBCA § 8.60(4). The comment to RMBCA § 8.61 emphasizes that the statutory approval procedures deal only with director personal interest or conflict of interest, and do not render the transaction invulnerable to attack on other grounds.

[107] See, e.g. RMBCA § 8.63(b) ('Qualified shares' defined to exclude those beneficially owned or controlled by a director with a conflicting interest or by a related person of the director).

[108] See, e.g. *Fliegler* v. *Lawrence*, 361 A.2d 218 (Del. Sup. Ct., 1976).

(1) What qualifications must the stockholder meet as a precondition to the initiation of a derivative suit?

(2) What conditions must be satisfied—or procedures followed—by the stockholder before the suit may proceed?

(3) What actions—if any—by the board of directors may terminate the suit?

The stockholder must have owned shares of stock in the corporation at the time of the complained-of wrong (the 'contemporaneous ownership' requirement) and must continue to hold shares as of the commencement of the derivative suit (the 'contemporary ownership' requirement).[109] With some exceptions, the stockholder must make demand on the board of directors to initiate the suit.[110] If, in response to this demand, the board initiates and pursues the suit, there is no further need for a derivative suit. If the board rejects the stockholder demand, the suit may either proceed or be substantively precluded, depending upon the nature of the claim, the procedure and character of the board's deliberations, and the status of the law in the jurisdiction.[111]

In some jurisdictions, the decision by a disinterested board or board committee not to proceed with the action results in a final termination of the proceeding. In other jurisdictions, the board or committee decision is subject to procedural or substantive review by the court.[112]

Recovery in a derivative suit flows to the corporation, though the plaintiff's expenses and legal bills are usually allowable by the court.[113] Most states require that discontinuance or settlement of a derivative suit be approved by the court.[114]

VII. Corporate Distributions

Corporate asset distributions to stockholders may be divided into two general categories; dividends, normally made pro-rata to the stockholders or to

---

[109] See, e.g. RMBCA §§ 7.40(2), 7.41(1).

[110] See, e.g. RMBCA § 7.42. Demand on the board of directors is excused in some jurisdictions when particular facts are pleaded creating a reasonable doubt that the directors are independent or disinterested. See, e.g. *Aronson* v. *Lewis*, 473 A.2d 805 (Del. 1984).

[111] See, e.g. RMBCA § 7.44, providing for dismissal of the action by the court following a majority vote of independent directors or of an independent committee.

[112] The standard of court examination varies by jurisdiction. New York examines only the independence and good faith of the board or committee. See *Auerbach* v. *Bennett*, 47 N.Y.2d 619, 419 N.Y.S.2d 920, 393 N.E.2d 994 (1974). By contrast, Delaware courts may examine the decision of the board or committee applying the court's independent business judgment. See *Zapata Corp.* v. *Maldonado*, 430 A.2d 779 (Del. 1981).

[113] See, e.g. RMBCA § 7.46.

[114] See, e.g. RMBCA § 7.45.

one or more classes of them, and acquisition by the corporation of its shares by means of redemption or repurchase.[115]

A. *Declaration of Dividends*

Dividends are declared by action of the board of directors which, under American law (apart from the legal limitations discussed below), has almost unlimited discretion on whether, when, and in what amounts to declare dividends.[116] Dividends may be in the form of cash, other assets, or stock of the corporation. Dividends of every kind, including those on preferred stock, become legal liabilities of the corporation only upon their declaration by the board.

B. *Legal Limitations on Corporate Distributions*

Corporate law limitations on dividend declaration and payment were clearly designed for the protection of creditors, and were originally based on the assumption that retention by the corporation of a certain asset base provides that protection. Recent revisions to several state corporation laws have rejected that assumption, and some have significantly changed the legal limitations on corporate distributions.

Within the United States, dividend limitations have three elements. First, they prohibit declaration or payment of dividends when they are prohibited by the terms of the articles of incorporation.[117] Secondly, most state corporation laws prohibit declaration or payment of dividends when the corporation is insolvent or would be rendered insolvent by virtue of the dividend.[118] Thirdly, dividends are permitted only when a balance sheet test is met. The test itself varies widely among jurisdictions.

The traditional balance sheet test restricts the corporation to making distributions not in excess of its 'surplus', calculated as the excess of its net assets

---

[115] The term 'redemption' usually refers to acquisition by the corporation pursuant to the terms of the shares, whereas 'purchase' or 'repurchase' refers to acquisition by market transactions or through negotiations with individual stockholders.

[116] See, e.g. *Eshleman* v. *Keenan*, 194 Atl. 40 (Del.Ch. 1937); *Gabelli & Co., Inc.* v. *Liggett Group, Inc.*, 479 A.2d 276 (Del. Sup. Ct. 1984). Compare *Miller* v. *Magline, Inc.*, 76 Mich.App. 284, 256 N.W.2d 761 (1977). The civil law procedure of stockholder approval (at the annual meeting) of proposed dividends does not exist in the United States.

[117] e.g. RMBCA § 6.40(a).

[118] e.g. RMBCA § 6.40(c)(1). Solvency, in the terms of these statutes, represents the ability of the corporation to pay its debts as they come due, and is not based on an asset test.

over its stated capital.[119] In some jurisdictions, such as Delaware, the resulting 'surplus' is fully available for dividends, subject to protection of the liquidation preferences of preferred stock.[120] In others, the 'surplus' is divided into two portions: 'earned surplus' represents that portion of the surplus equal to the accumulated and undistributed net income of the corporation, while 'capital surplus' or 'paid in surplus' represents the remainder. In these jurisdictions, only earned surplus is freely available for distributions. Capital surplus may be distributable subject to limitations, such as notice or perhaps stockholder approval.[121]

The actual calculation of the maximum permitted distribution under the balance sheet test varies among jurisdictions. For example, while most of the major corporate jurisdictions require application of 'book value' to the assets (usually determined in accordance with generally accepted accounting principles) the Revised Model Business Corporation Act accepts book or market value, calculated on any reasonable basis.[122]

Several important jurisdictions, beginning with California, have completely restructured the legal rules applicable to corporate capital, and in the process have significantly altered the legal tests for corporate distributions.[123] The key elements of that restructuring are elimination of the concept of stated or legal capital, elimination of the related concept of par value, and substantial alteration of the balance sheet test for corporate distributions. In the calculation of the permissible maximum amount of corporate distributions, these statutes do not require the subtraction of stated capital, and they therefore permit distributions to be made (with some limitations) to the full extent of net assets. The distribution provisions of the Revised Model Business Corporation Act, though broadly based on the California approach, are even more permissive. They require only that the corporation not be rendered insolvent by the distribution, and that post-distribution net assets exceed liabilities (as well as liquidating preferences of senior stock).[124]

---

[119] 'Net assets' are defined as the excess of the assets of the corporation over its liabilities. 'Stated capital' is defined as the aggregate par value of the outstanding shares. If the outstanding shares have no par value, stated capital is the amount of the consideration for the payment of the shares that has been designated as stated capital by the board of directors upon the issuance of the shares. See, e.g. NYBCL § 102(a)(9); Del. Gen. Corp. L. § 154.

[120] Del. Corp. L. § 170(a)(1). The references to 'surplus' have been placed in quotes to emphasize that they represent legal terms of art. While they carry accounting implications, they have been abandoned by the accounting profession. Readers of contemporary financial statements will encounter the more descriptive terms 'retained earnings' and 'additional paid-in capital', which often have essentially the same meanings, respectively, as the legal terms 'earned surplus' and 'capital surplus'. Some recently revised statutes use the contemporary terms.

[121] See, e.g. NYBCL § 510(c) (notice required).

[122] See RMBCA § 6.40(d) and comment to § 6.40: 'section 6.40 does not mandate the use of generally accepted accounting principles; it only requires the use of accounting principles and practices that are reasonable in the circumstances'.

[123] See Cal. Corp. Code § 500.   [124] See RMBCA § 6.40.

C. Redemption and Repurchase of Shares

In sharp contrast to the limitations of most civil law jurisdictions, corporations in the United States are permitted to reacquire their own shares by purchase (whether on the market or from individual stockholders) or redemption (normally by exercise of a right of redemption specified in the shares).[125] Payment for the reacquisition is subject to financial limitations, which are generally parallel to those for dividend distributions. Some recently revised statutes include share repurchases within the general concept of 'distributions',[126] with limitations identical to those on dividends.[127] Other more traditional statutes contain separate financial limitations for share repurchases, which are occasionally more permissive than the limitations on dividend distributions.[128]

D. Liabilities for Illegal Distributions

Violation of the legal restrictions on corporate distributions imposes the risk of joint and several personal liability of directors to corporate creditors.[129] In many states, stockholders who receive corporate distributions knowing that they were distributed in violation of the legal restrictions will be liable, to the extent of what they have received, either directly to the corporation or to the directors who have been held liable therefor.[130] The technical complexity of the distribution limitations has led to inclusion of provisions in most corporate statutes immunizing the directors from liability when their decision to make a distribution is based in good faith on the advice of experts, such as accountants and appraisers.[131]

VIII. Major Corporate Changes

A.   The Statutory Requirements

Four categories of major corporate change require special notice, disclosure, and approval procedures under state corporate law: amendment of the arti-

---

[125] See, e.g. RMBCA § 6.31. There is judicial support for imposition of a business purpose test on share repurchases, particularly when the shares are purchased from some, but not all, stockholders. See, e.g. *Cheff* v. *Mathes*, 199 A.2d 548 (Del. 1964); *Bennett* v. *Propp*, 187 A.2d 405 (Del. 1962); *Kors* v. *Carey*, 158 A.2d 136 (Del. Ch. 1960).

[126] See RMBCA § 1.40(6).   [127] See RMBCA § 6.40.

[128] See, e.g. Del. Gen. Corp. L. § 160 (impairment of capital).

[129] See, e.g. RMBCA §§ 8.30, 8.33.   [130] See, e.g. RMBCA § 8.33(b)(2).

[131] See, e.g. RMBCA § 8.30(b).

cles of incorporation; sale of all or substantially all of the corporate assets; merger or consolidation; and dissolution of the corporation. Although the procedures vary among the transactions, the requirements are similar:

(1) the board of directors must by resolution approve the proposed transaction or change;

(2) a meeting of stockholders must be called, with full notice of the proposal to be considered;

(3) at the meeting, the statutory majority of stockholders must vote in favor of the proposal;[132] and

(4) with respect to some of the corporate changes, special statutory protections are given to creditors and dissenting stockholders.

B. *Voting and Consent*

Most state corporation laws now require only a majority vote of stockholders to approve a major corporate transaction, but that majority is measured by the number of shares entitled to vote, not merely by the number present at the meeting or actually voting.[133] Some state laws retain larger majority requirements for certain transactions, such as a two-thirds majority for approval of a merger,[134] and all permit the articles of incorporation to provide for a greater than majority voting requirement.[135] The articles of incorporation may also grant shares of a particular class of stock the right to vote separately on the transaction, in which case the required majority vote must be obtained separately from each such class as well as from the remaining voting shares.[136] Most, though not all, statutes grant a statutory class vote to any class of shares, whether or not they vote by their terms, when the transaction or proposal affects adversely the rights, preferences, or privileges of that class.[137]

A variation on the voting process, allowed in every state, is approval by unanimous consent of the stockholders.[138] When a corporation has relatively few stockholders, and when notice and a meeting would be inconvenient or impracticable, written consents may be distributed and collected to obtain

---

[132] With respect to corporations the stock of which is registered under the Securities Exchange Act of 1934, the notice to stockholders as well as the vote would be regulated under the Proxy Rules under that act. This subject is discussed in Chapter 22 on securities regulation.

[133] See, e.g. RMBCA § 11.03(e) (merger); § 12.02(e) (sale of assets); § 14.02(e) (dissolution); § 10.03(e) (amendment of articles of incorporation).

[134] e.g. N.Y. Bus. Corp. L. § 903 (merger).   [135] See, e.g. RMBCA § 7.27.

[136] See, e.g. RMBCA §§ 7.25, 7.27.

[137] See, e.g. RMBCA § 10.04 (amendment of articles of incorporation); § 11.03(f) (merger).

[138] See RMBCA § 7.04.

and document the required stockholder approval. A few states have extended the consent procedure to non-unanimous approval.[139]

C. *Amendment of the Articles*

The first of the major corporate changes, amendment of the articles of incorporation, may be undertaken at any time, to add, delete or modify any permissible provision. State corporate laws reserve this power of amendment, and therefore no stockholder has a vested property right resulting from a provision of the articles.[140] The procedure for amendment requires approval by the board of a proposed amendment, notice to the stockholders, and favorable vote thereon, in most states by a majority of the outstanding voting shares.[141] A statutory class vote is usually extended to any class of shares the rights, preferences, or privileges of which would be adversely affected by the amendment.[142] The amendment becomes effective upon its filing with the state or on a later date as set out in the amendment itself.[143]

D. *Sale of Corporate Assets*

Although purchases and sales of corporate assets are normally within the authority of the board of directors, a disposition of substantially all the assets, not in the usual course of the corporation's business, is a major corporate change. The procedure for undertaking this transaction, like an amendment of the articles, requires a resolution of the board of directors and notice to the stockholders, followed by the favorable vote of a majority of the voting stock.[144] In addition, in many jurisdictions stockholders who vote against the sale of assets may choose to dissent from the transaction and demand that the corporation repurchase their shares at their fair value.[145] This right of dissent, usually called the 'appraisal remedy', is discussed in section VIII I below.

---

[139] See, e.g. Del. Gen. Corp. Law § 228 (transaction may be approved by majority consent and implemented prior to notifying non-consenting stockholders).

[140] See, e.g. RMBCA § 10.01.   [141] See RMBCA § 10.04.

[142] See, e.g. RMBCA § 10.04, containing an extensive detailing of such amendments. The Revised Model Business Corporation Act also grants an appraisal remedy to stockholders adversely affected by certain articles amendments. See RMBCA § 13.02(a)(4). Most state laws grant no such remedy with respect to articles amendments. The appraisal remedy is discussed in section VIII I below.

[143] See, e.g. RMBCA § 10.06.

[144] See, e.g. RMBCA § 12.02. Compare RMBCA § 12.01 (sales in the regular course of business). Since the sale of corporate assets does not, of itself, alter the rights, preferences or privileges of any class of stock, there is no statutory class vote in the absence of a provision in the share terms granting them such a right.

[145] See, e.g. RMBCA § 13.02(a)(3) (providing the appraisal remedy except with respect to a cash sale in which substantially all of the proceeds will be distributed within one year following the sale).

E. The Statutory Merger

The third of the major corporate changes—the statutory merger—generally requires resolution of the boards of directors, notice to the stockholders, and approval by affirmative vote of the stockholders of both corporations.[146] A class vote will be required on the plan of merger if it contains a provision that, if contained in an amendment to the articles of incorporation, would require a class vote.[147] Moreover, the appraisal remedy will ordinarily be available to the stockholders of each corporation who are entitled to vote on the plan of merger.[148] Following a statutory merger, the surviving corporation takes title to all the properties and rights of the merging corporation, but also becomes liable for all of its debts and obligations.[149] In its pure form, therefore, the statutory merger requires substantial statutory formality from both of the merging corporations, and it exposes the surviving corporation to potentially substantial (and possibly unknown) debts of the merging corporation. Among the most substantial of these are product and environmental liabilities, discussed in Chapter 18. In actual practice in the United States, the pure form of statutory merger has, principally for these reasons, become uncommon.

F. Alternative Forms of Business Combination

The corporate laws of most states provide alternative mechanisms for achieving the economic effects of a merger, while avoiding some of the statutory formalities and reducing exposure to liability. These include asset and stock acquisitions, share exchanges and three-party mergers. By the middle of this century, corporations in several jurisdictions achieved the effects of a merger by arranging for a sale of assets by the merging corporation in exchange for shares of stock of the surviving (or acquiring) corporation. Following the asset sale, the merging corporation was dissolved, and it distributed the shares received in the sale to its stockholders.[150] The economic effect of this two-step process (sale for shares, followed by dissolution) was essentially identical to that of a statutory merger. However, the corporate laws in most states required stockholder approval (and the appraisal remedy) only for the *selling* corporation; the purchase of assets by the acquiring corporation—

---

[146] See, e.g. RMBCA § 11.03(a).   [147] See, e.g. RMBCA § 11.03(f)(1).

[148] See, e.g. RMBCA § 13.02(a)(1).   [149] See, e.g. RMBCA § 11.06(a).

[150] When the selling corporation has several classes of shares outstanding, it is usually necessary not only to obtain approval for the sale and subsequent dissolution, but also for an articles amendment to alter the preferences of one or more classes. For a case in which these three votes were successfully combined, see *Goldman v. Postal Telegraph, Inc.*, 52 F. Supp. 763 (D.C. Del. 1943) (Delaware law).

though economically equivalent to a merger—was not subject to the statutory formalities of the merger process.

A second alternative to the statutory merger is an acquisition by the acquiring corporation of the stock of another corporation. As compared with the statutory merger and the asset acquisition, the stock acquisition has several advantages. Like the purchase of assets, the acquisition of shares requires no approval of the stockholders of the acquiring corporation. Moreover, since the *sellers* of the shares are individual stockholders rather than the corporation, the acquisition is made without a vote of the stockholders of *either* corporation. The shares may be obtained piecemeal by individual negotiations and purchases, and the timing, as well as the price and other purchase terms, may vary among stockholders. Finally, if the acquiring corporation does not dissolve the acquired corporation—i.e. if it retains the acquired corporation as a wholly or partially-owned subsidiary corporation—the acquiring corporation may avoid direct liability for the debts of the subsidiary.[151] The principal problem with this form of transaction is the difficulty, and occasional impossibility, of obtaining all (or the desired majority) of the shares through individual negotiations with many stockholders.[152]

These asset and share acquisition transactions were occasionally contested by disenfranchised stockholders of the surviving corporation, who sought voting and appraisal rights based on the theory that the combined steps of the transaction produced the effects of a merger. The 'de facto merger' doctrine was accepted in some cases and statutes, with the result that stockholders of the acquiring corporation were given voting or appraisal rights.[153] The doctrine was rejected in other jurisdictions,[154] and its status is unclear in several states. In California, the concept of 'reorganization' is broadly defined to include mergers, asset and share acquisitions, and multi-party transactions

---

[151] As suggested earlier, this factor alone may motivate the form of the acquisition, particularly if the acquired corporation may be subject to product liabilities, environmental liabilities, and other substantial contingent claims.

[152] This difficulty in the stock-purchase transaction has been addressed in a few states by the adoption of 'share exchange' provisions in the state corporation laws, providing for a mandatory exchange of shares following a vote of the stockholders. Under the Model Business Corporation Act a share exchange must be approved by the boards of directors of both corporations, and approved by an affirmative majority vote of the shareholders of the corporation the shares of which will be exchanged in the transaction. Following stockholder approval, the statutory share exchange is self-executing. The shares are deemed exchanged whether or not they are in fact tendered in return for new certificates, and they are treated thereafter as though they are the shares which were approved for exchange pursuant to the plan. RMBCA §§ 11.02, 11.03(a), 11.06(b).

[153] See, e.g. *Farris v. Glen Alden Corp.*, 393 Pa. 427, 143 A.2d 25 (1958) (reverse sale); *Rath v. Rath Packing Co.*, 257 Iowa 1277, 136 N.W.2d 410 (1965) (asset acquisition); *Applestein v. United Board & Carton Corp.*, 60 N.J. Super 333, 159 A.2d 146 (Ch.), *aff'd per curiam*, 33 N.J. 72, 161 A.2d 474 (1960) (stock acquisition).

[154] Delaware rejected the doctrine judicially in *Hariton v. Arco Electronics, Inc.*, 40 Del. Ch. 326, 182 A.2d 22 (1962), *aff'd.*, 41 Del. Ch. 74, 188 A.2d 123 (1963). Pennsylvania rejected the doctrine legislatively; the grounds for that rejection are explored in *Terry v. Penn Central Corp.*, 668 F.2d 188 (3d Cir. 1981).

with the same effect;[155] and the approval procedures and protections granted to all reorganizations are equivalent, irrespective of form.[156]

The widespread use of alternative merger forms gave rise to a statutory change in some states, permitting a statutory merger to be effected under certain circumstances without the vote of the stockholders of the surviving corporation. The Revised Model Business Corporation Act contains a typical provision, eliminating the need for a vote of the stockholders of the surviving corporation if four conditions are satisfied by the plan of merger with respect to the surviving corporation:

(1) the plan calls for no amendment to its articles of incorporation;
(2) there is no change in the terms of its previously outstanding shares;
(3) the number of voting shares outstanding immediately after the merger will be no more than 120% of the number of voting shares outstanding immediately prior to the merger; and
(4) the number of participating shares outstanding immediately after the merger will be no more than 120 percent of the number of participating shares outstanding immediately prior to the merger.[157]

G. Triangular Mergers

Mergers, like many other corporate transactions, may be used as components of larger multi-part business plans. The simplest triangular merger involves the merger of the acquired corporation into an existing or newly-created subsidiary of the acquiring corporation. The use of triangular mergers developed in response to the need to achieve certain results not obtainable by traditional combination or acquisition forms.[158] Neither a statutory merger nor an asset acquisition will, for example, insulate the acquiring corporation from the contingent product liabilities of the acquired corporation. As discussed above, a stock acquisition will achieve this result, but it may be difficult or impossible to acquire the desired majority of the stock of the acquired corporation from its individual stockholders.[159]

Use of the triangular merger in this setting is based on the description of the consideration permitted to be exchanged for the acquired corporation's stock, which includes not only stock of the acquiring corporation, but stock

---

[155] See Cal. Corp. Code § 181.   [156] See Cal. Corp. Code §§ 1200, 1201, 1300.

[157] RMBCA § 11.03(g). Voting shares are defined as those that vote unconditionally in election of directors, and participating shares as those that entitle the holders to participate without limitation in distributions. RMBCA § 11.03(h).

[158] Asset acquisitions and stock acquisitions can similarly be effected through subsidiary corporations. All of these forms can, as well, involve more than three corporations.

[159] This dilemma no longer exists in states that have adopted mandatory share-exchange provisions. See, e.g. RMBCA § 11.02, discussed in n.152 above.

of any other corporation.[160] In the triangular merger, the acquired corporation is merged into a subsidiary, but its stockholders receive stock of the parent (acquiring) corporation.

An interesting side-effect of the triangular merger is that, since the parent corporation is not merging with another corporation, its stockholders do not vote on the transaction.[161] Moreover, since the appraisal remedy with respect to corporate mergers is in most states granted only to stockholders entitled to vote on the transaction,[162] it is also denied to the stockholders of the parent corporation in the triangular merger. The triangular merger, as well as a variant form (the 'reverse triangular merger') in which the subsidiary is merged into the acquired corporation, has become among the most common forms of agreed business combinations in recent years.

H. Dissolution

The last form of major corporate change is dissolution, which, like the forms discussed earlier, must be authorized by board resolution, notice, and vote of the stockholders.[163] The effect of a dissolution, after filing by the corporation, is that the corporate existence continues only for the purpose of winding up and liquidating its business and affairs.[164] The corporation must pay or make provision for payment of its known and unknown claims, and distribute the remaining assets to its stockholders according to their interests.[165]

I. The Appraisal Remedy

The appraisal remedy extends in some states to certain amendments of the articles of incorporation in many states to sales of substantially all assets not in the usual course of business; and in most states to dissenting stockholders of both corporations that are parties to a statutory merger. Other major corporate changes, as well as dissolution, do not give rise to an appraisal remedy. In its operation, the appraisal remedy has been (and in many jurisdictions

---

[160] For example, the Model Business Corporation Act states that the plan of merger must set out: 'the manner and basis of converting the shares of each corporation into shares, obligations, or other securities of the surviving *or any other* corporation or into cash or other property in whole or in part'. RMBCA § 11.01(b)(3) (emphasis added).

[161] A few states by statute reject this analysis, and provide voting rights and the appraisal remedy to the stockholders of a parent corporation whose subsidiary is a party to a triangular merger. See Cal. Gen. Corp. Law §§ 1200, 1201, requiring board and shareholder approval by the corporation in control of any constituent or acquiring corporation, the 'parent party'.

[162] See RMBCA § 13.02(a)(1).   [163] See, e.g. RMBCA § 14.02.

[164] See, e.g. RMBCA § 14.05.   [165] See, e.g. RMBCA §§ 14.05(a), 14.06, 14.07.

remains) unwieldy, slow and expensive for both the dissenting stockholder and the corporation. The mechanical operation of the remedy varies widely among jurisdictions, but in general obtaining the remedy requires that the dissenting stockholder vote against the transaction, file his dissent with the corporation, and await a cash offer of fair value for his shares. If the offer is satisfactory, the corporation then purchases the shares at the stated price. If the offer is unsatisfactory, full litigation over the value may ensue.[166] The litigation in many jurisdictions is long and expensive; during its pendency, the dissenting stockholder in most jurisdictions retains his shares and receives no payment. Costs of the proceedings, with some exceptions, are borne separately by each of the parties.

More recent appraisal provisions, typified by the Revised Model Business Corporation Act formulation, have attempted to simplify the procedure and to facilitate resolution of the difficult valuation issue. The new provisions require that the corporation promptly pay to the dissenter the amount that the corporation estimates to be the fair value of the dissenter's shares, and provide financial information and an explanation of the basis for the valuation.[167] The dissenter is not bound by the corporation's valuation,[168] and costs of the appraisal proceeding are normally borne by the corporation, but the court may assess costs against the complaining stockholder if the stockholder acted arbitrarily, vexatiously or not in good faith in demanding additional payment.[169]

IX. Conclusion

The American law of corporations and other business associations is distinctive for its flexibility, its amenability to agreements by the parties, and its rapid and effective response to changes in business practices and in the market-place. The law is basically permissive, enabling the parties to establish the form of organization they desire and to tailor the details of organizational form and structure to suit the particular needs of their business. Corporate, partnership, and other business association statutes are often amended and occasionally rewritten to reflect changes in business and legal practices, with

---

[166] The problem of valuation, in appraisal as well as other contexts, remains particularly vexatious. For leading cases, see, e.g. *Weinberger* v. *UOP*, 457 A.2d 701 (Del. 1983) (abandoning the 'Delaware block' valuation approach, a weighted-average valuation method combining asset value, earnings value, and market value). Compare, e.g. *Piemonte* v. *New Boston Garden Corp.*, 377 Mass. 719, 387 N.E.2d 1145 (1979) (pre-*Weinberger* case applying the 'Delaware block approach'); *Leader* v. *Hycor, Inc.*, 395 Mass. 215, 479 N.E.2d 173 (1985) (reaffirming that the 'Delaware block approach', as applied in *Piemonte*, continues to be one of the acceptable methods of appraisal valuation, despite *Weinberger*).

[167] RMBCA § 13.25.   [168] RMBCA § 13.28.   [169] RMBCA § 13.31(a).

the result that the operative laws of business associations rarely stand in the way of organizing and operating legitimate businesses in the most efficient manner and in the best interests of the participants. Coupled with this flexibility is a well-developed body of statutory and decisional law protecting the interests of partners, stockholders, and other participants in business associations.

14

COMMERCIAL LAW

DONALD J. RAPSON

I. Introduction

'Commercial law', in its broadest sense, refers to the law governing all business transactions of any kind, including the body of law that affords special protections and rights to consumers. 'Consumer' transactions are generally those affecting personal, family, or household matters. In a narrower but still very broad sense, 'commercial law' means the *Uniform Commercial Code* ('UCC'), which is a state law that is in effect in all the states.

Commercial law in the broadest sense extends far beyond the UCC. Historically, its source is the judge-made common law, particularly that part known as the law merchant. As the American economy expanded and developed, the ever-increasing complexity and diversity of business transactions created the need for, and resulted in, the legislative enactment of numerous statutes at both the federal and state levels, which both provided special treatment for certain areas of commerce and were aimed at solving particular problems and concerns. Some examples of the scope of federal legislation are statutes dealing with agriculture,[1] aviation,[2] banking,[3] consumer credit protection,[4] payment systems[5] and transportation.[6] Many of these statutes are administered and enforced by federal regulatory agencies, which are given

---

[1] Packers and Stockyards Act, 7 U.S.C. §181 et seq.
[2] Federal Aviation Act, 49 U.S.C. §1401 et seq.
[3] Federal Bank Holding Company Act, 12 U.S.C. §1841 et seq.; National Bank Act, 12 U.S.C. §21 et seq.
[4] Consumer Credit Protection Act, 15 U.S.C. §1600 et seq.
[5] Federal Reserve Act, 12 U.S.C. §342; Expedited Funds Availability Act, 12 U.S.C. §4001 et seq.
[6] Interstate Commerce Act (Department of Transportation), 49 U.S.C. §101 et seq.

broad authority to promulgate rules and regulations,[7] have the force of law and must always be consulted in connection with a particular topic.

In addition, the states have enacted statutes on many of these subjects. As a matter of American constitutional law, a federal statute preempts a state law governing the same subject. Sometimes, however, the federal statute does not deal with a particular question[8] or expressly defers to state law,[9] in which event it is necessary to consult state law, either statutory or common law.

Although the range of federal and state statutes is very broad, there are still some commercial subjects that are governed by the common law. For example, common law tort rules generally govern the liability of manufacturers, distributors, and retailer-sellers for personal injury and property claims caused by negligence in the design, construction, manufacture, installation and marketing of goods and services. There is also a more recent common law doctrine known as 'strict liability in tort' which imposes liability in certain circumstances for putting defective products into the market-place, irrespective of whether there has been negligence. Another example of the effect of the common law on commercial transactions is the law governing guaranties and other arrangements for credit support known as 'suretyship'.

Accordingly, in researching and analyzing a question of commercial law, one must first determine whether there is an applicable federal statute. The next step is to review the statutes of the particular state to see if there is applicable legislation. If there is no federal or state statute covering the issue, it is then necessary to examine the common law of the jurisdiction. In some circumstances, there will be overlapping and simultaneous coverage of a particular subject, with a federal statute, a state statute, and the common law all having some applicability. In those instances, all three bodies of law must be considered and integrated. An important example is the subject of liability for defective goods where federal and state statutes provide for warranty liability, but the common law of tort and strict liability may also be applicable.

Even if a federal or state statute deals with the subject, it is often necessary to interpret, apply, and enforce that statute in accordance with common law principles. This means not only the substantive rules applicable to a particular topic, but also those principles of jurisprudence that are applicable to

[7] Federal Trade Commission Credit Practices Rules, 16 CFR Pt 444; Federal Reserve Board Regulation Z—Truth in Lending Regulations, 12 CFR Pt 226; Federal Reserve Board Regulation CC—Availability of Funds and Collection of Checks, 12 CFR Pt 29.

[8] e.g. neither the Securities Exchange Act of 1933, 15 U.S.C. §77a et seq. nor the Securities Exchange Act of 1934, 15 U.S.S. §78a et seq., set forth rules relative to the transfer of the rights that constitute securities. That subject is covered by UCC Article 8.

[9] e.g. under Section 705(g) of that part of the Consumer Credit Protection Act dealing with Equal Credit Opportunity, 15 U.S.C. §1691d(g), the law of a state providing for substantially similar or greater protections for credit applicants than the federal statute will govern.

American law generally, such as capacity to contract, equity, estoppel and good faith.

The UCC is comprised of separate Articles covering the following subjects: sales of goods (Article 2); leases of goods (Article 2A); negotiable instruments (Article 3); bank deposits and collections (Article 4); funds transfers, e.g. wire transfers (Article 4A); letters of credit (Article 5); warehouse receipts, bills of lading and other documents of title (Article 7); investment securities (Article 8); and secured transactions, including sales of accounts and chattel paper (Article 9). Article 1 contains general provisions applicable to all the Articles.

The underlying purposes and policies of the UCC are:

(a) to simplify, clarify and modernize the law governing commercial trans-
     actions;
(b) to permit the continued expansion of commercial practices through cus-
     tom, usage and agreement of the parties;
(c) to make uniform the law among the various jurisdictions.[10]

For the most part, the UCC's goal of uniformity has been achieved. The states and the District of Columbia have enacted the UCC with relatively few variations. Since 1984 the UCC has been under an on-going process of revision in order to bring it current with new technology and modern commercial practices. Articles 2A and 4A are new; Articles 3, 5 and 8 have been completely revised and Article 4 has been substantially amended; Article 6, which attempts to provide protections for creditors of sellers who dispose of their goods in bulk sales, has been repealed in most states because it has become functionally obsolete; and Articles 2 and 9 are currently in the process of being revised and modernized. Since the timing of the enactment process varies among the states, there is currently a lack of uniformity which will continue until all states have adopted these changes.

Even though the UCC contains separate Articles covering different topics, there is an over-all interrelationship among the various Articles. Indeed, at its inception the sponsors of the UCC stated:

> The concept of the present Act is that 'commercial transactions' is a single subject of the law, notwithstanding its many facets.
>
> A single transaction may very well involve a contract for sale, followed by a sale, the giving of a check or draft for a part of the purchase price, and the acceptance of some form of security for the balance.
>
> The check or draft may be negotiated and will ultimately pass through one or more banks for collection.
>
> If the goods are shipped or stored the subject matter of the sale may be covered by a bill of lading or warehouse receipt or both.

---

[10] UCC §1–102(2).

Or it may be that the entire transaction was made pursuant to a letter of credit either domestic or foreign.

Obviously, every phase of commerce involved is but a part of one transaction, namely, the sale of and payment for goods.

If, instead of goods in the ordinary sense, the transaction involved stocks or bonds, some of the phases of the transaction would obviously be different. Others would be the same. In addition, there are certain additional formalities incident to the transfer of stocks and bonds from one owner to another.

This Act purports to deal with all the phases which may ordinarily arise in the handling of a commercial transaction, from start to finish.[11]

Commercial law courses in most American law schools are structured around the Articles of the UCC, and familiarity with its provisions is essential to the practice of commercial law. Most of this chapter (section II) focuses on the UCC; section III discusses the related common law of suretyship and guaranty; and section IV describes the special treatment given to consumer transactions.

Despite the broad scope of the UCC, it is also necessary to integrate the UCC with the common law. A key provision states:

Unless displaced by the particular provisions of this Act, the principles of law and equity, including the law merchant and the law relative to capacity to contract, principal and agent, estoppel, fraud, misrepresentation, duress, coercion, mistake, bankruptcy, or other validating or invalidating cause shall supplement its provisions.[12]

This means that it is sometimes necessary to interpret and apply the provisions of the UCC in accordance with principles of the common law that are generally applicable to all areas of the law. For example, in determining whether one person is bound by or liable for the acts of another in connection with a transaction covered by the UCC, it is necessary to analyze the common law of agency. If, however, the provisions of the UCC deal expressly with an issue, it is usually inappropriate to go beyond the UCC and apply the common law. Thus, in determining whether a party has a security interest in goods, one should look only to Article 9 and not apply the 'equitable lien' concept of the common law.

In some instances the UCC expressly codifies common law concepts. An important provision of Article 1 states: 'Every contract or duty within this Act imposes an obligation of good faith in its performance or enforcement'.[13]

---

[11] General Comment of National Conference of Commissioners on Uniform State Laws and the American Law Institute, 1957 Official Text of the Uniform Commercial Code.
[12] UCC §1-103.   [13] UCC §1-203.

'Good faith' is an important concept in American commercial law, not limited to the UCC. It is generally defined to mean 'honesty in fact and the observance of reasonable commercial standards of fair dealing',[14] although the UCC in some instances limits the definition to 'honesty in fact'.[15] The doctrine of good faith is implied in all contracts and constitutes a standard of behavior by which the parties must perform and enforce that contract.

'Freedom of contract' is a principle that allows the parties to agree to express contractual terms that set forth their respective rights, powers, duties, and responsibilities in a manner different than the provisions of the statute or common law rule. The UCC specifically adopts that principle, subject to certain restrictions designed to prevent oppressive or capricious conduct. Thus, although the parties to an agreement may as a general rule vary the provisions of the UCC, they cannot disclaim 'the obligations of good faith, diligence, reasonableness and care' required by the UCC. The parties can, however, specify standards by which the performance of those obligations are to be measured, if those standards are not 'manifestly unreasonable'.[16]

The UCC is supplemented by Official Comments to each of its sections which explain the purpose and operation of the section, often in the context of specific examples. Although the Official Comments are not enacted as part of the statutory law, they are, nevertheless, very useful and persuasive in understanding the UCC and are relied upon extensively by lawyers and judges as aids in interpreting and applying its provisions.

II. The Uniform Commercial Code

A useful way to analyze the UCC is to do so in the context of a contract or lease to sell goods, examining the alternative arrangements and systems for obtaining payment of the buyer's obligations, and reviewing the laws governing those arrangements and systems. Although this approach examines the issues primarily from the perspective of a seller or lessor, most of these same issues can also arise from the perspective of a buyer, or from a lender who extends credit to a buyer to enable it to pay the seller.

---

[14] *Restatement (Second) of the Law of Contracts*, §205.
[15] UCC §§1-201(19), 5-102(a)(7).   [16] UCC §1-102(3).

A. *Article 2 Sales of Goods; Article 2A Leases of Goods*

In this analysis, it is first necessary to draw a distinction between 'goods' on the one hand, and 'real property' on the other, in order to determine whether the contract or lease is governed by the UCC or other law. Although some UCC Articles are not limited to transactions in goods,[17] Article 2 only applies to sales of goods.[18] Article 2A, which was recently adopted as a response to the rapid development of leasing as a means of marketing and distributing personal property, particularly equipment, is also only applicable to goods.[19] 'Goods' means things that are 'movable at the time of' the contract or lease,[20] which is another way of saying that Articles 2 and 2A do not apply to real property. It is not always easy, however, to determine whether a particular contract involves goods or real property. For example, a contract for the erection, installation, and sale of a radio tower involves the sale by the builder of many pieces of equipment which are clearly 'goods'. But because the contract is predominantly one for the construction of a structure on land, the radio tower would probably be treated as real property, and the performance and enforcement of the contract would not be governed by Article 2. The contract itself, however, would be characterized as personal property and, as such, could serve as collateral for a secured transaction governed by Article 9. Thus, although the law dealing with real property contracts would govern whether the builder had a right to be paid, that 'right' to be paid, for whatever it may be worth, is personal property under the UCC which the builder can use as a source of financing by selling or assigning it as collateral.

1. UCC sale or lease of goods; non-UCC contract for services

UCC Articles 2 and 2A only apply to contracts for the sale or lease of goods. An issue of current importance is whether contracts for computer programs that provide for software systems, together with back-up services and computer hardware, are for goods and covered by Article 2 or 2A. This is a 'mixed' contract involving both goods and services, and courts have rendered conflicting decisions. The pending revision of Article 2 is attempting to resolve this question by covering such transactions, but treating them as a separate category. A similar issue involves contaminated blood that is supplied by a hospital to a patient. Most courts hold that this involves services and not goods.

The distinction between goods and services is important because, if the

---

[17] e.g. UCC Articles 1, 3, 4, 4A, 5, 7, 8 and 9.   [18] UCC §2-102.
[19] UCC §§2A-102, 2A-103(1)(j).   [20] UCC §§2-105(1), 2A-103(1)(h).

contract or lease is not for goods, Articles 2 and 2A are not applicable. In that circumstance the general law of contracts governs, and the rules may be different. For example, there is generally no implied warranty of merchantability or fitness covering a contract for services as there is for goods under the UCC.[21] Where services are involved, it is, therefore, essential that a buyer obtain express contractual warranties covering the quality of the services to be furnished. Another difference is that the time in which a party to a contract must commence a lawsuit concerning that contract may be different in the case of services than for goods under the UCC.

2. Differences between an Article 2 'sale' and an Article 2A 'lease'

Although Article 2 governing sales and Article 2A governing leases have many parallel provisions, there are important differences, particularly the rights and remedies upon breach. In analyzing the distinction between 'sales' and 'leases', the fact that the parties expressly state that the agreement is a sale or lease is not determinative. Instead, the analysis focuses on the economic realities of the particular transaction.

To demonstrate the distinction, assume that Cella entered into two transactions with Byron, both of which were written as 3-year leases of equipment. Each lease provided for monthly rental payments of $10,000 totalling $360,000 over the 3-year term. The first lease was for a computer and the second for a newly designed high speed drill. Cella had purchased each piece of equipment from its manufacturer for $300,000. The $360,000 in rentals represented a return of Cella's investment in the piece of equipment plus a $60,000 'profit' or 'yield' on that investment. Cella expected that the computer would be functional but obsolete at the end of 3 years and gave Byron an option to buy it for $100 at the end of the term. In contrast, Cella expected that the drill would have a market value of $50,000 after 3 years. Although Cella was willing to give Byron an option to buy the drill at the end of the term, she required that the option price be $50,000.

Under the UCC the 'lease' for the computer is characterized as a sale governed by Article 2. Byron would most likely not return the computer if it were still operating after the 3 years. Instead, he would be economically motivated to exercise the option and buy it for $100, which would surely be a better price than he could find for a working computer, even if he had a relatively small need for it. Therefore, when Cella entered into the 'lease,' she could not have had a reasonable expectation of getting the computer back at the end of 3 years. Because Cella did not have a meaningful 'residual interest' in the

---

[21] UCC §§2-314, 2-315; 2A-212, 2A-213.

computer, the UCC treats Cella as a seller under Article 2 rather than a lessor under Article 2A.

In contrast, Byron would not be under any economic compulsion to buy the drill at the end of 3 years. He could, instead, buy a similar drill in the market-place without having to pay more than the option price, or not spend the money at all. Consequently, Cella entered into that lease expecting to get the drill (or $50,000) back at the end of the term, i.e. she had a meaningful residual interest. The UCC treats that transaction as a lease covered by Article 2A,[22] not because it was labelled as such, but because of its economic realities.

3. Comparison of remedies on breach of sale and lease

Whether a transaction is an Article 2 sale or an Article 2A lease is particularly important with respect to the remedies upon breach. If Byron made the required payments for both the computer and drill for 24 months, but then breached both 'leases,' leaving 12 unpaid payments of $10,000 totalling $120,000 under each lease, what would be his liabilities?

As shown above, Cella's interest in the computer was not that of a lessor. Despite being called a 'lease', the transaction was a sale. Cella, therefore, had the remedies of a seller under Article 2. Furthermore, if she had a right to repossess the computer on default, that right, even as a supposed 'lessor', would be treated as a 'security interest'.[23] The computer was collateral for Byron's obligation to pay the purchase price of $360,000. Article 9 would then be applicable[24] and gives Cella the right to repossess the computer.[25] Although she would also have the right to repossess the drill, her right in that instance would be as a 'true' lessor under Article 2A, not under Article 9.[26]

If Cella exercised her rights to repossess both pieces of equipment, sold both at public sales in a commercially reasonable manner, and received net proceeds of $100,000 for each, would Cella then be entitled to recover from Byron in each transaction a deficiency of $20,000 based on the unpaid balance ($120,000–$100,000)? Despite the similarities, the distinction between a 'sale' and a 'lease' produces different results under Articles 2 and 2A, as we now explain.

Inasmuch as the computer transaction was a sale under Article 2, Cella would have been entitled to recover the unpaid balance of $120,000 if she had not repossessed the computer.[27] However, because Cella enforced her Article 9 security interest in the computer and exercised her right to repossess and

---

[22] UCC §1-201(37).   [23] UCC §2-401(1).
[24] See the discussion of secured credit transactions in section II E below.
[25] UCC §9-503.   [26] UCC §2A-525.   [27] UCC §2-709(1)(a).

re-sell it, Byron was entitled to a credit for the $100,000 realized from the re-sale.[28] That left him liable for a deficiency of $20,000.

In the case of the drill a different analysis is required under Article 2A. Inasmuch as that transaction was a lease, Cella had a meaningful residual interest in the equipment at the end of 3 years even if Byron paid all $360,000 of the rentals. Therefore, Byron would not be entitled to a credit for the entire net proceeds of $100,000 because the value of Cella's residual interest was necessarily included in that $100,000. That value might even be more than the $50,000 value that Cella expected to get back after 3 years because the drill was repossessed one year earlier. Consequently, Article 2A uses a different measure: the present value of the $120,000 Byron was required to pay over the remaining one year of the lease, less the present value of what Cella might realize in the market-place from a re-lease of the drill to a new lessee for that one year.[29] Therefore, unless that market-place value was fairly close to the present value of $120,000, Byron's liability for the breach of the lease for the drill would probably be more than his $20,000 liability for breaching the 'lease' (recharacterized as a 'sale') of the computer.

This example not only demonstrates the difference between an Article 2 sale and an Article 2A lease, but also shows how a 'lease' that is in legal effect a 'sale' is treated as a sale on secured credit under Article 9. This, necessarily, leads to an examination of the differences between 'cash sales' and 'credit sales', and then to an analysis of the differences between 'credit sales' that are 'unsecured' and those that are 'secured'.

B. *Comparison of Cash Sales and Credit Sales*

1. Cash sales

Sales of goods are either 'cash sales' or 'credit sales'. In a 'cash sale,' payment is due on delivery of the goods; in a 'credit sale', payment need only be made in accordance with the terms agreed upon by the parties. In the absence of such an agreement, the general rule is that a seller is entitled to be paid upon tender of delivery to the buyer,[30] i.e. a 'cash sale'. If parties agree that payment should be 'C.O.D.' ('collect on delivery'), the sale is treated as a cash sale.

Historically, payment in a 'cash sale' was in legal tender. Payment was later broadened to include 'any means or in any manner current in the ordinary course of business [including checks] unless the seller demands payment in legal tender'.[31]

---

[28] UCC §9-504(1).   [29] UCC §2A-528(1).   [30] UCC §2-310(a).   [31] UCC §2-511(2).

2. Payment by check

A 'check' is an order from a customer to its bank to pay the person named on the check (or the person to whom the check is then 'negotiated') from the customer's funds at the bank. The order is in the form of a draft that is payable on demand.[32] Payment by check is a much less certain means of payment than cash, particularly if the check is issued by a buyer. If the seller gives possession of the goods to the buyer, there is a risk that the check may be dishonored by the drawee (payor) bank because of insufficient funds in the account or because the buyer has ordered the bank not to pay the check ('stop payment order').[33] Even though the buyer's right to retain possession of the goods in a cash sale is conditioned upon payment,[34] a dishonored check puts the seller at a considerable disadvantage because the buyer then has both the goods and the money. This means that the seller may have to institute a lawsuit in order to enforce its rights and remedies (the 'burden of litigation'). Consequently, a seller may bargain for a contract requirement that payment be made by a cashier's, teller's or certified check from a bank. Although still not completely risk-free,—the bank may fail—bank checks are generally more certain of payment than checks issued by buyers and are sometimes characterized as 'cash equivalents'. The legal rules governing the issuance of checks, a type of 'negotiable instrument', are in Article 3. The law governing their payment in the bank collection process is in Article 4.

3. Payment by wire transfer

In recent years the use of electronic funds transfers has become a more certain and expeditious means of payment than all kinds of checks. Sellers in commercial transactions regularly bargain for a contract requirement that payment be made in 'immediately available funds by wire transfer'. The dollar volume of wire transfer payments greatly exceeds that in any other payment system. Article 4A was added to the UCC in 1989 to provide rules governing electronic funds transfers, particularly the 'large dollar wire transfers' used in commercial transactions. The Federal Reserve System has incorporated Article 4A as part of its regulation governing the operation of its own wire transfer system known as 'Fedwire'.[35]

A 'cash sale' can be accomplished by requiring the buyer to make payment by wire transfer at the time the goods are delivered. In a wire transfer the buyer ('originator') gives a payment order to its bank ('originating bank') to

---

[32] UCC §3-104(f).   [33] UCC §4-403.   [34] UCC §2-507(2).
[35] Federal Reserve Board Regulation J—Funds Transfer Through Fedwire, 12 CFR Pt 210.25 et seq.

pay the required amount to the seller ('beneficiary') by transferring funds to an account at a bank specified by the seller ('beneficiary's bank'). When the message sending the payment order is received by the beneficiary's bank, it will then notify the beneficiary. At that point, the beneficiary's bank becomes liable to the seller-beneficiary for the amount of that payment order, and the buyer's obligation to the seller is simultaneously discharged.[36] An advantage of a wire transfer is that, upon receipt of the electronic message by the seller's bank, the money is immediately available to the seller; for that reason, when the buyer's bank sends the buyer's payment order, the amount is immediately deducted from the buyer's account, unlike a check which can take several days to clear.

4. Payment by commercial letter of credit

Although not customarily characterized as a 'cash sale', payment by a traditional ('commercial') letter of credit, governed by Article 5, accomplishes the same result. A letter of credit involves three interrelated, but independent contracts. First is the contract of sale in which the seller requires that payment of the purchase price be made by an irrevocable letter of credit issued by a bank satisfactory to the seller. Second is the contract between the buyer ('applicant') and that bank ('issuer') for the bank to issue a letter of credit in the required amount designating the seller as beneficiary. This contract between the applicant and the issuer sets forth the terms upon which (a) the issuer will pay the credit to the seller-beneficiary and (b) the buyer-applicant will then reimburse the issuer. Third is the letter of credit itself, issued by the issuer-bank to the seller-beneficiary, which specifies the terms and conditions, usually the presentation of designated documents evidencing shipment of the goods to the buyer, e.g. a bill of lading or other document of title[37], upon which the issuer will pay the beneficiary.

If the documents comply with the terms and conditions of the letter of credit, the bank must pay the seller-beneficiary. Payment is required whether or not the goods conform to the underlying contract for the sale of the goods.[38] This is known as the 'independence principle', which is fundamental to letter of credit law.

Article 5 governs some, but not all, rules and concepts of letters of credit. Historically, letters of credit were used primarily in international commercial transactions. Over the years, the International Chamber of Commerce

---

[36] UCC §4A-406.
[37] Article 7 covers documents of title but is preempted in export and interstate shipments by the Federal Bills of Lading Act, 49 U.S.C. §81 et seq.
[38] UCC §§5-103(d), 5-108(f).

developed uniform principles set out in the *Uniform Customs and Practice for Commercial Documentary Credits* (UCP).[39] The UCP, however, does not have the status of 'law'. Frequently, a letter of credit incorporates the UCP, and the UCC recognizes that its provisions can be supplemented by trade usage and practice, including specifically the UCP.[40] The revised version of Article 5 eliminates most of the inconsistencies between the UCC and UCP and provides rules for the resolution of any remaining inconsistencies.

In addition to the commercial letter of credit, a 'standby' letter of credit has emerged more recently. The standby letter of credit is a device which assures payment in the event of a default, such as the failure of a buyer to make required payments. Although standby letters of credit are also governed by the UCC and UCP, they are used in a different business context than commercial letters of credit. When there is a commercial letter of credit, the parties expect that the letter of credit will be the means of payment. In contrast, a standby letter of credit is the means to pay only when there is a failure to pay by the expected means, i.e. a default in paying according to the credit terms. As such, it serves the same economic function as a guaranty although as explained in section III, the law governing guaranties is significantly different.[41]

5. Credit sales

Although a sale of goods is a 'cash sale' in the absence of a contrary agreement, most commercial sales are 'credit sales' because of the economic realities of a competitive market-place. When supply exceeds demand, the seller usually agrees to extend credit to the buyer.

The terms upon which the seller extends credit to a buyer are, of course, a function of the bargaining powers of the parties. Credit terms come in a wide variety of forms and structures. Among the variable factors are the amount of any down payment or deposit; lump sum or installment payments; the period for installment payments; length of term of payments; interest rate or finance charge; 'interest-free' periods; events of default; conditions for acceleration of unpaid balance; requirements for guaranties or credit enhancements from secondary obligors; buyer's right to return goods or to revoke or rescind the payment obligation; discount for early payment; right to 'skip' payments in periods of seasonal downturns, etc. Just as when there is a bank loan, a critical term is whether the extension of credit is unsecured or secured.

---

[39] The version current at the date of publication is *ICC Brochure No. 500*, effective January 1, 1994.
[40] UCC §§1-102(2)(b), 5-116(c).
[41] See the discussion of the common law of suretyship and guaranty in section III below.

In an unsecured credit sale, there is no collateral securing payment of the buyer's obligation. A sale on unsecured credit is sometimes referred to as one on 'open account'. If the buyer breaches its obligation to pay, the seller does not have the right to repossess the sold goods or to seize other property of the buyer. Instead, the seller's remedy is to institute a lawsuit, obtain a court judgment against the buyer for the amount of the unpaid obligation, and then have a court officer ('sheriff' or 'marshall') seize property of the buyer ('levy') and sell it at a public sale ('execution sale'), applying the net proceeds to the payment of the judgment. This can be an expensive, time-consuming and difficult process, particularly if the buyer or its property are in a different state than the seller.

C. Receivables

The amounts due from buyers in credit sales are evidenced in many forms and are broadly referred to as 'receivables'. The UCC classifies 'receivables' into several categories. An 'account' is 'any right to payment for goods sold or leased or services rendered which is not evidenced by an instrument or chattel paper'.[42] Typically, an account would be reflected by a contract for the sale of the goods, a purchase order and acknowledgment, or an invoice, bill, or statement showing the sale and purchase price.

An 'instrument' includes a negotiable instrument covered by Article 3 and 'any other writing which evidences a right to the payment of money and is not itself a security agreement or lease and is of a type which is in ordinary course of business transferred by delivery with any necessary indorsement or assignment'.[43] A promissory note issued by a buyer to a seller, representing the unpaid balance of the purchase price, is an instrument. If the instrument qualifies as a 'negotiable instrument' under Article 3, it has special attributes which enhance its value.[44]

The remaining category of 'receivables' is known as 'chattel paper' which describes 'a writing or writings which evidence both a monetary obligation and a security interest in or a lease of specific goods'.[45] By definition there is no chattel paper when goods are sold on unsecured credit. Sales on unsecured credit result in an account or an instrument; if the account or note is supplemented by a security agreement for the buyer to provide collateral, the sale is on secured credit.

---

[42] UCC §9-106.   [43] UCC §9-105(1)(i).
[44] See the discussion of special attributes of negotiability in section II D2 below.
[45] UCC §9-105(1)(b).

1. Financing with receivables

Receivables represent a stream of future payments owed to the seller. A seller who needs immediate cash can use the receivables as collateral for a loan from a lending institution or can sell the receivables at a discount to that institution or to an investor. The use of receivables is an important source of commercial financing. In the textile and furniture industries, sellers frequently sell their accounts to 'factors' who purchase them 'without recourse'. In essence, factors assume the responsibility for collecting the accounts, as well as the credit risk of non-payment by the obligors on the accounts, for which they are paid a commission which is charged against the purchase price paid for the accounts.

2. Securitization of receivables

In recent years the acquisition of receivables has evolved into the business of 'asset securitization' also known as 'structured finance'. A seller owning a 'pool' of receivables, or a financial institution that has purchased a pool of receivables generated by a seller, sells interests in the pool to public or private investors through an intermediate 'bankruptcy remote' entity known as a 'special purpose vehicle'. These receivables consist of accounts, instruments, or chattel paper. The interests in the receivables sold to the investors are in effect 'securities'. The attraction to the investors is that the interest rate being paid on the receivables by the account debtors or obligors on the instruments is usually higher than the market rate paid on other investments. The attraction to the sellers is immediate liquidity, transfer of the credit risk to the investors and, frequently, the receipt of fee income earned by the sellers from continuing to administer and collect the receivables on behalf of the investors. 'Securitization' has come to be recognized as an increasingly important means of obtaining capital in the United States.

D. *Article 3 Negotiable Instruments*

1. 'Promises' and 'orders'

The value of a receivable is dependent upon the risk of its non-payment. If the receivable represents a sale on unsecured credit, the risk is generally greater than if sold on secured credit where there is collateral for the obligation. Another factor affecting risk is the extent to which the purchaser of a receivable is subject to the risk of non-payment due to problems with the sold goods, e.g., the goods fail to conform to express or implied warranties concerning quality or performance. If the receivable is in the form of a negotiable instrument, much of that risk is eliminated.

Article 3 defines a 'negotiable instrument' as 'an unconditional promise or order to pay a fixed amount of money' which is payable (1) to bearer or order (2) on demand or at a definite time and (3) does not state any other promise or order (with certain limited exceptions).[46] All instruments are like money in that they represent a right to payment and are transferred in the ordinary course of business from one party to another. It is essential that the parties be able to determine easily whether the instrument satisfies the Article 3 criteria so as to qualify for the special attributes of 'negotiability'. The concept is that a party should not have to look beyond the 'four corners of the instrument' to determine the terms and conditions for payment. The most critical criterion for negotiability is that the instrument be an 'unconditional promise or order' to pay the sum stated.

An instrument is either a 'promise' or an 'order'. A 'promise' is in the form of a note which is payable by the maker—a promise by a buyer to pay the seller. An 'order' is in the form of a draft drawn by a 'drawer' on a 'drawee' which is payable by the drawee, frequently a bank. The drawee acts upon the order by 'accepting' the draft. A check is one form of a draft, e.g. an order by the buyer ('drawer') to the bank ('payor bank') in which the buyer is a customer and maintains a checking account, to accept the order on demand by paying ('honoring') the amount of the check to the person entitled to enforce the check, i.e. the seller.[47] The customer's agreement with the payor bank is that the bank will honor genuine and valid checks, provided that there are sufficient funds on deposit in, or available for credit to, the customer's account. Checks can only be charged to the customer's account if they are 'properly payable',[48] i.e. not forged or altered. In commercial sales on credit terms, a seller may be the drawer and issue a draft ordering the buyer to make payment to the seller at a specified future date ('time draft'). In that case, the buyer is the drawee and evidences its agreement to pay the draft at that time by signing its 'acceptance' of the order on the draft. This is known as a 'trade acceptance'.

2. Special attributes of negotiability

The 'holder in due course' doctrine. The payee of an instrument issued by the maker of a note or drawer of a draft ('issuer') may transfer ('negotiate') it to a third party. If that transferee pays value, acts in good faith, and has no notice

---

[46] UCC §3-104(a).   [47] UCC §3-104(e) and (f).   [48] UCC §4-401(a).

of a claim to or defense on the instrument, it can enforce that instrument free from most claims or defenses that the issuer might raise against the payee, such as a defense that the goods sold by the payee were defective. The result is that the transferee gets better rights to the payment of the instrument than the transferor. This is known as the 'holder in due course' (HDC) rule.[49] It was developed by the law merchant in the nineteenth century as part of the 'good faith purchaser' doctrine designed to promote the 'security of the mar-ket-place'. By enabling transferees of instruments to obtain payment without being confronted with defenses arising out of the underlying transactions, the HDC rule enhanced the free flow of instruments ('commercial paper') issued in connection with commercial transactions. This allowed the instru-ments to be treated, in effect, as supplements to the supply of currency. For example, if a buyer of goods issued a note to the seller for the purchase price, the seller could get immediate cash by negotiating the note (usually at a dis-count) to a bank. If the bank qualified as an HDC, the buyer had to pay the instrument to the bank on the due date even though the goods did not con-form to the contract of sale.

The HDC rule served to lessen the discount factor (and ultimately the cost of credit) by minimizing the risk to the transferees of the instruments of the non-payment of the receivables they represented. Even if the buyer had a meritorious defense against the seller, it had to pay the instrument to the HDC. The buyer could not resist payment by asserting a defense to the HDC's claim for payment. Instead, the buyer had to pay the HDC and then institute a lawsuit against the seller to recover its damages. This is another example of how the allocation of the burden of ligation between the parties is affected by the legal rules governing payment.

The HDC rule had a particularly harsh effect on ordinary consumers by forcing them to pay even though they had been sold defective goods. Many of these buyers could not afford the burden of litigation, and often the breach-ing sellers were insolvent or had disappeared. In the 1960s the HDC rule was attacked as unfair and abusive to consumers. As a result of court decisions, new state statutes, and action by the Federal Trade Commission, the rule has been largely abrogated in consumer transactions.[50] In business transactions, however, the HDC rule continues to play an important role. It stands in sharp contrast to the regular contract rule that makes an assignee of rights under a contract subject to all claims and defenses that can be raised against the assignor, absent an express waiver by the account debtor of the right to assert such claims and defenses.[51] By using a negotiable instrument in a commer-

---

[49] UCC §§3-302(a), 3-305(a).

[50] Federal Trade Commission Holder-In-Due Course Regulations—Preservation of Consumers' Claims and Defenses, 16 CFR Pt 433.

[51] UCC §9-318(1).

cial transaction, the seller is able to reverse that rule by negotiating the instrument to an HDC.

Indorser liability. A second special attribute of 'negotiability' is that a party who signs its name to a negotiable instrument is presumed to have signed it as an indorser.[52] The consequence of being an indorser is that, if the instrument is dishonored by the principal obligor—the issuer of a note—the indorser is a secondary obligor which must then pay the amount due on the instrument. The indorser can prevent this result only by indorsing the instrument 'without recourse'.[53] Indorser liability also stands in sharp contrast to the regular contract rule that a party is not liable under a contract unless it has expressly agreed to accept such liability. Indorser liability provides another means for enhancing the value of instruments and encouraging their free flow in the market-place.

Automatic warranties. Another special attribute of 'negotiability' is that a party who transfers an instrument makes automatic warranties covering the genuineness, validity, and enforceability of the instrument, without the necessity of any special language to that effect.[54] For example, a seller may negotiate a note issued to it by a buyer, by selling the note to a financial institution, or by using that instrument as collateral for a loan by the institution. In doing so, the seller warrants as a matter of law to that institution that:

(1) the seller is authorized to enforce the instrument;
(2) there are no forgeries or alterations;
(3) the instrument is not subject to any claims against the instrument or defenses of the buyer; and
(4) the seller has no knowledge of any insolvency proceeding with respect to the buyer.

These automatic warranties by operation of law should be contrasted with the regular contract rule and practice with respect to transfers of receivables that are not negotiable instruments. In the latter circumstance, the transferee needs the protection of these kinds of warranties and must bargain for and obtain express written warranties from the seller covering these points. This attribute of negotiability is an additional enhancement to the value of negotiable instruments as a readily marketable form of receivable.

E. Secured Credit Transactions

In a secured credit sale there is collateral that provides additional protection against non-payment by the buyer. If the buyer defaults, the seller has the

---

[52] UCC §3-204(a).   [53] UCC §3-415(a) and (b).   [54] UCC §§3-416, 4-207.

right to take possession of the collateral, sell it, and apply the net proceeds of the sale to the payment of the buyer's obligation. The collateral may consist of the sold goods, other property owned by the buyer, or both. In some cases, another person ('secondary obligor') such as a guarantor, provides collateral.[55]

1. Scope of Article 9

The provision of collateral to secure payment of an obligation is a 'secured transaction'. If the collateral is real property, the secured transaction is called a mortgage or deed of trust, which is governed by the real property law of the jurisdiction where the property is located. If the collateral is personal property, Article 9 applies to most secured transactions in such property, including specifically 'goods, documents, instruments, general intangibles, chattel paper or accounts'.[56] Article 9 also covers secured transactions in fixtures, i.e. personal property which becomes so affixed or otherwise so related to real property that it becomes part of the real property, e.g. air conditioners and built-in washing machines in a building. The secured transaction can be in any form and may continue to use the pre-Article 9 descriptions such as 'pledge, assignment, chattel mortgage, chattel trust, trust deed, factor's lien, equipment trust, conditional sale, trust receipt, other lien or title retention contract and lease or consignment intended as security'.[57] In addition, Article 9 covers sales of accounts and chattel paper. As discussed above,[58] receivables in the form of accounts and chattel paper are frequently sold or used as collateral by the sellers who have generated such receivables from the sale of their goods. Whether structured as a sale or as a loan, either transaction is a commercial financing arrangement, and both are treated as secured transactions governed by Article 9.

Certain kinds of collateral are currently excluded from the coverage of Article 9, e.g. interests or claims concerning insurance policies,[59] real estate,[60] tort claims[61] and deposit accounts in banks.[62] Such property can and does serve as a valuable source of security for loan and commercial financing arrangements, but the rules governing their use as collateral are found largely either in the common law or in statutes governing real property mortgages. The pending revision of Article 9 may extend coverage to insurance policies and deposit accounts, but that decision will probably not be made before 1997.

---

[55] See discussion of the common law of guaranty and suretyship in section III below.
[56] UCC §9-102(1)(a).   [57] UCC §9-102(2).
[58] See the discussion of receivables in section II C above.   [59] UCC §9-104(g).
[60] UCC §9-104(j).   [61] UCC §9-104(k).   [62] UCC §9-104(l).

In addition, federal statutes govern, to varying degrees, secured transactions in ships,[63] aircraft,[64] copyrights, patents and trademarks.[65] Article 9 is preempted by those statutes to the extent that they deal with particular issues or topics, but Article 9 remains applicable to any gaps in coverage. This has resulted in some uncertainty as to which law is applicable in particular circumstances. The revision of Article 9 will attempt to resolve these difficulties.

2. Basic concepts

Article 9 applies to 'security interests created by contract'. A distinction is thus drawn between 'security interests' which arise by consent of the parties, and 'liens' which arise by operation of law as to which Article 9 is generally inapplicable. Article 9, which was largely drafted in the early 1950s, replaced a variety of laws, statutory and common law, which provided for numerous different security devices. Article 9 brought considerable clarity to secured transactions law by incorporating the different rules for these traditional security devices (and new ones that might be created) in one cohesive statute.

Secured transactions can take place in a variety of contexts: loans by lenders to borrowers; the extension of secured credit by sellers, suppliers or providers of goods or services to buyers and other end users of those goods and services; the conversion of unsecured debt to secured debt; and the sale of accounts and chattel paper to financers in the business of making such purchases. Under Article 9, the contractual agreement of the parties in all these instances is called the 'security agreement'[66]; the lender, creditor, seller, supplier or provider is called the 'secured party'[67]; and the borrower, debtor, buyer, end user or purchaser is called the 'debtor'.[68] Security interests are either possessory—the debtor 'pledges' collateral to the secured party by physically delivering property such as negotiable instruments, stock certificates or valuable jewelry—or non-possessory, with the debtor having the right, as long as it is not in default, to possess, use, and (in the case of inventory) sell the property in the ordinary course of business. Most security interests are non-possessory.

The emphasis in Article 9 is on specific rules and answers to the many practical issues and problems that can arise in secured transactions. The goal is to enable the parties to, or affected by, a secured transaction to properly structure the transaction and to guide themselves in accordance with these rules, knowing with relative certainty their respective rights, powers, duties, and

---

[63] Federal Ship Mortgage Act, 46 U.S.C. §911 et seq.

[64] Federal Aviation Act, 49 U.S.C. §1401 et seq.

[65] Copyright Act, 17 U.S.C. §101 et seq.; Patent Act, 35 U.S.C. §1 et seq.; Lanham Act (Trademarks), 15 U.S.C. §1501 et seq.

[66] UCC §9-105(1)(l).   [67] UCC §9-105(1)(m).   [68] UCC §9-105(1)(d).

obligations. Article 9 has worked very well. As a result, secured financing in the United States has grown and developed as a major and vital force in the economy. The structure of Article 9 allows for maximum creativity, flexibility, and ingenuity in fashioning a wide variety of financing transactions.

Collateral covered by Article 9 may be classified in three categories:

(1) tangible goods,[69] consisting of consumer goods,[70] equipment,[71] farm products[72] and inventory;[73]

(2) semi-intangibles, where the right to payment or to goods is embodied in a writing which, therefore, attains intrinsic value, i.e. chattel paper,[74] documents of title[75] and instruments;[76] and

(3) intangibles, consisting of accounts[77] and the catch-all category of 'general intangibles'.[78]

These three categories of collateral have different characteristics, and some of the Article 9 rules vary depending upon the particular category in which the collateral falls.

3. Secured financing of sales

Secured transactions under Article 9 are of major importance in facilitating the sale of goods. Secured financing takes place at several different levels. Initially, a manufacturer, supplier, or dealer may obtain its inventory of goods on a secured financing basis. It can enter into a secured transaction on credit terms either with the party from whom it is acquiring the goods, or by borrowing the acquisition price from a lender and using the inventory to secure repayment to that lender. This is known as 'inventory financing' or 'floor-planning'.

Alternatively, the manufacturer, supplier, or dealer can finance its operations by entering into a 'commercial financing' security agreement with a lender. Under such an arrangement, the lender agrees to advance funds from time-to-time over a period of time, in amounts based upon a specified percentage of (i) new acquisitions of inventory and (ii) accounts generated from the sale of that inventory. The manufacturer, supplier, or dealer, as borrower, is liable for interest on the outstanding amount of the advances. The inventory and accounts secure the repayment of those advances and, because the advances are only against a percentage (e.g. 70 percent) of the inventory and accounts, the lender should have a 'cushion' between the amount of the advances and the value of the collateral. Generally, the lender, rather than the borrower, actually collects the accounts either directly or through a 'lock-

---

[69] UCC §9-105(1)(h).   [70] UCC §9-109(1).   [71] UCC §9-109(2).   [72] UCC §9-109(3).
[73] UCC §9-109(4).   [74] UCC §9-105(1)(b).   [75] UCC §9-105(1)(f).
[76] UCC §9-105(1)(i).   [77] UCC §9-106.   [78] *Ibid.*

box',—a mail facility which it controls with a right to collect incoming payments. Sometimes the lender allows the borrower to do the collecting, but
then monitors the borrower's performance in making collections. The collected payments are used to 'paydown' the advances and interest. Inasmuch
as new advances are continuously being made, the outstanding balance will
fluctuate up or down. For this reason, this kind of financing is referred to as
'revolving credit'. At the end of the term of the financing agreement, the borrower must repay the outstanding balance.

The second level of secured financing takes place as the goods are sold in
the form of 'purchase money' financing of the buyers. If these sales are to
'buyers in the ordinary course of business', those buyers will acquire the
goods free of any security interest that the seller may have given.[79] This rule
implements the 'good faith purchaser' policy of protecting the security of the
market-place. The theory is that buyers should not have to be concerned
with the purchased goods being subject to a security interest held by the
financer of the seller. Indeed, the secured party that finances the seller *wants*
that seller to sell the inventory to these buyers in the ordinary course of business. The secured party is protected because the security interest extends to
the proceeds of the sales.[80] If these sales are 'cash sales,' the proceeds are
'cash'. Frequently, the cash received by the seller comes from the proceeds of
loans to those buyers by other lenders on secured credit terms, with the
goods, now in the hands of the buyer, securing the buyer's obligation to repay.
Alternatively, the sale to the buyer could be on secured credit terms from the
seller, i.e. a 'retail installment sale' with the goods securing payment. In either
instance, whoever is extending credit to the buyer has a 'purchase money
security interest' in the goods.

When the seller enters into a secured credit financing agreement with a
buyer in the ordinary course of business, the seller has a 'direct' purchase
money security interest in the goods. The security agreement with the buyer
is 'chattel paper'. This chattel paper is a 'proceed' of the inventory that
secures the secured financer of the seller. If the sale to the buyer is on unsecured credit, the resulting 'account' is also such a 'proceed'.

The third level of secured financing involves these proceeds, i.e. the chattel paper and the accounts arising from the sales of the goods. Even though
these receivables are proceeds of the security interest in the inventory held by
the seller's secured financer, the seller can use the chattel paper and accounts
as collateral for a loan by, or sell them to, that financer or a different financer.
'Factors' buy such accounts, and many financial institutions are in the business of purchasing chattel paper. If the loan or purchase is made by the

---

[79] UCC §9-307(1).   [80] UCC §§9-203(3), 9-306(1).

financer who had originally financed the seller's acquisition of the inventory, the proceeds of the loan or purchase will be applied to the repayment of that first secured financing. If the loan or purchase is made by a different financer, the seller is usually required to use the proceeds to repay that first financing. If the seller fails to do so, however, there will be conflicting claims to the chattel paper or accounts between the first secured financer and the financer making the later loan or purchase. The manner in which Article 9 resolves that conflict demonstrates the statute's emphasis on providing practical solutions to difficult problems.

Under Article 9 there is an express policy of encouraging the purchase of chattel paper, and as a general rule, the later financer of the chattel paper is given a 'super-priority' and will have a first right to the chattel paper. The theory is that secured financing of chattel paper, whether by loan or sale, enhances the ability of sellers to sell, and buyers to buy, goods in the marketplace.[81] The flow of funds from such loans or sales facilitates the ability of manufacturers, suppliers, and sellers to meet their financing obligations. At the same time, these loans and sales are, in effect, affording 'indirect' purchase money financing to the buyers. There is, however, no such 'super-priority' in the case of accounts, and the earlier financer will have a first right to the accounts. This disparate treatment of chattel paper and accounts is attributable to inherent differences in these two kinds of receivables and the manner in which they are used as collateral in the market-place.

4. The 'floating lien'

The flexibility and creativity in structuring secured financing arrangements under Article 9 is exemplified by its validation of the 'floating lien'. The three hallmarks of a security agreement in this kind of arrangement are:

(1)   the secured party receives a security interest in a broad range of collateral that not only includes property which is in existence, but also includes property subsequently created or acquired, known as 'after-acquired property';[82]

(2)   the security agreement secures not only present loans and advances, but also 'future advances or other value', whether or not the secured party is obligated to make such future advances,[83] and

(3)   the collateral in one transaction with the secured party secures ('cross-collateralizes') other transactions with the debtor so that a default in one constitutes a default ('cross-default') in the others.

By entering into such an arrangement, the parties are able to cover all their present and future financings in one security agreement. This gives the

---

[81] UCC §9-308.   [82] UCC §9-204(1).   [83] UCC §9-204(3).

secured party with the 'floating lien' that is perfected a first priority position that cannot be lost to other financers making loans or advances secured by the same collateral, even if made between the time that the parties enter the security agreement and the time that future advances are made.[84] The only exception to this rule is the super-priority given to financers providing 'purchase money' financing that enables the debtor to acquire new assets.[85] The 'commercial financing' or 'revolving credit' agreement described above is an example of a 'floating lien'.

5. Attachment of a security interest

In order for a security interest to be enforceable against the debtor, the security interest must 'attach'. The requirements for 'attachment' are:
(1) a security agreement describing the collateral which must be signed by the debtor in the case of a non-possessory security interest;
(2) value given to the debtor; and
(3) the debtor having 'rights in the collateral'.[86]

When all three requirements have been satisfied, the security agreement is then effective and enforceable against the debtor and unsecured creditors.[87]

6. Perfection of security interests

The secured party, however, will also want to be protected against third parties, such as purchasers or other transferees of the collateral (e.g. subsequent secured parties) and creditors who obtain judgment or execution liens against the collateral ('lien creditors').[88] In order to obtain such protection, the secured party must take the additional step of 'perfecting' the security interest. 'Perfection' is the legal procedure for giving third parties notice of the existence of the security interest.[89] The rules for perfection require careful study and attention, but are not difficult to understand or satisfy.[90]

Generally, the risk of most concern to the secured party is the bankruptcy of the debtor. It is in this circumstance that perfection is crucial. This is demonstrated by the following example: assume that a debtor has assets with a value of $100,000 and liabilities to ten creditors totalling $500,000. Nine of these creditors are unsecured with a total debt of $400,000; the other creditor is owed $100,000 and has a security interest in all of the debtor's assets. The debtor enters a 'Chapter 7 Liquidation' under the Bankruptcy Code.[91] If the

---

[84] UCC §9-312(7). [85] UCC §9-312(3) and (4). [86] UCC §9-203.
[87] UCC §9-201. [88] UCC §9-301. [89] UCC §9-302.
[90] See the discussion of methods for perfection in section II E7 below.
[91] See Chapter 17, Bankruptcy.

secured creditor's security interest is perfected, the secured party is entitled to have recourse to all $100,000 of the assets to fully satisfy its claim. This means that the remaining nine creditors receive nothing.

If, however, the security interest is 'unperfected', the results are dramatically different. In that circumstance, the secured creditor's security interest can be 'avoided' by the trustee in bankruptcy[92] or by the debtor-in-possession in a 'Chapter 11 Reorganization' (which has the rights and powers of such a trustee).[93] As a result, the status of the secured creditor is reduced to that of an unsecured creditor. This means that it must share the $100,000 in assets on a pro-rata basis with the other nine creditors and will only receive $20,000 on its $100,000 claim; the remaining nine creditors will now be able to apply the remaining $80,000 to their total claims of $400,000.[94]

7. Methods for perfection

The method for perfecting a security interest is determined by the type of collateral. In most cases, perfection may be accomplished by filing a one-page document called a 'financing statement' in a public office.[95] This is called 'notice filing'. A financing statement gives the names and addresses of the debtor and the secured party and 'contains a statement indicating the types, or describing the items of collateral'.[96] The particular office varies from state to state, usually based on the type of collateral. Some states require filing in a central office, e.g. the Secretary of State of that jurisdiction; others require local filing, such as in the county clerk's office; and still others require dual filing, i.e. centrally and locally. If the collateral is goods, the law of the state where the goods are physically located governs.[97] If the collateral is intangibles, such as accounts, the law where the debtor is located governs.[98] When the collateral is a motor vehicle, the security interest usually has to be noted on the certificate of title issued for that motor vehicle.[99]

As an alternative to filing, the secured party may perfect by taking possession of the collateral,[100] but that is impractical when the business needs of the

---

[92] Bankruptcy Code §544(a).

[93] See Chapter 17, Bankruptcy; Bankruptcy Code §1107(a).

[94] This results from the interplay of Article 9 and the Bankruptcy Code. Under Article 9 an unperfected security interest is subordinate to a 'lien creditor' which is defined to include a trustee in bankruptcy. UCC §9-301(1)(b). The Bankruptcy Code, in turn, gives the trustee in bankruptcy the rights that a lien creditor would have under Article 9 'whether or not such a creditor exists' (a 'hypothetical lien creditor'). Thus, because Article 9 makes the unperfected secured party subordinate to a lien creditor, who then has prior recourse to the assets, the trustee in bankruptcy gets the same rights of priority. This has the effect of reducing the secured party's status to that of an unsecured creditor.

[95] UCC §9-302.   [96] UCC §9-402(1).

[97] UCC §9-103(1) Under the proposed revision of Article 9, consideration is being given to changing the rule so that the law where the debtor is located would govern.

[98] UCC §9-103(3).   [99] UCC §9-302(3).   [100] UCC §9-305.

debtor are such that it must have possession. (How can a furniture maker make tables if the lender has the lathes, or sell those tables if they cannot be shown?) In that circumstance, the security interest has to be non-possessory and perfection will be by filing. If the collateral is an intangible, such as accounts, possession is never possible, and perfection must be by filing. On the other hand when the collateral is a document, such as a negotiable instrument that embodies the right to payment and is of the type frequently transferred from one party to another in the ordinary course of business by indorsement or assignment, perfection can only occur, as a general rule, if the secured party takes possession.[101]

There is a special rule for a purchase money secured financing of consumer goods, other than motor vehicles. In those instances perfection takes place automatically upon attachment, without more.[102] Security interests in TV sets, and household appliances are examples. The theory is that it is unlikely that this kind of collateral will be transferred to another party, or be relied upon by other financers as collateral, and so it is unnecessary to burden sellers and, in turn, consumers with the additional cost and fees attendant on preparing and filing a financing statement.

A recent revision to Article 9 uses the concept of automatic perfection in the circumstance of a security interest taken by a securities broker in a customer's account.[103] If the coverage of Article 9 is extended to cover bank deposits, the security interest of a bank in a customer's deposit account at that bank would similarly be automatically perfected. Although automatic perfection does not provide notice to third parties, the reasoning behind this concept is that third parties should generally be aware of the probability that these kinds of customer accounts are subject to a security interest of a securities broker or bank. In that circumstance, no useful purpose would be served by requiring the filing of a financing statement.

The drafters of the pending revisions are also giving careful attention to the modernization of the filing systems. It is generally recognized that manual filing systems are outmoded, impractical, inefficient, and too expensive. Electronic filing and information systems are increasingly being utilized in the light of advanced computer technology. In addition, there are suggestions for a national filing system in lieu of the various state systems, or at least an 'on-line' inter-connected system among the states.

8. Remedies on default

The Article 9 rules on default are very flexible. A secured party is not required to resort to the collateral securing the debtor's obligation. Instead, it may

---

[101] UCC §9-304(1).   [102] UCC §9-302(1)(d).   [103] UCC §9-115(4)(c).

institute suit against the debtor for the unpaid balance or enforce immediate payment from any guarantor or other secondary obligor who has provided credit support for the debtor's obligation.[104]

If the secured party decides to take possession of the collateral, it has the right to do so 'if this can be done without breach of the peace'.[105] Otherwise, the secured party can obtain a court order requiring the debtor to give up possession of the collateral ('writ of replevin'). If the collateral consists of accounts or instruments, the secured party may notify the account debtors and obligors on the instruments to make payment directly to the secured party.[106]

Upon obtaining possession of tangible or semi-intangible collateral, the secured party has two choices. It may propose to the debtor that the secured party keep the collateral in satisfaction of the obligation,[107] or it may sell the collateral at a public or private sale ('foreclosure sale').[108] The debtor has the right to require that there be a sale and ordinarily will do so if the value of the collateral is more than the amount of the debt. This is to protect the debtor's right to any surplus from a sale that produces proceeds in excess of the debt.[109]

If there is a foreclosure sale, the debtor must be given notice by the secured party of the time and place of a public sale, or the time after which a private sale will take place.[110] In addition, the secured party who is foreclosing ('senior secured party') must notify any subordinate secured party ('junior secured party') who has notified the senior of its interest. A foreclosure sale 'cuts-off' all rights in the collateral of the debtor and of any party subordinate to the senior secured party. If the required notice is not given to a party, that party has a right to recover from the senior secured party any loss caused by the failure to give notice.[111] A junior secured party can also enforce its security interest by a foreclosure sale. Because it cannot 'foreclose' the rights of a senior secured party if it sells the collateral, no notice need be given to the senior. In that circumstance, the purchaser at the sale of the collateral will receive a title that is still subject to the security interest of that senior secured party.

Every aspect of the foreclosure sale, 'including the method, manner, time, place and terms', must be conducted in a 'commercially reasonable manner'[112]. This is a very flexible concept, and the question whether the foreclosure sale was made in a 'commercially reasonable manner' is often disputed. A secured party must exercise care and good judgement in conducting such a sale. Although there is no hard and fast rule for satisfying the requirement of commercial reasonableness, the UCC states that the requirement is

---

[104] UCC §9-501(1).   [105] UCC §9-503.   [106] UCC §9-502(1).   [107] UCC §9-505 (2).
[108] UCC §9-504.   [109] UCC §9-504(2).   [110] UCC §9-504(3).   [111] UCC §9-507(1).
[112] UCC §§9-504(3), 9-507(2).

satisfied '[i]f the secured party . . . has otherwise sold in conformity with reasonable commercial practices among dealers in the type of property sold'.[113] The net proceeds of the sale must be applied to the satisfaction of the indebtedness (and then to any subordinate interest). If a sale produces net proceeds that are less than the outstanding debt, the debtor remains liable for any deficiency.

III. The Common Law of Suretyship and Guaranty

A crucial consideration in extending credit is the credit-worthiness of the debtor ('principal obligor'). Frequently, it is necessary to have additional credit support from a secondary obligor. This support can take many forms: guaranty; financial guaranty bond; assignment or transfer 'with recourse;' accommodation signature on a negotiable instrument; additional collateral to secure the obligation ('hypothecation agreement'); agreement to repurchase debt; establishment of a 'holdback' or reserve account; and other devices generally called 'credit enhancements'. These are 'suretyship' arrangements governed by the law of suretyship. The essence of suretyship is that an additional party ('surety'), or as called in this chapter, a 'secondary obligor', has assumed responsibility for the payment or performance of the obligations of the principal obligor. Issues concerning suretyship are generally governed by common law rules, rather than the UCC, although some states do have other statutes covering suretyship.

A 'standby' letter of credit serves the same economic function but is not governed by the law of suretyship. Rather, it is governed by the same law that governs the traditional or commercial letter of credit, i.e. Article 5 and the UCP.[114] In a typical standby letter of credit, the issuer agrees to pay the beneficiary upon the presentation of a document certifying to the default of the principal obligor. The issuer must pay the beneficiary if the document conforms to the stipulated language, even though the principal obligor may not actually be in default or may have a meritorious defense to the underlying obligation. In that circumstance, the effect is to place the burden of litigation upon the principal obligor to recover the payment from the beneficiary. Standby letters of credit are frequently required in contracts of sale requiring payment by a certain date. If payment is not made by that date, the seller can draw on the letter of credit and obtain payment by presenting a written statement that certifies to the buyer's failure to make that required payment.

---

[113] UCC §9-507(2).   [114] See the discussion of commercial letters of credit in section II B4 above.

In contrast, a 'secondary obligor' is generally required to pay or perform only upon proof of the underlying default itself. Suretyship law is distinctly different from letter of credit law in this respect, and this makes the assurance of payment somewhat less certain. Suretyship law is a doctrine which, historically, has been very protective of secondary obligors. In particular, there are special defenses called 'suretyship defenses' which can result in the discharge of the liability of the secondary obligor. Inasmuch as sellers, lenders, and creditors place important reliance upon the credit support provided by secondary obligors, familiarity with suretyship law is essential in order to assure that the agreement reflects the intent of the parties regarding the availability of suretyship defenses.

The UCC contains limited provisions dealing with suretyship, and these only cover secondary obligors who sign Article 3 negotiable instruments as accommodation parties;[115] otherwise it is necessary to apply the general law of suretyship. For example, even if the obligation of the principal obligor is contained in an Article 3 promissory note, if the secondary obligor has signed a separate guaranty agreement, the latter obligation is governed by the general law of suretyship. The American Law Institute has recently completed a Restatement of the Law of Suretyship and Guaranty in order to set out a modern compilation of the rules governing this important subject. Although the Restatement does not have the force of law, it will have an important and persuasive effect on issues involving the interpretation and application of the general law of suretyship, particularly where the general law is mostly contained in the common law.

Suretyship is also governed by contract principles. As a general rule, the consideration for the obligation of the principal obligor also supplies the consideration for that of the secondary obligor, without the necessity of any separate or independent consideration.[116] In addition, the secondary obligor may generally raise as defenses to its obligation the same defenses available to the principal obligor, with the important exception that defenses going to the fundamental reason for requiring a secondary obligor cannot be raised.[117] These defenses involve risks that the secondary obligor can be fairly assumed to have accepted, e.g. discharge in bankruptcy, infancy, or lack of legal capacity of the principal obligor.

Suretyship defenses, however, can only be raised by the secondary obligor, not the principal obligor. These defenses involve acts or failures to act by obligee-creditors that are considered harmful to secondary obligors. One important category of the suretyship defenses arises out of a material change

---

[115] UCC §§3-305(d), 3-419 and 3-605.
[116] *Restatement of the Law of Suretyship and Guaranty*, §9; UCC §3-419(b).
[117] *Restatement of the Law of Suretyship and Guaranty*, §34; UCC §3-305(d).

or modification[118] in the underlying contract made by the obligee and the principal obligor, without the consent of the secondary obligor, e.g. an extension of time for the principal obligor to pay or perform. The theory of this suretyship defense is that the secondary obligor only agreed to be liable for a particular obligation and that any material change in the terms of that obligation without its consent prejudices the secondary obligor. As a result, the secondary obligor is entitled to a discharge from liability. Under the common law the discharge was automatic and absolute, without any need for the secondary obligor to show that it actually suffered any harm or prejudice from the modification. The more modern view is that there should only be a discharge to the extent that there has, in fact, been harm or prejudice to the secondary obligor. The common law rule of absolute discharge continues to be applicable, however, in some states.

Another important suretyship defense is called 'impairment of collateral'.[119] This defense involves acts or failure to act by the obligee-creditor which have an adverse effect upon, or the right of recourse to, collateral that secures the obligation of the principal obligor. For example, impairment of collateral includes a failure to perform a duty to preserve the value of collateral or to perfect a security interest in the collateral. The rationale for this suretyship defense is based upon the equitable doctrine of subrogation. If the secondary obligor pays the obligee the full amount owed by the principal obligor, the secondary obligor has a right under suretyship principles to succeed (i.e. be subrogated) to all the rights that the obligee should have had as a perfected secured creditor in the collateral furnished by the principal obligor. If, however, those rights in that collateral have been impaired, the secondary obligor should be discharged from its liability.

For example, assume that a seller sold equipment to a buyer (i.e. the principal obligor) for $100,000 on secured credit, retaining a security interest in the equipment. X Co. guaranteed payment of the $100,000. The seller-secured party ('obligee') failed to file a financing statement, with the result that the security interest in the equipment was never perfected. The principal obligor failed to pay the debt when due and went into bankruptcy. The obligee then demanded payment from X Co., the secondary obligor, which refused to pay, raising the suretyship defense of impairment of collateral. X Co.'s contention would be that, because the security interest was not perfected, its right to be subrogated after payment to a perfected security interest in the equipment had been impaired. As a result, the security interest would be avoidable by, and be unenforceable against, the trustee in bankruptcy of the principal obligor.[120]

---

[118] *Restatement of the Law of Suretyship and Guaranty*, §§40 and 41; UCC §3-605(c) and (d).
[119] *Restatement of the Law of Suretyship and Guaranty*, §42; UCC §3-605(e) and (g).
[120] See the discussion of perfection of security interests in section II E6 above.

X Co. would succeed in this argument and would not have to pay the full $100,000. Under some interpretations of the common law, X Co. might even be completely discharged of any liability. The more modern view (and the one adopted by the Restatement of the Law of Suretyship and Guaranty) is that the secondary obligor is only discharged to the extent it has suffered loss from the impairment. For example, if the equipment was worth $100,000 and X Co., in its reduced status as an unsecured creditor would still be able to receive $15,000 in the bankruptcy proceeding, X Co. would then be discharged to the extent of $85,000. Or, if there were no funds available for distribution to unsecured creditors but the equipment was then only worth $60,000, X Co. would be discharged to the extent of $60,000.

IV. Special Treatment of Consumer Transactions

Many of the concepts, doctrines, structures, and rules described in this chapter are, unless modified, applicable to commercial transactions affecting consumers, i.e. those involving personal, family, or household matters, such as the sale of automobiles and household appliances by dealers to consumers. Nevertheless, since the 1960s there has been great sensitivity among the courts and legislatures (federal and state) to the need to protect consumers from perceived abusive or oppressive practices. As a consequence, there are numerous judicial decisions, statutes, regulations, and rules that restrict or limit the application or use of certain legal doctrines and practices, and establish new and special requirements in consumer transactions. These are generally referred to as 'consumer protection' laws.

In some instances, it is not easy to identify a consumer transaction or decide whether it should come within the scope of the consumer protection laws. For example, are these laws applicable to the sale of a luxury yacht that is used exclusively for pleasure purposes? Or, is a wealthy person's investment in stocks or bonds a consumer transaction entitled to special protection, in addition to those generally afforded by the securities laws?

In most instances, however, a consumer transaction is readily recognizable, and the seller in such a transaction, e.g. a dealer of consumer goods, should anticipate the need to comply with various consumer protection laws. For the most part, the UCC does not contain consumer protection provisions, but leaves the subject to other bodies of law. There are some exceptions: e.g. Article 2 makes unenforceable a provision in a contract for the sale of goods that limits a consumer's right to recover consequential damages for personal injuries caused by the goods,[121] and Article 9 prohibits the attachment of a security interest to consumer goods under an after-acquired property clause.[122]

The abrogation of the holder in due course doctrine in most consumer transactions discussed above is a classic example of consumer protection[123]. Many consumer protection laws invalidate or limit the effectiveness of certain kinds of contract provisions or require clear disclosures to the consumer of the nature and extent of his or her obligations. The Consumer Credit Protection Act[124] is an extensive statutory enactment replete with such requirements, having particular application to loans, credit cards, equal credit opportunity, fair credit reporting, debt collection practices, and other issues involving consumer credit. The Federal Trade Commission has issued *Credit Practices Rules* which, among other things require special disclosures to secondary obligors of consumer debt.[125] Many states have similar laws. There is also a *Uniform Consumer Credit Code* that has been enacted by several states. A recent development is the enactment in some states of laws requiring banks to provide inexpensive or no-cost checking accounts for low income consumers.

Although the UCC has not, in the past, dealt extensively with consumer protection issues, the on-going revisions of Articles 2 and 9 may alter that approach. Sales and secured transactions involving consumers are a major segment of American society and its economy. Protection of consumers is now an integral part of commercial law, and it is highly likely that a revised UCC will give more attention to these consumer concerns.

---

[121] UCC §2-719(3).　　　　　　　　　　　　　　　[122] UCC §9-204(2).
[123] See the discussion of the holder in due course doctrine in section II D2 above.
[124] 15 U.S.C. §1601 et seq.
[125] Federal Trade Commission Credit Practices Rules, 16 CFR Pt 444.

15

FAMILY LAW

MARTIN GUGGENHEIM*

I. Introduction

'Family law' is really a set of disparate subjects grouped under one heading. Taken as a whole, it is a complex field made especially difficult to describe because most of this vast body of law is state law and no two states treat the subject identically.

In recent years, however, the federal government has passed a wide variety of laws that have had a direct impact on local law. Because of this, more of family law today is uniform than at any time in American history. Fortunately, this 'federalization' of the subject allows a tidier discussion than was possible even 5 years ago.

In all areas of family law, the state invariably looms in the background. Of course, intimate relationships are formed outside the law's authority. However, law determines whether or not these relationships will be formally recognized. This determination can be of great significance. It may mean whether the law recognizes a parent-child relationship—as when a child is born out of wedlock and the mother, child, or putative father seeks to have the parent-child relationship formally acknowledged.[1] That determination, in turn, will affect a variety of vital matters including the child's right to inherit from the 'father', and the 'father's' right to visit with or obtain custody of the child or even to prohibit the child's adoption by others. To a

* The author gratefully acknowledges the many contributions to the material in this chapter of Alexandra Pylan Lowe and Diane Curtis.

[1] See, e.g., *Michael H.* v. *Gerald D.*, 491 U.S. 110 (1989).

corresponding degree, when the state refuses to recognize an intimate relationship (by making it unlawful for a couple to marry, for example), that determination has significant emotional and financial consequences. It can mean the difference between a person's having no entitlement to any part of another's property, and being entitled to half of all that person earned during the period of the relationship. In this sense, the state is omnipresent in the intimate affairs of Americans. But it looms in the background.

It is in the background in still another sense. Not only are intimate relationships formed without state involvement, they are dissolved that way as well. When relationships break up, the parties are free to agree between themselves on virtually anything about their affairs. Many of these agreements will never be reviewed by state officials. Others will be formally approved, but without meaningful scrutiny. The vast majority of all breakups are resolved by such private agreements. But these agreements, nonetheless, are made 'in the shadow of the law'.[2] What the law has to say on a certain topic is known by both parties and is, to a greater or lesser degree, taken into account in fashioning an agreement. In these senses, then, law is ubiquitous even in the most private of family affairs.

Because 'family law' covers so many subjects, it is necessary to divide it into categories. A useful, but imperfect, division is between public and private. 'Public family law' will refer to the formation and dissolution of families through direct state action. Included within this category is the law of child protection, foster care, state-initiated termination of parental rights, and adoption. 'Private family law' covers the formation and dissolution of family ties through private ordering. The principal topics in this category are marriage, divorce, custody and visitation disputes, and property distribution. As explained in the previous paragraphs, even 'private family law' matters invariably involve the state (law governs the conditions of marriage and divorce, and custody and property disputes in the wake of divorce commonly are decided by courts). A public–private distinction is nonetheless useful, with 'private' matters being characterized by people-initiated events, and 'public' matters involving state-initiated action.

Finally, a brief word is appropriate about the evolving nature of family law. The law's definition of 'family' changes as society's cultural norms and practices change. However, the law is always playing catch-up to behavioral changes in society. There are 3.5 million unmarried couples living together in the United States, over one-third with children.[3] A large number of children today are being raised by other than their biological parents. Almost one-

---

[2] Robert Mnookin and Lewis Kornhauser, 'Bargaining in the Shadow of the Law: The Case of Divorce', 88 *Yale L. J.* 950 (1979).

[3] U.S. Dept. of Commerce, *Statistical Abstract of the United States* 56 (114th ed. 1994).

third of American children are born to unwed mothers, and a slightly larger percentage live with a single parent.[4]

Many of these new families have obtained an important measure of legal protection. In addition, several state courts have recognized gay and lesbian relationships as the equivalent to state-sanctioned marriages, at least for limited purposes such as being able to keep a lease after a domestic partner has died.[5] Others allow gay and lesbian couples to adopt children. Extended families have been accorded legal significance in housing and child custody cases; unmarried heterosexual partners have had their unions legally validated; and discrimination against children born out of wedlock has repeatedly been held unconstitutional.

II. Constitutional Principles of Family Law—The Relationship of the Family and the State

Much of the constitutional law concerning family rights involves determining who should have the authority to decide how to raise children. American law has traditionally answered that question in favor of the child's biological parents. For this reason, much of the language regarding family rights is discussed in terms of parental rights. However, the term 'parental rights' encompasses a far broader idea than merely the power of a parent over his or her child. Rather, the term is a substitute for the basic notion that child rearing and family life are primarily private matters of intimate association of family members.

The state's power to regulate the lawful prerogatives of parents over their children or to intrude into the realm of family life is limited by the Constitution. The primacy of parental rights has remained fairly constant since the Supreme Court first considered the issue more than 70 years ago, although the Court has relied upon an amalgam of rights that, in combination, constitute 'parental rights'.

In 1923, for example, the Supreme Court struck down a Nebraska law that prohibited the teaching of a foreign language in state-run schools because 'the right of parents . . . to instruct their children' is protected by the due process clause of the Fourteenth Amendment to the Constitution.[6] In a 1944 opinion in a case involving a clash between state regulation of child labor and

---

[4] *Ibid.* at 66, 67.
[5] *Braschi v. Stahl Associates Company,* 74 N.Y.2d 201, 543 N.E.2d 49, 544 N.Y.S.2d 784 (1989).
[6] *Meyer v. Nebraska,* 262 U.S. 390, 400 (1923).

a parent's right to give a child religious training, the Court wrote, 'It is cardinal with us that the custody, care and nurture of the child reside first in the parents, whose primary function and freedom include preparation for obligations the state can neither supply nor hinder'.[7] In 1972, in a challenge to a compulsory education requirement, the Court reaffirmed the primacy of parental prerogatives to rear children by stating:

> The history and culture of Western civilization reflect a strong tradition of parental concern for the nurture and upbringing of their children. This primary role of the parents in the upbringing of their children is now established beyond debate as an enduring American tradition.[8]

Family rights, grounded in the Constitutional guarantee of privacy and liberty, are sometimes known as rights of 'family integrity'. The Supreme Court has determined that the right of family integrity exists, despite no specific reference to it in the Constitution, among the 'penumbra' of other rights protected by the Constitution. On several occasions, the Supreme Court has made clear that family rights are especially protected rights, superior even to other rights recognized by the Constitution. To cite only two of many illustrations, in 1953 the Supreme Court said that the custody rights of parents are 'far more precious . . . than property rights'[9] and in 1972, the Court stated,

> It is plain that the interest of a parent in the companionship, care, custody, and management of his or her children 'come[s] to this Court with a momentum for respect lacking when appeal is made to liberties which derive merely from shifting economic arrangements'.[10]

The right of privacy located in the Fourteenth Amendment's Due Process Clause was first secured in a 1965 case involving a challenge to a Connecticut statute prohibiting the sale of birth-control devices, even to married persons. The Court found the law unconstitutional, holding that a state may not interfere with marital privacy by prohibiting couples from using contraceptives. In a concurring opinion, Justice Goldberg wrote:

> The home derives its preeminence as the seat of family life. And the integrity of that life is something so fundamental that it has been found to draw to its protection the principles of more than one explicitly granted Constitutional right. . . . The entire fabric of the Constitution and the purposes that clearly

---

[7] *Prince* v. *Massachusetts*, 321 U.S. 158, 166 (1944).

[8] *Wisconsin* v. *Yoder*, 406 U.S. 205, 232 (1972).   [9] *May* v. *Anderson*, 345 U.S. 528, 533 (1953).

[10] *Stanley* v. *Illinois*, 405 U.S. 645, 651 (1972) (quoting *Kovacs* v. *Cooper*, 336 U.S. 77, 95 (1949) (Frankfurter, J. concurring)).

underlie its specific guarantees demonstrate that the rights to marital privacy and to marry and raise a family are of similar order and magnitude as the fundamental rights specifically protected.[11]

These constitutional protections mean that parents have superior rights to raise their children and to control the details of their rearing over state officials seeking to interfere with child custody or child rearing. State officials may not remove children from a parent's custody nor interfere with the manner in which parents raise their children without a 'compelling state interest'. When these principles are applied in real cases, there is an unclear line of demarcation between state laws designed to protect children from real or imminent harm and those that reach unnecessarily into realms of family life where the state has no justification to interfere. At the very least, however, states may not interfere with parental custody merely because state action is thought to be in a child's 'best interests'.[12] That standard—the best interests of the child—is used to decide custody between two parents who are equally entitled to custody, but not between a custodian with superior rights to custody and a third party, such as the state. Instead, when the state seeks to remove a child from a parent, it must demonstrate that the child would suffer harm unless removed.

These constitutional protections also mean that parents have superior rights to raise their children to those of other adults, even relatives, who have cared for them. As a general rule, the law presumes that children are best off when raised by their birth parents. However, the law recognizes a child's right to continuity of care by a long-term caregiver. For this reason, parents do not have an automatic right to obtain custody of their children after the children have lived with others. Three types of cases, in particular, frequently become contested matters:

(1) disputes between pre-adoptive parents and birth parents who oppose the adoption;
(2) disputes between foster parents and birth parents; and
(3) disputes between long-term caregivers and birth parents who had requested the caregivers to raise the children, but who now want the children back.[13]

---

[11] *Griswold* v. *Connecticut*, 381 U.S. 479, 495 (1965) (quoting *Poe* v. *Ullman*, 367 U.S. 497, 551–52 (1961) (Harlan, J. dissenting)).

[12] *Quilloin* v. *Walcott*, 434 U.S. 246, 255 (1978), quoting *Smith* v. *Organization of Foster Families*, 431 U.S. 816, 862–63 (1977) (Stewart, J. concurring). See also, *Moore* v. *City of East Cleveland*, 431 U.S. 494 (1977) (plurality opinion).

[13] For an example of the first line of cases, see *In the Interest of B.G.C.*, 496 N.W.2d 239 (Iowa 1992) (the 'Baby Jessica' case); *In re Clausen*, 442 Mich. 648, 502 N.W.2d 649 (1993), *stay denied sub nom. DeBoer* v. *DeBoer*, 114 S. Ct. 1 (1993). For an example of the second line of cases, see *Matter of Michael B.*, 80 N.Y.2d

In the first two disputes, the law favors the birth parents. Upon a showing that the parents did not abandon their children, did not give proper consent to their adoption, and are currently fit and able to care for them, they usually will succeed in regaining custody over the pre-adoptive or foster parents. Indeed, the foster family relationship was often formed for the explicit purpose of reuniting children with their birth families when those families are ready to have the children back. In the third dispute—between long-term caregivers and birth parents—a weaker form of preference towards the birth parents exists. In these cases, courts often will award custody to long-term caregivers even when parents are found to be fit and able to have custody when the bonding between the long-term caregivers and the children has become too firm to disrupt.

One important restriction on a parent's freedom to raise children is the requirement in every state that children receive an adequate education. In certain cases, however, a parent's religious beliefs may protect them from a claim that they violated compulsory education requirements. A 1972 Supreme Court case, *Wisconsin v. Yoder*,[14] held that a state could not compel Amish parents to send their children to school beyond the grammar school level. It is unclear how far this ruling may be extended. In *Yoder*, the Court was satisfied that the education that the children continued to receive outside of school by the Amish community adequately substituted for the education they would have received in school. Accordingly, *Yoder* may be seen simply as an application of the principle that parents may utilize their preferred form of alternative educational systems, which is an option available to parents in virtually every state.

Even extended family members who act like parents also have constitutionally recognized rights, though they are less firmly rooted in law. When state officials attempt to interfere with the relationship, courts tend to regard the extended family members as the equivalent of parents. As the Court said in a 1974 case:

> Ours is by no means a tradition limited to respect for the bonds uniting the members of the nuclear family. The tradition of uncles, aunts, cousins, and especially grandparents sharing a household along with parents and children has roots equally venerable and equally deserving of constitutional recognition.[15]

299, 604 N.E.2d 122, 590 N.Y.S.2d 60 (1992). For an example of the third line of cases, see *Bennett v. Jeffries*, 40 N.Y.2d 543, 356 N.E.2d 277, 387 N.Y.S.2d 821 (1976).

[14] 406 U.S. 205 (1972).   [15] *Moore v. City of East Cleveland* (n. 12 above) at 503–504, 506.

III. 'Public Family Law'—Child Protection, Foster Care, Termination of Parental Rights, and Adoption

A. Child Abuse and Neglect

An important restriction on a parent's liberty to raise children without interference are special laws to protect children from harm that is the intentional or negligent result of inadequate parenting. These laws, which exist in every state, are the legal system's way of balancing a parent's general right to raise children free from state interference and a child's right to protection when parenting is deficient.

In theory, the state bears a heavy burden to justify interference with a parent's liberty interest to raise children as he or she sees fit. In particular, because parents have constitutional rights to raise their children free from unnecessary interference, state officials must demonstrate a compelling interest to override parental decisions. Protecting children from danger, or potential danger, is considered a sufficiently compelling interest to justify intervention. To ensure that the state does not frivolously interfere, however, parents retain broad rights to raise their children. For example, although states may intervene in the case of child abuse, in virtually every state parents are permitted to punish their children corporally, so long as it is not 'excessive'.[16]

There are no reliable national statistics reporting the number of known abuse or neglect cases. However, the clear majority of these cases involve neglect. Neglect remains highly associated with poverty. Because race and poverty are so closely connected in the United States, the child protection system applies largely to the poor and to minorities.[17] Some believe that the powerful presumption in favor of privacy of the family is only applied vigorously in what this chapter refers to as the private family law area. In the public side, by contrast, these commentators suggest that the operating principles actually are derived from poor laws, which did not recognize weighty privacy rights of poor people and, for this reason, the presumption of familial privacy is substantially weakened or nonexistent.[18]

Every state has laws that create a mechanism for people to report their suspicions of child abuse and neglect. These laws are designed to bring cases of possible wrongdoing to the attention of public authorities who are in a position to help children and provide assistance to neglectful parents. Most state

[16] N.Y. Fam. Ct. Act § 1012(f)(i)(B) (McKinney 1983).

[17] See, e.g., *Smith* v. *Organization of Foster Families for Equality and Reform*, 431 U.S. 816, 833–34 (1977).

[18] See Jacobus ten-Broek, 'California's Dual System of Family Law: Its Origin, Development and Present Status', 16 *Stan. L. Rev.* 257 (1964), 16 *Stan L. Rev.* 900 (1964), 17 *Stan L. Rev.* 614 (1965).

laws require reporting from professionals who deal with children and may detect certain tell-tale signs of child abuse and neglect. These professionals often include doctors, nurses, police officers, welfare workers, and teachers. Persons not required to report suspected abuse or neglect are encouraged to do so.

These reports are used in two ways. First, they become the starting point for most investigations to determine whether coercive action will be necessary to protect a child. In addition, these reports are placed in a computerized statewide central register.[19] In most states, these records are used exclusively to aid authorities in the detection of abuse.

Most states have screening procedures for receiving a report. In these states, the person receiving the report will make an initial determination whether there is sufficient cause even to undertake an investigation. This determination is based on many factors, including how the reporter obtained the information and the seriousness and currency of the allegation. All states have laws that authorize police officers, doctors, or social-welfare agents to remove children from their home (or to keep them in hospitals) even when the parents object, if the person authorized by law believes that the child would otherwise die or be seriously injured.

The principal purpose of neglect and abuse laws is to protect children from future harm. This contrasts with the criminal law whose principal purpose is to punish wrongdoers for their past behavior. A parent's past behavior is relevant in child protection only to the extent that it reflects on a parent's capacity to raise children adequately in the future. When courts declare a child to be in need of protection, they are making a statement about the future likelihood of harm to the child.

Because of this non-punitive purpose, many of the constitutional rights of accused criminals are unavailable to parents in child protection cases. In addition, the laws defining child neglect are far more vague and broadly written than would be tolerated in criminal statutes; both the quality and the amount of evidence that is needed to prove allegations of neglect is lower than in criminal prosecutions; and the standard of proof needed to adjudicate a parent unfit is lower than in criminal cases.

No two states have laws that define child abuse exactly the same, but there are common aspects among them all. Virtually every state law considers the infliction of serious physical injury or sexual abuse upon a child by a parent or custodian to be child abuse. Many state child abuse laws are written broadly to permit child protection agencies to charge abuse when a parent creates a risk of serious physical injury or inflicts psychological abuse. Still

---

[19] See, e.g., N.Y. Soc. Serv. Law § 422 (McKinney 1992).

others consider the infliction of any injury to be abusive, whether 'serious' or not.

A typical definition of child abuse is found in the California law.

'[C]hild abuse' means a physical injury which is inflicted by other than acciden-tal means on a child by another person. 'Child abuse' also means the sexual abuse of a child or any act or omission . . . [of] (willful cruelty or unjustifiable punishment of a child) or . . . (unlawful corporal punishment or injury). 'Child abuse' also means the neglect of a child or abuse in out-of-home care, as defined in this article.[20]

It is sufficient to prove that parents have placed their children at serious risk to be found guilty of child abuse. If parents have permitted their children to be harmed or failed to take reasonable steps to avoid their harm, parents may be found guilty of abuse even when it is undisputed that the parent did not inflict the harm directly. However, parents are not strictly liable for injuries suffered by their children. Unless parents deliberately or negligently placed their children at risk, the parents have not fallen below the minimum level of care they owe their children. Parents who have not themselves inflicted injuries on their children and who are accused of abuse will be able success-fully to defend the charges if they can satisfy the court that they acted as rea-sonable parents would have acted in similar circumstances.

'Neglect' ordinarily refers to a lapse of care on the part of a parent, often involving some degree of willfulness. Generally, it covers situations in which parents do *not* do something that should be done, thereby placing the health and safety of their children in danger. Most states consider the failure of par-ents to supply their children with adequate food, shelter, clothing, and med-ical care to be child neglect. Abandonment and leaving a child without adequate supervision are also considered acts of neglect in most states.

Evidence of parental neglect or abuse of one child may result in an auto-matic finding of abuse or neglect of other children in the same household, even without any evidence of actual maltreatment of them. In addition, most laws hold parents and persons acting in the role of a parent responsible for the abuse or neglect of children under their care. For example, New York's law extends responsibility to 'a person legally responsible for a child's care',[21] and in Maryland, the law encompasses any 'person who has permanent or tem-porary care or custody or responsibility for supervision of a child, or any household or family member'.[22]

Generally, intentionally causing injury to anyone, including children, is a

---

[20] Cal. Penal Law § 11165.6 (West 1992).   [21] N.Y. Fam. Ct. Act. § 1012(a) (McKinney 1983).

[22] MD. Ann. Code, Family Law § 5-701(b)(i) (1991).

crime. For this reason, child abuse involving physical injury is usually also a criminal offense, as is sexual abuse whether or not it causes physical injury. Child neglect may or may not be a crime, depending on what type of behavior is involved. Since neglect encompasses a large scope of activities (and failures to act), some conduct might be criminal, while others, especially involving nonintentional inadequacies of parenting, might not. Even when authorities are empowered to file criminal charges in child abuse cases, they often choose to charge the parents civilly in family or juvenile court.

Many factors go into the decision whether to treat child abuse as a crime. The most significant is the degree of harm suffered by the child. A second prominent factor is the relationship of the abuser to the child. Although the criminal law makes no distinction between parents and non-parents in determining whether an act of abuse is or is not a crime, when the person responsible for the abuse is the parent, prosecutors are less likely to bring criminal charges, preferring to handle the matter civilly. When the abuser is someone other than a parent, for example, a day care worker or baby-sitter, commonly these matters are prosecuted criminally.

A frequent basis for neglect charges is a parent's failure to provide needed medical care for their children. In many cases of medical neglect, parents have refused, often on religious grounds, to consent to an operation for their child recommended by the treating physician. The right of a parent to practice religion does not include the liberty to expose the child to ill health or death.[23] There are many examples of cases in which courts have authorized medical care over a parental objection even when treatment was not required to save the child's life.[24] In virtually all cases in which court intervention is sought solely to order a particular treatment to which the parents are opposed, courts will issue a temporary order transferring authority to consent to the authorized medical procedure to some person other than the parents (often the treating physician), but otherwise not interfere with parental authority.

Generally, when a court declares a child to be neglected or abused, it may order that the child be placed in foster care for a specified period of time, usually a year at the start. Depending on the severity of the case, courts may prefer to place parents on probation for a period of time, during which they will be supervised and may be required to engage in a specific rehabilitative or educational program while the child remains with them in their home. When children are removed from parental care, the parents will be expected to take steps to correct whatever problems led to the removal. If parents fail to take these steps, the temporary removal may lead to permanent termination of parental rights.

[23] See, e.g., *People ex rel. Wallace v. Labrenz*, 411 Ill. 618, 104 N.E.2d 769, *cert. denied*, 344 U.S. 824 (1952).
[24] See, e.g., *In re Seiferth*, 309 N.Y. 80, 127 N.E.2d 820 (1955).

B. Foster Care

Foster care is a government-run system of providing 24-hour-a-day care for children who cannot live in their own homes, usually due to problems in the family. Foster children live away from their parents in a variety of settings including individual foster homes and group facilities. In some states, foster care is operated directly by the state government; in others, a state agency provides some form of supervision, regulation, or standard-setting, but counties, which are semi-autonomous subdivisions of the state, run the programs with varying degrees of state control.

In order to be allowed to take foster children into their home, foster parents enter into a contract with the agency. These contracts typically provide that the foster care agency retains the authority to make virtually all important childcare decisions, including the number of visits to be scheduled between the child and his or her parents and siblings, the length of time the child remains in care, and the ultimate decision whether to return the child to his or her family or to place the child with an adoptive family. Agencies also retain the contractual authority to visit and inspect the foster home to monitor the well-being of the child.

The foster parent–child relationship, viewed as temporary, is designed to provide the child with the benefits of living in a family setting (instead of institutionalized care) when residence outside of the child's original home is necessary. The theoretical goal of foster care is for the child to leave foster care within 1 or 2 years at most. While the child is in foster care, the state generally provides a variety of social services to the child's parent(s), such as parenting education, homemaker services, rehabilitation programs, job training, and respite care. These services are intended to alleviate the problems that necessitated the child's entry into foster care in the first place, so that the child can be reunited with his or her birth family.

When reunification is not a realistic possibility because the parent is plainly unable to care for the child or for some other reason, an alternative goal is to find a new permanent family for the child through adoption. When foster children are adopted, the adoptive parents may be the child's foster parents, members of the child's extended family, or other suitable adults. Unfortunately, many children spend years in foster care, unable to return to their birth families and yet still legally tied to them and thus unable to find a new permanent family through adoption.

Traditionally, protecting and caring for children was considered a matter of state rather than federal concern. However, faced with mounting evidence that children were being too readily placed in foster care and that, once placed, they were spending long periods of time in foster care 'limbo' without moving either toward reunification with their family of origin or toward adoption, Congress concluded that there was a need for federal action to change local practices.

In the landmark Adoption Assistance and Child Welfare Act of 1980,[25] Congress sought to limit the amount of time children spend in foster care, by requiring states to make 'reasonable efforts' to reunify children with their birth families, and if reunification is not feasible, to find a new permanent family for the child through adoption. To enforce these mandates, Congress conditioned the receipt of federal foster care funds on compliance with the new federal law. The Act also requires states that receive federal foster care money to take steps to prevent the unnecessary separation of children from their parents, to assure a careful monitoring of children who are separated, and to provide an infusion of services into the family to facilitate the return of children to their parents (where appropriate). Further, it makes funds available to encourage the adoption of hard-to-place children for whom reunification with their original family is not possible.

Although states are not obliged to obey these rules, a state's failure to implement them makes the state ineligible for any increase in federal foster care funds above the amount payable in 1979.[26] The most recent federal initiative in this area is the Family Preservation and Support Services Act of 1993.[27] Like the 1980 Act, it is based on the twin premises that it is best for children to be cared for by their birth parents and that many parents who have abused or neglected their children can, with the right combination of services and support, learn to become capable parents. The 1993 Act makes federal tax dollars available to the states for a variety of social service programs designed to allow children at risk of foster care placement to stay with their families.

Many states have statutes that express a preference for children being placed first with extended family members, if possible,[28] or in foster families instead of group facilities. Some children in foster care live with members of their extended family (such as grandparents, aunts, uncles or cousins) who become licensed foster parents under at least nominal supervision by the state child welfare agency, often called 'kinship foster care'.[29]

---

[25] P.L. 96–272 (1980), 94 Stat. 500, codified at 42 U.S.C. §§ 620–628, 670–679a (West 1991 and 1994 Supp.).

[26] For a discussion of the details of the federal legislation and strategies to assure its implementation, see Mary Lee Allen et al., 'A Guide to the Adoption Assistance and Child Welfare Act of 1980', in M. Hardin ed. *Foster Children in the Courts* at 575–611 (Butterworth, 1983); Abigail English, 'Litigating Under the Adoption Assistance and Child Welfare Act of 1980', in *ibid.* at 612–644.

[27] P.L. 103–66, 107 Stat. 649 et seq, 1993 U.S.C.C.A.N. 649, codified at 42 U.S.C. §§ 629 through 629e (West Supp. 1994).

[28] Cal. Welf. & Inst. Code § 16501.1(c)(West 1994); Colo. Rev. Stat. § 19–5–104(2) (1994); MO. Rev. Stat. § 210.565(1) (West 1994).

[29] See *Miller* v. *Youakim*, 440 U.S. 125 (1979).

In addition, some states have laws that either express a statutory preference for, or require matching children with, foster families of the same religious background as the child.[30] In interpreting New York's statute, a federal court ruled that religious matching was permissible only if it was not mandatory, took each child's interests into account, and did not result in discrimination.[31]

Many children who enter the foster care system cannot return to their parents, for a variety of reasons. Sometimes the parents' problems are too severe to be alleviated, even with services; sometimes services are not provided or the parents refuse to accept them; and sometimes the parents have abandoned the children. When children cannot be returned home, and other family members are not available to raise them, the goal of foster care is to find a new, substitute family for them through adoption.

C. Termination of Parental Rights

'Termination of parental rights' is the permanent severance of the parent–child relationship. After termination, the parent is no longer legally related to the child and possesses neither rights to nor responsibilities for the child. The principal purpose for seeking termination is to free the child to be adopted into a new family. The vast majority of the terminations are effected voluntarily, usually when parents relinquish a child to a child-care agency or place a child with an individual or couple chosen by the parents for adoption.

Children cannot be adopted without the consent of the living parent(s), unless there is a court order severing parental rights, so that a parent's consent is no longer required. In many foster care cases, the child's caseworker may decide that adoption is the appropriate goal to pursue for a child, often because the parent is not likely to be able to resume custody within a reasonable period of time. In those instances, caseworkers may attempt to persuade parents to surrender parental rights voluntarily or seek to have legal proceedings brought to sever parental rights.

In some cases, termination is sought because the child is believed to have bonded psychologically with the adult(s) with whom he or she has been living and the child's best interests are perceived to be advanced by terminating parental rights and thereby paving the way for the child's eventual adoption by his or her 'psychological parent'.[32] In other cases, termination is sought

---

[30] See e.g., N.Y. Soc. Serv. Law §373 (McKinney 1992).

[31] *Wilder* v. *Bernstein*, 848 F.2d 1338 (2d Cir. 1988).

[32] See Joseph Goldstein, Anna Freud, Albert Solnit, *Beyond the Best Interests of the Child* (The Free Press, 1973).

without regard to the actual prospects of the child's adoption because the agency has concluded that the prospects for reuniting with the parents are too remote.

Involuntary termination of parental rights usually requires proof of gross or long-standing neglect, including abandonment of parental obligations, repeated neglect or abuse, or parental incapacity or inability to care for children. Many states include mental illness, conviction of a crime affecting the fitness of a parent, and financial nonsupport as conditions justifying termination.

Often, these laws are rather complex, requiring the state agency to prove not only that the parents have been inadequate, but that the agency's efforts to correct deficiencies in the home were attempted without success. In New York, for example, the agency must prove that, despite its 'diligent efforts to encourage the parent–child relationship', a parent failed to 'maintain contact with or plan for the future of the child' for at least one year.[33] Many states, like New York, have passed laws that require proof that agencies have done everything in their power to assist the family before termination is permitted.[34] A few state courts have ruled that agencies must comply with all federal rules governing foster care before a termination of parental rights may be effected.[35]

For most of this century, courts have refused to terminate parental rights without a clear showing of neglect, unfitness, harm, or abandonment.[36] In the past two decades, however, courts in several states have authorized termination when children have not lived with their parents for a significant period of time and the agency can demonstrate that termination is in the child's 'best interests'.[37] Whether a 'best interests' showing suffices for termination under the Constitution is questionable.

Where a parent has failed to assume any responsibility for a child's care and support, the Supreme Court has ruled that a parent's right to the child's custody may be terminated. This commonly arises in connection with the rights of fathers. Although fathers have both a constitutional due process right and an equal protection right to the care and custody of their children,

---

[33] N.Y. Fam. Ct. Act § 614 (McKinney 1983); N.Y. Soc. Serv. Law § 384-b(7)(a) (McKinney 1992).

[34] See, e.g., Cal. Fam. Code § 7828 (West 1994); Conn. Gen. Stat. Ann. § 45a-717 (West 1993); N.Y. Soc. Serv. Law §§ 384-b(7)(a), (8)(a)(ii), (8)(b)(ii) (McKinney 1992); R.I. Gen. Laws § 15–7–7.

[35] e.g., *Matter of Burns*, 519 A.2d 638 (Del. 1986).

[36] See, e.g., *People ex rel. Portney* v. *Strasser*, 303 N.Y. 539, 104 N.E.2d 895 (1952); *Appeal of Renker*, 180 Pa.Super. 143, 117 A.2d 780 (Pa. 1955); *In re Clark's Adoption*, 38 Ariz. 481 1 P.2d 112 (1931).

[37] See, e.g., *In re Adoption of J.S.R.*, 374 A.2d 860 (D.C.App. 1977); *In re New England Home for Little Wanderers*, 367 Mass. 631, 328 N.E.2d 854 (1975); *In re William L.*, 477 Pa. 322, 383 A.2d 1228 (1978), *cert. denied sub nom. Lehman* v. *Lycoming County Children's Services*, 439 U.S. 880 (1978). See also, D.C. Code § 16–304(e) (1966); Mass. Gen Laws Ann. ch. 210, § 3(a)(ii) (West 1987); Wash. Rev. Code Ann. § 26.33.010 (West 1986).

'the mere existence of a biological link' between a biological parent and his child is not entitled to constitutional protection, in the absence of evidence that the parent had 'grasp[ed] the opportunity' to 'develop a relationship with his offspring' and to 'accept[ ] some measure of responsibility for the child's future'.[38]

Imprisonment may be considered grounds for termination because it falls into the definition of abandonment. But in most states, courts have ruled that imprisonment, by itself, cannot support a finding of abandonment since imprisonment does not establish a settled purpose to forego all parental duties. These states follow the rule that one's 'intention' to abandon must be proven, and, using it as a guide, incarceration cannot constitute abandonment since being sentenced to prison cannot be equated with a desire to forever abandon one's children.

Proof of grounds for termination of parental rights must be by at least clear and convincing evidence.[39] Some states use the even higher 'beyond a reasonable doubt' standard of proof. Similarly, proof beyond a reasonable doubt is required when a state seeks to terminate the parental rights of native Americans.[40]

As a general rule, relatives, such as grandparents and aunts and uncles, have few rights to be heard at the trial phase of a termination proceeding where the principal inquiry is whether there are legal grounds to terminate parental rights. However, at the dispositional phase of a termination case, where the court will decide whether to allow the child to be adopted, relatives commonly are permitted to intervene.

D. Adoption

Adoption is the legal recognition of a non-biological parent–child relationship. Adoptions may be ordered only by a court. Once an adoption order has been made, the adoptive parents assume identical responsibilities and enjoy rights identical to those of birth parents.

Children are ineligible to be adopted unless at least one of their birth parents is dead or has had his or her parental rights terminated. Most adoptions involve the voluntary relinquishment of parental rights (known as a 'surrender') at or near the time of birth. State laws carefully define the circumstances under which a surrender may be made (some states require it be done before a judge; others allow parents merely to sign a notarized document). These

---

[38] *Lehr* v. *Robertson*, 463 U.S. 248, 261–62 (1983).   [39] *Santosky* v. *Kramer*, 455 U.S. 745 (1982).
[40] *Indian Child Welfare Act*, 25 U.S.C. § 1912 (f) (1979).

laws also define when and how a parent may change his or her mind. In no State is an out-of-court surrender irrevocable when made. In some states, an in-court surrender is irrevocable. Most states, however, provide that a surrender is revocable for at least some period of time after being executed, although states differ as to what should happen when a parent revokes the surrender. Some states require that the child be returned to the birth parent once the surrender is revoked. Other states do not automatically return the child when the prospective adoptive parent opposes return. These states conduct a 'best interests' custody hearing to decide where the child should be placed.[41]

Adoptions are processed in one of two ways. 'Private placement adoptions' theoretically involve a birth parent choosing the person who will adopt the child. This actually occurs in many cases when relatives adopt, such as step-parents or grandparents. In other private placement adoptions, however, the parent does not actually choose the adoptive parent; more commonly, an intermediary for the parent—a doctor or lawyer, for example—locates a willing adoptive parent or parents for the birth parent.

'Agency adoptions' involve the use of licensed agencies that accept temporary care and custody of children when birth parents wish to surrender parental rights. These agencies also maintain a list of eligible adoptive parents whom they have screened and investigated. As new children come into their care, they choose an adoptive parent from their list. Many of these agencies are privately run; others are government-run. Parents often pay agencies a fee; however, the costs of private placement adoptions commonly are much higher, sometimes exceeding $25,000.

In the vast majority of adoptions, the child has been living with the prospective adoptive parent before the formal petition to adopt is filed with a court. When adoption papers are filed in court, it is common that the court will conduct an investigation to determine the fitness and suitability of the adoptive parents. Prospective adoptive parents do not have a 'right' to adopt that requires courts to grant their petition to adopt in the absence of a powerful reason to do otherwise. Nonetheless, most petitions are granted, if only because by the time the court is finally ready to decide the matter, the child has been living with the family for a significant period of time.

There is no requirement in any state that persons seeking to adopt be married. However, because agencies and courts have discretion whether to permit any adoption, it is often difficult for certain single people to adopt. In particular, cultural prejudice against gays and lesbians often makes it particularly difficult for them to adopt. However, only Florida and New Hampshire

---

[41] See, e.g., N.Y. Dom. Rel. Law § 115–b(4)(C) (McKinney 1992).

prohibit homosexuals from adopting.[42] In recent years, a few courts have even permitted gay or lesbian couples to adopt a child, resulting in a court order that a child has two mothers or two fathers.[43] Courts that have permitted such adoptions generally conclude that children are best served by having two legal parents rather than one legal parent and one de facto parent.

IV. 'Private Family Law'—Marriage, Separation, Divorce, and Related Matters

A. Marriage

Although marriage is among the most intimate of relationships, it is nonetheless highly regulated by law. All states generally require a license in order to enter into a formally recognized marriage contract. In many states, both parties must appear in person to obtain a license and provide information about themselves, including whether they were married before.

Many states also impose a waiting period after the application for marriage is sought and a physical examination, usually limited to a test for sexually transmitted disease. Many couples in a hurry to marry choose to do so in states that have the fewest restrictions, such as Nevada. These states perform thousands of out-of-state marriages each year. A marriage legally entered into by the laws of one state will be recognized by other states.

Though a number of states will recognize a 'common law' marriage—a long-term cohabiting relationship, usually including the couple's public declaration that they are married—even common law marriages must meet certain eligibility criteria. Every state places restrictions on those eligible to marry. The most common concern age (generally no one under 14 years old may marry, and young persons under 18 years of age must have parental permission); the relationship of the parties to each other (both incest—marriage between blood relatives of a certain degree—and same-sex marriages, for example, are prohibited); and current marital status (all parties must be single when they wish to marry—bigamy and polygamy are prohibited throughout the United States.)[44] In recent history, many states prohibited

---

[42] Fla. Stat. Ann. § 63.042(3)(West 1985); N.H. Rev. Stat. Ann. § 170–B:4 (1994).

[43] See *In re Jacob*, 1995 N.Y. Lexis 3579 (N.Y. Nov. 2, 1995); *Adoption of B.L.V.B.*, 160 Vt. 368, 628 A.2d 1271 (1993); *Adoption of Tammy*, 416 Mass. 205, 619 N.E.2d 315 (1993).

[44] *Reynolds* v. *United States*, 98 U.S. 145 (1878); *Maynard* v. *Hill*, 125 U.S. 190 (1888).

marriages between members of different races; however the Supreme Court ruled these miscegenation laws unconstitutional in 1967.[45]

No state recognizes marriages between two people of the same sex. However, in 1993, the Supreme Court of Hawaii held that a refusal to grant marriage licenses to same-sex couples may offend the state constitution.[46] When couples who wish to marry are unable to do so because of legal restrictions, they are denied opportunities and rights that married couples enjoy. These include such benefits as tax reductions for legal dependents or joint filings; inheritance rights when one partner dies without leaving a will; the right to sue for injuries to the other partner; employment-related health benefits; sick and bereavement leave; and survivorship rights to pension and insurance plans. A number of communities in the United States have passed domestic partnership ordinances which allow for a couple to register as partners, once they have met certain requirements.

B. *Divorce*

As changing cultural values in the United States over the past two generations have increasingly tolerated familial breakup and divorce, the laws of divorce in the various states have made it ever easier for couples to end their marriages. When divorce was frowned upon culturally—as it was until the middle of this century in the United States—law treated marriage as a life-long contract which could be breached only upon a few recognized grounds, such as abandonment; adultery; cruelty; or other marital 'fault'. In most states, unless one spouse engaged in conduct that served as grounds to sue for divorce, a couple could not obtain a divorce.

Today, divorce is a common fact of life in the United States, with over one million marriages ending in divorce each year.[47] Although only a few states have done away with fault-based grounds altogether, all fifty states have now added some form of no-fault provisions to their divorce laws. In most states today, it is sufficient that the parties have 'irreconcilable differences', or live separately from each other for a prescribed period of time, such as 1 year, to divorce.

As a result of these changes, there are relatively few legal battles fought in American courts about the propriety of the divorce. Instead, what legal battles are fought focus on three principal components of divorce: child custody and visitation; child support and alimony; and property distribution. In fact,

---

[45] *Loving* v. *Virginia*, 388 U.S. 1 (1967).   [46] *Baehr* v. *Lewin*, 74 Haw. 530, 852 P.2d 44 (1993).
[47] U.S. Commission on Interstate Child Support, *Supporting Our Children: A Blueprint for Reform* at 5 (1992).

relatively few divorces result in any contested dispute. Parents commonly decide custody arrangements on their own, with the help of a mediator or through a process of attorney-assisted negotiations. Mediation, an informal process using a neutral person to assist parties to reach their own agreement, usually is used to resolve custody and visitation matters, although it may also include alimony and property settlements. In some states, even when couples seek judicial assistance to resolve their disputes, court rules require them to use divorce mediation before being allowed to obtain a judicial hearing.[48]

C. Child Custody and Visitation

Because divorce formally requires state action (through the issuance of a judicial decree terminating the legal relationship of marriage), courts technically must approve many of the divorce-related agreements, even those consensually made. In particular, judges formally are called upon to ensure that an appropriate arrangement has been made for the custody and support of any minor children of the marriage. However, privately made agreements on these matters are routinely approved by courts in uncontested divorces.

Judicial resources to determine custody or visitation are preserved for cases when parents do not settle the matter privately. In many courts, judges engage psychiatrists, social workers, court-appointed guardians for the child, or other mental health professionals to assist the judge to reach the best result for the child. However, the question before the court is relatively narrow: how should the custody arrangements for the children be allocated between the parents?

Because parents have constitutional rights to raise their children free from all unnecessary intervention, courts may not remove children from either parent's care without first finding they have abused or neglected them within the narrow meaning of those terms. Since all but a tiny fraction of parents are minimally fit, the only choice available to judges is to award exclusive custody to one parent or establish a shared custody arrangement.

Exclusive custody, or 'sole custody', gives one parent (the custodial parent) primary authority to rear the child as s/he sees fit, on such matters as education, health care, discipline and religious training. When sole custody has been awarded, the non-custodial parent's rights usually are limited to fixed amounts of visitation with the child. In addition, the non-custodial parent may maintain some rights to be consulted about major child-rearing decisions.

---

[48] See, e.g., Cal. Fam. Code § 3170 (West Supp. 1993).

Because sole custody arrangements exclude the non-custodial parent from the larger part of parenting, the preferred custody arrangement in a majority of states today is a version of 'joint custody'. Joint custody does not necessarily mean shared physical custody. In fact, in many joint custody cases the physical custodial arrangements are similar to those in sole custody cases. When 'joint legal custody' is awarded, however, both parents retain an equal, shared decision-making authority over the major decisions affecting the child, even though physical custody may be awarded exclusively to one parent. In contrast, 'joint physical custody' attempts to fashion a relatively equal or truly shared custodial arrangement. A common joint custody arrangement is for the child to spend the school year with one parent and vacations with the other. Other parents who live near each other sometimes divide up the week, so that the children spend part of the week at one parent's home and part of the week at the other's. Over forty states have laws authorizing the award of joint custody.[49] Some jurisdictions use a presumption in favor of joint custody and even authorize the judge to award joint custody over a parent's objection.[50]

The trend towards joint custody has not been without controversy. As the more common non-custodial parent, men have gained increased opportunities to maintain a meaningful presence in their children's lives after divorce through the use of joint custody arrangements. Even so, not everyone agrees that joint custody serves children well. Some regard it as too difficult for a child to live in different homes and environments.[51] Many believe joint custody only works well when parents are capable of putting their child's interests ahead of their own conflicts, something that does not always happen.

In many states, custodial parents are not free to move out of state without obtaining the non-custodial parent's consent or the court's permission. Even in the absence of a statutory restriction, the non-custodial parent may be able to complain that a move would interfere with visitation rights. In some states, there is a presumption against a move, and the parent wishing to move must demonstrate that the child's best interests will not be infringed as a result. Other states presume that a custodial parent is entitled to move to another state unless the opposing parent can prove that the move is sought for the purpose of interfering with visitation.[52]

[49] Linda D. Elrod and Timothy B. Walker, 'Family Law in the Fifty States', 28 *Family L. Q.* 515 at 568, 586–88 (Winter 1994).

[50] See, e.g., Cal. Fam. Code §§ 3081, 3082 (West Supp. 1993); Iowa Code Ann. § 598.41(2)(West Supp. 1994).

[51] *Malone* v. *Malone*, 842 S.W. 2d 621 (Tenn. App. 1992). See generally, Judith S. Wallerstein and Sandra Blakeslee, *Second Chances: Men, Women and Children a Decade After Divorce* at 256–73 (Tichner & Fields, 1989).

[52] See, e.g., *Ballard* v. *Wold*, 486 N.W.2d 161 (Minn.App. 1992); *In re Marriage of Smith*, 491 N.W.2d 538 (Iowa App. 1992).

The bases upon which courts decide custody disputes have changed dramatically throughout the course of American history. In the nineteenth century, children were treated as their father's exclusive property. By the early part of this century, it was generally assumed that children, particularly those under the age of 7 years, were better off with their mother after a divorce. As recently as 1976, in more than thirty states the mother was to be awarded custody of her young children, so long as she was not unfit.[53]

By the 1970s, however, this legal rule, known as the 'maternal preference' or 'tender years doctrine', had come under attack by fathers' rights advocates and some feminists on the grounds that it perpetuated sex-based stereotypes and violated the Equal Protection provision of the Constitution. Most states now prohibit the explicit use of gender in deciding child custody cases. Instead, some courts use the open-ended 'best interests of the child' test, with no stated presumption in favor of either parent. Other states still retain a presumption, but have substituted the gender-neutral 'primary caretaker' test for the maternal preference, even though under either test women are awarded custody in the great majority of cases.[54] Even when a presumption is used, courts may consider other factors in determining the child's 'best interests'. If one parent is better able than the other to fulfill the child's emotional and psychological needs, for example, that parent may prevail over a primary caretaker. A prevailing presumption, also rebuttable in particular cases, is that siblings should remain together.

A complete discussion of custody matters must include enforcement provisions. In a federal system such as the United States, interstate custody disputes, including interstate flight by parents who take children with them, can create enormous complications. The most complicated issues arise when a parent who loses a custody case moves to another state and tries again by filing a new custody action. Under an exceptional doctrine in the law, custody decisions technically are never 'final', in the sense that they may always be modified to cover changed circumstances. For this reason, ordinary rules of civil procedure that would prohibit a second court from relitigating a judgment of a first court commonly are inapplicable in custody cases. As a consequence, a second state court is permitted to modify a prior court custody order, provided the second court otherwise has jurisdiction in the case. In this context 'jurisdiction' once only meant that a parent and the child be physically present in the state, a rule that encouraged interstate movement of parents who lost a custody case. The result was a morass of conflicting state court judgments, escalating costs of relitigation, and uncertainty in the outcome of a custody matter.

---

[53] Martin Guggenheim, Alexandra Lowe, Diane Curtis, *The Rights of Families* (Southern U.P., 1996).

[54] Judith S. Wallerstein and Joan B. Kelly, *Surviving the Breakup: How Children and Parents Cope with Divorce* 121 (Basic Books, 1980) (mother received custody in more than 80 percent of cases studied).

In light of these problems, Congress enacted the Parental Kidnapping Prevention Act.[55] This law eliminates any incentive to cross state lines to file a second custody action because the Act requires that the new state reject a custody petition and send the matter to the original state so long as the child had been in the original state within the past 6 months prior to filing the second case. The law allows the second state to modify the initial custody order only if the first state no longer has jurisdiction or has declined to exercise jurisdiction.

Since 1994, leaving the United States for the purpose of interfering with another's custody rights is a federal crime, punishable by up to 3 years' imprisonment.[56] In addition, the Hague International Child Abduction Convention, in effect in over forty countries,[57] requires the prompt return of a child who was removed from a country in violation of a parent's custody rights.

Not only parents may seek judicial orders to visit their children. Within the last 30 years, every state has enacted legislation granting grandparents the right to petition for visitation of their grandchildren under certain circumstances. Most of these statutes allow grandparents to petition for visitation only when the nuclear family has been disrupted in some way, for example, through divorce or death.[58]

Step-parents have lesser rights to custody or visitation than biological or adoptive parents. However, courts have looked for ways to preserve and protect the continuity of the child's relationship with a step-parent who has served as a significant caregiver. It is easier for a step-parent to obtain visitation than to win custody, and some states expressly authorize step-parent visitation in the event of death or divorce.

D. Child Support and Alimony

Parents are obliged to support their children whether or not they have custody of them, even if they never married the children's other parent. Legal disputes often arise when non-custodial parents fail to pay at least what a court would require. Unfortunately, these disputes arise all too commonly in the United States where fewer than half of the custodial parents who have child support orders actually collect the full amount they are owed.[59]

---

[55] 28 U.S.C. § 1738A (West 1994).   [56] 18 U.S.C. § 1204 (West Supp. 1994).
[57] Linda Silberman, 'Hague International Child Abduction Convention: A Progress Report', 57 Law and Contemp. Probs. (Summer 1994).
[58] See, e.g., Cal. Fam. Code § 3103 (Deering 1994).
[59] U.S. Bureau of the Census, Child Support and Alimony: 1989, Current Population Reports, Series P-60, No. 173, (U.S. Government Printing Office, 1991).

Moreover, this figure covers only those parents who have child support orders in the first place. According to Census data, only 72 percent of divorced mothers have support orders. Among never married mothers, the figure is far lower—only 24 percent have an award of support for their children.[60] By far the greatest problem in the child support area is ensuring that custodial parents receive support payments. This section discusses the principal issues and trends in the area of court-awarded child support.

Parents are, of course, free to provide their non-custodial children with more than the minimum to be awarded by courts. But children have the right to be supported, and custodial parents are authorized by laws in every state to bring an action for child support on the child's behalf when a non-custodial parent fails to pay adequate support. Child support, technically viewed as a child's right, must be made equally available to out-of-wedlock children and children born of a marriage.[61]

In most states, as a general rule parents must support their children until they are 18 years old. In some states, this age is 19 or even 21. There may be reasons to shorten the time that parents must support their children, such as when a child becomes 'emancipated' (for example, by marrying or becoming self-supporting after leaving the parents' home). There also may be reasons to lengthen the period, such as when children are in college.

As already indicated, enforcement of child support obligations is a significant problem in the United States. Like a number of other areas of law that were once the exclusive province of the states, important features of the law of child support have become federalized within the past 20 years through the passage of significant legislation by Congress. The principal purpose of these combined laws is to make it easier to collect child support from recalcitrant, non-custodial parents. These laws include the Social Services Amendments of 1974,[62] the Child Support Enforcement Amendments of 1984,[63] the Family Support Act of 1988,[64] and the Child Support Recovery Act of 1992.[65]

Federal law also aids in the collection of support payments by authorizing withholding of support from parents' wages and the interception of income tax returns to collect overdue support payments. Federal law also has eased complications in interstate collection by assisting in locating absent parents and, most recently, Congress made the willful failure to pay at least $5,000 in court-ordered child support a federal crime.[66]

---

[60] Ibid.   [61] See Pickett v. Brown, 462 U.S. 1 (1983); Trimble v. Gordon, 430 U.S. 762 (1977).

[62] Pub. L. No. 93-647, 88 Stat. 2337 (1974), codified in part as 42 U.S.C. §§ 651–669 (West 1991).

[63] Pub. L. No. 98-378, 98 Stat. 1305 (1984).

[64] Pub. L. No. 100–485, 102 Stat. 2343 (1988). See also 42 U.S.C. § 667(b)(2)(West 1991).

[65] Pub. L. No. 102–521, 106 Stat. 3403 (1992), codified at 18 U.S.C. § 228 (West Supp. 1994).

[66] Child Support Recovery Act of 1992, Pub. L. No. 102–521, 106 Stat. 3403 (1992), codified at 18 U.S.C. § 228 (West Supp. 1994).

To maximize the opportunity that all children receive support from their fathers, federal law requires states to develop a relatively easy method for establishing paternity for non-marital children. All states must permit paternity claims to be brought any time until the child's eighteenth birthday and require that the putative father submit to genetic testing.[67] In addition, states must provide a simple method for men to acknowledge paternity when a child is born.

Though various state schemes still differ in considerable detail, federal law requires each state to use child support guidelines that are uniform throughout the state for children of divorced, separated, and never married parents, which take into account all of an absent parent's income. Child support amounts are based principally on the parent's income. Different states have different formulae (there is no federal formula). Most guidelines, however, fall into one of two categories: some are based on a percentage of the non-custodial parent's income, while others establish the total appropriate amount of support for the child, and then apportion that amount according to each parent's income.[68] Child support obligations commonly require parents to pay from between 17 percent of income to over 35 percent, depending on the number of children to be supported.[69] Most states apportion support obligations by considering the combined incomes of both parents.

Parents may agree on an appropriate child support arrangement, including allocation of basic support, payment for the costs of health insurance and medical expenses, educational expenses, and child care costs. However, these agreements must be made part of the court papers upon which the divorce will be granted. Courts, therefore, insist that the agreement be consistent with the guidelines or contain valid reasons for deviating from them.

The duty to pay child support and the right to visitation are legally distinct from one another. A non-custodial parent may not withhold child support in retaliation for the custodial parent's interference with his or her visitation with the child. Conversely, a custodial parent may not interfere with the child's visitation on the grounds that the non-custodial parent has failed to pay child support.

'Alimony' or 'maintenance' is financial support to a former spouse. Once regarded as a right of the wife, it is awarded today on a gender-neutral basis.[70] Women continue to be the more likely recipient of alimony because they are more likely than men to have engaged in nonremunerative tasks during the marriage and, as a result, have diminished earning capacities. Despite this modern justification for its use, alimony is currently disfavored and awarded

---

[67] 42 U.S.C. §§ 666(a)(5)(A),(B)(West Supp. 1994).   [68] *The Rights of Families*, n. 53 above.
[69] See, e.g., New York Dom. Rel. Law § 240(1-b) (McKinney 1993).
[70] *Orr v. Orr*, 440 U.S. 268 (1979).

in only a minority of divorces.[71] It is now more commonly termed 'mainte-nance', 'spousal support', or 'rehabilitative' or 'transitional maintenance'. About half the states today impose time limits on these payments, commonly limiting them to 10 years or less.[72] These payments are taxable to the spouse who receives them and deductible from the income of the spouse who makes them. By contrast, child support payments are not deductible expenses or includable income, but are relevant in determining which parent may claim the child as a dependent on his or her tax return.

Marital fault, which has otherwise increasingly become an insignificant factor in divorce, may result in a reduction in the amount or length of an alimony award. Alimony is often reduced or eliminated when the person receiving payments chooses to live with another person. However, many courts will not reduce alimony under such circumstances if the person's income has not actually increased. As a general rule, alimony ends when the recipient remarries.

Traditionally, courts had been reluctant to recognize agreements between unmarried persons that try to replicate the financial obligations imposed by marriage. In a celebrated 1976 case, *Marvin v. Marvin*, the California Supreme Court held that, even in the absence of a written contract, an unmarried couple had entered into an implied contract of mutual support, obligating the man to share the income he earned during the period of the relationship with the woman.[73] Since then, courts in most states have adopted the ratio-nale of *Marvin* and regularly entertain so-called 'palimony' suits, although such suits do not succeed very often.

E. *Property Distribution*

There has been a minor revolution in the law of property distribution in the past 20 years or so in the United States. Courts today see the marital rela-tionship as an important economic relationship. As society has come to understand more completely the economic value of a non-income producing partner, especially when that partner is an active homemaker and parent, courts have vastly expanded the definition of 'marital property'—those pos-sessions and assets acquired between the period of marriage and divorce— and made it ever easier to give them to the non-working spouse after a break-up. The non-income producing partner—usually the wife in American society—has come to be regarded both in law and by society as a significant

---

[71] U.S. Census Bureau, Current Population Reports, Series P-60, No. 173, *Child Support and Alimony: 1989* at 12 (1991).

[72] *The Rights of Families*, n. 53 above.   [73] 18 Cal.3d 660, 557 P.2d 106, 134 Cal.Rptr. 815 (1976).

contributor to whatever tangible assets are accumulated by the other partner during the relationship.

This new conceptualization has allowed non-income producing partners to share all of the tangible assets accumulated during the relationship even when all of the money was earned by only one partner. Thus, for example, when a wife is the sole homemaker, and the husband is the sole business proprietor, courts today routinely include the worth of the business as martial property. In addition, and even more expansively, marital property has come to include a partner's intangible career assets, including such things as pensions and other retirement benefits, employee stock options, group medical and life insurance and, in some states, the value of a professional education or professional license. Moreover, by treating pensions as deferred compensation earned during the marriage, courts have included them as part of the property accumulated during the marriage.

One court, which held that professional degrees should be regarded as divisible marital property, reasoned:

> [F]ew undertakings during a marriage better qualify as the type of joint effort that the . . . economic partnership theory is intended to address than contributions toward one spouse's acquisition of a professional license. Working spouses are often required to contribute substantial income as wage earners, sacrifice their own educational or career goals and opportunities for child rearing, perform the bulk of household duties and responsibilities, and forego the acquisition of marital assets that could have been accumulated if the professional spouse had been employed rather than occupied with the study and training necessary to acquire a professional license.[74]

Separating parties are free to make whatever financial arrangements among themselves they choose. Regardless of how many assets a couple has, either party is free to waive all claims to shared property. Courts will not review provisions of property distribution unless they are asked to by one of the parties or unless the distribution is intertwined with issues concerning child support. Although parents cannot waive a child's right to support, they may agree to take less for themselves than a court would order if the matter were contested. In addition, couples occasionally sign contracts—called 'prenuptial' or 'antenuptial' agreements—before they marry that attempt to clarify which property owned by one person before the marriage is unavailable to the other person. In most states, courts will enforce these agreements if the court considers the agreement to be reasonable. However, courts will not enforce these agreements when they completely bar someone from seeking property earned during the marriage.

---

[74] *O'Brien v. O'Brien*, 66 N.Y.2d 576, 585, 489 N.E.2d 712, 716, 498 N.Y.S.2d 743, 747 (1985).

There are general rules by which courts will decide property distribution matters when separating parties bring such disputes to court. Although this section uses the phrase 'marital property', jurisdictions following *Marvin* v. *Marvin* (see section IV D above) may allow former partners in non-marital relationships to share assets acquired during the relationship and, for those states, the principles defining 'marital assets' also apply to non-marital relationships.

Until the 1970s, states distributed property on the basis of one of two distinctions. Some states recognized 'community property', which they defined as all property acquired by the spouses during the marriage. These states were ahead of the country in regarding marriage as an economic and social partnership in which each makes it possible for the other to accomplish their tasks, whether or not both are income producers. The more common method involved the technical concept of 'title'. Individuals could keep what they earned during a marriage by putting their assets in their own name. At the end of a marriage, each party kept what he or she owned and only jointly titled property, such as a house, or certain other obvious joint assets would be divisible by a court.

Over the past 20 to 25 years, the clear trend in the United States has been away from technical notions of title to an expansive definition of shared marital property. Eschewing the term 'community property', these states have changed their rules by invoking equitable principles that allow courts to distribute property acquired during a marriage without regard to title. 'Equitable distribution' authorizes courts to divide all property acquired during the marriage, regardless of who holds title to a particular asset. In most states, today, divisible marital property includes only property acquired as a result of the efforts of one or both spouses during the marriage. Property acquired prior to the marriage, property given as a gift to a spouse by a third party, and, at least in a majority of states, property inherited by the spouse during the marriage continue to be treated as separate property.

Only a very few states deviate from this arrangement. In some of these states, the court will divide all property owned by either spouse at the time of the divorce, regardless of how or when the property was acquired or permit division of even 'separate' property if one partner would end up with too little without the separate property being invaded.

Another significant change in this area concerns the purpose of property distribution. Formerly, courts only awarded property to 'worthy' parties. Persons who engaged in 'marital misconduct', such as adultery, could be excluded from sharing in property. Though a few states continue to consider fault when making property distribution determinations, the vast majority of states today distribute property on the basis of need and economic fairness.

Wrongful behavior that is directly related to finances still is commonly considered, such as a person's dissipating marital assets, but behavior that may have led to the marital break-up has no bearing on property distribution in most of the country.

Finally, federal law has also influenced the property distribution area. Recognizing the importance of retirement pensions in economic planning, the 1984 Retirement Equity Act requires private pension plans to comply with court-ordered divisions of pensions, and it permits all or part of a worker's pension and survivor benefits to be paid directly by the plan to a former spouse when a court enters such an order.[75] When a person receives a court-ordered division of the pension that specifies s/he is entitled to survivor benefits, the Act also protects that person's rights to those benefits. Finally, the Act prevents a married worker from opting out of survivor's benefits without the written consent of his or her spouse.

The cost of health care has become a very serious economic matter in the United States. Congress has further addressed the needs of people who divorce when it passed the Comprehensive Omnibus Budget Reconciliation Act of 1986 (COBRA) which requires that employers allow divorced spouses and children for 3 years following the divorce to remain paying members of the former spouse's group health insurance plan.[76]

V. Conclusion

Perhaps no area of the law is as sensitive to changing values and mores in culture as family law. In addition, this area of the law is influenced to a great extent by changing notions of social science, particularly psychology and the impact of behavior on the well-being of children. To the extent that all law is an experiment to develop rules of behavior that maximize the well-being of citizens, the one thing of which we can be certain is that family law will continue to change in the future as American society itself changes and as notions of the common good change.

[75] 29 U.S.C. § 1056(d)(3)(West Supp. 1994).
[76] 29 U.S.C. §§ 1161 through 1168 (West Supp. 1994).

III

FEDERAL LAW

16

ANTITRUST LAW

HARRY FIRST

I. Overview: Antitrust Statutes and Enforcement

A. *Basic Statutory Provisions*

Antitrust law in the United States has developed over a period of more than 100 years. The basic statutes are written in broad, general language. Their meaning has been developed by the courts, applying this broad language to a wide variety of business practices.

The oldest federal antitrust statute is the Sherman Act, enacted in 1890. Its main substantive provisions are Sections 1 and 2.[1] Section 1 prohibits contracts, combinations, or conspiracies 'in restraint of trade'. Section 2 prohibits monopolization or attempts to monopolize.

Early court interpretations of the rather vague statutory provisions of the Sherman Act led many to believe that the Sherman Act required further amendment if it were to be effective. The result was the passage in 1914 of the other two basic antitrust statutes, the Clayton Act and the Federal Trade Commission Act. The former contains provisions dealing with a number of specific business practices about which Congress was concerned, the most important being a provision dealing with mergers (Section 7).[2] The latter

---

[1] See 15 U.S.C. §§ 1, 2. Most States also have some form of antitrust legislation applicable to conduct that occurs within the state. These provisions are generally similar to federal law. This chapter will discuss only federal antitrust law.

[2] See 15 U.S.C. § 18. Other important provisions are Section 2, which prohibits price discrimination (charging a different price to different buyers for the same product) under certain circumstances, and Section 3, which prohibits exclusive dealing and tying agreements in certain circumstances. Exclusive dealing and tying agreements are discussed in section V D below.

established a regulatory agency, the Federal Trade Commission (FTC), which was given broad power to prevent 'unfair methods of competition'.[3]

B. Enforcement Structure and General Enforcement Trends

1. Government enforcement

There are two government agencies that have major responsibility for enforcing the antitrust laws, the Antitrust Division of the Department of Justice and the Federal Trade Commission. Each has somewhat different responsibilities and procedures.

The Department of Justice is part of the Executive Branch and is given the responsibility for representing the United States in court proceedings. The head of the Department (the Attorney General) and the head of the Antitrust Division are appointed by the President and are subject to Senate confirmation. The Antitrust Division is responsible for enforcing the Sherman and Clayton Acts. Enforcement is accomplished through litigation in the federal courts, using judicial procedures both for investigating facts and for determining whether violations have occurred. Under the Sherman Act the Antitrust Division can choose to invoke either civil remedies (for example, seeking to enjoin an illegal transaction) or criminal remedies (fines and imprisonment for the most serious violations). Remedies under the Clayton Act are exclusively civil.

The Federal Trade Commission (FTC) is an independent regulatory Commission consisting of five Commissioners appointed by the President, with the advice and consent of the Senate, for 7 year terms. To help assure independence, no more than three can be from the same political party, and Commissioners can be removed only for cause. The Commission is responsible for enforcing the Federal Trade Commission Act and the Clayton Act. The Commission investigates and adjudicates violations of these Acts through its own administrative procedures. These procedures are somewhat less formal versions of those followed in federal courts, although an FTC proceeding is presided over by a civil service appointee, rather than by a life-tenure judge, and is ultimately decided by the Commissioners themselves. The FTC's remedial powers are generally limited to cease-and-desist orders; it has no power to enforce the antitrust laws criminally.

There is considerable overlap in the statutory responsibilities of these two agencies. Not only do they both enforce the Clayton Act, but the FTC has

---

[3] Section 5, 15 U.S.C. § 45.

interpreted 'unfair methods of competition' to include any conduct which would violate the Sherman Act. As a general matter, however, the two agencies have tended to cooperate and share enforcement burdens rather than duplicate enforcement. They also have tried to agree on common enforcement approaches (for example, issuing joint horizontal merger guidelines in 1992). On occasion, however, one agency will investigate a matter in which the other agency has refused to proceed.

2. Private enforcement

Any person injured in their business or property by a violation of the Sherman or Clayton Acts may sue for three times their damages plus a reasonable attorney's fee.[4] This treble-damage action may be filed without regard to whether the government brings suit against the allegedly improper behavior. Courts have in the past emphasized the important public policy behind allowing private parties to supplement government antitrust enforcement resources and to act, in effect, as 'private attorneys general'. More recent court decisions, however, have shown some skepticism about the private right of action and reflect a concern that private litigants might use the private cause of action to achieve anticompetitive ends.

3. Jurisdiction

The Sherman Act covers restraints of trade 'among the several States, or with foreign nations'. The first clause relates to the central government's power in a federal system to regulate business transactions. The clause has been interpreted broadly to permit the federal courts to reach any transaction which might have an effect on interstate commerce. Those rare cases whose impact is so local as to be outside the jurisdiction of the Sherman Act are left to the exclusive jurisdiction of the states. The second clause relates to the foreign commerce of the United States, that is, to imports and exports. This part of the Sherman Act was amended in 1982 to limit jurisdiction over United States export trade to conduct that has a 'direct, substantial, and reasonably foreseeable effect' on United States domestic commerce or on import trade.[5]

There has been a continuing controversy over whether United States antitrust law should reach conduct that occurs abroad but which has some effect on domestic American markets or firms (this is often referred to as 'extraterritorial jurisdiction'). It was held in one landmark case that the

---

[4] See Clayton Act, Section 4, 15 U.S.C. § 15. This provision was originally enacted as part of the Sherman Act in 1890.

[5] 15 U.S.C. § 6a.

antitrust laws reach activity that occurs abroad which 'affects' United States commerce.[6] Other courts and commentators, however, have urged the exercise of discretion in taking jurisdiction over foreign transactions, to take account of the interests of foreign countries in the transaction in question.[7] Whatever the outer bounds of the Sherman Act's jurisdictional reach, however, it is clear that foreign firms that export goods or services to the United States would be wise to expect that their conduct will be subject to the Sherman Act, even if the allegedly improper conduct occurs entirely outside the borders of the United States.

4. Enforcement trends

Government antitrust enforcement in the United States has always been affected by politics. This effect has been felt in two ways. The first is the use of political influence to alter an enforcement decision in a particular case. The second, and more important, is the impact on antitrust enforcement that comes from the generally shifting current of American political and economic thought. Antitrust enforcement has continually been shaped by changing political value judgments regarding basic approaches toward economic structure and the government's regulatory role. Has big business become too powerful? Do we need more government action to control abusive corporate behavior, and should we favor the small entrepreneur? Or is a government policy of laissez faire more appropriate? Should we permit the growth of large companies because they are most efficient, trusting to the marketplace to self-correct?

In one way or another government enforcement patterns have reflected widely-shared changes in these basic political values. Weak antitrust enforcement during the laissez faire era of the 1920s was succeeded by increased government intervention in the 1930s and eventually more vigorous antitrust enforcement in the late 1930s and 1940s as the Roosevelt administration became concerned about cartel behavior. Enforcement moderated in the 1950s, but increased again in the 1960s, reflecting a renewed concern with corporate size; government enforcers embarked on an ambitious program which included major merger and monopolization cases. Enforcement in the 1970s shifted again, now toward greater use of criminal prosecutions against

---

[6] See *United States* v. *Aluminum Co. of America*, 148 F.2d 416, 444 (2d Cir. 1945).

[7] See, e.g., *Mannington Mills, Inc.* v. *Congoleum Corp.*, 595 F.2d 1287 (3d Cir. 1979). Most unsettled is the question whether the Sherman Act applies to conduct occurring in foreign countries which blocks American firms from exporting to foreign markets. There is some precedent for allowing such suits. See *Continental Ore Co.* v. *Union Carbide*, 370 U.S. 690 (1962) (conspiracy to exclude an exporter of vanadium products from the Canadian market; 'part of the conduct' occurred in a foreign country; jurisdiction upheld).

clear-cut violations of Section 1 of the Sherman Act (usually bid-rigging). After the election of Ronald Reagan in 1980, government enforcement by the Justice Department became very heavily oriented toward such prosecutions, reaching a high point in 1984 with 100 criminal prosecutions. At the same time, the government brought very few cases against the very large mergers which were then taking place. With the election of a new administration in 1992, enforcement shifted again, with more civil antitrust cases being brought against a wider array of potential violators and with a renewed concern for the connection between antitrust and its impact on innovation.

Private suits, on the other hand, are not directly affected by political pressure; the decision to institute such litigation is purely in private hands. Nevertheless, the level of private litigation is affected by political trends. For one, private cases often follow government litigation, taking advantage both of the government's investigative work and of the successful litigation outcome by the government. When enforcement is low, there are fewer such cases to follow. For another, the views of the courts toward antitrust litigation are affected by general political trends. In periods when courts look less favorably on antitrust, fewer cases will be brought.

From the enactment of the Sherman Act until roughly the early 1960s, the numbers of private cases filed were about the same as the number of cases filed by the Justice Department. This changed in the early 1960s, when private parties successfully sued the major electrical equipment manufacturers for price-fixing (following a criminal case brought by the federal government). In part as a result of favorable recoveries in that litigation, private antitrust litigation became much more popular. From the mid-1960s until 1980, there were approximately sixteen times more private cases filed than public cases. In the late-1970s, however, the courts began to be less receptive to antitrust plaintiffs, and in the 1980s the ratio of private to public cases dropped to approximately eleven-to-one.

Even with these changes in the level of private litigation, private enforcement continues to be an important component of antitrust enforcement in the United States. The possibility of recovering treble-damages and attorneys fees is a significant incentive for bringing such litigation, as is the general availability of class actions and jury trials.[8] For some business transactions, the possibility of enjoining a competitor from engaging in activity which competitively harms the plaintiff also provides strong incentive; these actions, likewise, require the defendant to pay the successful plaintiff's attorneys fees. It is the existence of this strong private action which is perhaps the most significant difference between the American antitrust system and antitrust systems in other countries.

[8] For further discussion of class actions, see Chapter 4, Litigation.

C. *Purpose of the Antitrust Laws*

Unlike more recently drafted antitrust legislation in other countries, United States antitrust law contains no statutory statement of its purposes. As a result, the task has fallen to the courts and commentators to articulate a set of purposes for antitrust which can be used in interpreting the statutes.

Two major schools of thought have emerged. The first takes the view that the antitrust laws have but one purpose, 'efficiency'. This view is loosely ascribed to the 'Chicago School'. Relying heavily on neo-classical economic theory, this approach seeks to promote a particular type of efficiency, 'allocative efficiency', which refers to making optimal use of the resources available in the economy so that the 'correct' amount of goods are produced. The amount that is 'correct' depends on consumer preference; it is in this sense that Chicago School theory seeks to maximize consumer welfare. Chicago School theory also makes extensive use of neo-classical economic theory to describe business behavior and to judge whether particular behavior will enhance efficiency or not.

The second major school of thought lacks a convenient label, but might be called 'pluralist'. Those who argue for that approach agree that the antitrust laws should seek to advance consumer welfare through an efficient industrial structure and efficient business practices. In addition, however, they argue that the goals of antitrust law also encompass political and social objectives which the mere pursuit of efficiency would not necessarily achieve. These political and social goals include:

(1)   the deconcentration of economic power;
(2)   the protection of market access and a fair opportunity to compete on the merits;
(3)   the promotion of consumer choice, considering price, quality, and service; and
(4)   the maintenance of a competitive market process.

Each of these four factors has an economic impact, but they are sought because they have social and political purposes as well.

As an historical matter, until the 1970s, antitrust interpretation was much closer to the pluralist school. At that time strong Chicago School criticism of the pluralist approach began to have an impact on the courts. With the arrival of the Reagan Administration in 1980, the Chicago School philosophy became dominant, both within the enforcement agencies and gradually in the courts. This has increased the importance of economic theory for analyzing antitrust issues, as well as generally leading to a greater tolerance for business practices that had traditionally been viewed as suspect. The critical role of economic theory will no doubt continue for the foreseeable future, even if courts once again begin to take a broader approach to the goals of antitrust.

II. Monopolization

A. Introduction

Section 2 of the Sherman Act prohibits monopolization. This prohibition implicates the core concerns of antitrust. For those who believe that the antitrust laws should be concerned only with efficiency, prohibiting the exercise of monopoly power is the major argument in favor of antitrust enforcement. Firms with monopoly power raise price and limit output, adversely affecting allocative efficiency. For those who take the pluralist approach, ending 'monopoly' becomes a primary goal of antitrust. Monopoly firms are the quintessential examples of concentrated economic power, carrying with them the potential for abusing consumers and for stifling the opportunities of competing entrepreneurs.

At the same time, bringing an antitrust case against a 'monopolist' often involves prosecution of a large and successful company. To those who believe that large firms are necessary for efficient industrial production and for national economic strength, the prohibition on monopolization is often translated as a simplistic attack on bigness. 'Big', critics argue, 'is not necessarily bad'.

To deal with these tensions, the courts have developed a two-part test for determining whether a firm has 'monopolized' in violation of Section 2. To prove a violation, the plaintiff must show:

(1)   the possession of monopoly power in a relevant market; and
(2)   the willful acquisition or maintenance of that power as distinguished from success caused by a 'superior product, business acumen, or historic accident'.[9]

This two-part test can also be viewed as an inquiry into (1) market structure and (2) conduct.

---

[9] *United States v. Grinnell Corp.*, 384 U.S. 563 (1966).

B. Market Structure

To show that a defendant possesses monopoly power in a relevant market requires answering two questions.

(1)   What is the definition of a 'market'?
(2)   What is meant by 'monopoly power'?

1. Market definition

Courts have defined the market from several different perspectives. The first and most frequently used is the consumer's perspective: what products might a consumer find 'reasonably interchangeable' in use? If the consumer has a good substitute for the seller's product, the seller would be subject to competition from that other product should the seller wish to raise price.

Using the test of consumer substitutability, the Supreme Court, in a famous monopolization case brought against the sole producer of cellophane, defined a market consisting of 'flexible packaging materials'.[10] This market included brown wrapping paper, wax paper, and aluminum foil, in addition to cellophane. The Court found that, if the seller raised the price of cellophane slightly, consumers would shift to these other products. In this broad market, the defendant was not a monopolist and therefore had not violated Section 2. Examples of other product market definitions are: virgin aluminum ingot and aluminum ingot made from recycled aluminum (separate markets); bottled reconstituted lemon juice and fresh lemons (separate markets); and 'rigid walled containers' (a market which includes glass and plastic bottles).

Courts have also defined the market from the seller's perspective. That is, courts have asked what decisions other sellers might make if the 'monopoly' seller of a particular product decided to raise its price. If those other sellers would alter their production process, and start to make an equivalent product, then the alleged monopolist would find itself in competition from those other sellers. In such a case, the courts have said, the 'market' must include the production capacity of the would-be competitors.

An example of such 'supply-side substitutability' came in a case brought by the manufacturers of computer equipment that plugged into IBM mainframe computers.[11] These manufacturers argued that the market consisted of 'plug-compatible' computer equipment because consumers could not substitute

---

[10] See *United States* v. *DuPont*, 351 U.S. 377 (1956).
[11] See *Telex Corp.* v. *IBM Corp.*, 510 F.2d 894 (10th Cir.), *cert. dismissed*, 423 U.S. 802 (1975).

computer equipment made by other companies that did not plug into IBM computers. The court disagreed with this product market definition, observing that it would be relatively easy for other competitors to change the 'plug' and make compatible equipment. As a result, the market was found to include all such equipment manufacturers (whether currently manufacturing compatible equipment or not).

Market definition includes a geographic component as well as a product component. In a sense, the geographic component of market definition examines the same issue that the product component does—what is the set of sellers competing for the buyer's business—but factors in the question of the geographic proximity of those competing suppliers. Thus, courts have defined a geographic market as the 'area of effective competition . . . in which the seller operates and to which the purchaser can practicably turn for supplies'.[12] In theory, this geographic area could be as small as a city or metropolitan area, or could be as large as the entire world.

To give some examples of geographic market definition: the Supreme Court has held that a banking market could be defined as a metropolitan area and its surrounding counties, even though some business customers might go elsewhere for large loans.[13] The Court chose this definition in recognition of the fact that this was the area in which most bank customers found it practical to do their banking business. In the landmark case of *United States v. Aluminum Co. of America*, brought against Alcoa for monopolizing virgin aluminum ingot, the court held that the market could be limited to the United States, even though foreign producers could and did export ingot to the United States in competition with Alcoa. The court stressed that this foreign competition was limited by tariffs and the cost of transportation. Within this limit Alcoa still had the power 'to raise its prices as it chose'.[14]

Actual court decisions defining product and geographic markets show that the process of market definition is ultimately a matter of judgment, not of science. Courts often attempt to get an appreciation of the business realities that affect buyer/seller relationships. In so doing courts understand that competition can take many forms and that each buyer and seller does not react identically. The ultimate goal of market definition, however, is to articulate a set of products whose control might give a particular seller (or group of sellers) the power to raise prices or exclude competition.

---

[12] *Tampa Elec. Co. v. Nashville Coal Co.*, 365 U.S. 320, 327 (1961).
[13] See *United States v. Philadelphia Nat'l Bank*, 374 U.S. 321 (1963).
[14] *United States v. Aluminum Co. of Am.*, 148 F.2d 416, 426 (2d Cir. 1945).

2. Possession of monopoly power

Once the market (product and geographic) is defined, the next question is whether the defendant possesses 'monopoly power' in that market. Courts have generally placed most emphasis on the defendant's market share as the way to answer this question. In the *Alcoa* case the court provided this rule of thumb: 33 percent of the market is certainly not sufficient for finding monopoly power, 60 percent is 'doubtful', but 90 percent is clearly enough. Although later cases have found the existence of monopoly power in the 60 percent range, the range suggested in *Alcoa* remains a useful guide.

Market share is not the only indication of monopoly power. Particularly in the contested range (over 50 percent but less than 80 percent), courts may give weight to a variety of other factors which might show whether the defendant in fact has monopoly power. These factors include an examination of profit rates, historical trends in market shares (for example, examining whether the defendant's market position is eroding), and the power of large or sophisticated buyers to keep price down.

C. *Conduct*

A major debate in the development of monopolization law is whether a defendant violates Section 2 of the Sherman Act simply by being a monopolist, or whether some additional improper conduct must be shown. Those taking the former view ('structuralist') argue that inevitably a monopolist will act in an economically inefficient way, that is, the monopolist will raise price and restrict output. The resulting allocative inefficiency is reason enough to condemn the monopolist. Those arguing in favor of examining the monopolist's conduct more closely believe that not every action by a monopolist is necessarily anticompetitive. They also argue that some monopolists achieve their position by virtue of being a superior firm; it would be foolish to condemn such a firm for its competitive success.

No United States court has ever adopted a complete structuralist viewpoint. The case that comes the closest is *Alcoa*, decided in 1945 (see section II B1 above). In *Alcoa* the court placed on the defendant the burden of proving that it had achieved its monopoly position through 'superior skill, foresight, or industry'. The court found that Alcoa was not entitled to this defense, despite the fact that the Government had not shown that Alcoa engaged in any improper behavior and despite the fact that Alcoa had, in the court's words, progressively embraced every opportunity to expand, bringing to bear 'the advantage of experience, trade connections and the elite of personnel'.[15]

Subsequent cases have given monopoly firms more latitude. For example, in the 1970s a number of private cases were brought against major American firms for conduct relating to the way in which these firms maintained their dominant positions. In these cases the courts were generally more receptive than was the *Alcoa* court to permitting these dominant firms to engage in competitive behavior, even if that behavior disadvantaged smaller rivals.

One such case involved the introduction by the Eastman Kodak Company of a new, smaller amateur camera and film.[16] The court found that Kodak had not violated Section 2 by bringing out the camera and film without providing advanced notice of the film's size to its camera competitors (these competitors were at a disadvantage because they needed to know the size of the film before they could produce a smaller camera). The court felt it was necessary to allow Kodak to reap the competitive advantages that flowed from its being an integrated company, bringing out an innovative product that consumers liked.

Another important area in which the courts have given dominant firms more latitude is in pricing. In one important case the plaintiff American television manufacturers alleged that the defendant Japanese manufacturers had attempted to monopolize the United States television market through predatory pricing, selling televisions at prices below market levels.[17] The Supreme Court dismissed the plaintiffs' case because the Court believed it was unlikely that the defendants could rationally have believed that they could recoup their losses through later monopoly pricing. In dismissing the case the Court showed skepticism about complaints relating to the pricing behavior of competitors. The Court refused to adopt antitrust rules that would unduly restrict the ability even of dominant firms to engage in competitive pricing.[18]

The increased tolerance for permitting aggressive conduct by monopoly firms reflects an underlying shift in attitude toward such firms. In 1945 the *Alcoa* court wrote:

> Congress . . . did not condone 'good trusts' and condemn 'bad' ones; it forbad all. Moreover, in so doing it was not necessarily actuated by economic motives alone. It is possible, because of its indirect social or moral effect, to prefer a system of small producers, each dependent for his success upon his own skill and

---

[15] *Ibid.* 148 F.2d at 431.

[16] See *Berkey Photo, Inc.* v. *Eastman Kodak Co.*, 603 F.2d 263 (2d Cir. 1979), *cert. denied*, 444 U.S. 1093 (1980).

[17] See *Matsushita Elec. Indus. Co., Ltd.* v. *Zenith Radio Corp.*, 475 U.S. 574 (1986).

[18] See also *Brooke Group Ltd.* v. *Brown & Williamson Tobacco Corp.*, 113 S.Ct. 2578 (1993) (even below cost pricing will not violate the antitrust laws if the seller is unlikely to recoup its losses through subsequent monopoly pricing).

character, to one in which the great mass of those engaged must accept the direction of a few.[19]

By contrast, in a 1979 case brought against IBM, in which the court held that it was not a violation of Section 2 to fail to predisclose design changes in the 'plug' between IBM central computers and peripheral equipment (even though competing peripheral makers were thereby disadvantaged), the district court wrote:

> It is an unwise policy for the law to coddle competitors, especially if the protection comes at the expense of destroying a larger firm's incentive to compete. Even companies that choose to enter dominated markets must be prepared to face competition on the merits. Where a monopolist chooses an alternative that does not unreasonably restrict competition, the law is not offended.[20]

The views of both of these courts were affected by the general political and economic concerns of their times. *Alcoa* was decided at a time when the United States was convinced of the connection between competitive economies and democracy; cartels and monopolies, after all, had led to authoritarian regimes in Germany and Japan. By the time the more recent cases were decided, many in the United States were becoming concerned that undue restrictions on large firms were hindering the competitiveness of American companies in international markets. Courts did not want the competitive instincts of the most innovative firms diminished, no matter how large such firms might be. Put otherwise, pluralist political concerns were giving way to Chicago School efficiency concerns.

To say that political value judgments have shifted does not mean that the courts are willing to permit a monopolist to engage in any behavior the monopolist deems appropriate. On the contrary, the Supreme Court has shown continuing interest in stopping monopolistic conduct aimed at excluding competitors 'on some basis other than efficiency'.[21] One such decision involved an attempt by a firm that dominated a skiing market to disadvantage its competitor in a way that reduced consumer choice; another case involved the effort of a firm that sold complex photocopy equipment to squeeze out independent companies that sought to service the equipment that it manufactured.[22]

---

[19] *United States* v. *Alcoa*, 148 F.2d at 427.

[20] *Transamerica Computer Co.* v. *International Business Machines Corporation*, 481 F.Supp. 965, 1022 (N.D. Cal. 1979), *aff'd*, 698 F.2d 1377 (9th Cir.), *cert. denied*, 464 U.S. 955 (1983).

[21] *Aspen Skiing Co.* v. *Aspen Highlands Skiing Corp.*, 472 U.S. 585, 605 (1985).

[22] See *Eastman Kodak Co.* v. *Image Technical Services, Inc.*, 504 U.S. 451 (1992) (attempt to exclude competition by independent service companies for service of machines made by defendant); *Aspen Skiing*, n. 21 above (monopolist of ski facilities refusing to permit joint ticketing with competitor for no valid business justification).

These two cases show that the Supreme Court is still receptive to at least one goal of the pluralist school, market access. This attention will likely continue because it is in line with emerging concerns of economists relating to the strategic use of monopoly power, and because it reflects the general international concern with market access in an internationalizing economy.

III. Mergers

A. *Introduction*

Mergers—consolidations of businesses, regardless of the legal form they take—raise concerns similar to those raised by monopolization. Rather than waiting for a firm to attain a monopoly position, however, merger law asks whether any limits should be placed on the ability of firms to grow by acquiring the assets of other companies. At what point might such growth create a market structure in which competition will be lessened?

The first merger case reached the Supreme Court in 1904.[23] Although the Court held the merger violative of the Sherman Act, the Court's opinion left many concerned that the Sherman Act would not be an effective tool for dealing with future mergers. This led to the inclusion of a stricter merger standard in Section 7 of the Clayton Act of 1914. Subsequent court opinions, however, gave this new provision a narrow interpretation, and by 1930 it had been rendered useless in preventing anticompetitive mergers. In 1950, Section 7 of the Clayton Act was amended to create what Congress hoped would be a more effective remedy. Although there have been minor subsequent modifications, the statute remains basically in its 1950 form.

In amending Section 7 in 1950 Congress sought a broad statute. The amended Section 7 was intended to cover all types of corporate acquisitions, whether the acquisition is classified as horizontal (between firms whose products compete with each other); vertical (between firms at different levels in the chain of distribution of the same product); or conglomerate (between firms whose products are unrelated). Congress wanted Section 7 to be used to stop the 'rising tide of economic concentration' that many believed was affecting the United States economy. As with Section 2 of the Sherman Act, this Congressional fear of concentrated economic power reflected a social and political concern about the exercise of such power, as well as a concern about the adverse economic effects of a non-competitive economy.

---

[23] See *Northern Securities Co.* v. *United States*, 193 U.S. 197 (1904).

Section 7 prohibits the acquisition of stock or assets where, in 'any line of commerce', in 'any section of the country', the effect of such acquisition 'may be substantially to lessen competition'.[24] The 'line of commerce' and 'section of the country' requirements are equivalent to the product and geographic market concepts discussed in section II B1 above in connection with monopolization. Although proper definition is quite critical to merger analysis, these terms raise no issues not already mentioned. What is unique about Section 7 is the competitive effects clause. This clause requires a court to predict the future impact that an acquisition might have on competition.

B. *Competitive Effects*

The first case to consider the meaning of the 1950 amendments, *Brown Shoe Co.* v. *United States,* was decided in 1962. In this case the Supreme Court wrote that Congress did not adopt any definite quantitative test for determining when a merger's effect 'may be substantially to lessen competition'. Rather, the Court stated that a merger had to be 'functionally viewed' in the context of its industry, with all factors examined.[25]

The following year, however, the Court decided the landmark case of *United States* v. *Philadelphia National Bank.* In this case the Court moved away from a broad economic investigation to a more focused approach. Drawing on industrial organization economic theory, which placed great emphasis on market structure factors, the Court adopted the following test: probable anti-competitive effect could be predicted where:

(1)   the merged firm controlled an 'undue percentage share' of the relevant market and

(2)   the merger resulted in a 'significant increase' in concentration in the relevant market.[26]

Once the plaintiff produced such market share evidence, the merger would have to be enjoined, at least in the absence of proof 'clearly showing' that there would not likely be any such anticompetitive effect.

The Court did not give precise guidance on what would be 'undue' or 'significant'. In cases decided over the next decade, however, the Court proved very receptive to government arguments that mergers should be

---

[24] Note that the statute is not technically limited to full mergers or consolidations, but covers the acquisition of any type of asset, or of stock, if the acquisition has the requisite anticompetitive effect.

[25] 370 U.S. 294, 321–22 (1962).

[26] See *United States* v. *Philadelphia Nat'l Bank,* 374 U.S. 321 (1963).

found to violate Section 7 even when the merged firm did not have an extremely high market share and even though the increase in concentration was slight. Perhaps the high-water mark for this view was *United States v. Von's Grocery*, involving the merger of the third and sixth largest grocery chains in Los Angeles.[27] The merged firm had only 7.5 percent of the market, and the share of the market held by the first four firms ('the four-firm concentration ratio') was 24.4 percent (only a 7.6 percent increase over the pre-merger ratio). In finding the merger unlawful, the Court underscored the Clayton Act's purpose 'to prevent economic concentration in the American economy by keeping a large number of small competitors in business'.[28]

The Court's willingness to give the government broad latitude changed in 1974. In *United States v. General Dynamics Corp.*, the Government challenged a coal company merger between the second and fifth-largest firm in a particular geographic market; the four-firm concentration ratio was 54 percent, the merged firm would be the largest in that market, with a 23 percent share, and the increase in concentration in the top two firms was 22 percent.[29] Although acknowledging that the market share and concentration figures were comparable to other cases in which it had found a violation of Section 7, the Court now disclaimed sole reliance on such data. The simple predictive link between increased market share and diminished competition was no longer compelling. Instead, the Court took a closer look at the industrial factors which had led to consolidations in the coal industry, as well as at the economic position of the acquired firm. The Court thus moved back toward the standard originally set out in *Brown Shoe*; many factors need to be examined before one could accurately predict the probable anticompetitive effect of a merger. Perhaps more importantly, the Court also moved away from a central focus on economic concentration, signalling a willingness to see competition as possible even in concentrated industries.

There have been no significant Supreme Court merger decisions since *General Dynamics*. There was a substantial merger wave in the United States in the late 1970s and the 1980s, but by this time merger enforcement by the government also changed, with the result that there were far fewer government merger challenges, although private parties did make some use of Section 7 as a tactical device in corporate takeover battles.

The new merger enforcement posture was made clear in 1982 when the Department of Justice in the Reagan Administration issued a new set of merger guidelines. There had been merger guidelines in effect since 1968, but the 1968 Guidelines reflected the economic and political philosophy of the *Philadelphia National Bank* era. The 1982 Guidelines, by contrast, substantially

---

[27] 384 U.S. 270 (1966).   [28] *Ibid.* at 275.   [29] 415 U.S. 486 (1974).

altered the government's economic approach to mergers, stating clearly the government's new view that most mergers were either 'competitively beneficial or neutral'.

The 1982 Guidelines changed merger analysis in three critical ways. First, the Guidelines articulated a single purpose for Section 7—to prevent the exercise of market power, defined as the power to raise price. Secondly, the Guidelines adopted a market definition that was related to this purpose. A market was defined as a set of products over which a hypothetical monopolist could exercise market power by profitably raising the price a 'small but significant and nontransitory' amount. That is, if a hypothetical monopolist of a group of products could raise price by 5 percent and hold the price for a year without attracting competitors to force the price back down, that set of products would constitute a 'market'; if competitors would be attracted in, those competitors would be considered as part of the market and the 5 percent test would be performed again.

Thirdly, the government would look at pre- and post-merger concentration in the market by use of the Herfindahl-Hirshman Index (HHI), a mathematical measure of market concentration which gives more precise weight to differing market structures than the previously-used four-firm concentration ratio. The Guidelines then gave ranges of post-merger HHIs within which a merger would either face no challenge, possible challenge, or certain challenge. These three thresholds were set at levels that permitted mergers creating substantially more concentrated markets than had been allowed in the 1960s and 1970s.[30]

The 1982 Guidelines also shifted the economic theory used for merger analysis away from simple industrial organization theory, which saw clear links between market structure and conduct, toward cartel theory. Cartel theory shows more skepticism about the ability of firms, even in concentrated markets, successfully to raise price and limit output. Under this theory, even firms in highly concentrated markets must devise some method for tacitly communicating among themselves regarding the terms to be followed on price and output. Further, even if communication can successfully be done, such cartels are viewed as inherently unstable and prone to cheating. Thus, the Guidelines look for indications beyond market share that firms in a particular market are likely to be able to form a tacit cartel and collude to raise price.

The Guidelines were subsequently amended in 1984 and again in 1992.

---

[30] The HHI is computed by summing the squares of the market shares of all the firms in the market. The safe harbor lower limit HHI was set at 1000, which could be a market of 10 firms each with 10 percent of the market, or a market where the four-firm ratio is approximately 50 percent. The upper limit, over which the government said a challenge was likely, was set at 1800, roughly a four-firm ratio of 70 percent.

The 1992 version moves even further away from the simple concentration-conduct paradigm. Mergers that fall in the highest range are still 'presumed' to create market power, but the presumption can be overcome by further analysis in three areas: competitive effects, entry, and efficiencies. With regard to competitive effects, the Guidelines require a more complete exploration of the exact mechanism of collusion, specifically 'the extent to which post-merger market conditions are conducive to [1] reaching terms of coordination, [2] detecting deviations from those terms, and [3] punishing such deviations'.[31] Entry conditions are likewise critical, because new entry can defeat price-raising behavior. The Guidelines state that entry will be considered easy if new entry 'would be [1] timely, [2] likely, and [3] sufficient in its magnitude, character and scope to deter or counteract the competitive effects of concern'.[32] Finally, the Guidelines call for an inquiry into manufacturing and distributional economies, as well as possible managerial economies arising from a merger.

Thus, current merger analysis shows the effects of the change in overall antitrust approach that resulted from the increasing influence of the Chicago School. Since 1982 the Guidelines have focused attention on one major area of economic concern, the power to raise price. Neo-classical economic theory has also been predominant, first as a skeptical counterweight to the notion that all concentrated industries are non-competitive, and then as a way to probe more deeply into whether particular firms in particular markets really will be able to raise price.

C. Conclusion

Despite the increased tolerance for mergers, merger enforcement continues to be an important part of antitrust law. Under the Hart-Scott-Rodino Antitrust Improvements Act of 1976, mergers over a certain asset size must be reported to the government, generally 30 days prior to consummation.[33] This pre-merger notification requires the parties to disclose substantial amounts of information to the government, thereby enabling the government better to decide whether to institute litigation. The pre-merger notification process also makes it easier for the government to convince the parties to modify a proposed merger where there are specific anticompetitive problems that may be easily cured without foregoing the entire merger. As a result of this statute, all substantial merger transactions are reviewed by private counsel and by government attorneys.

---

[31] 1992 Guidelines, § 2.1.   [32] 1992 Guidelines, § 3.0.   [33] 15 U.S.C. § 18a.

Merger enforcement in the 1980s reflected an economic and political judgment that prior merger enforcement had discouraged some beneficial mergers. Merger enforcement in the 1990s may reflect the view that prior non-enforcement was too permissive. As with changes in monopolization enforcement (see section II C above), changes in this area are not likely to return enforcement to a simple concern for large firm size. What is more likely is that enforcement agencies will make increasing use of economic theory that looks at the strategic efforts of firms to prevent new entry or to discourage innovation.

IV. Horizontal Agreements

A. *Introduction: Analytical Structure*

Section 1 of the Sherman Act deals with joint behavior (as opposed to single-firm monopolization), prohibiting contracts, combinations, or conspiracies 'in restraint of trade'. Unlike the more structurally-oriented provisions of Section 2 or Section 7 of the Clayton Act, Section 1 is most concerned with conduct, and conduct which is done by agreement, however transitory that conduct or agreement may be.

Once particular behavior is found to involve some agreement (joint action), the next question is whether the joint action in question should be evaluated under a 'per se' test or under a rule of reason. An agreement which is per se unlawful is one that is unlawful 'without more'. The court will not consider any defense or justification; the proof of the conduct, itself, is sufficient. By contrast, under the rule of reason, the court examines more of the economic circumstances surrounding the conduct in an effort to assess its competitive impact. The question whether to characterize particular types of agreements as per se unlawful has been a continuing issue of controversy in antitrust jurisprudence, as has the question of what factors a court should consider when judging an agreement under the rule of reason.

It has been customary to divide analysis of Section 1 problems into horizontal agreements (between competitors in the same market) and vertical agreements (between firms at different points in the production and distribution process), even though the statute, on its face, applies equally to both types of agreements. This analytical structure recognizes that different economic consequences may flow from whether an agreement is horizontal or vertical, and thus different rules have developed for determining legality in the two areas.

B. Price

The core rule under Section 1, about which there is no current dispute, is that horizontal agreements fixing price are illegal per se. This rule was most clearly articulated in 1940 in *United States v. Socony-Vacuum Oil Co.*, which involved an agreement among producers and refiners of gasoline to support prices in the gasoline market by buying up 'excess' gasoline that could not be sold at 'fair market prices'. The defendants argued that the program was justified by the distressed economic conditions facing the industry during the Depression. The defendants also pointed out that certain officers of the federal government knew about the program and 'tacitly approved'.

The Court rejected any justifications. Noting the importance to a free market economy of having untampered-with prices, the Court held: 'Under the Sherman Act a combination formed for the purpose and with the effect of raising, depressing, fixing, pegging, or stabilizing the price of a commodity . . . is illegal per se'.[34]

The Supreme Court's strict view of price-fixing agreements in *Socony-Vacuum* came after a period during which both the Court and the Congress had shown a willingness to allow price-fixing cartels in the face of the severe economic problems of the Depression. By 1940, however, the Depression had faded, and the Court was free to reject the idea that it was wise to organize the economy into cooperative cartels to avoid 'ruinous competition'. No doubt influenced by the contrast with the authoritarian regimes in Japan and Germany, where government-cartel cooperation was an important feature of the economy, the Court wrote that if such agreements were permitted, 'the Sherman Act would soon be emasculated; its philosophy would be supplanted by one which is wholly alien to a system of free competition; it would not be the charter of freedom its framers intended'.

The per se rule against price-fixing continues to be widely accepted, even though the political arguments against cartels are perhaps less compelling today than are the economic arguments as to the adverse effects of agreements to set prices. Indeed, so well-accepted is this hostility toward price-fixing and bid-rigging agreements that (as mentioned earlier) the Department of Justice will generally prosecute such agreements criminally, rather than merely seek civil remedies.[35]

To say that price-fixing is per se unlawful, however, does not mean that every agreement that has an effect on price will be characterized as

---

[34] 310 U.S. 150, 223 (1940). Subsequent cases have held that the rule applies to agreements setting maximum prices, as well as minimum prices. See *Arizona v. Maricopa County Med. Soc.*, 457 U.S. 332 (1982).

[35] The prohibition extends to services as well as to goods and includes elements of pricing (such as purchase credit terms) as well as the final price itself.

'price-fixing'. On the contrary, there is a substantial line of cases in which the Court has refused to condemn an agreement simply because the agreement has some effect on price. One of the most famous is *Chicago Board of Trade* v. *United States*, which involved a rule of the Board of Trade prohibiting trans-actions outside trading hours at any price other than the closing bid during the trading period (thereby 'fixing' the price). The Supreme Court held that the agreement was to be tested under the rule of reason. In an often-cited ver-sion of what factors are relevant to a rule of reason analysis, the Court stated that it was necessary to inquire into the 'history of the restraint, the evil believed to exist, the reason for adopting the particular remedy, [and] the pur-pose or end sought to be attained'.[36] Viewed as such, the Court held that the restraint was reasonable, and not violative of Section 1 of the Sherman Act.

More recent cases continue to apply the rule of reason to certain agree-ments among competitors that have an effect on price. The test for deter-mining whether a price related agreement will be subject to a rule of reason, or whether the agreement will be illegal per se, is 'whether the practice facially appears to be one that would always or almost always tend to restrict competition and decrease output . . . or instead [is] one designed to "increase economic efficiency and render markets more rather than less competi-tive" '.[37]

This test was articulated in a 1979 Supreme Court decision, *Broadcast Music, Inc.* v. *Columbia Broadcasting System, Inc.* (*BMI*). That case involved two 'performing rights societies', which are groups of authors, composers, and music publishers that license the performance of the copyrighted musical compositions of their members, collect and distribute royalties, and monitor compliance. Both societies insisted on providing only a blanket license of all the copyrighted works in their repertory, giving the licensee the right to use any work the licensee wanted. The plaintiff, a major broadcasting network, sought to license just individual works (thereby reducing its costs for music). When this request was refused, the plaintiff sued under Section 1 of the Sherman Act.

The lower court held the blanket license to be per se unlawful. By setting (in effect) a single price for all copyrighted works, the blanket license pre-vented price competition among the copyright holders and fixed the price. The Supreme Court disagreed, holding that the blanket license should be viewed under a rule of reason because it was designed to 'increase economic efficiency'. First, there were obvious transactional efficiencies in combining to provide a single source to whom music users could go when they want to use copyrighted music. The availability of such a source thus facilitated trans-

---

[36] 246 U.S. 231, 238 (1918).
[37] *Broadcast Music, Inc.* v. *Columbia Broadcasting System, Inc.*, 441 U.S. 1, 19–20 (1979).

actions that would otherwise have been much more costly. Secondly, by combining to produce the blanket license, the parties (who were otherwise competitors) produced a new product that no one of them could produce individually. The performing rights societies 'made a market' in which no individual copyright holder could have effectively competed.

The Court's willingness to recognize such integrative efficiencies is consistent with the view that the goal of antitrust law is to promote efficiency. Rather than mechanically condemning collaborative behavior among competitors, the Court will examine economic effects where a plausible case can be made that the behavior is designed to advance marketplace competition. It will not apply a rule of reason when the defense argument is that the price-related agreement was adopted to promote non-economic goals.

C. Division of Markets

A second type of horizontal restraint that the courts have held to be per se illegal is an agreement among competitors dividing markets. An example is *United States v. Topco Associates, Inc.* A group of regional supermarket chains had formed an association to engage in cooperative buying of various food items; these items were then distributed under a common trademark to each of the chains. Each of the supermarket chains that joined Topco operated in different cities. As part of the agreement, each supermarket chain was prohibited from expanding its operations into the territory of any other member.

The Supreme Court held that this territorial division was illegal per se. The Court refused to consider Topco's justification that territorial exclusivity was necessary for producing commonly trademarked goods which, in turn, were necessary if Topco's members were to be effective competitors against other supermarket chains. The Court stated that Congress did not give private groups of competitors the right to decide to sacrifice competition among themselves because they believed that their agreement would enable them to compete more vigorously with others. In so holding the Court emphasized the importance under the Sherman Act of securing to entrepreneurs the freedom to compete in any sector of the economy. 'Antitrust laws', the Court wrote, 'are the Magna Carta of free enterprise', as 'important to the preservation of economic freedom and our free-enterprise system as the Bill of Rights is to the protection of our fundamental personal freedoms'.[38]

---

[38] 405 U.S. 596, 610 (1972).

D. Boycotts

A boycott is a joint refusal by two or more parties to deal with another party or parties. This can cover a wide range of behavior, ranging from agreements whose goal is to exclude competitors from a market, to agreements that limit membership in cooperative production or marketing groups. Although the Supreme Court has often stated that boycotts are per se unlawful, the breadth of possible behavior that can possibly be characterized as a boycott has actually led the Court to a more varied treatment.

The cases in which the courts have generally used a per se approach have involved efforts by competitors to use a boycott as a coercive tactic either to exclude competitors who refused to follow the wishes of those participating in the boycott or to raise prices. An example of the former is *Fashion Originators' Guild* v. *Federal Trade Commission*.[39] The Guild was a group of firms that manufactured and distributed women's dresses. The designs of their dresses were not protected by any intellectual property rights, with the result that competitors were copying the dress designs and selling them at lower prices. To deal with this competition the Guild arranged an elaborate system to monitor the purchases of retailers and to boycott retailers that purchased copied designs.

The Federal Trade Commission found that the Guild's behavior violated Section 5 of the Federal Trade Commission Act as an 'unfair method of competition'. The Supreme Court agreed with the FTC, upholding the Commission's refusal to consider the Guild's asserted justification that the boycott was necessary to prevent the 'evils' of copying. Among the reasons the Supreme Court gave for condemning the boycott was its exclusionary impact on lawful competitors, and the restraints that the boycott imposed on the freedom of action of retailers. Again, the Court emphasized that groups of private competitors (cartels, in other words) did not have thr right to regulate competition and restrict the opportunities of competitors or customers. Even if the copying were illegal, a group boycott would not be the proper response.

A more recent case involved a boycott that enabled competitors to raise prices.[40] A group of lawyers who represented indigent criminal defendants were dissatisfied with the low rates that the government paid them for this work. The government was constitutionally required to provide lawyers to indigent defendants and was dependent on this group of lawyers to represent those defendants. The group decided to refuse to accept any more cases until

---

[39] 312 U.S. 457 (1941).
[40] *Federal Trade Comm'n* v. *Superior Court Trial Lawyers Ass'n*, 493 U.S. 411 (1990).

the government agreed to pay them more. Within two weeks of the institution of this boycott, the government capitulated and agreed to raise the rates that it would pay.

The Court held this boycott to be per se illegal. It rejected consideration of the defendant's justification that higher rates were necessary if indigent clients were to receive adequate representation and it did not require the FTC to show that the defendants possessed market power. As a horizontal arrangement among competitors, the agreement posed 'some threat to the free market'.

There are other boycott cases, however, in which the Court has refused to apply a per se approach to boycotting behavior. These have generally been cases where the defendants offered an efficiency justification for their behavior, which, under the test from *BMI*, will require application of a rule of reason.

For example, in *Northwest Wholesale Stationers, Inc. v. Pacific Stationery & Printing Co.*[41] the defendant was a purchasing cooperative of approximately 100 office supply retailers. By engaging in joint purchasing, the cooperative's members were able to achieve economies of scale and lower their purchasing costs for merchandise. The plaintiff was a former member that had been expelled for violating the rules of the cooperative. Because cooperative purchasing arrangements have the potential for enhancing competition, the Supreme Court rejected the plaintiff's view that its expulsion and the subsequent refusal to deal with it must be treated as a per se unlawful boycott.

Another important case involved the efforts by a group of universities to control television broadcast rights to their football games and limit the number of games that could be televised.[42] The universities were members of the National Collegiate Athletic Association (NCAA). When some of their members threatened to televise their games on a competing television network, the NCAA threatened disciplinary action against them, which would have affected sports in addition to football. To prevent this threatened boycott by the NCAA, several of the universities brought suit under the Sherman Act.

Because the NCAA could not produce its product of 'college football' without engaging in some degree of collaborative behavior, the Supreme Court held that the boycott could not be judged under the per se rule. The Court then applied the rule of reason to determine whether the anticompetitive effects of the NCAA's restrictions were outweighed by some procompetitive justification. The anticompetitive consequences were that individual competitors (the schools) lost their freedom to compete. Absent the agreement, there would have been more football games on television (output

---

[41] 472 U.S. 284 (1985).
[42] *National Collegiate Athletic Ass'n v. Board of Regents of the University of Oklahoma*, 468 U.S. 85 (1984).

would be increased), price would have been lower, and consumers would have had a wider range of choices (and would have been able to see the best teams more frequently). There were no procompetitive justifications to outweigh these harmful effects because the limitation on numbers of games was not necessary to sell television rights nor was the plan necessary to enable NCAA football to compete against other rivals (college football being a unique product for which there was no ready substitute).

E. Conclusion

There are some well-accepted categories of horizontal agreements that the courts will find to be per se illegal. What often remains uncertain is whether a court will place a particular agreement within one of those categories, or will be willing to examine the justifications for the agreement more closely. In recent years this decision has come to be made less mechanically, being influenced by the court's views as to whether the agreement might be efficiency-enhancing. This concern for efficiency, of course, is a reflection of current views about the goals of antitrust.

At the same time, the courts have not abandoned traditional concerns for consumer choice and entrepreneurial freedom. Indeed, as recent cases indicate, the courts are still quite concerned about the ability of cartels to regulate a market and block the entry and efforts of those who would compete in a different way.

V. Distribution Restraints

A. Introduction: Analytical Structure

Vertical restraints in the distribution process raise the same analytical issues as are raised by horizontal agreements. Under Section 1 of the Sherman Act, there must be joint, as opposed to individual, action. Once joint action is found, the courts will examine the question whether the joint action is to be judged under the per se test or under the rule of reason. If subject to the rule of reason, the competitive impact must be assessed.

Although the questions may be the same as those posed by horizontal agreements, the answers need not be. Distribution agreements involve transactions in which a manufacturer is attempting to get its goods to market, not a cartel of competitors attempting to regulate competition among themselves. Many economists argue that a manufacturer has an economic incentive to adopt agreements that are procompetitive, that is, that enhance its ability to compete with other sellers of comparable products ('interbrand competition'). This may not mean that every distribution agreement should be lawful, but it does at least caution against too-quick condemnation of distribution restraints.

B. Price

Vertical price-fixing (sometimes called 'resale price maintenance') occurs when a seller (whether a manufacturer or a wholesaler) requires the buyer to resell the purchased product at a set price. The Supreme Court has consistently held, from its earliest cases, that such vertical price-fixing is per se unlawful. The classic case is *Dr. Miles Medical Co.* v. *John D. Park & Sons*, decided in 1911.[43] Dr. Miles manufactured patent medicines and required its distributors to resell at stipulated prices. The Supreme Court held that the agreement was against public policy. The product had passed into the channels of trade, and further restraint on alienation could not be justified by any advantage the parties intended to get by charging higher prices to the consumer. The manufacturer had sold the product at satisfactory prices; the public was now entitled to the advantage of subsequent competition among the retailers.

Although this rule was well-accepted, a case decided eight years after *Dr. Miles* opened up a way for manufacturers to moderate its effect. *United States* v. *Colgate & Co.* was a criminal prosecution for setting resale prices. The Supreme Court dismissed the case because Colgate had not been charged with entering into any agreement. Stressing Section 1's statutory requirement of joint action, the Court pointed out that the Sherman Act does not restrict a trader from exercising its independent discretion in choosing the parties with whom it will deal; '[a]nd, of course, he may announce in advance the circumstances under which he will refuse to sell'.[44] Thus, after *Colgate*, a seller may suggest resale prices and can even refuse to deal with parties who will not follow these prices. Such conduct is viewed as unilateral behavior and hence outside the coverage of Section 1. It is only when the situation gets beyond simple notification by the seller, and acquiescence by the buyer, that joint action will be found.

---

[43] 220 U.S. 373 (1911).   [44] 250 U.S. 300, 307 (1919).

C. *Territorial and Customer Restraints*

Manufacturers often restrict distributors to sales within a given geographic territory; there are also occasions when manufacturers will restrict distributors to sales to particular customers or types of customers. Territorial restraints can also be accompanied by territorial exclusivity, that is, by an agreement by the manufacturer that the distributor will be the only distributor within the area.

In 1967, in *United States* v. *Arnold, Schwinn & Co.*, the Supreme Court faced the question of the legality of territorial and customer restraints. The Court ruled that such restraints were 'obviously destructive of competition'. In selling the goods, the manufacturer had parted with dominion over them; echoing the views of the Court in *Dr. Miles*, to permit post-sale restrictions would thus 'violate the ancient rule against restraints on alienation'.[45] The Court therefore held that post-sale restraints on customers or territories are per se unlawful.

The per se approach of *Schwinn* was much criticized and lasted only 10 years. In 1977 the Supreme Court decided *Continental T.V., Inc.* v. *GTE Sylvania, Inc.*, a case involving a territorial restriction placed by a small television manufacturer on its distributor. The Supreme Court overruled *Schwinn*, holding that post-sale territorial and customer restrictions (or, more broadly, non-price restraints) should be evaluated under a rule of reason.[46]

The Court changed its position because it concluded that such restraints on distribution could very well be procompetitive. The Court saw that a manufacturer had a legitimate interest in the activities of its distributors and might choose a competitive strategy that required a distributor to provide certain pre- or post-sale services to customers, services which might not otherwise be provided if the distributor were subject to competition from unauthorized sellers of the same brand.

For example, a manufacturer might want a distributor to provide expensive presale information about a product. If a discounter could easily obtain the product, it could open a nearby store and 'free ride' off the efforts of the authorized distributor (consumers would get the information from the authorized dealer and buy from the discounter). Such free riding would ultimately destroy the ability of the full-service retailer to provide the necessary information; this, in turn, would thwart the efforts of the manufacturer to make its products known and to compete for customers.

Two aspects of *Sylvania* are particularly important. First, *Sylvania* was the first Supreme Court decision clearly showing the Court's willingness to base

---

[45] 388 U.S. 365 (1967).   [46] 33 U.S. 36 (1977).

its reasoning on the economic arguments of the Chicago School, which had heavily criticized the Court's past decisions in the distribution area. Secondly, despite accepting the basic critique and theoretical approach toward distribution restraints advocated by the Chicago School, the Court in *Sylvania* did not take the Chicago School's position to its logical conclusion. It held only that these restraints were subject to a rule of reason analysis, not that distribution restraints were always lawful. It also clearly confined its decision to non-price restraints, emphasizing that vertical price restraints remained subject to the per se rule.

Despite these apparent limitations in *Sylvania*, it soon became clear that the basic Chicago School view of the beneficence of distribution restraints would make the courts very sympathetic to defense arguments in distribution cases. Many of the cases brought after *Sylvania* involved the termination of a price-cutting distributor, which the plaintiff would allege was done pursuant to an agreement between the manufacturer and a full-service retailer to maintain high resale prices. Although these cases appeared to involve a per se unlawful price restraint, courts have often refused to find liability.

Two Supreme Court cases have played a large role in narrowing liability in these circumstances. The first is *Monsanto Co. v. Spray-Rite Service Corp.*[47] In this case the Court stated that there could be no joint action under Section 1 where a manufacturer received a complaint from a distributor that a competing distributor was cutting its price, and the manufacturer subsequently terminated the price-cutter. In so ruling the Court stressed the view of distribution adopted in *Sylvania*; manufacturers and distributors share common interests in the distribution process, and manufacturers may need to protect the profits of distributors so that they can offer the services that manufacturers want them to provide.

The second case is *Business Electronics Corp. v. Sharp Electronics Corp.* In this case the manufacturer terminated a distributor, on the complaint of a competing distributor, for selling at prices below the manufacturer's suggested minimum retail price. The plaintiff argued that this was per se unlawful price-fixing. The Supreme Court disagreed, holding that this conduct would not be a per se violation unless the plaintiff could show that the agreement was to set a price or price level. In reaching its decision, the Supreme Court conceded that such proof would not be required in a horizontal price-fixing case, but the Court noted that *Sylvania* rejected the view that horizontal and vertical restraints are to be treated identically. The Court also emphasized that its decisions in *Sylvania* and *Monsanto* were designed to be 'market-freeing',

---

[47] 465 U.S. 752 (1984).

allowing manufacturers great freedom to construct their distribution systems. Liability rules under Section 1 were to be framed narrowly so as not to
chill the willingness of manufacturers and distributors to engage in 'legitimate and competitively useful conduct'.[48]

There have been frequent legislative proposals to change the results in
Monsanto and *Sharp*, but none of them has been enacted. The current state of
the law with regard to distribution restraints is thus rather clear:

(1) To come within Section 1 of the Sherman Act, more than a mere com-
    munication from a distributor (followed by action by a manufacturer)
    must be shown. There must be evidence that the complaining distribu-
    tor and the manufacturer had a 'conscious commitment to a common
    scheme designed to achieve an unlawful objective'.[49]
(2) Even if the conduct is within Section 1, unless there is proof of an agree-
    ment on a specified price or price level, the restraint will be viewed
    under the rule of reason.
(3) All non-price agreements will be viewed under a rule of reason analysis,
    which will likely give great weight to the manufacturer's legitimate
    efforts to engage in effective interbrand competition.

D. *Exclusive Dealing and Tying*

Exclusive dealing and tying are two types of conditioned sales. In an exclusive
dealing arrangement, the seller conditions the sale of its product on the
buyer's agreement to deal exclusively with that seller on that product and not
to buy it from someone else. In a tying arrangement, the seller conditions the
sale of one product (the tying product) on the buyer's agreement to purchase
a second product (the tied product) from the seller.

Exclusive dealing and tying arrangements are covered by two antitrust
statutes, Section 1 of the Sherman Act and Section 3 of the Clayton Act.
Although the Clayton Act provisions were passed to establish a stricter standard of liability than that provided by the Sherman Act, current interpretations of both statutes have diminished the separate importance of the
Clayton Act. This is because exclusive dealing agreements have come to be
viewed under a very generous rule of reason standard (under both statutes)
and because tying has been held to be a per se offense under Section 1 of the
Sherman Act, which is a stricter standard than the Clayton Act.

The two major exclusive dealing cases are *Standard Oil Co. of California* v.

---

[48] 485 U.S. 717 (1988).   [49] *Monsanto Co.* v. *Spray-Rite Service Corp.*, 465 U.S. at 764.

United States[50] and *Tampa Electric Co.* v. *Nashville Coal Co.*[51] In both cases the Supreme Court identified the economic problem as one of market foreclosure; that is, an exclusive dealing arrangement forecloses other sellers from selling to the particular buyer for a certain period of time. In *Standard Oil* the Supreme Court found the foreclosure of less than 7 percent of the market to be sufficient for purposes of Clayton Act liability. In *Tampa Electric*, however, the Court held lawful an exclusive supply contract of greater duration and dollar value, although of smaller market share, indicating that the legality of exclusive dealing agreements could not be mechanically evaluated but needed to take account of the effects such foreclosure might have on competition. Analysis of exclusive dealing after *Tampa Electric* has thus come to emphasize the efficiency-enhancing aspects of exclusive dealing contracts, which offer the parties important savings on transaction costs. As a result few challenges are currently brought to such agreements.

Tying, however, is still a matter of great antitrust controversy. Tying is per se unlawful if the plaintiff can show three things:

(1) that there is a conditioned sale of two products (the tying and tied products);
(2) that a not insubstantial volume of commerce is involved; and
(3) that the seller has sufficient economic power in the tying product market to impose the tie.

In holding that tying arrangements are per se illegal, the Court has traditionally stressed a number of factors. One is market foreclosure; a tying arrangement forecloses competitors of the seller in the tied product market from selling to the buyer. This diminishes 'competition on the merits' with respect to the tied product, possibly insulating an inferior product from effective competition. Tying may also raise barriers to entry in the tied product market; new entrants might need to enter both the tying and the tied products. Finally, consumer choice is diminished. The consumer is forced to buy the tied product from the seller of the tying product, when the consumer might prefer to buy the tied product from someone else.

Not everyone agrees, however, that tying arrangements should be viewed under a per se test. Drawing again on economic theory, and focusing exclusively on price-raising effects, many have argued that (except in some unusual circumstances) a seller with monopoly power who imposes a tie cannot thereby raise the price of the tied product. The seller will already be charging the monopoly price for the tying product, and any increase in the price for

---

[50] 337 U.S. 293 (1949).   [51] 365 U.S. 320 (1961).

the package of tied and tying product will actually lower the net profit. The only anticompetitive effect the monopolist might hope for is to gain control of the tied product market and thereby gain separate monopoly power in that market.

The difference between these two views of tying was demonstrated in *Jefferson Parish Hospital* v. *Hyde*.[52] This case involved a hospital which required patients who needed an operation (the tying product) to use the services of a specified anesthesiologist (the tied product). A five-member majority of the Supreme Court held that this agreement should be viewed under the per se test, although it found that the hospital lacked market power. Four members of the Court would have held that tying arrangements are subject to the rule of reason, to be condemned only if there is a substantial threat that the tying seller will acquire market power in the tied-product market.

Despite the sharp difference in views expressed in *Jefferson Parish*, subsequent cases have not revisited the question whether tying arrangements are more appropriately viewed under the rule of reason. Instead, the controversial issue has been whether the seller actually has sufficient economic power to impose the tying arrangement. The most recent such case, *Eastman Kodak Co.* v. *Image Technical Services, Inc.*,[53] involved Kodak's effort to require purchasers of parts for its photocopiers to also use Kodak service, rather than purchasing service from independent service organizations. Kodak argued that, although it might have monopoly power over its parts (it controlled their supply), it could not exercise that power and raise prices on service because it was subject to competition in the primary market for the original equipment. That is, if consumers know that Kodak will tie aftermarket parts and supplies (thereby raising the lifetime total price), consumers will factor this into their evaluation of whether to buy Kodak machines in the first place.

However plausible Kodak's argument might have been as a matter of economic theory, the Supreme Court was unwilling to say that the plaintiff's argument was necessarily implausible. Rather, the Court drew on economic theory to show how, despite competition in the primary market, consumers might still find themselves forced to take unwanted service in the secondary market. The Court observed that consumers, having purchased expensive equipment, were locked-in to that equipment and were unlikely to return to the primary market for new, expensive supplies. In addition, the Court pointed out that imperfections in the market for information make it difficult for consumers to know, when purchasing a long-lasting machine, exactly how much service might be necessary or what those costs might be. Finally, the Court noted that the service provided by the independent companies was

---

[52] 466 U.S. 2 (1984).   [53] 504 U.S. 451 (1992).

offered at a substantially lower price than Kodak's and was considered by some customers to be of higher quality. The Court thus remanded the case to the district court for trial, allowing both parties the opportunity to test their economic theories against the facts of the case.

The decision in *Kodak* illustrates some important points about the current state of antitrust jurisprudence. Economic theory is critical for analyzing antitrust problems and for determining which antitrust rule to choose. In using economic theory the courts are becoming ever more sophisticated, willing to move beyond the neo-classical views of the Chicago School. At the same time, the courts are not indifferent to how these theories actually work in the real world. They will give plaintiffs, who can present a plausible economic theory, the opportunity to show how the exercise of a seller's economic power in fact adversely affected competition and consumer choice.

VI. Conclusion

This chapter has reviewed the development of the major doctrines of United States antitrust law: monopolization; mergers; horizontal agreements (price; territory; and boycotts); and vertical agreements (price, territory and customer, exclusive dealing and tying). It has shown how the development of these doctrines has reflected the changes in the courts' views of the underlying objectives of the antitrust laws. At times, the courts have stressed a concern for concentrated economic power and a desire to promote an economy of small, independent firms. At other times, the courts have been more concerned with efficiency and have taken a more benign view both of corporate growth and of contractual arrangements between competitors or between manufacturers and suppliers.

In recent years, the courts have focused much more on efficiency. In this effort they have been aided by the insights of economic theory. This focus on efficiency is an accepted part of antitrust doctrine and is likely to continue, as is the use of economic theory. It is also likely, however, that the courts will pay more attention to at least one of the traditional objectives of the antitrust laws, the protection of market access. It is becoming widely accepted, both in the United States and elsewhere, that open markets are critical to a dynamic economy. Antitrust law, by depriving individual firms and cartels of their ability to control market access, may therefore come to play an increasingly important role in the development of the coming international economy.

17

BANKRUPTCY AND OTHER INSOLVENCY REMEDIES

LAWRENCE P. KING

I. Introduction

When credit of any sort is extended, such as a loan of money by a bank, or delivery of goods without payment, there is always the risk that the money will not be repaid on time, or at all, because the debtor—the one obtaining the credit—either will not or cannot do so. Normally this risk is recognized in two ways with the intention of reducing it as much as possible. First, the lender will make a business judgement concerning the creditworthiness of the borrower and, second, the lender may insist that the debtor pledge some of its property, known as collateral, that the creditor can sell to repay the obligation.

When no collateral is used, and the creditor relies exclusively on the promise of the debtor to repay, the lender has what is called an unsecured debt. Essentially, this means that, if the debt is not paid, the creditor has no rights against any specific property of the debtor from which to satisfy the debt. When, on the other hand, collateral is given by the debtor, either in real property, such as a real estate mortgage, or in personal property, by a security interest in stock, equipment, inventory or accounts receivable, if payment is not made, the creditor can sell that property to satisfy the debt. That is called secured credit. The creation, use, and enforcement of secured credit is generally governed by state law as distinguished from federal law.

In general terms, when a creditor has the right to use specific property to satisfy a debt, the creditor is said to have a *lien* on the property described in the mortgage or security agreement. The unsecured creditor has no lien at all, and to be able to sell the debtor's property to obtain repayment, it must obtain a lien.

In order to obtain a lien, the unsecured creditor can bring a lawsuit against the debtor in order to obtain a judgment from the court, establishing the exact liability of the debtor. That judgment, in and of itself, even though written and signed by the court, does not effectively put the money into the bank account of the creditor, now called a judgment creditor. Rather, it is necessary to use the laws of the state where the debtor has property, to collect the money owed under processes generally referred to as attachment, seizure, or, in the case of an individual who is owed wages or other money, garnishment. Methods vary from state to state and, for individuals, there may be exemptions that limit the property that can be taken.

These procedures can be used by an individual creditor without regard to any other creditors. The only exception would be if there were more than one lien on the same property, in which case, as a general rule, but subject to exceptions, the first lien filed will have priority. Another form of individual action may be one brought by an individual creditor in a state court to have a receiver appointed to take charge of the debtor's property; this is available in limited situations and is rarely used. It generally cannot be used simply to obtain repayment of a debt.

As distinguished from the individual remedies of creditors, the law, both state and federal, permits collective actions by creditors. With respect to a business entity, it is possible either under state statutory law or common law to have an 'assignment for the benefit of creditors'. This consists of the debtor in fact assigning all of its property to a named individual or organization who sells the assets and distributes the proceeds on a pro rata basis among the creditors. The assignment procedure is purely voluntary on the part of the debtor. It has been used in a limited number of industries, and even within those it is only rarely used.

The most common of all collective actions is known as bankruptcy. While the term is a generic one, it most commonly refers to a court-supervised proceeding in which the assets and liabilities of the debtor come within the control of the court through a trustee, who is responsible for converting the assets into money and distributing the money according to the priorities set forth in the statute.

Pursuant to the United States Constitution, Article I, section 8, clause 4, Congress is given the express power to enact a uniform law of bankruptcy. Although some states have bankruptcy statutes, since Congress has enacted a federal law, the state laws are preempted, and thus any state laws remaining on the books are of no effect.

The substantive law of bankruptcy in the United States is located in the federal Bankruptcy Code, which is title 11 of the United States Code.[1] The Bankruptcy Code ('the Code') contains five chapters that offer different forms of relief to various types of persons who have financial difficulties. The word 'person', as used in the Code, means an individual, a partnership or a corporation.[2]

Chapter 7 of the Code is called 'Liquidation' and, under it, all of the debtor's property is sold and the proceeds distributed pro rata to the debtor's unsecured creditors, after providing for secured creditors and those entitled to priority of payment according to the Code.[3] Under Chapter 7, a trustee is appointed, and his or her duties are, among others, to take control of the debtor's property as of the date the case was commenced, and then to sell it.[4] The trustee is not a government official; private individuals, usually attorneys, are appointed as Chapter 7 trustees by a government office known as the Office of United States Trustees.

The other essential aspect of a Chapter 7 case is that it results in a discharge of the debtor from unpaid liabilities.[5] Because there is no connection between the amount of the payment received by creditors, and the right to a discharge, even a debtor who has no property obtains a discharge. Thus, in many Chapter 7 cases, creditors receive little or no payment on their debts; nevertheless, the individual debtor may obtain a discharge from the total amount owed.

In general, there are two limitations on the right to an absolute discharge. First, if the debtor has committed any one of several acts listed in the Code, the discharge may be denied.[6] These acts, for the most part, involve dishonesty of one sort or another; in addition, an individual debtor may not obtain a Chapter 7 discharge more frequently than once in 6 years. Neither a partnership nor a corporation is entitled to a discharge.[7] The reasoning behind

---

[1] There is a fair amount of statutory procedural and jurisdictional law located in the Judicial Code (28 USC) and in the Federal Rules of Bankruptcy Procedure (FRBP). See 1 *Collier on Bankruptcy* (Matthew Bender, 15th edn.) c. 3.

[2] 11 USC §101. Hereinafter all section number references are to 11 USC ('the Bankruptcy Code' or 'the Code').

[3] Secured creditors are entitled to be paid first from the proceeds of their collateral, that is, the property securing their debt. See Section 725. Section 507 specifies the order of payment (priorities) among unsecured creditors.

[4] §§ 701, 702, 704.   [5] See § 727, FRBP 4004.   [6] § 727.

[7] § 727(a)(1).

this provision is that these types of business entities have no need for a discharge because, after a Chapter 7 liquidation, they will go out of business, unlike an individual who may have future earnings from which the non-discharged debts could be paid.

The other limitation on the right to a discharge is that even if a discharge is granted, there are certain types of debts which the Code renders non-dischargeable.[8] This list includes, among other types of debts, family obligations of child support and alimony, certain taxes, debts incurred by various fraudulent means, and, in general, education loans.

Chapter 11 is entitled 'Reorganization', and its basic purpose is to assist a financially distressed business so that it can become profitable once again. Chapter 11 is the focus of this chapter. It is a form of relief that is available to individuals, partnerships and corporations, except banks and insurance companies which may be liquidated under other laws.[9]

Finally, similar to Chapter 11 is Chapter 13 which is available only to individuals whose debts do not exceed a certain amount and who have regular income out of which repayment may be made.[10] Chapter 13 permits the debtor to propose a plan to pay as much of the debt as can be paid from his or her disposable future income over a 3-year period, which may be extended to 5 years.[11] On completion of the plan, the debtor will receive a discharge from any unpaid amounts.[12]

II. Some General Considerations

A. *Property of the Estate; Exemptions*

1. Property

When a petition commencing a case under the Code is filed, an 'estate' is created.[13] The estate operates under the supervision and control of the trustee in a Chapter 7 case and of the debtor, if no trustee is appointed, in a Chapter 11 case.[14] The estate, whether under Chapter 7 or Chapter 11, is comprised of all of the debtor's legal and equitable interests in property as of the date the petition was filed. As a general rule, property that the debtor acquires after the filing of the petition does not become property of the estate and is not available for distribution to creditors in a Chapter 7 case. For example, if the debtor is a wage earner and filed a Chapter 7 petition on May 14, her unpaid

---

[8] § 523(a).   [9] § 109(d).
[10] § 109(e). 'Family farmers' may use Chapter 12 which is similar to Chapter 13.
[11] § 1322(c).   [12] § 1328(a).   [13] § 541.   [14] § 1107.

salary from May 1 to May 14 has been earned and is property of the estate even though she will not actually receive it until June 1. However, any salary earned after May 14 does not become property of the estate and, when paid, belongs to the debtor.

2. Exemptions

An individual debtor may claim an exemption for certain property of the estate that the law provides is not available to pay the claims of a debtor's creditors. In the United States, there are two sets of exemption laws. One is the statutory law of the various states, each having its own set of exemptions.[15] The other is Section 522 of the Code, which sets out the exemptions any debtor may claim in a bankruptcy case, regardless of where he or she resides. The laws are different, but the underlying policy of them all is that a financially distressed debtor, even one unable to pay the outstanding debts, should be able to retain certain kinds of property. For example, all laws permit the debtor to have a family homestead exemption, i.e. a place to live. In many states the homestead exemption is limited in amount so that, for example, in the State of New York, the debtor's house could be sold to satisfy creditors, but the debtor would be entitled to retain the first $10,000 from the proceeds of the sale. In Florida, however, there is no dollar limit, and some debtors have moved to Florida to take advantage of this very favorable law for debtors.

Section 522 provides that a debtor may either claim the exemptions in that section, or the exemptions permitted by the state of the debtor's domicile. However, Section 522 also provides that the state law may restrict such a debtor to claiming only the exemption law of the state, and over half of the states have such laws.

Whatever property is properly claimed as exempt is given over to the debtor by the trustee. It may not be used for payment of the creditors' claims, either in a Chapter 7 case or outside of it.

B. *Priorities*

While the basic policy of the bankruptcy law is to provide for an equitable (pro rata) distribution of an insolvent debtor's assets among its creditors, Congress has determined that certain types of creditors should be paid before other types of creditors. Section 507 lists the order in which unsecured claims

---

[15] There is no uniform exemption law applicable in all of the states.

should be paid. But note, pursuant to Section 725, the secured creditor is entitled to be paid first from the proceeds of its collateral; in this way, secured debt and the rights of the secured creditor are specifically protected by the bankruptcy law.

Section 507 requires the costs and expenses of administering the bankruptcy estate to be paid first. Other priorities exist for the debtor's employees, to the extent they have not been paid for the 90 days before the filing of the petition, up to a maximum of $4,000 per employee. After that come priorities for a creditor who gave a deposit for the purchase of consumer goods, up to a maximum of $1,800 per individual consumer. Another priority is for governmental taxes owed for the preceding 3 years. There are, in all, nine groups of priorities listed in Section 507, not all of which will apply in any one case. After these priorities are paid, the remaining unsecured creditors will share in what is left of the estate. If there is not a sufficient amount of assets to pay any priority category, those entitled to the priority share pro rata, and no creditor with a lesser or no priority will receive anything. This priority scheme applies in Chapter 7, 11, 12, and 13 cases.

C. Governmental Claims

As mentioned above, taxes owed the state and federal governments are, to the extent provided for in Section 507, entitled to priority in payment. The same taxes that are entitled to priority are also non-dischargeable debts of an individual debtor in a Chapter 7, 11, 12, or 13 case.[16]

Other types of debts owed to the government are, for the most part, treated the same as debts owed to private parties. For example, if a company borrowed money from the Small Business Administration of the federal government, the Small Business Administration is not placed on any different footing from any other general creditor.

III. Introduction to Chapter 11

Chapter 11, the reorganization chapter, essentially provides the incentives and machinery for the parties to arrive at a voluntary plan for the financial restructuring of the debtor.[17] As will be explained in greater detail below, there are various provisions that encourage the parties to negotiate a settle-

---

[16] § 523(a)(1).   [17] See 5 *Collier on Bankruptcy* (Matthew Bender, 15th edn.) cc. 1101–1146.

ment that will afford some return to creditors and also permit the survival of the business. Of course, not every business that commences a case under Chapter 11 will survive; this is because, in part, some businesses should have filed Chapter 7 petitions and gone out of business and, in part, because some have thought it possible to reorganize, but subsequently found it impossible to do so, principally because there was not enough business to permit it to survive. Nevertheless, the theory of Chapter 11 is to help the business survive if survival is possible, and this is done through the construction of a plan of reorganization that ultimately obtains court approval.

A. Eligibility for Chapter 11 Relief

As mentioned, Chapter 11 may not be used by banks or insurance companies. In addition, it may not be used by stock brokers or commodity brokers for whom there are special subchapters in Chapter 7 of the Code which only permit these businesses to liquidate and not to reorganize.[18] Individuals, partnerships, and corporations may commence a case under Chapter 11 on a voluntary basis and need not claim that they are insolvent or unable to pay their debts. This does not mean that a healthy business will consider using Chapter 11. It is too drastic and risky a proceeding. It does mean that a business with problems can use Chapter 11 but does not also have to be insolvent.

It is also possible for a business to be placed into Chapter 7 or Chapter 11 by means of an involuntary petition filed by its creditors.[19] It is necessary, however, for the creditors to be able to prove either that the debtor generally is not paying its debts as they become due, or that some other person has taken control over substantially all of the debtor's property within 120 days before the petition was filed.[20] If the debtor has twelve or more creditors, three creditors are required to join in the involuntary petition; if there are fewer that twelve creditors, one creditor alone may properly file the petition.[21] Because of the harshness of this remedy, if the creditors are not able to prove their case, the judge may award damages to the debtor, including its attorney's fees.[22]

In practice, there are few involuntary petitions filed. One problem is that it is not a simple matter to obtain the agreement of three creditors to act together. A further problem is the substantial financial risk inherent in filing

---

[18] Subchapter III of Chapter 7 provides for the liquidation of a stockbroker (defined in § 101) and subchapter IV provides for the liquidation of a commodity broker (defined in § 101). Pursuant to § 109, the Code is not available to failing banks and insurance companies.

[19] § 303.   [20] § 303(h).

[21] § 303(b). In addition, the petitioning creditors must be owed, in total amount, at least $10,000 in unsecured debt.

[22] § 303(i).

an involuntary petition that the bankruptcy court may dismiss the petition because its allegations are not well founded.

B. The Players

There are several parties in a Chapter 11 case who, pursuant to the theory of the chapter, are the key participants or players. First is the debtor in possession. Under the American system, when a Chapter 11 case is commenced, the debtor, whether it is an individual, partnership or corporation, remains in possession of and continues to manage its property.[23] In essence, this means that the governing body of the debtor's business, such as the officers and directors of the debtor corporation, continue to operate its business; there is no automatic or immediate change in such governance.

Another way of expressing this very important concept and result is that neither a trustee nor a receiver is automatically appointed to take over the operation of the business or control of its assets.[24] Interested parties, such as a creditor or a committee of creditors, can ask a court for an order directing that a trustee be appointed if they can establish that there is cause for such an appointment. Examples of cause are listed in the Code and include incompetence of current management, lack of current management, fraudulent acts by current management, and the like.[25] Accordingly, unless there is a specific reason to the contrary, the debtor will remain in possession and control of its business.

The other key player in the Chapter 11 process is the committee of unsecured creditors. This committee is regarded as such an important part of the process that the Code *requires* the appointment of such a committee, generally composed of the unsecured creditors holding the seven largest claims.[26] The number seven is only a statutory suggestion, and, in practice, it varies both up and down.

In cases involving larger companies, there will often be different types and layers of unsecured creditors, having different interests. For example, the debtor may have issued bonds that are specifically made inferior, or 'junior', to a different series of bonds ('senior bonds') that it previously issued. The terms of the bond indentures would provide that the holders of the junior bonds are not entitled to payment until the obligations to the senior bondholders have been met. Or, an agreement may provide that a type of debt,

---

[23] §§ 1101, 1107, 1108. See 5 Collier on Bankruptcy, c.1101 (Matthew Bender, 15th ed.).

[24] The Code does not permit the appointment of a receiver in any circumstance. § 105(b).

[25] § 1104.

[26] § 1102(a)(1),(b)(1). The court may order that a committee not be appointed for a small business debtor, that is, one whose debts do not exceed $2,000,000.

such as a bank loan, must be paid before another type of debt. Thus, in each layer, there may be both senior and junior unsecured debt. There may also be different types of creditors, having the same rights against the debtor, but having different economic interests. Thus, there may be both trade debt, which is generally short term, and bank debt, which is often longer term, and so may wish to have their own committee. Finally, shareholders may desire to have a committee appointed so that their interests can be protected if the company survives. Committees representing these other interests may be appointed, but only if the court orders their appointment.[27]

Parties may form their own committees without court order, but this practice is not routinely followed. A major difference between the statutorily required committee or the court ordered committee (the official committees), and the informal committee organized by the parties themselves, is that only the first two may automatically have their professionals such as an attorney, an accountant, and an investment banker[28] paid from the assets of the Chapter 11 estate. Court approval is necessary for the employment of professionals and for their compensation, which comes from the estate, not the committee employing them. Professionals employed by an unofficial committee may also obtain compensation from the estate, if they can show that they made a 'substantial contribution' to the case,[29] which is not an easy showing.

The most important responsibilities of the official committees are to negotiate a plan of reorganization with the debtor and to oversee the operation of the business by the debtor in possession.[30] A committee may move for the appointment of a trustee, if that is justified, and the debtor in possession should consult with such committees when it contemplates taking any action outside the ordinary course of business, such as the sale of assets other than ordinary sales of inventory.

Another possible player in the Chapter 11 case is the examiner, who may be appointed only if the debtor is retained in possession.[31] The Code provides that a party in interest may move for the appointment of an examiner for cause. Additionally, if there is such a motion, and if the unsecured bank debt is at least $5,000,000, the court is required to appoint an examiner. Under the Code, the examiner's function is to investigate the debtor and its officers to determine if there are any claims that the estate may make against any of them or any one else. In practice, courts have used examiners for various purposes unconnected with such an investigation.

What makes Chapter 11 a difficult process for management of the debtor is that the business is being operated under very public scrutiny. The

---

[27] § 1102(a)(2).   [28] See §§ 330(a), 1103, 503(b), 1103(a).

[29] § 503(b)(3),(4).   [30] § 1103(c).   [31] § 1104(c).

bankruptcy court has general jurisdiction over any disputes that may arise,[32] and the committees will be 'looking over the shoulder' of management on a regular basis. Operating reports must be given to the committee or committees, and important business decisions should be brought to the committee before they are finalized. At the same time that management is trying to keep the business operating, it is also trying to deal with and solve the very problems that caused the Chapter 11 filing in the first place, and also to negotiate a plan of reorganization.

C. Case Administration

At the outset of a Chapter 11 case, there is often a flurry of activity on several fronts. When the Chapter 11 case is initiated, an estate is created composed of all of the debtor's legal and equitable rights in property at the date of the filing of the petition.[33] This property normally will be used in the business, and the debtor in possession must be able to continue to exercise control over it. On the other hand, the property may be subject to the rights of secured creditors whose debts are in default. The Code offers solutions to these seemingly incompatible needs.

D. Automatic Stay

The Code creates what is called an automatic stay when either a voluntary or involuntary Chapter 11 petition is filed.[34] This stay prevents third parties from disposing of the estate's property, even if they are secured creditors, and bars *all* creditors from using *any* means to collect their claims from the debtor or from the property of the estate.[35] One example of the effect of the stay is that a secured creditor, even one in possession of the property serving as collateral, may not take any action to enforce its security interest whether it is a pledge, mortgage, or other type of security device. Another example is that all lawsuits involving the debtor are halted immediately, until and if the bankruptcy court allows them to proceed.

The most important purposes of the automatic stay are to prevent creditors from trying to disassemble the debtor's property on a piecemeal basis and to grant the debtor an opportunity to try to reorganize.[36] In keeping with

---

[32] 28 USC §§ 1334(b),157(a).   [33] § 541.

[34] In fact, the stay arises when a petition commencing any case under the Code is filed. § 362(a) lists all of the actions and activities that are stayed and § 362(b) sets out those acts that are excepted from the automatic stay. In addition, the court has power under § 105(a) to issue specific injunctions.

[35] See 2 *Collier on Bankruptcy* (Matthew Bender, 15th edn.) c.362.   [36] *Ibid.*

this last purpose, if a secured creditor were able to foreclose on its collateral and sell it to satisfy its debt, the debtor would not have the very property necessary to continue to operate the business. If it cannot operate the business, there is no hope for reorganization; the business will be liquidated and closed down instead.

The Bankruptcy Code recognizes the seeming dilemma between the rights of the secured creditor and the concept of permitting reorganization. It provides that the creditor may request relief from the bankruptcy court by way of an order lifting the automatic stay and granting permission to seize the property and sell it. Such relief will be granted if the debtor does not offer the creditor what is called 'adequate protection'.[37] The idea behind this rule is that, if the debtor is allowed to continue to use the property, and if the property will decline in value over the time of its use, the creditor should be protected from that decline in value. Thus, the debtor may be ordered to make periodic payments to the creditor to offset this depreciation in value. The Code allows other means of offering adequate protection, but the purpose is the same. The court should also lift the stay if the debtor has no equity in the property (the secured debt equals the value of the property) and if it is not needed for an effective reorganization.[38]

E. *Post-petition Financing*

It is not unusual, at the outset of a Chapter 11 case, for a debtor in possession to need working capital to operate the business. It may, for example, have money for its regular overhead expenses, but need money to purchase inventory. To obtain financing after the filing of a Chapter 11 petition, the Code requires approval from the bankruptcy court, but it also provides incentives for lenders to agree to grant such financing.[39] The most important incentive is the ability of the lender to obtain what may be called a 'super priority', or even a 'super-duper priority' and a lien or security interest on the estate's free assets.[40] In effect, these mean that the lender of post-petition money will be entitled to have that loan repaid before payment to any other unsecured creditors.

This priority is so valuable that it enables the lender to be paid ahead of others who are also entitled to be paid first because their debts arose in the course of the Chapter 11 case. For example, attorneys, accountants, and other professionals representing the debtor in possession and the official committees are given what is called a first priority because their fees are

---

[37] §§ 362(d)(1) and 361 (which gives examples of how adequate protection can be structured).
[38] § 362(d)(2).   [39] § 364(a)–(d).   [40] § 364(c).

expenses incurred in the administration of the Chapter 11 case. However, the post-petition lender may be given a priority even ahead of these professional expenses. Then, if the reorganization attempt is unsuccessful, and if there is not enough money from a liquidation of the assets to pay even all of the administration expenses, the post-petition lender will be paid first. Accordingly, there is little risk for the post-petition lender, and such lending is regarded as a rather lucrative business.

F. *Cash Collateral*

Similarly, it is possible that a secured creditor will have a security interest in the proceeds of the property serving as its collateral which will come into being during the course of the Chapter 11 case. These proceeds are called 'cash collateral'.[41] A debtor in possession may not use such cash collateral for any purpose without either the consent of the secured creditor or a court order.[42] To obtain either, it may be necessary for the debtor in possession again to offer some form of adequate protection to protect the secured creditor against loss through the use of such property.

G. *Executory Contracts*

Most debtors have entered into a variety of contracts before the filing of the Chapter 11 petition. If these contracts remain unperformed when the petition is filed, they are called 'executory contracts', and a special section in the Code determines a variety of issues with respect to them.[43] Included within the term are both leases of real and personal property, as well as labor contracts. However, in Chapter 11 cases, a collective bargaining agreement is treated specially by the Code in Section 1113. For the protection of employees, the debtor must make a showing of need in order to modify a labor contract.

The debtor in possession is given the power to decide whether to perform (assume) executory contracts or not to perform (reject) them. Except for labor contracts, the determination is based on the exercise of reasonable business judgement by the debtor in possession. The decision to assume or reject is, nevertheless, subject to the approval of the bankruptcy court.[44]

The Code also provides that any provision in the contract which would limit the debtor in possession in making this determination is of no effect.

---

[41] § 363(a).   [42] § 363(c)(2).   [43] § 365.   [44] § 365(a).

This means that, if the contract states that if a party to the contract commences a case under the Bankruptcy Code, the contract is automatically terminated, such a provision is of no force or effect. The debtor in possession may still assume or reject it.[45]

If the contract is assumed, the debtor in possession must perform it as written and may not change any of its terms.[46] If there is a subsequent breach during the case, the ensuing damages are entitled to a first priority in payment as an expense of administration.[47] If, however, the debtor in possession decides to reject the contract, the Code indulges in a fiction and deems the rejection to give rise to a pre-petition claim for damages, and it is treated the same as other pre-petition unsecured claims with no higher priority.[48]

There are, however, special protective provisions, applicable only in Chapter 11 cases, for employees whose collective bargaining agreements may need modification.[49] There are also special protective provisions in Chapter 11 cases for retiree health benefit plans.[50] Before it can attempt to modify such a contract or plan, the debtor in possession must provide financial information to the union or other representative and both sides must negotiate in good faith. When negotiations fail, the motion to modify or reject the contract or plan will be heard by the bankruptcy court which is required to 'balance the equities' when reaching a decision.

H. Claims

In order for a creditor to vote in the plan and to receive a distribution under it, the creditor must file a proof of claim. In some instances a claim scheduled by the debtor need not be filed by the creditor.

When a proof of claim is filed, it constitutes prima facie evidence of the validity and amount of the claim. If the debtor disagrees either with the claim of liability or the amount, it must object to the claim, and a court hearing will follow. At times, it is necessary to vote on a plan of reorganization before these disputes can be settled; the Code and Rules permit the court to allow a claim temporarily for the purpose of voting.

I. Interest on Claims

Interest that has accrued on a claim before the filing of a bankruptcy case, for example, pursuant to the debtor-creditor agreement, becomes part of the prin-

---

[45] § 365(e).
[46] See 2 *Collier on Bankruptcy* (Matthew Bender, 15th edn.) c.365.
[47] See § 365(g)(2)(A).
[48] §§ 365(g)(1), 502(g).
[49] § 1113.
[50] § 1114.

cipal claim for which proof is filed and on which distribution may be made. However, interest accruing after the filing of the petition is not recoverable.

Exceptions to the rule exist. In a Chapter 7 liquidation case, if the debtor is solvent, Section 726 requires post-petition interest to be paid to creditors before any assets may be returned to the debtor. The law is not clear whether this same result will occur in a Chapter 11 case because of different language in the applicable provisions. Another exception concerns secured claims. If the collateral of a secured claim is of a value that is more than the underlying debt, the secured creditor is entitled to post-petition interest.

J. Voidable Preferences

As mentioned, one theory of the bankruptcy law is to provide for an equitable distribution of the debtor's assets among its unsecured creditors. One way of accomplishing this goal is to place restrictions on the debtor's ability to treat one or more creditors better by paying them shortly before the debtor files a petition under the Bankruptcy Code. Section 547 of the Code sets out the conditions under which pre-bankruptcy transfers to creditors may be avoided by the trustee (or debtor in possession in a Chapter 11 case); that is, recovered and treated as part of the bankrupt estate.

A transfer is voidable if it was made to a creditor, within 90 days before the filing of the petition, to pay or reduce a past due debt, when the debtor is insolvent. Section 547(f) creates a rebuttable presumption of insolvency during the 90–day period. The 90–day period is extended to one year if the creditor is an insider, such as an officer, director or relative. No improper intent of any kind is necessary to prove an avoidable preferential transfer. The transfer must also have the effect of giving that creditor more than it would otherwise receive in a hypothetical Chapter 7 liquidation. Thus, normally, a payment to a fully secured creditor (where the collateral is worth at least as much as the debt) would not be voidable because that creditor would have been entitled to full payment out of its collateral in any event. There is a list of exceptions in Section 547(c) limiting the power of the trustee in certain circumstances. For example, payments made in the ordinary course of business, on debts incurred in the ordinary course of business, may not be voided.

K. Fraudulent Conveyances

In addition to voiding preferential payments to creditors, the Code also permits the trustee to recover fraudulent transfers as described in Section 548.

Such transfers may be made with an actual intent to hinder, delay, and defraud creditors, or they may be inferentially fraudulent. An inferred fraudulent transfer does not require a showing of any fraudulent intent, but occurs when an insolvent debtor makes a transfer for which it does not receive a reasonably equivalent value.

In either case, the transfer, to be voidable, must have been made within one year before the filing of the petition. If a similar type of transfer was made more than one year earlier, the trustee may be able to use Section 544(b) to void it because that sub-section incorporates the fraudulent conveyance law of the state which will generally have a longer statute of limitations.

IV. The Plan of Reorganization

A. *Proposal of Plan*

When the Code was being drafted, there was a difference of opinion as to whether only the debtor could propose a plan, or whether any party in interest should be able to do so. The compromise that was reached was to permit the debtor a period of time when only it could file a plan. If one was not timely filed or if a trustee was appointed, any party in interest, in addition to the debtor, could file a plan. As a result, for the first 120 days only the debtor may file a plan, and if it does so, then this period of exclusivity is extended to 180 days.[51] Both time periods can be shortened or extended by the bankruptcy court for cause.[52]

Quite often, 120 days is not long enough for a debtor to be able to propose a plan; it may be so involved in running the business that it is unable to be in a position to file a plan in that time. It may also be in extensive and difficult negotiations with its creditors, particularly with the creditors' committee. The debtor often, therefore, seeks an extension of the period when it has the exclusive right to file a plan. It is for the court to decide whether the circumstances warrant an extension, and there have been instances where the court has granted several extensions.

It should be noted that, even if the debtor loses the exclusive right to file a plan, it does not lose the right to file a plan; it only means that other parties may also file a plan. If there are multiple plans, and they all are voted on, those voting may accept more than one plan; and they may express their preferences among the plans they accept. But the court may confirm

---

[51] § 1121(b),(c)(3). The exclusive period is shorter if the debtor elects to be considered a small business.
[52] § 1121(d).

(approve) only one plan, taking into consideration, but not being bound by, the preferences expressed by those voting.[53]

Only infrequently will a party other than the debtor want to file a plan. Most of the effort in the typical Chapter 11 case is spent in negotiating a plan with the debtor, and when the negotiation is successfully concluded, the parties will work together to get the plan accepted by the creditors and the court.

B. *Contents of Plan*

While there is a provision in the Code which specifies mandatory and discretionary matters that go into a plan of reorganization,[54] they are not the essence of the plan, which is the payment terms: what can creditors expect to receive as a result of the reorganization process? These terms are left by the statute to the imagination of the negotiating parties who indeed often have a great deal of imagination.

One might think that payment would come only in a monetary form. For plan purposes, that is not so at all. When the Code speaks of payment, except for limited instances, it phrases it in terms of property. And property can take different forms.

The plan may provide for creditors to receive payment in money at or near the time of confirmation; it may provide for the creditors to receive notes or bonds that will not become due for several years; or it may provide for the distribution of stock in the reorganized company in exchange for all or part of the debt. The plan can provide for any one of these methods of disposing of the debt or any combination of them. The critical factors are what the reorganized company can afford to do and what the creditors are willing to accept. There is no one magic formula and no one method or combination required or even suggested by the Code.

In addition, the plan of reorganization is really a contract entered into by the debtor. There can be many terms and conditions contained in it, such as matters concerning corporate governance, and a multitude of non-monetary considerations.

C. *Voting on the Plan*

A key element in the Chapter 11 process is the vote on the plan in which, if a majority outvotes a minority, the minority will be bound by the terms of the plan. For instance, if the plan proposes to pay unsecured creditors one-third

---

[53] See § 1129(c).   [54] § 1123.

of the debt that is owed to them, and the plan is accepted by the required majority of unsecured creditors voting, the minority who voted against the plan will receive only the one-third payment, and the balance of two-thirds of the debt will be discharged.

There are two aspects of plan voting that merit attention. First, the Code requires a vote by classes. Persons with different rights and interests are placed in different classes. It is possible that senior creditors and junior creditors may be placed in different classes, but this may not always be true.[55] Secondly, or a plan to be a consensual plan, it must be accepted by the required majority of each class that is entitled to vote, which occurs when a class is 'impaired'.[56]

1. Impairment

The Code establishes rules to determine if a class of claims or interests is unimpaired.[57] If one is not unimpaired, it is impaired. A class is unimpaired if its legal and equitable rights are not going to be changed by the plan. If, for example, the class consists of the holders of a bond, and the terms of the bond are not changed in any respect by the plan, the class is unimpaired. The same payment terms must remain in effect, as well as the maturity date and all other terms and conditions of the bond. It does not matter if a change is for the better; any change will cause that class to be impaired. If the class is impaired, it has the right to vote on the plan; if the class is unimpaired, it cannot vote.[58]

2. Requisite majorities

The required majorities for acceptance of a plan are two-thirds in dollar amount of the creditors in the class and over one-half in number of creditors in that class.[59] A double majority is required so that the power to determine the outcome will not rest either in a large number of creditors holding small claims, or a small number of creditors holding very large claims. If equity interest holders are to vote, the requisite majority is two-thirds in amount of the interests.[60]

In both cases, the majorities are based on the votes that are actually cast. If a creditor does not cast a ballot, that creditor is deemed not to have voted, and its claim is not counted in any way.

---

[55] The subject of classification is treated generally in § 1122.
[56] § 1129(a) which is discussed more fully in section IV E below.
[57] § 1124.   [58] § 1126(a),(f).
[59] § 1126(g).   [60] § 1126(d).

If a class is to receive nothing under the plan, i.e. it is wiped out, that class is deemed to have rejected the plan.[61] For example, if shareholders are not going to retain their current ownership interests, they are deemed to reject the plan. The consequences of such rejection will be described in section IV E below discussing confirmation of the plan.

D. Disclosure Statement

Before a plan can be submitted for a vote, a disclosure statement must first be filed with and approved by the bankruptcy court.[62]

The disclosure statement is supposed to contain appropriate information to enable a reasonable investor, typical of the holders of claims and interests of the debtor, to make an informed judgement when voting on the plan.[63] The detail and complexity of the disclosure statement is supposed to depend on the case and the plan that is involved. In a simple restructuring of unsecured debt, the essence of the statement may only be to compare what creditors will receive under the plan with what they would get if the debtor were liquidated.

The court does not, prior to a vote, have the duty to approve the plan itself. It is only concerned with whether those being asked to vote are given sufficient information on which to make a reasoned judgement.

When the court approves the disclosure statement, the statement and the plan, or a court approved summary of the plan, are sent to the impaired classes.[64] At this point, those interested in obtaining the favorable votes, including the debtor and usually the official creditors' committee, will help to obtain that vote. Of course, those opposed to the plan, which is not too frequent, may seek to obtain rejections of the plan.

After the vote is taken, a hearing on the confirmation of the plan will be held in the bankruptcy court.[65]

E. Confirmation of the Plan

The whole thrust of Chapter 11 is to produce a reorganization plan, hopefully through a voluntary settlement that is contained in the plan which will be confirmed by the court. Confirmation is basically another word for

---

[61] § 1126(g).

[62] § 1125(b). If the debtor elects to be considered a small business, the hearing on final approval of the disclosure statement and confirmation may be combined.

[63] § 1125(a).   [64] FRBP § 3017(d).   [65] § 1128.

approval; in effect, when the court orders that the plan is confirmed, it has approved the plan as meeting the requirements of Chapter 11 and any other provisions in the Code related to it.[66]

There are two ways in which the court can confirm a plan; these may be called the easy way and the hard way. If all classes consent to the plan by the required majorities, confirmation is easy.[67] In addition to some formal and routine requirements, the only real finding that the court must make is that the impaired classes will receive under the plan at least as much as they would receive in a hypothetical liquidation of the business.[68] This requirement is for the protection of those who vote against the plan but who are outvoted. Their legal entitlement is to receive only what a liquidation would give them; if the plan provides at least that much, this requirement is satisfied.

If fewer than all classes accept the plan, it is more difficult to confirm it, but it is still possible. In that case, the plan may be confirmed if it is 'fair and equitable' or is consistent with the absolute priority rule.[69] The Code defines fair and equitable to mean that if a class of unsecured creditors or equity holders rejects the plan, it may still be confirmed if the rejecting class receives full payment of its allowed claim or, if not, no class junior to it will receive anything.[70] This option is called the 'cram down' of the plan over the rejection of one or more classes.

A difficulty with using the cram down is the possibility that a court hearing will be required to determine what the entitlement is of the rejecting class. In making this determination, it becomes important to ascertain the solvency or insolvency of the reorganized debtor because it is necessary to know to what level in the hierarchy of claims the reorganization plan must pay claims. The solvency issue is not based on any current financial information with respect to the business but, rather, what the business will be like in the future. In other words, solvency or insolvency is based on the value of the debtor as a going concern, which will be determined, at least in part, by guess work. Various investment banking experts will testify, creating disagreement and controversy as to the worth and value on a going concern basis and, relying on such testimony, the court will have to make a judgment. Part of the problem is that much time can be consumed in such hearings and court appeals.[71]

Accordingly, the Code places pressure on the parties to negotiate a plan that can be confirmed the easy way, i.e. by getting all classes to consent.[72] A method used to achieve this result is for senior classes to be willing to give up

---

[66] See § 1129. [67] The basic, formal requirements are set out in § 1129(a).

[68] § 1129(a)(7). [69] § 1129(b). [70] § 1129(b)(2)(B),(c).

[71] For full discussion of cram down and going concern valuation problems, see 5 *Collier on Bankruptcy*, (Matthew Bender, 15th edn.) ¶1129.03.

[72] § 1129(a)(8).

some of their share to the junior class, whether it be a junior class of creditors or an equity class. When the junior class receives something under the plan, it can vote on the plan; it is not deemed to reject it automatically. The vote can be an acceptance and obviate the need to cram down the plan.

The incentives are for the senior class, by giving something up, to avoid the going concern value dispute and obtain a distribution at an earlier time. For the junior class, there is the incentive to accept what is being offered because, if the plan had to be crammed down, the business might be found to be insolvent, and the junior class not entitled to receive anything. Most plans are confirmed the easy way.

F. Secured Creditors and the Plan

Because of the nature of their claims, secured creditors are specially treated. Absent their consent to be treated otherwise, the secured creditor is entitled to retain its lien on the collateral, but the plan can provide for payment on the claim over a period of time and at an interest rate that will give the secured creditor the present value of its claim.[73]

Some secured creditors are called non-recourse creditors. This means that they can look only to the property securing the debt for payment; the borrower is not personally liable for any deficiency that may arise from the sale of the property. For example, if the property is worth $10,000 and the outstanding debt is $15,000, the creditor will only receive $10,000; no one is liable to that creditor for the unpaid unsecured balance of $5,000.

There is a special provision in the Code, in a Chapter 11 case only, for automatically converting a non-recourse debt into a recourse debt.[74] Therefore, in the above example, the secured creditor would have an unsecured claim against the Chapter 11 debtor for $5,000. Often, the size of this claim will be large enough for the secured lender to control the vote of the unsecured creditor class and reject the plan. It puts that creditor in a strong bargaining position and, absent its consent, practically bars the debtor's shareholders from retaining their ownership interest.

V. Discharge

The Code provides that confirmation of the plan discharges the debtor from any unpaid claims that arose prior to confirmation and binds all persons to

---

[73] § 1129(b)(2)(A).   [74] § 1111(b).

the terms and conditions of the plan.[75] It also provides that, on confirmation, the property of the estate revests in the debtor or reorganized entity as set out in the plan.

Of necessity, the discharge is an important ingredient in the Chapter 11 process. Without it, there would not be any utility in Chapter 11. With it, the reorganized debtor has the ability to come out of Chapter 11 with perhaps a smaller operation, a revised and better balance sheet through the reduction of debt, and the opportunity to become economically viable once again.

If the debtor is able to remain in business instead of being liquidated and closed, there is a greater benefit to the local or larger community of which the debtor may be a part. These benefits reach the employees who can retain jobs, governmental units who can retain a solvent taxpayer, suppliers who can retain a valuable customer, landlords who retain lessees in their property, and the like. Closing down a business results in the corresponding disadvantages to these same economic groups. While reorganization certainly is not possible for every business, it serves a valuable function when the circumstances support its use.

---

[75] § 1141.

18

ENVIRONMENTAL LAW

RICHARD B. STEWART

In the United States, as in other nations, environmental law is a new field that has mushroomed over the past 30 years in response to rising public and political concerns over environmental degradation. The field is comprised of three basic components: control of pollution, wastes, and other side-effects of industrial processes and products; management of natural resources; and regulation of land use, infrastructure, and development. While the basic goals of environmental protection have enjoyed broad public support, the means for achieving them have proved controversial.

The United States has a highly developed and complex system of environmental law.[1] Over 35,000 United States lawyers specialize in environmental law. United States environmental law relies heavily on administrative regulation, a strong federal government role, and the use of procedural formalities, public participation, and court review to control administrative decision-making and ensure that legislative mandates for environmental protection are carried out. The growth of United States environmental law has been stimulated by important legal innovations, including environmental impact assessment, the use of rule-making procedures that rely on public comment to help develop administrative standards and regulations, sweeping liability

---

[1] For a more detailed overview of United States environmental law, see P. Menell and R. Stewart, *Environmental Law & Policy* (Little, Brown, 1994); W. Rodgers, *Environmental Law* 2nd ed. (West Pub., 1994); C. Campbell-Mohn, B. Breen & W. Futrell, *Environmental Law: From Resources to Recovery* (West Pub., 1993).

programs to deal with toxic wastes and oil spills, and the grant by courts, statutes, and regulations of broad rights to environmental advocates to participate in agency decision-making procedures and obtain judicial review. Many of these innovations have been followed by other nations.

United States environmental programs have made considerable progress in protecting health and the environment. At the same time, they have been strongly criticized in recent years as overly legalistic, excessively costly, unduly rigid, and productive of conflict and litigation rather than cooperative problem-solving. There is increasing recognition of the limits of the dominant 'command and control' system of centralized regulation, and growing interest in the use of alternative approaches, including economic incentives for environmental protection.

I. The Origins of Contemporary Environmental Law

A. *The Common Law*

The judge-made common law of the several states of the United States has provided some protection to private plaintiffs suffering personal or property damage as a result of environmental disruption. Common law doctrines allowing recovery in trespass, nuisance, negligence, and in some instances strict liability enabled a private plaintiff to recover damages when a given defendant's conduct caused the plaintiff identifiable, serious injury. But private litigation has proven wholly inadequate to deal with many of the wide-scale environmental problems posed by industrialization and development. For example, a given defendant's air pollution may potentially affect millions of individuals throughout an air basin. While each may suffer some increased risk of harm as a result of exposure, it is virtually impossible to show that such pollution has caused a particular individual's illness or property damage. Moreover, pollution is often created by dozens or hundreds of sources, making the problem of establishing causal responsibility even more difficult. Litigation is very costly, the individual plaintiff's stake is often small, and class actions are cumbersome and expensive means of pooling interests. Case-by-case court litigation is also a poor means for resolving recurring scientific, economic, and engineering issues presented in environmental controversies. Damage remedies are often inadequate because of the difficulties in tracing and quantifying injury. And, perhaps most important, the public demands prophylactic measures to prevent harm from occurring in the first place. Case-by-case court litigation is ill-suited to ensuring coordinated and consistent management of preventive measures aimed at a wide range of pollution sources and other agents of environmental degradation.

Some courts have attempted to respond to the limitations of the private law system by relaxing traditional standards of proof, encouraging class actions, and devising creative new remedies. These innovations, however, strain the courts' traditional institutional role and have proven controversial.

B. Regulation as a Solution to the Failures of the Market and the Common Law

The limitations of the common law and growing public concern over environmental problems generated strong political demands for legislative adoption of ambitious new environmental protection measures. Environmental problems can be viewed as instances of market failure which occur because the market price system fails to reflect and internalize to firms the costs to society of pollution, wastes, and other environmental externalities which firms generate in competing for consumer favor. In theory, the common law could solve this failure by making firms pay compensation to those injured by these externalities. For reasons already noted, however, the private litigation system is in practice institutionally unsuited to this task.

There are a variety of techniques which legislatures might select to deal with the failures of the market and the common law and protect the environment. For example, the government could impose a tax or fee on pollution. The government could issue a limited number of pollution rights and allow them to be bought and sold in the market. The government could subsidize measures to reduce pollution. It could disseminate information regarding firms' environmental performance to consumers and investors who might use their market power to reward firms with superior environmental performance and punish those with poorer records. These alternatives have, until recently, played little or no role in environmental policy. In the United States, as elsewhere, the overwhelming instrument of choice has been command and control regulation. Pursuant to legislation, government agencies adopt specific prohibitions or requirements relating to pollution, wastes, resource management, land use, and development. These regulations are enforced against firms and individuals through licensing and permit requirements, enforcement actions, and sanctions for violations.

Regulation appeals to legislators for several reasons. It responds to the public perception that environmental degradation is evil and should be prohibited. Regulation promises the public that effective action is being taken to prevent harm from occurring in the first place. Regulatory programs, at least in their initial phases, are relatively easy to construct, implement, and enforce. For example, polluters can be required to install available technology for reducing pollution and sanctioned if they fail to do so. As explained below, however, experience with regulation has made clear some of the limitations of the command and control approach and stimulated interest in alternatives. Nonetheless, regulation remains the bedrock of environmental law in the United States.

C. The Dominant Role of the Federal Government

States and local governments have long engaged in certain forms of health, sanitary, and environmental regulation. Since the outpouring of public concern over environmental issues began in the mid-1960s, the federal government has taken the lead role, enacting comprehensive statutes that authorize ambitious programs of federal regulation to deal with pollution, wastes, and other industrial hazard,s and protect natural resources. The commerce clause in the United States Constitution gives Congress nearly unlimited authority to enact such measures. Some federal legislation is also constitutionally supported by Congress's power to spend money for the general welfare and to adopt legislation for property of the federal government. The Constitution imposes few constraints on Congress' use of these broad powers or on the states' exercise of similar powers.[2] The Constitution does not recognize a right to environmental quality, and the courts have refused to imply one.[3] In certain instances, environmental regulation has been held to be a 'taking' of private property for which compensation must be paid.[4] These instances are, however, exceptional.

If it chose to do so, Congress could establish an exclusively national system of regulatory law administered solely by the federal government, preempting any and all state law or role. But practical and political considerations have, in most instances, led Congress to adopt a mixed system. Under it, the federal government takes a strong leadership role, establishing uniform national minimum standards of environmental protection administered by powerful

---

[2] But see *New York* v. *United States*, 502 U.S. 1023 (1992) (invalidating portions of the Low-Level Radioactive Waste Act forcing states to assume ownership of privately-generated nuclear wastes or adopt and enforce federal requirements for private disposal, as violative of state autonomy protected by the Tenth Amendment to the Constitution).

[3] See *Tanner* v. *Armco Steel Corp.*, 340 F. Supp. 532 (S.D. Tex. 1972).

[4] See generally *Lucas* v. *South Carolina Coastal Comm'n*, 112 S. Ct. 2886 (1992).

federal bureaucracies, such as the Environmental Protection Agency (EPA), but state and regional governments are given an important role in implementing the federal regulatory program. In addition, federal legislation generally leaves states and local regions free to adopt their own laws and programs. As a result, environmental law in the United States is a complex mosaic of federal, state, and local statutes, regulations, administrative rulings, and court decisions. Further complexity is generated by the division of regulatory authority among different administrative agencies within each level of government. As a result of these dispersions of authority, owners or developers of major facilities and projects are often subject to dozens of government authorities and must secure separate permits or approvals from each.

The resort to federal regulation reflects a political judgment that regulation by the several states will not secure effective environmental protection. This judgment rests on several concerns.[5] Fear has been expressed that state competition for industry will lead to a 'race to the bottom', in which many or all states will adopt inadequate standards. Also, some states may lack the administrative resources or political commitment to ensure effective environmental protection. Transboundary spillovers of pollution or wastes from one state to another may also impair the effectiveness of a decentralized system of state regulation.

Economic rivalries among states and regions nonetheless play an important role in the design and fate of federal regulatory programs. For example, industrialized, heavily-polluted states in the northeast and midwest successfully supported congressional legislation imposing special strict limitations on additional pollution in lightly-polluted areas of the south and west in order to limit the ability of such regions to attract industrial development.[6] Similarly, the more industrialized states backed provisions in the Clean Water Act providing for nationally-uniform technology-based controls on water pollution discharges, even if such controls were more stringent than necessary to meet water quality standards, in order to limit competition from states with less polluted waters.[7] In both instances, these legislative initiatives were also supported by environmental groups. Congressional legislation to deal with acid rain was blocked for many years by political deadlock between midwestern states where major sulfur-emitting sources are located and northeastern states where sulfur compounds created by those emissions are deposited.

[5] See Revesz, 'Rethinking the "Race to the Bottom" Rationale for Federal Environmental Regulation', 67 *N.Y.U. L. Rev.* 1216 (1992); Stewart, 'Pyramids of Sacrifice? Federalism Problems in Mandatory State Implementation of Federal Environmental Controls', 80 *Yale L.J.* 1196 (1977).

[6] Prevention of Significant Deterioration of Air Quality provisions of the Clean Air Act, Sections 160–169B, 42 U.S.C. §§ 7470–7492. See P. Pashagian, 'Environmental Regulation: Whose Self-Interests Are Being Protected', 22 *Economic Inquiry* 551 (1985).

[7] Clean Water Act, Sections 301, 304, 33 U.S.C. §§ 1311, 1314.

II. The Subjects of Environmental Law and Regulation

A. *Regulation of Industrial Products and Processes*

During the 1970s Congress enacted comprehensive regulatory statutes to deal with air pollution (Clean Air Act[8]), water pollution (Clean Water Act[9]), and hazardous and other wastes (Resource Conservation and Recovery Act[10] (RCRA)). Other statutes deal with oil spills, pesticides, chemicals, ocean dumping, drinking water, occupational hazards, and radioactive hazards. The EPA administers all of these statutes except those governing occupational hazards and radioactive hazards, which are administered respectively by the Labor Department and the Nuclear Regulatory Commission.

These regulatory programs require the responsible federal agency to adopt standards and regulations through rule-making procedures. Industry, environmental groups, states, and other interested parties have the right to submit evidence, analysis, and views through written comments. The agency must justify its final standard or regulation on the basis of the administrative record created by agency studies, other documents, and outside comments. The rule-making proceedings often take years to complete and, more often than not, the final standard or regulation adopted is challenged in court, in many cases by several different parties. These regulations and standards establish national uniform requirements for a given type of pollution, waste, product, or other problem. States are generally free to adopt additional, more stringent, requirements and they often do so.

The standards and regulations adopted through rule-making are then applied to individual facilities through licenses or permits. The terms of permits are often the subject of dispute and litigation between the government and the facility. New facilities are subject to special regulatory requirements and approval procedures. The government monitors compliance through inspections and by requiring regulated facilities to file regular and extensive reports on discharges, wastes, and other aspects of operations with the government. Such reports are available to the public, as are almost all other similar documents in the government's possession.

Implementing and enforcing national regulatory programs in a country the size of the United States is a formidable task. There are hundreds of thousands of industrial and commercial facilities subject to federal air and water pollution regulation and nearly a million regulated waste generators. It is,

---

[8] 42 U.S.C. §§ 7401–7671q.   [9] 33 U.S.C. C. §§ 1251–1387.   [10] 42 U.S.C. §§ 6921–6939e.

therefore, not surprising that Congress has often authorized delegation by EPA of much of the implementation process and enforcement, including issuance of permits and enforcement, to states that have regulatory programs which satisfy federal standards.[11] Even when EPA has made a delegation, it retains authority to bring enforcement actions if a state fails to do so, or to revoke a delegation if a state fails persistently to carry out federal law.

Congress and the states have used a variety of different command and control regulatory strategies to advance environmental protection. Sometimes regulators are directed to use case-by-case screening, applying broad general standards, to approve or disapprove particular products or projects. For example, legislation requires EPA to approve or disapprove use of a given pesticide based on whether it causes 'unreasonable adverse effects'[11] to health and the environment.[12] More commonly, the legislature mandates that agencies adopt specific standards that fix requirements in quantitative terms. There are two types of such standards.

First, environmental quality standards specify the maximum permissible amount of a pollutant or other potential hazard in a given environmental medium, such as the air, water, or soil. For example the National Ambient Air Quality Standard for Sulfur Oxides adopted by EPA provides that concentrations of sulfur dioxide shall not exceed 365 micrograms per cubic meter (24 hour average) anywhere in the United States. State environmental regulatory agencies then adopt specific limitations on discharges from individual sources in order to ensure compliance with the ambient standard.

Secondly, emission or effluent standards limit the amount of pollution discharged by a given source or facility. For example, the effluent standards for meat-packing plants adopted by EPA under the Clean Water Act provide that such plants' effluent discharges may not contain more than 9 milligrams of ammonia per liter of discharge. Emission or effluent standards are often based on the level of environmental performance that can be achieved by application of the best available pollution control technology in a given industry. These two types of standards have various advantages and disadvantages with respect to ease of standard-setting; ease of monitoring and enforcement; cost of achieving pollution reductions; effects on competition; dealing with industrial growth; and the geographical pattern of environmental quality. The major federal environmental regulatory statutes, including the Clean Air Act, Clean Water Act, and RCRA, generally use a combination of environmental quality standards and emission standards.

Whatever strategy is chosen, the process of establishing standards is a complex and often controversial exercise involving highly technical scientific,

---

[11] See, e.g. Clean Water Act, Section 402(b), 33 U.S.C. § 1342(b).
[12] Federal Insecticide, Fungicide, and Rodenticide Act, Section 3(c)(5), 7 U.S.C. § 136a(c)(5).

engineering, and economic issues. A recurring issue of debate is the extent, if any, to which the costs of compliance should be considered by agencies in setting environmental quality standards. Environmental advocates claim that protection of health and the environment is paramount, and that costs should not be considered. They also maintain that if the government sets ambitious standards and insists on compliance, it can 'force' industry to develop technology to achieve compliance at reasonable cost.[13] Economists and business point out that, in most instances, total elimination of all risk from industrial activities and products is impossible. They argue that the social and economic costs of reducing risk should be explicitly considered in standard-setting in order to strike a sensible balance, and that government regulation should target societal resources on those risks that can be reduced at relatively less cost.

Another recurrent debate is how stringently to regulate risks that are, because of limits to current scientific knowledge, highly uncertain. In setting environmental quality standards, or selecting the required level of control in technology-based standards, regulators must consider the weight to be given economic considerations on the one hand and the reduction of uncertain risks on the other. Because most environmental statutes give regulatory agencies substantial discretion in applying screening standards and setting specification standards, these debates figure prominently in agency rule-making and licensing decisions and in subsequent litigation challenging the agency's decision.

B. *Natural Resource Management*

Although Congress could use its commerce power to regulate virtually all private use of natural resources, including land, water, and other resources such as forests and minerals, such regulation has been and still is regarded as a state and local function. Nonetheless, the federal role in resource management is extremely important, by virtue of the federal government's ownership of nearly one-third of all land in the United States.[14] The federal lands are located primarily in the western states and Alaska and include many national parks and forests and other scenic and wilderness areas. During the nineteenth century the federal government followed a consistent policy of divesting itself of its vast property holdings, which had been acquired by purchase or conquest, and turning them over to private ownership or to the states. In

---

[13] For discussions of 'technology-forcing', see La Pierre, 'Technology-Forcing and Federal Environmental Protection Standards', 62 *Iowa L. Rev.* 771 (1977).

[14] See E. Moss, *Land Use Controls in the United States* (Dial Press, 1977).

the early twentieth century, under the leadership of President Theodore Roosevelt, the conservation movement succeeded in reversing this pattern, insisting that these lands continue to be owned, preserved, and managed in the national interest by the federal government. In addition, the federal government controls the biological and mineral resources of the territorial seas and the outer continental shelf.

By the late 1960s it was widely perceived that federal land management agencies often disregarded environmental and preservation values in favor of private development and exploitation of public lands and other resources. These policies benefitted politically powerful economic interests: the oil, gas, mining, and timber industries, and agricultural and ranching interests. In response, Congress classified large portions of the public lands as wilderness areas, in which only the most limited development is permitted.[15] It also amended many of the federal land and other resource management statutes to require more explicit consideration of environmental and preservation values.[16] Concern about federal land management practices also helped propel the enactment in 1969 of the National Environmental Policy Act (NEPA),[17] discussed more fully in section III A below, which requires federal officials to prepare an environmental impact assessment before they undertake, finance, or license activities that significantly affect the environment.

These laws nonetheless left federal agencies with considerable discretion to balance environmental and other values of particular resource management decisions. Such flexibility may be inevitable as well as desirable, although critics attribute the latitude afforded by statutes to federal land management agencies to the political influence of development interests and their allies in Congress and the federal bureaucracy. Congress, however, abandoned flexibility when it enacted the Endangered Species Act (ESA) of 1973. The Act forbids the federal government from undertaking, financing, or licensing any activity that will destroy the critical habitat of a species that has been listed as either threatened or endangered.[18] In *Tennessee Valley Authority v. Hill*, 437 U.S. 153 (1978), the Supreme Court affirmed that the statutory prohibition is absolute, and at the behest of environmental groups, enjoined completion of a federal dam on which $100 million had already been spent to protect the snail darter, a small endangered species of fish. Critics have sharply attacked the ESA's failure to balance preservation goals against social and economic concerns, contending that the Act blocks many beneficial development activities in order to protect obscure species that are of no value or interest. Environmental advocates insist that species

---

[15] Wilderness Act of 1965, as amended, 16 U.S.C. §§ 1131–1136.
[16] See, e.g. Federal Land Policy and Management Act, 43 U.S.C. §§ 1701–1784.
[17] 42 U.S.C. §§ 4321–4370d.
[18] Endangered Species Act, Section 7, 16 U.S.C. § 1536, 30 U.S.C. §§ 1201, et seq.

preservation is an ethical imperative, and decry the administrative delay in listing species as endangered or threatened.

In a few instances Congress has also abandoned its traditional deference to state and local government in the regulation of privately-owned lands and resources. For example, the Surface Mining Control and Reclamation Act[19] regulates mining on private as well as federal lands. In addition to imposing broad constraints on the federal government, the ESA prohibits private 'taking' of members of an endangered species.[20] The Supreme Court has recently upheld the Department of Interior's position that 'taking' includes private activities that adversely affect habitat, indirectly causing losses of individual members of an endangered species.[21] Such a prohibition could significantly curtail private development. The Court's decision has fuelled proposals in Congress to amend the ESA. The notion of 'national land use planning' remains politically quite unpopular.

C. Land Use Regulation, Infrastructure, and Development

Congress also has the constitutional authority to control much zoning and land use; the location and design of highways, transport, water supply, sewage collection, and most other basic infrastructure; and most development projects. Again, however, it has decided to leave these responsibilities primarily to state and local government. These regulations are discussed in Chapter 11, Property. Nonetheless, federal spending and regulatory programs have a significant impact on such activities, and Congress has taken steps to ensure that these programs take environmental considerations into account.

There is extensive federal financial assistance to state and local governments for highway and airport construction; transit service; sewage treatment and housing; and more general forms of assistance for other forms of infrastructure. NEPA requires that federal officials assess the environmental consequences of a given project before providing funds for it. In addition, particular statutes, such as the federal transportation acts, often contain provisions designed to ensure protection of the environment. For example, a federally-funded highway may not be routed through an existing park unless there is no 'feasible and prudent' alternative.[22] Municipalities receiving sewage treatment grants have been required to use them to achieve a specified level of pollution removal in treatment works.

---

[19] 30 U.S.C. §§1201 et seq.   [20] ESA Section 9, 16 U.S.C. § 1538.

[21] *Babbit* v. *Sweet Home Chapter of Communities for a Great Oregon*, 115 S. Ct. 2407 (1995).

[22] See *Citizens to Preserve Overton Park* v. *Volpe*, 401 U.S. 402 (1971) (construing and enforcing statutory limitations on highway routing through parkland).

Federal environmental regulatory statutes, most notably the Clean Air Act, often have an important indirect effect on land use and development patterns. For example, federal clean air regulation influences the siting of new industrial facilities. The EPA is engaged in a controversial effort to force states to limit automobile use and place greater reliance on mass transit in order to achieve air quality goals.

III. Distinctive Elements of United States Environmental Law

A. Environmental Impact Assessment: The National Environmental Policy Act

The 1969 National Environmental Policy Act was the first of the current generation of federal environmental statutes. It differs sharply from most of the statutes which followed, which are regulatory in character, focus on a particular environmental medium or problem, aim at controlling private conduct, and contain lengthy and complex provisions. NEPA is generic, brief, and aimed at ensuring that federal administrators give greater consideration to environmental values in making decisions. Congress enacted NEPA because it believed that federal agencies slighted environmental values in the pursuit of their primary bureaucratic missions such as building highways, promoting oil development on the outer continental shelf, or approving new energy projects.

NEPA requires that federal administrators integrate environmental considerations in their decision-making. It requires responsible federal officials to prepare a 'detailed report', known as an environmental impact statement (EIS) on the environmental impacts of 'major Federal actions significantly affecting the quality of the human environment' and on alternatives to the proposed action.[23]

Despite the absence in NEPA of any provision for judicial review, the courts have held that private litigants threatened with environmental injury from a proposed federal action may bring suit to challenge either the adequacy of a federal agency's EIS or its failure to prepare one. When courts find that NEPA's EIS requirements have not been satisfied, they typically grant an injunction against the project in question until an adequate EIS is prepared. The courts have construed 'federal' actions for which an EIS must be

---

[23] NEPA Section 102(c), 42 U.S.C. § 4332(c).

prepared to include not only projects directly undertaken by federal agencies—including the launching of space shuttles, the transport by the army of chemical weapons, and timber sales—but also federal decisions to grant regulatory approval to private projects, and federal grants of funds for state and local government projects such as construction of highways or prisons. At the same time, the courts have largely refused to enforce other provisions of NEPA that are arguably more substantive in character, but also far more nebulous, such as the responsibility to 'fulfill the responsibilities of each generation as trustee of the environment for succeeding generations'.[24] Instead, they have focussed on the EIS provision and insisted that NEPA is 'essentially procedural'.[25]

As a result of court decisions in the more than 2,000 NEPA cases that have been brought, federal agencies have developed the administrative capability to produce lengthy impact statements on a regular basis, churning out hundreds each year. Draft statements are made available for public comment; the final versions respond to the comments received. In addition to describing, often in great detail, the environmental impacts of the proposed action, the EIS also evaluates alternatives to the proposed action, including doing nothing. NEPA litigation has declined somewhat in recent years, but private plaintiffs still institute nearly 100 lawsuits each year,[26] seeking to stop projects because of asserted non-compliance with NEPA. For example, environmental groups recently challenged, unsuccessfully, the Clinton administration's failure to prepare an EIS on its submission to Congress of legislation approving the North American Free Trade Agreement.[27]

The extent to which NEPA has fulfilled its basic objective of ensuring greater consideration of environmental factors is much debated.[28] Some critics contend that the EIS process is nothing more than a bureaucratic paper exercise, and that agency decisions are still driven by mission-oriented political and bureaucratic considerations. Other critics complain that NEPA has been exploited by environmental groups to kill projects by delaying them, and that NEPA should therefore be abolished. Others would have courts review more closely the substantive balance between environmental and other considerations reached by an agency in deciding to go forward with a project. Defenders contend that the current process has promoted environ-

---

[24] NEPA Section 101(b) (1), 42 U.S.C. § 4331(b)(1).
[25] See, e.g. *Strycker's Bay Neighborhood Council* v. *Karlen* 444 U.S. 223 (1980).
[26] See U.S. Council on Environmental Quality, *Environmental Quality—22nd Annual Report* 137 (1992).
[27] *Public Citizen* v. *United States Trade Representative*, 5 F.3d 549 (D.C. Cir. 1993). The court based its decision on the ground that, in the circumstance of the case, the claim of NEPA violation had to be asserted against the President, and that the President is not subject to suit under the Administrative Procedure Act.
[28] For varying assessments of NEPA, see Sax, 'The (Unhappy) Truth About NEPA', 26 *Okla. L. Rev.* 239 (1973); Friesura and Culhane, 'Social Impacts; Politics, and the Environmental Impact Statement Process', 16 *Nat'l Res. J.* 339 (1976); Turner, 'The Legal Eagles', *Amicus J.* 25 (Winter 1988).

mental protection by exposing and sensitizing agencies to environmental considerations, creating a vehicle for public awareness and influence, and holding up environmentally destructive projects that, on further consideration, have often been dropped or significantly modified.

B. *The Role of Legal Proceedings and the Courts in Controlling Administrative Decision-Making*

Although administrative regulation has displaced common law litigation as the United States legal system's primary means of dealing with environmental degradation, the courts continue to play a important role. The United States has developed an elaborate system of administrative law to control administrative decision-making. During the past 25 years environmental disputes have been the focus of innovations in administrative law, with the federal courts taking the lead role.

Traditional principles of administrative law generally limited the right to participate in formal regulatory agency proceedings and seek judicial review to individuals and firms subject to regulatory controls and sanctions. The collective interests of environmentalists or consumers were supposed to be protected by the political process. Regulatory agencies relied primarily on case-by-case adjudication against specific persons and businesses to define and enforce the law. Judicial review was primarily directed at ensuring that agencies followed proper adjudicatory procedures; that agency fact-finding was supported by substantial evidence in the record generated by the administrative proceedings; and that the agency's action was within its statutory authority.

Beginning in the late 1960s, dramatic changes in these traditional arrangements occurred.[29] As a result of court decisions and statutory changes, the right to participate in agency decision-making procedures was extended to individuals and groups representing environmental, consumer, and other 'public' interests. This change was fueled by widespread perceptions that Congress often delegated broad discretion to regulatory agencies; that regulatory choices were dictated less by bureaucratic expertness than by policy choices and the influence of political and economic interests; and that for a variety of reasons agencies were more responsive to the interests of the industry they regulated than to the less well-organized public they were supposed to protect. The extension of participation rights and standing to secure

---

[29] See Stewart, 'The Reformation of American Administrative Law', 88 *Harvard L. Rev.* 1669 (1975).

judicial review was designed to redress this imbalance by giving 'public' interests access to legal fora where their concerns could be heard and protected.

In the case of standing, for example, the right to judicial review is available to any person who will suffer 'injury in fact' as a result of the government action in question, if the person is 'arguably within the zone' of interests protected or regulated by relevant statutes.[30] Injury in fact includes impairment of environmental, recreational, and aesthetic interests, and a person does not lose standing because many others share the same injury, such as exposure to air pollution.[31] Organizations generally have standing if their members do.[32] Although the Supreme Court has recently somewhat tightened the required showing of 'injury in fact',[33] environmental plaintiffs in most cases have no difficulty in challenging government actions or failures to regulate that threaten environmental harm.

In reviewing agency decisions, courts have not only sought to ensure that agencies obey relevant statutes, but have also reviewed administrators' exercise of discretion, requiring a detailed agency explanation, supported by the administrative record, of why an agency chose a given alternative and why it rejected others advocated by those challenging its decision. In short, courts have attempted to ensure that agencies take a 'hard look' at the evidence, analysis, and considerations of policy, as well as the legal arguments advanced by the contending interests, and justify the policy choices that they make.[34] At the same time, courts generally refuse to dictate a particular choice unless it is rather plainly required by the relevant statute. If an agency fails adequately to justify its discretionary policy choices, the usual remedy is a remand for further administrative proceedings.

Another major innovation has been the shift by agencies from case-by-case adjudication to rule-making as the basic vehicle for developing regulatory policy. Many of the major federal environmental regulatory statutes mandated this shift by requiring EPA and other agencies to use rule-making to develop standards and other regulatory requirements. This shift was motivated in part by considerations of administrative efficiency. It would simply take too long to formulate and implement an effective regulatory program through the cumbersome process of case-by-case adjudication. Moreover,

---

[30] See *Association of Data Processing Service Organization* v. *Camp*, 397 U.S. 150 (1970). The Court stated that the 'injury in fact' requirement was necessary to satisfy Article III of the Constitution, which limits the jurisdiction of Article III federal courts to 'cases or controversies'. The 'zone of interests' requirement was the Court's interpretation of Section 702 of the Administrative Procedure Act, which extends the right to judicial review of agency actions to persons 'suffering legal wrong because of agency action, or adversely affected or aggrieved by agency action within the meaning of a relevant statute'.

[31] See *Sierra Club* v. *Morton*, 405 U.S. 727 (1972).

[32] See *Hunt* v. *Washington Apple Advertising Comm'n*, 432 U.S. 333 (1977).

[33] See *Lujan* v. *Defenders of Wildlife*, 112 S. Ct. 2130 (1992).

[34] See *United States* v. *Nova Scotia Food Products Corp.*, 568 F.2d 240 (2d Cir. 1977).

rule-making serves Congress' insistence that regulatory requirements and protections be uniform throughout the United States.

Prior to 1970, procedural requirements for most forms of rule-making had been modest, following a legislative model of decision-making. The agency was required to provide notice of a proposed rule and provide opportunity for public comment, but could rely on whatever materials or considerations that it wished. The relevant matters considered did not have to be marshalled in a formal record, and the agency was required to give only a brief explanation for the final rule or standard. Under these circumstances, judicial review was necessarily highly deferential.

These modest procedures were not compatible with the courts' growing desire to ensure more effective representation of a wide range of affected interests and to review more closely agencies' exercise of discretion. In the early 1970s, the federal courts prodded agencies into developing a 'paper hearing' procedure, in which the agency must make available to the public all of the documents in its possession that are relevant to its rule-making proposal.[35] Under the new procedures, interested persons, including industry, environmental groups, and others, are able to submit informed comments on the proposed rule. These comments often make detailed criticism of the agency proposal and the adequacy of its documentary support, and are often accompanied by extensive documentation containing supporting evidence and analysis. Often these criticisms expose major weaknesses in the proposal, forcing the agency to develop additional factual and analytical materials which must, in turn, be subject to a fresh round of comment. At the close of the comment period, all of the documentation generated by the agency and by commenters becomes the administrative record which forms the basis for the agency's decision and the court's review of it. Courts are no longer satisfied by cursory agency explanations for choices made, but demand detailed justification, supported by the administrative record, for the decision made and for the rejection of alternatives favored by the commenters. Aided by the litigants, courts often test these justifications by closely examining the administrative record.[36]

Taken together, these innovations represent a notable effort to develop an interest representation model of administrative law, designed to ensure that the extensive powers exercised by regulatory bureaucracy are responsive to the range of interests and values affected by its choices, and that those choices are fairly supported by fact and reason. These measures to promote effective access to justice in environmental, health, and safety cases have been applied

---

[35] See Stewart, '*Vermont Yankee* and the Evolution of Administrative Procedure', 91 *Harv. L. Rev.* 1805 (1978).
[36] See *Motor Vehicle Mfts. Ass'n* v. *State Farm Mutual Automobile Ins. Co.*, 463 U.S. 29 (1983).

by the courts to other areas of government decision-making, including health care administration, public housing, social insurance programs, and the administration of other social welfare programs.

Despite intimations to the contrary in some early decisions, the courts have not given environmental values any preferred status in this judicially-developed surrogate for the legislative process. Under the current system, business' interests have equal or even greater success than environmental plaintiffs in overturning agency decisions as factually unsupported or inadequately explained. This result is hardly surprising, given that businesses generally have greater litigation resources. At the same time, the new model has undoubtedly given environmental interests more power and influence than they had under the traditional model, where they largely lacked any legal rights.

Despite its achievements, the new model of administrative law has its drawbacks. Rule-making proceedings are protracted and cumbersome; litigation often follows. For example, EPA issues several dozen major rules each year; over 90 percent are challenged in court. In a substantial number of these cases the court finds that the agency has failed to justify at least some portion of its decision, and remands for a second rule-making proceeding, which is often followed by a second round of judicial review. This process also tends to diffuse governmental responsibility and impair coordination of regulatory policy by treating each decision in relative isolation. Two basic alternatives to the present system have been proposed. One is to follow an even more explicitly legislative model of decision-making by promoting informal regulatory negotiation of rules by agencies and affected interests, subject to only limited judicial review.[37] Experiments with 'regneg' have, thus far, achieved only limited success. The other alternative, discussed further in section IV A below, is greater White House control and coordination of agency regulation.

C. *Environmental Advocacy*

Directly related to the increased role of law and the courts is the fact that environmental advocacy organizations, following the precedent set by civil rights groups, have used litigation as a tool to reform law and government policy.[38] Environmental groups dedicated to legal advocacy arose in the late 1960s and early 1970s. Their financial support has come from modest contributions from large numbers of interested citizens, from wealthy individuals,

---

[37] See Susskind and McMahon, 'The Theory and Practice of Negotiated Rulemaking', 3 *Yale J. Reg.* 133 (1985).

[38] See, Turner, 'The Legal Eagles', *Amicus J.* 25 (Winter, 1988).

and from foundations. This funding has been encouraged by the American tradition of voluntary association observed by de Tocqueville, and the tax incentives provided by the Internal Revenue Code. Presently there are a dozen major national environmental organizations and myriads of state and local groups.

The national organizations pioneered the developments in administrative law summarized in section III above by bringing litigation to seek the right to participate in agency proceedings; seek judicial review; force agency adherence to statutory obligations to protect the environment; give enforcement teeth to NEPA; and persuade courts to review agencies' exercise of discretion. The courts' favorable response to these initiatives, in turn, enabled these groups to trumpet their success to donors and expand their revenues and operations. The largest environmental groups have from 50,000 to over 500,000 members and annual budgets in excess of $20 million. These groups have attracted the services of able young professionals and command great influence with the media and Congress.

Congress has encouraged and enlisted the energies of these groups by adopting 'citizen suit' provisions in most of the major federal environmental regulatory laws.[39] These provisions entitle 'any person' to bring private enforcement actions in federal court against firms or other persons subject to regulatory requirements in order to enjoin compliance, and impose civil penalties, which are paid to the federal Treasury. In both types of proceedings, the statutes authorize courts to require the opposing party to pay a successful plaintiff's attorneys' fee.[40] These provisions also authorize suits against EPA and other federal agencies for failure to carry out non-discretionary duties imposed by statute. Congress frequently imposes such duties by enacting statutory deadlines for EPA issuance of standards or regulations and other 'action forcing' mandates designed to galvanize the bureaucracy. When EPA fails to carry out these mandates in a timely fashion, environmental groups often bring suit to obtain a judicial order requiring agency compliance.

These provisions have given environmental groups a powerful role in ensuring effective implementation of environmental regulatory statutes. During the early 1980s, for example, the Reagan administration EPA sought, in effect, to repeal many environmental regulatory requirements by simply not enforcing them. Environmental groups closed the enforcement gap by bringing numerous citizen suits against regulated firms for violation of pollution control requirements. Critics, however, complain that citizen suit

---

[39] See, e.g. Clean Air Act, Section 304, 42 U.S.C. § 7604.
[40] The provision for award of a fee is an exception to the general 'American rule' that each party is responsible for its own litigation costs.

provisions unjustifiedly delegate governmental authority to private groups, enabling them to pick and choose which measures to enforce. Critics also contend that the deadlines and other mandates imposed by Congress are often arbitrary and unrealistic, particularly given that EPA's budget is quite limited relative to its extensive responsibilities.[41]

D. Enforcement Techniques

No system of regulation is better than its monitoring and enforcement component. The strictest standards in the world will not protect the environment if they are not obeyed. The lesson from capitalist and socialist nations alike is that government, and or private enterprises will shirk costly regulatory requirements unless there are sanctions or other incentives to ensure compliance. During the 1970s, United States governmental agencies devoted much energy to adopting rules and standards and incorporating them into facilities' permits. In the 1980s and 1990s, the problem of enforcing these requirements has attracted steadily increasing attention.

Both federal and state environmental regulatory statutes provide for administrative, civil, and criminal enforcement of environmental requirements. Administrative agencies such as EPA are generally authorized to issue administrative orders to require compliance and impose administrative penalties of as much as $10,000 per violation. The government can also file civil actions in court to enjoin further violations, require remediation of past ones, and seek substantial civil penalties. The penalties sought by EPA are calculated to recoup the economic savings the violators enjoyed as a result of non-compliance, and also include an additional 'gravity' component, based on the seriousness of the violation. EPA has succeeded in recovering millions of dollars in penalties in cases involving repeated violations. Finally, criminal enforcement is being pressed with increased vigor. Under the federal Sentencing Guidelines, individuals (including corporate employees and officers) can expect to serve time in jail for a 'knowing' violation of environmental regulatory requirements. Corporate violators have been sentenced to pay multi-million dollars fines. EPA and the U.S. Justice Department have devoted greatly increased resources to all forms of enforcement activity.

The federal environmental laws provide for a three-tier enforcement system; the federal government; state governments, which generally have authority to enforce federal requirements; and environmental groups, who can also bring civil enforcement actions pursuant to the citizen suit

---

[41] For discussion of congressional use of deadlines in environmental regulatory laws, see Melnick, 'Pollution Deadlines and the Coalition for Failure', 75 *Public Interest* 123 (1984).

provisions discussed in section III C above. If one enforcement authority shirks its duties, the others can take up the slack. Enforcement is also promoted by the extensive reporting requirements imposed on regulated firms. These firms must file regular submissions with the government, recording their pollution discharges and waste generation. These reports are available to the public and are often used in citizen suits to establish violations.

In the past few years, business firms have sought to avoid exposure to increasingly heavy environmental sanctions and liabilities by developing corporate environmental auditing and compliance programs. These programs are designed to monitor the firm's compliance with environmental requirements, take actions to correct violations, and take other management steps to promote compliance by the corporation and its employees. Given the inevitable limitations of government monitoring and enforcement resources, there are significant reasons to encourage corporate self-policing to monitor and deter employee violations of the law. The federal government has sought to provide such encouragement by promising leniency in its prosecutive and sanctioning decisions to firms with strong programs.[42]

E. New Forms of Liability

Although command and control regulation has been the principal instrument selected by legislators to deal with environmental problem, the challenge of toxic waste clean-up led Congress to adopt a sweeping program that places the costs of remediating waste problems on those responsible for creating the problems. The 1980 Comprehensive Environmental Remediation Compensation and Liability Act (CERCLA or 'Superfund')[43] imposes strict, retroactive, joint and several liability on present and past owners and operators of a hazardous waste site and on transporters and generators of the waste taken to the site, requiring them to pay for clean-up of the site.[44] The federal EPA supervises the Superfund program, either cleaning up the sites itself and securing reimbursement from the responsible parties, or forcing them to undertake the clean-up directly. Several thousand sites have been designated for clean-up at an average cost of $30–40 million, with some clean-ups costing hundreds of millions of dollars. Many states have adopted similar programs. Many cases involve dozens or even hundreds of defendants who

---

[42] See United States Department of Justice, *Factors in Decisions on Criminal Prosecutions for Environmental Violations in the Context of Significant Voluntary Compliance or Disclosure Efforts.*

[43] 42 U.S.C. §§ 9601–9675.

[44] The Superfund program also imposes a tax on chemical feedstocks and on business corporations generally to help pay for clean-up, but the revenues generated by the taxes are small relative to total clean-up requirements.

have shipped their wastes to or had some other involvement with a site. Superfund defendants have also brought many cases against their insurance carriers as a result of disputes over insurance coverage for Superfund liabilities. Litigation costs are, not surprisingly, high. The Oil Pollution Act[45] adopts a similar program of clean-up liability for oil spills.

In addition to providing funding to clean up waste problems, the Superfund system provides powerful incentives to firms and individuals to minimize generation and ensure proper treatment and disposal of hazardous wastes. Purchasers of industrial and commercial properties now carefully investigate possible hazardous waste problems to ensure that they are not acquiring clean-up liabilities. Lenders make similar inquiries. As a result, sellers and borrowers are under pressure to avoid creating hazardous wastes problems and to clean up those that already exist.

Both CERCLA and the Oil Pollution Act also authorize a similar system of liability for natural resource damages. Federal, state, and native american tribal authorities with ownership or management authority over public resources are empowered to bring actions against those responsible for hazardous substance releases or oil spills and recover the cost of restoring the injured resources. Natural resource damages are a rapidly expanding field of liability. In the *Exxon Valdez* case, Exxon was forced to pay the federal government and Alaska nearly $1 billion for restoration of Prince William Sound.

Another emerging area of environmental liability consists of 'toxic tort' actions brought under state law by private litigants for personal and property injuries attributed to exposure to hazardous substances and other toxic agents. Although courts have generally adopted a rule of strict liability, rather than negligence, in such cases, plaintiffs seeking recovery for health injuries often face formidable problems in establishing that their cancer or other malady was attributable to exposure to a particular substance generated by defendant rather than diet, heredity, exposure to other toxic agents, or other causes, known or unknown. These difficulties are exacerbated in many cases by the long latency period between exposure and the onset of illness. Some state courts have sought to deal with this problem by relaxing traditional requirements for proof of causation by plaintiffs or recognizing innovative remedies, such as recovery for fear of contracting illness as result of an exposure, or imposing the costs of regular monitoring of the medical condition of those exposed on the polluter.[46]

---

[45] 33 U.S.C. §§ 2701–2761.

[46] See *Elam* v. *Alcoa, Inc.*, 765 S.W. 2d 42 (Mo. App. 1988), *cert. denied*, 493 U.S. 817 (1989) (relaxing causation standards); *Potter* v. *Firestone Tire & Rubber Co.*, 274 Cal. Rptr. 885 (Cal. App. 6 Dist. 1990) (recovery for emotional distress); *Ayers* v. *Township of Jackson*, 525 A.2d 287 (N.J. 1987) (recovery for medical monitoring costs).

IV. Current Topics in United States Environmental Law

A. White House Control of Regulation

It may seem unremarkable that the President, as the Chief Executive, has sought to control the adoption of important regulations by the federal departments and agencies under his supervision. Nonetheless, the subject has excited considerable controversy. President Reagan, by executive order,[47] directed federal agencies to conduct regulatory impact analyses (RIAs) of the cost and benefits of major new regulations and of alternative means of accomplishing regulatory objectives, and, to the extent permitted by the particular statutes governing the regulatory decision, to follow cost-benefit principles in making regulatory decisions. The order also provided for review by the White House Office of Management and Budget (OMB) of agencies' RIAs and proposed and final regulations to ensure that the executive order had been followed. This directive was prompted by the perception that federal regulatory agencies, particularly EPA, were overly 'regulation minded' and gave insufficient consideration to the costs and impacts on industrial competitiveness of the requirements that they adopted. The concern was also expressed that EPA gives too much weight to the views of the congressional environmental committees and to environmental activists. The executive order also responded to the perceived need systematically to monitor and review the cumulative economic impact of regulatory requirements.[48] For example, the EPA found that in 1992 it would cost the United States $115 billion annually to achieve compliance with federal environmental regulatory requirements, and that by the year 2000 annual costs would rise to $185 billion, assuming full implementation of existing laws.[49]

OMB regulatory review under the Reagan and Bush administrations was sharply criticized by congressional Democrats and environmental groups. Some maintained that the President did not have the authority to control EPA issuance of regulations because the environmental regulatory statutes generally vest authority in the Administrator of EPA, not the President. Others protested the use of cost-benefit analysis, including the assignment of dollar figures to the benefits of saving lives.[50] It was also claimed that OMB

---

[47] Executive Order 12,291 (1981).

[48] See De Muth and Ginsburg, 'White House Review of Agency Rulemaking', 99 *Harv. L. Rev.* 1075 (1986).

[49] U.S. Environmental Protection Agency, *Environmental Investments: The Cost of a Clean Environment* 2-1 (1990).

[50] See S. Kelman, 'Cost-Benefit Analyses: An Ethical Critique', *Regulation*, Jan./Feb. 1981, 33.

review was being used to delay or block the adoption of regulations. Much criticism was directed at procedural issues. For example, the 'secrecy' of OMB review and the fact that OMB received, off the record, information and analysis from businesses opposed to proposed regulations was claimed to undermine the 'paper hearing' notice and comment rule-making process.[51] OMB has taken steps to meet these procedural criticisms. For example, it makes publicly available materials received from persons outside the government and logs its meetings with them.

Although the Republican administrations were attacked as biased against regulation, when President Clinton took office he retained, with minor modifications, the OMB review process.[52] Many people believe that some form of centralized review is necessary to counteract the powerful dispersion of power and accountability that results from a congressional form of government and the creation of a vast federal bureaucracy. Some would like to see the OMB review process become more systematic and professionalized, drawing on science as well as economics, evolving into an American version of the French *Conseil d'Etat*. Such an institution might well relieve courts of the felt necessity to supervise agencies' exercise of discretion as closely as they do under current 'hard look' standards of review. But others dismiss such a possibility, arguing that such an institution would be entirely incompatible with American political structures and cultural traditions.

B. Cost–Benefit Analysis, Risk Assessment and Regulatory Priorities

OMB review of agency regulations is part of a large debate over the extent to which environmental regulatory decisions should be based on cost–benefit analysis. Environmental advocates have long maintained that environmental quality standards should be based on protection of health and the environment, without considerations of costs, and that regulated firms should also be required to install best available control technology, without balancing the costs of such controls against the environmental benefits. These positions have long been challenged by economists, policy analysts, and the business community.[53] The executive orders described above have sought to promote greater use of cost–benefit analysis in environmental regulatory decision-making. However, the executive orders require agencies to follow such

---

[51] Olson, 'The Quiet Shift of Power: Office of Management and Budget Supervision of Environmental Protection Agency Rulemaking Order Executive Order 12,291', 4 *Va. J. Natl. Res. L.* (1984).

[52] Executive Order 12,866 (1993).

[53] See, e.g. W.J. Baumol and W.E. Oates, *The Theory of Environmental Policy* (Cambridge U.P., 1988).

analysis in making decisions only to the extent that the particular statute governing the decision in question allows for weighing of costs, or a balancing of costs and benefits. Many environmental regulatory statutes preclude considerations of such factors. In addition, courts are without jurisdiction to enforce compliance with the executive orders. Legislation has been introduced in Congress to impose a 'supermandate'—a generic measure that would override particular environmental, health, and safety regulatory statutes, require all regulatory decisions to be made in accordance with cost–benefit principles, and authorize private parties to enforce compliance with this requirement through litigation in the courts. Such legislation passed the House but has thus far failed to pass the Senate.

A related debate revolves around the use of risk analysis to set regulatory priorities and make regulatory decisions. Critics have claimed that regulatory agencies fail to follow consistent principles of risk assessment, and often use unduly conservative assumptions and procedures that seriously overestimate the risks in question. In an influential book, Supreme Court Justice Stephen Breyer has strongly criticized much environmental regulation on the ground that it focuses on trivial risks and ignores other, more pressing regulatory and public health priorities.[54] He would establish an expert body within the executive branch to ensure consistent and appropriate risk assessment, and reorder regulatory priorities accordingly. The House recently passed legislation that would mandate use of specific risk assessment principles and methods by environmental, health, and safety regulatory agencies, and make these requirements judicially enforceable. This legislation, however, has also failed to pass the Senate.

C. Alternative Strategies for Environmental Protection

Although the regulatory programs enacted by Congress in the 1970s had some important successes, the limitations of the command and control strategy are becoming increasingly apparent. Achieving ever more ambitious environmental goals, while maintaining economic prosperity, will in large part depend on the development of innovative new processes and products that are resource efficient and minimize adverse environmental side effects. The command and control system is effective in requiring industry to adopt existing technologies, but the incentives that it provides for innovation are, at best, uneven and often counterproductive. The detailed requirements and short deadlines for compliance that are characteristic of command style

---

[54] S. Breyer, *Breaking the Vicious Circle: Toward Effective Risk Regulation* (Harvard U.P., 1993).

regulation tend to stifle innovation by depriving firms of flexibility in meeting environmental goals. The proliferation of ever more detailed regulations has created other problems characteristic of central planning: information overload, rigidity, lack of coordination and consistency among different requirements, and economic inefficiency. In the United States, these dysfunctions are exacerbated by the legal formalism of the regulatory process and the enormous amount of litigation that it spawns.[55] Not only industry and academics, but also some environmentalists, have recognized the need for fundamental rethinking of environmental protection strategies.

Economists have long favored the use of emission fees and taxes, on the ground that they would give firms both the incentive and the flexibility to develop and adopt the most cost-effective means of reducing pollution or achieving other environmental objectives and thereby greatly reduce the cost to society of achieving a given level of protection. This approach has, however, generated little support. Industry is opposed to new taxes; under regulation, the emissions that industry is allowed to generate are 'free'. Environmentalists have opposed taxes as a 'license to pollute', questioned whether the taxes likely to be levied will be sufficient to induce adequate levels of control, and raised concerns about monitoring and enforcement. There has however, been some use by states and local governments of charges on household waste and consumer deposits on beverage containers to encourage recycling, which operate like a tax on pollution.

Another market-based approach that has many of the advantages of a tax system, but without some of its drawbacks, is a system of tradeable pollution rights.[56] In such a system, the government limits the total amount of pollution that can be emitted, but allows pollution rights to be bought and sold by companies that are actual or potential polluters. If the market functions properly, firms with lower abatement costs will reduce their pollution and sell their excess rights to those with higher costs, resulting in a lower cost to society of achieving a given overall level of control. All firms also have an incentive to find more environmentally beneficial ways of doing business, because if they do so, they can earn a profit by selling their excess pollution rights. Business opposition can be reduced by giving pollution rights to existing firms in proportion to their existing regulatory rights to pollute, rather than requiring firms to purchase them. Reductions in the overall level of pollution can be achieved by depreciating the rights over time. A system of tradeable rights is, however, not without problems. It may be difficult to establish a well-functioning market. There is a need for monitoring and enforcement to ensure that facilities' emissions do not exceed the amount permitted by the

---

[55] See Stewart, 'Madison's Nightmare', 57 *U. Chi. L. Rev.* 335 (1990).
[56] See B. Ackerman and R. Stewart, 'Reforming Environmental Law' 37 *Stan. L. Rev.* 301 (1985).

rights that they possess. Additionally, many environmentalists have ethical reservations about the use of market mechanisms to advance environmental goals.

EPA pioneered the use of tradeable permits to introduce greater flexibility in air pollution regulation and to phase out lead in gasoline. These programs have saved hundreds of millions of dollars without sacrificing overall environmental quality. In the 1990 Amendments to the Clean Air Act, Congress adopted an ambitious program of tradeable rights as part of a program to reduce sulfur emissions from electric generating plants by 50 percent over a 10-year period.[57] The cost savings anticipated from this approach was a determinative factor in adoption of the program. The program is barely underway, and questions remain as to whether a well-functioning market in sulfur rights will emerge, but the experience thus far shows enormous cost savings. If the program continues to succeed, it will undoubtedly encourage Congress to use the tradeable permit approach in other contexts.

Increasing attention is being paid to other economic incentive systems. Interest has been expressed in the system of environmental contracts and covenants being developed in the Netherlands and some other European nations.[58] Under this approach, government contracts with industry for a specified reduction in total pollution and waste over an extended period of time, such as 10 years. Industry enjoys the flexibility and lead time to achieve such reductions in innovative, cost-effective ways. The government, in turn, requires that industry achieve a substantially greater overall reduction than would be required under otherwise applicable regulations. There is also growing interest in eco-labelling programs, under which environmentally superior products would carry a logo or seal of approval, and in other environmental information strategies designed to elicit consumer and investor demands for environmentally progressive products and firms.

D. Environmental Justice

The distributional impact on racial minorities and low-income groups of decisions to site industrial facilities and regulatory enforcement practices has received increasing attention in recent years. Environmental and civil rights groups point to empirical studies which assertedly show that hazardous waste landfills and other environmentally hazardous facilities are disproportionately located in neighborhoods with racial and ethnic minority or low-

---

[57] See Clean Air Act, Sections 401–416, 42 U.S.C. §§ 7651–7651o.

[58] See J. van Dunné, ed., *Environmental Contracts and Covenants: New Instruments in a Realistic Environmental Policy?* (Vermande Lelystadt, 1993).

income residents. It is also asserted that government environmental enforcement and clean-up efforts are less vigorous in such neighborhoods. These disparities are attributed to the relative lack of political access and influence by such neighborhoods or to 'environmental racism'.[59] Questions have been raised, however, about the extent of the statistical correlation between environmentally hazardous facilities and poor or minority residents, and, to the extent that there is such a correlation, whether it is due not to the fact that such facilities are sited disproportionately in such neighborhoods but rather that such facilities depress local property values, leading wealthier residents to move and poorer persons to relocate to such areas.[60]

V. Conclusion

The United States has created an ambitious and highly developed system of environmental law in 25 years. The system has achieved substantial progress in environmental protection. It has also generated some remarkable legal innovations, including the extension of rights to participate in agency decision-making procedures and obtain judicial review; the development of new procedures for regulatory decision-making and new approaches to judicial review; the citizen suit; and statutory liability for toxic waste clean-up and natural resource damages. At the same time, the system is cumbersome, costly, and contentious. One study found that overall environmental quality in the United States was essentially the same as in the United Kingdom, which has a system of environmental law that relies far less on adversarial processes and is far less costly. The command and control regulatory system may also be approaching the limits of its ability to secure additional improvements in environmental quality at reasonable cost. Accordingly, United States environmental law is now ripe for basic reconsideration and rethinking.

[59] See R.D. Bullard, ed., *Confronting Environmental Racism: Voices from the Grassroots* (1993).
[60] See V. Been, 'Locally Undesirable Land Uses in Minority Neighborhoods: Disproportionate Siting or Market Dynamics?' 103 *Yale L.J.* 1383 (1994).

19

INTELLECTUAL PROPERTY LAW

ROCHELLE COOPER DREYFUSS

I. Introduction to Intellectual Property

This chapter describes the provisions of American law that create exclusive rights in the fruits of the intellect, principally inventions, designs, writings, technical know-how, and marketing symbols. These laws include patent law, which protects inventions and designs; copyright law for the protection of writings; trademark law for marketing symbols; and state trade secrecy and contract law for the protection of know-how. Collectively, these are referred to as 'intellectual property law'. However, it is important to stress from the outset that, although this phrase uses the word 'property', this branch of the law is very different from the law that deals with tangible property.

There are at least three features that highlight the differences between tangible and intangible property law. One has to do with supply. Much of property law deals with natural resources, such as land and minerals. These are fixed: there is, for instance, a finite amount of land on the globe and no way to replace a piece that is despoiled. The law of tangible property, therefore, is partly aimed at encouraging creative management and conservation. There are, however, infinite possibilities for new ideas and no need to conserve them for the future. To the contrary, one innovation can open doors to many others, so that the sooner and more fully an idea is discovered and utilized, the faster the knowledge base expands.

This interrelatedness is the second feature that distinguishes the laws of tangible and intangible property. With regard to natural resources, demand and supply are in some ways discrete concepts. For example, using zinc cannot increase the world's supply of zinc. But using ideas does create more ideas. The cumulative nature of innovation means that intellectual property law must be fashioned with an eye toward the duality of ideas as input and output. It must be structured to simultaneously reward the producer of an invention and protect other inventors' access to the building blocks of knowledge.

The third, and most important, difference between tangibles and intangibles has to do with the ability to share. Tangible property lawyers talk about the 'tragedy of the commons'. If, for example, every farmer has the right to graze sheep on a piece of land, the grass will be chewed to its roots. When the grass dies, all the sheep starve. Establishing exclusive rights to property solves the problem because private ownership gives individual farmers the ability and incentive to graze the flock in a manner that maintains the grass. There is, however, no tragedy of the commons with regard to intellectual property because it can be shared. That is, once an invention is perfected, or a manuscript completed, the creator's ability to use it for its intended purpose—to read a research report, or to operate a machine—is usually not diminished by the use made of that same invention by others. Instead, as each utilizer enjoys the benefits of the innovation (and as each utilizes the invention as a source for other ideas), social welfare increases.

The effect, then, of creating substantial rights in intellectual property appears to be a social disutility. These rights are, after all, essentially monopolies in that they control the 'supply' of a product, in this case, information. Like other monopolies, they have the potential for raising prices and lowering output. In addition, they can produce deadweight social loss as people who could profitably use the innovation, were it priced competitively, forgo purchasing it at the monopolist's price.[1] Thus, the imposition of a private-rights system must be justified, and the justification must be based on some ground other than the tragedy-of-the-commons idea that supports the laws of tangible property.

Several rationales have been suggested. The *natural rights theory* holds that the creator has a moral right to the fruits of his labor, including the benefits produced by his intellect. Although many nations' intellectual property laws are at least partially premised on this rationale, American law has largely rejected it, the theory apparently being that creativity is its own reward.

[1] Of course, the degree to which, say, a copyright or patent functions as a monopoly depends on the extent to which unprotected inventions can function as substitutes for the copyrighted or patented one. In many cases, near-complete substitution is possible, and so it is never correct to assume from the existence of a patent or copyright that its holder possesses monopoly power.

Four other rationales exert more of an influence on intellectual property law; three to a lesser extent and one to a greater extent. The lesser theories include the *exchange-for-secrecy rationale*, which states that, without a legal right to prevent others from copying his invention, the creator may be tempted to keep it secret. If he does, others may unknowingly duplicate the effort that went into creating it. Moreover, no one will be able to use its ideas to push the frontiers of knowledge further. Even though creating an exclusive right in the innovation raises costs, the increase is offset by the benefits of disclosure. The *quality-control principle* looks at the exclusive right as a method for protecting the innovation once it is released. By giving the holder of the right the power to control how the innovation is used, exclusive rights enable him to maintain its integrity. He can, for example, use this right to prevent others from distorting or mutilating his work, thereby diluting its quality. The *prospecting theory* shares some of these quality-promotion elements. It argues that one value in a system of exclusive rights is that it concentrates research. Like a miner who owns her mining claim, the holder of an exclusive right has the incentive to fully develop her ideas. And since anyone else who wants to pursue work in that field must seek her authorization, the holder comes to possess comprehensive knowledge of how the field is unfolding and can help maintain an 'orderly market' in its further development.

The *profit-incentive theory*, which has the most dominant influence on the shape of American intellectual property law, takes the most utilitarian approach. It argues that a period of exclusivity is necessary to protect the innovator from copiests. This protection is needed because the costs of copying are lower than the costs of innovating, and so the copiest/freerider could easily capture the entire market for the product and prevent the innovator from earning back the costs of producing the invention. Since most inventors cannot afford to donate their services to the public, the optimum level of innovation will not be achieved without exclusivity. Of course, government could solve the freerider problem by subsidizing innovative efforts, but exclusivity works better because market mechanisms generate a reward that, more or less, mirrors the benefit the public sees in the invention. Presumably, others will be induced by this profit to channel their innovative efforts into areas the public especially values.

As the following pages will demonstrate, the question whether exclusivity is justified in a particular case, and if so on what theory, is at the heart of many of the pivotal disputes underlying American intellectual property law. How these questions are resolved—and what power, as a constitutional matter, the states and Congress have to resolve them—determines whether a particular endeavor will receive legal protection at all, and whether it will receive that protection under the patent system, the copyright laws, trademark law, or some other state or federal regime. In the end, the choice of justification shapes both the rights of creative individuals and the quality (and quantity) of the product that passes to the public.

II. Sources of Intellectual Property Law

A. *Federal Law*

Article I, § 8 of the United States Constitution gives Congress authority to 'promote the Progress of Science and Useful Arts, by securing for limited Times to Authors and Inventors the exclusive Right to their respective Writings and Discoveries'. Using this authorization, Congress has enacted copyright and patent legislation. The Patent Act[2] deals with the discoveries of inventors. Last recodified in 1952 (but amended several times since), it conforms to the Paris Convention for the Protection of Industrial Property, to the Patent Cooperation Treaty, and to the Agreement on Trade Related Aspects of Intellectual Property Rights of the General Agreement on Tariffs and Trade (the TRIPS Agreement). The Copyright Act[3] is concerned with the writings of authors. The 1976 recodification executes the United States' undertakings under the Universal Copyright Convention. Conforming changes were made after 1988, when the United States acceded to the Berne Convention for the Protection of Literary and Artistic Works and to the TRIPS Agreement. As a signatory of these major world intellectual property conventions, the United States has agreed to extend to the citizens of other signatories the same copyright and patent rights available to Americans. There are also some bilateral treaties that contain national treatment provisions.

The language of the 'Copyright Clause' cited above carries several important implications. First, the 'limited times' provision requires Congress to create copyrights and patents of finite duration. Secondly, the 'authors and inventors' language allows Congress to vest rights only in creators: producers of noncreative works cannot receive this protection. Importers, manufacturers, and such are also barred from initial ownership of these rights, although they can own them by assignment. Thirdly, the clause as a whole is interpreted as reflecting the profit-incentive theory. As we saw, this theory argues that rewarding creators is not an end in itself. Rather, profits are intended to encourage the creation of works that enrich the public. Thus,

---

[2] 35 U.S.C. §§ 1–376.   [3] 17 U.S.C. §§ 101–1010.

when situations arise in which the public's interest in access conflicts with the creator's interest in profits, it is the public that usually wins. Furthermore, the emphasis on profits means that the dignity interests encompassed by some of the other rationales receive only secondary recognition.

The limitations in the Copyright Clause are also interpreted to mean that it cannot support legislation to protect trademarks since these are not considered writings or discoveries. Instead, Congress protected the goodwill merchants invest in their marks by enacting trademark legislation (the Lanham Act)[4] under its constitutional authority to regulate commerce between the states. Like the Patent Act, the Lanham Act, which was last recodified in 1946 (but has been amended), conforms to the Paris Convention and to the TRIPS Agreement.

In some ways, dependence on the Commerce Clause gives Congress more flexibility than it would have had under the Copyright Clause: Congress can protect works that lack a creative element and can establish rights of unlimited duration. Furthermore, it can rely more explicitly on those justifications for intellectual property protection that are outside the ambit of the Copyright Clause (as it is currently understood). Thus, quality-control and dignity interests have traditionally received greater support in trademark law than they have in either copyright or patent law.

Trademark law has, however, read into the Commerce Clause limitations of its own. Thus, although the Commerce Clause receives a very broad interpretation when Congress enacts civil rights and antitrust legislation, courts have always interpreted it as giving Congress trademark authority only with regard to works actually involved in, or about to be involved in, interstate commerce. That is, trademarks must be in use—and in use in more than one state—to qualify for federal registration. Indeed, it is sometimes said that trademarks are not created under federal law: they are created in the states, and then receive national recognition when they are used interstate and registered federally.[5]

In addition to enacting copyright, patent, and trademark legislation, Congress has also used the Copyright and Commerce Clauses as authority to protect other forms of intellectual property. For example, the Semiconductor Chip Act[6] protects the layouts of semiconductor chips from copiests; the

---

[4] 15 U.S.C. §§ 1051–1127.

[5] It is worth noting that this view may be out of date. This issue was last considered in 1932, and then by a lower court, *A. Leschen & Sons Rope Co.* v. *American Steel and Wire Co.*, 55 F.2d 455 (C.C.P.A. 1932). That decision was based on the Supreme Court's definitive rejection of national trademark legislation under Copyright Clause authority (Trade-Mark Cases, 100 U.S. 82 (1879)), as well as pointed dicta in several subsequent (but old) Supreme Court opinions. At the same time, however, the Supreme Court's recent decision in *United States* v. *Lopez*, 115 S.Ct. 1624 (1995), makes the reach of the Commerce Clause uncertain. Besides, the two-tiered (state/federal) approach taken by virtue of these decisions has solidified and, as the text notes, offers some distinct advantages.

[6] 17 U.S.C. §§ 901–914.

Plant Variety Protection Act[7] gives an exclusive right to breeders of novel varieties of sexually reproduced plants; and the Orphan Drug Act[8] creates a short term right in drugs used to treat illnesses that afflict small populations.

B. State Law

Because federal authority to protect intellectual property is limited, gaps are sometimes filled by state law. In the case of trademarks, the state's power is extensive[9]. Thus, whereas federal legislation protects mainly against the use by others of confusingly similar marks or trade dress (that is, configuration and packaging) on similar goods, states protect marks and trade dress from becoming diluted through use on goods that are dissimilar to the trade-marked goods (for example, a roadside diner's use of the name of a famous perfume). Most states also have rights of action to prevent other misappropriations of goodwill.

The situation is more complicated for potentially patentable and copyrightable subject matter. The constitutional goal of protecting the public is read as even protecting the public from interference by the states. Accordingly, state laws regarding uncopyrighted and unpatented works are considered preempted when their effect undermines federal goals. Despite congressional efforts to define the scope of preemption,[10] its boundaries remain unclear. State laws that protect subpatentable works on the same profit-incentive theory that is thought to underlie the Copyright Clause have been held preempted, as have state laws creating copyright-like rights in uncopyrightable materials. States have, however, been on firmer ground when using justifications other than the profit-incentive theory. They can establish trade secrecy laws that bar competitors from using valuable information gathered by improper means, such as bribery and industrial espionage. They are also permitted to enforce promises of confidentiality and contracts not to compete, both of which prevent employees from appropriating their employer's discoveries. In addition, many states have rights of publicity that give people control over the use of their names and likenesses in advertising, and rights of privacy that protect personal information. These rights vary from state to state, and are best considered in connection with tort law.

---

[7] 7 U.S.C. § 2402.   [8] 21 U.S.C. §§ 360aa-dd.   [9] 15 U.S.C. § 1121.
[10] See, for example, 17 U.S.C. § 301.

III. Patent Law

A. Introduction

Patent law protects what are commonly regarded as inventions. It creates, for 20 years, exclusive rights against all who make, use, offer to sell, or sell the protected invention, including independent inventors. In exchange, the patent is published so that the ideas in the invention go into the public domain immediately, where they can be used to create other innovations.[11] Patent protection is the strongest form of intellectual property protection, and it is the hardest to obtain.

B. Requirements for Patent Protection

There are seven requirements for patent protection. The invention must be patentable subject matter; it must be useful; novel; original; non-obvious; and the applicant must not have engaged in barred conduct. In addition, the patent document must specify the invention so that the public knows exactly what is protected, how it is made, and how it is best practiced.

1. Patentable subject matter

Under §§ 101, 161, and 171,[12] the following subject matter can be patented: processes, machines, manufactures, compositions of matter (collectively, 'utility' inventions), designs, and plants. These provisions are interpreted to reach 'anything under the sun that is made by man'.[13] Excluded, however, are scientific principles and works of nature, such as living things. The distinction can be difficult to draw. The patentability of computer programs, for example, is in doubt because courts have characterized them as reciting algorithms, which can be understood as scientific principles. Similarly, purified natural substances, such as genetic sequences, straddle the line between compositions of matter and works of nature. The remainder of this chapter deals with utility patents; design and plant patents are beyond the scope of this book.

---

[11] Congress is currently considering changing the law so that patent applications would be published 18 months after they are filed.

[12] Unless otherwise noted, all statutory citations are to 35 U.S.C.

[13] *Diamond* v. *Chakrabarty*, 447 U.S. 303, 309 (1980).

2. Usefulness

In recent years, § 101's utility requirement has been interpreted as requiring only that the invention have an end-use. This marks a distinction from earlier case law, which sometimes barred inventions, such as gambling machines, that lacked a socially beneficial use. The thinking now is that the agency that administers patent law, the Patent and Trademark Office (PTO), is not the appropriate institution of government to police the market place for detrimental products.

3. Novelty

Subsections 102(a), (e), and (g) set out the definition for novelty. Section 102(a) is the principal safeguard that patents issue only for truly innovative inventions. It provides that an invention cannot be patented if, prior to the applicant's date of invention, it was known or used by others in the United States, or patented or described in a printed publication in the United States or abroad. A publicity requirement is usually interpolated into the 'known' and 'used' provisions so that only information accessible to the public can interfere with patenting. Similarly, publications are considered relevant ('effective') only if they were available publicly before the invention was made.

The other novelty subsections are of minor significance. Subsection 102(e) prevents delays in the patent office from creating exclusive rights in information that would have gone into the public domain. Under this provision, an invention cannot be patented if it was described in a United States patent application that was filed before the applicant's date of invention and eventually results in a patent. The novelty provision of § 102(g) prevents a patent from issuing if the same invention was in continuous use by someone else before the applicant's date of invention. Since both § 102(g) and § 102(a) deal with inventions made prior to the applicant's invention date, they are somewhat similar. However, the publicity requirement of § 102(a) is not read into § 102(g). Thus, the latter makes even secret inventions effective—so long as they are actually in use.

4. Originality

Only inventors can apply for patents (§ 116). If the information that led to the invention was derived from others, the patent is denied under § 102(f).

5. Non-obviousness

Much of the reported patent litigation concerns the perception that more than mere novelty should be required to merit patent protection; that even if an invention is not wholly contained in a prior work, it is effectively already a part of the public domain if it could have been invented easily—if it was an *obvious* extension of earlier knowledge. This perception, codified into § 103 when the patent law was revised in 1952, was explained in *Graham v. John Deere Co.*:[14]

> [T]he scope and content of the prior art are to be determined; differences between the prior art and the claims at issue are to be ascertained; and the level of ordinary skill in the pertinent art resolved. Against this background, the obviousness or non-obviousness of the subject matter is determined.

In practice, this test has led to unpredictable outcomes and subjective determinations. The Court of Appeals for the Federal Circuit (CAFC), which hears patent appeals from all over the nation, has therefore required lower courts to look also at objective factors. These so-called 'secondary considerations' include commercial success; longfelt but unmet need; failure of others; and acquiescence in the patent by competitors.

6. Statutory bars

In addition to affirmatively meeting the requirements for a patent, inventors must not have engaged in certain barred activities. The principal provision here is § 102(b), which prevents patentees from expanding the patent term by utilizing their inventions for a period of time before they apply for patents. This provision bars patents on inventions that were in public use or on sale in the United States, or patented or described in a printed publication anywhere for more than a year before the application was filed. This provision is similar to ones found in the patent laws of most nations, except that it gives the patentee a one-year grace period. The justification for this grace period is that allowing the inventor to discuss the invention with others while the application is being prepared promotes the dissemination of information and helps the inventor perfect the invention. Along the same lines, courts have created an 'experimental use' exception which exempts activities that could be classified as public uses or sales, but which are mainly designed to perfect the invention.

---

[14] 383 U.S. 1, 17 (1966).

There are two other bars: § 102(d) is aimed at encouraging foreign inventors to file in the United States quickly. If a patent application is filed abroad more than a year before the United States application is filed, and the foreign patent issues before the PTO issues the United States patent, the United States patent is barred. Section 102(c) bars an inventor from receiving a patent on an invention if he earlier abandoned the invention (interpreted as, abandoning the intent to procure a patent).

7. Specification

Section 112 requires, among other things, that the patentee enable others to practice the invention and make it, describe the best mode for using the invention, and 'distinctly claim' (clearly announce) that which he regards as his property. The first two provisions, enablement and best mode, reflect the exchange-for-secrecy rationale of intellectual property law and insure that the public is able to make and use the invention in the manner that the inventor deems most efficacious. The claiming requirement protects the public domain, for it forces the inventor to set forth the metes and bounds of the invention. Only inventions precisely described by the language of the claims will be considered literally infringing; all other information within the patent document can be used by the public without authorization.[15]

C. Priority

If more than one inventor meets all the requirements for receiving a patent and applies for patent protection, the PTO will declare an interference, § 135. The priority rule of § 102(g) will determine which inventor is awarded the patent right.

The United States is considered rather unique among the nations of the world in that it awards priority to the first to invent rather than the first to file. However, the Act contains complexities that bring it somewhat closer to first-to-file than is generally recognized. First, the first to invent can, under § 102(g), be divested of priority for lack of diligence. That is, if the first to conceive the idea that underlies the invention stops working on it, and during the period of inactivity, another conceives the same idea and is then the first to make the idea work ('reduces the invention to practice'), it is the second inventor who will receive the patent. In this way, the law mainly rewards concep-

---

[15] In addition to meeting the statutory requirements for a patent and avoiding the statutory bars, there are equitable doctrines that may make the patent unenforceable. These are discussed in section III F below.

tion, but does encourage inventors to continue to engage in the activities necessary to make their inventions usable. Secondly, the first to file has a distinct advantage in a priority dispute in that the later applicant bears the difficult burden of proving that it was she who invented first. Finally, § 104 prevents an inventor from establishing a date of invention with activity that occurred outside the United States or one of the countries that is a signatory of the North American Free Trade Agreement or the TRIPS Agreement. Inventors who conducted their work in non-NAFTA, non-TRIPS countries must use the date on which they filed their applications as the date of invention.[16] Thus, for them, the priority rule effectively awards the patent to the first to file.

D. Rights

The holder of a utility patent receives the right to prevent others from making, using, offering to sell, or selling the patented invention in the United States (§ 271(a)); the right to prevent others from inducing domestic infringements (§ 271(b)); the right to prevent domestic contributory infringements (§ 271(c)); the right to prevent others from selling components for assembly of the patented invention abroad (§ 271(f)); and the right to prevent others from importing into the United States articles manufactured with a patented process (§ 271(g)). It is important to note that there are no affirmative patent rights: the patentee has no right to sell, use, or make the invention in the face of restrictive regulatory law. At the same time, however, other than paying fees to the PTO, there are no requirements for maintaining a patent, such as working the invention or licensing others to do so.

For utility patents, the duration is 20 years from the time the patent application is made, unless extended by Congress or subject to restoration provisions that compensate for the time the invention is subject to certain pre-market clearance procedures (§§ 154–156).[17]

E. Infringement

Infringement suits are within the exclusive jurisdiction of the federal courts (28 U.S.C. § 1338). There are two kinds of infringement, literal and infringe-

[16] Under the Paris Convention, this may be the date on which the inventor's home country application was filed.

[17] Prior to the United States' adherence to the TRIPS Agreement, the term of a United States patent was 17 years from the time the patent issued. Because of various transition provisions, there will be a period of time when some inventions will be protected for whichever term is longer: 17 years from issuance, or 20 years from application. Special remedies are applicable to inventions governed by this transition rule.

ment under the doctrine of equivalents. Literal infringement is determined in a two-part test. First, the claims are interpreted; secondly, the court determines whether all of the elements of the claimed invention can be found in the accused product (the 'all elements' test). In a jury-tried case, the court will interpret the claims, and the jury will determine whether the accused product infringes them.

Under the doctrine of equivalents, infringement is found when the accused product and the patented invention 'do the same work, in substantially the same way, to accomplish substantially the same result', *Graver Tank & Mfg. Co. v. Linde Air Products Co.*[18] The purpose of this doctrine is to prevent copiests from depriving the inventor of her market by making unimportant and insubstantial changes to the invention.

There is also a doctrine called the 'reverse doctrine of equivalents' which was also enunciated in *Graver Tank*, but is in the nature of a defense. Thus, 'where a device is so far changed in principle from a patented article that it performs the same or a similar function in a substantially different way, but nonetheless falls within the literal words of the claim', the infringement action fails.

F. Defenses

Because infringement is a continuing activity, there is no statute of limitations for these actions. However, damages cannot be collected on infringements that are more than 6 years old (§ 286). In addition, laches and estoppel prevent patentees who have fostered reliance interests in others from asserting their patent rights.

In the main, there are four strategies for defending against infringement. First, the validity of the patent can be challenged as not meeting the requirements discussed above. Only the claims that are successfully challenged will be stricken; if the accused device is covered by a claim that is still considered valid after the challenge, the device will be considered to infringe (§ 288).

Secondly, the defense can be made that the patent is unenforceable for inequitable conduct in the PTO. Because examination is not an adversary proceeding, courts are sensitive to the adequacy of the information the PTO receives. If it can be shown that the applicant knowingly withheld information that a reasonable examiner would have regarded as material, the patent is unenforceable in its entirety, both as to claims to which the inequity applied and as to all other claims in the patent.

---

[18] 339 U.S. 605 (1950).

Inequitable conduct outside the PTO is the third avenue for defending a patent suit. The doctrine of patent misuse renders the patent unenforceable when it is thought that the patentee is using her power over the patented product as leverage to expand her monopoly. For example, if the patentee forces a licensee to promise to pay royalties beyond the time when the patent is in force, the patent will not be enforced in its entirety until the misuse is purged (e.g., the patentee disclaims post-expiration royalties). Misuse sometimes takes the form of resale price maintenance, or tying sales of unpatented materials to sales of the patented product ('tie-ins'), or other activities that violate the antitrust laws. In such circumstances, a defendant may be able to both defend the patent infringement action on the ground of misuse, and counterclaim for treble damages under antitrust law.

Finally, the alleged infringer can claim that his activity is excused as repair or experimental use. Under the doctrine of repair, purchasers are permitted to do whatever construction is necessary to maintain their purchased embodiment, but not so much that they have essentially reconstructed the invention. Thus, for example, replacing a blade on a patented scalpel may be considered repair; reshaping the scalpel after the sterilizer melts it will be considered reconstruction. The common law doctrine of experimental use permits non-competitors to conduct pure research on the invention.[19] Under the statutory experimental use provision, competitive research on drugs and medical devices can be undertaken during the patent period if it is aimed solely at preparing submissions required by the Federal Food, Drug, and Cosmetics Act[20]. For example, testing a generic drug to determine whether it has the same effect, dose for dose, as a patented drug is permissible because the Food and Drug Administration (FDA) requires generic drug makers to demonstrate bioequivalence.

G. *Remedies*

The principal remedy sought in patent infringement actions is the injunction (§ 283). Preliminary injunctions are relatively difficult to secure as the patentee needs to prove that the injury cannot be remedied with a monetary award and that there is very little likelihood that the patent will be declared invalid. Permanent injunctions are awarded more readily. Compulsory licensing is unknown under the patent statute, and so most courts will not deny an injunction at the end of the case. However, when significant public interests are at stake, such as failure to meet a reasonable level of demand for a vital product, courts have occasionally refused to issue injunctions.

---

[19] This is an extremely limited doctrine and does not apply to inventions that are mainly intended for research use.

[20] 35 U.S.C. § 271(d).

Monetary damages are generally awarded as compensation for past infringements (§ 284). The usual measure is lost profits. However, if these are difficult to demonstrate, the court will impute a reasonable royalty or consider the defendant's illicit gain. Damages are calculated from the time the defendant receives notice of the patent. Patentees can mark their product, 'pat.' followed by the patent number to provide constructive notice. In the absence of marking, the patentee will have to demonstrate actual notice (§ 287). Interest, both pre- and post-judgment, is available.

In exceptional cases, other monetary relief is also available. Willful infringement is punished with an award of treble damages (§ 284). Contrary to general practice in lawsuits in the United States, attorneys fees are sometimes available in patent cases. However, they are awarded only when the losing party has engaged in disfavored behavior (§ 285). Finally, the patentee has the right to have infringing goods excluded at the border of the United States (19 U.S.C. § 1337) so long as there is a domestic supply of the invention or efforts toward creating that supply are under way.

H. *The Application Process*

Applying for a patent is a complicated task and is generally undertaken with the help of a lawyer or a patent agent who is admitted to practice before the PTO after the successful completion of a rigorous examination (§§ 131–135). Applications for a patent are always made in the name of the inventor, even if the patent is subject to a right of assignment and even if the invention was made on an employer's premises and therefore subject to a 'shop right' (a right in the employer to use the invention consistent with his business) (§§ 116, 261). Parties dissatisfied with the decisions of the PTO have a right to appeal to the Board of Patent Appeals and Interferences (an administrative tribunal within the PTO), and then to the federal courts (in most instances, the Court of Appeals for the Federal Circuit) (§§ 134–146). Defective patents can be reissued (§§ 251–256), and can be reexamined at the request of anyone (including the Commissioner of Patents) who believes the PTO failed to consider certain relevant material (§§ 301–307).

The significance of the application process does not end with the issuance of the patent. All documents generated during the examination become part of the patent's prosecution history (or 'file wrapper'), which is consulted whenever the patent is the subject of litigation. The information will be used to resolve ambiguities in the language of the issued claims. Furthermore, the doctrine of 'prosecution history estoppel' prevents the patentee from contradicting statements made in the course of prosecuting the application, which underscores the importance of hiring an experienced lawyer or a patent agent.

IV. Copyright Law

A. Introduction

Copyright protects what are commonly considered writings, as well as sound recordings and some technical materials such as computer programs. Copyright protection is weaker than patent protection in that only copying is actionable. Independent creation of the same product is not regarded as infringement. Copyright, however, endures for longer than patents: depending on the work, it lasts for approximately 75 years.[21] It is also much easier to acquire a copyright than a patent.

This section is mainly aimed at describing works protected under the 1976 Copyright Act, which governs works created after January 1, 1978 ('1976 Act works'). Works produced before that time were subject to the Copyright Act of 1909, and in many respects, it is the 1909 Act that determines whether such works currently enjoy copyright protection.

B. Requirements for Copyright Protection

There are four requirements for copyright: the work must be fixed in a tangible medium of expression; it must be copyrightable subject matter; it must be original; and it must be a work of 'authorship'.

1. Fixation

Under § 101,[22] works must be fixed in a tangible medium of expression under authority of the copyright owner. Fixation is a term of art: in most cases it means that the work is written down or recorded. However, even ephemeral renditions of the work on a computer can count as fixation.

2. Copyrightable subject matter

Section 102 sets out a non-exclusive list of the categories of works considered copyrightable: literary works; musical works; dramatic works; pantomimes

---

[21] The duration issue is discussed in greater detail in section VI C below.
[22] Unless otherwise noted, all statutory citations are to 17 U.S.C.

and choreographic works; pictorial; graphic; and sculptural works; motion pictures and other audiovisual works; sound recordings; and architectural works. Compilations and derivative works are also copyrightable (§ 103). Sections 102(b) and 101 make clear, however, that it is only the expression in these works that is copyrightable, not the ideas, principles, concepts, procedures, and processes expressed. Should the idea in a work fuse with the expression—that is, should there be only a limited number of ways to express a particular idea—then the doctrine of 'merger' will bar copyright in both the idea and the expression. A similar merger doctrine applies to facts, which are regarded as part of the public domain and therefore not suitable for copyright protection.

The line between idea and expression (or fact and expression) is often a difficult one to draw. For example, although the Act expressly protects computer programs (§§ 101, 117), courts have struggled to find a way to define the scope of protection in a manner that puts the programming ideas into the public domain. Similarly, stock literary figures (for example, the hard-boiled detective); standard plotlines (e.g. boy loves girl, angers family, and dies); and stock literary devices ('*scenes à faire*', such as using a diary to initiate a flashback) are considered ideas, facts, or in the public domain and are not copyrightable.

3. Originality

Originality means only that the work is created by the author. There is no requirement that a work be novel in the patent law sense. Thus, if two people paint the same tree, and each paints it absolutely accurately, each is entitled to copyright his work. Two copyrights in two identical works would then subsist.

4. Authorship

To qualify for copyright protection, a work does need to include some spark of creativity or individuality, which is sometimes referred to as 'authorship'. (Confusingly, some courts call this 'originality'). Imaginative works, such as novels and songs, rarely encounter a challenge on this ground. However, factual works, such as databases and histories, and works constrained by physical requirements, such as architecture and computer programs, do sometimes raise authorship concerns. Even if such works are found copyrightable, the copyright will be considered 'thin'. Very similar works will often escape infringement on the ground that only public domain materials (the facts in the database, for example) were taken, or because the similarity was due to the fact that both authors were guided by the same restrictions. (Thus, the two paintings in the tree example would not be considered to infringe each other even though they are identical).

C. Duration

The duration of copyright depends on a number of factors. For works created after January 1, 1978 by identified individuals, the basic rights subsist for the life of the author (or in the case of joint works, the longest living author) plus 50 years (§ 302). However, those rights that derive from quality-control and dignity interests, such as the author's right to have her name attached to works she created, or removed from works she did not create ('rights of attribution'), as well as the author's right to prevent the mutilation of her work ('rights of integrity'), subsist for only the life of the author (§ 106A). For anonymous and pseudonymous works, as well as for works made in the course of employment ('works made for hire'), the basic term is 75 years from the date of publication or 100 years from the date of creation, whichever expires first (§ 302).

As noted above, works created prior to the effective date of the 1976 Copyright Act were initially protected under a different regime. They received an initial term of 28 years' protection with the right to renew for an additional 28 years. While Congress was pondering the longer term provided for in the bill that led to the 1976 Act, it was considered unfair to allow subsisting copyrights to expire. Congress therefore extended the term of protection for these works in a series of interim measures, culminating in a complicated provision in the 1976 Act which has the effect of giving all works in which copyright subsisted on January 1, 1978, a term of 75 years of protection (§ 304). Furthermore, works that were fixed tangibly, but not published by that date, were brought into the federal system. State common law copyright had given such works perpetual protection. However, Congress is constitutionally obligated to limit the term of copyrights. Under the 1976 Act, such works are to be protected for the same term as works created after January 1, 1978, except that if such a work is published before December 31, 2002, it will remain copyrighted until at least December 31, 2027 (§ 303).

In addition to considering the term of protection, those utilizing copyrighted works must keep the termination provisions in mind. These provisions—§§ 203 (for 1976 Act works) and 304 (for 1909 Act works)—provide a window of opportunity, opening roughly 35 years after publication, to copyright holders and their heirs to terminate any licensing arrangements granted by the author. The purpose is to provide an author whose work has increased in value with an opportunity to capture some of the increase. Termination means that no new works can be prepared under the terminated license; works created while the license was in effect can continue to be used in accordance with the terms of the original grant. For example, consider a playwright who licenses a film producer to utilize her play. The producer can exploit any film produced during the term of the license, so long as he obeys the terms of the agreement. Even after termination, the original film can be exploited under the license terms. However, after termination, the producer cannot do a remake without entering into new negotiations with the playwright.

D. Rights

Sections 106 and 106A set out the rights in copyrighted works. Once again, the statute differentiates among works. Thus, all authors enjoy exclusive rights to reproduce their works, prepare derivative works, and distribute copies of their works. Authors of literary, musical, dramatic, choreographic works, pantomimes, and audiovisual works also have the exclusive right to perform their works, while authors of literary, musical, dramatic, choreographic works, pantomimes, pictures, and sculptures have exclusive display rights; authors of certain works of visual art have rights of attribution and integrity. In addition, the Supreme Court has, through analogy to patent law, held that authors can sue those who contributorily infringe these rights.

Despite their seemingly broad scope, these rights are rather limited. First, the categories are strictly construed. There is, for example, no performance right in a sound recording. That is, although unauthorized *sale* of, say, a *Two Live Crew* CD will infringe the music copyright owned by the composer, as well as the sound recording copyrights owned by the performers and their producers, *playing* the CD in public will infringe only the composer's copyright. Congress did not choose to give performers and producers of sound recordings the right to prevent others from playing lawfully purchased copies in public, even though it did wish composers to have this right. Similarly, rights stemming from justifications other than profit-incentive (such as the right to prevent mutilation) are limited to those works where quality and dignity interests are especially salient.

Secondly, each of these rights is limited by §§ 108–120, which create a series of royalty-free and compulsory licenses that bring down the cost of certain favored usages. For example, library archiving, classroom performances, and transmissions to the handicapped are exempted from infringement. Retransmissions of broadcast signals by cable companies, secondary transmissions by satellites, and performances of musical works that have been recorded are subject to complex compulsory licensing schemes. With certain exceptions, the first sale of a copy of a copyrighted work exhausts the copyright holder's interest in that copy. Thus, for example, one who purchases a copy of a novel can resell it without the copyright holder's permission because the Act gives the copyright holder rights in only the initial transaction.

Most significant to copyright holders, however, is the open-ended limitation of § 107, the fair use provision. Enacted in part to safeguard First Amendment interests in free speech, in part to keep down the costs of transacting copyright licenses, and in part to correct for market failures, the fair use provision permits certain unauthorized uses. Four factors determine which uses are entitled to fair use protection.

First is the purpose and character of the use. In general, it is easiest to make out a claim for fair use if the use is non-commercial and for such purposes as news reporting, teaching, scholarship, and research. The idea here is that these are important activities aimed at expanding the knowledge base. If no profit is earned, the user will not have funds to pay the copyright holder for permission. Rather than require the public to forgo the use, the statute permits unauthorized use. However, sometimes even commercial uses have an important public purpose, such as social commentary. In such cases—one example is a song parody—the court may find fair use, if the other factors favor such a finding.

The second factor is the nature of the copyrighted work. Works in which copyright is thin—factual works such as histories are examples—are more likely to be considered fair-used than other works because of the importance of assuring public access to that part of the work that is not suitable for copyright protection. Some courts also look to the way in which the copyright holder utilized the work. The more secret she kept it, the less likely the court is to find unauthorized public utilization fair.

The third and fourth factors, the amount and substantiality of the portion used and its effect on the market, deal with economic considerations. Although the public may enjoy a significant public benefit from free utilization of a work, the profit-incentive justification for copyright law would be undermined if this utilization deprived authors of the economic motivation to continue to produce. For example, although education is a prime fair-use purpose, the right to fair-use high school textbooks would soon end the practice of publishing them. Thus, the more clear it is that a copyright holder is losing a significant market, the less likely a court will be willing to find fair use.

E. Infringement

Infringement actions are in the exclusive authority of the federal courts (28 U.S.C. § 1338). Since copyrights are infringed through copying (§ 501), a copyright holder must in theory show that the defendant copied his work. However, most infringers operate in secret. Consequently, courts infer copying from a showing of access and substantial similarity. The substantiality of the similarity is also relevant to the question whether the copying was extensive enough to cause injury. Traditionally, expert witness testimony is admissible on the question of copying, but not on the question of whether the copying was substantial enough to injure the copyright holder. There, the real issue is whether the lay audience, thinking the works are the same, will purchase from the infringer rather than the copyright holder. Thus, only lay impressions matter. However, courts have been increasingly willing to admit expert testimony in the case of technologically complex material, such as computer programs.

The most difficult infringement cases are those involving 'thin' copyrights: factual works and works constrained by physical requirements. In these cases, courts generally employ a filtration method to remove from consideration ideas, public domain materials, and any expression that has merged with ideas or facts. It is only after filtration that such works are compared. In many cases, the outcome is a finding of no infringement, with the result that these works can, in effect, by copied with impunity. The Supreme Court has considered the problem of under-rewarding the authors of such works, but has decided that copyright is not intended to protect the 'sweating brow', that is, works that require labor but not creativity.

F. Defenses

Section 507(b) requires that civil actions be commenced within three years of the accrual of the claim. Laches and estoppel also limit rights of action. Although the doctrine of copyright misuse is not as advanced as the analogous patent misuse doctrine, there have been cases where copyright holders have been unable to pursue claims because they were using their copyrights to restrain others improperly.

The main strategy for defending against copyright actions is reliance on §§ 107–120. Some courts call these provisions defenses to infringement; others call them limitations on copyright. But in either event, success under them results in no liability or liability capped by the compulsory license fee.

Copyright actions can also be defended by challenging the validity of the copyright. In addition, defendants sometimes claim that their free speech rights under the First Amendment are violated if they cannot utilize a copyrighted work. In the main, this claim is not successful because the fair use provision of § 107 is thought to reconcile copyright and First Amendment values. However, there are instances where the concern for free speech leads a court to deny injunctive relief and requires the copyright holder to accept monetary compensation. Additional protection is afforded by the limits the Act places on the damages that can be awarded against certain favored users, such as publishers, librarians, and educators.[23]

G. Remedies

The principal remedy is the injunction, with both preliminary and permanent injunctions readily available (§ 502) along with orders to impound and destroy infringing articles (§ 503), and the equipment with which they were manufactured (§ 509). Monetary damages include the amount necessary to compensate for actual injuries and the infringer's profits (double counting is not permitted) (§ 504). When it is difficult to evaluate injury and profit, the copyright holder can request statutory damages, which can reach $100,000 per work for willful infringement. The court has discretion to award the winning party in copyright litigation (be it plaintiff *or* defendant) costs and attorneys' fees (§ 505).

Copyright owners can also have infringing goods excluded at the borders of the United States (§§ 602–603). In extreme cases, there are criminal sanctions for certain kinds of copyright infringement (§ 506; 18 U.S.C. §§ 2318–2319).

H. The Application Process

For 1976 Act works, there is no required application process: as soon as a work is fixed in a tangible medium of expression under authority of its creator, copyright attaches (§ 102(a)). But even though there are no required formalities, it is recommended that works be registered with the Copyright Office; that copies of the work be deposited with the Library of Congress; and that works be marked with the name of the copyright owner, the date of first publication, and a (P) or a (C) for sound recordings or other works, respectively (§§ 401–407). Complying with these requirements is

---

[23] See, e.g. § 504(c).

advantageous in infringement actions as they create a presumption of copyrightability, establish defendant's notice of copyright, and are sometimes prerequisites to relief (§§ 408–412).

Registration is, in general, a simple affair (§ 409). It is made in the name of the 'author', which has a somewhat technical meaning under the statute in that an employer is considered the author of works prepared in the course of employment or pursuant to a signed writing establishing employer-authorship (§ 201(b)) ('works for hire').[24] The Copyright Office furnishes registration kits easily understood by laymen (§ 707). Thus, legal advice is usually not needed to perfect copyright protection. Should registration be denied (a rare occurrence), an action against the Register lies in federal court.

It is important to understand that this regime marks a substantial change from the 1909 Act. Under that statute, works that were not published were 'copyrighted' if at all, under state law (so-called 'common law copyright'). At publication, state rights ended and federal protection became available if, and only if, the author complied with strict registration, deposit, and notice requirements. In addition, until July 1, 1986, works published in English had to be manufactured in the United States or Canada (§ 601). Failure to comply with these requirements divested the work of copyright. Thus, some 1909 Act works may ostensibly be copyrighted. If, however, the issue of copyright becomes important, the facts surrounding publication must be investigated with care. Except as to manufacture, this is never necessary for 1976 Act works.[25]

V. Trademark Law

A. *Introduction*

Trademark law protects the goodwill that merchants invest in their products by creating exclusive rights in the markings that purchasers use to identify the goods they wish to buy. To maintain an unambiguous avenue of communication between supplier and purchaser, no two trademarks can be so similar

[24] Works made for hire are subject to special treatment by the Act. The term of protection is 75 years from the date of publication or 100 years from the date of creation, whichever expires first (§ 302); there are no rights of attribution and integrity for such works (§ 106A); nor are they subject to termination (§ 203). The film industry is largely responsible for this special treatment. It was concerned that, if those who contributed to the production of a film were given the rights normally associated with writings, films would not be fully exploitable as every 'author' could veto exploitation decisions made by the others.

[25] To complicate matters further, the North American Free Trade Agreement and the TRIPS Agreement require the United States to create new copyright protection for certain foreign 1909 Act works that fell into the public domain.

that members of the public will be confused. Thus, the standard for determining infringement is consumer confusion, and not copying or use. Trademarks endure for the time in which they are being used to denote a particular source and quality.

B. Requirements for Trademark Protection

There are five requirements for trademark registration: proper subject matter; use; use in commerce; distinctiveness; and non-functionality.

1. Subject matter of trademarks

Only words and symbols used to denote source or origin are protectable. They must be registered in connection with specific goods ('trademarks') (§ 1052);[26] services ('service marks') (§ 1053); as designation of membership in specific organizations ('collective marks') (§ 1054); or achievement of particular established standards ('certification marks') (§ 1054). There are no rights in words or symbols standing alone ('in gross'). Goods can, however, have more than one registrable mark. For example, it is not uncommon to protect a word associated with a product, as well as its configuration and the packaging in which it is sold.

2. Use and use in commerce

Use and use in commerce are two distinct requirements, although they often occur together. A trademark can be established through its use on goods sold only in a single state. However, because federal trademark law is based on a restrictive reading of Congress's Commerce Clause powers, to be federally registrable, a mark must be used on goods involved in at least one interstate transaction.

Marks established in countries other than the United States are treated differently in this regard. Because the United States can enact domestic legislation to conform to treaties it has entered, the United States' ability to protect foreign trademarks is not limited by the Commerce Clause. Under the Paris Convention, any mark that is recognized in a signatory country is subject to federal registration immediately (if other requirements are substantially met), even if no use was required in the home country (§ 1126).

This has caused substantial difficulties for Americans. There are several

---

[26] Unless otherwise noted, all citations are to 15 U.S.C.

cases in which an American who used a mark first lost his rights to a foreign trademark holder who had never used the mark, but had qualified for registration abroad. To put Americans on an even footing with foreigners, the Lanham Act now permits registrants to establish a priority date by filing an 'intent to use' application (§ 1051(b)). Use in commerce must begin within 6 months (§ 1051(d)), at which time the mark is registered.[27]

3. Distinctiveness

Because trademark law is intended to protect investments in goodwill by providing sellers with a means to communicate with consumers, marks must be distinctive. A mark cannot function unambiguously to indicate the source or origins of a particular good if it is confusingly similar to a mark already in use on like goods. Nor can it so function if it is just a description, accurate or otherwise, of the goods or services for which registration is sought. Section 1052 therefore prohibits registration of such marks, as well as marks that are scandalous or immoral; that spuriously suggest connections with people, places, or institutions; or that are deceptive. Pursuant to the TRIPS Agreement, § 1052 was recently amended to prohibit the use of certain geographic misdescriptions, especially in connection with wines and spirits. For purposes of these provisions, marks in foreign languages are usually translated into English.

In implementing § 1052, the PTO and courts have divided marks into four classifications: coined, suggestive, descriptive, and generic. Coined words, such as EXXON for petroleum products, and suggestive marks, such as CHEERIO for a cute o-shaped oat cereal, are immediately registrable. Since these words had no real former meaning, they cannot run afoul of § 1052. In contrast, generic marks, such as 'Noodles' for noodles, can never be registered because every seller of the product needs to be able to use the same word.

Descriptive marks, such as International Business Machines for business equipment in world wide use, fall between these other categories. Although they are not needed by every seller, their immediate association is with contents rather than source or origin. However, if over time, consumers begin to associate the mark with the trademark holder—that is, the mark develops 'secondary meaning'—it will be accepted for federal registration. For instance, most consumers actually associate the words 'International Business Machines' with a particular company (IBM). It is for that reason that these words are federally registrable.

---

[27] The statute does provide for extensions on this time limit in certain circumstances.

The PTO maintains a supplemental register for words that are capable of acquiring secondary meaning. The supplemental register does not create the same federal rights as the principal register on which federal trademarks are maintained, but it does provide documentation that these marks are in use. A presumption of secondary meaning arises after 5 years, at which time the mark can be transferred to the principal register (§ 1052(f)). This procedure can also be used to correct certain other defects, such as non-geographic misdescriptions, if they are not actually deceptive.

4. Non-functionality

Shapes, colors, and numbers are all eligible for registration as trademarks, subject to the doctrine of functionality. Thus, if a shape or a color has unique value to a product, it will not be registrable as a mark for the product on the theory that the trademark would, in effect, create a patent-like right. Some courts also rely on a doctrine of aesthetic functionality to prevent trademark law from creating rights in popular design features.

C. Duration

Trademarks endure for as long as there is continuing use. Section 1058 requires periodic filings of affidavits of continuing use; § 1059 requires periodic renewals. Trademarks can be sold or assigned (§ 1060). However, rights will terminate upon naked assignment or sale—that is, alienation without an agreement that insures continuing quality. The justification is that trademarks are protected, in large part, on the quality-control principle. Thus, it is only because—and when—marks convey a consistent message to consumers that trademark rights are legally cognizable.

D. Rights

The Lanham Act creates three types of rights. First, registration on the principal register establishes constructive notice of use, giving the registrant the ability to prevent anyone from adopting similar marks for similar goods (§ 1115). Secondly, after 5 years on the principal register, a trademark becomes incontestable: some of the defects that would have prevented the initial registration or would have supported cancellation can no longer be asserted.

Curiously, the third right to prevent consumer confusion (§ 1114) is, in a sense, extended to all trademark holders, whether their marks are federally registered or not. Under § 1125 of the statute (Section 43(a) of the Lanham Act), any person who uses a mark in a manner that is likely to cause confusion, to misrepresent a product, or to falsely suggest an association between a product and a manufacturer, is liable to the holder of the mark for damages. In the main, challenges to comparative advertising are brought under this provision. Since the Act makes only misstatements actionable, true comparative ads are not considered violations of trademark law unless they in fact mislead consumers.

E. Infringement

Infringement actions are within the exclusive jurisdiction of the federal courts. Actions under state law arising from the same conduct can be asserted as supplemental claims (§ 1114; 28 U.S.C. §§ 1338, 1367). Marks do not have to be identical to be considered infringing. Rather, the standard is the *likelihood* of confusion, and courts will consider both the way the mark sounds and its visual impact. Nor do the marks have to be used on identical products. If the trademark holder can show that consumers will believe the trademark holder likely to make the leap from selling the goods or services for which the mark is registered to the goods or services for which the mark is used, infringement will be found. Similarly, although the trademark holder cannot bring an infringement action in a geographic area where he is not using the mark, an action will lie if it is likely that consumers will nonetheless be confused.

The 'likelihood' standard is also used in Section 43(a) claims. Thus, even if a statement about trademarked goods is accurate, it will be actionable if there is a likelihood that consumers will misunderstand it.

F. Defenses

The Lanham Act does not contain a statute of limitations, although it does make laches and estoppel available as defenses (§ 1115(b)(8)). To determine the timeliness of a trademark infringement suit, a federal court will look to the law of the state in which the action is brought, and use the statute of limitations for analogous causes of action.

Registration on the principal register is prima facie evidence of validity, and, as noted above, 5 years' registration makes the mark incontestable in some respects. However, infringement actions can be defended on the ground that the mark was procured by fraud; that it is being used deceptively;

that it has been abandoned or subject to a naked assignment; or that it is being used to violate the antitrust laws. In addition, it can be argued that, through use, the mark has become the generic word for the product (§ 1115). Examples of marks lost through 'genericide' include aspirin, cellophane, and thermos.[28]

The Act and the courts are also concerned that trademark rights not interfere with free speech values in violation of the First Amendment. Section 1114 creates a category of innocent infringers, such as newspaper publishers, who cannot be sued for monetary damages. Even injunctive relief is limited so that deliveries of such writings as newspapers are not delayed. Section 1115(b)(4) sets up a kind of fair use defense allowing an individual to use his own name, even if the name is a protected mark. (For example, a restauranteur named McDonald can use his name, but not McDonald's other trademarks, in connection with his services.) This provision also permits marks to be used in their natural meanings, to describe goods, services, and geographic origin ('Juicy Fruit' is registered for candy, but can be used nonetheless to describe oranges). Courts sometimes entertain First Amendment defenses, but usually manage to avoid a conflict between First Amendment and trademark law by finding that the mark in question is not being used in a manner likely to confuse consumers. Parodies are an example: courts often find that the consumers 'got the joke', and so are not confused into thinking the owner of the registered trademark is the source of the parody.

G. Remedies

As in other areas, the usual remedy is the injunction (§ 1116), although rights are limited with respect to innocent infringers. Trademark holders can have infringing articles and the means for making them destroyed (§ 1118), and can also recover the costs of the action as well as damages and defendant's profits (no double counting) (§ 1117). These monetary awards run from the time of actual notice unless the trademark is displayed with the words, 'Registered in the U.S. Patent and Trademark Office', or the symbol (R) (§ 1111). When damages are difficult to prove, the court has discretion to enter an award for the amount it considers just, and may, in exceptional cases, award attorneys' fees (§ 1117). Some cases of willful infringement are considered a crime—trafficking in counterfeit goods, 18 U.S.C. (§ 2320), which is punishable by fines, imprisonment, and in a civil action for treble damages

---

[28] To avoid genericide defenses, trademark holders are wise to use the word 'brand' after their mark and to provide consumers with another word for their product. Johnson & Johnson, for example, has popularized phrases like 'adhesive bandage' to avoid losing the trademark 'bandaid'. Similarly, when the word 'sanka' became popular, labels were changed to read 'Sanka brand decaffeinated coffee'.

(§§ 1116(d), 1117(b)). Goods bearing infringing marks can, in some instances, be excluded at the border (§ 1124).

H. The Application Process

Trademarks are administered by the PTO, which maintains a separate trademark division, including an agency court, the Trademark Trial and Appeal Board, to hear appeals from the decisions of examiners (§ 1070). Appeals from the Board are generally to the Court of Appeals to the Federal Circuit, although actions against the Commissioner of Trademarks can be instituted in federal district court (§ 1071).

Applications for trademarks, which are made in the name of the trademark owner, are relatively straightforward to execute, although the assistance of an experienced trademark lawyer is advised. The verified application contains a drawing of the mark; a description of the goods on which the mark is to be used; the date of the applicant's first use of the mark on these goods; affirmation that the mark is used in commerce; and affirmation that to the best of the applicant's knowledge, there is no one else with prior right to use the mark in a way that will confuse consumers (§ 1051).

The fact that the application focuses only on the applicant's knowledge of prior users does not mean that a rigorous search for prior users is unnecessary. Federal registration creates only constructive notice to future users of a superior right in the registrant; it does not create a national right to a trademark. That is, it does not create a right to prevent those who used a mark before it was registered from continuing in their use (§ 1115(b)(5)). Since the registered owner will not be allowed to confuse consumers, she will be barred from using the mark in the geographic area of the prior user. Thus, failure to fully investigate may result in investment in a mark that can never be utilized throughout the United States.

The application process is generally *ex parte*, although the statute does provide for a right to oppose registration (§ 1063). The public interest in being free of unregistrable marks is, however, more often vindicated through cancellation proceedings (§ 1064). In addition, invalidity can sometimes be asserted as a defense to infringement (§ 1115). If two parties apply to register the same mark, an interference will be declared (§ 1066). In the wholly domestic context, the first to use the mark in commerce is entitled to priority. The Commissioner can, however, register both marks concurrently. Concurrent registrations place geographic or product limits on each usage so that consumers are protected from confusion (§§ 1068, 1051).

20

LABOR AND EMPLOYMENT LAW

SAMUEL ESTREICHER

I. Rationales for and Structure of Employment Regulation[1]

As a generalization—and certainly in comparison to the laws of other industrialized nations—the employment relationship is not pervasively regulated
in the United States, even to this day. Absent a specific statute or express contract, employment in the United States is considered 'at will'; both the
employee and employer are free to terminate the relationship with or without cause. The theory behind the 'at will' rule is that reliance on market
forces will best serve the joint interests of employers and workers.
Employers, it is argued, face lower costs in hiring workers because they can
easily terminate the relationship if it proves unsatisfactory. Workers also
benefit from a system which allows them to quit at any time. An unfair
employer will not succeed in retaining able workers and will have trouble
recruiting new ones. Such an employer also must deal with the threat that
workers dissatisfied with their conditions will form trade unions. (As discussed in section IV below, United States law protects the rights of workers

[1] This chapter deals primarily with labor and employment law issues affecting employees in private
firms. Although many of the laws discussed here also affect employees in the public sector, other bodies
of law beyond the scope of this chapter—such as the Constitution, civil service systems and public-sector
labor relations statutes—play an even more important role in the work lives of government workers.

to form independent trade unions and engage in collective bargaining with their employers.)

Over the course of the twentieth century, however, public policy in the United States has shifted in favor of a system that mixes reliance on market forces with regulation. Three rationales are often offered for government intervention. The first is a concern that contracts formed between employers and individual workers will systematically favor employers because of the limited bargaining power of workers. Under this view, workers often will endure long hours, unsafe conditions, and poor pay because they are dependent on employers for their livelihood, and are not able easily to move to seek opportunities elsewhere. Indeed, for unskilled workers, there may be few such alternative opportunities. Regulation is thought to be needed *to correct this imbalance of bargaining power* by protecting the right of workers to form unions and engage in collective bargaining, and by writing minimum terms into every employment contract, such as minimum wages, maximum hours of work, limits on the use of child labor, and guarantees of safe and sanitary workplaces.

A second rationale for regulation is that society can properly insist that employment take place only in conformity with *evolving social norms of fair conditions*. This justification would also apply to maximum hours, child labor, and occupational safety laws. Rules barring discrimination on account of race, religion, sex, age or handicap can also be viewed as an expression of social value judgments about the permissible grounds for evaluating human beings.

Another formulation of this argument for regulation is that the law may be seeking to alter the values or preferences of workers and firms. For example, occupational safety laws may encourage workers to change their expectations of the proper trade-off between wages and safe conditions—expectations which form a new baseline for employment contracts. Similarly, the discrimination laws have forced employers to re-evaluate early assessments of the costs of hiring black and female workers because anticipated adverse reactions of customers or co-workers did not materialize.

A third justification for regulation is *to correct deficiencies in the operation of labor markets*. Under this view, labor markets are not perfectly competitive, and some forms of regulation may actually improve efficiency in labor markets. Unemployment insurance and adjustment assistance laws require employers to absorb some of the costs of their termination decisions; in the absence of such laws, these costs would be imposed on society. The mobility of workers, and hence their ability to pursue market options, can be enhanced by laws making pensions and other benefits transferable with them to their new jobs, rather than dependent on continued service with the same employer. Collective bargaining laws can also be viewed as a mechanism for producing 'collective goods', such as grievance systems; in individual bargains, such terms may be omitted because the costs to the firm of such systems (which cannot be confined to individual workers) may be greater than the benefits to the individual worker. However, such a system may be something the workers collectively would seek if they could bargain on a collective basis.

However, regulation is not costless. There are the costs of administering the scheme (including the risk that fear of liability may discourage employers from making socially desirable judgments). Moreover, employers will attempt to shift the costs of regulations to workers, in the form of lower wages or smaller wage increases. To the extent such cost-shifting occurs, and mandatory minimum terms do not capture well what workers want, these workers may be worse off than they would be in the absence of regulation. Even when such laws benefit those who have jobs, they may create disincentives to hire additional workers. Imposing excess costs on employers may also affect the competitiveness of American products and services in world markets.

This chapter examines three dimensions of the labor and employment law system in the United States:

(1) employment law (or what in many other countries is called individual labor law);
(2) discrimination law; and
(3) collective bargaining and union organization law.

Regulations in the first two categories apply to all workers; regulations in the third category affect principally workers who have chosen, or are seeking, to be represented by unions. Historically, the American labor movement distrusted state intervention and preferred self-help through union organization and collective bargaining to promote the welfare of workers. This preference was reflected in a labor and employment law that emphasized protections for collective bargaining over mandatory minimum terms of employment. However, with the decline of union organization in private firms from a high point of 35 percent of private workers in 1954 to under 12 percent today, and the rise of civil rights movements challenging racial and other forms of discrimination, legal intervention increasingly takes the form of expansions of employment law and discrimination law.

Regulation of the employment relationship in the United States is divided between the federal government and the states. The federal government's authority to regulate the behavior of private parties is limited to matters affecting interstate commerce. Since 1937, however, Congress' power to legislate under the Commerce Clause of the Constitution has received an expansive reading so that Congress could, if it chose to do so, regulate virtually every aspect of the employment relationship in the United States. Several federal statutes affect employment, including:

(1)   the National Labor Relations Act of 1935 (NLRA),[2] which governs the rights of workers to form unions and engage in collective bargaining;

(2)   the Fair Labor Standards Act of 1938 (FLSA),[3] which regulates minimum wages, overtime pay and child labor;

(3)   the Employee Retirement Income Security Act of 1974 (ERISA),[4] which imposes minimum funding levels, fiduciary operating standards, and reporting requirements for employee pension benefit plans seeking favorable treatment under the tax laws;

(4)   the Occupational Safety and Health Act of 1970 (OSHA),[5] which provides for a 'general duty' to maintain safe conditions and authorizes the Department of Labor to impose minimum safety and health standards;

(5)   Title VII of the Civil Rights Act of 1964,[6] which prohibits discrimination in employment decisions on account of race, color, religion, national origin, and sex;

(6)   the Age Discrimination in Employment Act of 1967 (ADEA),[7] which prohibits discrimination in employment decisions on account of age;

(7)   the Americans with Disabilities Act of 1990 (ADA),[8] which, among other things, prohibits discrimination in employment decisions on account of disability;

(8)   the Worker Adjustment and Retraining Notification Act of 1988 (WARN),[9] which requires 60 days' advance notice of plant closings and mass lay-offs; and

(9)   the Family and Medical Leave Act of 1993 (FMLA),[10] which requires employers to provide job-protected unpaid leaves of absences for certain family and medical reasons.

Because Congress has regulated only in certain defined areas, the states play a very important role in filling out the terms of the employment relationship. States administer the unemployment insurance and workers' compensation systems; maintain their own safety, minimum wage, overtime, and maximum hours rules; and set the terms for hiring and firing workers. Even where Congress has legislated in the area, with the exception of a few laws like the NLRA and ERISA, which broadly preempt all state laws affecting similar subject matter, most federal statutes allow the states to enact laws that are more protective of workers than the federal law.

---

[2] 29 U.S.C. § 151 et seq.   [3] 29 U.S.C. §§ 201–219.
[4] This statute is codified in various places in the Internal Revenue Code and at 29 U.S.C. § 1001 et seq.
[5] 29 U.S.C. § 651 et seq.   [6] 42 U.S.C. § 2000e et seq.   [7] 29 U.S.C. § 621 et seq.
[8] 42 U.S.C. § 12101 et seq.   [9] 29 U.S.C. §§ 2101–2109.
[10] 29 U.S.C. §§ 2601–2654.

II. Substantive Employment Protections

A. Job Security

As discussed above, employment in the United States continues to be based on the 'at will' principle. Absent a specific contract or statute restricting terminations, employers can fire workers without notice or justification, and workers are free to quit at any time. Accordingly, neither the federal government nor the states (with the exception of Montana[11]) have enacted general laws limiting the situations in which a worker can be discharged. In the public sector, civil service laws and constitutional due process standards require a hearing before discharge and a substantive showing of misconduct or unsatisfactory performance.[12] But for private firms, the principle of 'just cause' applies only where a union is recognized and a collective bargaining contract (which typically contains such protection) is in place.

However, despite the formal adherence to the employment 'at will' doctrine, the courts of many of the states have recognized important limitations on the power of employers to discharge employees. The majority of the states will require employers to adhere to the procedures and policies contained in their application forms and employee or personnel manuals.[13] Employers are free to alter or abandon such rules prospectively,[14] but have to take into account adverse effects on employee morale as well as the threat of unionization. An employee who is discharged in violation of such procedures or policies can bring a lawsuit for past and future earnings losses; reinstatement and other damages are normally not available remedies.

In addition, an ever-increasing number of states recognize a tort action for terminations that are in violation of 'public policy'. Thus, an employer can be sued, for example, if it discharges an employee because the employee indicates his/her availability for jury duty,[15] refuses to commit perjury,[16] or declines to act in violation of certain professional standards.[17] A number of states have also enacted statutes that protect 'whistleblowers', who report violations of laws by their employers, from retaliatory discharge.[18]

[11] Montana Wrongful Discharge from Employment Act, Mont. Code Ann. §§ 39–2–901 to –914 (1987).

[12] See, e.g. Civil Service Reform Act of 1978, as amended, codified in various sections of 5 U.S.C.; N.Y. Civ. Serv. Law §§ 75–76 (McKinney 1983 and Supp. 1995).

[13] See, e.g. *Woolley v. Hoffman-La Roche, Inc.*, 99 N.J. 284, 491 A.2d 1257 (1985); *Toussaint v. Blue Cross and Blue Shield of Michigan*, 408 Mich. 579, 292 N.W.2d 880 (1980).

[14] See, e.g. *Bankey v. Storer Broadcasting Co.*, 432 Mich. 438, 443 N.W.2d 112 (1989) (*en banc*).

[15] See *Nees v. Hocks*, 272 Or. 210, 536 P.2d 512 (1975).

[16] See *Tameny v. Atlantic Richfield Co.*, 27 Cal.3d 167, 164 Cal.Rptr. 839, 610 P.2d 1330 (1980).

[17] See *Pierce v. Ortho Pharmaceutical Corp.*, 84 N.J. 58, 417 A.2d 505 (1980).

[18] See, e.g. Cal. Lab. Code § 1102.5 (West 1989); Mich. Comp. Laws Ann. §§ 15.361–15.369 (West 1994); N.J. Stat. Ann. § 34:19–1 et seq. (West 1988); N.Y. Lab. Law, § 740 (McKinney 1988); Pa. Stat. Ann. tit. 43, § 1421 et seq. (1991). Some federal health and safety laws also contain 'whistleblower' protections.

Employers face other sources of liability for wrongful termination. Many states allow an employee who has difficulty obtaining new employment to sue his/her former employer for defamation because of dissemination of an erroneous discharge that affects the employee's reputation.[19] Moreover, for individuals covered by federal and state discrimination laws—e.g. all employees over the age of 40 are within the protected class of federal age discrimination law—the absence of a persuasive justification for a discharge may give rise to a finding of discrimination.

Thus, unlike the situation in Western Europe and Japan, the United States does not nominally provide for generalized protection against wrongful termination. As a practical matter, however, the various exceptions to the 'at will' doctrine place employers at a significant risk of liability for discharges not based on some valid reason. Typically, these actions are tried before juries, and liability can be quite open-ended and unpredictable.[20]

B. Unemployment

Unlike the situation in Western Europe, there are no 'redundancy' laws in the United States. Employees covered by collective bargaining contracts typically are protected by a seniority principle that requires lay-offs to occur in reverse order of length of service; very few labor agreements prohibit lay-offs outright. In 1988, Congress passed the WARN statute which requires 60 days' advance notice of plant closings and mass lay-offs. The theory of the statute is that advance notice will help affected workers (and communities) to adjust to the dislocations resulting from such decisions. The statute applies to businesses with at least 100 employees, and requires advance notice of any facility shutdown causing at least 50 employees to lose their jobs within a 30-day period; a 'mass layoff' occurs when, at a single site, either 500 employees or 50 employees representing at least 33 percent of the work force are terminated or laid-off within a 30-day period.

The WARN law does not require payment of severance to workers who are laid-off or terminated for economic reasons. Although a few states mandate severance pay on account of plant closings,[21] this is generally a matter governed by contract. Where an entitlement to termination pay is based on a unilateral employer policy, businesses have substantial latitude to modify or eliminate such entitlements prospectively.

[19] See, e.g. *Lewis* v. *Equitable Life Assurance Soc'y*, 389 N.W.2d 876 (Minn. 1986).

[20] See generally Samuel Estreicher, 'Unjust Dismissal Laws: Some Cautionary Notes', 33 *Am.J.Comp.L.* 310 (1985); James N. Dertouzos and Lynn A. Karoly, *Labor-Market Responses to Employer Liability* (Rand Instit. 1992).

[21] See, e.g. *Fort Halifax Packing Co.* v. *Coyne*, 482 U.S. 1 (1987) (upholding Me. Rev. Stat. Ann. Tit. 26, § 625–B, against a challenge based on ERISA and NLRA preemptions).

Unemployment insurance is funded through a payroll tax under a cooperative arrangement between the federal and state governments. Employees who voluntarily quit or who are terminated because of 'misconduct' are not entitled to unemployment benefits. By European standards, benefits are modest (up to one-half of pay) and normally expire after 26 weeks. During periods of economic distress, Congress has passed emergency legislation extending the benefit period. Also, employees suffering trade-related job loss may be entitled to extended unemployment benefits and training assistance.

C. Benefits

As a general matter, the United States does not mandate provision of employee benefits. Other than modest social security payments for retirees and disabled workers (funded by a payroll tax) and the minimum wage, maximum hour, and overtime protections provided by the FLSA and state laws, benefits are a matter of contract. Most private employers, whether unionized or not, do provide a fairly extensive array of benefits, the most important of which are pensions and health insurance. Tax laws favor employer provision of such benefits by allowing employers to deduct their cost and employees to receive them on a tax-free or tax-deferred basis. Under federal ERISA legislation, employee pension benefits become 'vested' after 5 years and thus cannot be forfeited even with change of employment; the statute also contains disclosure and minimum-funding requirements and imposes fiduciary standards on administrators and advisers handling employee pension funds. Other benefits, such as medical insurance, severance pay and the like, are not subject to minimum-funding and vesting requirements. Entitlement to such 'welfare' benefits is determined by contract.

Increasingly, the federal government has shown an interest in expanding regulatory involvement in the employment arena through employer mandates. The WARN and FMLA statutes are the most recent examples. WARN is described in section II B above. The FMLA, enacted in 1993, applies to firms with 50 or more employees. The statutory purpose is to require employers to permit flexible work schedules for employees who need to attend to health problems or major events like the birth of a child. Eligible employees—those employed by firms with fifty or more employees who have worked for at least one year and for at least 1250 hours during the 12 months preceding their leave request—are entitled to take job-protected leaves of absence of up to 12 weeks (a) upon the birth or adoption of a child, (b) to take care of a family member with a 'serious health condition', or (c) because of the employee's own 'serious health condition' rendering him/her unable to perform the job.

The FMLA does not require employers to pay salary during the period of the leave, but it does require employers to maintain health benefits in place prior to the leave. The law also entitles the employee to reinstatement at the end of the leave, unless the individual is among the highest paid 10 percent of the employees at the facility or within 75 miles thereof.

In 1993, President Clinton proposed universal health insurance for all employees, which would be financed through an employer mandate. This proposal was not enacted by Congress in part out of concern that employer mandates will depress levels of employment.

D. Health and Safety

The federal Occupational and Safety Act of 1970 (OSHA) requires employers to meet minimum safety and health standards. Under OSHA's 'general duty' clause, employers are required to maintain a safe workplace. In addition, the Department of Labor promulgates substantive standards (e.g. setting permissible exposure levels to particular substances) and inspects workplaces for violations.[22] The law also requires disclosure of hazards to workers and union representatives. Under Labor Department regulations, employees may refuse to perform work assignments where there is insufficient time to correct the hazard through regular statutory channels, and the employer has not corrected the condition.[23]

The states also regulate safety practices in the workplace. In addition, states have enacted workers' compensation laws that provide a no-fault compensation system for workplace injuries in place of a civil tort action against employers for negligence.[24] The rationale for such laws is that barriers to recovery in civil actions failed to deter unsafe practices, and that an insurance scheme would do a better job of promoting workplace safety and compensation objectives. Workers' compensation laws are financed by mandatory employer contributions, with premiums set in accordance with the employer's claims 'experience' rating. Advocates for injured workers criticize such laws because of the growing disparity between the limited compensation available under the statutory compensation schedules and the more substantial jury verdicts available in civil tort actions. Employers also face mounting premiums because of fraudulent claims.

---

[22] See generally Wayne B. Gray and John T. Scholz, 'Does Regulatory Enforcement Work? A Panel Analysis of OSHA Enforcement', 27 *Law & Soc'y Rev.* 177 (1993).

[23] See *Whirlpool Corp.* v. *Marshall*, 445 U.S. 1 (1980) (sustaining 29 C.F.R. § 1977.12).

[24] See generally Lawrence M. Friedman, *A History of American Law*, ch. 14 (1973); Richard A. Epstein, 'The Historical Origins and Economic Structure of Workers' Compensation Law', 16 *Ga.L.Rev.* 775 (1982).

E. Workplace Privacy

Workplace privacy is an area of emerging concern. Advocates of privacy regulation argue that workers should have the right to preserve areas of privacy even when on the job. Such protections are common in the government sector, and some have suggested that similar rules be extended to the private workplace. Congress has passed laws restricting use of polygraphs (lie detectors)[25] and interception of telephone calls[26] as tools for investigating employee misconduct. In recent years, bills have been introduced in every session of Congress to regulate electronic surveillance of employees while at work.

Drug testing of employees is an increasingly common practice. For government employees, the fourth amendment of the United States Constitution and statutes in some states restrict random testing and require 'reasonable suspicion' of illegal drug use—unless the employees work in certain safety- or security-sensitive positions.[27] Employees in the private sector do not have such protections unless they are covered by a collective bargaining contract or work in a state which has enacted a law regulating drug testing.[28]

III. Employment Discrimination Law

A. Title VII

A very important area of federal and state regulatory involvement in the American workplace is discrimination. The central statute is Title VII of the Civil Rights Act of 1964, which was amended by the Civil Rights Act of 1991 to provide additional protections for claimants of discrimination. The law was passed in response to a civil rights movement in the 1960s of black Americans protesting racial segregation. Discrimination is viewed both as unfair to individuals and as imposing unnecessary costs on a society by restricting otherwise qualified workers from competing on an equal basis for

---

[25] See Employee Polygraph Protection Act of 1988, 29 U.S.C. §§ 2001–2009.

[26] See Title III of the Omnibus Crime Control and Safe Streets Act of 1968, as amended by the Electronic Communications Privacy Act of 1986, 18 U.S.C. §§ 2510–2520.

[27] The leading Supreme Court decisions in this area are *Skinner* v. *Railway Labor Executives' Ass'n*, 489 U.S. 602 (1989); *National Treasury Employees Union* v. *Von Raab*, 489 U.S. 656 (1989).

[28] See, e.g. Conn. Gen. Stat. Ann. §§ 31–51t–aa (West 1995); Vt. Stat. Ann., tit. 21, §§ 511–20 (1987). Some courts have found workplace privacy rights as a matter of state public policy. See, e.g. *Luedtke* v. *Nabors Alaska Drilling Inc.*, 768 P.2d 1123 (Alaska 1989).

employment opportunities. The law also seeks to promote the economic advancement of previously discriminated-against groups.

The federal law covers all employers with 15 or more employees, and prohibits discrimination on account of race, color, religion, national origin, and sex. The law prohibits two forms of discrimination. The first is intentional discrimination. Because direct evidence of discriminatory motive is often lacking, employees/job applicants are also permitted to mount a case through circumstantial evidence attacking the reasons for the challenged decision articulated by the employer,[29] or statistical proof of a 'pattern or practice' of discrimination.[30]

Title VII also authorizes challenges to neutral practices that have a disproportionately adverse effect on members of a statutorily protected group. This is called the 'disparate impact' theory of discrimination. If an employer is unable to show 'business necessity' for such practices, a violation is found even where there is no evidence of intentional discrimination. The rationale for regulation here is that such practices reduce employment opportunities for such groups without advancing important goals of the firm; hence, if we ignore significant administrative costs (including the competence of courts and agencies to second-guess employer needs) regulation can 'costlessly' improve economic opportunities for previously disadvantaged groups. Utilizing the disparate-impact theory plaintiffs have successfully overturned practices in particular circumstances such as aptitude tests[31] and height and weight requirements.[32] Although there was some question whether the 'disparate impact' approach could be used to challenge subjective hiring and promotion practices,[33] such doubts have been laid to rest as a result of the Civil Rights Act of 1991.[34]

Title VII has been interpreted not to reach sexual orientation discrimination against gay and lesbian individuals,[35] although some local laws prohibit such discrimination. Title VII also does not prohibit discrimination on account of citizenship status, apart from racial and national origin distinc-

---

[29] See McDonnell Douglas Corp. v. Green, 411 U.S. 792 (1973); Texas Dept. of Community Affairs v. Burdine, 450 U.S. 248 (1981); St. Mary's Honor Center v. Hicks, 113 S.Ct. 2742 (1993).

[30] See Teamsters v. United States, 431 U.S. 324 (1977); Hazelwood School Dist. v. United States, 433 U.S. 299 (1977).

[31] See Griggs v. Duke Power Co., 401 U.S. 424 (1971); Albemarle Paper Co. v. Moody, 422 U.S. 405 (1975).

[32] See Dothard v. Rawlinson, 433 U.S. 321 (1977).

[33] The Supreme Court's decision in Watson v. Fort Worth Bank and Trust, 487 U.S. 977 (1988), permitted such challenges, but its ruling a year later in Wards Cove Packing Co. v. Atonio, 490 U.S. 642 (1989), appeared to undermine the disparate-impact theory of discrimination altogether.

[34] Express authorization of disparate-impact challenges is found in Section 703(k) of Title VII, as amended by the 1991 law. Section 703(k)(1)(B)(i) provides that the plaintiff must show that a 'particular' employment practice causes a disparate impact, 'except that if the complaining party can demonstrate to the court that the elements of a respondent's decisionmaking process are not capable of separation for analysis, the decisionmaking process may be analyzed as one employment practice'.

[35] See, e.g. DeSantis v. Pacific Tel. & Tel. Co., 608 F.2d 327 (9th Cir. 1979); Smith v. Liberty Mutual Ins. Co., 569 F.2d 325 (5th Cir. 1978).

tions which are forbidden.[36] However, Section 102 of the Immigration Reform and Control Act of 1986 (IRCA)[37] prohibits such discrimination against any 'intending citizen' (either a resident alien or an alien seeking legalization under IRCA's amnesty program or lawfully admitted under the refugee and asylum provisions of federal immigration law). IRCA reaches only intentional citizenship status discrimination, and does not authorize a disparate-impact challenge.

B. Foreign Companies Doing Business in the United States

As a general matter, foreign companies doing business in the United States are subject to federal discrimination law, and preferences for citizens of the foreign country for posts in the United States would constitute national-origin or citizenship discrimination. There are two exceptions to this general rule. First, the foreign company might be able to prove that being a foreign national is a 'bona fide occupational qualification' (BFOQ) for executive positions. The BFOQ exception is a narrow one, and would require a showing that a preference for nationals is necessary to ensure that executives are familiar with the culture, custom and practices of the home country. Secondly, some treaties, such as the Friendship, Commerce, and Navigation (FCN) Treaty between Japan and the United States, permit 'companies of either Party . . . to engage, within the territories of the other Part, . . . executive personnel . . . of their own choice'. The Supreme Court has ruled that this treaty does not apply to United States-incorporated subsidiaries of a Japanese corporation, but presumably does apply to a true 'company of Japan'.[38] Also, United States subsidiaries controlled by their parent corporations may be able to assert the treaty rights of the parent to defeat liability for national-origin discrimination under Title VII where the parent 'dictates' the conduct in question, and that conduct involves preferences for citizens of the parent protected by the FCN.[39]

C. Extra-territorial Application

As a result of the Civil Rights Act of 1991, Title VII (and the Americans with Disabilities Act of 1990 (ADA)) protects the employment of citizens of the

---

[36] See *Espinoza* v. *Farah Mfg. Co.*, 414 U.S. 86 (1973).   [37] 8 U.S.C. §§ 1324a–1324b.

[38] See *Sumitomo Shoji America, Inc.* v. *Avigliano*, 457 U.S. 176 (1982).

[39] See *Fortino* v. *Quasar Co.*, 950 F.2d 389 (7th Cir. 1991); *Papaila* v. *Uniden America Corp.*, SI F. 3d 54 (5th Cir. 1995). Such an argument may, however, expose the parent corporation to suits in other areas seeking to 'pierce the corporate veil'. See Eileen M. Mullen, 'Rotating Japanese Managers in American Subsidiaries of Japanese Firms: A Challenge for American Employment Discrimination Law', 45 Stan.L.Rev. 725 (1993). Also, the EEOC disagrees with the *Fortino* and *Papaila* rulings.

United States employed by some American businesses operating in foreign countries.[40] If a covered employer 'controls' a corporation incorporated in a foreign country, any violation of Title VII (or the ADA) engaged in by the foreign corporation is presumed to be engaged in by the employer. The determination of whether an employer 'controls' a foreign corporation is based on a consideration of four factors: the interrelation of operations; common management; centralized control of labor relations; and common ownership or financial control. However, it is not unlawful for an employer to take any action that would otherwise be unlawful under Title VII (or the ADA) with respect to an employee working in a foreign country if compliance with Title VII (or the ADA) would cause the employer to violate the law of the country in which the employee works. A similar provision is contained in the federal age discrimination law.

D. *Administrative Procedure and Remedies*

A Title VII claimant must first file a charge with a federal agency, the Equal Employment Opportunity Commission (EEOC), or the state agency with similar responsibilities. The administrative agency then investigates the charge and has the option of filing suit on behalf of the claimant. If the EEOC declines to proceed further, the Title VII claimant may go to court; the agency's disposition cannot block a private lawsuit unless the agency agrees to sue on the claimant's behalf. If a violation is found, the court may award back-pay and reinstatement, or front-pay in lieu of reinstatement, to put the employee in the position he/she would have been had the discrimination not occurred. (In one celebrated case, a female employee of a major accounting firm, who was discriminatorily denied a partnership promotion, was awarded partnership status as a remedy.[41]) As a result of the 1991 amendments, jury trials are available in Title VII actions challenging intentional discrimination, and plaintiffs may seek compensatory damages for future economic loss and non-economic loss (such as damages for 'pain and suffering') as well as punitive damages. Such damages are capped at levels ranging from $50,000 to $300,000 depending on the size of the defendant's workforce.

E. *Gender Discrimination*

Gender discrimination is outlawed by Title VII. Like racial discrimination, gender discrimination, which can be raised by both men and women, is

---

[40] See Section 109 of the Civil Rights Act of 1991, Pub. L. No. 102–166, Nov. 21, 1991, 105 Stat. 1071 et seq., amending Sections 701(f) and 702 of Title VII of the Civil Rights Act of 1964 and Sections 101(4) and 102 of the Americans with Disabilities Act of 1990.

[41] See *Hopkins* v. *Price Waterhouse*, 920 F.2d 967 (D.C. Cir. 1990), on remand from 490 U.S. 228 (1989).

viewed as unfair to individuals, creating obstacles to equal opportunity, and as unnecessary, if not harmful, to a productive economy. Gender discrimination includes use of stereotypes that involve different standards of job performance and demeanor for women than for men,[42] and the making of unwanted sexual offers and other sexual harassment as a condition for obtaining a job, a promotion or a raise or simply as part of the workplace environment.[43] Since 1978, Title VII also requires employers to treat pregnancy on the same terms as they would any other disability under their benefit plans.

Employers are permitted a limited defense to show that the use of sex in employment decisions is a 'bona fide occupational qualification' (BFOQ). This BFOQ defense is narrowly interpreted to reach only those practices implicating the firm's 'business essence', such as hiring women as cocktail waitresses in a 'Playboy Club' or persons of Chinese national origin to preserve a sense of authenticity in an ethnic restaurant. The BFOQ defense is not available to permit an airline to hire women only as flight attendants, even where this caters to customer preferences,[44] or to exclude women who might become pregnant from jobs, whose conditions might endanger an unborn child, except in rare circumstances where reproductive potential prevents actual performance of job duties.[45]

In the Equal Pay Act of 1963,[46] formally amending the Fair Labor Standards Act of 1938, Congress established the principle that men and women must receive equal pay for 'equal work on jobs the performance of which requires equal skill, effort, and responsibility, and which are performed under similar working conditions . . .'. Title VII prohibits intentional sex-based discrimination in compensation and benefits,[47] including the use of gender-based actuarial classifications in pension and insurance plans.[48] However, neither the Equal Pay Act nor Title VII authorizes what is called a 'comparable worth' challenge, under which the employer would have to provide equal pay for different jobs that are deemed to be of 'comparable worth' in some objective sense.[49]

---

[42] See *Price Waterhouse* v. *Hopkins*, 490 U.S. 228 (1989).

[43] See *Meritor Savings Bank, FSB* v. *Vinson*, 477 U.S. 57 (1986); *Harris* v. *Forklift Systems, Inc.*, 114 S.Ct. 367 (1993).

[44] See, e.g. *Diaz* v. *Pan American World Airways*, 442 F.2d 385 (5th Cir.), *cert. denied*, 404 U.S. 950 (1971).

[45] *Cf. International Union, UAW* v. *Johnson Controls, Inc.*, 499 U.S. 187 (1991).

[46] 29 U.S.C. §§ 206(d), 216–17.

[47] See *County of Washington* v. *Gunther*, 452 U.S. 161 (1981).

[48] See *Arizona Governing Committee* v. *Norris*, 463 U.S. 1073 (1983); *Los Angeles Dept. of Water & Power* v. *Manhart*, 435 U.S. 702 (1978).

[49] See, e.g. *American Federation of State, County, and Municipal Employees, AFL-CIO* v. *Washington*, 770 F.2d 1401 (9th Cir. 1985). See generally Paul Weiler, 'The Wages of Sex: The Uses and Limits of Comparable Worth', 99 Harv.L.Rev. 1728 (1986).

F. Religious Discrimination

Title VII also prohibits discrimination on account of religion. The statutory prohibition extends beyond intentional discrimination to include employer refusals to extend 'reasonable accommodation' to the religious practices of employees. Employees assigned to work on days of religious observance have a qualified right to request that the employer readjust their work schedules to accomodate their religious practices. However, the required level of accommodation does not entail disturbing the seniority or contractual rights of other employees.[50]

G. Age Discrimination

By virtue of the Age Discrimination in Employment Act of 1967 (ADEA), the anti-discrimination principle also applies to employees over the age of 40 complaining of age-based discrimination. This statute presents difficulties not present in Title VII because age-based rules may promote legitimate employer objectives (as in the design of retirement benefit plans), and increasing age may be associated with legitimate employer considerations, such as years 'out of school', and declining performance levels.

ADEA prohibits intentional discrimination where the employer is found to treat older workers differently because of their age. Despite lower court precedent, however, it remains an open question whether the statute authorizes challenges on a disparate-impact theory of discrimination.[51] As a result of later amendments to ADEA, mandatory retirement is generally unlawful in the United States. (In Japan, by contrast, mandatory retirement rules are lawful.) A narrow exception (Section 12(c)(1) of ADEA) permits the mandatory retirement at age 65 or later of employees who are entitled to a non-forfeitable annual retirement benefit of $44,000 or more and who, for 2 years prior to retirement, were 'employed in a bona fide executive or high policy-making position'.[52] In a case resulting in a $200,000 verdict, a corporation's chief labor counsel (with supervisory authority over the firm's labor lawyers) was held not to be a 'bona fide executive' or in a 'high policymaking position' within the meaning of this exemption.[53]

---

[50] See *Trans World Airlines* v. *Hardison*, 432 U.S. 63 (1977).

[51] See *Hazen Paper Co.* v. *Biggins*, 113 S.Ct. 1701, 1706 (1993) (Kennedy, J., concurring); *Markham* v. *Geller*, 451 U.S. 945, 948 (1981) (Rehnquist, J., dissenting from denial of certiorari).

[52] 29 U.S.C. §631(c)(1).

[53] See *Whittlesey* v. *Union Carbide Corp.*, 567 F.Supp. 1320 (S.D.N.Y. 1983), *affirmed*, 742 F.2d 724 (2d Cir. 1984). See generally the EEOC's interpretation of the exemption in 29 C.F.R. § 1625.12.

Employers seeking to reduce workforce levels have established incentive programs, such as enhanced early retirement benefits, to encourage employees to retire voluntarily. Such programs are lawful provided they do not confer more valuable benefits on younger workers while withholding such benefits from older workers. Employers have also attempted to trade specially enhanced severance packages in return for agreements to waive ADEA claims. Such waiver agreements are lawful provided they are 'knowing and voluntary'. Under the Older Workers Benefit Protection Act of 1990 (OWBPA),[54] Congress stipulated minimum requirements for such agreements. For individual agreements, Congress requires a written agreement, expressly waiving ADEA rights or claims (but not claims or rights arising after the agreement); additional consideration for the waiver; written advice from the employer to consult with an attorney; a 21-day waiting period to consider the agreement; and a 7-day period to revoke the agreement. For agreements 'requested in connection with an exit incentive or other employment termination program offered to a group of employees', Congress requires a longer waiting period (45 days instead of 21 days). In addition, employers must disclose any eligibility factors for individuals covered by the program and 'the job titles and ages of all individuals eligible or selected for the program' and the ages of all individuals 'in the same job classification or organizational unit' who were not selected for the program. OWBPA also requires that age-based distinctions in benefit plans generally conform to an equal-contribution or equal-cost rule.

ADEA has generated considerable litigation resulting in large verdicts for plaintiffs, who are typically white, relatively well-off professionals or managers.[55] Jury trials are available in ADEA actions, which authorize back-pay and reinstatement or front-pay in lieu of reinstatement as customary remedies. Damages are doubled in cases involving 'willful' violations.[56] The extraterritorial reach of ADEA is similar to that of Title VII (see section III C above).

H. Disability Discrimination

The anti-discrimination principle also applies to discrimination against individuals with disabilities. Like race discrimination, adverse treatment of individuals on account of disability or handicap violates norms of fairness,

---

[54] Pub. L. No. 101–433, Oct. 16, 1990, 104 Stat. 978 et seq., amending, inter alia, Section 7 of ADEA.

[55] See generally Michael Schuster and Christopher S. Miller, 'An Empirical Assessment of the Age Discrimination in Employment Act', 38 *Indus. & Lab. Rel. Rev.* 64 (1984).

[56] See *Trans World Airlines* v. *Thurston*, 469 U.S. 111 (1985); *Hazen Paper Co.* v. *Biggins*, 113 S.Ct. 1701 (1993).

reduces opportunities for disadvantaged groups, and may reflect uninformed stereotypes of the limits of the abilities of a disadvantaged worker. However, unlike race and gender discrimination, employer resistance to hiring individuals with disabilities is often based, at least in part, on the costs related to such hires (e.g. physical modifications of the workplace and higher premiums for health and other benefits), rather than dislike or other form of prejudice.

Although some state laws barred handicap discrimination prior to the enactment of the Americans With Disabilities Act of 1990 (ADA),[57] only federal sector employers and government contractors were under a duty, as a matter of federal law, not to discriminate against otherwise qualified employees on account of their disability. With the passage of the ADA, all private and public employers with 15 or more employees are barred from disability-based discrimination. ADA represents an extensive regulation of the workplace. The statute bars both intentional and disparate-impact discrimination. All employment standards having an adverse impact on individuals with disabilities must be 'job-related and consistent with business necessity'. Employers may also not require medical examinations prior to making offers of employment (except for tests for illegal drug use); post-offer examinations must be job-related and follow strict rules of confidentiality.

In a departure from the equal-treatment rule of most other employment discrimination laws, the ADA also imposes affirmative obligations on employers by requiring them to provide 'reasonable accommodation' of 'qualified individuals with a disability'. The reasonable-accommodation duty may in particular circumstances include 'making existing facilities used by employees readily accessible to and usable by individuals with disabilities' and 'job restructuring, part-time or modified work schedules, reassignment to a vacant position, acquisition or modification of equipment or devices, appropriate adjustment or modifications of examinations, training materials or policies, the provision of qualified readers or interpreters, and other similar accommodations for individuals with disabilities'.[58] The rationale for this reasonable accommodation duty is twofold. First, it is hoped that some of the costs anticipated in employing disabled individuals will turn out to be minimal, and employers will then reassess the desirability of such hires in the future. Secondly, it has been argued the statute seeks to advance a social norm of 'mainstreaming' disabled individuals, whether or not the costs of accommodation exceed some proportion of the value of the job as measured by the salary it commands.

The accommodation duty is not limitless. Employers can show that the proposed accommodation is not 'reasonable' or entails an 'undue hardship'—a term defined in the statute as 'an action requiring significant

---

[57] 42 U.S.C. § 12101 et seq.　　[58] Section 101(9) of the ADA, 42 U.S.C. § 12111(9).

difficulty or expense, when considered in light of certain factors, such as the cost of the accommodation; the overall financial resources of the facility in question; the overall financial resources of the employing entity; and the type of operation of the covered entity.[59]

ADA's coverage is quite extensive. The term 'disability' means an individual with 'a physical or mental impairment that substantially limits one or more of the major life activities of such individual', or with 'a record of such impairment', and includes someone who is erroneously 'regarded as having such an impairment'.[60] Individuals with contagious diseases, including individuals who test positive for the HIV virus,[61] are protected by the ADA.[62] However, employers may maintain requirements that an individual not pose 'a direct threat to the health or safety of other individuals in the workplace'.[63] Individuals 'currently engaged in the illegal use of drugs' are excluded from the protected class of 'qualified individuals with a disability'. Such exclusion does not extend, however, to individuals who have successfully completed a supervised drug rehabilitation program, are currently in such a program and not engaged in drug use, or are 'erroneously regarded as engaging in' illegal use of drugs.[64] The ADA does not exclude even current alcoholics from coverage, although employers may hold alcoholics (as well as drug users) to the same job standards as applied to other employees.

An employer's benefit plans may not treat individuals with disabilities differently than other employees. However, the statute does not prohibit insurers or health care organizations that administer benefit plans from 'underwriting risks, classifying risks, or administering such risks that are based on or not inconsistent with State law'—or self-insured employers making similar risk classification decisions—provided that such decisions are 'not used as a subterfuge to evade the purposes' of the ADA. A June 1993 administrative guidance from the EEOC interprets this provision to allow universal, non-disease-specific restrictions on coverage, such as limits on 'mental/nervous' conditions or 'eye care', blanket exclusion of preexisting conditions, or caps on annual benefits for the treatment of any physical condition. But disease-specific provisions must be justified 'by legitimate actuarial data, or by actual or reasonably anticipated experience', and must treat conditions with 'comparable actuarial data and/or experience' in the same fashion.[65]

---

[59] Section 101(10) of the ADA, 42 U.S.C. § 12111(10).

[60] Section 3(2) of the ADA, 42 U.S.C. § 12102(2).

[61] See, e.g. *Chalk* v. *U.S. District Court*, 840 F.2d 701 (9th Cir. 1988).

[62] See *School Board of Nassau County* v. *Arline*, 480 U.S. 273 (1987) (elementary school teacher suffering from tuberculosis).

[63] Section 103(b) of the ADA, 42 U.S.C. § 12113(b).

[64] Section 104(a)–(b) of the ADA, 42 U.S.C. § 12114(a)–(b).

[65] See EEOC *Interim Guidance on Application of ADA to Health Insurance*, (BNA) Daily Lab. Rep., No. 109, June 9, 1993, E-1 ff.

IV. Union Organization and Collective Bargaining Law

Although once the fountainhead of American employment law, union organizing and collective bargaining have receded in importance with the decline of union representation in private firms from 35 percent of the workforce in 1954 to under 12 percent today.

A. *Underlying Premises*

The American labor relations system differs from its European counterparts in a number of ways. First, the system is based on an adversarial model. In most cases, unions obtain bargaining rights in contested elections administered by a federal agency. In such elections, management has a right to, and often does, speak out in opposition to the union.[66] Companies may not have a role in initiating or supporting 'labor organizations', a term that is broadly defined to include any mechanism by which employees 'deal with' their employer on terms and conditions of employment.[67] The labor laws are based on a fundamental division of interest between labor and management: unions can seek bargaining authority on behalf of non-managerial and non-supervisory workers, but managers and supervisors are deemed representatives of the firm who have no right to form unions or insist on collective bargaining.[68] The scope of bargaining also reflects this division between spheres of influence: the parties must bargain over wages, hours and working conditions, but decisions involving the disposition of assets and the strategic position of the firm, including plant closings, are deemed to be part of management's realm of unilateral action; management must bargain over the effects of such decisions but not the decisions themselves.[69]

Secondly, collective bargaining is highly decentralized. Unions acquire bargaining authority on a plant-by-plant basis, often among a subgroup of workers in the plant. Unlike the German, French and Swedish systems,

---

[66] See Section 8(c) of the NLRA, 29 U.S.C. § 158(c)—the so-called 'employer free speech' provision.

[67] See Section 2(5) of the NLRA, 29 U.S.C. § 152(5), for the definition of 'labor organization'. Employer interference with or domination of such organizations is barred by Section 8(a)(2), 29 U.S.C. § 158(a)(2). See generally Samuel Estreicher, 'Employee Involvement and the "Company Union" Prohibition: The Case for Partial Repeal of § 8(a)(2) of the NLRA' 69 N.Y.U.L. Rev. 101 (1994).

[68] The statutory exclusion of supervisors is contained in Section 2(11) of the NLRA, 29 U.S.C. § 152(11). The Supreme Court recognized an implied exclusion for 'managerial' employees in *NLRB* v. *Bell Aerospace Co.*, 416 U.S. 267 (1974). Faculty of institutions of higher education are considered 'managerial' employees if they play a role in the formulation or administration of educational policy for their employers. See *NLRB* v. *Yeshiva University*, 444 U.S. 672 (1980).

[69] See *First National Maintenance Corp.* v. *NLRB*, 452 U.S. 666 (1981).

regional bargaining between labor federations and multi-employer organizations in the United States is exceptional; multi-employer bargaining units are formed only by consent and in many industries they have unravelled. Coalition bargaining among unions representing different units of the same employer can occur only with the employer's consent. Unions attempt to maintain 'pattern' settlements across firms competing in the same product market, but are finding this increasingly difficult in the face of a growing non-union sector and the competitive pressures of global markets.

Thirdly, unions are predominantly multi-employer organizations representing employees of competing firms. Unlike Japan's enterprise unions, employee associations representing only the employees of a particular firm are rare are in the United States, and tend over time to affiliate with national labor organizations that are members of the central labor federation, the American Federation of Labor—Congress of Industrial Organizations (AFL-CIO). Enterprise-based works councils—found in most continental European countries—are non-existent in the United States. American unions typically negotiate agreements with single companies, often applicable only to a particular facility, while making every effort to ensure that such agreements conform to the national 'pattern' for that industry.

The fact that American unions are multi-employer associations makes it difficult for firms to share non-public financial information with their unions, and to secure terms at variance with the national bargaining goals of the union.

Finally, American unions are institutionally insecure. The unions' vulnerability comes from the growing non-union sector and from various legal mechanisms that are designed to ensure union responsiveness to the rank-and-file employees. These mechanisms include decertification elections; the employer's ability to test the union's continued majority support by withdrawing recognition; duty of fair representation suits brought by employees complaining of the union's representation in grievances or collective bargaining; the rights of non-union members to seek rebates of union dues used for non-collective bargaining purposes; and union democracy requirements for the conduct of internal union election and union discipline. As a result of these pressures, union leaders must be politically attuned to the preferences of median voters within bargaining units—typically, long-service workers who are protected from lay-off by seniority rules.

B. *Statutory and Administrative Framework*

The principal labor law is the National Labor Relations Act of 1935 (NLRA or Wagner Act). The NLRA applies to all employers in private industries 'affecting commerce', with the exception of the railroad and airlines industries. Labor relations in the latter industries are regulated by the Railway Labor Act of 1926 (RLA).[70] Both the NLRA and RLA broadly preempt all state regulation of labor relations in the industries they cover. The states have enacted 'mini Wagner Acts' for industries not regulated by federal law, and public sector labor relations laws for the employees of state and local governments. The federal government has a separate labor relations statute for its employees.

Government agencies play an important role in the administration of the federal labor laws. In the case of the NLRA, the National Labor Relations Board (NLRB) has exclusive authority over the representation procedures and unfair labor practice provisions of the NLRA. The role of the courts is limited to judicial review of final NLRB orders in unfair labor practice cases and suits to enforce collective bargaining agreements.[71] In the case of the RLA, the National Mediation Board (NMB) conducts representation elections and plays an important role in mediating disputes.

Under the NLRA, charges of unfair labor practices (ULPs) are filed with regional offices of the NLRB. If, after investigation, the charges are believed to be meritorious, the General Counsel issues a complaint on the government's behalf. An adversarial, trial-type proceeding is conducted before an administrative law judge (ALJ), who hears the testimony and reviews the evidence, and makes initial findings of fact and conclusions of law. If no appeal is taken, the ALJ's determination becomes the ruling of the agency. If a party appeals, the NLRB considers the record and briefs and, on rare occasions, hears oral arguments. The final decision of the NLRB is reviewable in the federal courts of appeals. The reviewing court must uphold the agency's decisions if its findings of fact are supported by 'substantial evidence' on the record 'considered as a whole' and its rulings of law are in conformity with the NLRA. By contrast, under the RLA, the NMB's adjudicative authority is limited to representational disputes; the parties go directly to the federal district court to enforce other statutory obligations.

Both statutes are based on the principles of *exclusivity* (only the representatives chosen by a majority of the employees in a unit may bargain, to the exclusion of individual employees or representatives of a minority); *a legally mandated duty to bargain* (both the exclusive bargaining representative and the employer are legally obligated to bargain in 'good faith'); *free collective bargaining* (after exhaustion of the duty to bargain, the parties are free to press their disagreements in the form of strikes and lock-outs); and, *arbitration of*

---

[70] 45 U.S.C. §§ 151–188.
[71] See Section 301 of the Labor-Management Relations Act, 29 U.S.C. § 185—a 1947 amendment to the NLRA.

disputes arising under collective bargaining agreements (if the parties have agreed to arbitration).

C. Selection of Exclusive Bargaining Representative

Although 'members only' unionism is permissible under both statutes, unions typically seek exclusive bargaining status either by securing voluntary recognition from the employer upon a showing of majority support, or petitioning the NLRB or the NMB to hold a secret-ballot representation election. Such petitions require a preliminary showing of interest (the NLRB requires that 30 percent of the employees in an appropriate unit sign cards requesting a representation election). The agency conducts a hearing to resolve contested issues, if any, concerning the scope of the bargaining unit, eligibility of voters, etc., and then schedules an election to determine if a majority of employees desire union representation. (The NLRB requires that a majority of employees voting affirmatively select union representation; the NMB requires that a majority of the eligible electorate cast valid ballots.) After the election is held, the agency considers challenges based on the conduct of the election campaign. If the petitioning union was selected by a majority of the employees, and the agency has rejected challenges to the conduct of the campaign, the agency certifies the union as the exclusive bargaining representative.

In the election campaign, the employer is permitted to voice his opposition to unionism in general and to the particular union. The employer may not, however, discharge or discipline employees because of their support of the union, engage in threats of reprisal, or change the terms and conditions of work for the purpose of affecting the election outcome. Such conduct would provide grounds for setting aside the election (if the majority of employees voted 'no union') or holding the employer to have engaged in unfair labor practices. Under the NLRA, if employers are guilty of egregious unfair labor practices that so mar the environment that a fair rerun election cannot be held, the NLRB may order the employer to bargain with a union that previously demonstrated majority support on the basis of authorization cards signed by a majority of the unit.[72]

D. The Process of Collective Bargaining

Under the NLRA, once the union has been certified, the parties are under a duty to meet and confer at reasonable times and engage in 'good faith'

[72] See *NLRB v. Gissel Packing Co.*, 395 U.S. 575 (1969).

bargaining. There is no legal obligation to make concessions or reach agreements. The duty to bargain is limited to 'wages, hours and other terms and conditions of employment'. These are considered 'mandatory' subjects over which the parties must bargain (and provide information to substantiate bargaining positions) and are free to press their disagreements to the point of 'impasse'. Bargaining is not required over subjects like plant closings, advertising budgets, and capital investments that are considered to lie within the realm of 'entrepreneurial control'; subjects that affect the union's relationship with its members such as strike and contract ratification votes; or subjects that alter the established framework of negotiations, such as proposals to bargain with coalitions of unions or to submit disagreements over the content of labor contracts to arbitration. These are considered 'permissive' subjects over which the parties have no duty to bargain and may not be a basis for deadlock over mandatory subjects.[73]

If the parties have reached an 'impasse' over mandatory subjects, the NLRA permits resort to self-help after notice is given to the Federal Mediation and Conciliation Service (FMCS) and a 60-day 'cooling off' period has expired. The employer may lock-out its employees and/or unilaterally implement its final offer to the union. The union may exercise its right to strike, which is legally protected. Although the employer may not discharge striking workers, it can, in the interest of maintaining operations, hire permanent replacements even without a showing that it could not maintain operations by other means.[74] Even if permanent replacements have been hired, strikers remain 'employees' and have preferential rights to job openings as they occur, once the strikers have offered unconditionally to return to work. If the strike is in protest over the employer's unfair labor practices, the employer may not hire permanent replacements and returning strikers will displace replacement workers. Also, if the employer resorts to a lock-out, locked-out employees may not be permanently replaced.

Although employers have had the right to hire permanent replacements as a means of staying in business, the decade of the 1980s witnessed a significant increase in the use of this bargaining tactic. Bills have been pending in Congress for several years to outlaw the hiring of permanent replacements, but so far they have not been enacted.

The framework for collective bargaining in the railroad and airline industries resembles that of the NLRA but differs in at least two important respects. First, bargaining occurs on a carrier-wide (in airlines) or system-wide (in rail) basis. Secondly, there are substantial statutory impediments to changing agree-

[73] See *NLRB* v. *Wooster Division of Borg-Warner Corp.*, 356 U.S. 342 (1958).

[74] See *NLRB* v. *Mackay Radio & Telegraph Co.*, 304 U.S. 333 (1938). See generally Samuel Estreicher, 'Collective Bargaining or "Collective Begging"'?: Reflections on Antistrike Breaker Legislation', 93 Mich. L. Rev. 577 (1994).

ments. The parties to a collective bargaining agreement are under a statutory duty 'to exert every reasonable effort to make and maintain agreements'. A party commences the process of seeking changes in agreements by serving the other side with what is called a 'Section 6 notice' containing its proposals. The parties are then obligated to engage in direct negotiations. If no agreement is reached, either party may request mediation by the NMB, or the agency can intervene on its own. The NMB has the authority to prolong bargaining (virtually free of judicial review), as long it believes further talks may be productive. As a practical matter, the NMB determines when the parties are at an impasse by making an offer of binding arbitration of the dispute; if the offer is refused, the agency declares that its mediation efforts have failed. The parties are then obligated to maintain the status quo for 30 days, in order to permit the President to establish an emergency board. If the President does not do so, the parties are free to engage in a strike or lock-out to pressure the other side. Emergency boards are common in rail disputes, but have seldom been appointed in airline disputes since the 1960s.

E. The Process of Administering the Labor Agreement

Once the parties have entered into a collective bargaining agreement, some mechanism is needed to resolve disputes arising under the agreement—of necessity, a general document that cannot contain rules for all disputes that might develop. Such disputes often involve discharges and other terms of discipline challenged by the union under the 'just cause' provisions of the labor agreement, or disagreements over the meaning of particular terms governing seniority, overtime assignments, and use of subcontractors. The preferred mechanism under United States labor law for resolving such 'rights' disputes is a contractual grievance machinery involving, in the first instance, stages of negotiations between union and management representatives, and, should disagreements persist, arbitration before a neutral arbiter. Typically, unions agree not to strike over 'rights' disputes during the life of the agreement, in exchange for which employers agree to 'final and binding' grievance arbitration.

Arbitrators are chosen by the parties. Some agreements provide for regular resort to the same arbitrator or a panel of arbitrators. More commonly, arbitrators are selected on an ad hoc basis from rosters compiled by either the Federal Mediation and Conciliation Services, the state labor relations agency, or the American Arbitration Association, a private organization providing arbitration services. Under the RLA, the parties are required to establish boards of adjustment to hear grievances (in rail, the statute establishes an industry-wide grievance apparatus, the National Railroad Adjustment Board).

Hearings before arbitrators are considered more informal, quicker, and less costly than proceedings in court. Although some unions (like the International Association of Machinists (IAM)) continue to use non-lawyer staff in arbitrations, the process is becoming increasing judicialized, and reliance on lawyers is now common.

The arbitrator's award is considered a 'final and binding' resolution, with the legal bases for challenging an award quite limited. Absent bias, an indefinite award, or a strong showing that the arbitrator clearly exceeded his or her authority under the contract, the court must enforce the award.

In three rulings issued the same day in 1960[75]—the so-called '*Steelworkers Trilogy*'—the Supreme Court established rules strongly supportive of labor arbitration. The High Court announced a 'presumption of arbitrability' under which any facially plausible claim of a contract violation within the scope of the arbitration clause of the agreement—even if of dubious merit— is presumed arbitrable, absent clear evidence in the agreement that the parties intended to exclude a particular subject from the promise to arbitrate. The Supreme Court also made clear that, since the parties bargained for their own special dispute-resolver and contract-interpreter, the courts may not set aside an award absent clear proof that the arbitrator strayed beyond his or her contractual authority. Even where an award is claimed to be inconsistent with 'public policy', the Court has insisted that, in order to overturn an award, the award must be in direct conflict with other 'laws and legal precedents', rather than simply in tension with an assessment of 'general considerations of supposed public interests'.[76]

There can be situations where a challenge to an employer's decision, such as a discharge, can be framed both as a breach of the collective bargaining agreement, as well as an unfair labor practice under the NLRA. The National Labor Relations Board's policy in such cases is to require the union, which is the exclusive representative of employees for all claims under the labor contract, to exhaust the contractual grievance procedure before the agency will exercise its statutory jurisdiction. After completion of the grievance procedure, the agency will generally defer to the results of the labor arbitration if the statutory claim involves the same facts as the contractual claim, and the arbitration award is not 'clearly repugnant' to the policies of the labor law.[77]

---

[75] See *United Steelworkers of America* v. *American Mfg. Co.*, 363 U.S. 564 (1960); *United Steelworkers of America* v. *Warrior & Gulf Navigation Co.*, 363 U.S. 574 (1960); *United Steelworkers of America* v. *Enterprise Wheel & Car Corp.*, 363 U.S. 593 (1960).

[76] See *United Paperworkers Int'l Union* v. *Misco, Inc.*, 484 U.S. 29 (1987).

[77] See *Olin Corp.*, 268 N.L.R.B. 573 (1984); *United Technologies Corp.*, 268 N.L.R.B. 557 (1984).

F. Individual Rights and the Collective Agreement

Once the employees have selected an exclusive bargaining representative, their ability to negotiate individual employment contracts is severely curtailed—unless the collective agreement allows individual bargaining.[78] Workers also may be discharged if they engage in concerted action to compel bargaining with groups other than the exclusive representative.[79]

Concerning disputes arising under the labor agreement, individual workers file grievances with their union representatives. The union ultimately controls which grievances are taken up through the process to arbitration. If a grievance is taken to arbitration, the arbitrator's award will generally be preclusive of any court action by the employee against his or her employer for breach of contract. Even if a grievance is not taken to arbitration, its resolution by the contractual process is 'final and binding' and precludes a court action. There are two exceptions to the preclusive effect of the contractual dispute resolution process. The first is where the employee convinces a court that the union breached its duty of fair representation. The exclusive representative, as a matter of law, is under a duty to fairly represent all employees in the bargaining unit. If a breach of this duty is shown, a court action for breach of contract against the employer may proceed.[80] The second exception is where the employee's claim is based on a public law creating individual rights not waivable by the collective bargaining representative, such as Title VII or other anti-discrimination laws.[81]

G. Union Democracy

Federal labor law does not require workers to become members of labor unions even in firms where unions are the exclusive bargaining agency. Indeed, the law prohibits 'closed shops', i.e. agreements requiring workers to become union members as a condition of being hired for a position. However, 'union shop' clauses are lawful (except in states which have enacted 'right to work' laws barring such provisions). Under a typical 'union shop' clause, the employer is permitted to hire whomever it wishes, but the individual hired must within 30 days pay dues that cover the costs of collective representation. This is a financial obligation rather than obligation to join the union as such.

---

[78] See *J.I. Case* v. *NLRB*, 321 U.S. 332 (1944).
[79] See *Emporium Capwell Co.* v. *Western Addition Community Organization*, 420 U.S. 50 (1975).
[80] See *Hines* v. *Anchor Motor Freight, Inc.*, 424 U.S. 554 (1976); *Vaca* v. *Sipes*, 386 U.S. 171 (1967).
[81] See *Alexander* v. *Gardner-Denver Co.*, 415 U.S. 36 (1974).

For individuals who are union members (and most represented employees become members), the federal Labor-Management Reporting and Disclosure Act of 1959 (LMRDA or 'Landrum-Griffin Act')[82] imposes rules of internal union democracy. Under the LMRDA, union members have enforceable rights of free speech at union meetings and to run for union office free of unreasonable restrictions in fairly conducted elections. The NLRA also limits the bases on which unions can discipline their members, and ensures minimum standards of fairness in any such disciplinary proceedings. Union members can be subject to fines but cannot lose their jobs because of a violation of internal union rules. They also have the right to resign their union membership even in the midst of a strike.[83]

H. Labor Law and Business Change[84]

As a general matter, companies seeking to merge with other firms or to sell all or part of their assets are under no duty to bargain over the decision itself, although there is a duty to bargain over the 'effects' of the decisions. 'Effects' bargaining must be in time to permit 'meaningful' bargaining, but can take place after the decision is made.[85] There may, however, be restrictions in the labor agreement requiring the employer to secure a purchaser who will assume the obligations of the unexpired agreements. Such restrictions are enforceable in arbitration, and unions may seek court injunctions to preserve the status quo pending arbitration.

In mergers and sales of stock, the surviving entity or purchaser will generally be held to assume the obligation to bargain with the union and to comply with the terms of the unexpired labor agreement—absent a strong showing that employment conditions with the surviving entity or stock purchaser will so radically alter the preexisting employment relationship that the union cannot be considered any longer to be the exclusive representative of the workers in an appropriate unit.[86]

In the case of asset purchases, however, the purchaser's obligations are substantially relaxed. The purchaser is free to hire an entirely independent workforce, absent proof of refusal to hire the seller's workers because of their

---

[82] 29 U.S.C. §§ 153, 158–60, 186, 401–531.

[83] See *Pattern Makers' League of North America* v. *NLRB*, 473 U.S. 95 (1985).

[84] See generally Samuel Estreicher and Daniel G. Collins (eds.), *Labor Law and Business Change: Theoretical and Transactional Perspectives* (Quorum Books, 1988).

[85] See *First National Maintenance Corp.* v. *NLRB*, 452 U.S. 666 (1981).

[86] See *John Wiley & Sons* v. *Livingston*, 376 U.S. 543 (1964) (surviving entity in merger remains subject to duty to arbitrate); *Clothing Workers* v. *Ratner Corp.*, 602 F.2d 1363 (9th Cir. 1979) (employer bound by collective bargaining agreement despite stock transfer coupled with reorganization as holding company).

union status.[87] The purchaser is under no obligation to assume the predecessor's labor contract[88]—unless possibly if it hires substantially all of the predecessor's employees without predicating offers on changes in terms and conditions and without making substantial changes in the operation.[89] The purchaser is also under no obligation to bargain with the predecessor's union unless a majority of the purchaser's employees come from the ranks of the predecessor's workforce. This determination is made at the time the purchaser hires a 'substantial and representative' complement, rather than the later point when its 'full' complement has been hired.[90] However, a purchaser who buys a business with knowledge of the seller's unremedied unfair labor practices is subject to the NLRB's remedial authority.[91]

V. Conclusion

United States labor and employment law presents a mix of reliance on market forces and regulation. With private-sector unions and collective bargaining in decline, public policy has shifted away from an emphasis on private bargaining to a regulatory model in pursuit of public objectives in the employment arena. The areas of growth and change in the law are employment discrimination law and the common law of wrongful discharge. Nominally, United States law is more protective of management prerogative and skeptical of state intervention than European law. As a practical matter, however, employers face significant litigation costs and risk of liability in personnel decisions.

[87] See *NLRB* v. *Burns International Security Services, Inc.* 406 U.S. 272 (1972).
[88] See *Howard Johnson Co.* v. *Detroit Local Joint Executive Board*, 417 U.S. 249 (1974).
[89] See *Howard Johnson*, 417 U.S. at 258; *United Steelworkers of America* v. *United States Gypsum Co.*, 492 F.2d 713 (5th Cir.), *cert. denied*, 419 U.S. 998 (1974); *Canteen Co.*, 317 N.L.R.B. No. 153 (1995).
[90] See *Fall River Dyeing & Finishing Corp.* v. *NLRB*, 482 U.S. 27 (1987).
[91] See *Golden State Bottling Co.* v. *NLRB*, 414 U.S. 168 (1973).

21

REGULATION OF BANKS

MICHAEL KLAUSNER

I. Introduction

The legal regime governing banks in the United States is comprised of two separate bodies of law. One body consists of the law governing the transactions in which banks are involved: loans, mortgages, deposits, payments by check, payments by wire, letters of credit, and a variety of other transactions. Those transactions are governed by the *Uniform Commercial Code*, as adopted by the states, and additional bodies of state commercial law. Chapter 14 addresses that area of law. The second body consists of the law limiting the businesses in which banks may engage and regulating how they conduct their business. That area of law, commonly referred to as 'bank regulation', is covered in this chapter. Because of the complexity of the bank regulatory system and the nature of this book, this chapter will address only the major elements of the system.[1]

There are bank regulatory agencies in each of the fifty states and three federal regulatory agencies that are directly involved in regulating banks.[2]

---

[1] For an excellent classroom text designed largely around the American 'casebook' model, see Jonathan R. Macey and Geoffrey P. Miller, *Banking Law and Regulation* (Little, Brown, 1992). For a more straightforward text, see Joseph Jude Norton and Sherry Castle Whitley, *Banking Law Manual* (Matthew Bender, updated through 1994).

[2] In addition to the three federal agencies described in section III below, the Office of Thrift Supervision, an office of the Treasury Department, regulates nationally chartered 'savings associations', and the National Credit Union Administration regulates 'credit unions'. Savings associations (often called

Together, they pervasively constrain the business of banks. Some elements of the regulatory regime represent a sound policy response to the economics of banking and associated failures of market forces. Other elements, however, can only be explained as the product of historic, political, and bureaucratic forces. In the last decade, members of Congress and the executive branch have made several attempts at comprehensive reform of the bank regulatory system, with only limited success to date.[3] As this chapter is being completed, Congress is considering comprehensive reform once again. Therefore, a word of warning is in order: much of what is described here could become obsolete with a single congressional enactment.

II. Policy Overview

In a market economy most businesses are not regulated, at least not to any substantial extent. The first step in understanding and evaluating bank regulation is to identify how banks differ from other businesses and to determine why those differences might warrant regulation. One common answer to the question of why banks are so heavily regulated is that they are 'important' to the economy. While that is certainly true, it is not a reason to regulate. Indeed, some would say that it is a reason *not* to regulate. A stronger justification is required.

The primary justification for bank regulation lies in the role banks play in the economy and, as a consequence of that role, in the potential spillover effects that the failure of a bank can have on local and regional economies, and possibly on the national economy as well.[4] Banks are the conduit though which monetary policy is implemented in the United States. The Federal Reserve System adds to and subtracts from the money supply by controlling the funds that banks have available to lend. For this mechanism to work effectively, banks must be sufficiently solvent to make loans when the Federal Reserve System pumps funds into the banking system.

'Savings and Loans') and credit unions perform many of the same functions that banks perform. For simplicity, however, this chapter addresses only the law governing banks, sometimes referred to as 'commercial banks'.

[3] See, e.g. Financial Institutions Safety and Consumer Choice Act of 1991, S.713, 102d Cong. 1st Sess., 137 Cong. Rec. S3712 (daily ed. Mar 20, 1991); H.R . 1505, 102d Cong., 1st Sess., 137 Cong. Rec. H1912 (daily ed. Mar. 20, 1991) (comprehensive reform bill proposed by the Bush Administration). For an analysis of that proposal and of bank regulatory reform generally, see Michael Klausner, 'An Economic Analysis of Bank Regulatory Reform: The Financial Institutions Safety and Consumer Choice Act of 1991', 69 *Wash. U. L. Q.* 695 (1991).

[4] An additional justification for certain types of regulation is the importance of certain banking services to individuals and society's interest in promoting their availability beyond the scope that market forces would dictate.

Banks are also responsible for processing the payments of their customers. Hundreds of billions of dollars in payments are made through the banking system every day. At any point in a day, a bank may be a net payor or payee of billions of dollars. By the end of the day, however, all accounts must be reconciled. If one bank finds itself with insufficient funds to make good on its depositors' payment obligations, a chain of interdependent transactions would have to be unwound.[5] Not only would this be a costly process, but it would undermine confidence in the payment system, which could increase the cost of transactions generally in the economy.

Finally, banks are important (though not exclusive) providers of credit. They provide credit not only to individuals and businesses for investment, but also to other financial institutions whose liquidity promotes liquidity and growth in the economy. The loss of substantial lending capacity as a result of bank failures could impair such liquidity and growth.

Not only is the social cost of bank failure potentially higher than the social cost of other business failures, but the likelihood of bank failure may be higher as well. Because of their financial structure, banks may be more vulnerable to failure than other firms. Banks' assets, consisting largely of loans to clients, are generally illiquid. Their value to the originating bank may be high, but they cannot easily be sold at an amount approaching that value. In contrast, a bank's liabilities are highly liquid. They consist primarily of deposits payable on demand or in a short period of time. Consequently, if many depositors were to demand their funds at the same time—a phenomenon referred to as a 'run'—a bank would have to liquidate its assets rapidly at below-market prices to pay its depositors, which ultimately could result in its insolvency. What is most startling is that this could occur even if the bank is healthy—that is, the value of its assets prior to the run exceeded its liabilities. For this reason, it is important to preserve the public's confidence in banks. Government regulation of the risks that banks undertake is one means of promoting such confidence.

In 1933, following 3 years of widespread bank runs and failures, the United States instituted federal deposit insurance as a means of ensuring depositor confidence in the banking system. Deposit insurance, which is provided explicitly or implicitly in all industrialized countries, essentially eliminates the risk of a bank run. It does so, however, at a cost; it weakens a potential source of market discipline on bankers to operate their banks prudently. Holders of insured deposits have no incentive to consider the solvency or riskiness of their bank. Moreover, deposit insurance places the taxpayer in the

---

[5] For instance, Bank A's ability to pay $1 million may be dependent on its receipt of payments from Banks B, C, and D, which in turn may be dependent on their receipt of funds from Banks E and F, and so on.

position of potentially paying the cost of bank failures. It thus creates an additional justification for using government regulation to control bank risk-taking.

III. The Allocation of Regulatory Responsibility

Both state and federal government agencies charter and regulate banks. This 'dual banking system', however, was not created by design; it is largely an accident of history. Banks were originally subject only to state regulation.[6] In 1863, however, Congress passed the National Bank Act, which created a new class of banks that would be chartered by the new federal agency called the Office of the Comptroller of the Currency ('the Comptroller'). Congress's original plan was to have all banks become federally chartered and to have the Comptroller replace the state banking agencies as the sole bank regulatory authority. History evolved differently, however, and the ranks of the state-chartered banks eventually grew.[7]

Ultimately, Congress brought state-chartered banks under the federal regulatory umbrella. In 1913, Congress enacted the Federal Reserve Act, which created the Federal Reserve System (FRS). The FRS would serve two roles: it would serve as the country's central bank; and the FRS's governing body, the Federal Reserve Board, would regulate state banks that chose to become members of the FRS. Then, in the Banking Act of 1933, Congress created the Federal Deposit Insurance Corporation (FDIC), which would also serve two roles: it would provide deposit insurance to all national banks and, in its discretion, to state banks; and it would regulate state banks that purchased its insurance, but that were not members of the FRS. The result today is a regime of confusing and overlapping, and, many people believe, inefficient regulatory jurisdiction.[8]

---

[6] Prior to 1863, there were three banks chartered by the federal government. In 1781, the Bank of North America was established under a national charter. In 1785, however, Congress repealed its national charter, and the bank continued operation under a Pennsylvania charter. Then, in 1791, Congress issued a 20-year charter to the First Bank of the United States. At the end of its 20-year charter, that bank dissolved. Finally, in 1816, Congress chartered the Second Bank of the United States. It too ceased operation at the end of 20 years, when Congress declined to extend its charter. In addition to providing commercial banking services, these banks served as central banks.

[7] At that time, banks issued notes that served as legal tender. Congress expected that the establishment of uniform notes issued by national banks would force state banks out of the note-issuing business and pressure them to convert to national charters. In 1865, to add a further push, Congress levied a 10 percent tax on state bank notes. In response, however, state banks developed checking accounts, which served as an alternative method of payment, escaped taxation, and kept state banks in existence.

[8] For an overview of the historical development of the U.S. bank regulatory system, see Macey and Miller, n. 1 above, at 1–36.

The basic allocation of regulatory responsibility is thus as follows. If a state banking agency charters a bank, that bank is subject to the regulation of the chartering state's banking authority and, most likely, to the regulation of a federal banking authority as well. If the bank is a member of the FRS (a status that was once necessary to obtain certain central bank services but today has little functional meaning), the bank is regulated by the Federal Reserve Board, the governing body of the FRS.[9] If the bank is not a member of the FRS, but it is insured, it is subject to the regulation of the FDIC.[10] Essentially all state non-member banks today are insured by the FDIC, although historically that was not true. To further complicate the picture, if the state-chartered bank is controlled by a corporation (a 'bank holding company'), that holding company is subject to Federal Reserve Board regulation, regardless of whether the bank is a member of the FRS. State banks that are members of the FRS are referred to as 'state member banks'. Those that are not members of the FRS are referred to as 'state non-member banks'. If a bank is chartered by the Comptroller, it is referred to as a 'national bank' and is subject to the Comptroller's regulation.[11] As in the case of a state bank, however, if a national bank has a holding company, the Federal Reserve Board regulates the holding company.

The following summarizes the federal agencies' primary regulatory jurisdiction:

Type of Bank	*Primary Federal Regulator*
State member banks	The Federal Reserve Board
Insured state non-member banks	The FDIC
National banks	The Comptroller
All holding companies	The Federal Reserve Board

To add a further complication, the FDIC insures the deposits of all national banks, all state member banks, and, as stated above, essentially all state non-member banks. Consequently, the FDIC has a secondary role in chartering and regulating nearly all banks.

Despite this division of regulatory responsibility, there is a high degree of uniformity in the regulations governing national banks and state member banks. State non-member banks of some states are treated somewhat differently, but again, the similarities in regulation are greater than the differences.

There is little policy justification for this crazy-quilt pattern of regulatory responsibility. Over the last 15 years, Congress and the executive branch have

---

[9] Federal Reserve Board regulations are located at 12 C.F.R. Parts 200–299.
[10] FDIC regulations are located at 12 C.F.R. Pts 300–399.
[11] The Comptroller's regulations are located at 12 C.F.R. Pts 1–199.

periodically considered consolidating regulatory responsibility, and indeed as this book goes to press, Congress is considering such a reorganization. So far, however, these efforts have failed due to political and bureaucratic opposition.

Before moving on to discuss the regulation of banks, a bank-like institution—the 'savings and loan institution'—deserves mention. Savings and Loans (also called 'S & Ls', 'thrifts', and a variety of other terms) collect deposits, just as banks do, but unlike banks, they are required to invest those deposits primarily in residential mortgage loans. Savings and Loans are regulated by their own federal agency;[12] they are subject to their own rules and regulations; and, while they are insured by the same federal agency that insures banks, this is a new development and their insurance pool is still segregated from that of the banks.

Savings and Loans are best known today for their widespread failures during the 1980s and early 1990s. These failures, which entailed well over $100 billion in losses, were the product of several factors. To a large extent, however, they were the product of a misguided regulatory regime. Savings and Loans were historically required to make 30–year fixed-rate mortgage loans, thereby exposing them to massive losses when interest rates rose in the 1970s. In an attempt to allow Savings and Loans to make up these losses, Congress enacted a law allowing them to invest in a wide range of assets, including corporate equity and real estate, with which neither the Savings and Loans nor their regulators had prior experience. Adventures with these new investment powers led to further losses. Finally, Savings and Loans were not allowed to expand across state lines. This exposed them to further losses as certain regions of the country, particularly the Southwest, were struck by severe recessions. This chapter will not address Savings and Loans regulation. The experience of the Savings and Loans, however, provides an instructive lesson in the dangers of mis-regulation.

IV. The Chartering Process

In the United States, except for certain professions requiring special education and licenses (such as the legal and medical professions), there is no need to obtain government approval before a business may begin operation. The organizers may simply start. If they choose to operate in the form of a corporation (with limited liability and other privileges that attend incorpora-

---

[12] The Office of Thrift Supervision, which is part of the Department of the Treasury, regulates Savings and Loans.

tion), they merely file a 'charter' or 'certificate of incorporation' with a state agency. If the organizers choose to operate as a partnership or as a sole proprietorship, there are no formalities whatsoever.

To enter the banking business, however, governmental approval is necessary. As discussed in section III above, an application to form a bank may be submitted either to the Comptroller or to the state banking authority of the state in which the proposed bank would be located.

In considering an application, the Comptroller considers the following factors:

(1) the financial history and condition of the bank (if it previously operated under a state charter);
(2) the adequacy of its capital structure;
(3) the bank's future earnings prospects;
(4) the general character and fitness of its management;
(5) the risk the bank presents to the federal insurance fund;
(6) the convenience and needs of the community to be served;
(7) whether the bank has complied with all provisions of the law and whether its proposed operations are consistent with the policies underlying the banking laws.[13]

These considerations are obviously so open-ended that the Comptroller has a great deal of discretion in granting a charter, especially when the bank has no prior operating record under a state charter.

State laws regarding the issuance of a bank charter are generally similar to federal law. In addition, however, almost all states require that applicants obtain federal deposit insurance from the FDIC, and in making its decision whether to provide such insurance, the FDIC considers the factors listed above.[14] In effect, therefore, the FDIC shares chartering authority with the state banking authorities. (A national bank automatically receives deposit insurance if the Comptroller grants a charter.)

V. Regulation of the Bank's Business

The core business of a bank involves taking deposits, making loans, and processing its customers' payments (by check or wire). As the financial services sector has evolved, however, banks have felt increasing competitive pressure to provide additional services. This evolution has run headlong into a bank regulatory regime that was designed in an earlier era. Whereas an ordinary

---

[13] 12 U.S.C. §1816; 12 C.F.R. §5.20(c).   [14] 12 U.S.C. §1816.

corporation in the United States can engage in any lawful business, a bank may engage only in businesses that the law affirmatively permits. Accordingly, all of a bank's services are subject to regulation, as is the geographic location at which a bank operates.

A. *Regulation of Deposits*

Compared to the other aspects of a bank's business discussed below, the collection of deposits is relatively free of regulation. Historically, interest paid on all deposits was subject to governmentally-imposed ceilings, but today banks are free to set interest rates on most accounts at whatever level the market demands. The only accounts now subject to interest rate limits are demand deposit accounts held by businesses.[15] By shifting funds between checking and other accounts, however, businesses are able to minimize this disadvantage.

The government's primary involvement in the deposit side of the banking business is as provider of deposit insurance.[16] Federal law requires that all national banks, state member banks, and state non-member banks owned by holding companies purchase deposit insurance from the FDIC. In addition, nearly all states require that their non-member banks do so, and even in states without a requirement, banks typically choose to purchase FDIC insurance.

The FDIC's insurance covers accounts of up to $100,000. Depositors may obtain coverage of more than that amount, however, by spreading their funds among more than one bank. Accounts in different banks are not aggregated for purposes of the $100,000 limit. In addition, a joint account or a trust account is accorded separate coverage up to the $100,000 limit, even if the joint account holders or the trust beneficiaries have individual accounts at the same bank.[17]

Historically, banks paid a flat-rate premium to the FDIC for this insurance. Beginning in 1993, however, the FDIC has attempted to charge rates related to the estimated risk of a bank's failure. It remains to be seen how successful risk-related premiums will be, both in deterring banks from taking risks and in protecting the FDIC's insurance fund.

---

[15] 12 C.F.R. Pt 217.
[16] 12 U.S.C. §1821(a). The FDIC's deposit insurance coverage rules are contained in 12 C.F.R. Pt 330.
[17] 12 U.S.C. §1821(a)(1).

B. Regulation of Assets

Although traditionally a bank's assets consisted primarily of loans, as the financial system has evolved, banks have sought to invest in other assets, particularly in real estate and securities. In the United States, however, banks are subject to severe restrictions with respect to assets other than loans and to less severe restrictions with respect to loans. The general objective of asset regulation is to limit the riskiness of a bank's asset portfolio.

1. Investment in real estate

While banks commonly secure their loans with real property, they are generally not permitted to hold real estate for investment purposes. National banks and state member banks may hold real estate that they acquire in satisfaction of a debt or in a foreclosure sale, but they generally must dispose of such property within 5 years. In addition, they may own the buildings in which they conduct their business.[18] In the past, state non-member banks enjoyed greater freedom to invest in real estate. Today, however, FDIC regulations subject state non-member banks to restrictions similar to those applicable to national banks.[19]

2. Investment in securities

One of the central features of the bank regulatory system in the United States is the set of restrictions that it imposes on banks' involvement with corporate securities. The primary targets of those restrictions are underwriting and dealing in securities, which are addressed in section C, below. Passive investment in securities, however, is restricted as well.

National banks and state member banks are permitted to invest in bonds issued by the federal, state, or local governments; the national or provincial governments of Canada (as a result of the North American Free Trade Agreement); and certain quasi-governmental organizations. In the case of certain government securities that are not backed by the full taxing authority of the issuing government, there are limits on the quantity of the bonds that a bank may hold. National and state member banks may also invest in investment grade corporate bonds for which an active market exists. They may not, however, invest in equity securities or in risky or illiquid bonds.[20]

State non-member banks are governed by state laws and by the regulations

---

[18] 12 U.S.C. §§29, 371d.   [19] 12 U.S.C. §1831a; 12 C.F.R. Pt 362.
[20] 12 U.S.C. §§24 (Seventh), 335.

of the FDIC. Most states have rules that parallel those described above. Some states, however, allow banks to invest more broadly in corporate securities. The FDIC does not restrict these investments via any broadly applicable regulation, but it has the authority to require individual banks to divest securities that threaten the solvency of the bank.[21]

3. Regulation of lending

Restrictions on lending fall into three categories. First, there are qualitative limits on lending to insiders—including officers, directors, and major shareholders[22]—and quantitative limits on the volume of loans that can be made to any single borrower.[23] These rules are intended to prevent self-dealing and to promote portfolio diversification.

Secondly, there are usury laws in some states that establish ceilings on the interest rates that banks may charge on certain loans. The law of a particular state is applicable to that state's banks and, in most cases, to national banks operating in the state. Usury rules create complications when loans are extended across state lines (for instance, when a credit card is issued to a resident of another state). The general rule is that the usury law of the state in which the bank is located applies.[24]

Thirdly, there is a group of rules designed to expand the availability of credit to individuals and communities that may otherwise have difficulty gaining access to the credit market. The Equal Credit Opportunity Act prohibits discrimination in lending on the basis of race, color, religion, national origin, sex, marital status, or age.[25] This law, in its intent and its operation, parallels laws prohibiting discrimination in employment, housing, and in other contexts. The Community Reinvestment Act goes a step further by affirmatively encouraging banks to make loans in low and moderate income neighborhoods.[26] The sanction for a bank that fails to make such loans is that the federal regulators may withhold their approval of transactions that they are empowered to approve or disapprove (e.g. opening a new branch, or a merger of two banks).[27]

---

[21] 12 U.S.C. §§1818(a), 1831a.   [22] 12 U.S.C. §§375a, 375b.
[23] 12 U.S.C. §84.
[24] See, e.g. *Marquette National Bank of Minneapolis* v. *First of Omaha Service Corp.*, 439 U.S. 299 (1979).
[25] 15 U.S.C. §§1691–1691f.   [26] 12 U.S.C. §§2901–2906.
[27] This author and others have advocated a more market-oriented form of intervention to facilitate the provision of credit to these communities. Michael Klausner, 'Letting Banks Trade CRA Obligations Would Offer Market-Based Efficiencies,' *American Banker*, January 21, 1994; Jonathan A. Neuberger and Ronald H. Schmidt, 'A Market-Based Approach to CRA', *FRBSF Weekly Letter*, No. 94–21, May 27, 1994.

C. Activities Restrictions

Under the National Bank Act, national banks may engage in traditional banking activities—receiving deposits, making loans, and processing customers' payments—as well as 'incidental' activities that are 'necessary to carry on the business of banking'.[28] Especially in recent years, the Comptroller has interpreted this language broadly, allowing banks to expand into non-traditional activities, including for example certain types of leasing; issuance of municipal bond insurance; issuance of insurance related to repayment of a loan; the provision of management services to banks; the provision of data processing services related to bank operations; assisting customers in preparing tax returns; and foreign exchange trading. The Supreme Court has recently held that the Comptroller has broad discretion in interpreting this language, and that the courts should defer to its exercise of that discretion so long as it is 'kept within reasonable bounds'. The only hint given regarding the scope of the Comptroller's discretion is the Court's statement that '[v]entures distant from dealing in financial investment instruments—for example, operating a general travel agency—*may* exceed those bounds' (emphasis added).[29]

Banks have been particularly interested in getting into the insurance business, both as underwriters and sales agents. At this point, national banks are generally not permitted to underwrite insurance (nor are they permitted to affiliate with insurance underwriters). The law on insurance agency activities, however, is more permissive, and peculiar—again reflecting the history and politics of banking regulation. There is a separate section of the National Bank Act that allows national banks located in towns of no more than 5,000 people to sell insurance as agents.[30] This rule was designed to give struggling national banks in small towns an additional source of revenue. The Comptroller recently ruled that national banks in these towns could sell insurance to people outside the town, with no geographical limit. This ruling was recently upheld by a court of appeals.[31]

State banks are generally subject to the same activity restrictions that apply to national banks. The FDIC, however, may allow a well-capitalized state bank to engage in additional activities if it finds that such activities 'pose no significant risk' to the deposit insurance fund.[32] In the area of insurance activities, state banks generally may not underwrite insurance, but about half the

---

[28] 12 U.S.C. §24 (Seventh) (national banks may exercise 'all such incidental powers as shall be necessary to carry on the business of banking').
[29] *Variable Annuity Life Insurance Co.* v. *NationsBank of North Carolina*, 115 S. Ct. 810, 814 n. 2 (1995).
[30] 12 U.S.C.(1946 ed.) § 92.
[31] See *Independent Insurance Agents of America* v. *Ludwig*, 997 F.2d 958 (D.C.Cir. 1993).
[32] 12 U.S.C. §1831a.

states allow their state-chartered banks to sell insurance as agents to some extent.[33]

In addition to limiting banks' activities generally to those 'incidental' to core banking services, the law also prohibits banks from underwriting or dealing in corporate securities. They are permitted, however, to underwrite and deal in United States Treasury securities, and state and local government securities, and Canadian national and provincial government securities supported by the taxing power of the issuing entity (as opposed to bonds to be repaid out of the proceeds of a particular project). In addition, banks are permitted to underwrite and deal in certain other government and quasi-government securities subject to quantity limitations. Finally, they are allowed to provide investment advice, stock brokerage services,[34] and certain private placement services.[35]

Other industrialized countries allow banks to provide a full range of securities services. The origin of these restrictions in the United States was the stock market crash of 1929 and the Great Depression of the 1930s, when approximately one-third of all American banks failed. At the time, there was a general perception that a major cause of the crash and the bank failures was the involvement of banks in securities underwriting and dealing. In response, Congress enacted the Banking Act of 1933, which dramatically altered the way banks were regulated. Among the changes included in the Act were restrictions on securities activities. Those parts of the Act that impose these restrictions are commonly referred to as the 'Glass-Steagall Act', named for their well-known congressional sponsors.

Recent research has raised substantial questions regarding the role that securities activities actually played in the bank failures of the 1930s,[36] and additional research has suggested that banks could be both safer and more profitable if they (or their affiliates) were permitted to provide securities services.[37] In response to this research and to the pressures of the evolving financial market-place, bank regulators have eased restrictions on securities activities to the extent that the Glass-Steagall Act permits. Congress is cur-

---

[33] A small number of state banks currently underwrite insurance, but current federal law prohibits others from doing so.

[34] Under the National Bank Act, banks are permitted to sell securities 'upon the order, and for the account of, customers'. 12 U.S.C. §24.

[35] See *Securities Industries Association* v. *Board of Governors of the Federal Reserve System*, 807 F.2d 1052 (D.C. Cir. 1986), *cert. denied*, 483 U.S. 1005 (1987). For an exhaustive treatise on securities activities of banks, see Melanie Fein, *Securities Activities of Banks* (Prentice Hall, updated through 1993).

[36] George Benston, *The Separation of Commercial and Investment Banking: The Glass-Steagall Act Revisited and Reconsidered* (Oxford University Press, 1990); Milton Friedman and Anna Schwartz, *A Monetary History of the United States 1867–1960* (Princeton U.P., 1963); Flannery, 'An Economic Evaluation of Bank Securities Activities Before 1933', in *Deregulating Wall Street* (Ingo Walter ed., Wiley, 1985); Kelly, 'Legislative History of the Glass-Steagall Act' in *ibid*.

[37] Robert Litan, *What Should Banks Do?* (Brookings 1987).

rently considering repealing Glass-Steagall's separation between banking and securities activities.

D. Capital Requirements

The investment and activity restrictions described in section V A–C above are intended to limit the risk that a bank will become insolvent and thereby impose losses on the FDIC's insurance fund and on depositors with deposits above the $100,000 limit. Additional regulatory instruments aimed directly at bank solvency are 'capital requirements'. These requirements are complex, but the basic idea is simple: banks must maintain a minimum amount of 'capital', which roughly means shareholders' equity, plus some forms of debt that are subordinated to the claims of the FDIC and depositors.

Banks must comply with two capital requirements: a 'risk-based' capital requirement and a leverage requirement. The risk-based capital requirement was developed jointly by the banking authorities of twelve major industrialized countries in a document known as the 'Basle Accords'. It is designed to force banks to hold capital that is roughly proportionate to the size and credit risk of their asset portfolio. (An additional requirement is currently being developed that will link capital to interest-rate risk as well.) The way this requirement basically works is as follows. Different weights are assigned to different categories of assets (e.g. home mortgages, government securities), based on their general riskiness. A bank's weighted assets are then added together to construct its 'risk-weighted assets'. Similar calculations are performed for off-balance-sheet obligations, such as letters of credit and loan commitments.[38] Next, capital is calculated and adjusted in two different ways, one more restrictive than the other. Finally, two ratios of capital to risk-weighted assets are constructed. The regulations provide that each of these ratios must be above a specified level.

In addition to these risk-based capital requirements, banks must meet a leverage requirement. This is a more crude measure of bank risk, because it is unadjusted for the riskiness of the bank's portfolio. It consists of the ratio of a bank's equity to its assets, each adjusted in various ways. Bank regulators have discretion to impose between a 3 percent and 5 percent leverage requirement on a bank, depending on the regulator's assessment of the bank's condition.[39] The leverage requirement serves as a backstop for the risk-based requirement.

[38] The risk-based capital regulations are the same for all banks. They are published separately for each type of bank: 12 C.F.R. Pt 3, App A (national banks); 12 C.F.R. Pt 325, App A (state non-member banks); 12 C.F.R. Pt 208, App A (state member banks).

[39] These regulations are also the same for all types of banks: 12 C.F.R. §3.2 et seq (national banks); 12 C.F.R. Pt 208, App B (state member banks); 12 C.F.R. §325.5.

E. *Geographic Location*

Historically, most states prohibited banks from operating out of more than one office; branches were not permitted, either within the chartering state or in other states. When Congress authorized the chartering of national banks, they too were subject to this restriction. Beginning in the twentieth century, however, these geographical restrictions were reduced. This liberalization culminated in 1994 with the passage of federal legislation essentially eliminating these restrictions. After a phase-in period, unless a state imposes its own restrictions, banks will be permitted to branch freely.

VI. Regulation of Banks' Affiliates

Not only are banks themselves subject to restrictions on their business, but the affiliates of banks are restricted as well. There are two justifications for these restrictions. First, there is a concern that a bank may be used to support a failing affiliate. Secondly, if a bank's affiliates are strong, they will be better able to support the bank if it encounters financial difficulties. A company that controls a bank is termed a 'bank holding company'. The Federal Reserve Board regulates bank holding companies and their non-bank subsidiaries.

The primary source of restrictions on bank holding companies and their non-bank subsidiaries is the Bank Holding Company Act, which was enacted in 1956 and expanded in 1970. That Act provides that bank holding companies and their subsidiaries may engage in non-banking activities only to the extent that those activities are 'so closely related to banking or managing or controlling banks as to be a proper incident thereto'.[40] The Federal Reserve Board divides this legal standard into two parts: whether an activity is 'closely related to banking', and whether it is a 'proper incident' thereto. The first test requires consideration of the following factors: (a) whether banks generally have provided the service in question; (b) whether banks generally provide services that are so similar that they are well suited to provide the proposed service; and (c) whether banks provide services that are so integrally related to the proposed service as to require them to provide the proposed service. The 'proper incident' test requires a balancing of the social benefits of a particular bank engaging in a proposed activity and the social costs of its doing so. The statute explicitly provides, however, that almost all insurance underwriting and agency activities are not 'proper incidents' to banking.

---

[40] 12 U.S.C. §1843(c)(8).

The Federal Reserve Board has issued a regulation termed 'Regulation Y', which lists activities the Board has determined generically to be 'closely related to banking'.[41] The board adds to this list from time to time. An activity's inclusion in Regulation Y does not bear on the issue of whether the activity meets the 'proper incident' test, which the Board applies on a case-by-case basis. Some of the activities currently included in Regulation Y are: performing trust services; acting as a financial adviser; providing data processing and transmission services; performing appraisals on real estate; providing securities brokerage services; providing foreign exchange services; providing tax planning and preparation services; and operating a credit bureau. For a bank holding company to enter a business not included in Regulation Y, it must apply to the Federal Reserve Board for an individual ruling on whether the proposed business meets the 'closely related' test.

The Glass-Steagall Act (see section V C above) also restricts the securities underwriting and dealing activities of bank holding companies. Section 20 of that Act provides that national banks and state member banks may not affiliate with a company that is 'principally engaged' in underwriting or dealing in securities. As the Federal Reserve Board and the courts have interpreted this provision, banks' affiliates are not barred from underwriting and dealing in government securities.[42] Moreover, they are not barred from underwriting and dealing in corporate securities so long as they are not 'principally engaged' in doing so. Pursuant to this interpretation, bank holding companies may apply to the Federal Reserve Board to establish subsidiaries that earn up to 10 percent of their revenues by underwriting and dealing in corporate securities. The formation of these 'Section 20 affiliates' must be approved by the Board, however. In addition, their operations are subject to restrictions, especially regarding transactions with their affiliated banks and communications with the public.

VII. International Banking

The regulations described above relate to the domestic operations of banks chartered in the United States. Different rules govern both the foreign operations of United States banks and the American operations of foreign banks. Foreign banks operating in the United States are subject to their home country laws as well as United States law. Similarly, American banks operating

---

[41] 12 C.F.R. §225.4.

[42] Recall that under Section 16 of the Glass Steagall Act, banks themselves may engage in these activities. See section V C above.

abroad are subject to both United States law and the laws of the countries in which they operate. Entire books are devoted to international banking.[43] The following discussion provides a brief overview.

A. United States Banks Abroad

When American banks and bank holding companies operate abroad, they often compete with banks whose regulators allow them much greater freedom than that generally available to United States banks. Most importantly, banks in other countries are commonly permitted to provide a wide range of financial services, including underwriting and dealing in securities. Accordingly, federal law accommodates American banks operating abroad by allowing them to engage in activities that are 'usual' to the business of banking in a host country.[44] Similarly, bank holding companies are given more freedom abroad than in the United States. The law, however, still imposes limits on the expanded powers of banks and their holding companies when operating abroad. It requires banks to obtain regulatory permission before opening a foreign branch or beginning to engage in an activity not listed by regulation as generally permissible; and it requires their holding companies to obtain permission before beginning major foreign operations or making large investments abroad.

B. Foreign Banks in the United States

There are two policy concerns underlying the law governing foreign banks operating in the United States: maintaining the solvency of these banks; and promoting competitive equality between foreign banks and their American competitors. Accordingly, a foreign bank seeking to operate in the United States must apply to the Federal Reserve Board. In ruling on the application, the Board considers competence, experience, and integrity of the bank's management and the financial resources of the bank. In addition, the Board must be assured that the bank is 'subject to comprehensive supervision and regulation on a consolidated basis' by the banking authority of the applicant bank's home country.[45] Once a foreign bank obtains approval to operate in the United States, it is subject to essentially the same regulations that govern national banks.[46]

---

[43] See, e.g. Michael Gruson and Ralph Riesner, *Regulation of Foreign Banks* (Butterworth, 1991).
[44] 12 U.S.C. § 601; 12 C.F.R. §211.3(b).   [45] 12 U.S.C. § 3105(d)(2).
[46] 12 U.S.C. §§3102(b), 3105(h).

VIII. Examinations and Enforcement

The enforcement of bank regulations requires that the regulator have detailed information regarding a bank's operation. Without this information and without the authority to impose penalties when violations are uncovered, the voluminous bank regulations would be of little use. Federal bank regulators obtain information primarily from two sources. First, each bank must file reports containing detailed financial information. One report, referred to as the 'Report of Condition' or 'call report', contains information regarding the bank's assets and liabilities. This report is due quarterly. Another report, the 'Report of Income', is due quarterly from large banks and semi-annually from smaller banks, and contains information regarding the bank's income. Secondly, employees of the federal regulators make on-site visits to every bank, termed 'examinations'. During these visits, the 'bank examiner' is given free access to the bank's files and may question its management and employees. No other business in the United States is subject to such a thoroughgoing examination by a government agency. Congress has recently instructed the regulators to conduct examinations of every bank above a minimum size once a year (and the smallest banks once every year and a half), but it remains to be seen whether agency personnel can maintain such a pace. State banks are subject to a similar examination regime carried out by state banking authorities.

At the conclusion of a bank examination, the examiners assign a bank a set of numerical scores designed to reflect the bank's condition. Scores, ranging from '1' to '5', are given for each of the following criteria: capital adequacy, asset quality, management quality, earnings, and liquidity. In addition, they assign a composite score, which need not equal the average of the individual scores. This scoring system is commonly referred to by the acronym CAMEL, which is derived from the first letter of each criterion. A composite rating of '1' reflects strong performance, and a rating of '5' indicates that the bank that is at high risk of imminent failure. Intermediate ratings, particularly of '3' or '4', may require remedial action.[47]

Neither the CAMEL ratings nor any other information uncovered in a bank examination is made available to the public. The reasons for this are straightforward. First, this information could be used by a bank's competitors in a manner that would impair market competition. Secondly, information indicating the weakness of a bank could trigger a bank run of uninsured deposits, which can result in the loss of asset values and failure. Although information

---

[47] FDIC, *Manual of Examination Policies, Basic Examination Concepts and Guidelines*, 1.1–1 to 1.1.3 (1990).

regarding a bank's condition would be valuable to a bank's customers in deciding whether to continue doing business with the bank, they must instead rely on the interest and ability of the bank's regulator to preserve its viability.

Regulators give heightened scrutiny to a bank with a poor CAMEL rating, especially if its capital is low. Under a system termed 'prompt corrective action', the regulators are required to impose increasingly strict limits on a bank's operations and management as its capital declines. For instance, if a bank's capital is below specified levels, the regulators may require it to submit a plan for the restoration of its capital, prohibit it from paying dividends or increasing executive salaries, limit its growth, or even replace its managers.[48]

Even if a bank's capital is not low, the regulators have the authority to enter into formal and informal arrangements by which a bank agrees to improve its performance or to limit the risks it assumes. Under the threat of formal enforcement action or in order to obtain a regulatory approval of some new action, a bank may commonly enter into a written agreement with a regulator under which the bank promises to modify its business in a manner designed to enhance its performance or reduce its risk. These informal arrangements constitute an important part of the enforcement regime. If informal action is unsuccessful, or if circumstances require more severe measures, the regulator has the authority to order a bank to take or refrain from taking any action, or to alter its business in any way necessary to bring the bank into compliance with the law and to alleviate any unsound condition. If contested, these orders, referred to as 'cease and desist' orders, require formal notice and hearing procedures within the regulatory agency. Once an order is final, the bank may challenge it in court, but the courts review these orders under standards that are highly deferential to the regulators. If necessary, the regulator can have its order take effect immediately pending litigation regarding its validity.

Additional regulatory tools available to the banking authorities include the imposition of monetary penalties on banks and bank managers; suspension of deposit insurance; placement of the bank in a conservatorship; charter termination; and criminal prosecution. Any of these actions may be challenged in court.

IX. Bank Failures

Despite strict regulation and intensive examinations, bank insolvencies occur. Indeed, during the last decade, such insolvencies have been more numerous than at any other time since the Great Depression of the 1930s.

---

[48] 12 U.S.C. §1831o.

When a bank fails, it is not subject to the normal bankruptcy process described in Chapter 17. Instead, bank failures are governed by a separate regime administered primarily by the FDIC. The FDIC performs two functions in 'resolving' a bank failure. First, it serves as the receiver for the bank. In that capacity, the FDIC has a wide range of authority, including most basically the authority to liquidate the bank's assets and to process its creditors' claims.[49] Secondly, as the deposit insurer, the FDIC is the bank's primary claimant.

When a bank fails, the FDIC is required to make funds available to its depositors as soon as possible, at which point the FDIC is subrogated to the rights of the depositors against the bank.[50] The FDIC may provide these funds either by making direct payments to depositors, or by transferring the deposits to another bank and making a payment to that bank. At that point, the FDIC may liquidate the failed bank, sell off its assets, and repay the bank's uninsured claimants and itself out of the proceeds. More commonly, however, the FDIC facilitates a merger between the failed bank and a healthy bank, or it sells the failed bank to a bank holding company. Typically, the FDIC subsidizes such a transaction, either by making a cash payment to the acquiror or the merged bank, by guaranteeing the value of the failed bank's assets, or by similar means. The FDIC is permitted to engage in this type of transaction only if it is the least costly means of disposing of the failed bank. This is often the case, however. By continuing the operation of a failed bank, rather than liquidating it, the FDIC saves the administrative costs of liquidation, and it may preserve the going concern value of the bank, for which an acquiring bank is often willing to pay a premium. One common by-product of this type of transaction is that deposits above the $100,000 insurance limit are preserved in the merged or acquired bank.

If a failed bank is part of a bank holding company, the FDIC may be able to reduce its losses by obtaining funds from the holding company. This can occur in either of two ways. First, the law allows the FDIC to obtain funds from other banks within the holding company of the failed bank.[51] This legal arrangement is unusual in that separately incorporated businesses outside the banking sector generally do not have obligations to the creditors of their affiliates. Secondly, as a bank approaches the point of failure, the bank's federal regulator can induce its holding company to agree in advance to guarantee the solvency of the bank up to an amount equal to 5 percent of the bank's total assets.[52]

---

[49] 12 U.S.C. §§ 1821, 1822.   [50] 12 U.S.C. § 1821(f), (g).   [51] 12 U.S.C. §1815(e).
[52] 12 U.S.C. §1831o(e)(2).

X. Conclusion

This chapter has only discussed the highlights of a very complex topic. The bank regulatory statutes and regulations fill several volumes, and that does not even include the court cases interpreting them. The allocation of regulatory responsibility is byzantine, and today many restrictions are indefensible as a matter of policy. But many elements of the underlying scheme are sensible. Because banks play crucial roles in the implementation of monetary policy, the provision of credit, and the processing of payments, bank failures can have costly spillover effects. Consequently, it makes sense for banks to be subject to regulation aimed at controlling the incidence of bank failures and minimizing the social costs of such failures.

22

FEDERAL REGULATION OF SECURITIES

HELEN S. SCOTT

I. Introduction to the United States Securities Markets

The capital markets of the United States provide mechanisms for the purchase and sale of instruments, broadly known as securities, which represent claims of a contractual nature against the company that sells or issues the instrument and which is generally referred to as the 'issuer'. Equity and debt instruments which can have standardized characteristics, and thus can be widely traded by the public,[1] are used by business enterprises[2] as sources of funds.[3]

[1] While it is theoretically possible to have public markets for unique instruments, the necessity of fully explaining the unusual characteristics of each instrument would substantially limit the number of such transactions by making them too costly.

[2] Most business enterprises in the United States which issue securities to fund operations are organized in corporate form. However, there is no requirement that an issuer of securities to the public be a corporation, and many issuers are not in corporate form, for example, trusts or limited partnerships. Under the various state corporate laws, shareholders are the owners of the corporation, and the value of their interests fluctuates with the fortunes of the company. This is in contrast to debt-holders, whose interest in the issuer is fixed by contract. The market value of debt generally varies by the interest rate it bears (as compared to the rate of return available on other investments) and the credit-worthiness of the issuer.

The state statutes also provide for limited liability for shareholders. Since the holders of common stock

The use of securities represents one of the available financing devices to corporations generally, regardless of whether the instruments are publicly tradable. There are many marketable (but not widely traded) securities that have terms which are individually tailored to particular transactions or interests. Because one or more classes of security (usually stock) will also possess the power to vote, securities may also be designed and issued for the purpose of allocating control of the entity.[4]

There are several different types of public markets for securities in the United States. Stock exchanges are the oldest public markets. They are private enterprises, with members who buy their memberships in the form of 'seats'. The issuer of securities which are to be traded on a stock exchange must meet the listing requirements of the exchange, enter into a contract with the exchange, called a 'Listing Agreement', and pay listing fees to the exchange. Listing requirements typically include a minimum amount of assets, a minimum number of shares outstanding, and certain governance structures.[5]

Public trading of securities off the exchanges is done in the 'over-the-counter' (OTC) market. The principal OTC market is NASDAQ, the National Association of Securities Dealers Automated Quotation System, which is divided into several tiers, the largest of which is the National Market System. NASDAQ is run by the NASD, which is a trade association composed of virtually all the brokers and brokerage houses in the United States The stock exchanges and the NASD support themselves by member fees and 'listing fees' paid by companies whose securities they trade.

The primary source of profits to members of both the stock exchanges and the NASD is the money they make from trading securities, either for their customers or for their own accounts. The greater the number of listings a

---

are the residual claimants in a corporation's capital structure, without limited liability the price and characteristics of common stock could not be as easily standardized. Different shareholders with differing levels of wealth, which without limited liability would be fully exposed to the debts of the corporation, would demand different prices and different safeguards in exchange for their investment. Without standardized prices and terms, public trading of these instruments would be extremely cumbersome. See Frank H. Easterbrook and Daniel R. Fischel, 'Limited Liability and the Corporation', 52 *U. Chi. L. Rev.* 89, 92 (1985). On state corporate laws, see generally Chapter 13.

For convenience, this chapter refers to the issuer of securities as the 'corporation', 'company', or 'issuer' interchangeably.

[3] There are also a variety of instruments which can be standardized sufficiently to be traded publicly whose value varies with either another instrument or a company's performance, but which do not represent claims on the underlying company, which are known as 'derivatives'. A simple example is the stock call option, which is a right (but not an obligation) to purchase shares of a company's stock at a fixed price at a time in the future. The company whose stock value will determine whether or not that option will be exercised need not be involved in the creation, purchase or sale of the option. The option is a contract between its issuer and its purchaser, and does not represent a claim on the company at all. Many companies do issue such options, particularly in connection with executive compensation plans.

[4] F. Hodge O'Neal and Robert B. Thompson, *O'Neal's Close Corporations* (3rd edn. 1986) §§ 3.17–3.18.

[5] See, e.g. New York Stock Exchange, Inc., *New York Stock Exchange Listed Company Manual* § 102.01 (June 1989).

market has, or the bigger the listings in terms of company size and market capitalization,[6] the greater the trading volume is likely to be, and the more money the members will make. As a result, there is considerable competition among the various markets for listings.

The stock exchanges, of which the New York Stock Exchange is the largest in the United States, are called 'auction' markets. All buyers' and sellers' orders are brought together in a single place and are matched in an auction-type setting, resulting (theoretically, at least) in the best price to the parties, and in the least volatility in prices because any particular price change should be only an incremental change from the prior price. To facilitate this auction, the exchanges have firms called 'specialists' through whom all buy and sell orders flow. Each listed security is assigned to a particular specialist. Although the specialist doesn't have to be involved in all matches between buyers and sellers, it can be and it must be there to 'create an orderly market' when there are temporary order imbalances. Thus, if there are more buyers than sellers for a few hours, the specialist is required to sell shares of the stock as a principal (rather than a broker) to keep the market from swinging wildly. Most transactions on the exchanges, however, are done by brokers who act as agents for customers and are paid through commissions on the sales. Transactions on the exchanges are reported as they occur, so the actual sales price for the last prior transaction is easily available.

Unlike the exchanges, the over-the-counter markets do not have a centralized trading location. Instead, transactions are executed over phone lines and on computer screens. These markets are 'dealer' markets, because each trade is executed with a dealer (a market professional acting as a principal) on one side, whose profit is not a commission, but a 'spread'.[7] NASDAQ has moved to real-time trade reporting, so trades are reported as they are on the exchanges.

The role of the specialist is roughly filled in OTC markets by the 'market maker', a dealer that holds itself out as willing to buy and sell a particular security, on which it issues bid and asked quotes. There can be many market makers for a particular security, because securities are not assigned as they are

---

[6] 'Market capitalization' refers to the value of a company's equity securities, measured by the price at which the securities are trading at the time the measure is being taken, multiplied by the number of units outstanding.

[7] The spread is the difference between the bid price and the asked price, or the difference between the price paid for the security and the price it is sold for. Spreads are not limited in amount the same way as brokerage commissions are, although there are regulations governing the way in which broker-dealers must deal with their customers. See rules 15c1-1 to c3-3, 17 C.F.R. §§ 240.15c1–1 to c3–3 (1993). On the exchanges, only the specialist can act as a dealer; the other people on the floor, acting for customers, must act as brokers only. Of course, all the brokerage houses and financial institutions do a considerable amount of 'proprietary trading' (trading for their own accounts) where they are acting as principals.

on the exchanges where there are rarely more than two specialists assigned to any security.[8]

The increasing presence of institutional investors has dramatically affected the United States capital markets. The term 'institutional investor' generally describes an entity that 'manage[s] the combined assets of many investors'. A non-comprehensive list of types of institutional investors includes banks; insurance companies; pension plans; foundations; universities; trust funds and investment companies (including mutual funds).[9] Institutions, by their size, are far better able to negotiate the commission or spread on a transaction when trading in traditional markets. More important, institutions buy in sufficient volume and with sufficient frequency that companies are increasingly selling their securities directly to institutions, eliminating brokers, dealers, underwriters—all the usual intermediaries.

For the public markets, increased participation by institutions means increased trading volume requiring new facilities to keep up with the paperwork; increased speed of transactions, which means increasingly sophisticated computerization; and increased size of average trades. Combining all these factors can lead to increased volatility in the form of more dramatic price swings over a shorter time period.

Increasing institutional trading also means decreased direct participation by the small and individual investors, who have traditionally been the purchasers of smaller or more risky issues, and have been longer-term holders. In addition, institutional capital is highly mobile, and institutional money managers look for investment opportunities on a global basis.

II. The Systems of Regulation

The major federal statutes regulating the United States securities markets are the Securities Act of 1933[10] ('the 1933 Act') and the Securities Exchange Act of 1934[11] ('the 1934 Act'). Four other statutes are also considered part of the federal regulatory scheme in the securities area: the Investment Company

---

[8] Market makers are not subject to the same requirements as specialists are to use their own capital to maintain an orderly market. On October 19, 1987 (the day the market dropped over 500 points), many specialist firms went bankrupt trying to maintain an orderly market with their own capital; some market makers just dropped out of the market during the turmoil. Robert J. Cole, 'Market Turmoil: The Professionals' Day', *N.Y. Times*, October 22, 1987, at D14.

[9] New York Stock Exchange, Inc., *Fact Book: 1992 Data* 3 (1993). At the end of the first quarter of 1993, institutions held 47 percent of the total equities outstanding in the United States Board of Governors of the Federal Reserve System, *Flow of Funds Accounts: Flows and Outstandings* 112 (June 8, 1993).

[10] 15 U.S.C. §§ 77a–77aa (1988).

[11] 15 U.S.C. §§ 78a–78ll (1988).

Act,[12] the Investment Advisors Act,[13] the Trust Indenture Act,[14] and the Public Utility Holding Company Act.[15]

The basic purposes of the 1933 and 1934 Acts are the same: disclosure of information and prevention of fraud.[16] Both statutes are administered by a federal government agency known as the Securities and Exchange Commission (SEC).[17] The statutes were passed as part of the federal government's response to the economic situation in the 1930s and the stock market crash of 1929. While stock market practices were not cast as the sole causes of the Depression of the 1930s, Congress clearly felt that the markets encouraged unduly speculative activity, were rife with conflicts of interest, and had proved unable to police themselves.

The 1933 and 1934 Acts speak to different aspects of the capital markets. The 1933 Act is concerned with the process of capital formation through the public sale of securities. The Act refers to the 'distribution' of securities and is concerned with the process by which securities get from a company (or other issuer) into the hands of the investing public.[18] It proceeds from two concepts: first, that sound investment decision-making requires the investor to have certain information at the time of purchase; and secondly, that when the seller of the securities is the issuer, its agent, or a person who controls the issuer, the issuer is the most appropriate (and the lowest cost) provider of that information.

---

[12] 15 U.S.C. §§ 80a–1 to 80a–64 (1988). The Investment Company Act, which has assumed increasing importance over the last few years, defines and regulates 'investment companies' which, broadly speaking, means any company the bulk of whose business consists of investing in securities. Mutual funds are obvious examples of investment companies. Individuals increasingly make their securities investments through intermediary entities, and as a result, investment companies are prominent among the institutional investors whose importance to the United States markets has been growing rapidly.

Once a minimum number of investors is exceeded, the investment company must register under the Act, and becomes subject to extensive regulation of its dealings with its investors, corporate governance, investment management relationships and financial disclosures.

[13] 15 U.S.C. §§ 80b–1 to 80b–21 (1988). The Investment Advisors Act regulates persons who hold themselves out as rendering investment advice to more than a minimum number of clients. This Act also involves registration and disclosure requirements.

[14] 15 U.S.C. §§ 77aaa–77bbbb (1988). The Trust Indenture Act regulates certain terms of the contract between a company issuing debt to the public and the trustee acting on the public's behalf in connection with that debt. Various clauses are mandated, and certain rights are conferred by statute.

[15] 15 U.S.C. §§ 79–79z-6 (1988). The Public Utility Holding Company Act was passed in response to the development of a certain pyramidal holding company structure in the public utility business. It is rarely invoked today.

[16] "The basic policy is that of informing the investor of the facts concerning securities to be offered for sale in interstate and foreign commerce and providing protection against fraud and misrepresentation'. S. Rep. No. 41, 73d Cong., 1st Sess. (1933).

[17] See Section 4 of the 1934 Act, 15 U.S.C. § 78d (1988).

[18] The entire 'distribution process' may involve several steps and numerous participants. For example, a typical sale of stock will involve the company that issues it in exchange for money; the distributors with whom it contracts to sell the securities (known as 'underwriters') who receive a per share payment for each share; sub-distributors (known as 'dealers') who also receive a per share payment; and the investors to whom the shares are ultimately sold.

The conceptual center of the 1933 Act is Section 5, which prohibits any person from offering or selling a security using the facilities of interstate commerce without a registration statement.[19] The document around which the 1933 Act is centered is the registration statement, which contains within it the prospectus or selling brochure. These documents are prepared by the issuer and contain numerous lengthy disclosures about the company, its business operations, its finances, its owners, the securities being offered, and the distributors of those securities.

There are a number of exemptions from the registration requirement contained in Sections 3 and 4 of the 1933 Act.[20] The broadest exemption is in Section 4(1) for transactions by persons 'other than an issuer, underwriter or dealer'. It is this exemption that permits the ongoing public trading markets to exist, by exempting members of the investing public from the registration requirements. 'Issuer', 'underwriter' and 'dealer' are technical terms defined in the statute in such a way as to capture all those who participate, directly or indirectly, in the transaction or series of transactions by which securities travel from the issuer into the hands of the public. It is the incentive to push the securities onto the public, which can create the risk of misrepresentations or unwarranted pressure on potential buyers, that the statute is meant to regulate. The 1933 Act also exposes sellers to liability for material misstatements in connection with offers or sales, or for violations of Section 5.[21]

The 1934 Act talks, in the broadest sense, about the trading markets. The SEC was created by the 1934 Act[22] which also contains its remedial and enforcement powers.[23] The 1934 Act regulates market professionals, including the stock exchanges, brokers and dealers, and dealers in government securities (governments themselves are exempt). The 1934 Act also regulates companies whose securities are publicly traded (including changes in control of those companies effected by purchases and sales of stock),[24] and extensions of credit by lenders for the purpose of purchasing securities.[25] The 1934 Act proceeds by the same method as the 1933 Act: registration of the regulatees, and a raft of regulations concerning the conduct of their business.

The SEC is an independent regulatory agency which is charged with acting 'in the public interest and for the protection of investors'. Its five Commissioners are appointed by the President and confirmed by the Senate;

---

[19] Technically, no offers can be made until a registration statement (in preliminary form) is filed, and no sales can be made until the registration statement is declared effective by the SEC.

[20] 15 U.S.C. §§ 77c, 77d (1988).   [21] See section IV below.

[22] Section 4(a), 15 U.S.C. § 78d(a) (1988).

[23] See Sections 21, 21A, 21B, and 21C, 15 U.S.C. § 78u, 78u-1, 78u-2, 78u-3 (1988).

[24] See Sections 12, 13 and 14, 15 U.S.C. §§ 78l, 78m, 78n (1988), and discussion in section III C below.

[25] The 'margin rules', authorized by Section 7 of the 1934 Act, 15 U.S.C. § 78g, are issued by the Board of Governors of the Federal Reserve. Generally, a buyer may borrow no more than 50 percent of the purchase price of securities.

no more than three Commissioners can come from the same political party. Administering and enforcing these statutes is an enormous undertaking for the SEC. In 1992, $702.1 billion of public offerings of securities filed with the SEC; over 99.6 billion shares were traded that year on a range of exchanges and over-the-counter.[26]

The SEC has both extensive rule-making and broad adjudicative enforcement authority. Rule-making is generally of the 'notice and comment' variety.[27] When rules are properly promulgated, they have the force of law: a violation of a rule constitutes a violation of the statutory section under which the rule was promulgated. When the SEC brings an administrative enforcement action, it is the five Commissioners who issue the complaint, making a determination as prosecutors. Once the action is commenced by the staff of the Division of Enforcement, communication with the Commission itself is highly restricted. This is because the case is decided at the trial level by an administrative law judge, and appeal from that decision lies to the Commission sitting as a five-judge appellate court. Appeals from the Commission's decisions go directly to the federal courts of appeal. The SEC also brings cases as a plaintiff in federal court, seeking injunctions and various other remedies, like treble damages in certain insider trading cases. It is represented in those actions by the Office of the General Counsel of the SEC.

In examining United States securities regulation, it is extremely important to remember that the statutes did not create the securities markets, nor, with the exception of the SEC itself, the institutions of those markets, like stock exchanges. Instead, the laws were imposed on an already existing and highly developed, if somewhat arcane, industry.

The 1933 and 1934 Acts were the subject of intense lobbying by the securities industry at the time of their enactment. This can help explain some of the prominent features of the acts.[28] The 1934 Act relies heavily on self-regulatory organizations (SROs). Instead of direct regulation of stock exchanges or NASD members by the SEC, the statutory scheme first involves the adoption of rules by the SRO which are subject to SEC review and approval and, secondly, enforcement of those rules by the SRO against its members in the first instance.[29] These structures, originally adopted at the urging of the industry, now serve to conserve the SEC's resources, while giving it tools for broad surveillance of the markets and back-up enforcement powers when needed. Both the 1933 and the 1934 Acts rely on disclosure as a principal regulatory tool. Disclosure is a comparatively mild form of regulation and is not intended to control the fairness of the transactions involved.

[26] United States Securities and Exchange Commission, *1992 Annual Report* 32, 154–155 (1993).
[27] See discussion in Chapter 13.
[28] See generally James D. Cox et al., *Securities Regulation: Cases and Materials* 17–18 (1991).
[29] Section 19 of the 1934 Act, 15 U.S.C. § 78s (1988).

Concurrent with federal regulation of securities transactions and market professionals is the system of state regulation,[30] commonly called 'blue sky' laws.[31] Each state has such a law. The statutes generally cover similar ground, but can vary greatly in their details. A major distinguishing feature of many state blue sky laws is that the state securities administrator has the authority to review the substantive fairness of an offering, rather than being limited to the type of disclosure review the SEC performs.

The securities markets regulated by the SEC form only a part of the public capital markets in the United States The trading of United States government securities,[32] which by dollar volume greatly exceeds all other markets, is subject to oversight by the Department of the Treasury.[33] Treasury securities are sold by the Federal Reserve Bank of New York through an auction process. Bidders in a Treasury auction submit offers for the dollar amount of securities they wish to buy and the interest rate they are willing to pay on those securities. After all the bids are received, the Federal Reserve Bank begins selling securities to the bidder asking for the lowest interest rate, then to the bidder asking the next lowest interest rate, and so on until all the securities being offered are sold, thus securing the best 'price', i.e. lowest cost for the financing needs of the government.[34] Until very recently only so-called 'primary dealers' were permitted to participate in this auction.[35]

The market for municipal securities, which generally means securities issued by state, regional, and local governmental entities,[36] is also very large. Like the market for Treasury securities, there is little public participation in the trading market. Unlike the Treasury, many issuers of municipal securities are of questionable creditworthiness. Nevertheless, while municipal securities dealers are regulated by the Municipal Securities Rulemaking Board,[37] the issuers of the securities are largely unregulated by the securities laws, and the SEC has no authority to mandate disclosures in this area.[38]

Finally, securities regulation does not reach trading in commodities or financial futures although it does reach trading in stock options. The futures markets, for which there are organized exchanges (e.g. the Chicago

---

[30] Section 18 of the 1933 Act, 15 U.S.C. § 77r (1988).

[31] The term 'blue sky' law refers to the nature of the interests that some promoters were selling before regulation; they were characterized as being nothing more than 'so many feet of blue sky'. *Hall* v. *Geiger-Jones Co.*, 242 U.S. 539, 550 (1917), reprinted in Cox, n. 28 above, at 28.

[32] See definition in Section 3(a)(42) of the 1934 Act, 15 U.S.C. § 78c(a)(42) (1988).

[33] Section 15C(a)(4) of the 1934 Act, 15 U.S.C. § 78o-5(a)(4) (1988).

[34] See generally, Richard W. Jennings et al., *Securities Regulation: Cases and Materials* (7th edn. 1992) 7–9.

[35] In 1991, due to activities of one of the 39 investment firms which qualified as primary dealers, the Treasury decided to increase competition in this market by opening up the auctions to additional securities dealers who were not primary dealers.

[36] Section 3(a)(29) of the 1934 Act, 15 U.S.C. § 78c(a)(29) (1988).

[37] Section 15B(b) of the 1934 Act, 15 U.S.C. § 78o-4(b) (1988).

[38] See Jennings, n. 34 above, at 10–11.

Mercantile Exchange), are regulated by the Commodities Futures Trading Commission (CFTC), another federal agency, which was established by the Commodity Exchange Act.[39] While there is a central antifraud provision in the Commodity Exchange Act, the commodities regulatory scheme and the securities regulatory scheme differ substantially, as do the structure of the markets in which these instruments are traded.[40] Given the rapid development of new and hybrid instruments in today's markets, the jurisdictional line between the SEC and the CFTC can often become blurred.

III. Federal Regulation of Companies Under the 1933 and 1934 Acts

A. Disclosure Philosophy

The 1934 Act sets up a system of periodic reporting obligations applicable to companies whose securities are publicly traded. Companies become subject to these requirements either by having a class of securities listed for trading on an exchange,[41] or by issuing securities to the public pursuant to a registration statement,[42] or by having both a class of equity securities held by 500 or more persons and total assets exceeding $5,000,000.[43] Reporting companies are required to file and distribute reports annually, quarterly, in connection with stockholder meetings, and upon the occurrence of specified events.[44]

From a company's perspective, both the 1933 and 1934 Acts are primarily disclosure-mandating schemes. Not surprisingly, they often mandate disclosure on identical matters. Until 1983, however, the specific requirements for

---

[39] 7 U.S.C. §§ 1–26 (1988 & Supp. V 1993). Futures originally became subject to regulation in the Future Trading Act of 1921, 42 Stat. 187 (1921), which was renamed and substantially amended several times, the most recent of which was in 1992.

[40] See Jennings, n. 34 above, at 11–15.

[41] Section 12(b) of the 1934 Act, 15 U.S.C. § 78l(b) (1988).

[42] Section 15(d) of the 1934 Act, 15 U.S.C. § 78o(d) (1988).

[43] Section 12(g) of the 1934 Act, 15 U.S.C. § 78l(g) (1988).

[44] The statutory authority for these reports is Section 13 of the 1934 Act, 15 U.S.C. § 78m (1988). The reports are the Annual Report on Form 10–K, Fed. Sec. L. Rep. (CCH) ¶¶ 31,101–31,107 (Feb. 16, 1994); the Quarterly Report on Form 10–Q, Fed. Sec. L. Rep. (CCH) ¶¶ 31,031–31,035 (Apr. 21, 1993); the Proxy Statement on Schedule 14A, 17 C.F.R. § 240.14a-101 (1993); and the Current Report on Form 8–K, Fed. Sec. L. Rep. (CCH) ¶¶ 31,001–31,004 (Sep. 9, 1992).

Different forms are available to 'Small Business Issuers' (defined in rule 12b-2, 17 C.F.R. § 240.12b-2 (1993), as a United States or Canadian issuer, not an investment company or a majority-owned subsidiary, with both revenues and an aggregate market value of securities held by non-affiliates not exceeding $25,000,000) and foreign private issuers. These forms modify or abbreviate certain of the disclosures required in the more generally applicable forms.

disclosures on the same matters varied from one act to the other. This forced issuers to generate large disclosure documents each time they went to market under the 1933 Act and at regular intervals under the 1934 Act, all of which were extremely costly. In addition, issuers were afraid of exposure to liability for making different statements in each document about the same matter.

In 1983, the SEC responded to these issuer concerns and, based in part on the increasing presence of institutional investors and the increasing use by individuals of intermediary investment vehicles such as mutual funds, adopted an integrated disclosure system for both statutes. This system is based on the assumption that at least some United States securities markets are 'efficient'. Briefly, the market is efficient with respect to information disclosure where the prices of securities reflect all available public information about the securities and where newly available information is immediately reflected in the price.[45]

Relying on this assumption, the integrated disclosure system provides that one disclosure on a particular matter is all a company need ever make (unless updating is required).[46] The technique for implementing this one-time disclosure rule is called 'incorporation by reference'. All disclosure documents filed under the 1933 and 1934 Acts are eligible to be incorporated by reference in subsequent filings in whole or in part. That is, once the information has been disclosed, it is deemed to be present for all subsequent investment decisions because the assumption that the market is efficient means that the information remains embedded in the price of the security. When the stock price already takes into account the market's view of the effect of that information on the 'value' of the company, the information is 'there' and need not be repeated in subsequent disclosure documents. Since the SEC acts for the protection of investors, this theory also depends for its regulatory validity on the assumption that what investors are interested in can always be expressed as price and what they must be protected from is misinformation that affects price.

The market does not work 'efficiently' for all individual companies. In order to sort out those companies to whose securities this theory could be

---

[45] FASB, *The Efficient Market Hypothesis: Tentative Conclusions of Objectives of Financial Statements of Business Enterprises* ¶¶ 122–130 (1976), reprinted in Cox, n. 28 above, at 33–37. 'If the stock market is an efficient market, individual investors can gain no advantage by analyzing public information, either about the history of a stock's market price or about the enterprise that issued the stock. A significant implication of the hypothesis is that neither technical analysis of past stock prices nor fundamental analysis of individual business enterprises is likely to help investors "beat the market". At any time, the market price is, on the average, the best estimate of the stock's value'. *Ibid.* at 34.

[46] The integrated disclosure system codified the vast majority of substantive disclosure requirements for both 1933 and 1934 Act documents in Regulation S-K, 17 C.F.R. §§ 229.10-.915 (1993). Financial disclosures were codified in Regulation S-X, 17 C.F.R. §§ 210.1-01 –.12-29 (1993).

applied, the SEC has used two tests: the length of time that the company has met the reporting requirements of the 1934 Act, and the 'aggregate market value of the voting stock held by non-affiliates of the [company]'.[47] The result of these tests is that the SEC has adopted a graduated disclosure system: the very largest or most actively traded companies in United States markets, which are those companies whose stock is closely followed by the greatest number of investors, brokers, investment advisors, security analysts, portfolio managers, etc., are the ones that may take the greatest advantage of integrated disclosure and incorporation by reference.[48]

B. Disclosure Triggering Events Under the 1933 Act

The 1933 Act centers on the public sale of securities. As discussed, Section 5 requires all offers or sales of securities to be made pursuant to a registration statement. The preparation and dissemination of a registration statement is a time-consuming and expensive undertaking. In addition, issuers and certain other parties are exposed to liability risks for any material misstatement in a registration statement.

The prohibitions of Section 5 attach from the moment a company is 'in registration'. From that moment, no offers to sell or solicitations of offers to buy may be made by or on behalf of the issuer until a registration statement in preliminary form is filed.[49] When a particular company goes into

---

[47] Form S-3 under the 1933 Act, General Instruction I.B.1., 17 C.F.R. § 239.13(b)(1) (1993). This value is also referred to as the 'float'.

'Affiliate' is defined as 'a person that directly, or indirectly through one or more intermediaries, controls or is controlled by, or is under common control with, the person specified'. Rule 405 under the 1933 Act, 17 C.F.R. § 230.405 (1993).

[48] This theory of market efficiency contains within it a paradox: only if there are numerous people evaluating information as soon as it becomes available and making investment decisions on that basis can the securities market operate efficiently. In effect, then, the efficiency of the market depends on enough investors and analysts doubting its efficiency. FASB, n. 45 above.

This reliance on market professionals to act as agents, in effect, for investors as a whole in translating information into price, has substantial ramifications for liability concepts under the securities law. See section IV below.

[49] Section 5(c), 15 U.S.C. § 77e(c) (1988). The registration statement that is initially filed will be incomplete because information accurate as of the effective date will not yet be available, and the securities will not have been priced. The price of the securities will be determined as close to the sales time as possible. Under the statute, a registration statement will automatically go effective 20 days after it is filed. Section 8(a), 15 U.S.C. § 77h(a) (1988). In order to delay the effective date, an amendment may be filed, which will start the 20-day period again. In practice, in order to control the time at which the registration statement is declared effective and therefore to control when the security is priced, amendments are nominally filed whenever the 20-day period is about to expire. When the issuer is ready to go to the market, 'acceleration' of the effective date is requested from the SEC. During the period between filing and effectiveness, the SEC has the opportunity to review the document and make comments. See generally, Cox, n. 28 above, at 258–269.

registration with respect to a particular offering is a question of fact.[50] Once a registration is filed, oral offers may be made subject to antifraud limitations, but no writings except the preliminary prospectus from the registration statement may be used.[51] After the registration statement is declared effective, all other materials may be used, provided that the investor has been previously furnished with a copy of the final version of the prospectus.[52]

As a result of the complexity, costs, and risks associated with a registered public offering, many issuers prefer to sell their securities in a transaction exempt from registration. In addition, many issuers, particularly start-up companies or foreign companies, may not wish to become subject to the reporting requirements of the 1934 Act, which can result from a registered public offering.[53] There are numerous exemptions from registration.[54] Probably the most widely used issuer exemption is for transactions 'not involving any public offering'.[55]

The question of what constitutes a 'public' offering has a long judicial and administrative history. The principal factor on which the exemption turns is whether the investors involved need the protections afforded by the registration statement.[56] This concept, also expressed as whether the investors can 'fend for themselves' or whether they are 'sophisticated', involves a calculus of elements: who the investor is, how wealthy the investor is, how much information the investor possesses about the particular company and offering involved or how easily the investor can obtain the information, and how capably the investor can evaluate the information either alone or with a representative.

While the statutory language itself creates the exemptions from registra-

---

[50] See 'Publication of Information Prior To or After the Filing and Effective Date', *Exchange Act Release* No. 33–5009, [1969–70 Transfer Binder] Fed. Sec. L. Rep. (CCH) ¶ 77,744 (Oct. 7, 1969).

[51] Section 5(b), 15 U.S.C. § 77e(b) (1988). Only prospectuses that comply with section 10 of the 1933 Act, 15 U.S.C. § 77j (1988), are permitted during this period. The Section 10 prospectuses are the preliminary prospectus, a summary prospectus (where permitted by the registration form) and the final or statutory prospectus which is not available at this time. The term 'prospectus' is broadly defined in section 2(10), 15 U.S.C. § 77b(10) (1988), to cover all writings and all broadcasts which 'offer' a security for sale or confirm the sale of a security.

[52] Section 2(10)(a), 15 U.S.C. § 77b(10)(a) (1988). It is unlawful to complete the sale of a security before a registration statement with respect to that sale is in effect. Section 5(a), 15 U.S.C. § 77e(a) (1988).

[53] Foreign private issuers which do not wish to enter the United States market have been exposed to securities acts risks in the past if they made offers of securities to United States persons. In 1990 the SEC adopted Regulation S, comprising Rules 901–904 under the 1933 Act, 17 C.F.R. §§ 230.901–.904 (1993), which exempts from section 5 foreign offerings, essentially as long as there is no substantial United States market interest in the securities or issuer and there are no selling efforts directed at or sales made to United States persons. This Regulation represents a considerable retreat from the SEC's prior position on the extra-territorial reach of the United States securities laws.

[54] See Sections 3 and 4, 15 U.S.C. §§ 77c, 77d (1988), and the rules thereunder. The burden of proof on each element of an exemption from registration is on the person claiming the exemption.

[55] Section 4(2), 15 U.S.C. § 77d(2) (1988). These transactions are widely known as 'private placements'.

[56] *SEC v. Ralston Purina Co.*, 346 U.S. 119 (1953).

tion,[57] the SEC has over the years carved out pieces of the overall exemption for treatment as 'safe harbors' in the form of rules. In the private placement area, the SEC promulgated a series of Rules, known as Regulation D, which replaced and integrated a number of earlier rules, while codifying a variety of administrative interpretations in the area.[58]

The question of who is sophisticated for private placement purposes is addressed by Regulation D in the definition of 'accredited investor'.[59] Accredited investors include institutional investors like banks, insurance companies, pension and other employee benefit plans and foundations with assets over $5,000,000. Individuals with high net worth or high income over several years qualify. In addition, officers and directors of the issuer qualify as accredited investors.

Since accredited investors are deemed to be sophisticated, an issuer may sell to an unlimited number of such investors without turning the transaction into a public offering. The issuer also is relieved of any obligation to supply such investors with information. It is presumed that such investors know what information they need, and have the ability to obtain it from the issuer should they want it.

Other investors can be made sophisticated through a combination of information disclosure and purchaser representatives. However, the issuer is limited to thirty-five such non-accredited investors in any transaction. Any non-accredited investor must be given a variety of information by the issuer.[60] Other safeguards in Regulation D, which prevent an exempt offering from being made to the 'public', are a ban on general solicitation of purchasers,[61] and a requirement that purchasers be informed that the securities cannot be freely resold without registration or an exemption from registration.[62]

[57] The only exemptive provision which contains no substantive description is Section 3(b), 15 U.S.C. § 77c(b) (1988), which authorizes the SEC to promulgate rules creating exemptions 'if it finds that the enforcement of [the registration provisions] with respect to such securities is not necessary in the public interest and for the protection of investors' so long as the aggregate amount offered under any such exemption does not exceed $5,000,000. The SEC has issued rules creating three of these 'small issues' exemptions: Regulation A (comprising rules 251–263, 15 U.S.C. §§ 230.251–.263 (1993)), and Rules 504 and 505 in Regulation D, 17 C.F.R. §§ 230.504, .505 (1993).

[58] 17 C.F.R. §§ 230.501–.508 (1993). Regulation D does not occupy the entire field covered by Section 4(2), 15 U.S.C. § 77d(2) (1988). Compliance with its provisions will, however, ensure an issuer the exemption. Many issuers may still choose to structure a transaction to comply with Section 4(2) itself, in order to avoid some of Regulation D's requirements, principally the filing requirement of Rule 503, 17 C.F.R. § 230.503 (1993), which requires a variety of information about the transaction and the purchasers be made publicly available. There are important differences between the elements of a Section 4(2) transaction and a Regulation D transaction. For example, the issuer in a section4(2) transaction has the burden of proving the requisite sophistication on the part of each of its offerees as well as its purchasers, while Regulation D limits proof of sophistication, where required, to purchasers.

[59] Rule 501(a), 17 C.F.R. § 230.501(a) (1993).

[60] Rule 502(b), 17 C.F.R. § 230.502(b) (1993).

[61] Rule 502(c), 17 C.F.R. § 230.502(c) (1993).

[62] Rule 502(d), 17 C.F.R. § 230.502(d) (1993). The reasons for this limitation are both statutory and practical. A purchaser who buys securities from an issuer and resells them shortly thereafter meets the

Here again, the increasing presence of institutional sources of capital has resulted in some recent changes to the rules and the regulatory philosophy. Purchasers of privately placed securities have traditionally sold them pursuant to Rule 144 which permits sales, after a 2-year holding period, of limited amounts of securities issued by companies about which there is current information publicly available, through a broker or to a market maker into the public trading markets. However, for many securities there is no public trading market in the United States, and the volume limitations and holding period requirements make reselling a large block of securities extremely costly. These problems are most severe where institutional portfolios are concerned.

Many institutional investors acquired large blocks of securities in companies which were not publicly traded in the United States, either because they were not United States companies, or because they were start-up or development stage companies, for which institutions are a major source of seed capital. In addition, many institutions traded privately with each other on a regular basis, but these transactions were costly: there was no central clearing facility, and there were considerable Securities Acts risks associated when these resales involved restricted securities.

In response, in 1990 the SEC adopted Rule 144A[63], which is a attempt to create a kind of 'free trading zone' for large institutional investors.[64] To the extent that there is any group of investors who are 'sophisticated' for all purposes under the Securities Acts, and for whom the benefits of registration are too remote, it is these investors. The rule is an attempt to lower the transactions costs of sales to and among these institutions, and thereby to increase liquidity for these investors and lower the cost of capital for issuers that sell to them by facilitating resales. The rule is also an attempt to provide an opening into this highly desirable segment of our capital markets for non-American issuers, by encouraging them to privately place securities with institutions without United States Securities Acts risks.

---

statutory definition of 'underwriter' in Section 2(11), 15 U.S.C. § 77b(11), ('purchased from an issuer with a view to . . . distribution') thereby jeopardizing the issuer's exemption. Similarly, permitting the free resale of securities issued without a registration statement would open a loophole through which securities could enter the public trading markets without the information disclosure the statute requires. These securities are known as 'restricted' securities, and their resale is a very complex subject which has been addressed on a number of occasions by the SEC. See Rules 144 and 144A, 17 C.F.R. §§ 230.144, 230.144A (1993).

[63] 17 C.F.R. § 230.144A (1993).

[64] Rule 144A exempts certain sales to 'qualified institutional buyers' the definition of which is limited to entities which each 'in the aggregate owns and invests on a discretionary basis at least $100 million in securities of issuers that are not affiliated with the entity'. Rule 144A(a)(1)(i), 17 C.F.R. § 230.144A(a)(1)(i) (1993).

C. Disclosure Triggering Events Under the 1934 Act

The usual disclosure events for companies under the 1934 Act are the reports that companies file on a periodic basis. As a result, within 45 days after the end of each fiscal quarter, and 120 days of the end of each fiscal year, a reporting company must publicly disclose all material information about the company then in its possession, including financial statements. Audited financial statements are required in the annual report. If, during any fiscal quarter, a change in control of the company occurs; the company acquires or disposes of a significant amount of assets; the company goes into bankruptcy or receivership; or changes the accounting firm it uses to certify its financials, it must file an interim report.[65]

The stock exchanges and the NASD also require companies to make public disclosures, in the form of press releases, upon the occurrence of material events, or material changes in previously disclosed information.[66] Finally, companies are subject to the antifraud provisions of the Securities Acts at all times, which may require that they issue a public statement even when no periodic filing is then required, because of the risk of liability for a material misstatement or omission.[67]

The shareholders of most public corporations are extremely numerous and geographically widely dispersed, and do not attend shareholders' meetings in person but instead vote by proxy.[68] Section 14(a) of the 1934 Act prohibits the solicitation of any proxy with respect to a class of securities registered under Section 12 of the 1934 Act, except in compliance with rules promulgated by the SEC. As a result, a significant piece of a company's reporting obligations occurs whenever the company seeks a vote of the holders of such a class.[69] The rules under Section 14(a), known as the Proxy Rules,

---

[65] Form 8–K, Fed. Sec. L. Rep. (CCH) ¶¶ 31,001–31,004 (Sep. 9, 1992). A company may choose to, but is not required to, file an interim report for any other events it considers important. *Ibid.*, item 5, ¶ 31,003, at 21,994.

[66] Both the stock exchanges and the NASD have extremely sophisticated market surveillance programs. Any unusual activity in a company's securities will result in a call from the exchange or NASD to the company seeking an explanation. In unusual circumstances, or at the company's request, the exchange or NASD will stop trading in the company's securities pending a public announcement by the company. New York Stock Exchange, Inc., *New York Stock Exchange Listed Company Manual* §§ 202.03–.07 (July 1992); National Association of Securities Dealers, Inc., *NASD Manual* ¶ 1806A (1994).

[67] The determination of whether a company must issue a public statement, and when such a statement is required (outside of the periodic reporting system) is an extremely difficult one. See discussion in section IV below regarding antifraud liability.

[68] The term 'proxy' refers to the authorization by a shareholder of another person to cast his votes at a meeting. Voting by proxy is a matter of state not federal law, e.g., Del. Code Ann. tit. 8, § 212 (1974).

[69] The matters on which shareholders must vote, and the circumstances under which shareholder meetings must be called, are largely governed by the corporate law of the state in which the company is incorporated. Once a shareholder vote is sought by a company, whether required or not, the Proxy Rules impose procedural and disclosure requirements on the process.

implement the federal interest in the process of shareholder communication and voting.[70] The principal document involved in a proxy solicitation is the Proxy Statement, which requires extensive information about the issues to be voted on; the persons making the solicitation; and the background, experience, and performance of directors and executive officers (if any directors will be elected at the meeting). The Proxy Statement must be filed with the SEC and mailed to all the shareholders.[71] Large parts of the information required by the Proxy Rules are also required in the company's annual report to its shareholders. If the annual report is up-to-date, that information can be incorporated by reference into the Proxy Statement, and so most shareholders' meetings of public corporations are scheduled to occur shortly after the annual reports have been sent out.

Management is rarely defeated, or even opposed, when it seeks a shareholder vote.[72] This is frequently explained by the small economic interest that any single shareholder has in the company, so that the easiest way for a shareholder in a public company to express its dissatisfaction with management is to sell its shares in the market. If a shareholder were to oppose management, and wanted to seek the votes of other shareholders in opposition, it would have to comply with the Proxy Rules, which apply to all solicitations of proxies regardless of who does the soliciting. The wide dispersion of shareholders makes communication among shareholders expensive, and the added expense of Proxy Rule compliance makes coordinated shareholder actions opposing management even less likely.

The Proxy Rules were intended to facilitate shareholder democracy in public corporations. To help achieve that goal, Rule 14a-8 requires corporations to include in their proxy statements certain proposals that shareholders want to be voted on at the meeting. However, the rules also made communication among smaller groups of shareholders extremely difficult.[73] Again,

[70] 'Underlying the adoption of Section 14(a) of the [1934] Act was a Congressional concern that the solicitation of proxy voting authority be conducted on a fair, honest and informed basis'. 'Regulation of Communications Among Shareholders', *Exchange Act Release* No. 34-31326, [1992 Transfer Binder] Fed. Sec. L. Rep. (CCH) ¶ 85,051, at 83,355 (Oct. 16, 1992).

[71] There are special disclosure instructions regarding compensation of officers and directors; compensation plans; authorization of new securities; the modification or exchange of existing securities; mergers or acquisitions; charter amendments; and various other matters to the extent issues regarding those matters are to be the subject of action at the meeting.

[72] Contesting an election of directors is a technique for acquiring control of a corporation. This technique, called a 'proxy fight' or 'proxy contest', has ebbed and flowed in popularity depending on economic conditions and the legal status of other acquisition techniques. For example, in the late 1980's, it became increasingly difficult to finance a hostile tender offer (an acquisition technique involving an offer to purchase a company's outstanding stock) with high yield securities (known as 'junk bonds') because of problems in that market, an overall economic contraction, and the increasing use of legal obstacles like state antitakeover statutes. As a result, there was an increase in the occurrence of proxy fights, a technique that had, during the previous decade, fallen largely into disuse.

[73] Before the recent amendments to the Proxy Rules discussed below, communications among shareholders were likely to be deemed 'solicitations' and, if more than ten shareholders were contacted, were not exempt from the Proxy Rules and the requirement to prepare and send out a Proxy Statement.

this problem was aggravated by the increasing presence of institutional investors, for whom simply exiting the company by selling their stock is often an insufficient remedy. Many such institutions own blocks of stock large enough to make resale disruptive to the market, and have few comparable investment alternatives that are not already in their portfolios. In addition, the size of these investments gives institutions a larger economic stake in improving the performance of the corporation, although not large enough to warrant a proxy contest over performance issues. Nor are such investors likely to be interested in running the corporation by replacing its board of directors. Finally, with investments of this size, the number of shareholders that must be coordinated to be effective is much lower, and those shareholders are easily identifiable.

The SEC responded to the desire of large shareholders to have a low-cost method of communicating with each other regarding their investment with a series of amendments to the Proxy Rules in 1992. One major effect of the amendments is to exempt from the Proxy Rules communications to shareholders where the communicator is not seeking proxies and has no real interest in the subject matter other than as a shareholder.[74]

Another set of disclosure requirements in the 1934 Act revolves around changes in control of public companies. In 1968, in response to the perception that corporate takeovers were being effected by quick, secret accumulations of stock, purchased from shareholders with neither the time nor information necessary to make informed decisions, Congress amended Sections 12, 13 and 14 of the 1934 Act. In broad outline, these amendments, which are known as the 'Williams Act', require public reporting of any accumulation of any equity security registered under Section 12 once it exceeds 5 percent,[75] including identifying information about the beneficial owner, its source of funds, plans, and intentions.[76] The commencement of a tender offer for such a security triggers the application of extensive disclosure requirements to the bidder[77] and a requirement for a response and recommendation from the target company.[78] The procedure by which the tender offer must be conducted is the subject of a number of regulations to ensure equal access and price to all tendering shareholders. The SEC's position regarding hostile takeovers has been to favor neither bidders nor targets. However, the federal law in this area largely regulates bidders, since the target company's actions, particularly when resisting a takeover, primarily

---

[74] 'Regulation of Communications Among Shareholders', n. 70 above, at 83,356. All communications remain subject to the antifraud provisions of the 1934 Act.

[75] Section 13(d), 15 U.S.C. § 78m(d) (1988).

[76] Schedule 13D, 17 C.F.R. § 240.13d-101 (1993).

[77] Section 14(d), 15 U.S.C. § 78n(d) (1988), and Schedule 14D-1, 17 C.F.R. § 240.14d-100 (1993).

[78] Rule 14e-2, 17 C.F.R. § 240.14e-2 (1993), and Schedule 14D-9, 17 C.F.R. § 240.14d-101 (1993).

involve questions of the fiduciary duties of target company directors, a matter of state corporate law.

IV. Antifraud Liability for Reporting Companies

Liability under the federal Securities Acts for companies, their officers, and directors is largely based on concepts of fraud, except where the underlying claim is for failure to register when required.[79] The principal antifraud provisions of the 1933 Act are Sections 11 and 12(2). Both impose liability for 'an untrue statement of a material fact or [a failure] to state a material fact required to be stated therein or necessary to make the statements therein not misleading'. Section 11 is only available where the defect was in a registration statement at the time it became effective; Section 12(2) applies to any offers or sales 'by means of a prospectus or oral communication'.[80] Potential plaintiffs in a Section 11 case include all purchasers, including remote purchasers, of the securities which were the subject of the registration statement; available defendants are listed in Section 11(a). All defendants except the issuer, which is strictly liable, have a defense available to them if they exercised sufficient care in the preparation of the registration statement; their liability is negligence-based.[81] The remedy under Section 11 is damages, calculated as set out in Section 11(e). Purchasers are also potential plaintiffs in a Section 12(2) case, but the available defendants for each purchaser are only his 'sellers',[82] and the remedy is rescission. A seller may defend against a Section

---

[79] Section 12(1) of the 1933 Act, 15 U.S.C. § 77*l*(1) (1988), creates liability in a seller to its purchaser for violations of the registration requirement of Section 5, 15 U.S.C. § 77e (1988). This liability is strict in that neither negligence nor any level of *scienter* must be shown in the defendant. Merely showing a violation of the requirement to register an offering of securities, within the statute of limitations contained in Section 13 of the 1933 Act, 15 U.S.C. § 77m (1988), will entitle a buyer to return the securities to its seller and receive its purchase price back (less any money already received). This rescissionary remedy in effect creates a 'put' in the purchaser. Should a seller seek to qualify its sale under an exemptive provision and fail to satisfy the burden of proof on the elements of the exemption, the result is a violation of Section 5. But see Rule 508 of Regulation D (see section III B above), which provides that a claim may not be based on an insignificant and inadvertent failure to meet the requirements of that exemption.

[80] In a case involving a privately negotiated contract to sell securities, the Supreme Court rejected the claims that this language covers both public and private sales transactions, and interpreted it to be limited to transactions involving public solicitations to buy securities. *Gustafson* v. *Alloyd Co, Inc.*, 115 S.Ct. 1061 (1995).

[81] Section 11(b)(3), 15 U.S.C. § 77k(b)(3) (1988), contains this so-called 'due diligence' defense, which requires that the defendant prove 'he had, after reasonable investigation, reasonable ground to believe and did believe', that the registration statement was true and complete. Section 11(b)(3)(A), 15 U.S.C. § 77k(b)(3)(A) (1988). The defense is somewhat easier to maintain in connection with statements in the registration statements made on the authority of experts other than the defendant. Section 11(b)(3)(C), 15 U.S.C. § 77k(b)(3)(C) (1988).

[82] The term 'seller' for Section 12 purposes includes but is not limited to the person who transfers title. See *Pinter* v. *Dahl*, 486 U.S. 622 (1988).

12(2) action by proving that 'he did not know, and in the exercise of reasonable care could not have known, of such untruth or omission'. Both Sections 11 and 12(2) are subject to a short statute of limitations.[83]

The principal antifraud provisions of the 1934 Act, which apply to purchasers as well as sellers, are in Sections 10(b) and Rule 10b-5 thereunder, the general antifraud provisions; rule 14a-9, which prohibits fraud in the proxy area and was promulgated pursuant to Section 14(a); and Section 14(e) and Rule 14e-3 thereunder covering fraud with respect to tender offers. Sections 10(b) and 14(e), in addition to the typical material misrepresentation or omission language, include language prohibiting the use of manipulative or deceptive acts or practices.[84]

Fraud under the securities laws is a disclosure, rather than a fairness, based concept. In interpreting the general antifraud provisions of the 1934 Act, the Supreme Court has twice made clear that, without a disclosure defect, there is no claim for fraud under the securities laws.[85] As a result, antifraud liability depends on a finding that there has been an actionable misrepresentation or omission made.

A threshold issue in any disclosure case is whether the omitted or misrepresented information was 'material'. The classic definition of materiality was announced by the Supreme Court in a Rule 14a-9 case, *TSC Industries, Inc.* v. *Northway, Inc.*[86] and was explicitly adopted for Section 10(b) and Rule 10b-5 purposes in *Basic, Inc.* v. *Levinson*:[87] 'An omitted fact is material if there is a substantial likelihood that a reasonable shareholder would consider it important in deciding how to vote'. The purpose of the materiality requirement is to further the statutory purpose of informed investment decision-making. Without all reasonably significant information, investors would not be sufficiently informed; if the materiality threshold is set too low, however, investors would be inundated with too much information of little importance. Many of the most difficult materiality judgments are in the area of contingent or speculative information and soft data (like opinions), as opposed to

---

[83] Section 13, 15 U.S.C. § 77m (1988). Suit must be brought within one year of when the untruth or omission is discovered or should have been discovered by the exercise of reasonable care, but cannot be brought more than 3 years after the sale of the security.

[84] 'It shall be unlawful for any person, directly or indirectly, by the use of any means or instrumentality of interstate commerce or of the mails, or of any facility of any national securities exchange . . . (b) To use or employ, in connection with the purchase or sale of any security registered on a national securities exchange or any security not so registered, any manipulative or deceptive device or contrivance . . .'. Section 10(b), 15 U.S.C. § 78j(b).

'It shall be unlawful for any person to . . . engage in any fraudulent, deceptive, or manipulative acts or practices, in connection with any tender offer . . .'. Section 14(e), 15 U.S.C. § 78n(e) (1988).

[85] See *Santa Fe Industries* v. *Green*, 430 U.S. 462 (1977) (interpreting Section 10(b) and Rule 10b-5 thereunder, 17 C.F.R. § 240.10b-5 (1993)); *Schreiber* v. *Burlington Northern, Inc.*, 472 U.S. 1 (1985)(interpreting Section 14(e)).

[86] 426 U.S. 438 (1976).   [87] 485 U.S. 224, 231–232 (1988).

historical facts. With respect to contingent or speculative information, like the kind of negotiations which were the subject of the *Basic* case (negotiations which may or may not result in a merger), 'materiality "will depend at any given time upon a balancing of both the indicated probability that the event will occur and the anticipated magnitude of the event in light of the totality of the company activity" '.[88] Opinions may also be actionable, but only if they are opinions 'with respect to . . . material facts'.[89] In order for such an opinion to be actionable under the antifraud provisions, it must 'misstate the speaker's reasons and also mislead about the stated subject matter'. Both aspects, the belief and the subject matter, must be misstated in order for an opinion to generate liability.

Materiality judgments are, therefore, extremely fact-specific and are subject to no bright-line standards.[90] Further, making a determination that a matter is material does not end the disclosure inquiry. With respect to an omission, in order for liability to result, there must also have been a duty to disclose the information, which was breached.[91] Some duties to disclose are straightforward: the periodic reporting requirements give rise to duties to disclose; if the company has made a public disclosure on which the market is currently relying and the information has materially changed, there is a duty to correct; if the company is aware that insiders of the company are trading on material non-public information, there is a duty to disclose that information.

Outside of those areas, the duty to disclose remains unclear. There appears to be room for competitive or business justifications for non-disclosure. For example, if a mining company makes a significant ore discovery, absent another duty to disclose, it may keep that information confidential in order

---

[88] 485 U.S. 224, 231–232 (1988) at 238, quoting *SEC* v. *Texas Gulf Sulphur Co.*, 401 F.2d 833, 849 (1968), *cert. denied*, 394 U.S. 976 (1969).

[89] *Virginia Bankshares, Inc.* v. *Sandberg*, 111 S. Ct. 2749, 2757 (1991). In that case, which involved a recommendation to shareholders that they vote in favor of a proposed merger, the plaintiff challenged the directors' statement of opinion that the merger price represented a 'high' value for the shares. Plaintiff claimed that the directors did not believe the price was 'high' and recommended the merger to keep their jobs.

Opinions that are not regarding material facts are not actionable because, the Court said, the resulting litigation would be about the 'impurities' of a director's 'unclean heart'. *Ibid.* at 2760. On the other hand, opinions with respect to material facts are subject to independent verifiable proof—'evidence of historical fact outside a plaintiff's control'. *Ibid.* at 2758. As a result, misrepresenting the fact that you hold the opinion, 'mere disbelief or undisclosed motive', is not actionable. *Ibid.* at 2760.

[90] In addition, if the judgment becomes subject to review, it will be in the context of a litigation taking place at a much later time, where the facts which existed earlier will be viewed with 'twenty-twenty hindsight'.

[91] With respect to a misrepresentation, there may have been no duty to speak at the time, but if the company chooses to speak, it is obligated to disclose fully and accurately. The question of how a company remains silent in the face, for example, of a stock exchange inquiry, was addressed by the Supreme Court in *Basic* where it said '[s]ilence, absent a duty to disclose, is not misleading under Rule 10b-5. "No comment" statements are generally the functional equivalent of silence'. 485 U.S. at 239 n.17.

to buy up the land under which it believes the ore exists at the cheapest price, even though the discovery is clearly material to the company.[92] This example illustrates that there should be limits on disclosure policy, regardless of the market's interest in the information, if the information is necessary to enable the company to conduct its essential operations. It also illustrates that any disclosure decision has two sides: it will advantage one set of investors, including shareholders of the company, and disadvantage another.[93] Therefore, a misrepresentation or omission that was material and made in breach of a duty is an actionable disclosure defect for Securities Acts antifraud purposes.

However, the broad language of the general antifraud provisions has required the federal courts to define the elements of the cause of action further.[94] First, the plaintiff must be a purchaser or seller of the securities to sue under Rule 10b-5,[95] or must be a shareholder to sue under Section 14(a). Secondly, the courts have developed the antifraud action as analogous to an action in tort, requiring the private plaintiff to prove behavior in breach of a duty; *scienter* on the part of the defendant;[96] causation; reliance; and damages.[97] The SEC can bring any of these actions as well, without having to be

---

[92] This example is taken from the facts of *SEC* v. *Texas Gulf Sulphur Co.*, 401 F.2d at 833, in which the court indicated that, absent the insider trading it found, the company would not have been liable for non-disclosure.

[93] All sellers who sold before disclosure of, in this case, positive information, may have sold for less money than they would have received had the information been made public; all of their buyers, on the other hand, will therefore have paid less. This is characteristic of disclosure decisions by a public company where there is an active trading market in the company's shares.

The two-sided nature of disclosure decisions where there is a public trading market also suggests that finding a securities law duty to delay disclosure, in order to maximize shareholder welfare, is not workable. In a public company, the identity of the shareholders changes daily, and their preferences as to the timing of any disclosure by the company will depend on the timing of their own investment decisions.

[94] The antifraud provisions do not themselves create causes of action for private parties. Compare Sections 11 and 12 of the 1933 Act, 15 U.S.C. § 77k, 77l (1988). The courts early on created such an implied cause of action under Section 10(b) of the 1934 Act and Rule 10b-5 in *Kardon* v. *National Gypsum Co.*, 69 F. Supp. 512 (E.D. Pa. 1946), which was finally affirmed by the Supreme Court in *Herman & MacLean* . *Huddleston*, 459 U.S. 375 (1983), and under section 14(a) of the 1934 Act in *J.I. Case Co.* v. *Borak*, 377 U.S. 426 (1964). More recently, the Supreme Court refused to find a private right of action available under the general antifraud provision of the 1933 Act, Section 17(a), 15 U.S.C. 77q(a) (1988), in *Touche Ross & Co.* v. *Redington*, 442 U.S. 560 (1979).

[95] *Blue Chip Stamps* v. *Manor Drug Stores*, 421 U.S. 723 (1975).

[96] For the purposes of Section 14(a) and Rule 14a-9 thereunder, negligence appears to be the standard applied to the corporate issuer, *Gerstle* v. *Gamble-Skogmo, Inc.*, 478 F.2d 1281 (2d Cir. 1973). The applicable standard for other parties has not been definitively established. See, e.g. *Adams* v. *Standard Knitting Mills, Inc.*, 623 F.2d 422 (1980), *cert. denied*, 449 U.S. 1067 (1981), where the Sixth Circuit found that negligence was insufficient to find the issuer's certified public accountants liable for violations of Section 14(a) and Rule 14a-9 in the company's proxy materials.

With respect to Section 10(b) and Rule 10b-5, in *Ernst & Ernst* v. *Hochfelder*, 425 U.S. 185 (1976), the Supreme Court held that proof of negligence was insufficient to give rise to liability, and that some level of *scienter* in the defendant was required. While the Court expressly reserved the question of whether 'recklessness' would suffice, most lower courts have accepted the recklessness standard and have not required proof of intentional fraud.

[97] A private plaintiff may also or instead seek injunctive relief.

a purchaser or seller. In addition, the SEC is not required to prove damages. While it may, in the appropriate case, obtain civil penalties which are monetary, it also has a range of other remedies available to it.[98]

Although causation and reliance are often said to be two separate elements of a plaintiff's case, the courts have not developed a clear articulation of either the difference between the two, or the functions each fulfills in antifraud jurisprudence.[99] Reliance involves proof by each individual plaintiff that defendant's allegedly fraudulent behavior was sufficiently connected to the plaintiff's decision to go forward with the transaction it is now challenging. In other words, the plaintiff must prove that he would not have gone ahead with the transaction on the same terms had there been full disclosure.

Causation adds to the analysis a requirement that the plaintiff prove that the defendant's fraudulent acts gave rise to the harm the plaintiff is alleging. While the plaintiff may well have relied on defendant's misrepresentation in going forward with the transaction and may have suffered a monetary loss, the defendant's misrepresentation may not have been the source of that loss. For example, the stock market overall may have declined in the same percentage as defendant's stock price. Conversely, while the defendant's misrepresentation may have caused a loss that plaintiff suffered when it engaged in a transaction, it may be that plaintiff did not rely on the misrepresentation. In other words, the plaintiff might have engaged in the transaction even had the truth been known. These requirements, especially where there are many injured investors, cause a number of problems in recovery which are discussed below.

In the proxy area, the statute and rules are aimed at the process by which shareholders decide how to vote their shares. The population which would be harmed by a disclosure defect in that process is thus easily identifiable. In that setting, the Supreme Court has ruled that a materiality finding will also satisfy the element of reliance.[100] Causation, however, will only be found when the votes of the shareholders challenging the disclosure defect were necessary in order for the transaction to be approved.[101]

The ordinary purpose of the causation and reliance requirements is to narrow the potentially limitless scope of liability by requiring plaintiffs to

---

[98] See, e.g. Section 21A(a)(2), 15 U.S.C. § 78u-1(a)(2) (1988), where the SEC can seek three times the 'profit gained or loss avoided' for certain insider trading violations. See also Section 21C, 15 U.S.C § 78u-3 (1988), giving the SEC cease and desist authority, and Section 21(d)(1), 15 U.S.C. § 78u(d)(1) (1988), giving the SEC the power to seek injunctions.

The SEC has no power to bring criminal prosecutions, but it does refer matters to the Department of Justice (DOJ). The DOJ can also bring cases on its own motion. Civil securities law violations can become criminal if they are 'willful'. Section 32(a), 15 U.S.C. § 78ff(a) (1988).

[99] See generally Cox, n. 28 above, at 784–789.

[100] *Mills* v. *Electric Auto-Lite Co.*, 396 U.S. 375 (1970).

[101] *Virginia Bankshares, Inc.* v. *Sandberg*, 111 S. Ct. 2749 (1991).

demonstrate a sufficiently close relationship to the wrong. A disclosure defect in the form of a misrepresentation into or an omission kept from the public trading market by a company whose securities are being traded can implicate the entire market for the company's securities. Should such a misrepresentation or omission cause a loss, it will be experienced by a large number of investors or shareholders, each one of which may have suffered a relatively small loss. As a result, open market securities fraud cases are generally pursued in the form of class actions.[102] In addition, the public markets are anonymous markets since investors generally do not know the identity of the party on the other side of their trades.

Plaintiffs may use materiality as a surrogate for causation in the open market case,[103] but they are still required to show reliance by each member of the plaintiff class. This individualized proof requirement is not only extremely burdensome for plaintiffs,[104] but it greatly diminishes the usefulness of the class action device by requiring substantial time be devoted to individual rather than group evidence.

Recently, the Supreme Court adopted a theory of liability, called 'fraud on the market', pursuant to which a presumption of reliance may be created in such a case.[105] In order to get the benefit of this presumption, plaintiff must show public material misrepresentations by the defendant; that the securities which are the subject of the case were traded in an efficient market;[106] and that plaintiff traded the shares after the misrepresentation was made, but before the truth was disclosed.[107]

In order to eliminate individual proof of reliance, fraud on the market theory rests on the assumption that the plaintiffs all relied on the same thing, that is, they all relied on the integrity of the market price. If the market price should be an accurate reflection of all public information about the company, then it follows that, when the market price is infected with false statements,

---

[102] Many securities fraud cases would be economically unfeasible absent the class action device, since the expense of litigation vastly exceeds any single plaintiff's economic loss.

The availability of the class action device, or the requirements for bringing such an action, are beyond the scope of this chapter.

[103] *Affiliated Ute Citizens of Utah v. United States*, 406 U.S. 128, *reh'g denied*, 407 U.S. 916, *reh'g denied*, 408 U.S. 931 (1972).

[104] 'Requiring plaintiff to show a speculative state of facts, i.e. how he would have acted if omitted material information had been disclosed, or if the misrepresentation had not been made, would place an unnecessarily unrealistic evidentiary burden on the Rule 10b-5 plaintiff who has traded on an impersonal market.' *Basic, Inc. v. Levinson*, 485 U.S. 224, 245 (1988).

[105] *Basic, Inc. v. Levinson*, 485 U.S. 224 (1988). The 'fraud on the market' theory was first adopted in 1975 by the Ninth Circuit in *Blackie v. Barrack*, 524 F.2d 891, *cert. denied*, 429 U.S. 816 (1976). See generally Jennings, n. 34 above, at 1241–1245.

[106] Which markets qualify as efficient for this purpose remains a question for further judicial development. Some courts have defined an efficient market as one 'in which security prices reflect all available public information about the economy, about financial markets and about the specific company involved'. *In re Laser Arms Corp. Securities Litigation*, 794 F. Supp. 475, 490 (S.D.N.Y. 1989).

[107] *Basic*, 485 U.S. at 248 n.27.

the integrity of the market on which plaintiff is relying is damaged. For federal securities law purposes, the fraud occurs when the plaintiff makes an investment decision based on a deception, and it is actionable fraud when the plaintiff suffers economically.

V. Insider Trading: A Species of Antifraud Liability

There are three provisions in the 1934 Act where personal liability can result from trading while in possession of material non-public information.[108] While all of these are 'insider trading' violations, the most prominent cases have arisen under the general antifraud provision in Section 10(b) and Rule 10b-5. Insider trading law, like other Rule 10b-5 law, is judge-made. Many attempts have been made to codify insider trading jurisprudence in legislation, but none has been passed.[109]

Since fraud is a disclosure-based concept under the securities laws, insider trading cases can be seen as omission cases. A failure to disclose, even information which is material, is not itself sufficient for liability to result. The rule against insider trading has been characterized as a 'disclose or abstain' rule. Because corporate officers or directors, or indeed outside counsel or even financial printers, would be prohibited from disclosing material non-public information, by state fiduciary concepts or by contract, the Rule, in effect, requires them to abstain from trading instead. Only omissions which are made in violation of a duty to disclose are actionable.[110] As a result, many insider trading cases turn on whether or not a duty existed which was breached by the trade.[111]

Three strands of insider trading analysis have been developed. Traditional insider trading theory requires that the trader owe a duty to the party on the other side of the transaction which is breached by the trade. Because of the anonymous nature of the public trading markets, this duty will not be found

---

[108] Section 10(b) and Rule 10b-5 thereunder; Section 14(e) and Rule 14e-3 thereunder (prohibiting and preventing fraudulent practices in connection with a tender offer); and Section 16, 15 U.S.C. § 78p (1988), which requires reporting of all trades in a company's stock by officers, directors, and holders of 10 percent or more of the company's securities, and provides a cause of action in favor of the company to recapture all profits from 'short swing' trades (a purchase and sale or a sale and purchase) by those persons within a six month period. While the Section 16 case does not depend on proof of fraud, the section embodies a Congressional presumption that it is more likely than not that insiders are benefitting from their superior information when they engage in short-term trades.

[109] The SEC has resisted attempts to define insider trading, on the grounds that such a definition would be too easy to evade. As a result, however, it can often be difficult to determine in advance, particularly in cases at the margin, what conduct is prohibited.

[110] 'When an allegation of fraud is based upon nondisclosure, there can be no fraud absent a duty to speak.' *Chiarella* v. *United States*, 445 U.S. 222, 235 (1980).

[111] Indeed, the definition of 'insider' depends on the presence of such a duty. *Chiarella* v. *United States*, 445 U.S. 222 (1980).

except where the person with whom the insider is trading is someone to whom a duty is owed, which means that officers and directors trading in the stock of their own company are almost the exclusive defendants under this theory.[112] This analysis may be extended to find liability in persons who received information from the insider illegitimately ('tippees') and traded on it, but their violation is entirely derivative of the insider's.[113]

The second strand of insider trading theory grows out of the first. Because tippees of insiders cannot be liable unless the insider breached his duty by tipping, persons who acquire material non-public information from insiders for legitimate corporate purposes would seem to be free from liability for their trades as well. However, in footnote 14 to the *Dirks* case, the Supreme Court noted that certain relationships, like outside counsel or accountant, give rise to an obligation of confidentiality to the corporation. Those persons are 'temporary insiders', which means that they take on the same duties as insiders with respect to information conveyed in the confidential relationship.

The third strand of insider trading theory grew out of the separate concurring and dissenting opinions in *Chiarella* in which several Justices raised the possibility that a theory based on the taking of information owned by another might give rise to insider trading liability even absent a fiduciary relationship.[114] This analysis, now known as the 'misappropriation' theory, is the one most frequently used in criminal prosecutions.[115] As developed by the federal courts of appeal[116], misappropriation theory can apply to any

---

[112] In *Chiarella*, the defendant was a financial printer whose employer was hired by an acquiring corporation to print the required documents in connection with its tender offer for another corporation. Chiarella purchased the stock of the target, on which he made profits after the tender offer was announced. Because Chiarella had no duty to the persons on the other side of the transaction (selling target shareholders), he breached no duty by trading without disclosure and was found not liable.

[113] *Dirks* v. *SEC*, 463 U.S. 646 (1983). Dirks was a securities analyst who received negative information about a company from an officer of that company. Dirks and his clients traded before the information was made public. Because Dirks was not himself an insider, his liability depended on the 'tip' from the insider being a breach of the insider's duty. Since the 'tip' was not made for his 'personal benefit', the insider did not breach his duty not to disclose. As a result, Dirks could not be found in violation of the insider trading prohibitions. Had the insider breached a duty to disclose, Dirks would have been liable if it had been shown that he 'knew or should have known of the breach'.

[114] See 445 U.S. at 238 (Stevens, J., concurring); 445 U.S. at 239 (Brennan, J., concurring); 445 U.S. at 240–44 (Burger, J., dissenting); 445 U.S. at 245 (Blackmun, J., dissenting).

[115] The misappropriation theory has never been upheld by the Supreme Court. In *Carpenter* v. *United States*, 484 U.S. 19 (1987), in which the misappropriation theory was the basis for a criminal conviction, the Court split 4–4 on the securities law counts, and upheld the conviction on mail and wire fraud grounds.

[116] The theory has been adopted by the Second, Seventh and Ninth Circuit Courts of Appeal, see *U.S.* v. *Newman*, 664 F.2d 12 (2d Cir. 1981), *aff'd* after remand, 722 F.2d 729 (2d Cir.), *cert.denied*, 464 U.S. 863 (1983); *U.S.* v. *Chestman*, 947 F.2d 551 (2d Cir. 1991) (*en banc*), *cert. denied*, 503 U.S. 1004 (1992); *SEC* v. *Cherif*, 933 F.2d 403 (7th Cir., 1991), *cert. denied*, 502 U.S. 1071 (1992); *SEC* v. *Clark*, 915 F. 2d 439 (9th Cir. 1990), and rejected only by the Fourth Circuit, *U.S.* v. *Bryan*, 58 F.3d 933 (4th Cir. 1995). In *Bryan*, the Court held that a criminal conviction based on the misappropriation theory cannot be based on a misappropriation of information in breach of a fiduciary duty unless the party to whom the duty was owed was a purchaser or seller or was otherwise connected with a securities transaction.

situation in which a person involved in a relationship, which is fiduciary in nature, trades on information received in that relationship which is intended to be confidential. The breadth of the relationships to which this obligation can attach is enormous.[117] However, few non-government cases can be brought under this theory because private plaintiffs will only have standing if, first, they are the parties to whom the duty breached was owed,[118] and secondly, they satisfy the purchaser or seller requirement for Rule 10b-5 suits generally.[119]

VI. Conclusion

The 1933 and 1934 Acts, as well as the SEC itself, recently celebrated their 60th birthdays. While the capital markets of the 1990s bear little resemblance to those of the 1930s, both in size and complexity, the securities laws and the SEC are generally considered a regulatory success. The United States model of securities regulation relies primarily on the 'remediation of information asymmetries',[120] that is, it intervenes to provide information, not to affect the substantive terms of a transaction. This assumption—that given sufficient information, investors are best left to make their own (even incorrect) decisions—is deeply related to our political and economic philosophy. It is not the only kind of system of securities regulation which can work to curb abuses, while not impeding the functioning of capital markets, but it has worked and

[117] See, e.g. *SEC* v. *Materia*, 745 F.2d 197 (2d Cir. 1984)(employer-employee, financial printer), *cert. denied*, 471 U.S. 1053 (1985); *Carpenter* v. *United States*, 484 U.S. at 19 (employer-employee, *Wall Street Journal* reporter); *United States* v. *Reed*, 601 F. Supp. 685 (S.D.N.Y.) (father–son), *rev'd on other grounds*, 773 F.2d 477 (1985); *U.S.* v. *Willis*, 778 F. Supp. 205 (S.D.N.Y. 1991) (doctor–patient).

The courts continue to try to define the kind of relationships to which this securities law duty attaches. *United States* v. *Chestman*, 947 F.2d 551, 556–57 (2nd Cir. 1991), *cert. denied*, 112 S. Ct. 1759 (1992). The breadth of the misappropriation theory can convert breaches of a variety of relationships governed under other law into Securities Act cases. If, for example, an employee steals pencils, or even trade secrets, from his employer, he might be liable for theft or misappropriation of assets, but he wouldn't be liable for securities fraud, with all its additional remedies. If instead the employee 'steals' his employer's material non-public information to the extent of trading in securities (which neither deprives the employer of the use of the information nor makes it public), he is arguably guilty of theft, and he may face securities law charges as well.

[118] *Moss* v. *Morgan Stanley*, 719 F.2d 5 (2d Cir. 1983), *cert. denied*, 465 U.S. 1025 (1984).

[119] There is a private cause of action for insider trading, but it is limited by the elements of proof required in other Rule 10b-5 cases. Although the allegedly illegal trade usually suffices to prove *scienter* on the part of the trader, plaintiff still has to prove materiality, causation, reliance and damages.

Causation concepts have been used to substantially narrow the class of potential plaintiffs—anyone selling from the time the insider or misappropriator starts buying until the material information is made public—to those trading 'contemporaneously' with the violator. See *Wilson* v. *Comtech Telecommunications Corp.*, 648 F.2d 88, 94–95 (2d Cir. 1981); *Fridrich* v. *Bradford*, 542 F.2d 307, 326 (6th Cir. 1976) (Celebrezze, J., concurring).

[120] Seligman, 'Agency Born Amid Scandals', *Nat'l L.J.*, July 18, 1994, at C4.

worked well, over dramatic changes in the markets, market participants, and market practices.

The greatest current challenge to the adaptability of the laws and the SEC is, of course, the increasing globalization of capital markets. We can expect to see further accommodations by the SEC of other schemes of securities regulation, and further refinements and limitations on the SEC's assertion of extra-territorial jurisdiction.

If history is any guide, these changes will be worked into the system of securities regulation over time, and the result will be the continuing success and viability of the markets.

23

TAXATION

DEBORAH H. SCHENK

I. Overview of United States Tax System

In the United States, taxes are imposed at multiple levels for a number of purposes. The government levies the vast majority of taxes in order to provide revenue to operate. But the tax system also can be utilized to compensate the government for using certain of its facilities ('user fees'), to provide incentives to engage in certain activities, or to penalize those who take certain actions.

The federal government of the United States is the world's largest taxing authority, raising hundreds of billions of dollars in taxes every year. The chief source of revenue is the federal income tax imposed on individuals and certain entities. Other federal taxes include estate and gift taxes, excise taxes, and social insurance taxes. The latter, which is now 15.3 percent of salary (one-half paid by the employer and one-half paid by the employee) is used to fund the social security program, to which all employees and employers contribute to provide retirement security and medical insurance. Excise taxes are imposed on many goods, such as tobacco, alcohol, gasoline, telephone service, airplane tickets, and luxury goods. Although a gift tax theoretically is levied on all completed gifts, and an estate tax is levied on the value of property transferred at death, there are very large exemptions, and, thus, those taxes apply only to the very wealthy. Unlike many other industrialized countries, the United States does not have a value added tax. It also does not levy a property tax, a wealth tax, or a sales tax.

Each of the fifty states has the power to tax. Most states have an income tax similar to the federal income tax. In addition, many states also impose real property taxes, excise taxes, inheritance taxes and sometimes wealth taxes. State sales taxes are also a significant source of revenue. Many large cities also impose income taxes, as well as sales taxes. Each state or city can impose its own taxes as well as develop its own rules. Most states also tax corporations. Sometimes the tax is an income tax, but often it is a franchise tax, based on the right to be chartered in the state.

Although taxes at all levels are significant and may affect how and where business is done, the federal income tax is the most important. It affects not only all United States citizens, residents, and businesses, but also foreign individuals and businesses who have some connection with the United States. Thus, most of the remainder of this chapter is devoted to that tax. The federal estate and gift taxes, which impose taxes on transferred wealth, are described in section XII below.

II. Sources of the Law

The federal income tax law, passed by the Congress, is a massive law, occupying thousands of pages and is probably the most complex American law. It is found in the Internal Revenue Code and is amended almost every year. The Treasury Department has the authority to issue regulations interpreting the law, and it has done so for almost every section of the Code. These regulations are also massive, totalling six volumes. Although not the 'law', the regulations are treated as law unless a court rules that a regulation has exceeded the power granted by Congress, a very rare occurrence.

The amount each taxpayer pays in income tax is largely self-assessed. Once a year, those subject to the law's provisions file a return reporting their income and deductions, and assessing a tax on themselves. Much of this tax is paid in advance, either through wage withholding or through payments of estimated tax on a quarterly basis.

The income tax is administered by the Internal Revenue Service (IRS), a very large bureaucracy. It is responsible not only for collecting the tax and assuring compliance, but also for interpreting the law and assisting taxpayers in meeting their obligations. It issues forms and instructions for filing returns, as well as rulings interpreting the law as applied to specific transactions.

Most disputes with the IRS are settled administratively. They may be initiated either because a taxpayer believes he has made a mistake in filing a return and seeks a refund, or much more likely, because the Service has audited a return and asserted a deficiency in the taxes paid. Most cases, particularly large corporate cases involving millions of dollars, are settled before reaching a court. These cases are heard in one of three federal courts: either the federal district court (a court of general jurisdiction), or the Claims Court (a specialized court), both requiring the taxpayer to pay the assessment and sue for a refund, or the Tax Court, a specialized court hearing only cases where the government asserts a tax deficiency which a taxpayer wishes to challenge without paying first. If a court orders the taxpayer to pay additional taxes, or the government to make a refund, interest is added automatically, thereby decreasing the effect of a difference in payment times. Appeals from these courts lie in the Circuit Courts of Appeal and ultimately in the Supreme Court, although the latter hears very few tax cases. Judicial gloss is much less important with regard to tax law than in other areas; it is almost entirely a statutory subject.

III. General Framework for Taxing 'Citizens' and 'Aliens'

Unlike most other countries in the world, the United States taxes 'U.S. persons' on their worldwide income. A 'U.S. person' is a citizen or resident of the United States. 'Resident' is defined very broadly to include those who are present in the United States for a significant period of time during the taxable year, generally one-half of the year, but sometimes less if there has been a significant presence in prior years. For example, a French citizen, who is present in the United States for 7 months during the year would be taxed on his entire income, no matter where it was earned. A U.S. person (citizen or resident) is subject to tax on his worldwide income even if it is subject to tax by another country, although he may have a credit against American tax for taxes paid to the other country. Thus, for example, a United States citizen is subject to United States tax on rents earned from an apartment building he owns in Sweden, or interest earned on a Japanese bond.

Even if a nonresident alien is not subject to United States tax on worldwide income, he may be subject to tax on income connected in some manner with the United States. This would include, for example, salary earned while present in the United States, dividends paid by American corporations, or income attributable to United States business. These rules often are modified by bilateral treaties and are discussed further in section XI below.

IV. Federal Income Taxation of United States Individuals

A. *Fundamental Concepts*

The taxable unit in the United States is the individual. (Certain entities are taxed as well, and discussion of this tax follows in sections V to VII below.) The United States does not tax the family unit. One exception to this rule is that a husband and wife are entitled to combine their income on one return. This is generally, but not always, advantageous. Generally, a child pays her own taxes, but the tax rate on the unearned income of a minor child (under age 14) is the same as the rate on the parent's income.

In the United States, the tax base is 'income', which is defined very broadly. It includes not only all receipts that are 'consumed' by the taxpayer, but also the change in the taxpayer's wealth during the taxable period. Although a tax based solely on consumption is favored by many scholars, it has never been considered seriously by Congress.

The tax is a percentage of the taxable income during a given period. For almost all taxpayers, this is one year. For individuals, generally the income is calculated at the end of the calendar year; for businesses, it usually is determined at the end of the fiscal year, which may, but need not be, the calendar year.

In order to determine what income is attributable to which taxable period, an accounting method must be used. Most individuals use the cash method of accounting. Income is included when it is actually or constructively received (that is, when the taxpayer has the *right* to possession even if he choses not to), and deductions are taken when paid. Businesses, on the other hand, use an accrual method of accounting. Although this is often very similar to the method used to keep their records for financial purposes, it is not identical. Generally, income is reported when all the events have occurred to fix the right to receive it. Deductions usually are taken when the obligation to pay is fixed, but sometimes the deduction is delayed until payment has been made or until the services have been performed or property has been delivered for which payment is being made.

B. *Defining the Base: Gross Income*

The statute defines gross income as income from whatever source derived. This is a very broad definition, in some cases broader than mere receipt of funds, but narrower than economic income. Congress has chosen to exempt certain items from the tax base, even though they clearly represent an economic benefit to the recipient. The courts also have determined that some receipts are not within the definition of 'income'. Finally, the United States has long exempted some items out of a concern for administrative convenience.

The single largest source of income is wages or salary paid to employees or independent contractors. The amount paid as compensation for services rendered is taxable regardless of the form it takes. For example, payment in cash, stock, or other property, or the discharge of an employee's liability are all taxable compensation.

Where the employee receives noncash property, the amount of taxable income is the fair market value at time of receipt. If, however, the property is nontransferable or is subject to a substantial risk of forfeiture, the employee can elect to report the value on receipt or alternatively to report the value when the restriction is lifted. Suppose, for example, that the employer transfers stock to an employee who must forfeit the stock if he leaves the employer within 5 years. The stock is worth $1,000 when transferred and $30,000 at the end of 5 years. The employee can report $1,000 now or $30,000 in 5 years. If he should resign in 3 years, he would report nothing, assuming he did not elect to report the stock on receipt. As will be explained later (see section IV D below), the choice will determine the 'basis' in the stock and, hence, the size of the gain (or loss) when it is sold.

The United States has a very complicated set of rules dealing with contributions to pension plans, designed both to encourage retirement savings and to regulate private plans. In general, a limited amount of salary contributed by both the employer and the employee to a qualified plan is not subject to current tax. Furthermore, the amount contributed is permitted to grow tax-free until the employee retires, when the entire amount is taxed. This treatment makes this type of investment very attractive for both employer and employee. As a result, a significant amount of capital in the United States is invested in private pension plans. This is not without a cost, however. The government imposes very strict limitations on private qualified plans to prevent discrimination in favor of highly paid employees and to monitor the plan, and many employers consider these restrictions and their accompanying paperwork quite burdensome.

Fringe benefits received in connection with employment may be taxable. If they are primarily for the benefit of the employer, they are not taxable. For example, books, computers, and supplies furnished by an employer are not subject to tax. Meals and lodging provided on the business premises for the employee and his family for the convenience of the employer are exempt.

Thus, a hotel manager who is given a free apartment in the hotel, or an office worker whose lunch is supplied so that she can continue to work during the lunch hour, has no taxable income. On the other hand, many not dissimilar fringe benefits are taxable. For example, if the employer provides an automobile that the employee may use at any time, the value of the use of the car would be included in the employee's income.

Congress has chosen to favor certain fringe benefits by exempting them from tax. Because of their tax-free status, they are quite common and valuable. The most important of these is health insurance. Payment of all or a portion of the premium on health and accident insurance is not taxable to the employee; neither are the amounts paid by an employer directly to health care providers, nor reimbursements from the plan to pay for medical expenses. As a result, many businesses participate in group health insurance plans funded largely by employers. Employers also may provide up to $75,000 in group term life insurance that is nontaxable to the employee. Amounts received as compensation for sickness or injuries (for example, a judgment in a personal injury action) are also not taxable. Finally, employers may transfer certain goods or services to their employees on a tax-free basis.

Another large source of income is dividends and interest. Dividends in cash or property paid on corporate stock are taxable except in the case where the corporation has no profits (see section V C below), or in some cases where the dividend is in the stock of the company (see section V E below). Most interest that is paid or accrues during the taxable year on a debt obligation is taxable. This includes personal as well as business interest, interest on installment sales obligations, and original issue discount. Note that the receipt of a loan is itself not a taxable event on the theory that there is an offsetting liability and thus, the taxpayer's net worth has not increased. Accordingly, the repayment of the loan does not trigger a deduction, because, although there has been a decline in assets, there has also been a decrease in liabilities. Where, however, a loan is discharged without payment, there is income to the extent the liability has been cancelled. An exception to this inclusion rule applies where the debtor is insolvent or is involved in a bankruptcy proceeding. Another important source of taxable income is rent received for the use of either real or personal property.

In general, transfer payments received from the government are not subject to tax. This is true for benefits that all citizens receive—such as police and fire protection—as well as those that are means tested—such as welfare or Legal Aid services. However, benefits that may be received by certain citizens but not others, as a substitute for wages, are generally included in income. For example, unemployment compensation (paid for a period after an employee loses a job) is taxable, as is a portion of social security benefits at middle and upper income levels.

Some receipts that clearly are an economic benefit nevertheless are excluded from tax. Congress has chosen to exempt the interest paid on bonds issued by states and municipalities. This enables the local governments to issue bonds with a rate of interest less than that offered on commercial bonds. In effect, by forgoing the tax, the federal government subsidizes a portion of the cost of the bond to the local government. In order to receive the subsidy, the proceeds of the bond must be used for public purposes. Private purpose or industrial development bonds may not be tax-exempt, or the local government may be limited in the amount they can issue.

Gifts and inheritances also are not included in the federal income tax base of the recipient. The cash or property is taxed in the hands of the donor or decedent, but is not taxed again in the donee's or beneficiary's hands. The converse rule applies to alimony. Alimony or maintenance payments generally are income to the recipient, and the payor obtains a deduction unless the divorced parties agree to reverse the treatment. Thus, the payments are taxed only once, either to the recipient or the payor. Transfers that are labelled as child support are not alimony and are not taxable, even if received by the former spouse for the children's benefit.

Some items are exempt from tax because they are too difficult to value, or it is impossible to require compliance. The most important of these is imputed income from services or the use of property. The use of a residence owned by the taxpayer, for example, does not produce taxable income. This is a significant exemption. Similarly, when a taxpayer performs services for herself, there is no taxable income. A taxpayer who remains at home and cares for children or provides domestic services for the family has no taxable income, whereas a taxpayer who enters the workforce and uses her salary to pay for childcare and domestic services is taxed on the full amount of her salary, with virtually no deduction for the cost of the service.

After computing gross income, a taxpayer is entitled to deduct certain expenditures. Tax is levied on the net amount, known as 'taxable income'. There are currently five brackets ranging from 15 percent to 39.6 percent. Because Congress has permitted some deductions as incentives for certain activities, it is possible for a taxpayer to owe no taxes, even though he has significant economic income. To some extent, this possibility is lessened by the 'alternative minimum tax'. Certain high-income taxpayers are required to pay the greater of their 'regular' tax liability or their alternative liability, computed at 28 percent on a much broader base.

A basic tenet of the federal income tax system is that the tax should be levied on those who have an ability to pay, after taking allowable deductions.

But many people in lower income brackets don't have deductions to take, and so the law permits every taxpayer to take a 'standard deduction'. This amount roughly compensates for minimal living expenses, and a taxpayer need not offer any proof of expenses in order to take this deduction. In addition, every taxpayer is entitled to an exemption (currently about $2,000) for himself, his or her spouse (if filing jointly), and for every dependent. A dependent is generally a relative or someone who lives with the taxpayer who has a minimum amount of income and for whom the taxpayer provides more than one-half of her support. Only a taxpayer whose income exceeds the standard deduction and the exemption would be subject to tax, and then only on the amount of that excess.

As an alternative to the standard deduction, taxpayers may take 'itemized deductions', in addition to business-type deductions (discussed in section IV C below). The former are generally personal expenditures and are subject to numerous restrictions. They are as follows:

(1)   Medical expenses. A taxpayer may deduct unreimbursed medical expenses only to the extent they exceed 7.5 percent of adjusted gross income. Adjusted gross income (AGI) is gross income minus certain deductions (generally business related). Reimbursements from a medical insurance plan are totally tax-exempt, although out-of-pocket medical expenses are deductible only if they are extraordinarily large.

(2)   Casualty losses. A casualty loss occurs when a taxpayer suffers a sudden or unexpected loss to property. Such net losses (after insurance or other payment) are deductible, however, only to the extent they exceed 10 percent of adjusted gross income.

(3)   Taxes. Taxpayers may deduct state and local income and real property taxes paid during the year. Note that federal taxes, as well as other local taxes, such as sales taxes, are not deductible.

(4)   Charitable deductions. Amounts contributed to a recognized charity, such as religious organizations or educational institutions, are deductible. The deduction is the amount of the cash or the fair market value of the property contributed. Taxpayers are not permitted to avoid paying all income taxes by contributing large amounts to charity. Amounts exceeding 50 percent of AGI are not deductible, although they can be carried over to a future year.

(5)   Employee business expenses. Employee business expenses reimbursed by an employer are ignored for tax purposes. Although an employee can deduct business expenses he pays personally, only the expenses that exceed 2 percent of AGI are deductible, which effectively prevents most deductions.

(6) Interest. Taxpayers can no longer deduct personal or consumer interest, such as that paid on a personal line of credit or a car loan. A major exception to this rule is that the interest on a home mortgage remains deductible (subject to certain limits). The fact that home mortgage interest and real property taxes are deductible, even though Congress has cut back on deductions in recent years, is evidence of the importance ascribed to home ownership in the United States.

Taxpayers also may deduct investment interest to the extent they have offsetting investment income. Investment interest is interest on debt used to purchase investment assets such as stocks and bonds. Investment income includes the interest and dividends received on such assets, as well as any gain on the sale of the assets. Interest on debt used to purchase or carry tax-exempt assets, such as municipal bonds, is nondeductible.

These complicated rules, which limit the deduction of interest in certain circumstances, but not in others, make it necessary to trace the proceeds of borrowed funds. Because, however, money is fungible, taxpayers often engage in complicated transactions designed to insure that borrowed funds are used for 'good' purposes (i.e., the interest will be deductible) and non-borrowed funds are used for less desirable (not deductible) purposes.

C. Business Income

Business income is like other income. What is different are the deductions allowed, which generally apply to all forms of business, whether a sole proprietorship, a corporation, or a partnership.

1. General business expenses

The ordinary and necessary expenses of carrying on a trade or business are deductible in calculating adjusted gross income. Expenses are ordinary and necessary if a reasonable business person would have expended those funds with the hope of producing a profit. This would include salaries, rent, supplies, interest, utilities, advertising, and so on. These expenses are deductible in full, except that the deduction for business meals and entertainment is limited to 50 percent of the amount expended.

Businesses also may deduct service fees—such as those paid to lawyers and accountants—licensing fees, and royalties, provided they are ordinary and necessary. Almost all taxes relating to the conduct of a trade or business are deductible, except federal income taxes. These include state and local income taxes, real property taxes, sales taxes, franchise taxes, and social security taxes. Foreign taxes are deductible as well, provided a foreign tax credit is not claimed.

A business may not, however, deduct expenses that are thought to violate public policy, even if they are directly related to the business. For example, a business could not deduct a 'bribe' paid to a foreign official even if that is customary or required in the country in which it is doing business. Also nondeductible are any illegal payments, fines and penalties, political contributions, and certain lobbying expenses.

2. Depreciation

Amounts paid for assets, such as a machine or a building, which have useful lives of several years or more, are considered 'capital' costs and are not deductible immediately. However, individuals and businesses are permitted to take an annual depreciation deduction for the decline in value of business or income-producing property. For many years, the United States has used a depreciation system that employs schedules that bear almost no relation to the actual decline in value or the wear and tear on business assets. Tangible personalty is depreciated using a modified declining balance method, applied to the cost of the asset over an arbitrary period, ignoring salvage value. Although use of this accelerated depreciation system is elective, almost everyone chooses to use it because it permits a faster write-off of the asset, thereby reducing current taxable income. Alternatively, a taxpayer can use a straight line method of depreciation over a longer useful life. Realty and assets leased to nonresident individuals or entities can only be depreciated using a straight line method.

In order to be eligible for depreciation, an asset must be placed in service in a business or income-producing activity and must have an expected useful life. Certain intangibles, such as goodwill, may be depreciated over a 14-year period using the straight line method. Other intangibles that do not dissipate, such as stock, or assets that do not decline in value, such as land and antiques, are not depreciable.

In order to promote investment in small companies, an individual or business can elect to expense—immediately deduct— the entire cost of an asset even if it is still useful at year end, up to $17,500 of tangible personal property placed in service during a taxable year, provided that no more than $200,000 of such property is acquired during the year.

Property located in a foreign country can only be depreciated using the straight line method and then over a longer period. Property is generally considered as sited in a foreign country if it is used outside the United States, although exceptions are made for certain items, such as airplanes operating out of the United States. Mining and drilling businesses take a deduction similar to depreciation that is referred to as a 'depletion allowance'. The basis for the deduction is the historical cost, although the amount of each year's deduction is based on the income produced.

3. Development costs

Research and development costs incurred in a trade or business are generally deductible, provided they are not capital in nature. Alternatively, a taxpayer can elect to deduct the costs over a longer period. Similarly, expenses incurred in the exploration or development of mineral deposits are deductible, subject to an election by the taxpayer to deduct them over a longer period.

The start-up costs of a new trade or business are not deductible because they are capital in nature and are attributable to producing income over a long period. Congress, however, has permitted taxpayers to write off these costs over a 5-year period if they elect to do so.

4. Inventory

Businesses that manufacture or sell goods usually are required to use special accounting methods to determine the cost of the inventory sold. Very complicated rules have been developed to determine cost of goods sold and when and how inventory turns over.

D. Acquisition and Disposition of Property

1. Calculation of gain or loss

A major characteristic of the federal income tax system is that it does not tax increases or decreases in value as they accrue. Appreciation and depreciation (except on business property) is taken into account only on the disposition of the property when the gain or loss is determined ('realized'). This realization requirement means that, although a taxpayer's assets have increased in value, no tax is due until the assets are sold, exchanged, or otherwise disposed of. This ability to defer tax on appreciation is extremely important, and many transactions are designed to take advantage of this rule. In recent years, Congress has become increasingly conscious of transactions in which taxpayers enjoy the economic gain on an asset without 'realizing' it, and thus it has begun to tax the appreciation in value on the more egregious or sophisticated transactions, even though the gain has not yet been realized.

When a taxpayer purchases an asset, he acquires a 'basis' in the asset equal to his cost. He has a gain on the disposition of the asset only if the 'amount received' exceeds the basis, and a loss if his basis is greater than the amount received. Because the basis represents the cost that is unrecovered for tax purposes, it is decreased by any depreciation permitted, and increased by any additional costs.

Basis can be obtained without purchasing an asset. A gift is not a taxable event to either the donor or donee, and therefore neither pays income tax on any appreciation in the transferred property. The donee, however, takes the donor's basis as his own, and thus, on a subsequent sale, would report the appreciation during both the period he held the asset and the period the donor held the asset. A transfer at death is also not a taxable event, but the beneficiary does not carry over the decedent's basis. Instead the beneficiary's basis is the fair market value at the decedent's death. This has the effect of exempting all appreciation on inherited assets from income tax. This is a major 'loophole' and results in taxpayers holding on to their assets until death in order to take advantage of this provision.

2. Liabilities

Most businesses and some individuals acquire assets with debt (for example, a building with an existing mortgage, or borrowing money to buy the building), and the treatment of liabilities substantially complicates the tax law. In general, a taxpayer is given a cost basis in an asset equal to the full price of the asset even if he acquired the asset with debt. This is extremely beneficial because the taxpayer can take depreciation deductions based on the full price, including the mortgage, even though he has not yet made any principal payments. He thus creates a tax deduction without any cash expenditure. This is true even if the mortgage is nonrecourse (the lender can reclaim the property, but not sue the owners), and he is not personally liable. The *quid pro quo* is that an assumption of a mortgage by the purchaser is treated as an amount realized. Similarly, if the property declines in value and the mortgagor defaults, the amount of the outstanding mortgage that is discharged is treated as income. Where, however, a taxpayer mortgages property that he already owns, the basis of the property is not increased, because the mortgage is not part of the cost of acquiring the property. The owner has no taxable income even though the cash received may exceed his original cost for the property. Thus, even though the taxpayer is able to enjoy the appreciation in value (by borrowing against it), he is not taxed on that economic income until he sells the property.

3. Nonrecognition transactions

Congress has created certain statutory exceptions to the general rule, and no gain or loss need be reported even if there is a sale or exchange. The most important of these nonrecognition provisions for individuals permits the gain on a primary residence to escape tax so long as the sales proceeds are invested within a limited period of time (2 years) in a new residence. Once the taxpayer reaches age 55, the residence can be sold and up to $125,000 of the gain is exempt from tax even if the proceeds are not reinvested. The net effect of these two provisions is that appreciation on residences is almost never taxed in the United States. Gain on an asset subject to a casualty (such as a fire) or an involuntary conversion (such as condemnation by the government) also is deferred provided the proceeds from the insurance or the government are invested in similar property. Finally, a transfer from one spouse to another incident to a divorce is not a taxable event.

The most significant nonrecognition provision for businesses defers the gain on an exchange of like kind properties. These are generally business or income-producing assets (other than inventory or stock) that are exchanged for similar property. The gain on the transferred property is not taxed, but is preserved in the newly acquired property, which takes as its basis the basis of the original property.

4. Deductible losses

Other than the nonrecognition transactions, all gain that is realized is subject to tax, including gain on investment, business, and personal property. Losses, however, are subject to certain restrictions (more fully discussed in section IV D6 below). Individuals may deduct only losses on business or investment property (or in limited cases on personal property where the loss is due to a casualty). Thus, a loss on a personal automobile is not deductible. This reflects the view that dollars spent on consumption are never deductible.

5. Capital gain preference

One of the most complicating features of the United States income tax is that not all recognized gains and losses are treated alike. So-called 'capital gains' are subject to tax (unlike the treatment in some countries), but at a reduced rate. Currently, for example, the maximum rate on capital gains is 28 percent, whereas the maximum rate on 'ordinary gains' is approximately 40 percent. This rate differentiation causes an enormous amount of complexity. First, the term 'capital asset' is not self-defining, and both Congress and the IRS have developed very complex rules to distinguish capital and ordinary assets. These rules are often subject to litigation. Secondly, because the rate differential is so important, taxpayers and their advisers spend an inordinate amount of time trying to structure transactions to produce capital gains. Some of these transactions would not otherwise be economic, but because the after-tax rate of return on capital assets may exceed that on ordinary assets, there is an incentive to invest in these transactions.

Although there was one short period in our recent history when all gains were treated alike, Congress has been unable to resist the lure of providing special tax treatment for capital gains. There are a number of justifications. First, inflation generally is not taken into account in determining federal tax liability. Thus, if T purchases an asset for $100 and holds it for one year when there is 10 percent inflation, and then sells it for $110, T will pay tax on $10 gain even though the gain is entirely due to inflation. This failure to index is crucial, but a capital gains preference only roughly counteracts it because it is the same regardless of the actual amount of inflation or the period the asset is held.

The second justification stems from the fact that the United States has a progressive tax system, meaning that the rates are not proportional, but increase as income increases. This reflects our notion that the wealthy have more ability to pay taxes and that an income tax can be used to redistribute wealth. This means, however, that if income is bunched in one year (as it would be with appreciation that is reported only when an asset is sold), the taxes may be higher than they would be if the appreciation were reported on an annual basis. Again, the preference is too broad because it applies even if 'bunching' is not present. The third justification stems from our classical corporate tax system, discussed in section V below, that imposes a 'double tax' on corporate profits. Those who object to this system see the capital gains preference as a partial offset to the double taxation of dividends.

By far the best justification for the preference is as a response to the 'lock-in' problem, that is the incentive to hold on to assets to defer the gain, often until death when the gain is exempt from tax. The preference is thought to encourage taxpayers to sell their assets and thus to direct capital to its highest and best use. Congress also often justifies the preference by arguing that it is an incentive for businesses, particular start-up businesses or venture capital. It is thought by some to spur economic growth although, given the growth of the global open economy, this argument is less convincing.

While capital gains are given preferential treatment, capital losses are treated harshly. In order to limit a taxpayer's ability to report only her losses and defer her gains, she can deduct capital losses in any one year only to the extent she has matching capital gains, plus $3,000. Corporations can deduct capital losses only if they have matching gains. Ordinary losses, however, are deductible in full.

In general, capital assets are all assets except

(1) inventory or property held primarily for sale to customers;
(2) depreciable or real property used in a trade or business;
(3) copyrights, literary, artistic or musical works produced by the taxpayer;
(4) accounts receivable acquired from the sale or inventory;
(5) United States government publications; and
(6) property integrally related to a business.

Because the incentive is so powerful, Congress is constantly changing the definition and has special rules for various industries and assets.

6. Limitation on losses

Other types of losses, in addition to capital losses, are limited as well. For example, a loss on a sale to a related party, such as a family member, is not deductible. The theory is that the family unit otherwise would be able to enjoy the tax deduction while simultaneously retaining its investment in the asset. A similar concern motivates the 'wash sale' rules under which a loss on the disposition of publicly traded stock is disallowed if the shares are repurchased within 30 days of the sale creating the loss. Straddles are yet another example of an attempt to deduct a loss when, in fact, there is no overall loss in the transaction. In a straddle, the taxpayer would close the loss position before year end and report the gain position in the following year, enjoying the benefit of the deduction for a year although there was no economic loss. Under current law, the taxpayer can only deduct the loss leg to the extent it exceeds the gain on the open position.

In the 1980s, Congress became concerned with the proliferation of tax shelters, which were marketed widely and created significant tax losses. In a tax shelter, a taxpayer would acquire an investment interest (typically through a limited partnership) with very little cash and a significant amount of debt, generally nonrecourse. The activity would produce large depreciation and interest deductions that vastly exceeded the taxpayer's cash investment. The deductions would be used to 'shelter' the taxpayer's salary or other investment income.

Two provisions were adopted to limit what Congress perceived to be artificial losses. The first limits the taxpayer's deductions in certain activities to the amount 'at risk'. This is primarily aimed at nonrecourse debt, which is not considered an amount at risk. It does not apply, however, to nonrecourse debt acquired from a commercial bank to purchase real estate. The second is much more broadly based. It limits losses attributable to 'passive activities', generally an investment in an activity in which the taxpayer does not 'materially participate'. This roughly means that the taxpayer is not employed by the activity or does not spend a significant amount of time in connection with the activity. If the activity produces a net loss, the taxpayer cannot deduct it until such time as he disposes of the activity. Although the passive loss rules effectively shut down tax shelters, they did so in a broad brush way that also affects many legitimate activities that temporarily produce economic losses.

V. Federal Taxation of United States Corporations

The United States has a classical system of corporate taxation, that is corporate profits are subject to taxation twice, once at the corporate level and once at the shareholder level. There is no system of integration except for a limited pass through approach applied to so-called 'S corporations' (described below). Partnership income, however, is taxed only to the partners (see further section VI below).

Thus, the first step is determining whether an entity is, in fact, a corporation subject to tax. To be taxed as a corporation, an entity must have at least three of the following characteristics:

(a)   continuity of life,
(b)   central management,
(c)   free transferability of interests, and
(d)   limited liability.

A United States corporation, taxed on its worldwide income, is one that is incorporated in the United States, regardless of where it does business or is managed. The source of the income is irrelevant.

A. *Corporate Level Tax*

Corporations are subject to tax on net income, computed very similarly to the way business income is calculated for individuals. There are four brackets ranging from 15 percent to 35 percent. Corporations are also subject to the corporate alternative minimum tax (AMT), which is designed to ensure that a corporation with a significant amount of income pays some tax even though it has a number of exclusions, deductions, and credits. The AMT is imposed on a broader base at a lower rate and is due if it exceeds the regular tax.

B. Incorporation

A contribution of property to a corporation is generally a nontaxable event to the shareholder if the contributors together own 80 percent or more of the stock, and if they receive stock or securities in exchange for the property. The gain or loss inherent in the contributed property carries over to the corporation, which assumes the contributors' bases in the property. Similarly, the contributors take the basis of the contributed property as their basis in the stock or securities received. To the extent the shareholders receive property that is not stock or securities, they must include the value in income. A corporation never recognizes gain or loss on the issuance of its stock.

A subsequent contribution of property to a corporation by a noncontrolling shareholder is a taxable event. The shareholder recognizes gain or loss equal to the difference between the fair market value of the stock received and the basis in the property.

C. Dividend Distributions

A corporation obtains no deduction for distributions of dividends to its shareholders, which are generally taxable to them. Interest paid by the corporation to bondholders is, however, deductible. Thus, there is a substantial tax incentive for a United States corporation to raise capital through debt rather than equity. Particularly in the 1980s, purchases of corporations were accomplished through leveraged buyouts—the purchasers borrowed heavily and subsequently sold assets to provide funds to make interest payments.

Individual shareholders are taxed on ordinary dividend distributions to the extent they represent corporate 'earnings and profits'. A corporate shareholder is entitled to exclude anywhere from 70 percent to 100 percent of a corporate dividend. This prevents triple taxation of corporate profits.

Unlike the treatment in many other countries, a distribution from a United States corporation could be either a taxable dividend, a nontaxable return of capital, or a capital gain. A distribution is taxable to the extent it represents the 'earnings and profits' (E&P) of the corporation. E&P is similar to retained earnings, although there are significant differences. One major difference is that current earnings are considered first. If a corporation with a net loss in previous years makes a profit in the current year, a distribution of an amount equal to the current year's profits is a taxable dividend. To the extent the corporation distributes more than its current and accumulated E&P, the distribution is treated as a return of capital and is not taxable to the extent of the shareholder's adjusted basis (generally historical cost) in the stock. Any excess is a capital gain. These rules are applied even if the shareholder purchased his shares from another shareholder, directly in a secondary market (as is often the case) rather than from the corporation and thus literally has no capital invested in the corporation.

These rules apply not only to a distribution of cash, but also to a distribution of property, which is more common for smaller corporations. Because distributions are not deductible to the corporation, but salary and interest are, a corporation may try to disguise a dividend as some other type of payment. The IRS may recharacterize debt as equity or determine that a salary payment is really a 'constructive dividend' and thereby eliminate the corporate deduction.

Where a corporation distributes cash either as a dividend or in exchange for its stock, no gain or loss is recognized. On the distribution of appreciated property, however, the gain must be reported. This creates parity with a sale of the asset. Because a loss is recognized on the sale of a corporate asset, but not on a distribution, corporations almost never distribute depreciated property.

D. *Redemptions*

A redemption of a shareholder's stock also may be treated as a dividend distribution or a return of capital. The repurchase of shares is treated as a dividend unless the shareholder has either completely terminated or substantially decreased his interest in the corporation. A pro rata repurchase is always treated as a dividend, unless the corporation is partially liquidating. Generally, a non-pro rata repurchase of the shares of a public corporation is treated as a return of capital, which means that any excess over the shareholder's basis is a capital gain. On the other hand, a partial repurchase of a shareholder's interest in a closely held corporation is often an ordinary income dividend. Finally, a distribution in partial liquidation, which is a contraction of the corporation's business, is treated as a return of capital rather than a dividend.

E. Stock Dividends

The distribution of a debt obligation is treated just like a cash dividend. A distribution of a corporation's own stock, however, may be tax-free. Generally, a distribution of common stock (or a stock split), or of preferred stock to common stockholders is a nontaxable event. The shareholders' historical cost basis is now split between the two blocks of stock. Other stock dividends are taxable. These include:

(1) a dividend where the shareholder can elect to take cash or stock;
(2) distributions where some shareholders receive common stock and others receive preferred stock;
(3) stock dividends on preferred stock;
(4) distributions of convertible preferred stock, and
(5) other disproportionate distributions.

F. Liquidations

A complete liquidation of a corporation (where the corporate assets are distributed in exchange for all of the stock) is a taxable event. Generally, the sale of assets produces gain or loss taxable at the corporate level. Alternatively, a distribution of those same assets to the shareholders would produce gain or loss. The shareholders also are taxed on the difference between the amount received (either cash or the assets) and their cost basis, producing a capital gain or loss. Their basis in the assets received on the liquidation is the fair market value at the time of the liquidation.

A subsidiary (defined in this context as 80 percent control) may be liquidated into its parent on a tax-free basis. The subsidiary reports no gain or loss on the distribution of its assets to its parent, and the parent reports no gain or loss on the exchange of the stock. The parent takes the subsidiary's basis in the acquired assets, which means that the parent has inherited any gain or loss on the assets. Where the parent recently purchased the stock of the subsidiary, its cost basis for the stock may be much higher than the subsidiary's historical cost basis in the assets, either because of years of depreciation or because the assets have appreciated. The parent can elect to 'step up' the basis of the subsidiary's assets by treating the subsidiary as if it had sold its assets in a taxable transaction, and the parent's basis in the assets then becomes the fair market value.

G. *Reorganizations*

When a corporation seeks to acquire another corporation, it can do so by either acquiring the assets or the stock of the target. Furthermore, it can do so in a taxable or nontaxable way. Although many of the corporate 'mergers' in the United States are structured on a tax-free basis, some are not, usually out of choice, but sometimes not, because the rules describing nonrecognition reorganizations are quite complex and rigid. The extraordinary tax advantages in completing a nontaxable reorganization dramatically affect corporate restructuring in the United States. For example, in the 1980s, a significant restructuring of corporations was based largely on a corporation's ability to deduct interest and to reorganize without paying taxes.

The acquisition by one corporation of the stock or assets of another corporation for cash is a taxable event. The acquiring corporation has a basis equal to the fair market value in either the stock or the assets. If assets were sold, the target reports gain or loss on their sale, and assuming a subsequent liquidation, the target's shareholders have taxable gain or loss on the exchange of their shares. If the shareholders sold their stock directly to the acquirer, they report gain or loss. Another important consequence of a 'sale' is that the tax characteristics of the target disappear. The most important of these is any 'net operating loss' that the target may have incurred in prior years and that has not yet been deducted for tax purposes is eliminated.

There are seven basic types of nonrecognition reorganizations. All are premised on the notion that the surviving corporation must be a continuation of the target corporation and that the stockholders still own the same (or similar) entities. That is reflected in two general requirements:

(1)   there must be a continuation of the business of the target by the surviving corporation, and
(2)   the target shareholders must continue to have an ownership interest in the survivor.

Each type of reorganization has additional requirements that must be followed; a failure to abide by the form results in taxation.

A statutory merger or consolidation (known as a 'Type A' reorganization) is a union of two corporations under the laws of one of the states. The shareholders of the target corporation(s) must receive stock; receipt of bonds would not satisfy the continuity of interest requirement. The merger can be accomplished directly or by using a subsidiary that merges with the target, or a subsidiary can be created into which the acquirer transfers the assets of the target.

In a stock-for-stock reorganization (a 'Type B' reorganization), the acquirer obtains control of a target by transferring its stock directly to the target's shareholders in exchange for at least 80 percent of the stock of the target. The consideration must be voting stock of the acquirer or the acquirer's parent. The target's stock may be transferred subsequently to a new subsidiary of the acquirer or its parent.

In a stock-for-assets reorganization (a 'Type C' reorganization), the acquiring corporation must obtain substantially all of the assets of the target corporation in exchange for voting stock of the acquirer or its parent. The acquirer can acquire up to 20 percent of the target's assets with cash or other property and also may assume the target's liabilities. The target must subsequently liquidate, distributing the acquirer's shares to its shareholders. Stock of a subsidiary of the acquiring corporation may be used to acquire the target's assets, and the assets can be transferred to a new subsidiary of the acquirer or its parent.

An assets for stock reorganization (a 'Type D' reorganization) generally is used to split up a corporation. A corporation transfers all or part of its assets to a corporation that is controlled by the transferor, in exchange for the shares of the transferee that subsequently must be transferred to the transferor's shareholders. For example, A corporation operates two businesses and for nontax reasons wishes to spin off one business to a separate corporation. It transfers one business to a new subsidiary B in exchange for B stock that it then distributes to the A shareholders. Some or all of the A shareholders continue to own the business, but through a new corporation.

A corporation can also alter its capital structure in a tax-free way. A recapitalization (a 'Type E' reorganization) is generally a stock-for-stock, bond-for-bond or bond-for-stock exchange. A stock-for-bond exchange, however, does not qualify because it lacks the necessary continuity of interest.

A reincorporation merely to change the name, form or place of incorporation (a 'Type F' reorganization) can be accomplished tax-free so long as only one corporation is involved.

Finally, a tax-free reorganization can be accomplished as part of bankruptcy (a 'Type G' reorganization). One corporation must transfer assets to another corporation as part of a bankruptcy reorganization in which shares of the second corporation are distributed.

All types of statutory reorganizations result in the same tax treatment. An exchange of stock and securities in one corporation for stock and securities in another is tax-free to the participating shareholders. Because the basis in the old shares becomes the basis in the new shares, taxation of any gain or loss is postponed. If, however, the shareholders receive cash or other property, it is taxed, sometimes as an ordinary income dividend and sometimes as a capital gain. The corporation transferring property in exchange for shares recognizes no gain or loss, but the acquirer eventually reports the gain or loss as it takes the target's basis in the assets. The acquirer also obtains various tax attributes of the target, such as the earnings and profits account or any net operating loss (NOL). Very complex rules, however, limit the acquirer's use of a target's NOL in order to prevent trafficking in loss corporations.

H. *Consolidated Taxation*

To a limited extent, the United States employs a fiscal unity concept by permitting related corporations to file a consolidated return. That is, corporations under common control are treated as a single tax entity on the theory that, although one unified business has been split into separate corporations for business reasons, it can be treated as one entity for tax purposes. The decision to file a consolidated return is an election and generally is irrevocable. All affiliated members are jointly and severally liable for the tax liability that is based on their combined income.

To qualify to file a consolidated return, a common parent must own 80 percent of at least one subsidiary, and 80 percent of all other corporations must be owned by one or more other corporations in the group. The combined income is calculated without taking into account intra-group transfers, income, and loss. The chief advantage of filing a consolidated return is that the NOL of one corporation can be used to offset profits from another corporation. An extraordinarily complex set of rules has been developed to calculate total group income and to maintain the current basis in shares.

VI. Federal Taxation of United States Partnerships

A partnership is an unincorporated organization through which a business is carried on. In the United States, a partnership is not a taxable entity. Rather, it is treated as a 'pass through entity', one in which the income or loss produced by the entity flows through and is taxed solely to the owners. It is possible, however, to be a partnership under local law, but to be taxed as a corporation. To be a partnership for federal income tax purposes, an entity may have no more than two of the following characteristics:

(a)   continuity of life;
(b)   central management;

(c)   free transferability of interests; and

(d)   limited liability.

There are two kinds of partnerships: a general partnership, in which each partner is liable for all the debts of the partnership and a limited partnership, which has two types of partners, general and limited, the latter having no personal liability for the partnership debts.

A. *Formation and Contributions*

The transfer of cash or property to a partnership in exchange for a partnership interest is a nontaxable event for both the partnership and the partner. The partner's basis in the contributed assets becomes the basis in her partnership interest and the partnership's basis in the assets.

Partnership liabilities, including nonrecourse debt, increase a partner's basis in her partnership interest. For example, if a partnership asset is subject to a nonrecourse liability, each partner increases the basis in her partnership interest by her share of the liability. Conversely, the satisfaction of a partnership liability reduces each partner's basis.

B. *Taxation of Partnership Income*

Although the partnership is not subject to tax, it must compute its income, gain, deductions, losses, and credits generally as an individual does, but with certain exceptions. Because certain items have varying tax consequences in the hands of certain partners, they must be 'separately stated'. For example, because there is a limit on the amount of capital losses that can be deducted in any taxable year, a partnership's capital losses must be separately stated so that a partner can combine them with his own capital losses to determine the amount of his deduction. All other items are lumped together as 'nonseparately stated' income. The partnership then passes through its separately stated and nonseparately stated income.

Where a partner enters into a business transaction with the partnership, not in his capacity as a partner, but rather, as an employee or lender, the transaction is treated under the usual rules. For example, if a partner performs services for the partnership, whether legal, accounting, or painting a building, his compensation is deductible by the partnership and taxable to the partner. An anti-abuse rule prevents a partner from using the partnership to disguise a sale of property.

Partners must report their share of the income, regardless of whether it is actually distributed. A partner's distributive share is based on the partnership agreement. A particular item of income or deduction may be 'specially allocated', provided the allocation has a substantial economic effect. Thus, for example, a partner could be allocated 60 percent of the losses if he actually bears the economic risk of loss. Special allocations provide flexibility, which is one of the hallmarks of a partnership, but they also provide the potential for abuse. Much of the complexity surrounding the use of partnerships involves a determination of whether a special allocation will be recognized by the IRS.

A partner's deduction for partnership losses cannot exceed his basis in the partnership interest. Recall, however, that the basis includes the partner's share of partnership liabilities, including nonrecourse liabilities. This rule permits a partner to take significant deductions (such as interest and depreciation) with no cash outlay. A partner's basis is increased by his share of the partnership's income and decreased by his share of partnership losses.

C. Distributions

A distribution of cash to a partner is taxable only to the extent that it exceeds the basis in his partnership interest. A distribution of property is not taxable except in a partnership liquidation. The partner's basis in the partnership interest is reduced by the cash or the basis of the property. The basis of the property received cannot exceed the basis of the partnership interest.

D. Sale or Acquisition of Partnership Interest

Although generally the sale of a partnership interest does not affect the partnership, when more than 50 percent of the interest in partnership capital and profits is transferred within a 12-month period, the partnership terminates. This is not a taxable event to the partnership, but it is treated as if it distributed all its assets to the partners, which may result in taxation to the partners. The seller of a partnership asset generally recognizes a capital gain or loss, except to the extent the partnership has accounts receivable or inventory. His share of those items must be reported as ordinary income in order to prevent use of a partnership to avoid ordinary income. The buyer of the interest has a basis equal to the price paid. The basis of the partnership assets does not change unless the partnership elects to increase part of the basis of the assets to reflect the taxable sale. This complicated election benefits the incoming partner, who has paid market value for his share of assets that may have a lower basis. Continuing partners are not affected.

VII. Federal Taxation of Other Flow Through Entities

A. 'S Corporations'

Although the United States has a system of double corporate taxation, it does have a limited form of integration. Certain corporations, known as 'S corporations', are taxed on a pass through basis, like partnerships, so that the corporate income is taxed only to the shareholders at their rate.

Only certain corporations may make a subchapter S election. An S corporation can have no more than 35 shareholders; can have as a shareholder only an individual (who is not a nonresident alien) or an estate or certain types of trusts; can have only one class of stock (either voting or nonvoting); and cannot be a member of an affiliated group. Furthermore, an S corporation cannot engage in certain kinds of activities. These restrictions limit the election to non-publicly traded corporations with a simple capital structure. Nevertheless, many 'small' corporations in the United States make this election.

An S corporation calculates its income much the same way a partnership does and passes the separately and nonseparately stated income, gains, losses, deductions, and credits through to the shareholders who report them. A shareholder cannot deduct losses that exceed the basis in his stock or corporate debt. Unlike a partner, his basis is not increased by his share of entity-level debt, making an S corporation a less attractive investment vehicle than a partnership. The shareholder reports the income regardless of whether it is actually distributed and increases the basis in the S corporation stock accordingly. When the income is distributed, it is taxable only to the extent it exceeds the shareholder's basis in the stock.

Because an S corporation previously might have operated as a 'C corporation' (i.e. one that does not have an S election in effect), there are a number of complications. First, a C corporation keeps an accumulated earnings and profits (E&P) account to reflect the income that has been subject to tax at the corporate level, but not at the shareholder level. An S corporation, however, does not need such an account because all earnings, whether or not distributed, are taxed immediately at the shareholder level. When a C corporation with earnings and profits makes a subchapter S election, it must carry over the E&P so that when distributed, its prior earnings are subject to tax a second time. Secondly, a sale of assets by a C corporation is subject to tax at the corporate level and again when the proceeds are distributed to the shareholders. In order to prevent the use of an S election to avoid the second level of tax on appreciated assets, a former C corporation is subject to tax on the built-in gain on any assets held at the date of the election that is recognized during the 10 years following the election.

Another key difference between a partnership and an S corporation is that the latter actually is a corporation and thus can enter into certain corporate transactions, such as redemptions and tax-free reorganizations. A complicated set of rules has been developed to deal with the complexities that arise when a pass through entity uses these corporate provisions.

B. RICs, REITs, REMICs

The United States also provides pass through treatment for a number of special purpose corporations. A regulated investment company (RIC) is a domestic corporation that obtains 90 percent of its gross income from dividends, interest, security gains, futures, options, and currency transactions, and at least 50 percent of its asset value is represented by cash and securities. A RIC avoids corporate tax by distributing dividends that are taxable in the hands of the shareholders.

A real estate investment trust (REIT) is a corporation owned by more than 100 people that derives at least 75 percent of its gross income from real property rents, gains, and mortgage interest, and at least 95 percent of its gross income from rents and other passive income. A REIT receives a dividends paid deduction, provided that substantial dividends are paid, resulting in tax only at the shareholder level.

A REMIC is a 'real estate mortgage investment conduit' whose assets consist entirely of real estate mortgages. It is not subject to tax, but its debtholders (those who are entitled to a stated principal amount plus interest) report a distribution as interest, and shareholders report the REMIC's income much as a partnership does.

C. Trusts

A trust is an entity under which one or more people (the trustees) hold the legal ownership of property, but the beneficial ownership (the income) is payable to another. Trusts, which are commonly used in the United States for estate planning purposes or to make charitable gifts, are subject to two tax regimes. A simple trust (one that does not accumulate income) is entitled to deduct all income distributed to beneficiaries, who are then subject to tax. Thus, the trust has zero income and is not taxed. A complex trust, one that can accumulate income, is a taxable entity. To the extent the income is distributed, it is deductible. Thus, the taxable income of a complex trust is the accumulated income. The distributed income is taxed to the beneficiaries.

D. Estates

When a person dies, a separate entity, known as an estate, is created to manage the decedent's property until it can be passed on to the heirs. As such, the estate becomes a separate, albeit temporary, taxable unit. An estate is generally taxed as a complex trust during the period of administration. Any income accumulated during the year that is not distributed is taxed to the estate.

VIII. Taxation of United States Persons with Foreign Income

As noted above, the United States taxes its citizens and residents on worldwide income—gross income, no matter where earned, is subject to United States tax. Because this rule is not widely used in other nations, it is possible for a United States citizen to be taxed on income twice. For example, a United States citizen who is a resident of a foreign country may be subject to tax on his earnings both by the foreign country and by the United States. A United States resident who holds shares in a foreign corporation may be subject to tax on dividend distributions both by the country where the corporation is sited and the United States.

There are two avenues of relief. If the United States has a tax treaty with the foreign country, the income may be exempt from tax in that country. (A tax treaty would never exempt a United States person from United States tax). In the absence of such a treaty, the United States may grant a 'foreign tax credit' as relief from international double taxation. That requires rules to determine whether income is 'U.S. source', and thus not eligible for relief, or 'foreign source' and creditable. These 'sourcing' rules are also used to determine whether a foreign person's income is nevertheless subject to United

States tax. No relief is granted by U.S. tax laws for double taxes on income earned in the United States but the country where the foreign taxpayer is a citizen may do so.

A. Sourcing Rules

The Code contains an arbitrary set of sourcing rules that vary with the nature of the income. What follows are the general rules, but keep in mind that there are a number of technical exceptions that apply to avoid abuse (that is United States taxpayers attempting to take a foreign tax credit based on U.S. source income, or foreign taxpayers attempting to avoid United States tax on U.S. source income).

Interest income generally is sourced by the identity of the lender: interest on an obligation issued by a United States resident or a domestic corporation is U.S. source. Dividends paid by a domestic corporation (or by a foreign corporation with a significant amount of United States income) are U.S. source. Rents and royalties from property located within the United States is U.S. source, as is gain from the sale of American real property. Compensation for services performed within the United States is U.S. source regardless of the identity of the payor.

Although income from the sale of personal property is generally sourced by the residence of the seller, there are a number of exceptions. The most important of these is the rule for inventory. Generally inventory sold within the United States is U.S. source. Inventory sold outside the United States is generally foreign source unless an office or other fixed place of business is maintained in the United States and the income is attributable to that office. Income from the sale of inventory that is produced in the United States and sold outside (or vice versa) must be allocated. A sale is deemed to take place where title passes. Gain on depreciable property is allocated to where the depreciation deductions were taken.

B. Foreign Tax Credit

The basic purpose of the foreign tax credit is to offset double taxation, while at least subjecting the worldwide income of a United States person to tax at the American rates. The credit applies to foreign *income* taxes paid either directly or through withholding.

Under current law, the foreign tax credit is subject to an overall limit (as opposed to a per country limit) designed to limit the credit to reducing the foreign tax (and not the United States tax) on United States income. The credit cannot be used to reduce U.S. tax on U.S. source income or to offset higher taxes imposed by a foreign country, because there is double tax only to the extent of the United States and foreign taxes overlap.

In addition, the United States imposes separate limits for several income categories (known as 'baskets'). The rules are quite complex, but in general they are designed to avoid manipulation of foreign source and United States source income, to avoid a credit for income that usually bears no foreign tax, or to avoid mixing income that bears an unusually high rate of tax with low-taxed income. If the foreign taxes exceed the credit limitation in any one basket, they can be carried back 2 years and then forward 5 years in the same basket. There are special rules allocating foreign and United States losses.

IX. Taxation of United States Corporations with Foreign Income

A United States corporation (one incorporated in the United States) is taxed on its worldwide income, regardless of where earned. Similarly, losses are allowed on a worldwide basis. Where, however, an American business has a foreign loss that reduces the United States taxable income, the loss must be 'recaptured' when there are subsequent foreign profits; the profits are reported as U.S. source income. This rule results because some countries do not permit a loss carryover to offset subsequent income, with the result that it would be subject to foreign tax and be creditable.

A. Foreign Tax Credit

In addition to the general foreign tax credit, a United States corporation is permitted to take a credit (the deemed paid credit) for foreign income taxes paid by a subsidiary where the parent receives a dividend distribution. The parent must own at least 10 percent of the stock of the foreign subsidiary. The parent recalculates ('grosses up') the dividend to include the proportionate share of the taxes paid and then is given a credit for those taxes. The deemed paid credit applies as well to second- and third-tier subsidiaries.

B. Outbound Asset Transfers

An outbound transfer of assets to a foreign corporation on an incorporation, reorganization, or liquidation is taxable to the extent of the gain. Losses are not recognized. This avoids deferring the gain or re-sourcing the income by transferring the asset to a foreign source. In some cases, the rule does not apply to a transfer of property to be used in business by a foreign corporation. A transfer of an intangible is treated as the sale of the intangible for contingent payments, thus leaving open the purchase price.

C. Transfer Pricing

One of the most contentious issues in American international taxation is transfer pricing. This refers to the taxation of taxable transactions between domestic corporations and foreign affiliates that would not be subject to United States income tax. Suppose that a United States corporation manufactures goods and sells them to a foreign subsidiary at cost (thus, reflecting no United States profit subject to United States tax). If the foreign subsidiary in turns sells the products at a profit, that profit would not be subject to United States tax until the subsidiary repatriated it to the United States parent in the form of a dividend. The IRS has the authority to reallocate income and deductions by revising the 'transfer price' to reflect a reasonable profit. The controversy is created because the statute does not specify a standard for determining what is a reasonable profit. The regulations take the position that 'the standard to be applied in every case is that of an uncontrolled taxpayer dealing at arm's length with another uncontrolled taxpayer'. The assumption is that an arm's length standard produces the correct tax liability; the difficulty arises in trying to determine an arm's length price. Although this problem generally only involves large, multinational corporations, it is an issue of real importance because of the significant amount of revenue involved.

X. Anti-abuse Rules

The United States has adopted a number of anti-abuse rules that overrride other provisions. Because they have been adopted incrementally, they are often overlapping and sometimes conflicting. In most cases, the United States is exerting extra-territorial jurisdiction over persons or entities that otherwise would not be subject to United States tax. The United States is quite unusual in this respect.

A. *Foreign Personal Holding Companies (PHCs)*

Where a United States person invests in a foreign corporation, the profits are not subject to United States taxation until such time as they are repatriated through a dividend. Thus, the United States tax is deferred indefinitely. The PHC rules ignore the foreign corporate entity and tax the American shareholders on its income. Each shareholder includes his ratable share of the PHC's income.

In order to be a PHC, the foreign corporation must have more than 50 percent of its stock held by five or fewer United States persons, either directly or through attribution. At least 60 percent of the foreign corporation's income must be passive, i.e., dividends, interest, royalties, gains from the sale of stock, personal service contract income, rent paid by a significant shareholder, or, if they are less than 50 percent of total income, foreign passive income from a second-tier PHC.

B. *Controlled Foreign Corporations (CFCs)*

The United States subsequently extended the PHC rules to active businesses. This reflects an increasing concern that United States citizens or corporations are investing overseas in a manner designed to avoid United States tax. The CFC rules prevent the indefinite deferral of tax through use of a controlled foreign corporation.

Under the so-called 'Subpart F rules', the undistributed income of a CFC is subject to tax in the hands of its United States shareholders, even though they do not actually receive it. In order to be classified as a CFC, United States persons owning at least 10 percent of the stock must own more than 50 percent of the stock of a foreign corporation, either directly or indirectly. If the effective rate of tax on certain kinds of income is less than 90 percent of the United States shareholder's highest marginal tax rate, the shareholder's pro rata share of that income is taxed at United States rates as if a dividend had been distributed. The income to which the rule applies is:

(1) foreign sales income and foreign service income from related parties outside the country of incorporation;

(2)   foreign shipping income;

(3)   foreign oil-related income;

(4)   foreign PHC income; and

(5)   foreign insurance income.

C. Passive Foreign Investment Company Income (PFIC)

Yet another anti-abuse rule applies to what Congress perceived to be offshore tax shelters. A foreign corporation is a PFIC if 75 percent or more of its gross income is passive income or, on average, 50 percent of more of its assets produce passive income. For this purpose, passive income is dividends; interest; rents and royalties; annuities; gains from the sale of non-income producing property; gains from futures, commodities, or options; and foreign currency gains. Unlike the PHC and CFC rules, the current income of the PFIC is not taxed to the United States shareholders. Rather, when the shares are sold, the United States shareholder is subject to an interest charge, to compensate the government for the value of the tax deferral.

XI. Taxation of Foreign Persons with United States Income

The United States taxes nonresident aliens and foreign businesses on certain income connected to the United States. Generally, there are two forms of tax. Investment income is subject to a withholding tax; business income arising in the United States is subject to the regular United States income tax.

A. Investment Income

Nonresident aliens are subject to a 30 percent withholding tax on United States income, that is 'fixed or determinable periodic or annual gains, profits or income', known as FDAP income. This would include interest, dividends, royalties, rents, salaries, premiums, and annuities. Any FDAP income that is effectively connected with a United States trade or business is not subject to the withholding tax, but rather is subject to the general tax discussed in section XI B below. No deductions are permitted in calculating the withholding tax. In general, the tax applies to those types of income for which imposition of a tax on gross receipts is appropriate.

There are a number of exceptions to the withholding tax, designed to counteract the negative effect United States taxes have on foreign investment. The first is that the tax does not apply to portfolio interest, which is interest paid by a United States obligor on a registered obligation (or an unregistered one designed to be sold to a non-United States person). Interest paid to a related party, i.e. to a 10 percent owner, and interest received by a bank in the normal course of business are not covered by the exception. Also exempt from the withholding tax are interest-bearing deposits in United States banks. Finally, interest and dividends paid by '80/20' corporations are not subject to tax. An 80/20 corporation is one that derives 80 percent of its income from foreign business activities during a three-year period. To the extent dividends represent such foreign business income, they are not subject to United States tax because they are, in essence, foreign profits. Similarly, interest paid by such a corporation is not treated as U.S. source income.

An extreme example of the extra-territorial reach of the American taxing system is the imposition of the withholding tax on dividends paid to a non-resident shareholder by a nonresident corporation where the corporation receives 25 percent or more of its income from the United States during a 3-year period. The importance of this provision, however, has been diminished by the branch profits tax (discussed in sectioni XI B below).

The United States taxes nonresident aliens and foreign corporations on United States business income. Unlike other countries, the basis for this tax is not a permanent establishment within the United States, but rather the existence of 'effectively connected business income'. This rule is often modified by treaty, thereby limiting the application of the tax to those foreign businesses with a permanent establishment.

The tax applies only if the individual or corporation has a United States trade or business. Only a minimal amount of activity is required to create a trade or business. A sales office or a manufacturing unit clearly rises to that level. Even absent an office, substantial sales of inventory within the United States, either by employees or agents, is a business. The performance of services within the United States is almost always a business. A United States business does not include trading in stocks or securities through a resident broker, so long as the nonresident taxpayer does not maintain an American office to direct the trading.

Income attributable to a United States trade or business is effectively connected and subject to tax. Under a limited 'force of attraction' rule, U.S. source FDAP is treated as effectively connected if it is derived from assets used in the business, or if the activities of the business were a material factor in the realization of the income. If a nonresident has a fixed place of business in the United States, some foreign source income is considered effectively connected.

In computing effectively connected income, deductions are matched with income and source. If a deduction is attributable to the overall business, it is allocated, first to classes of income and then more generally. Interest expense and research and development expenses are subject to special rules that are complex and very controversial. Only deductions allocated to effectively connected income are taken into account in determining taxable income. The tax imposed is the regular rate for corporations or individuals.

B. *Branch Profits Tax*

The branch profits tax is a tax on a hypothetical dividend from a branch paid to its nonresident parent. It was adopted to achieve parity between a foreign business operating a branch in the United States and one using a subsidiary to conduct its business. The profits of the United States business would be subject to tax in any event, but a repatriation of the dividend from the subsidiary to the parent would be taxable whereas a transfer from a branch would not. To rectify this difference, a second tax is imposed on the 'dividend equivalent amount'. This represents the branch's profits minus the United States taxes paid, which, in theory, is the amount that could be distributed. This sum is decreased by any increase in the branch's net equity (i.e. the amount deemed to have been reinvested in the branch) and increased by any decrease in the net equity (the amount deemed to be transferred to the head office). In addition, branches are subject to a 30 percent branch interest withholding tax on actual and deemed interest payments made by the branch. Once again, the purpose of the tax is to create parity between United States subsidiaries and branches of foreign corporations.

C. *Real Property Income*

Although rental income is considered a type of FDAP and thus subject to the 30 percent withholding tax, a nonresident alien can elect to treat it as effectively connected with a United States trade or business. This election is usually made because even though a higher tax rate might be used (for example 35 percent or 39 percent rather than 30 percent), it is levied against net taxable income, and a rental activity often has significant deductions, unlike dividend or interest income.

The gain from the sale or exchange of United States real property is treated as connected with a United States business and thus subject to the regular tax. In order to avoid hiding the gain in a holding company, the United States taxes the gain on the transfer of a 'U.S. real property interest'. This includes not only the real property, but also an interest in an entity that holds the U.S. real property. A United States corporation is a real property holding company if the fair market value of its United States real property is at least 50 percent of the fair market value of its business assets and real property at any time during the preceding 5 years. Thus, a sale of the shares of the holding company by a nonresident alien would produce United States taxable gain. A gain on a sale by a nonresident corporation is taxed to the corporation.

XII. Federal Estate and Gift Taxes

The United States imposes a tax on the donor of a completed gift and on a decedent on the value of his estate at his death. These taxes generally apply only to the very wealthy, however, because each contains significant exemptions and exceptions. Many states also imposes taxes at death, although generally on the beneficiaries rather than the decedent, and a few states imposes gift taxes as well.

The gift tax is levied on all transfers without consideration, whether in money or property, directly or indirectly. Transactions required by law and incomplete transfers are not subject to tax. A donor is permitted an annual exclusion of $10,000 per year per donee. A gift made by a husband or wife is considered as one-half made by each; thus, a couple can transfer up to $20,000 a year tax-free to each donee. In addition, all gifts to qualified charities, to a spouse, to an educational institution for tuition payments, or to a health care provider for medical care for a donee, are not subject to gift tax. Because the gift tax applies to indirect gifts, there are special rules for transfers by a power of appointment, transfers pursuant to a divorce or separation, and transfers accomplished through a disclaimer of an interest in property left under a will.

The federal estate tax is levied on the fair market of the decedent's gross estate at the date of death, or if the estate elects, 6 months after death. The estate includes any interest that the decedent held at the time of his death. In order to eliminate the possibility of avoiding the estate tax on lifetime transfers of property that the decedent actually enjoys until death, certain transferred property is brought back into the gross estate. For example, where a donor transfers property subject to a retained life interest, the entire value of the property is included in the gross estate. Similarly, a power to alter, amend, or revoke a transfer of property results in taxation of the property. Other special rules are provided for property subject to a power of appointment; life insurance; annuities; and property transferred incident to a divorce or separation.

Deductions are permitted for funeral and administrative expenses, claims against the estate, and indebtedness. In addition, all transfers to a qualified charity by the estate are deductible. There is also an unlimited deduction for a qualified bequest to a surviving spouse.

The gift and estate tax rates are progressive and are applied cumulatively to lifetime gifts and the gross estate. Each donor is entitled to a credit of $192,800, which means a taxable estate of $600,000; thus only taxable gifts and/or a taxable estate exceeding that amount are subject to tax. The rates range from 18 percent to 50 percent. By making significant lifetime annual gifts, or by transferring property to a spouse or charity, many taxpayers are able to avoid the federal transfer taxes altogether.

INDEX

Printed in the United States
1097400003B/22-1209